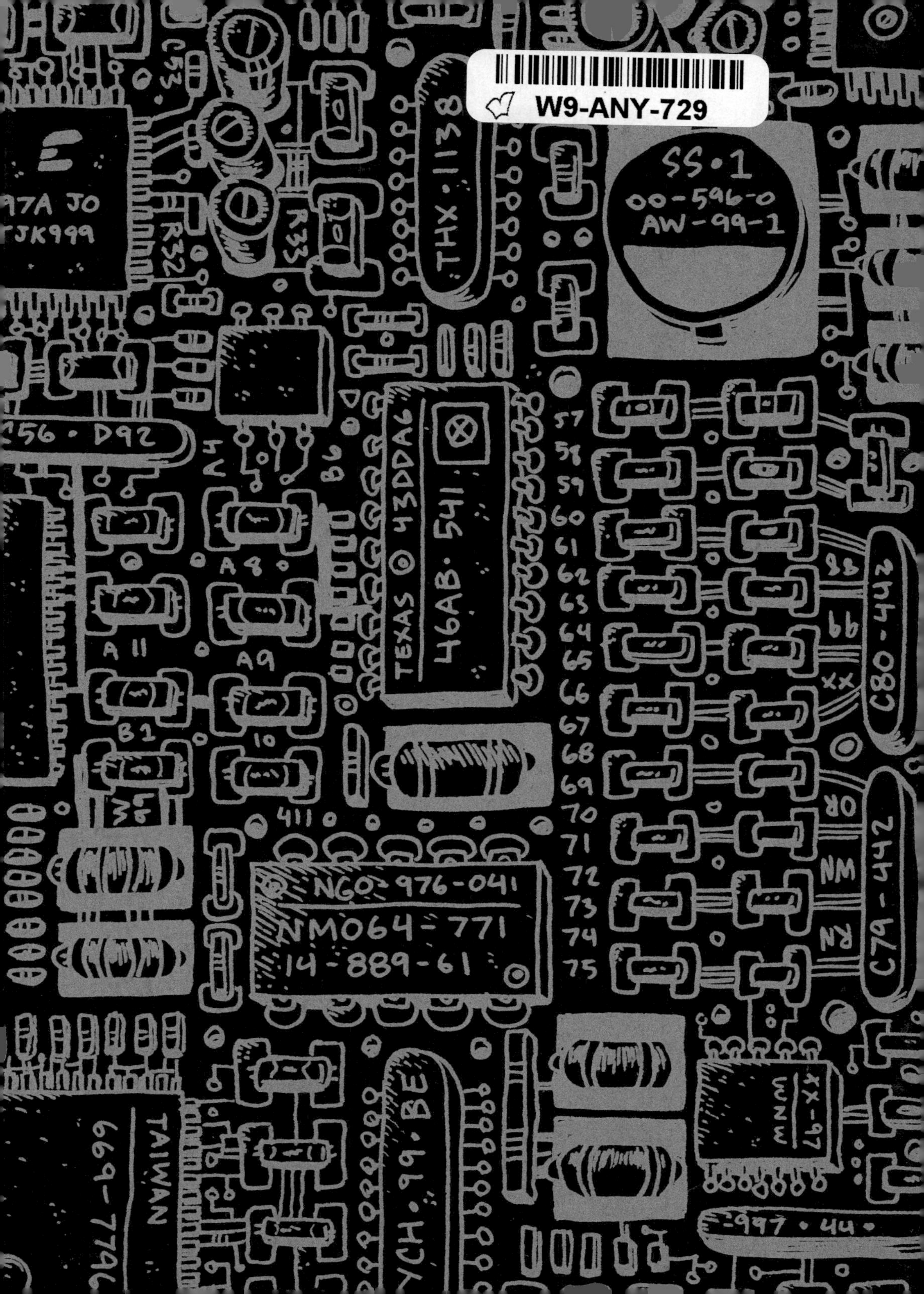
SS•1
00-596-0
AW-99-1
THX•1138
C53
R32
R33
TJK999
D92
A4
B6
A8
A11
A9
B1
10
411
TEXAS
43DDA6
46AB•541
57
58
59
60
61
62
63
64
65
66
67
68
69
70
71
72
73
74
75
88
99
XX
OR
NM
RN
C80-442
C79-442
NGO-976-041
NM064-771
14-889-61
TAIWAN
669-7796
YCH•99•BE
XX-97
WNW
997•44

WIZZYWIG

ED PISKOR

TOP SHELF
PRODUCTIONS

DEDICATED TO YOU, THE READER

BECAUSE YOU ARE LITERALLY AND FIGURATIVELY
HOLDING MY PAST, MY PRESENT, AND MY
FUTURE IN THE PALMS OF YOUR HANDS.

CHAPTER 1

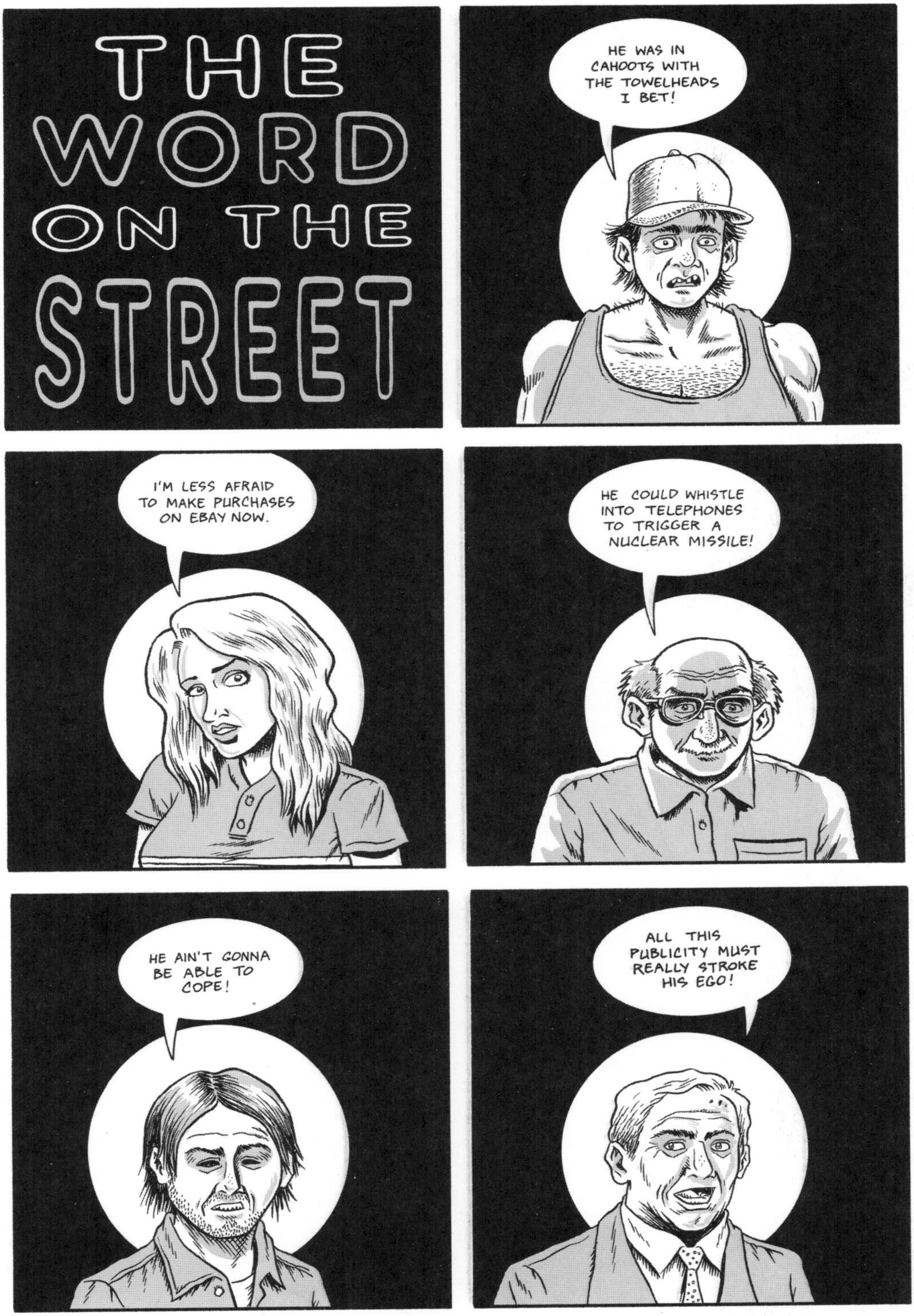
THE WORD ON THE STREET
HE WAS IN CAHOOTS WITH THE TOWELHEADS I BET!
I'M LESS AFRAID TO MAKE PURCHASES ON EBAY NOW.
HE COULD WHISTLE INTO TELEPHONES TO TRIGGER A NUCLEAR MISSILE!
HE AIN'T GONNA BE ABLE TO COPE!
ALL THIS PUBLICITY MUST REALLY STROKE HIS EGO!

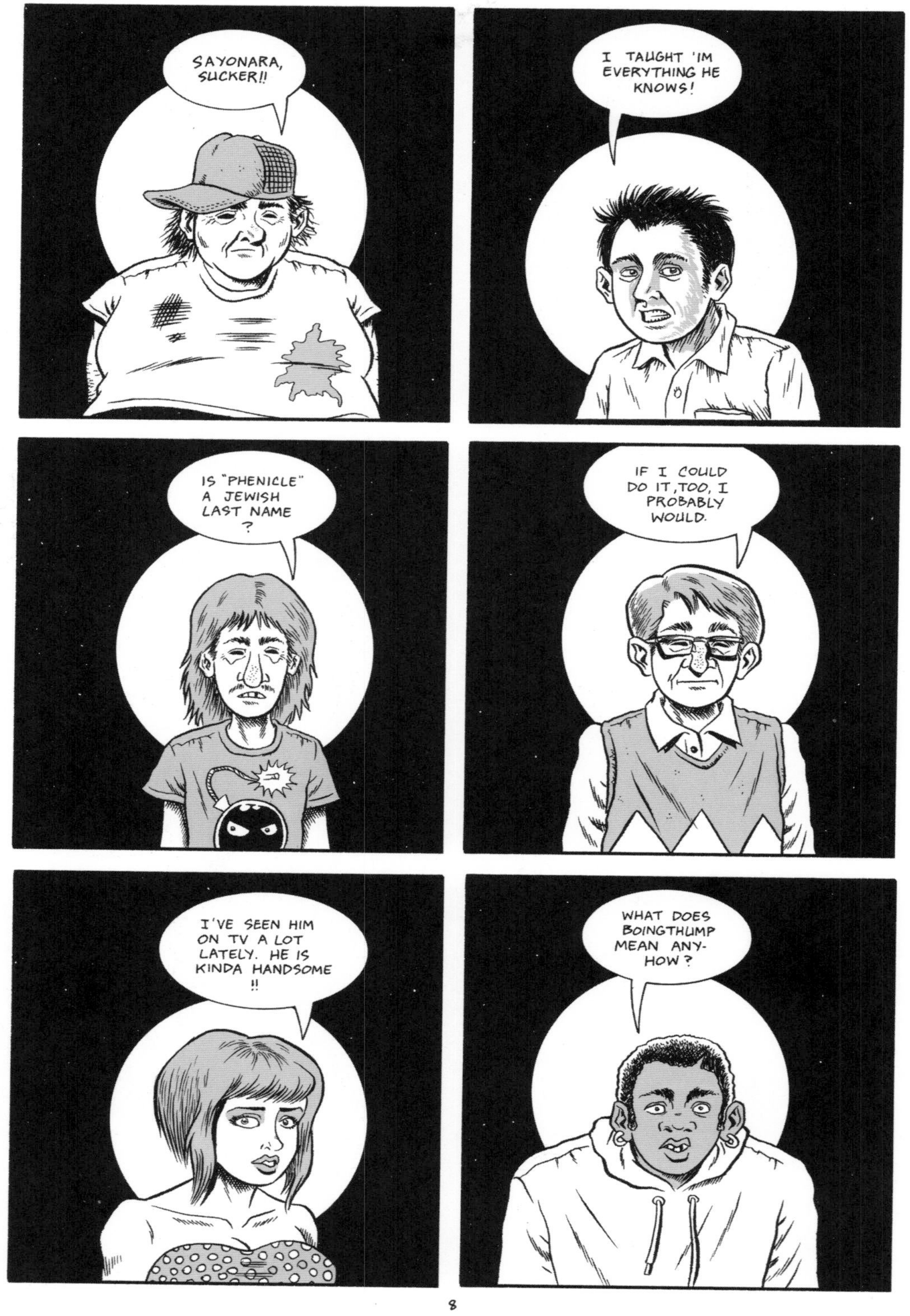
SAYONARA, SUCKER!!
I TAUGHT 'IM EVERYTHING HE KNOWS!
IS "PHENICLE" A JEWISH LAST NAME ?
IF I COULD DO IT, TOO, I PROBABLY WOULD.
I'VE SEEN HIM ON TV A LOT LATELY. HE IS KINDA HANDSOME !!
WHAT DOES BOINGTHUMP MEAN ANY-HOW ?

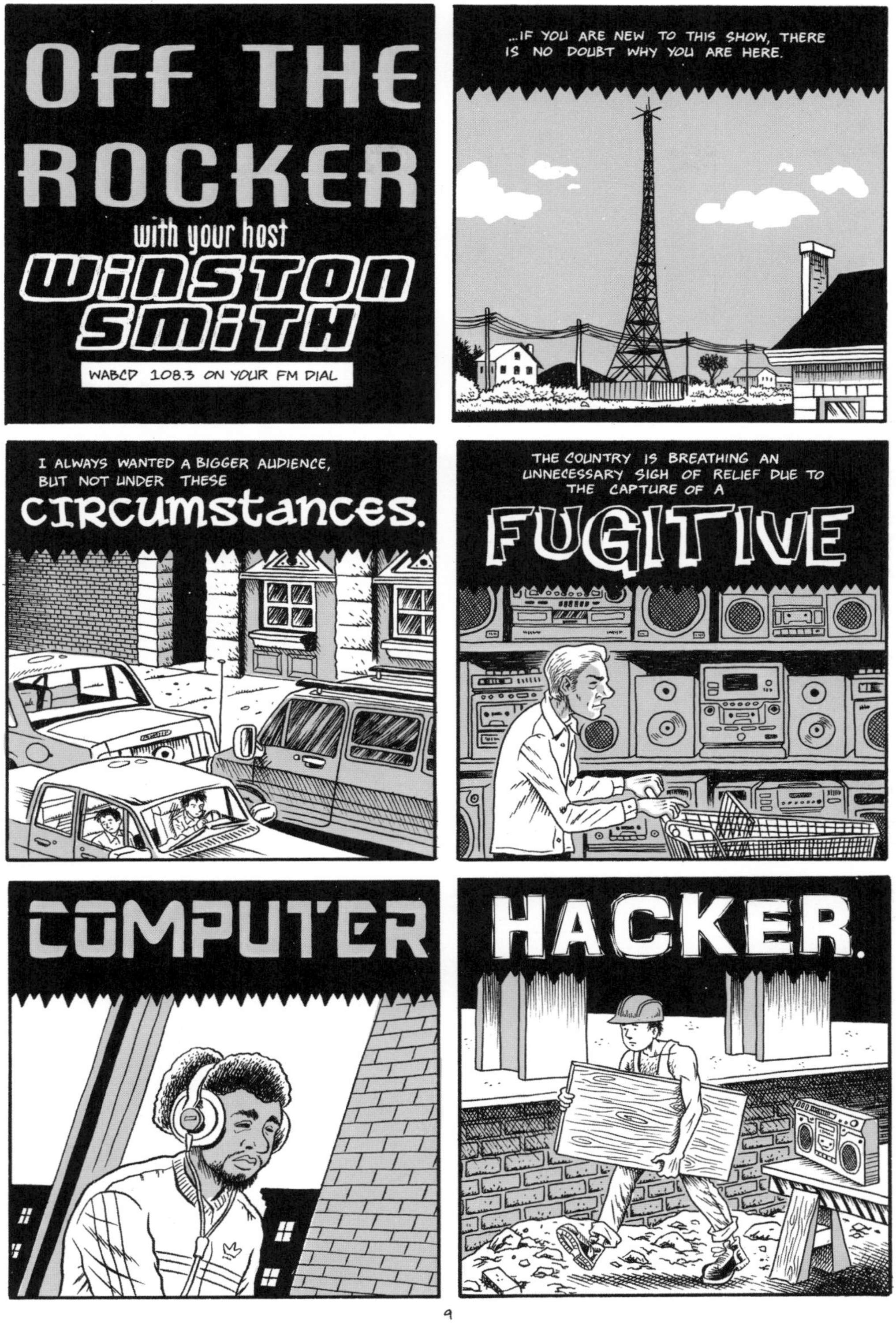
OFF THE ROCKER
with your host
WINSTON SMITH
WABCD 108.3 ON YOUR FM DIAL
...IF YOU ARE NEW TO THIS SHOW, THERE IS NO DOUBT WHY YOU ARE HERE.
I ALWAYS WANTED A BIGGER AUDIENCE, BUT NOT UNDER THESE
CIRCUMSTANCES.
THE COUNTRY IS BREATHING AN UNNECESSARY SIGH OF RELIEF DUE TO THE CAPTURE OF A
FUGITIVE
COMPUTER
HACKER.

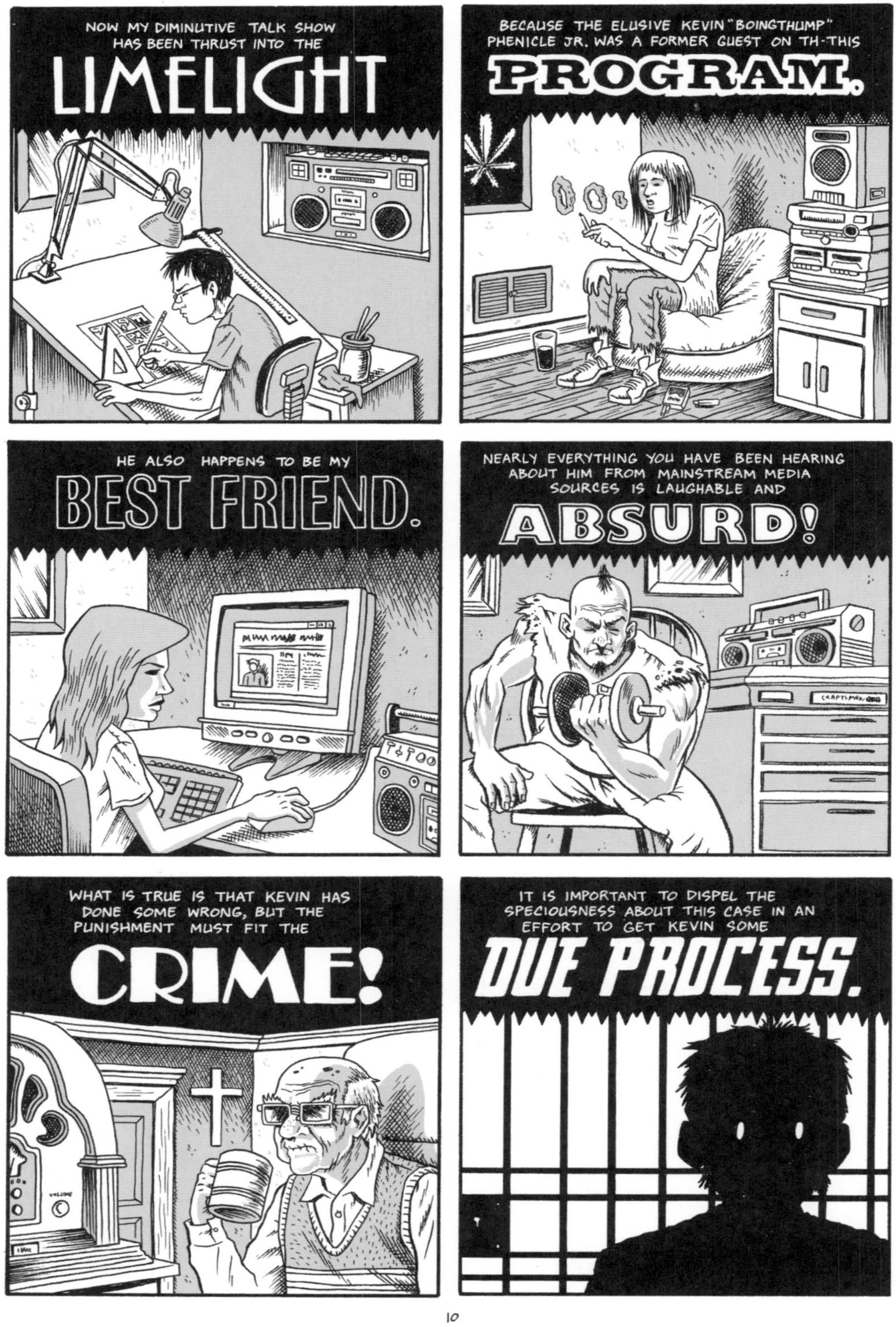
NOW MY DIMINUTIVE TALK SHOW HAS BEEN THRUST INTO THE
LIMELIGHT
BECAUSE THE ELUSIVE KEVIN "BOINGTHUMP" PHENICLE JR. WAS A FORMER GUEST ON TH-THIS
PROGRAM.
HE ALSO HAPPENS TO BE MY
BEST FRIEND.
NEARLY EVERYTHING YOU HAVE BEEN HEARING ABOUT HIM FROM MAINSTREAM MEDIA SOURCES IS LAUGHABLE AND
ABSURD!
WHAT IS TRUE IS THAT KEVIN HAS DONE SOME WRONG, BUT THE PUNISHMENT MUST FIT THE
CRIME!
IT IS IMPORTANT TO DISPEL THE SPECIOUSNESS ABOUT THIS CASE IN AN EFFORT TO GET KEVIN SOME
DUE PROCESS.

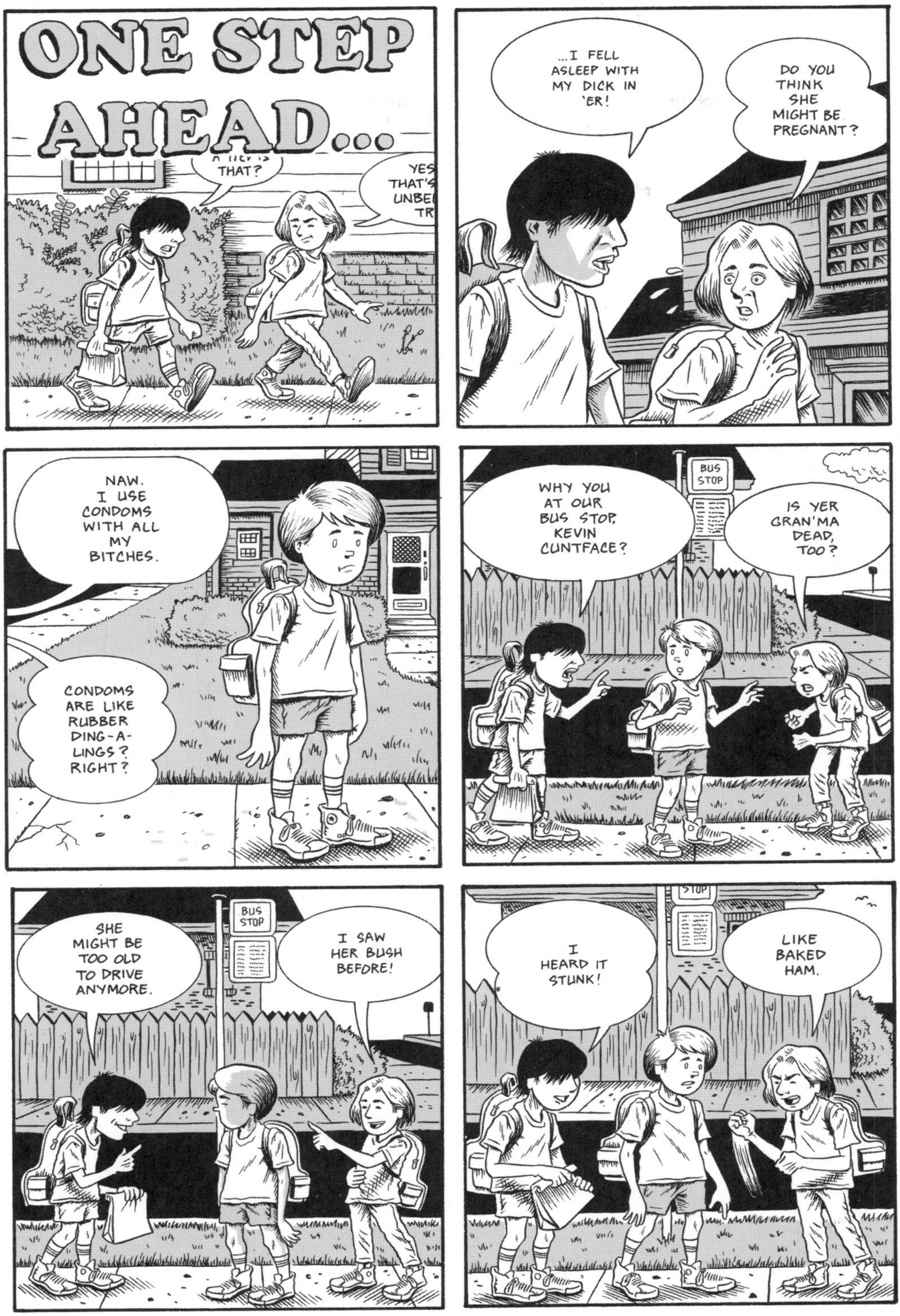
ONE STEP AHEAD...
THAT?
YES
...I FELL ASLEEP WITH MY DICK IN 'ER!
DO YOU THINK SHE MIGHT BE PREGNANT?
NAW. I USE CONDOMS WITH ALL MY BITCHES.
CONDOMS ARE LIKE RUBBER DING-A-LINGS? RIGHT?
WHY YOU AT OUR BUS STOP, KEVIN CUNTFACE?
BUS STOP
IS YER GRAN'MA DEAD, TOO?
SHE MIGHT BE TOO OLD TO DRIVE ANYMORE.
BUS STOP
I SAW HER BUSH BEFORE!
I HEARD IT STUNK!
STOP
LIKE BAKED HAM.

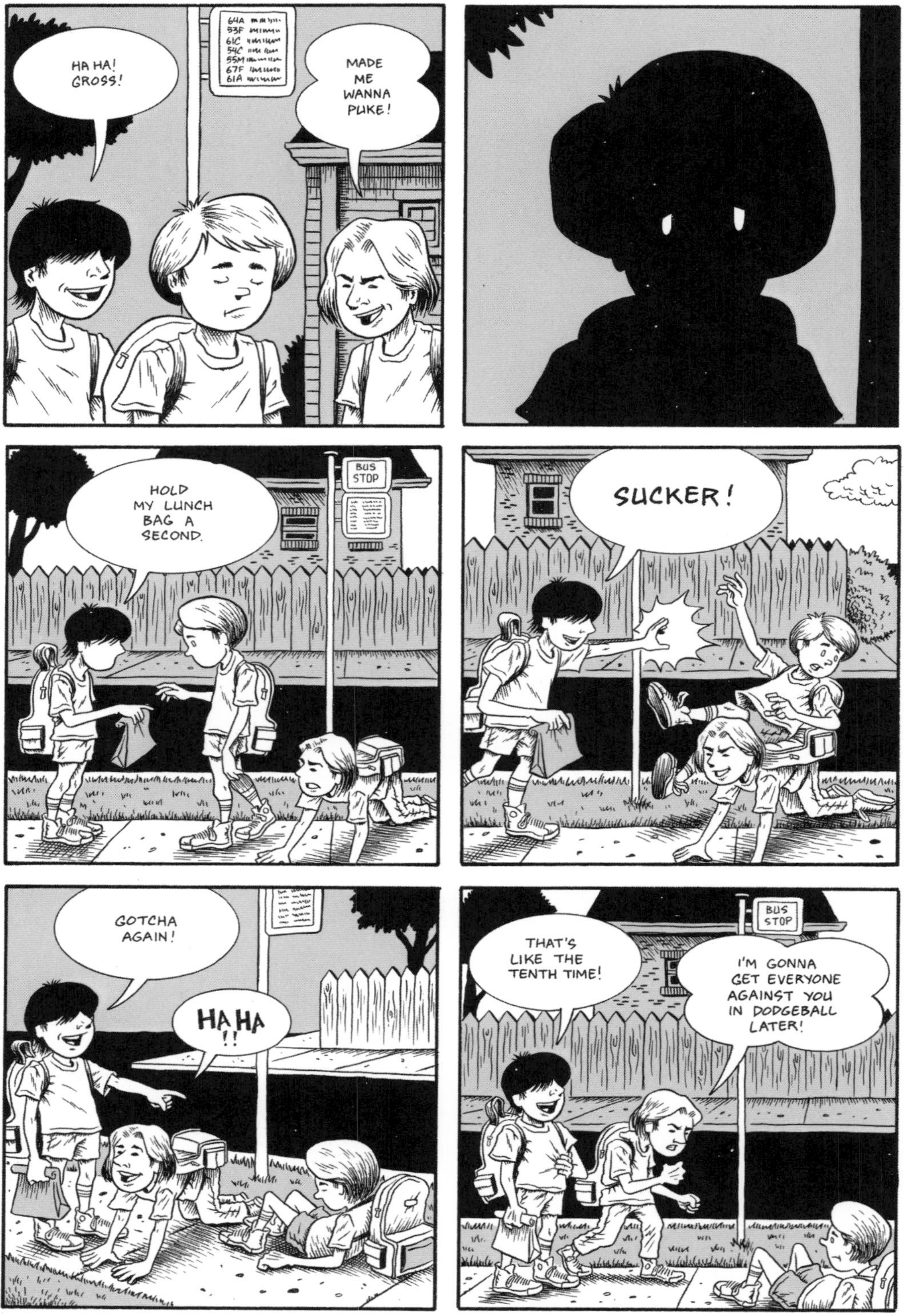
HA HA! GROSS!
64A
53F
61C
54C
55M
67F
61A
MADE ME WANNA PUKE!
HOLD MY LUNCH BAG A SECOND.
BUS STOP
SUCKER!
GOTCHA AGAIN!
HA HA !!
BUS STOP
THAT'S LIKE THE TENTH TIME!
I'M GONNA GET EVERYONE AGAINST YOU IN DODGEBALL LATER!

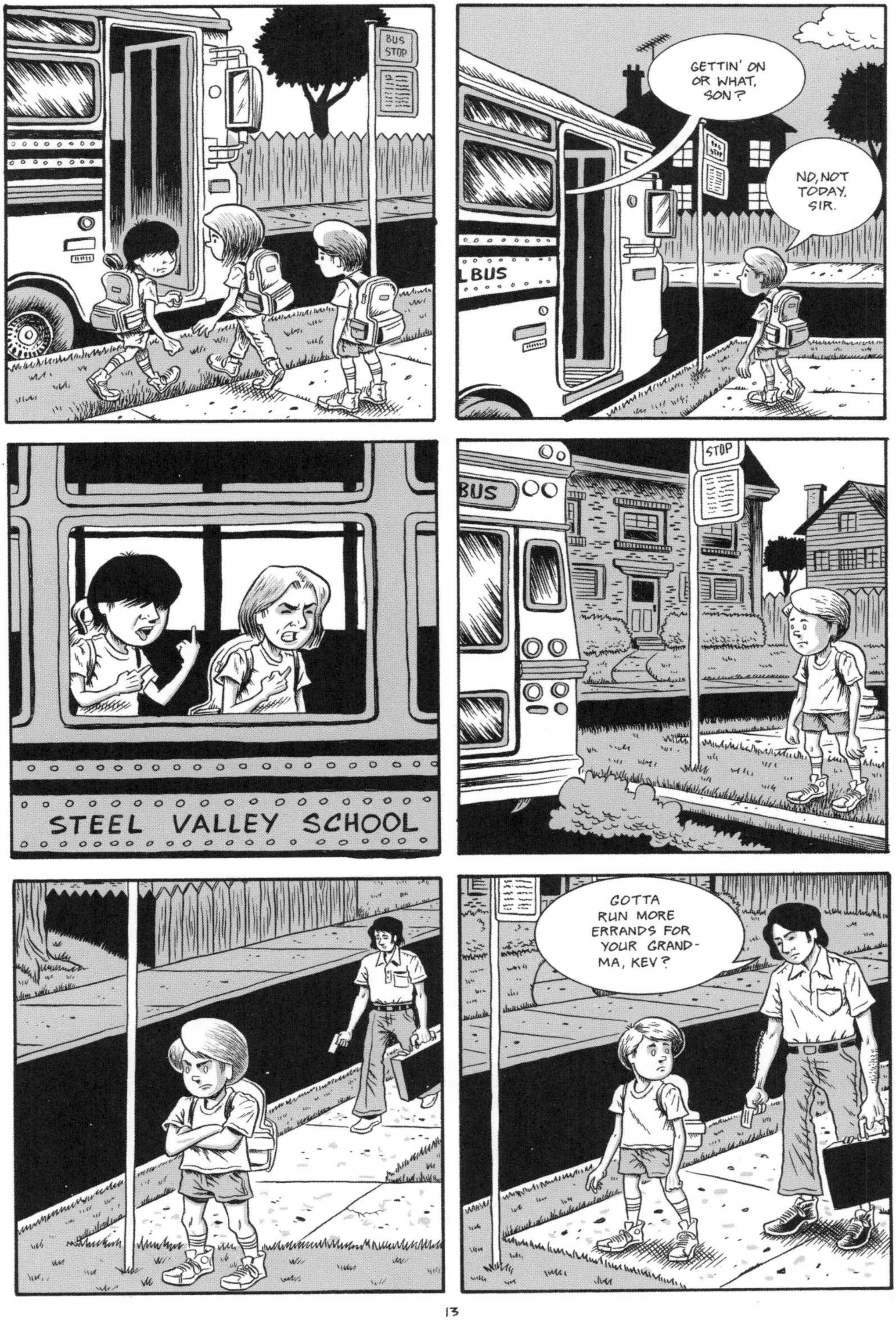
BUS STOP
GETTIN' ON OR WHAT, SON?
NO, NOT TODAY, SIR.
BUS
STEEL VALLEY SCHOOL
BUS
STOP
GOTTA RUN MORE ERRANDS FOR YOUR GRAND-MA, KEV?

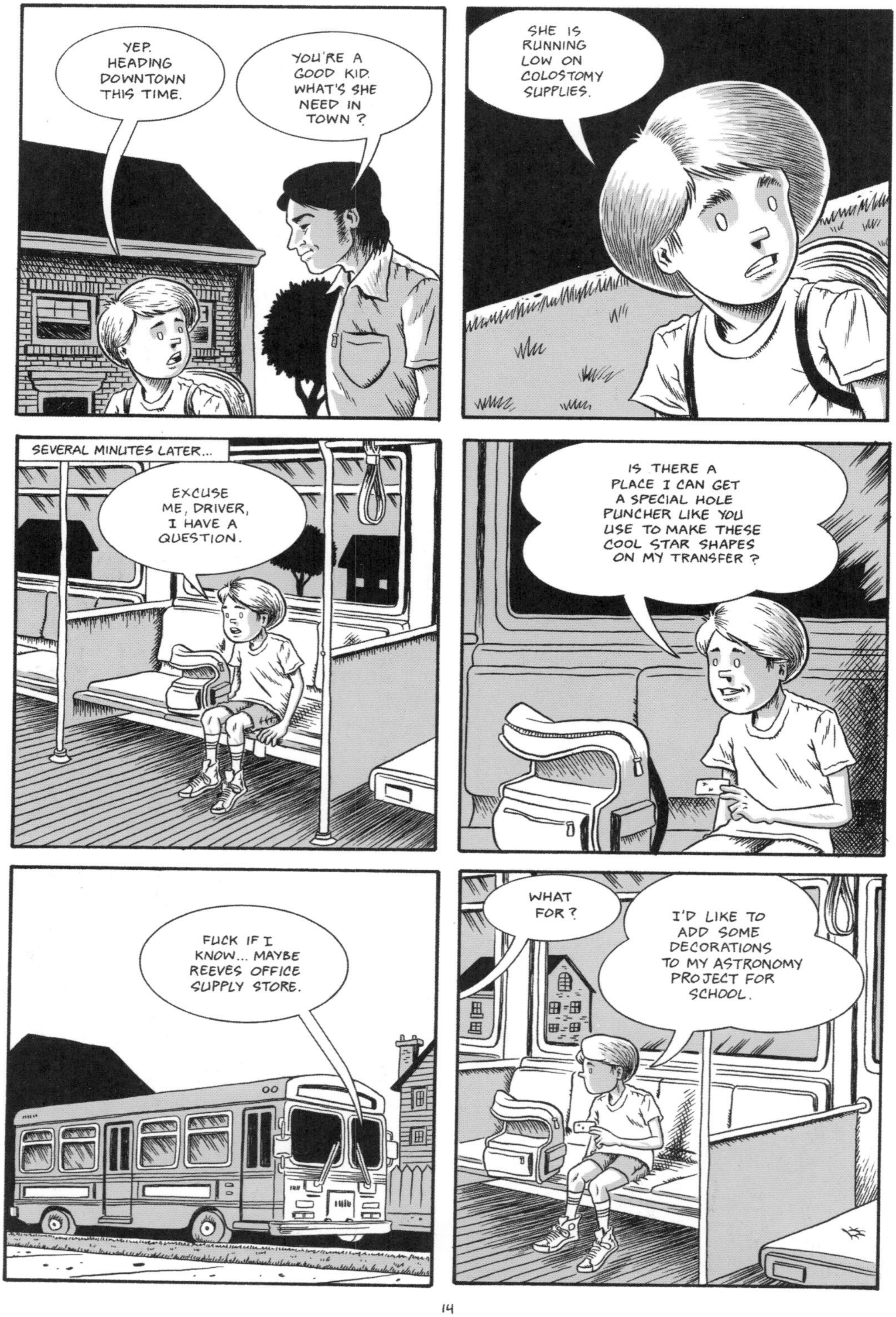
YEP. HEADING DOWNTOWN THIS TIME.
YOU'RE A GOOD KID. WHAT'S SHE NEED IN TOWN ?
SHE IS RUNNING LOW ON COLOSTOMY SUPPLIES.
SEVERAL MINUTES LATER...
EXCUSE ME, DRIVER, I HAVE A QUESTION.
IS THERE A PLACE I CAN GET A SPECIAL HOLE PUNCHER LIKE YOU USE TO MAKE THESE COOL STAR SHAPES ON MY TRANSFER ?
FUCK IF I KNOW... MAYBE REEVES OFFICE SUPPLY STORE.
WHAT FOR ?
I'D LIKE TO ADD SOME DECORATIONS TO MY ASTRONOMY PROJECT FOR SCHOOL.

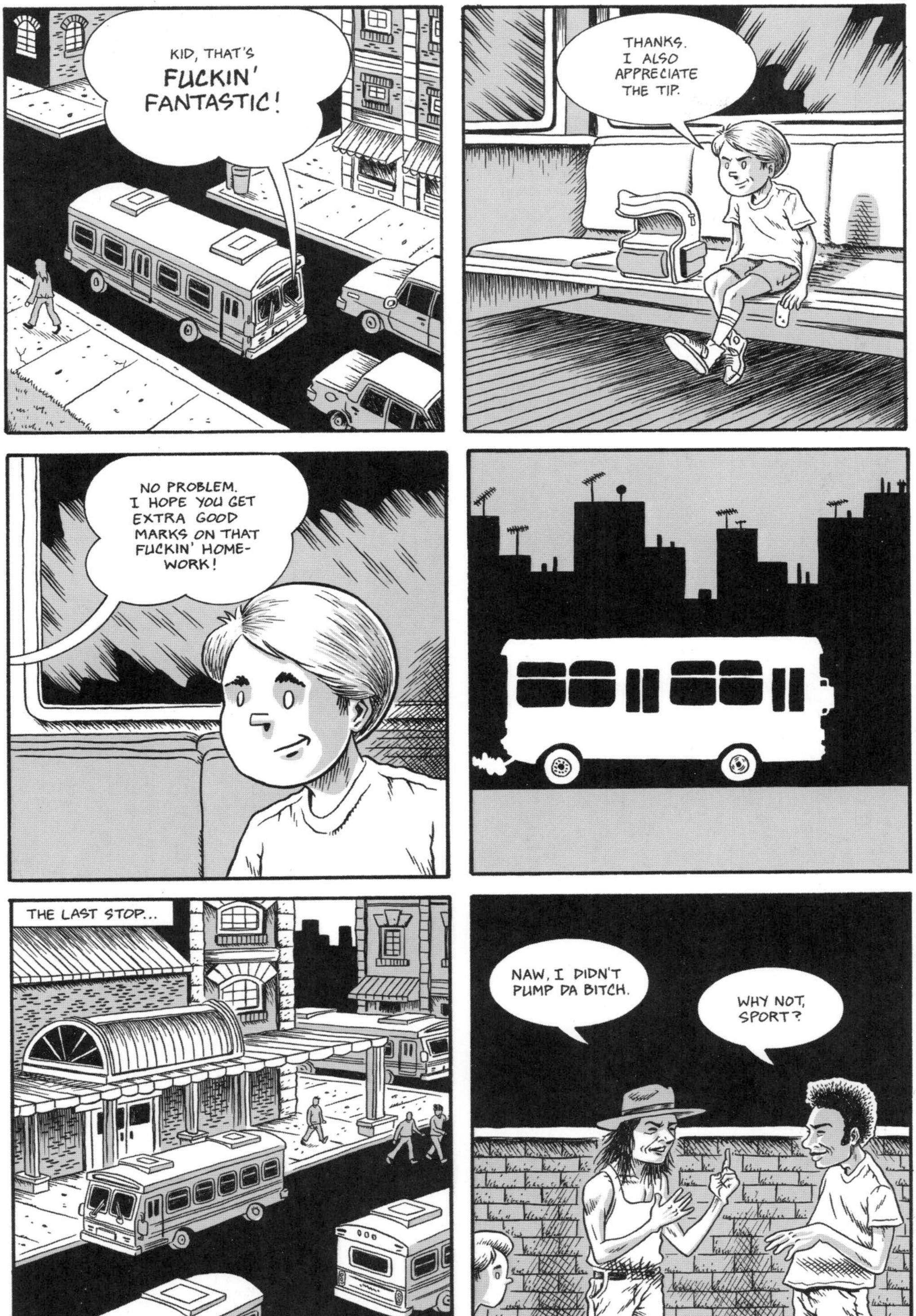
KID, THAT'S FUCKIN' FANTASTIC!
THANKS. I ALSO APPRECIATE THE TIP.
NO PROBLEM. I HOPE YOU GET EXTRA GOOD MARKS ON THAT FUCKIN' HOME-WORK!
THE LAST STOP...
NAW, I DIDN'T PUMP DA BITCH.
WHY NOT, SPORT?

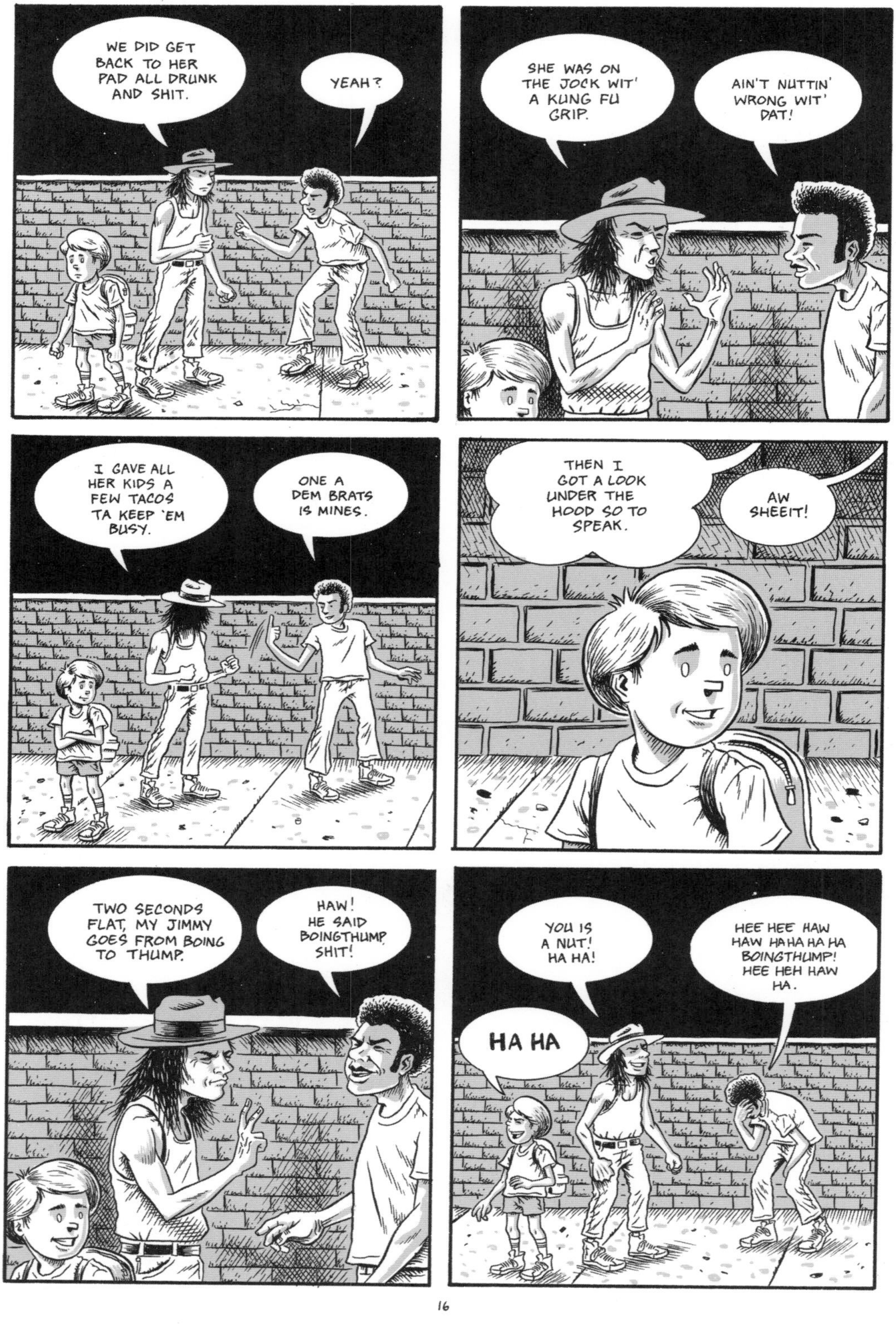

WE DID GET BACK TO HER PAD ALL DRUNK AND SHIT.
YEAH?
SHE WAS ON THE JOCK WIT' A KUNG FU GRIP.
AIN'T NUTTIN' WRONG WIT' DAT!
I GAVE ALL HER KIDS A FEW TACOS TA KEEP 'EM BUSY.
ONE A DEM BRATS IS MINES.
THEN I GOT A LOOK UNDER THE HOOD SO TO SPEAK.
AW SHEEIT!
TWO SECONDS FLAT, MY JIMMY GOES FROM BOING TO THUMP.
HAW! HE SAID BOINGTHUMP. SHIT!
YOU IS A NUT! HA HA!
HEE HEE HAW HAW HA HA HA HA BOINGTHUMP! HEE HEH HAW HA.
HA HA

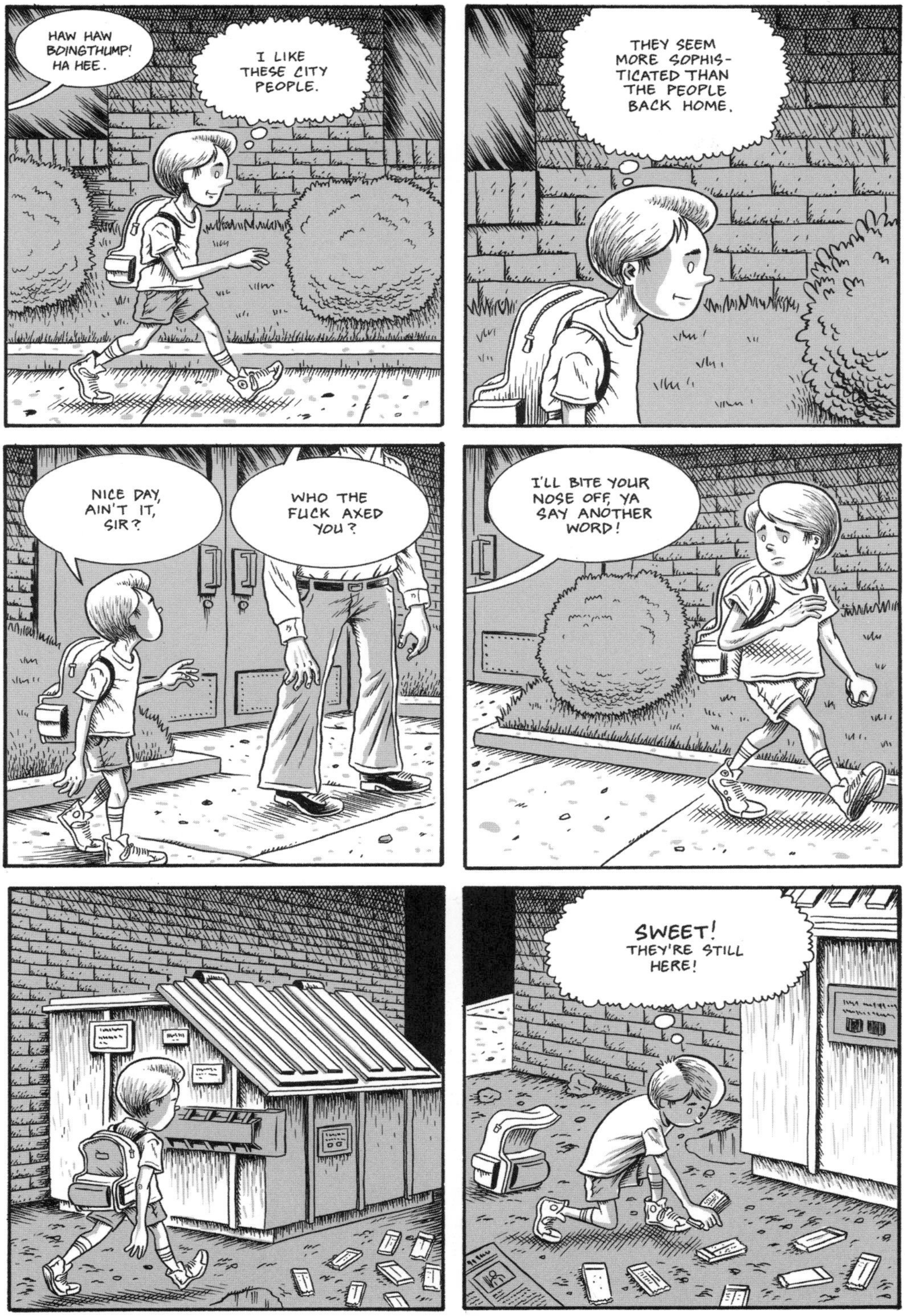
HAW HAW BOINGTHUMP! HA HEE.
I LIKE THESE CITY PEOPLE.
THEY SEEM MORE SOPHISTICATED THAN THE PEOPLE BACK HOME.
NICE DAY, AIN'T IT, SIR?
WHO THE FUCK AXED YOU?
I'LL BITE YOUR NOSE OFF, YA SAY ANOTHER WORD!
SWEET! THEY'RE STILL HERE!

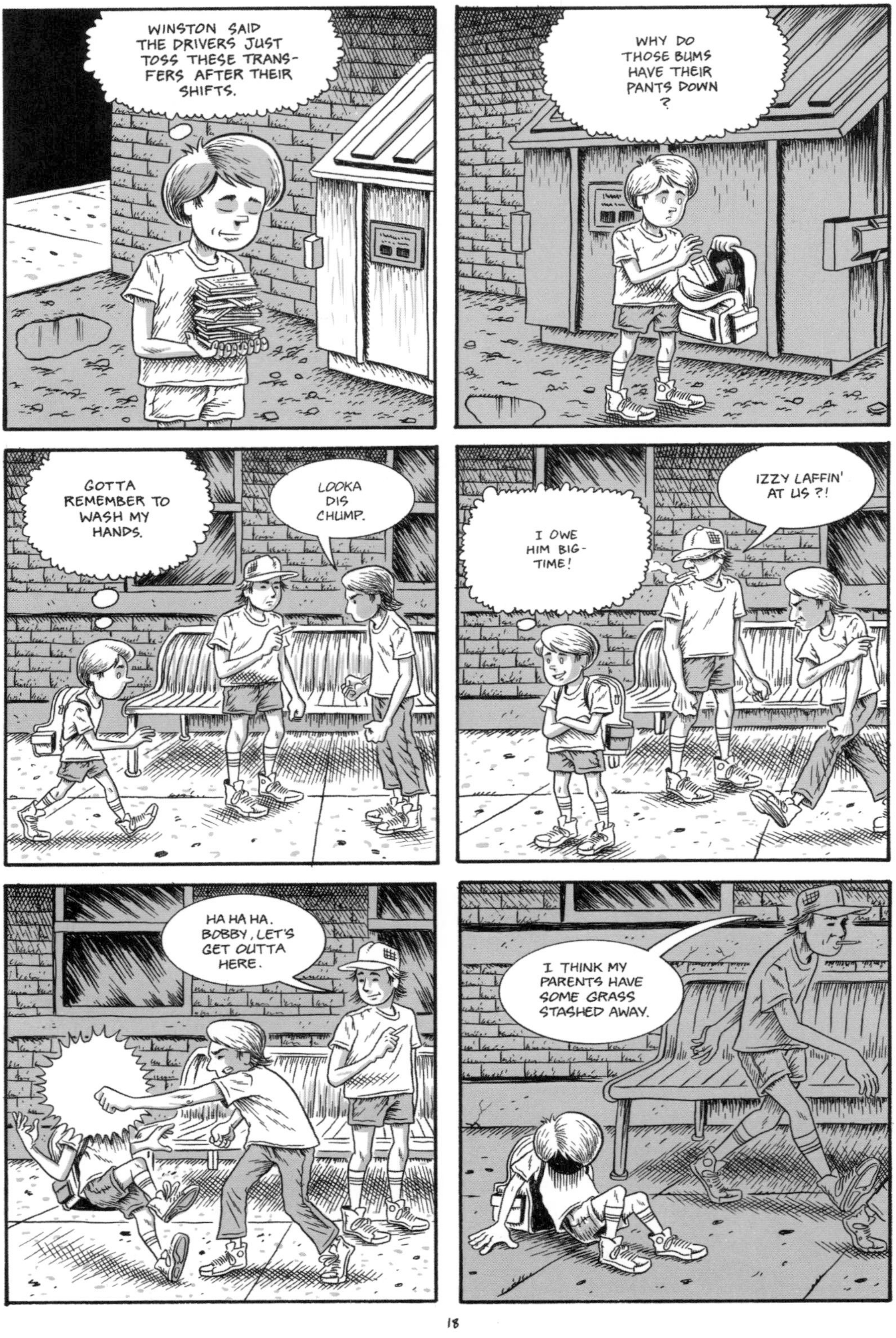
WINSTON SAID THE DRIVERS JUST TOSS THESE TRANSFERS AFTER THEIR SHIFTS.
WHY DO THOSE BUMS HAVE THEIR PANTS DOWN ?
GOTTA REMEMBER TO WASH MY HANDS.
LOOKA DIS CHUMP.
I OWE HIM BIG-TIME!
IZZY LAFFIN' AT US ?!
HA HA HA. BOBBY, LET'S GET OUTTA HERE.
I THINK MY PARENTS HAVE SOME GRASS STASHED AWAY.

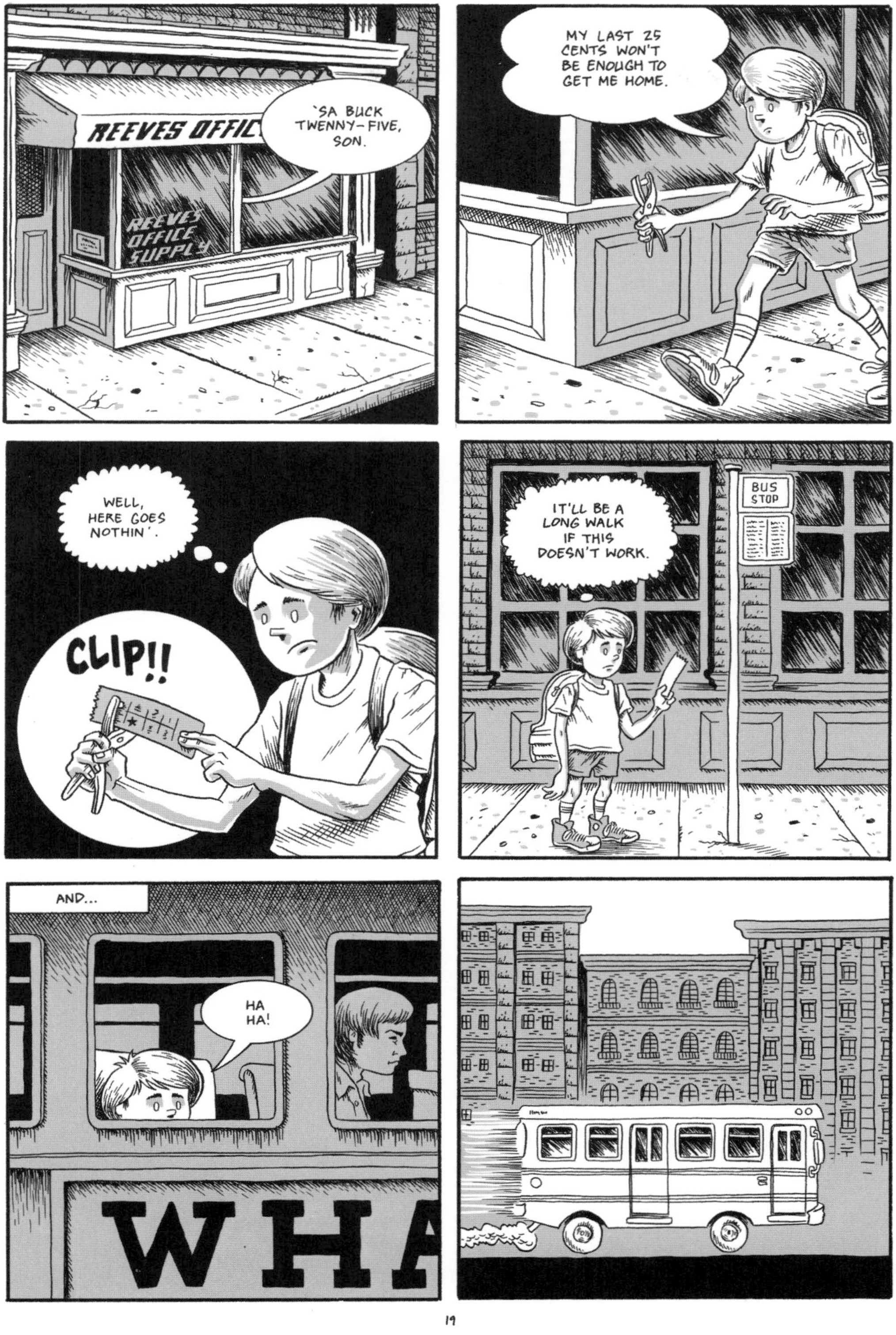
REEVES OFFIC
REEVES OFFICE SUPPLY
`SA BUCK TWENNY-FIVE, SON.
MY LAST 25 CENTS WON'T BE ENOUGH TO GET ME HOME.
WELL, HERE GOES NOTHIN'.
CLIP!!
BUS STOP
IT'LL BE A LONG WALK IF THIS DOESN'T WORK.
AND...
HA HA!
WHA

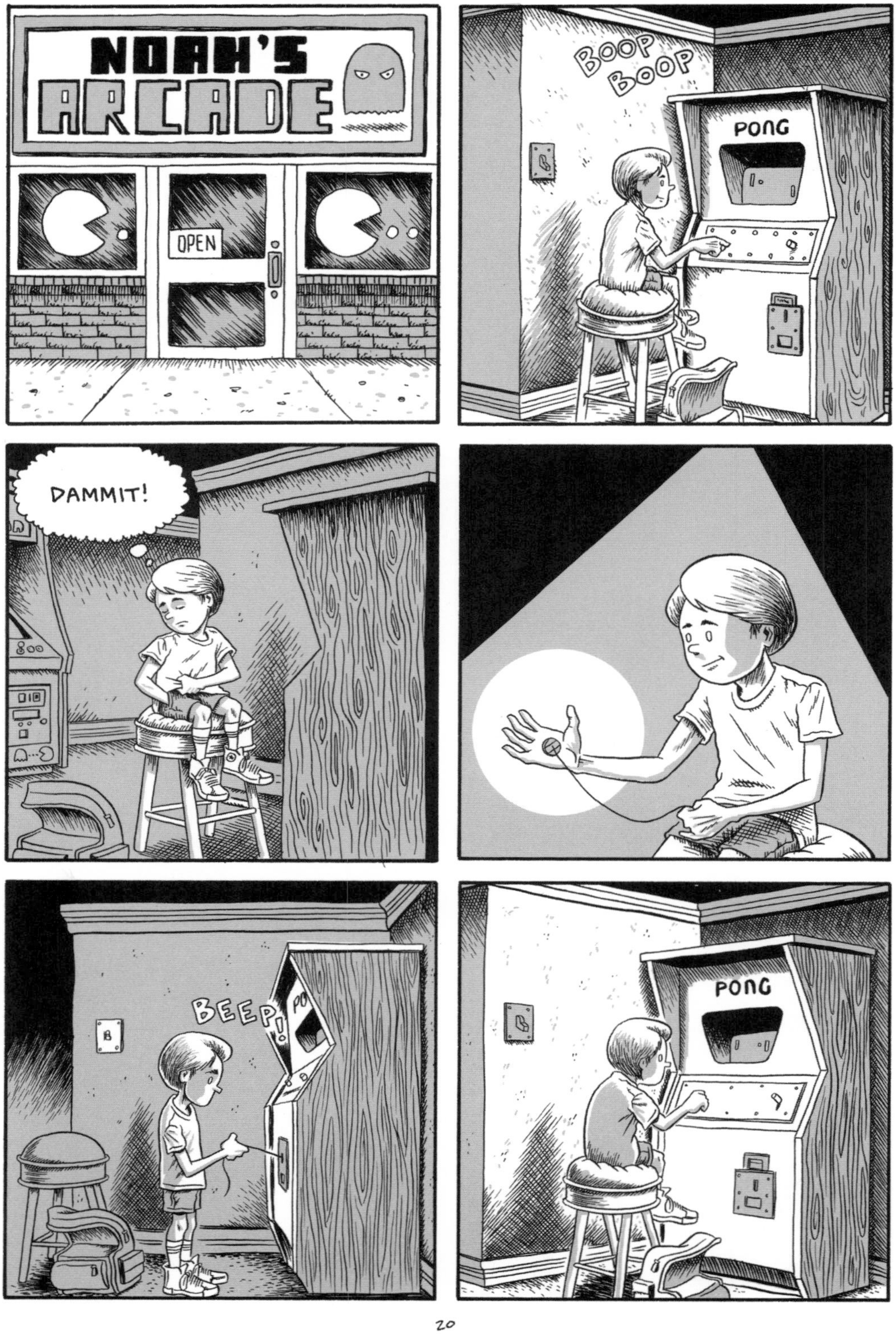
NOAH'S ARCADE
OPEN
BOOP BOOP
PONG
DAMMIT!
BEEP!
PONG

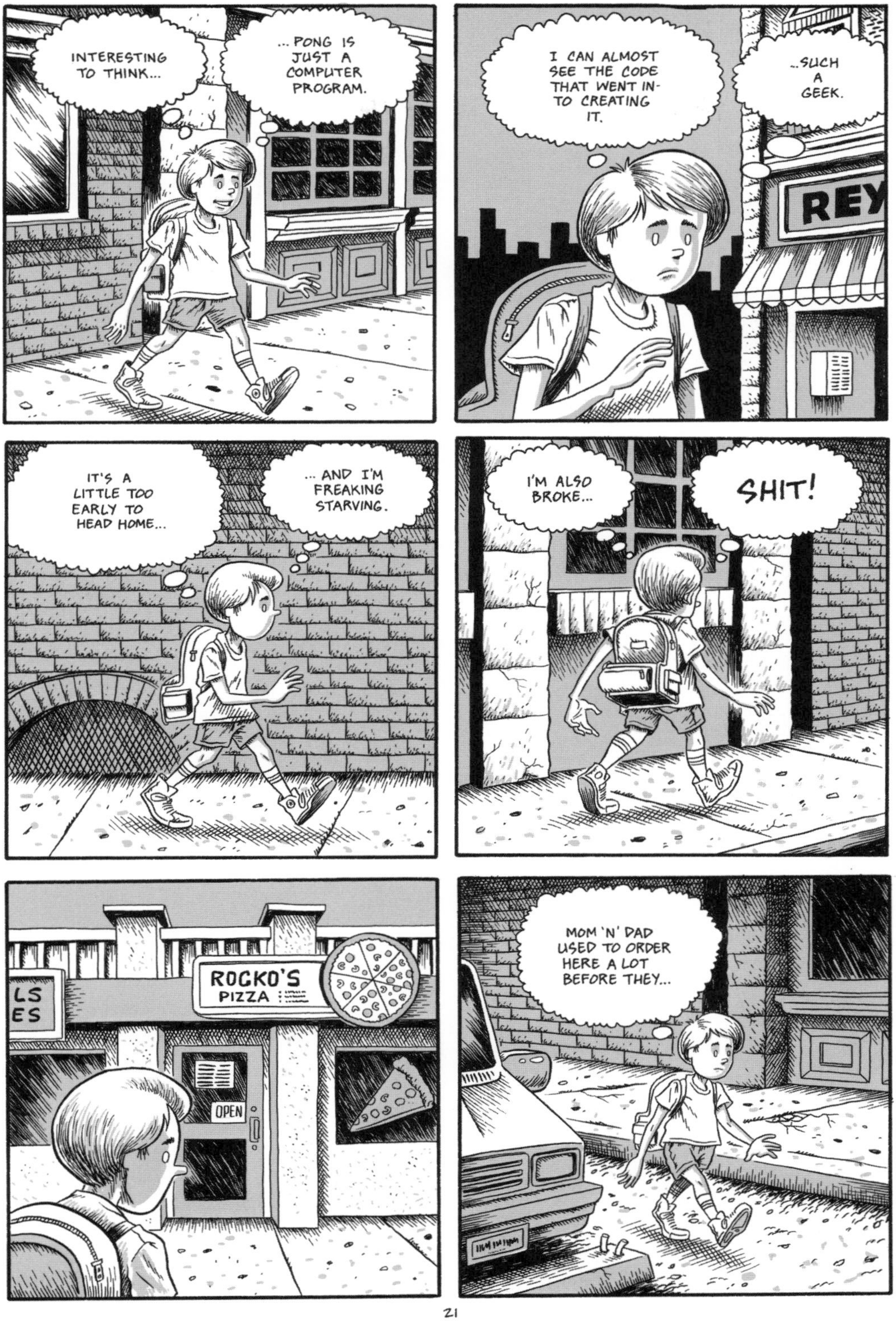
INTERESTING TO THINK...
...PONG IS JUST A COMPUTER PROGRAM.
I CAN ALMOST SEE THE CODE THAT WENT INTO CREATING IT.
..SUCH A GEEK.
REY
IT'S A LITTLE TOO EARLY TO HEAD HOME...
...AND I'M FREAKING STARVING.
I'M ALSO BROKE...
SHIT!
ROCKO'S PIZZA
OPEN
MOM 'N' DAD USED TO ORDER HERE A LOT BEFORE THEY...

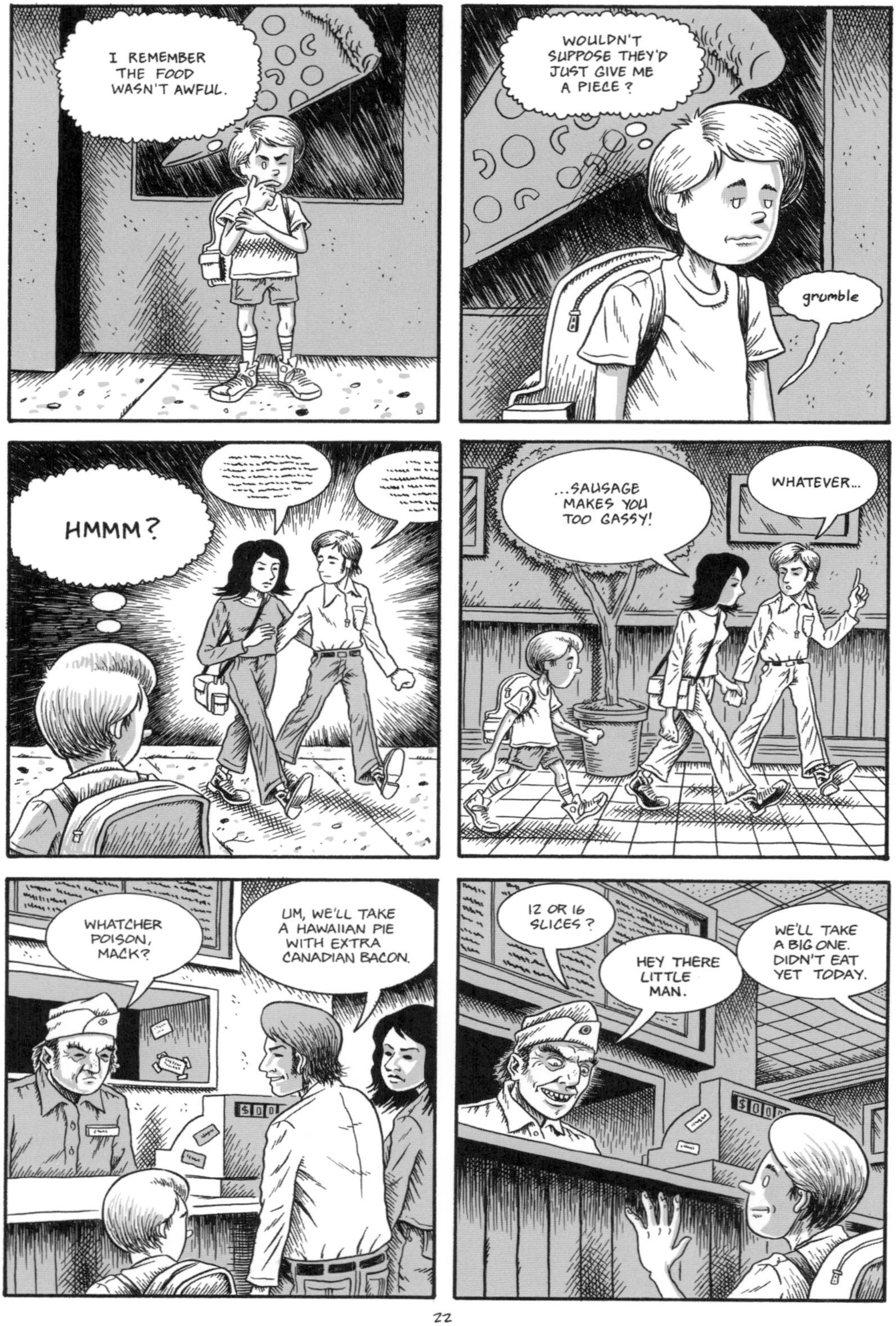
I REMEMBER THE FOOD WASN'T AWFUL.
WOULDN'T SUPPOSE THEY'D JUST GIVE ME A PIECE?
grumble
HMMM?
...SAUSAGE MAKES YOU TOO GASSY!
WHATEVER...
WHATCHER POISON, MACK?
UM, WE'LL TAKE A HAWAIIAN PIE WITH EXTRA CANADIAN BACON.
12 OR 16 SLICES?
HEY THERE LITTLE MAN.
WE'LL TAKE A BIG ONE. DIDN'T EAT YET TODAY.

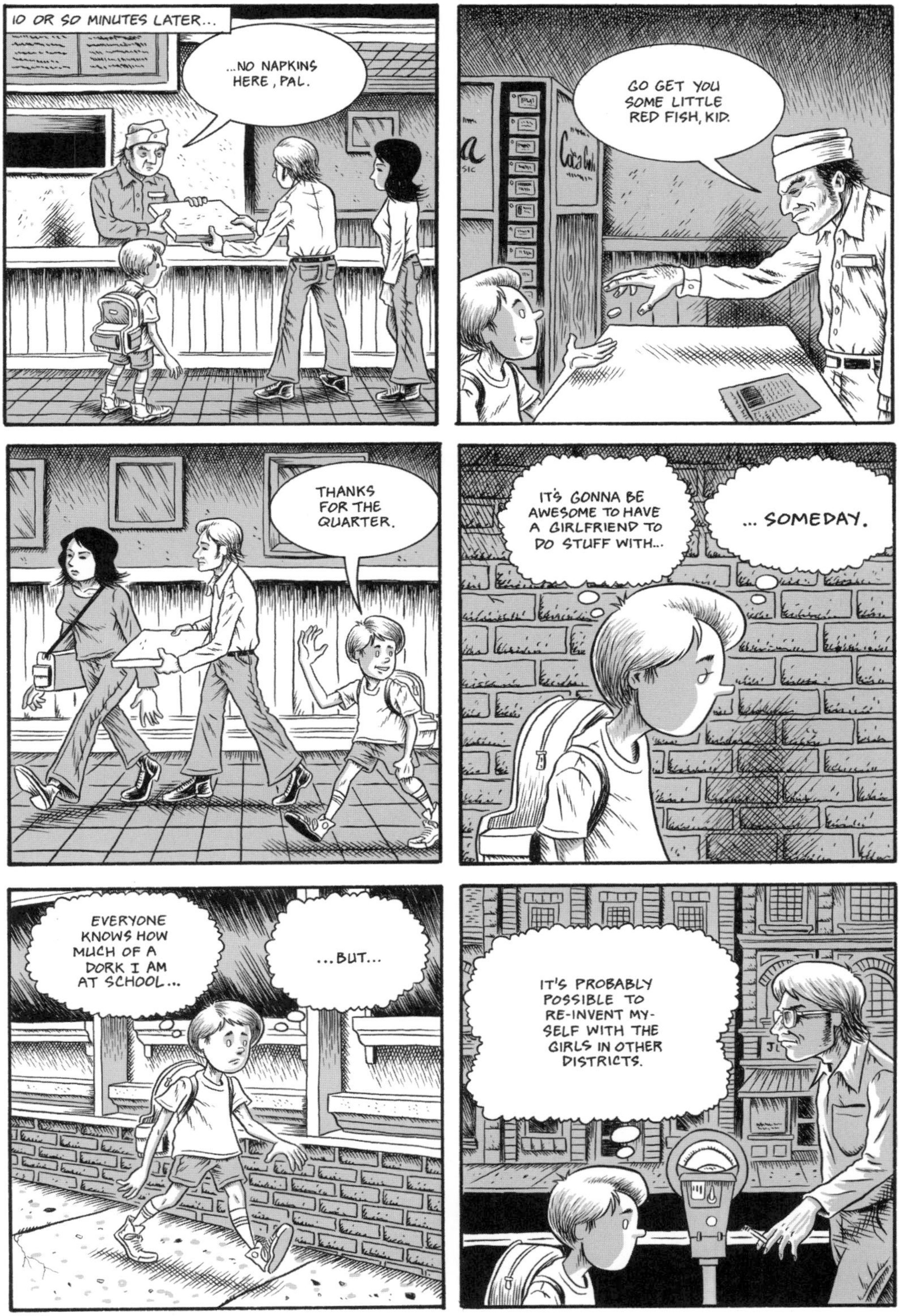
10 OR SO MINUTES LATER...
...NO NAPKINS HERE, PAL.
GO GET YOU SOME LITTLE RED FISH, KID.
THANKS FOR THE QUARTER.
IT'S GONNA BE AWESOME TO HAVE A GIRLFRIEND TO DO STUFF WITH...
... SOMEDAY.
EVERYONE KNOWS HOW MUCH OF A DORK I AM AT SCHOOL...
...BUT...
IT'S PROBABLY POSSIBLE TO RE-INVENT MY-SELF WITH THE GIRLS IN OTHER DISTRICTS.

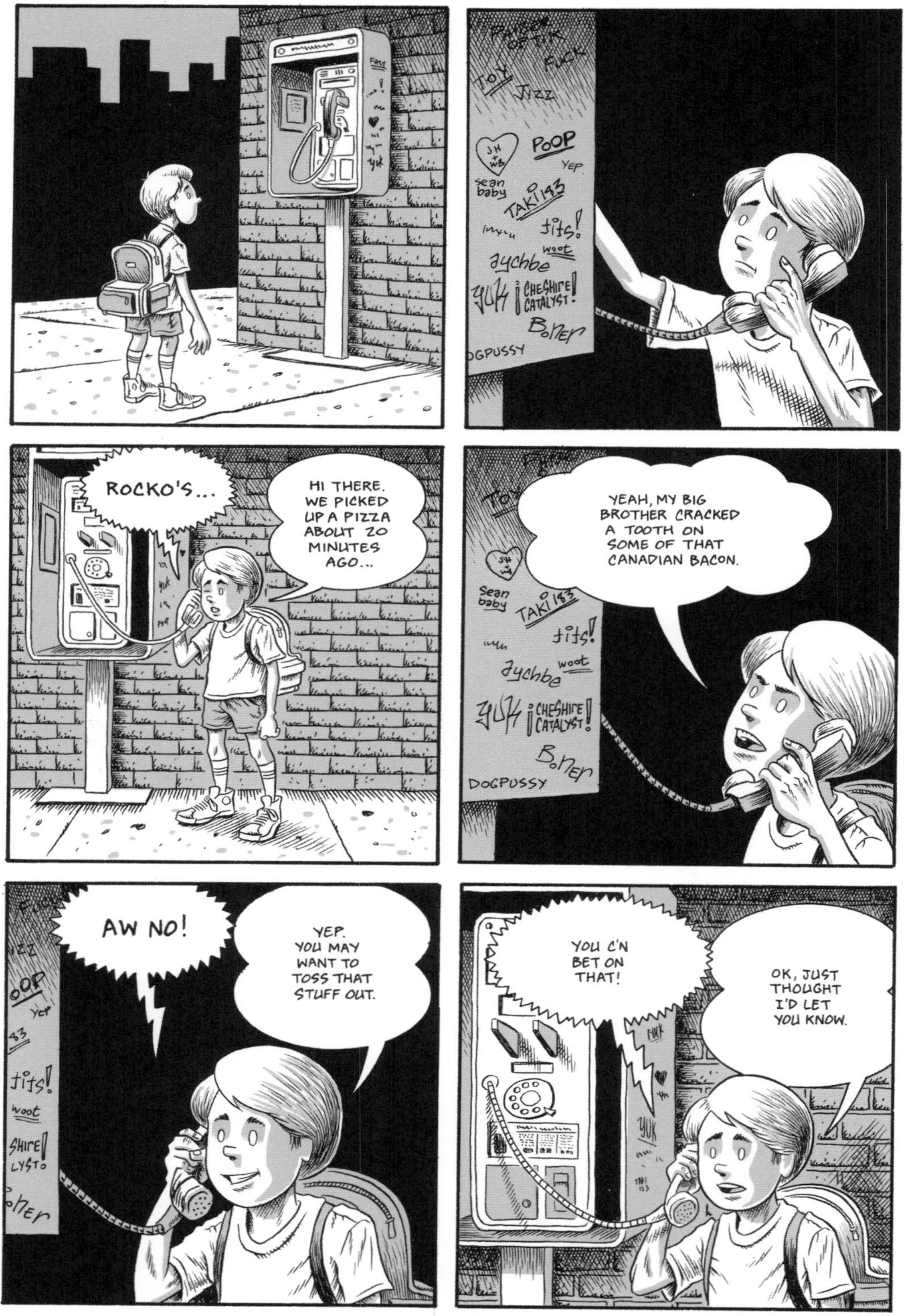
TOY
FUCK
JIZZ
POOP
YEP
sean baby
TAKI 143
tits!
woot
aychbe
YUK
¡CHESHIRE CATALYST!
BONER
DOGPUSSY
ROCKO'S...
HI THERE. WE PICKED UP A PIZZA ABOUT 20 MINUTES AGO...
YEAH, MY BIG BROTHER CRACKED A TOOTH ON SOME OF THAT CANADIAN BACON.
AW NO!
YEP. YOU MAY WANT TO TOSS THAT STUFF OUT.
YOU C'N BET ON THAT!
OK, JUST THOUGHT I'D LET YOU KNOW.

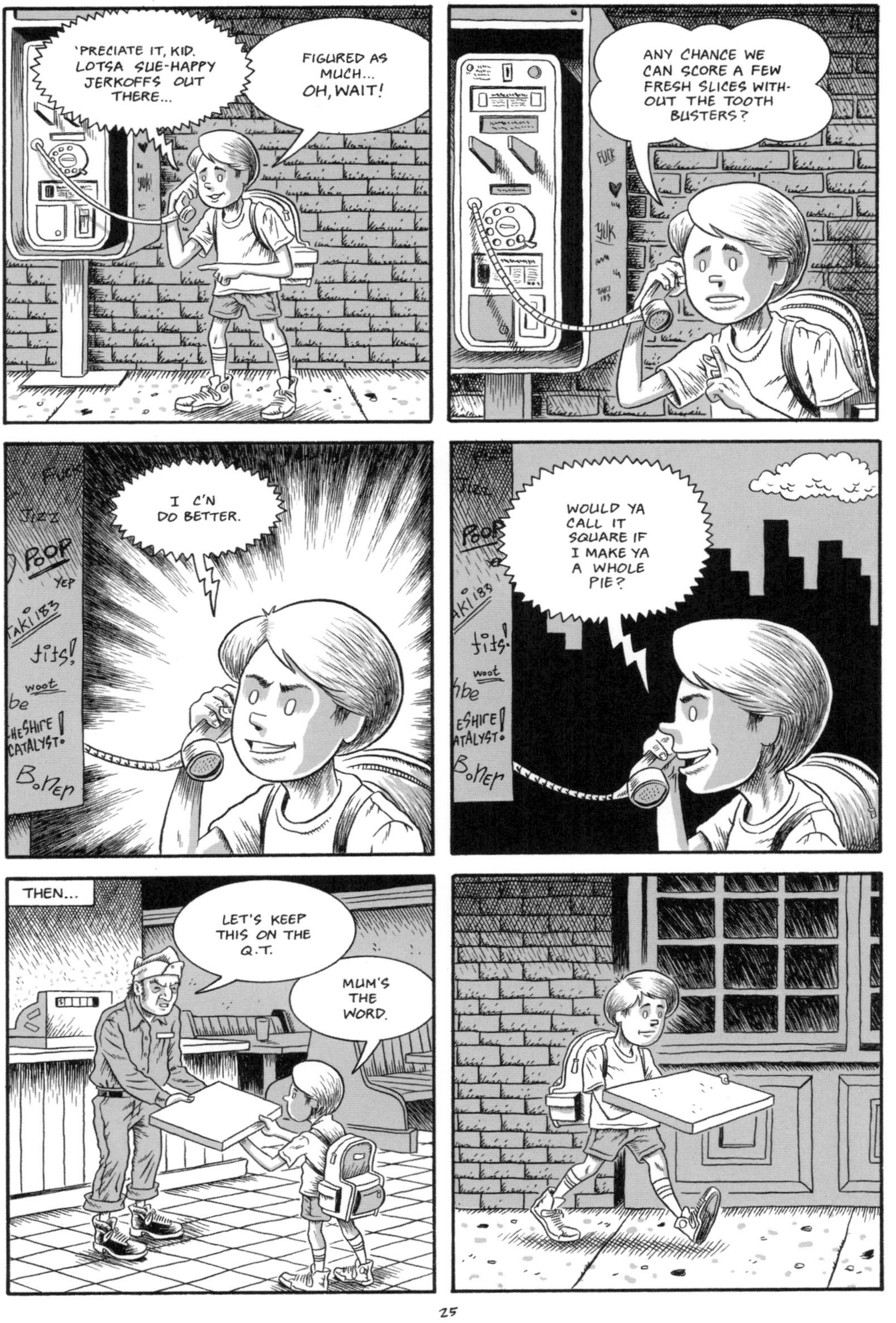

'PRECIATE IT, KID. LOTSA SUE-HAPPY JERKOFFS OUT THERE...
FIGURED AS MUCH... OH, WAIT!
YUK!
ANY CHANCE WE CAN SCORE A FEW FRESH SLICES WITHOUT THE TOOTH BUSTERS?
FUCK
YUK
TAKI 183
I C'N DO BETTER.
Jizz
POOP
YEP
TAKI 183
tits!
woot
CHESHIRE CATALYST!
Boner
WOULD YA CALL IT SQUARE IF I MAKE YA A WHOLE PIE?
THEN...
LET'S KEEP THIS ON THE Q.T.
MUM'S THE WORD.

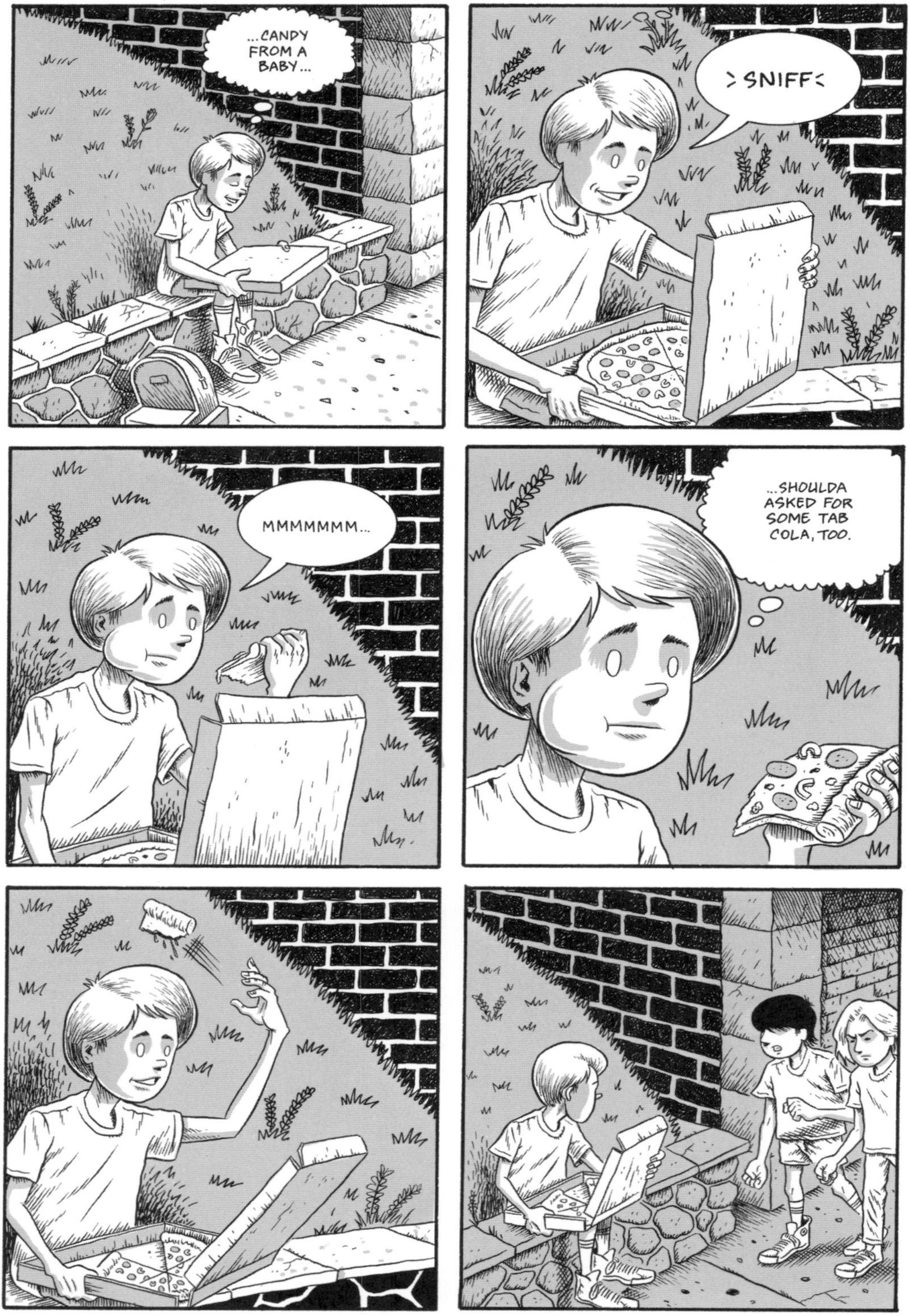
...CANDY FROM A BABY...
>SNIFF<
MMMMMMM...
...SHOULDA ASKED FOR SOME TAB COLA, TOO.

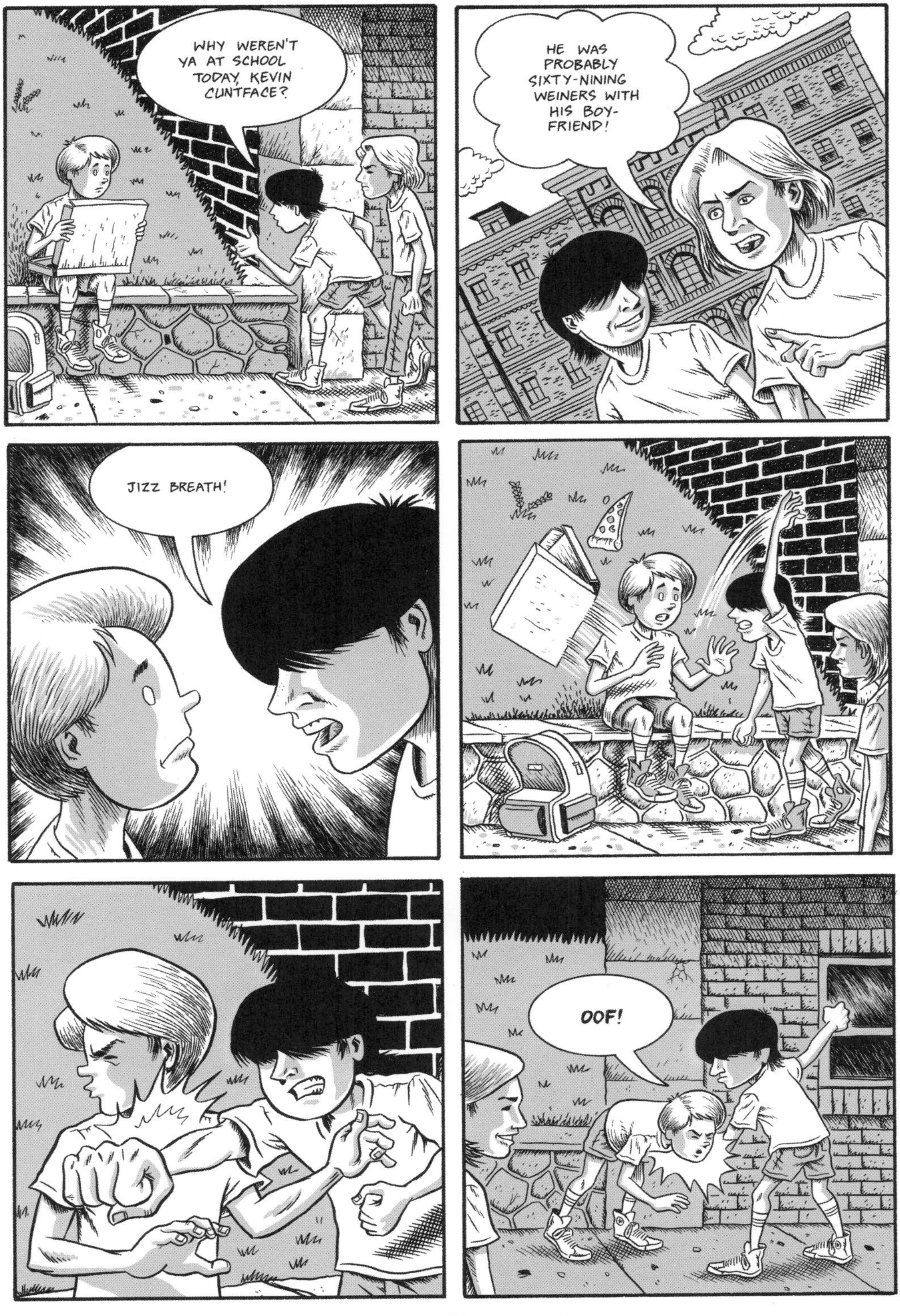
WHY WEREN'T YA AT SCHOOL TODAY, KEVIN CUNTFACE?
HE WAS PROBABLY SIXTY-NINING WEINERS WITH HIS BOY-FRIEND!
JIZZ BREATH!
OOF!

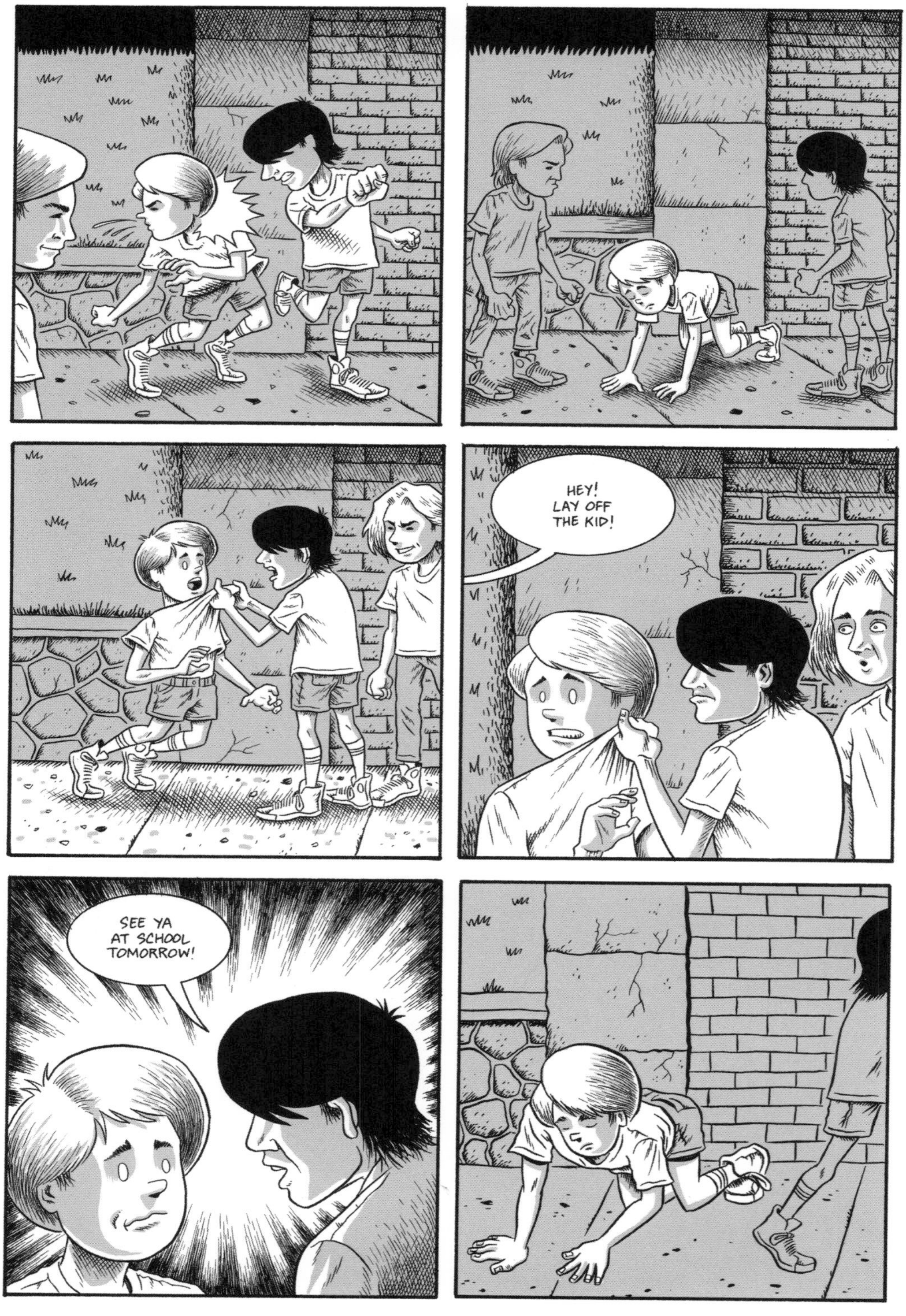
HEY! LAY OFF THE KID!
SEE YA AT SCHOOL TOMORROW!

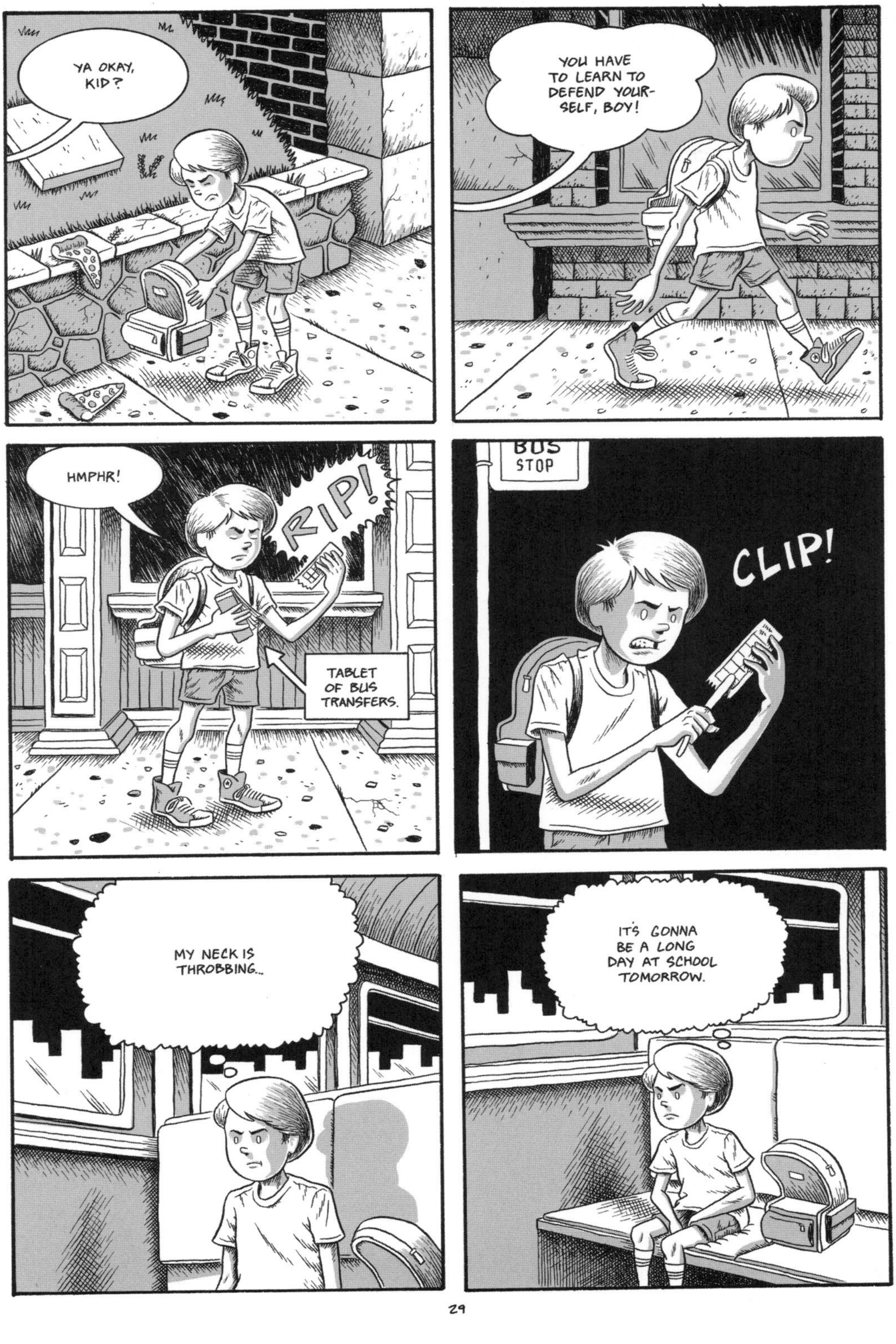
YA OKAY, KID?
YOU HAVE TO LEARN TO DEFEND YOUR-SELF, BOY!
HMPHR!
RIP!
TABLET OF BUS TRANSFERS.
BUS STOP
CLIP!
MY NECK IS THROBBING...
IT'S GONNA BE A LONG DAY AT SCHOOL TOMORROW.

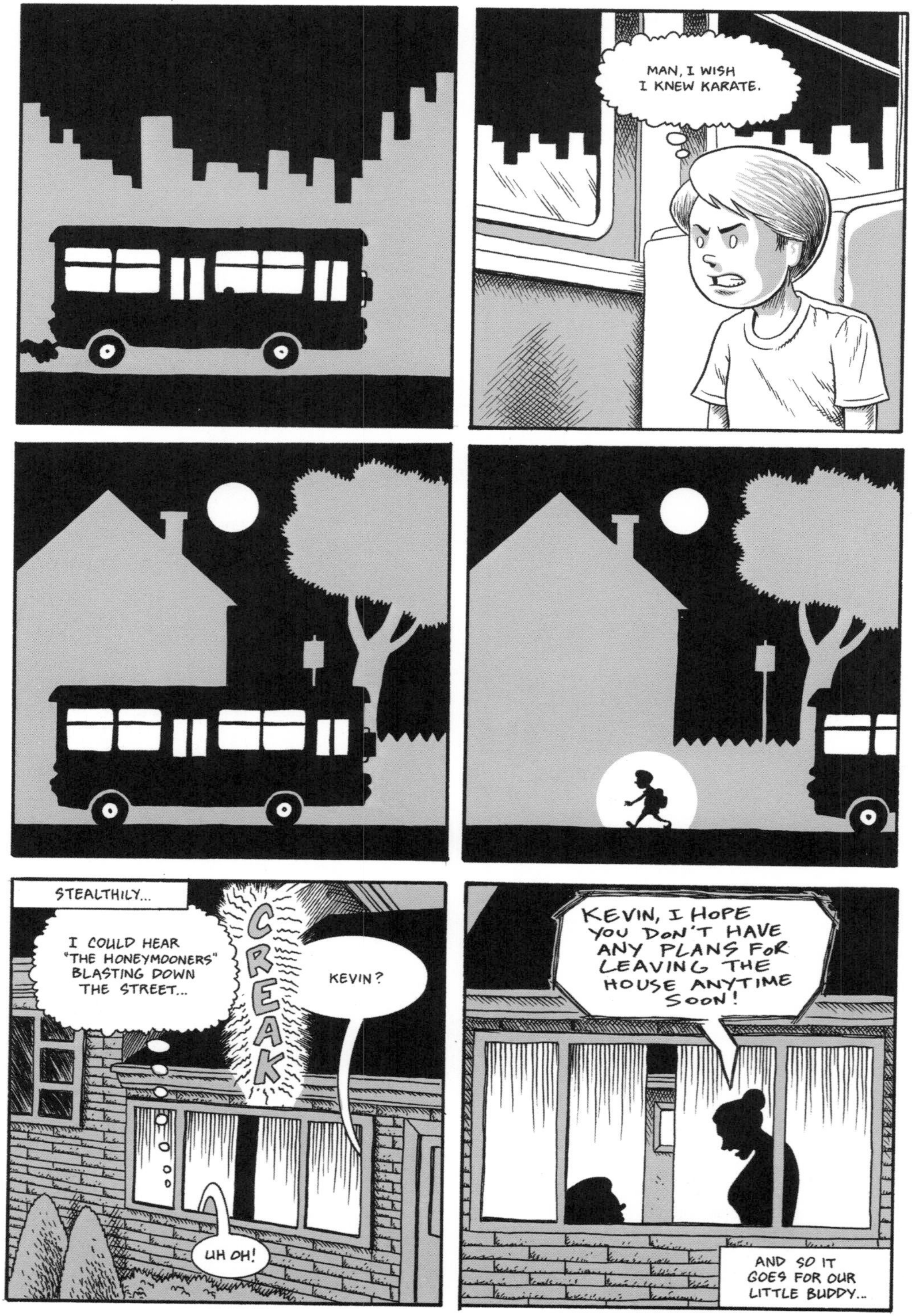
MAN, I WISH I KNEW KARATE.
STEALTHILY...
I COULD HEAR "THE HONEYMOONERS" BLASTING DOWN THE STREET...
CREAK
KEVIN?
UH OH!
KEVIN, I HOPE YOU DON'T HAVE ANY PLANS FOR LEAVING THE HOUSE ANYTIME SOON!
AND SO IT GOES FOR OUR LITTLE BUDDY...

KEYS TO THE KINGDOM

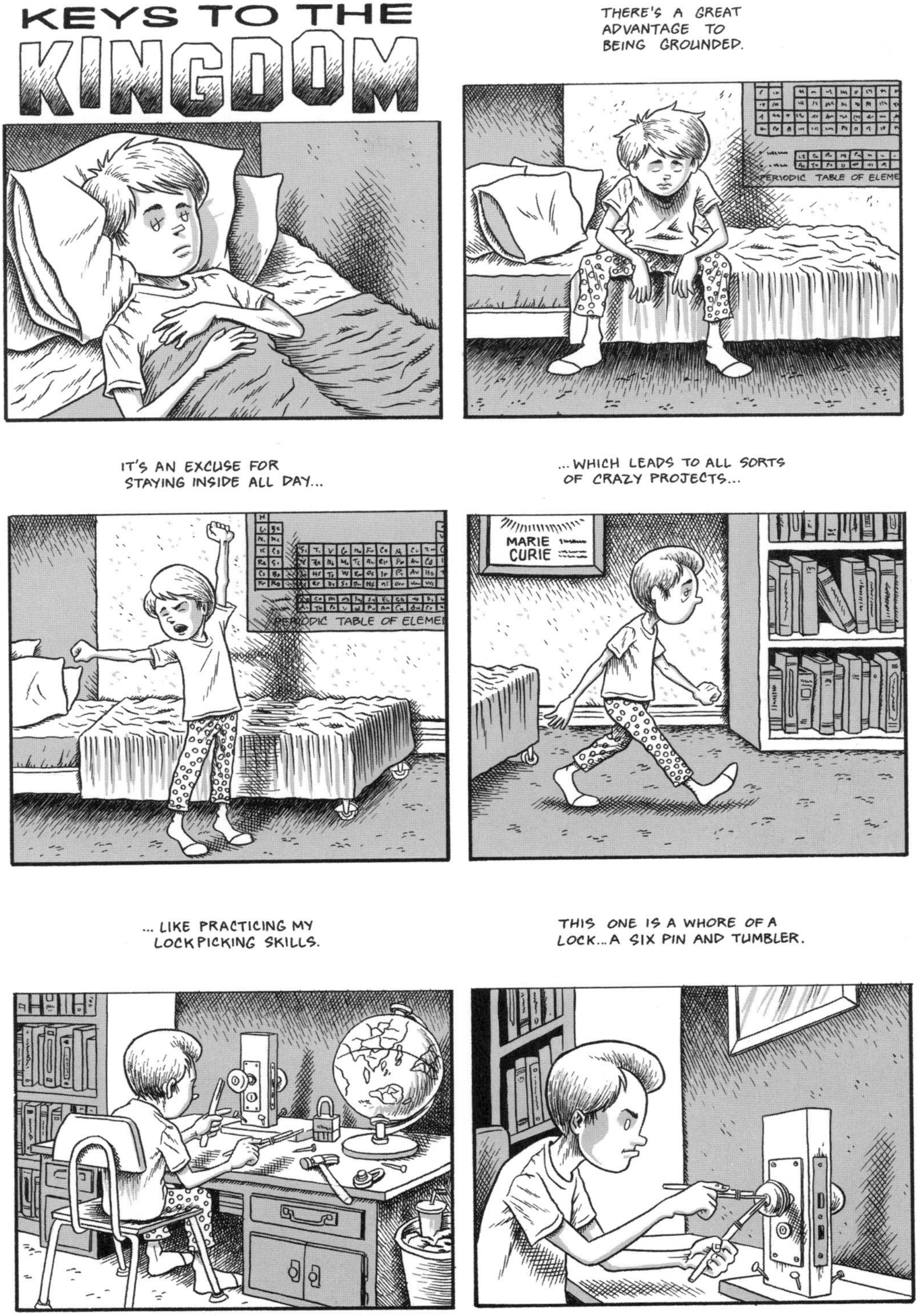
THERE'S A GREAT ADVANTAGE TO BEING GROUNDED.
PERIODIC TABLE OF ELEME
IT'S AN EXCUSE FOR STAYING INSIDE ALL DAY...
PERIODIC TABLE OF ELEME
...WHICH LEADS TO ALL SORTS OF CRAZY PROJECTS...
MARIE CURIE
... LIKE PRACTICING MY LOCKPICKING SKILLS.
THIS ONE IS A WHORE OF A LOCK...A SIX PIN AND TUMBLER.

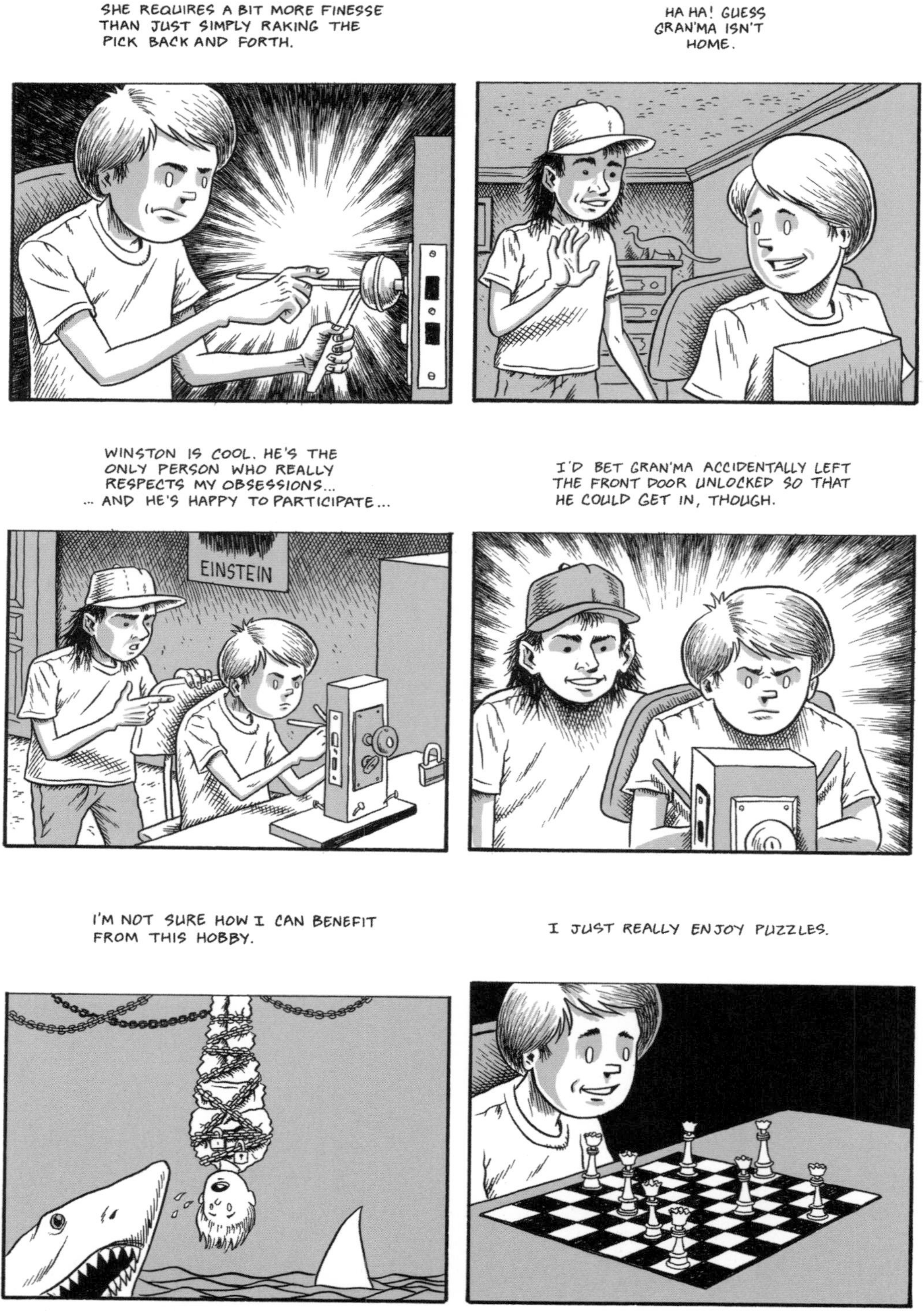
SHE REQUIRES A BIT MORE FINESSE THAN JUST SIMPLY RAKING THE PICK BACK AND FORTH.
HA HA! GUESS GRAN'MA ISN'T HOME.
WINSTON IS COOL. HE'S THE ONLY PERSON WHO REALLY RESPECTS MY OBSESSIONS...
... AND HE'S HAPPY TO PARTICIPATE...
EINSTEIN
I'D BET GRAN'MA ACCIDENTALLY LEFT THE FRONT DOOR UNLOCKED SO THAT HE COULD GET IN, THOUGH.
I'M NOT SURE HOW I CAN BENEFIT FROM THIS HOBBY.
I JUST REALLY ENJOY PUZZLES.

THIS LOCK REQUIRES A LEVEL OF CONCENTRATION THAT I CAN'T ACHIEVE WITH COMPANY.

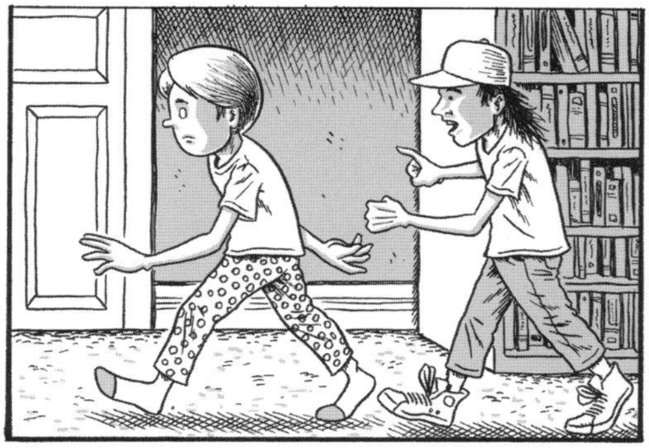

THE CONVERSATION SHIFTS OVER TO A PUZZLE THAT WE BOTH ENJOY... THE PHONE SYSTEM.

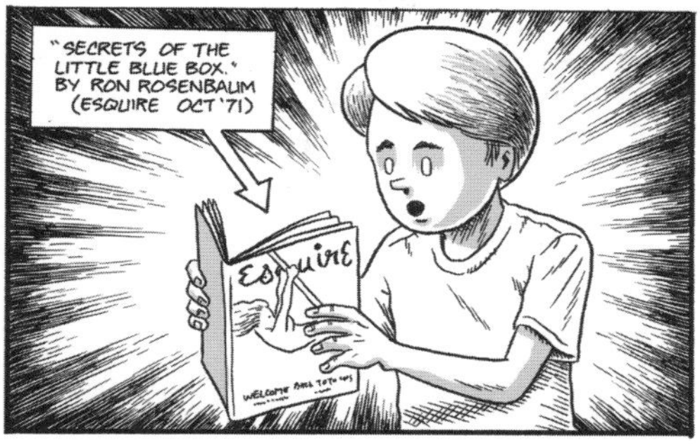
"SECRETS OF THE LITTLE BLUE BOX." BY RON ROSENBAUM (ESQUIRE OCT '71)
Esquire

WINSTON'S LACK OF KNOWLEDGE IS COMPENSATED FOR BY HIS ENTHUSIASM.

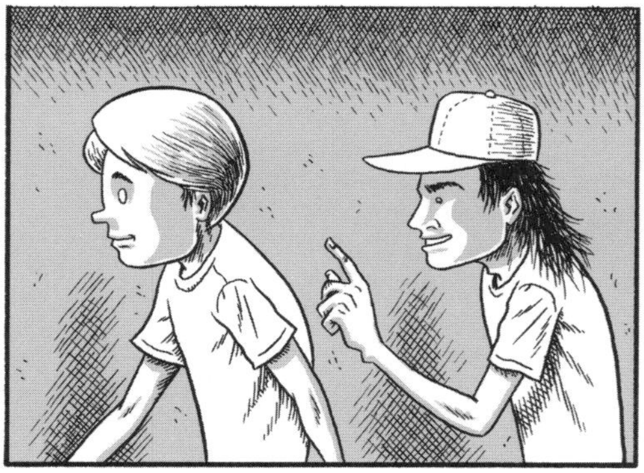

TURNS OUT A LITTLE WHILE AGO SOME PEOPLE FIGURED OUT HOW TO MAKE LONG DISTANCE PHONE CALLS FOR FREE.

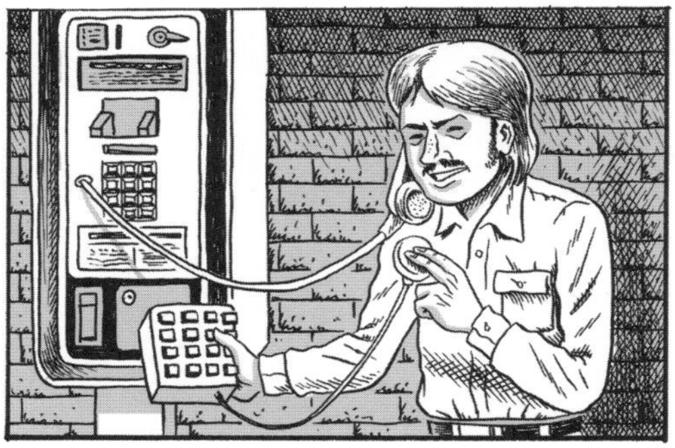

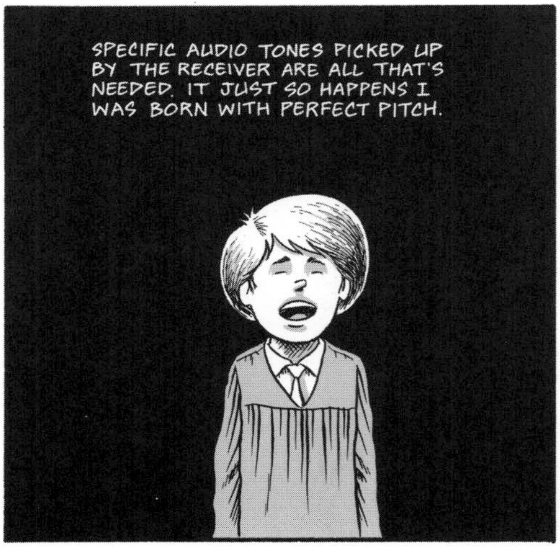
SPECIFIC AUDIO TONES PICKED UP BY THE RECEIVER ARE ALL THAT'S NEEDED. IT JUST SO HAPPENS I WAS BORN WITH PERFECT PITCH.

IT ISN'T HARD FOR ME TO MIMIC THE NECESSARY 2600HZ TONE BY WHISTLING INTO THE PHONE.

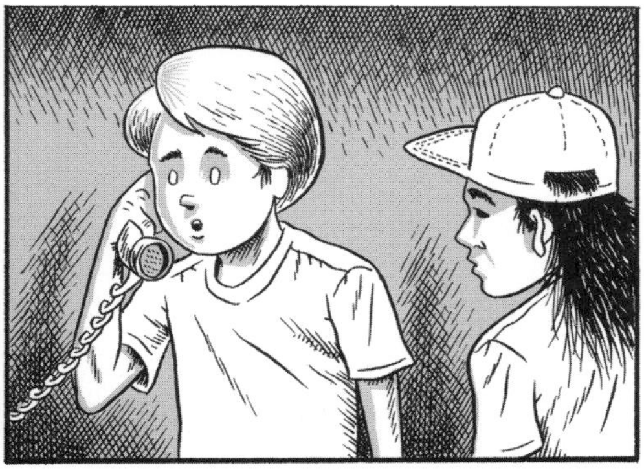

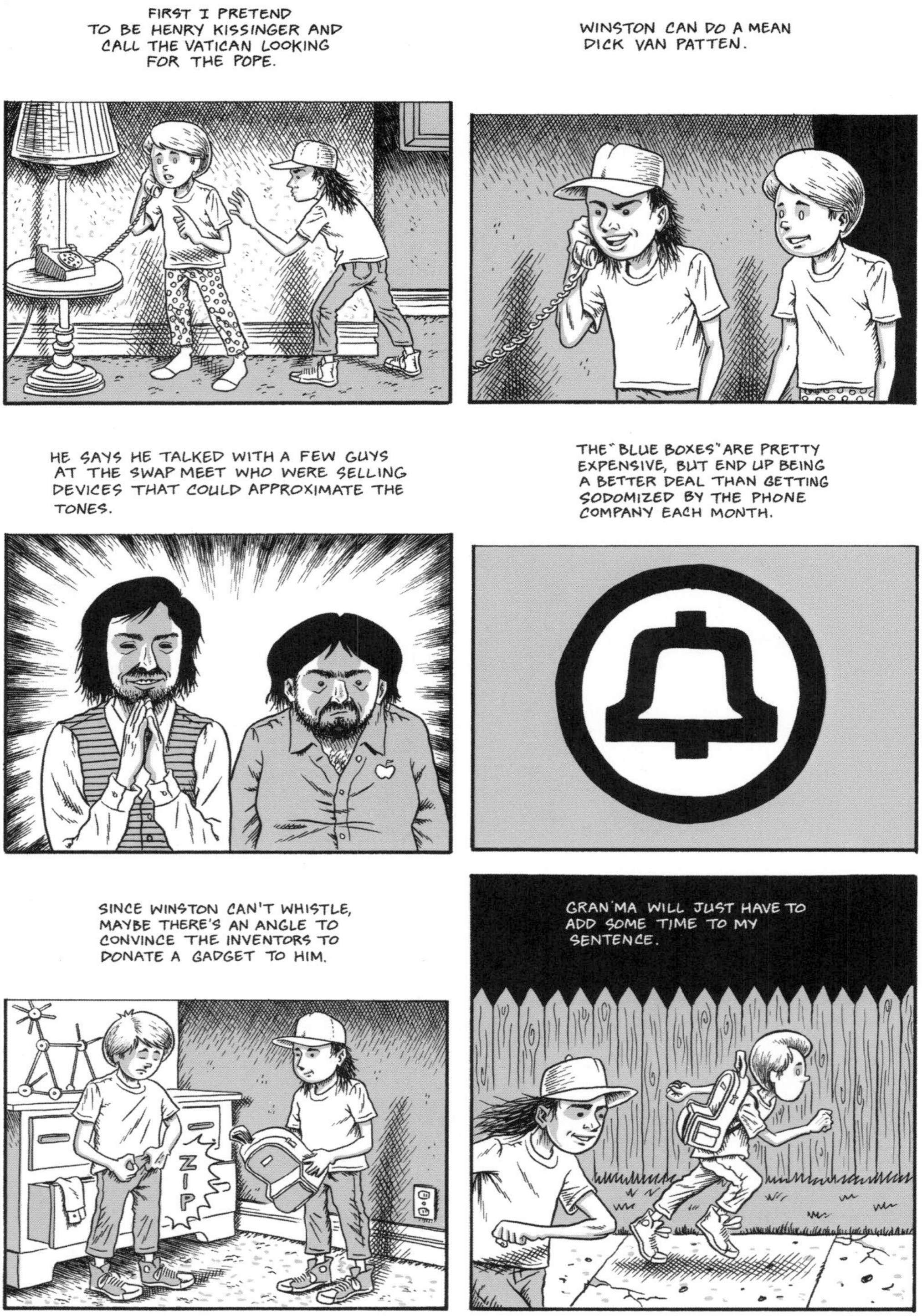
FIRST I PRETEND TO BE HENRY KISSINGER AND CALL THE VATICAN LOOKING FOR THE POPE.
WINSTON CAN DO A MEAN DICK VAN PATTEN.
HE SAYS HE TALKED WITH A FEW GUYS AT THE SWAP MEET WHO WERE SELLING DEVICES THAT COULD APPROXIMATE THE TONES.
THE "BLUE BOXES" ARE PRETTY EXPENSIVE, BUT END UP BEING A BETTER DEAL THAN GETTING SODOMIZED BY THE PHONE COMPANY EACH MONTH.
SINCE WINSTON CAN'T WHISTLE, MAYBE THERE'S AN ANGLE TO CONVINCE THE INVENTORS TO DONATE A GADGET TO HIM.
ZIP
GRAN'MA WILL JUST HAVE TO ADD SOME TIME TO MY SENTENCE.

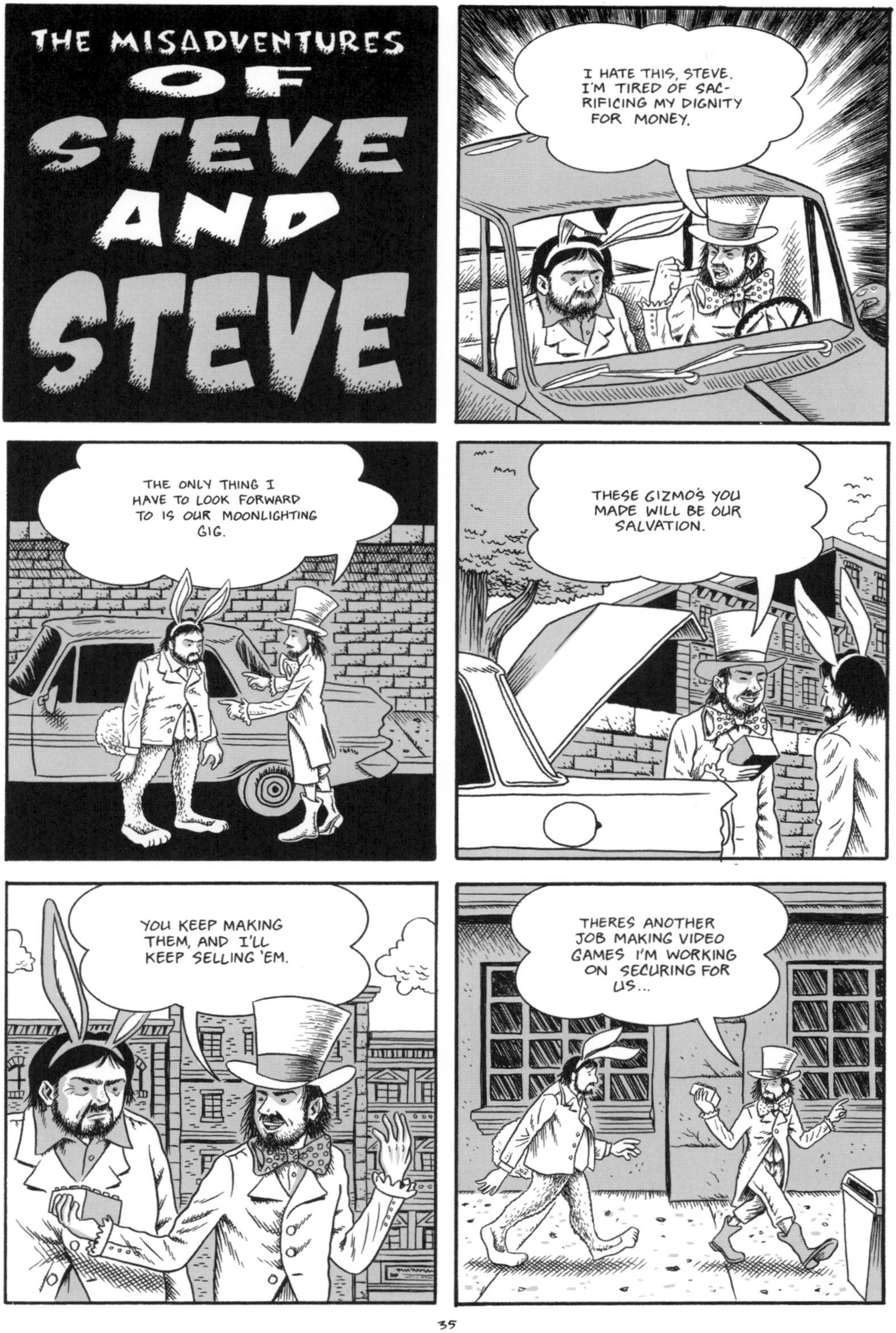
THE MISADVENTURES OF STEVE AND STEVE
I HATE THIS, STEVE. I'M TIRED OF SACRIFICING MY DIGNITY FOR MONEY.
THE ONLY THING I HAVE TO LOOK FORWARD TO IS OUR MOONLIGHTING GIG.
THESE GIZMO'S YOU MADE WILL BE OUR SALVATION.
YOU KEEP MAKING THEM, AND I'LL KEEP SELLING 'EM.
THERES ANOTHER JOB MAKING VIDEO GAMES I'M WORKING ON SECURING FOR US...

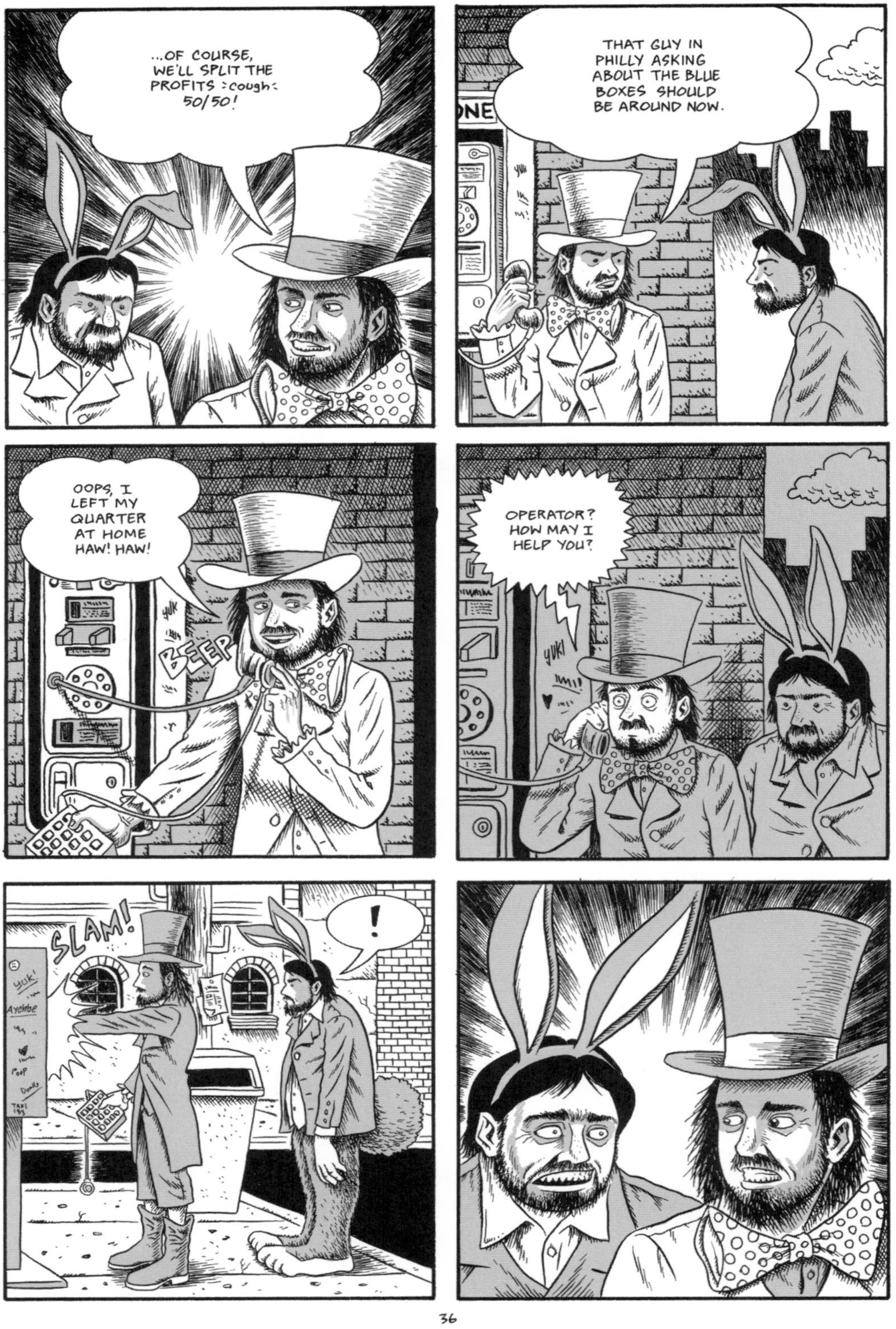
...OF COURSE, WE'LL SPLIT THE PROFITS :cough: 50/50!
THAT GUY IN PHILLY ASKING ABOUT THE BLUE BOXES SHOULD BE AROUND NOW.
OOPS, I LEFT MY QUARTER AT HOME HAW! HAW!
YUK
BEEP
OPERATOR? HOW MAY I HELP YOU?
YUK!
SLAM!
!
YUK!
Poop

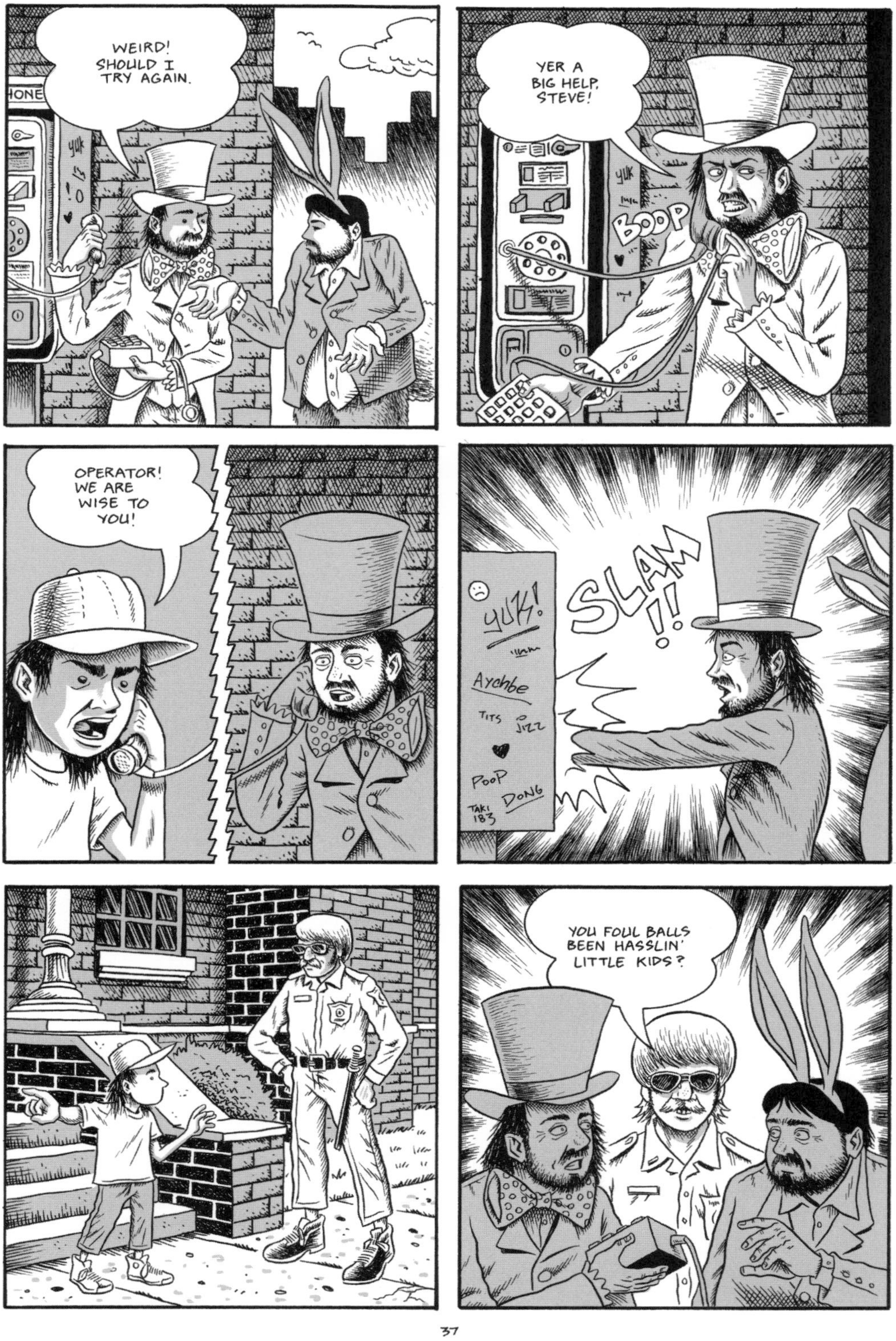
WEIRD! SHOULD I TRY AGAIN.
YUK
YER A BIG HELP, STEVE!
BOOP
YUK
OPERATOR! WE ARE WISE TO YOU!
SLAM!!
YUK!
Aychbe
TITS
JIZZ
POOP
DONG
TAKI 183
YOU FOUL BALLS BEEN HASSLIN' LITTLE KIDS?

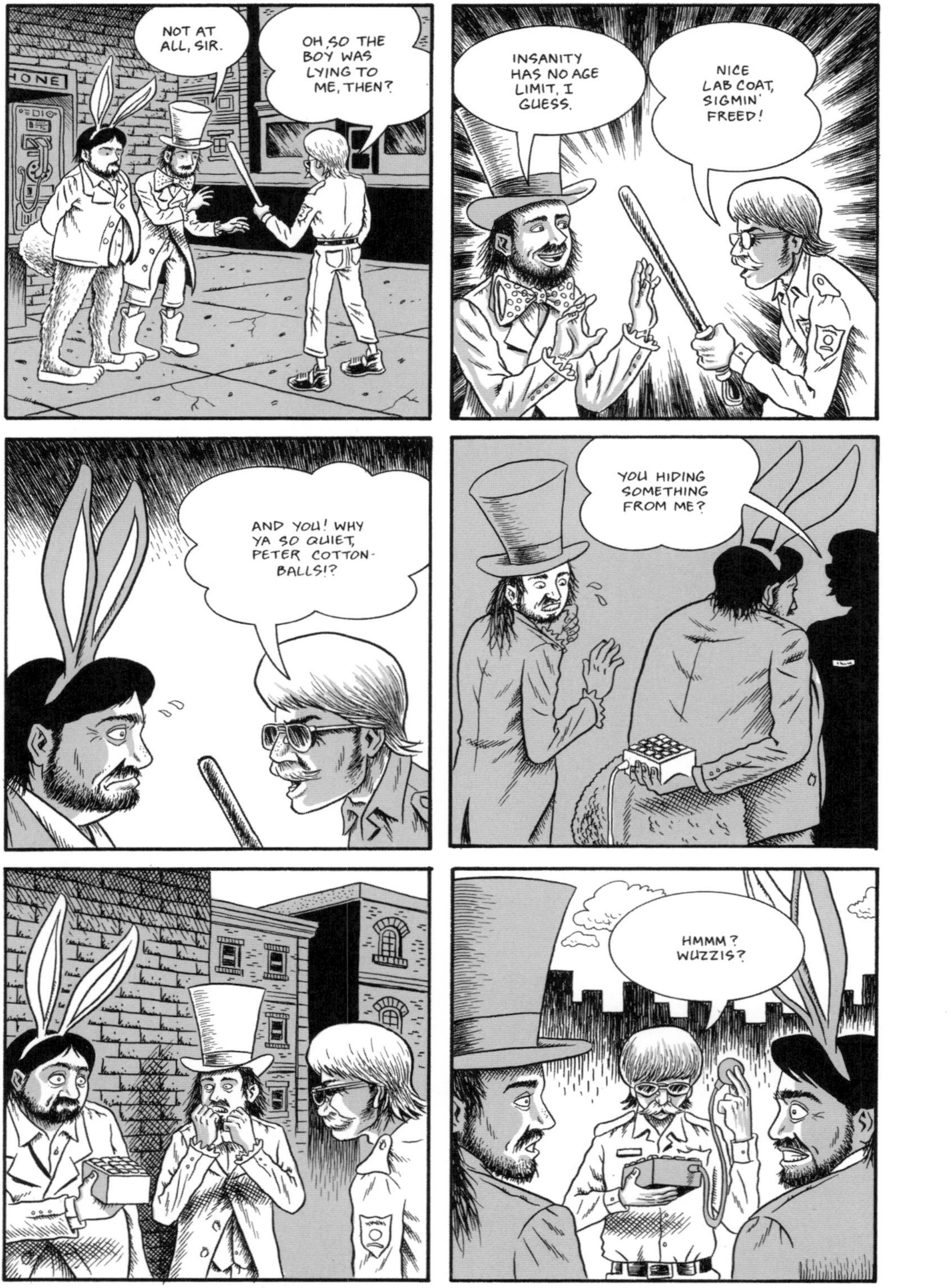
HONE
NOT AT ALL, SIR.
OH, SO THE BOY WAS LYING TO ME, THEN?
INSANITY HAS NO AGE LIMIT, I GUESS.
NICE LAB COAT, SIGMIN' FREED!
AND YOU! WHY YA SO QUIET, PETER COTTON-BALLS!?
YOU HIDING SOMETHING FROM ME?
HMMM? WUZZIS?

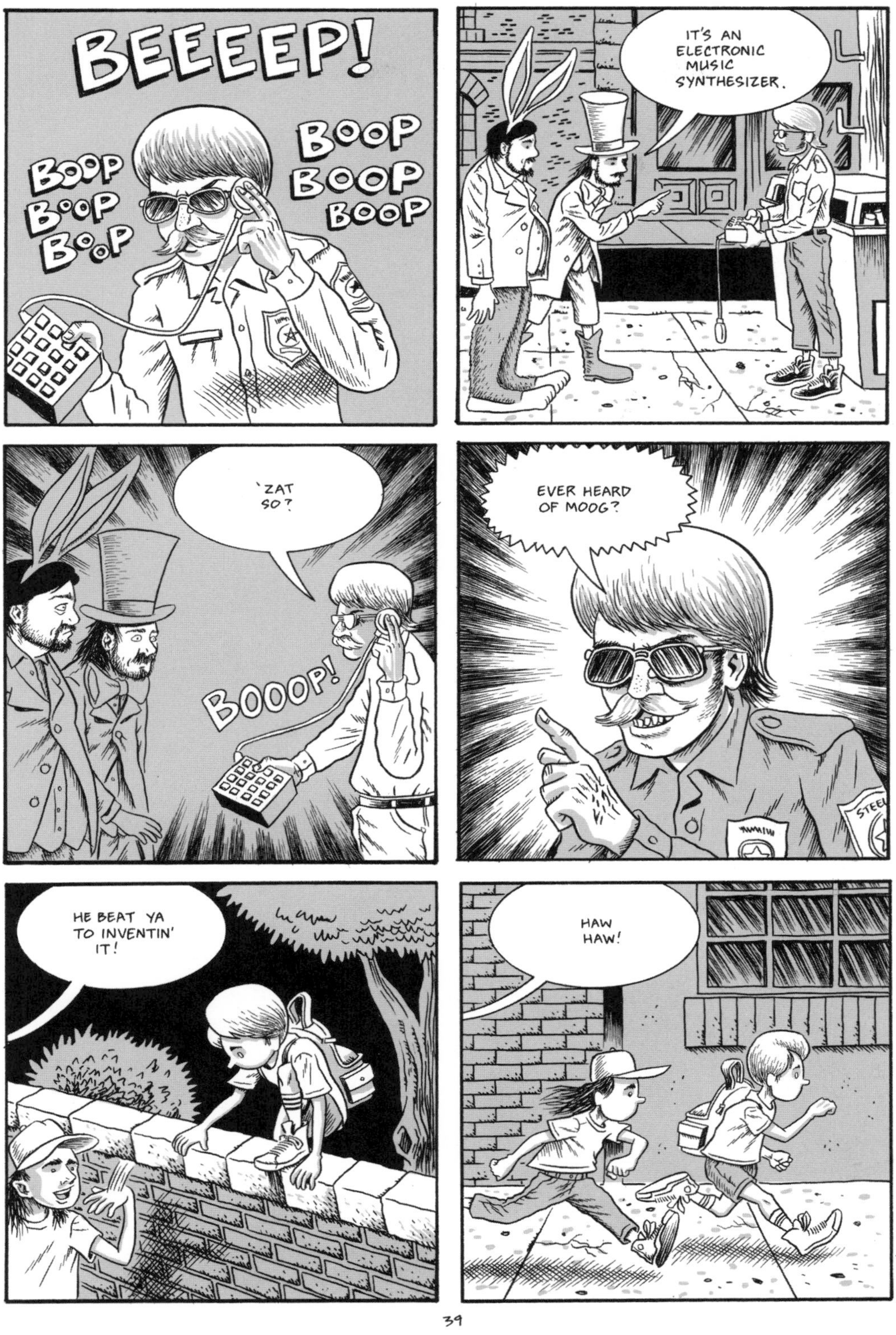
BEEEEP!
BOOP BOOP BOOP
BOOP BOOP BOOP
IT'S AN ELECTRONIC MUSIC SYNTHESIZER.
`ZAT SO?
BOOOP!
EVER HEARD OF MOOG?
HE BEAT YA TO INVENTIN' IT!
HAW HAW!

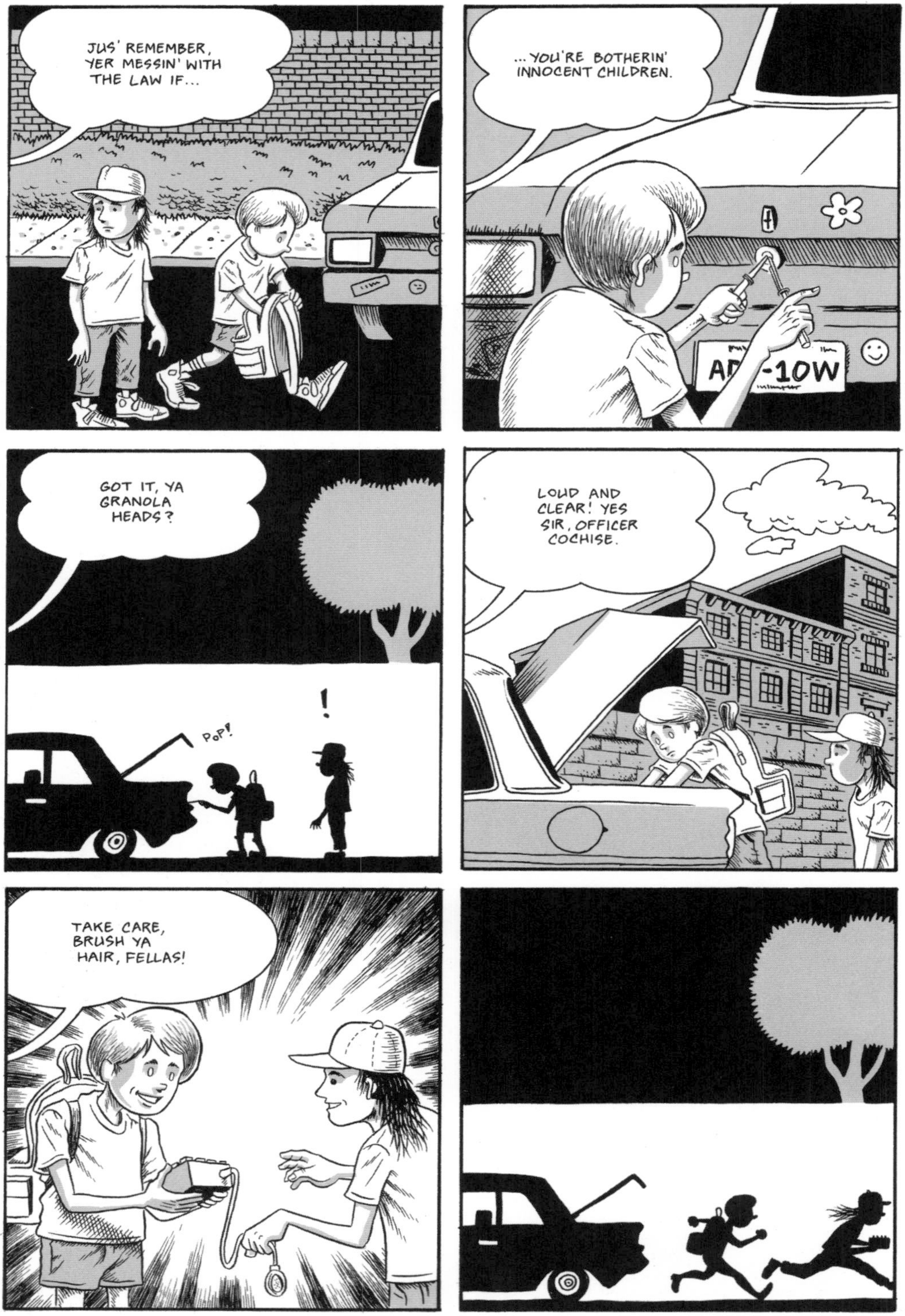
JUS' REMEMBER, YER MESSIN' WITH THE LAW IF...
...YOU'RE BOTHERIN' INNOCENT CHILDREN.
AD -10W
GOT IT, YA GRANOLA HEADS?
POP!
!
LOUD AND CLEAR! YES SIR, OFFICER COCHISE.
TAKE CARE, BRUSH YA HAIR, FELLAS!

CHAPTER 2

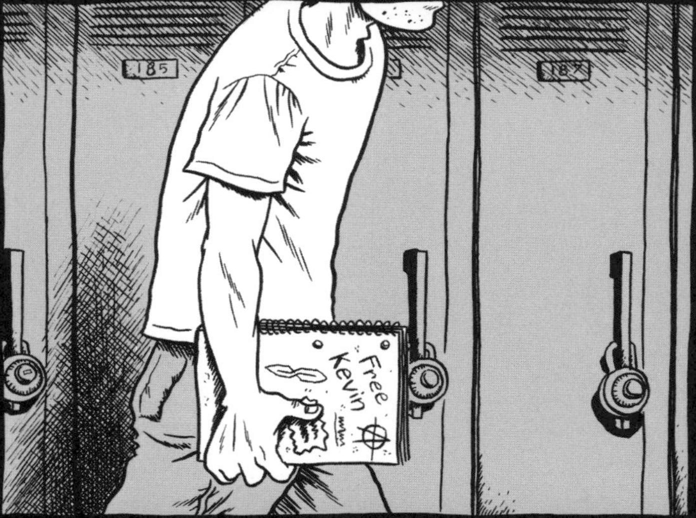
185
187
Free Kevin

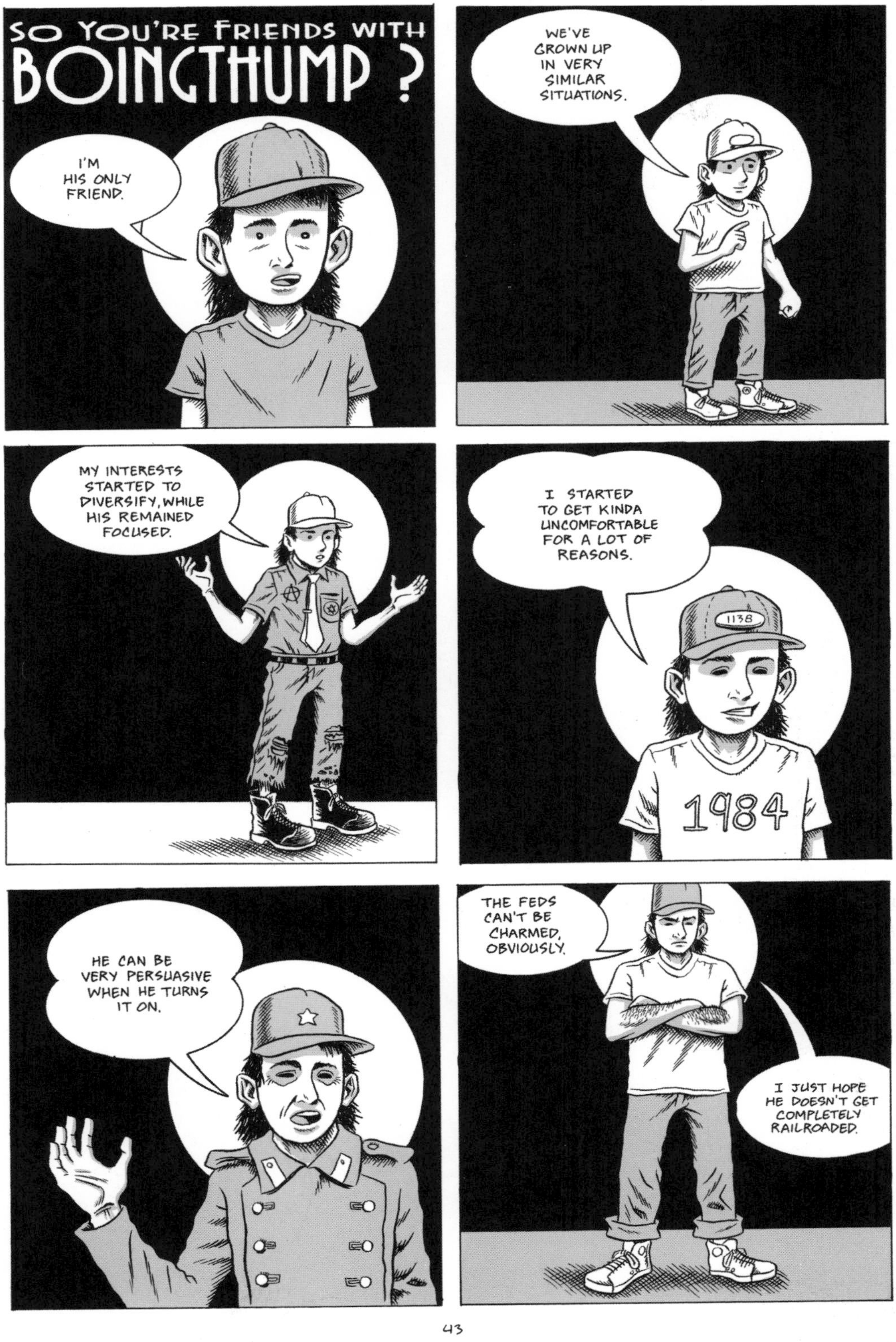
SO YOU'RE FRIENDS WITH BOINGTHUMP ?
I'M HIS ONLY FRIEND.
WE'VE GROWN UP IN VERY SIMILAR SITUATIONS.
MY INTERESTS STARTED TO DIVERSIFY, WHILE HIS REMAINED FOCUSED.
I STARTED TO GET KINDA UNCOMFORTABLE FOR A LOT OF REASONS.
1138
1984
HE CAN BE VERY PERSUASIVE WHEN HE TURNS IT ON.
THE FEDS CAN'T BE CHARMED, OBVIOUSLY.
I JUST HOPE HE DOESN'T GET COMPLETELY RAILROADED.

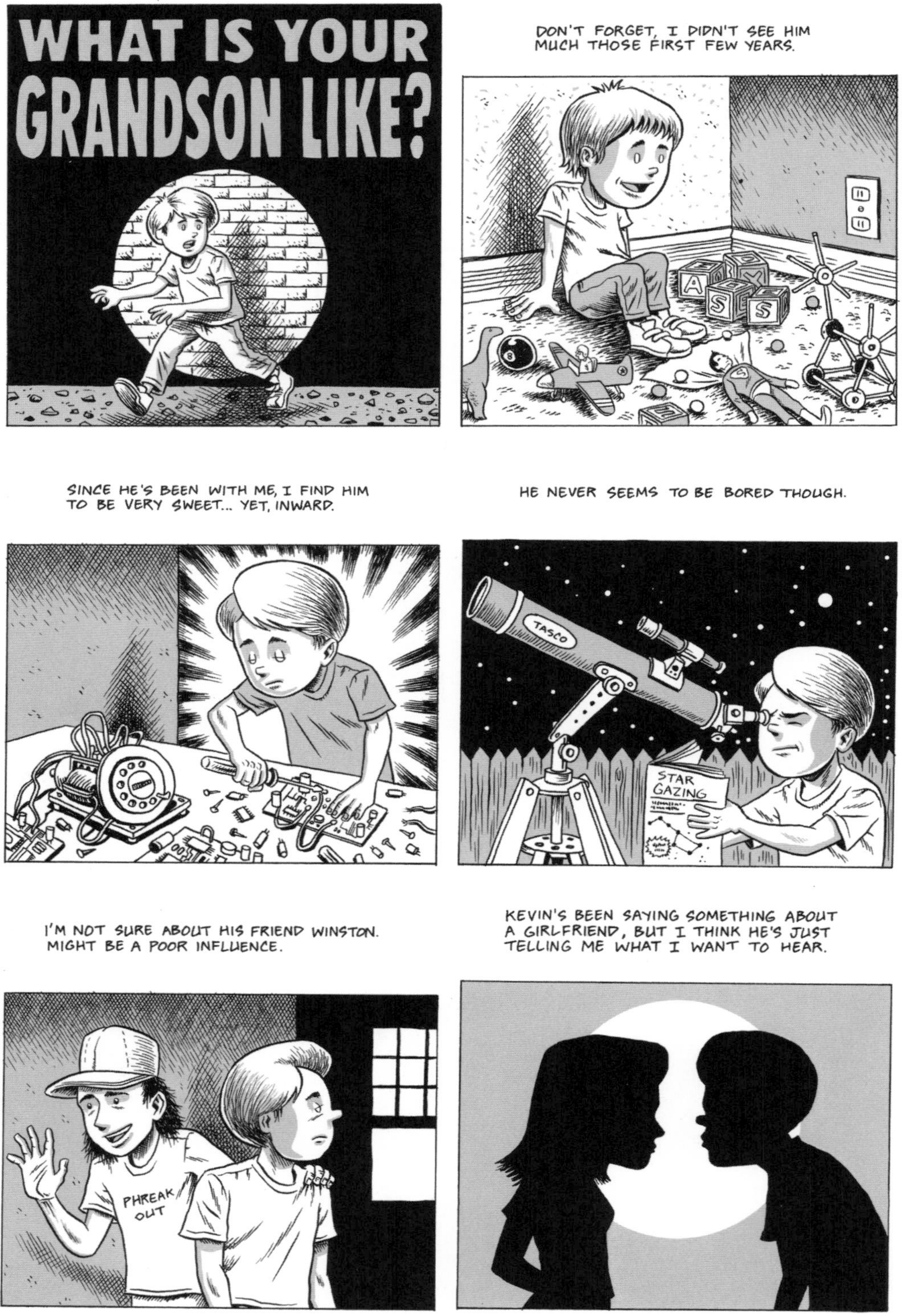
WHAT IS YOUR GRANDSON LIKE?
DON'T FORGET, I DIDN'T SEE HIM MUCH THOSE FIRST FEW YEARS.
A
S
SINCE HE'S BEEN WITH ME, I FIND HIM TO BE VERY SWEET... YET, INWARD.
HE NEVER SEEMS TO BE BORED THOUGH.
TASCO
STAR GAZING
I'M NOT SURE ABOUT HIS FRIEND WINSTON. MIGHT BE A POOR INFLUENCE.
PHREAK OUT
KEVIN'S BEEN SAYING SOMETHING ABOUT A GIRLFRIEND, BUT I THINK HE'S JUST TELLING ME WHAT I WANT TO HEAR.

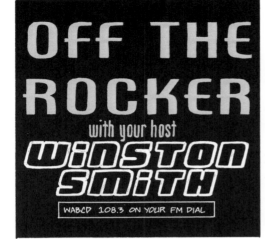

OFF THE ROCKER

with your host

WINSTON SMITH

WABCD 108.3 ON YOUR FM DIAL

IT'S ALL GOING DOWN THE WAY I EXPECTED IT WOULD.

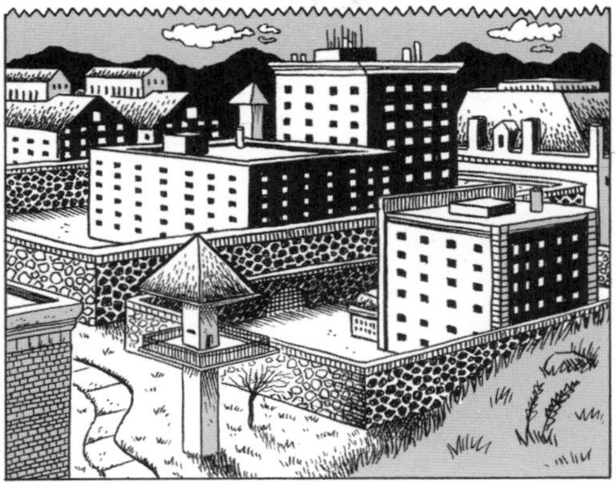

HE'S BEEN IN THERE FOR SIX MONTHS BY MY CALENDAR.

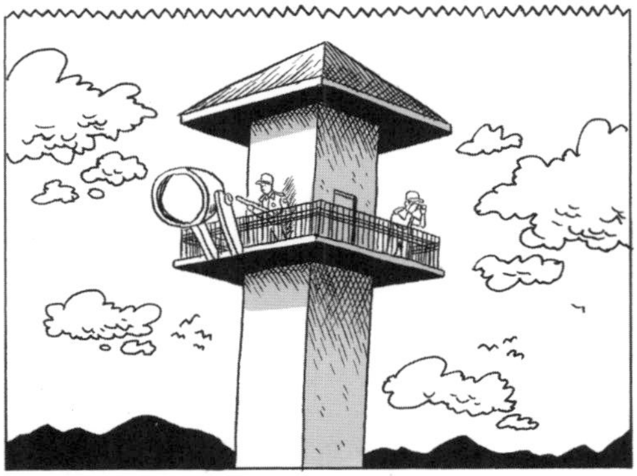

KEVIN STILL HASN'T BEEN FORMALLY CHARGED WITH A CRIME.

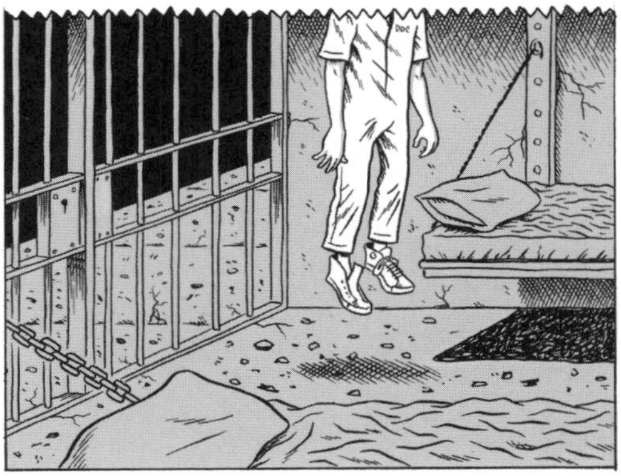

THEY KEEP SAYING THINGS ABOUT THE CASE BEING TOO COMPLICATED.

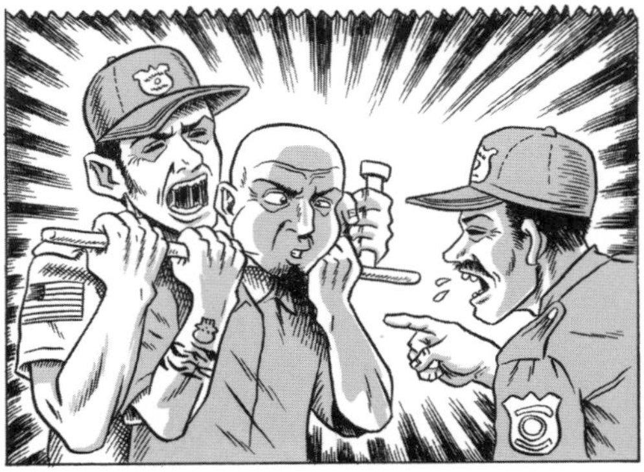

IT'S B.S.!! THEY WANT HIM TO FESTER! THEY WANT US TO FORGET HIM!

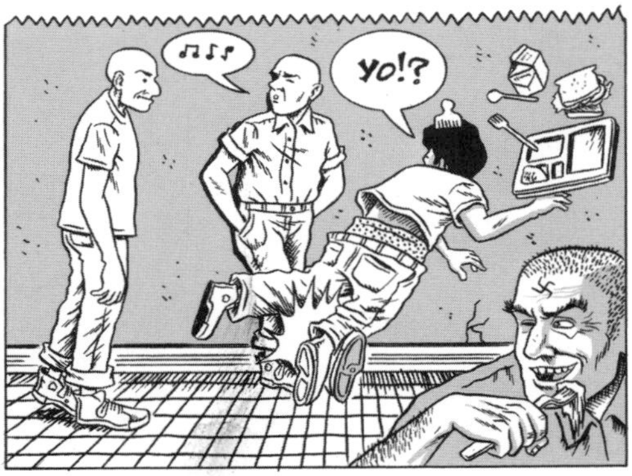
YO!?

HE WAS ABLE TO ELUDE THE AUTHORITIES FOR YEARS, AND THEY HAVE EGG ON THEIR FACES.

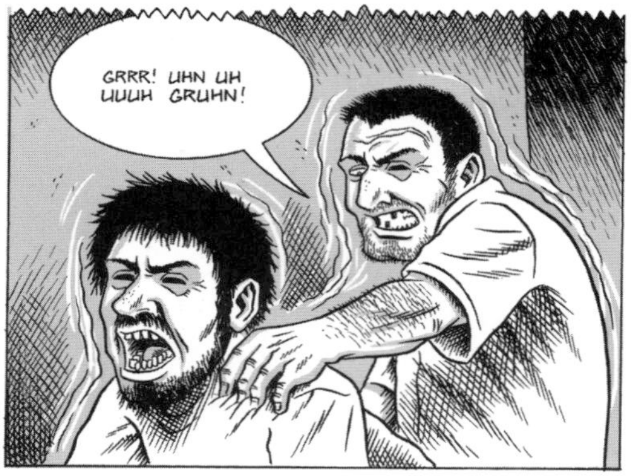
GRRR! UHN UH UUUH GRUHN!

THEY WANT TO MAKE AN EXAMPLE OUT OF HIM.

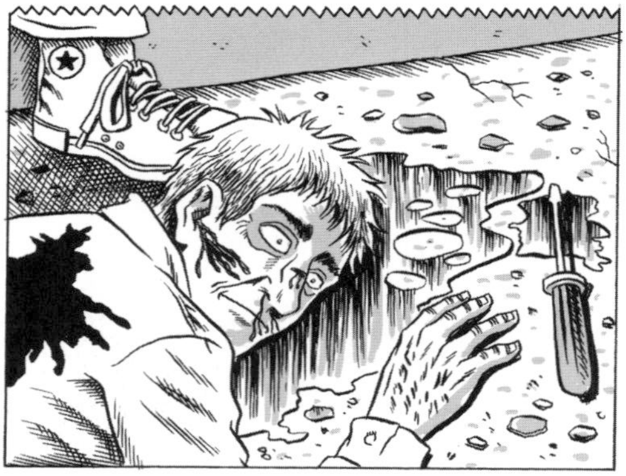

WITH THE CURRENT MEDIA BIAS AGAINST HACKING, IT WILL NOT BE HARD FOR THEM TO ACHIEVE THIS.

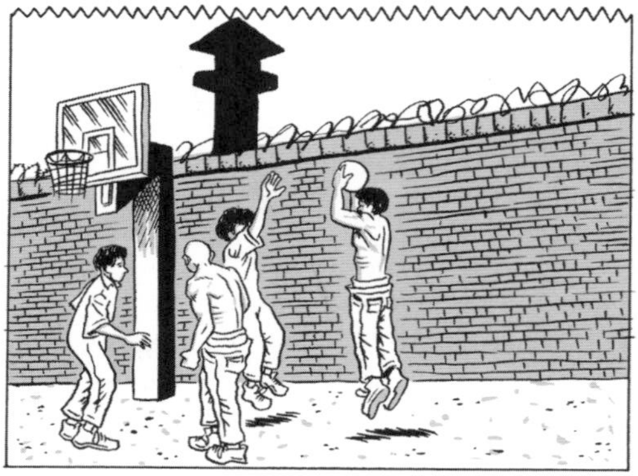

PHENICLE'S KNOWLEDGE COULD BE SO HELPFUL TO OUR NATIONAL SECURITY.

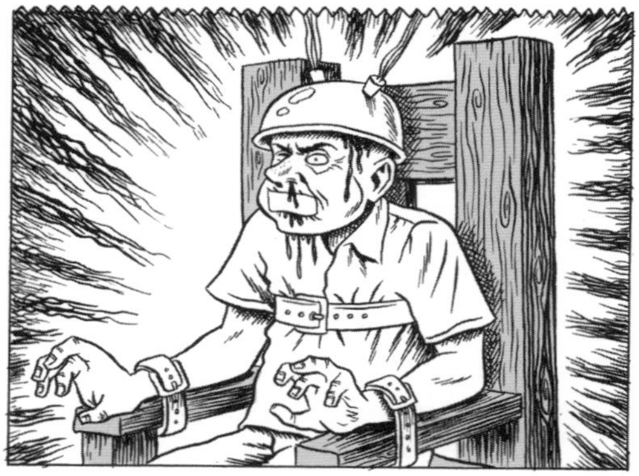

I GUESS THEY'D RATHER HAVE KILLERS AND RAPISTS PICK HIS BRAIN FOR SUCH INFO.

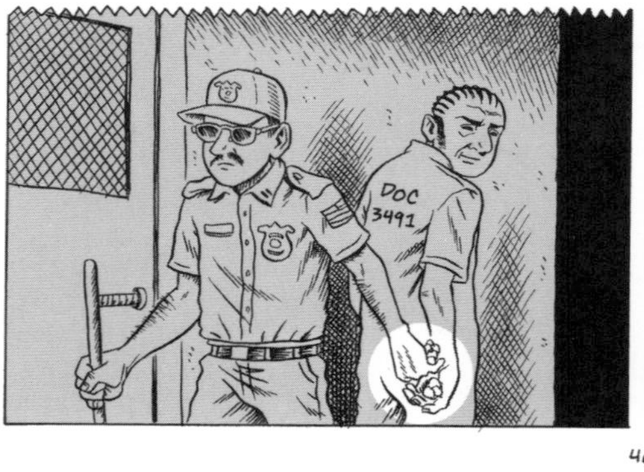
DOC 3491

I CAN GO ON, BUT LET ME GIVE YOU KEVIN'S ADDRESS TO SEND HIM BOOKS AND MAGAZINES BEFORE I FORGET.

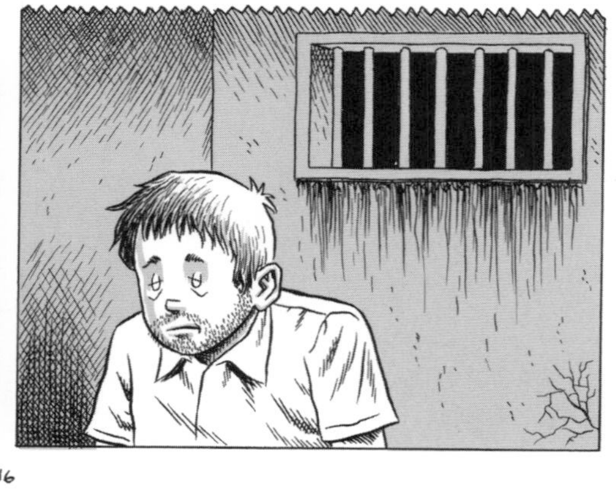

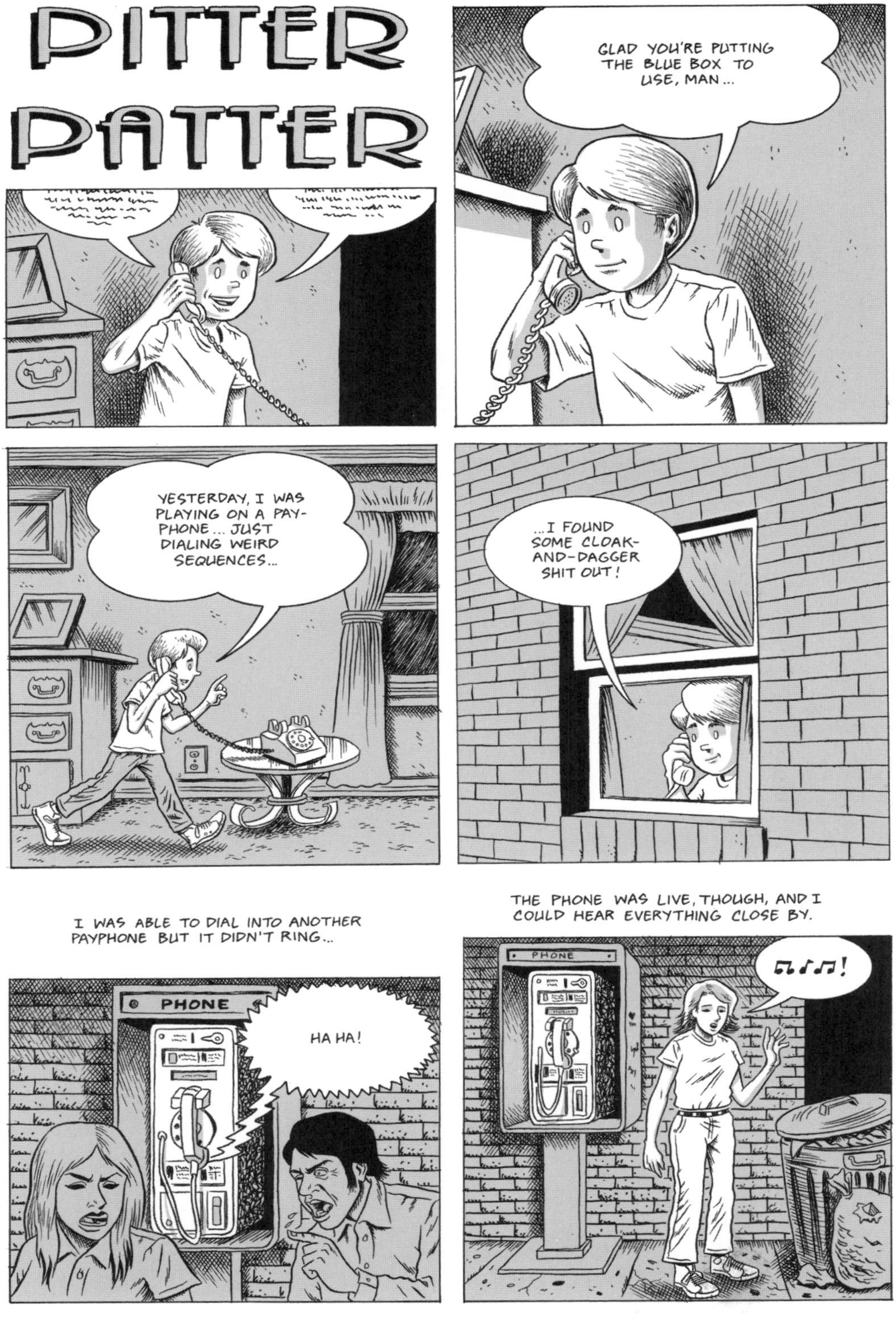
PITTER PATTER
GLAD YOU'RE PUTTING THE BLUE BOX TO USE, MAN...
YESTERDAY, I WAS PLAYING ON A PAY-PHONE... JUST DIALING WEIRD SEQUENCES...
...I FOUND SOME CLOAK-AND-DAGGER SHIT OUT!
I WAS ABLE TO DIAL INTO ANOTHER PAYPHONE BUT IT DIDN'T RING...
PHONE
HA HA!
THE PHONE WAS LIVE, THOUGH, AND I COULD HEAR EVERYTHING CLOSE BY.
PHONE

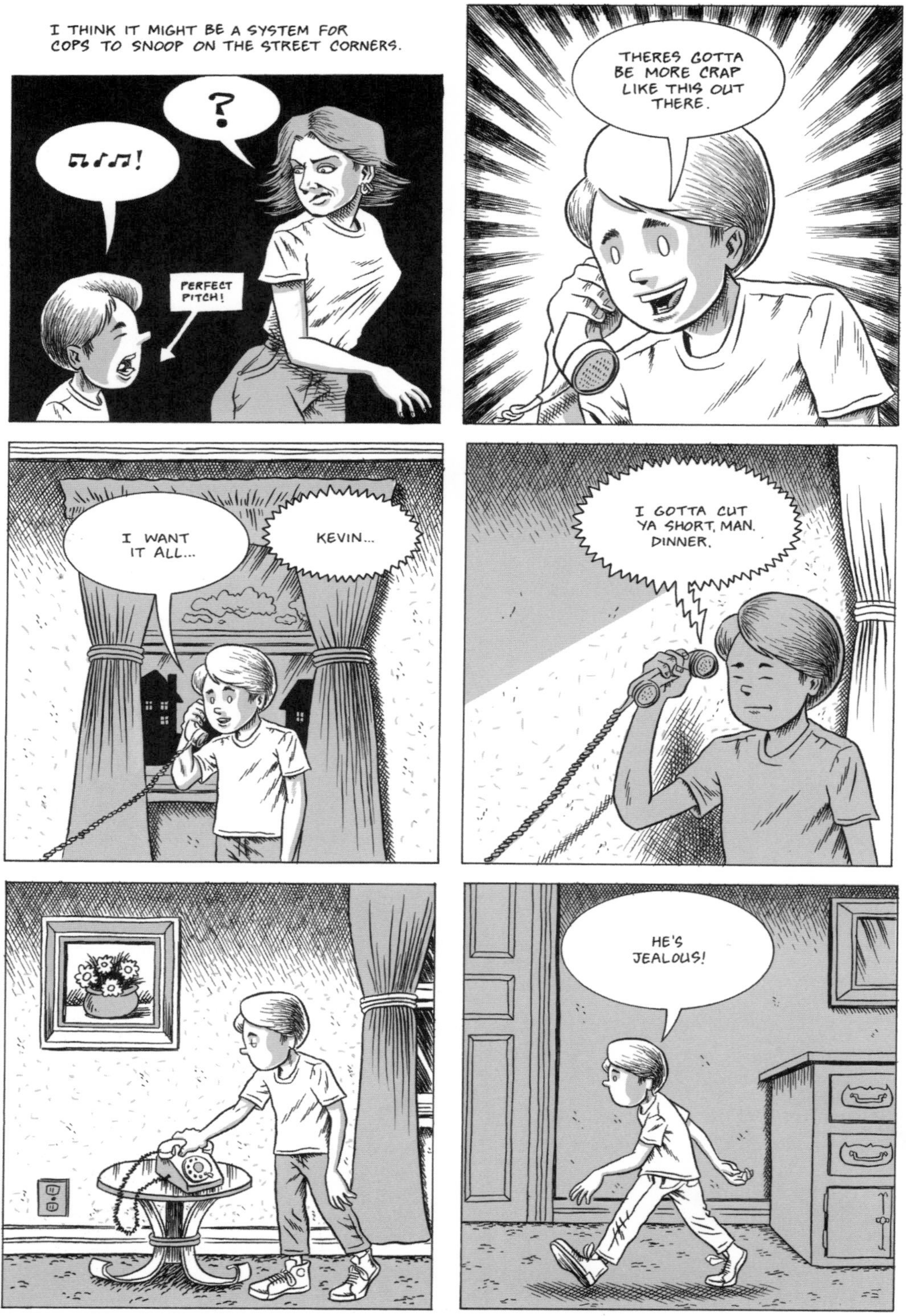
I THINK IT MIGHT BE A SYSTEM FOR COPS TO SNOOP ON THE STREET CORNERS.
♫♪♫!
?
PERFECT PITCH!
THERES GOTTA BE MORE CRAP LIKE THIS OUT THERE.
I WANT IT ALL...
KEVIN...
I GOTTA CUT YA SHORT, MAN. DINNER.
HE'S JEALOUS!

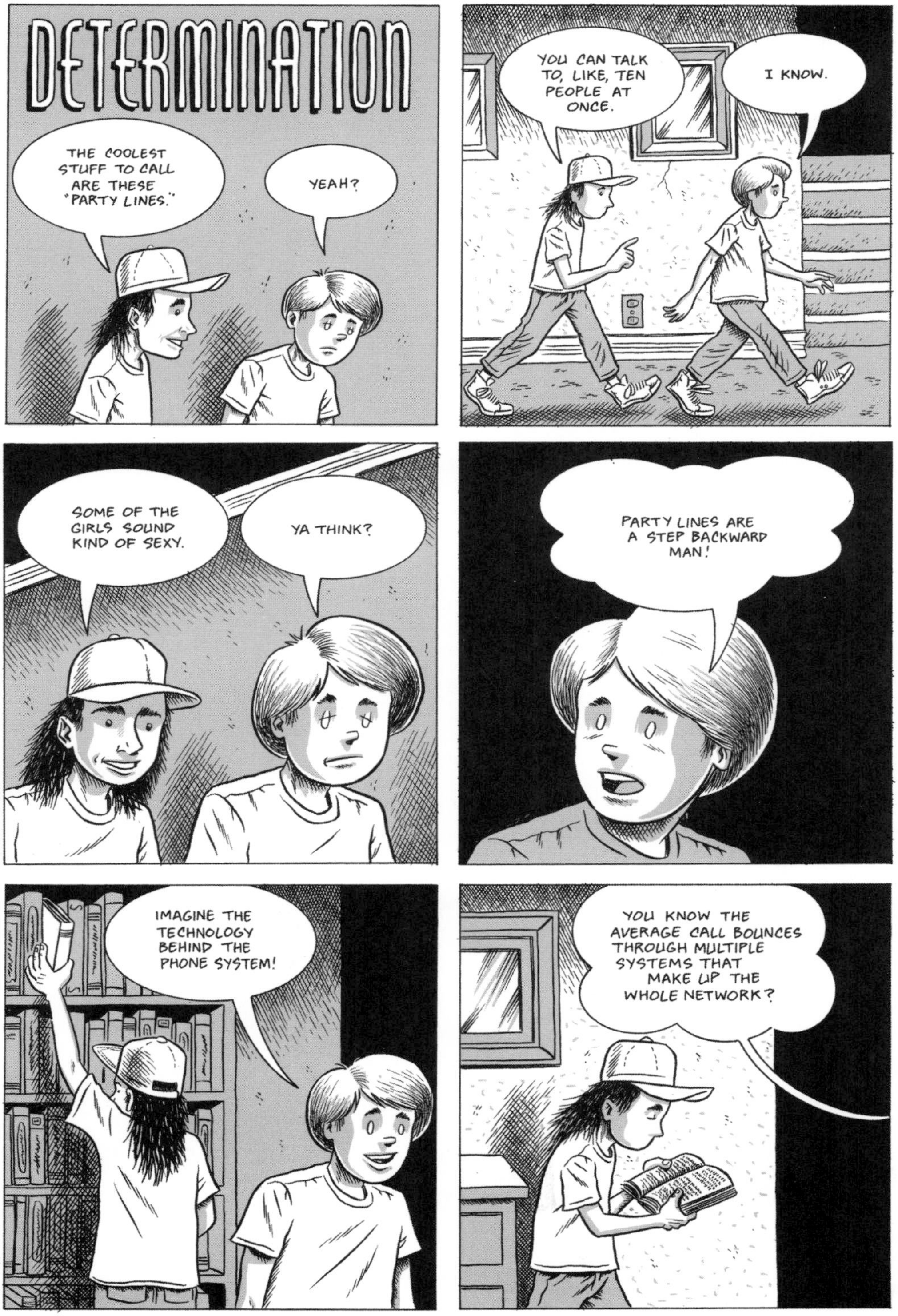
DETERMINATION
THE COOLEST STUFF TO CALL ARE THESE "PARTY LINES."
YEAH?
YOU CAN TALK TO, LIKE, TEN PEOPLE AT ONCE.
I KNOW.
SOME OF THE GIRLS SOUND KIND OF SEXY.
YA THINK?
PARTY LINES ARE A STEP BACKWARD MAN!
IMAGINE THE TECHNOLOGY BEHIND THE PHONE SYSTEM!
YOU KNOW THE AVERAGE CALL BOUNCES THROUGH MULTIPLE SYSTEMS THAT MAKE UP THE WHOLE NETWORK?

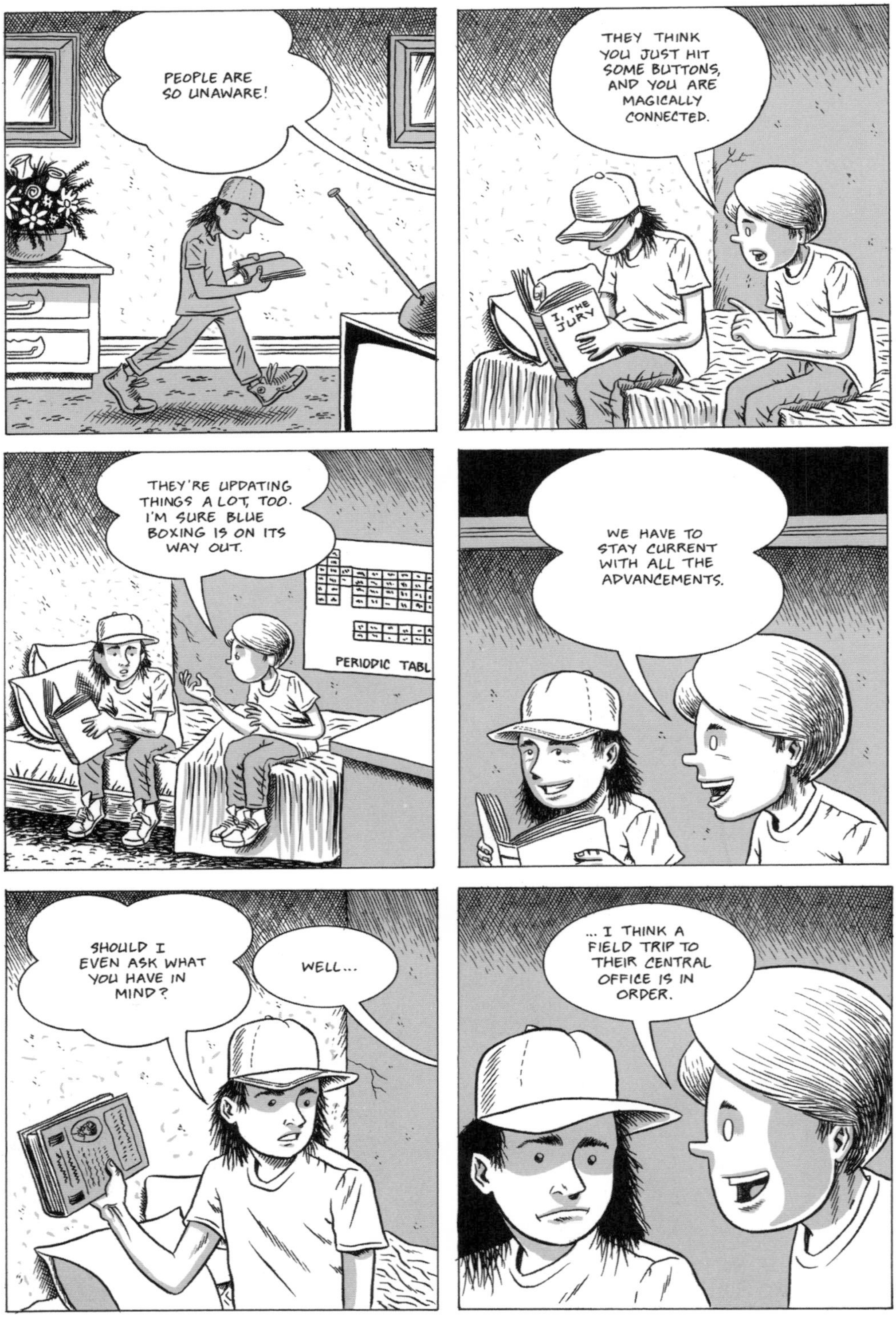
PEOPLE ARE SO UNAWARE!
THEY THINK YOU JUST HIT SOME BUTTONS, AND YOU ARE MAGICALLY CONNECTED.
I, THE JURY
THEY'RE UPDATING THINGS A LOT, TOO. I'M SURE BLUE BOXING IS ON ITS WAY OUT.
PERIODIC TABL
WE HAVE TO STAY CURRENT WITH ALL THE ADVANCEMENTS.
SHOULD I EVEN ASK WHAT YOU HAVE IN MIND?
WELL...
... I THINK A FIELD TRIP TO THEIR CENTRAL OFFICE IS IN ORDER.

LISA

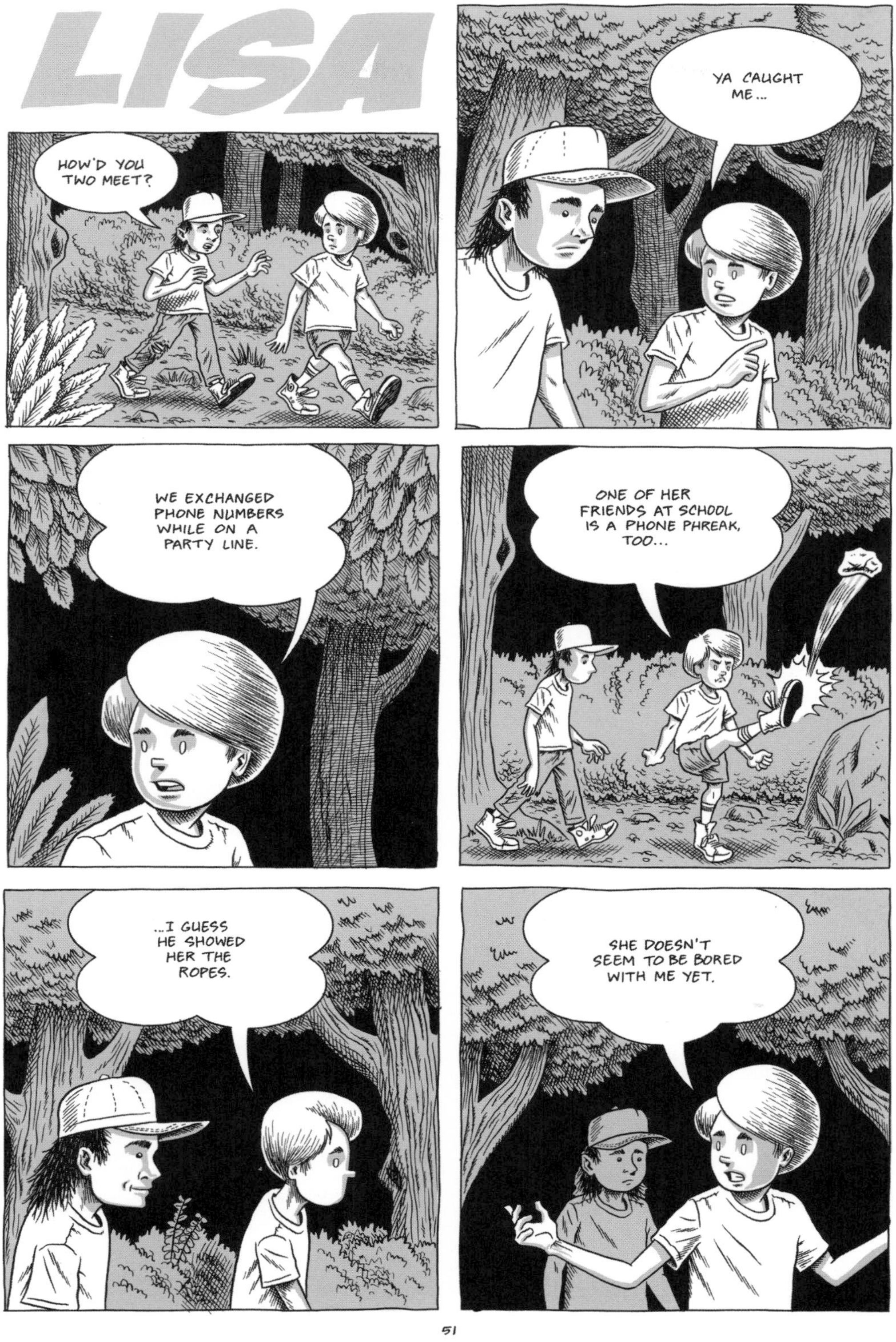
HOW'D YOU TWO MEET?
YA CAUGHT ME...
WE EXCHANGED PHONE NUMBERS WHILE ON A PARTY LINE.
ONE OF HER FRIENDS AT SCHOOL IS A PHONE PHREAK, TOO...
...I GUESS HE SHOWED HER THE ROPES.
SHE DOESN'T SEEM TO BE BORED WITH ME YET.

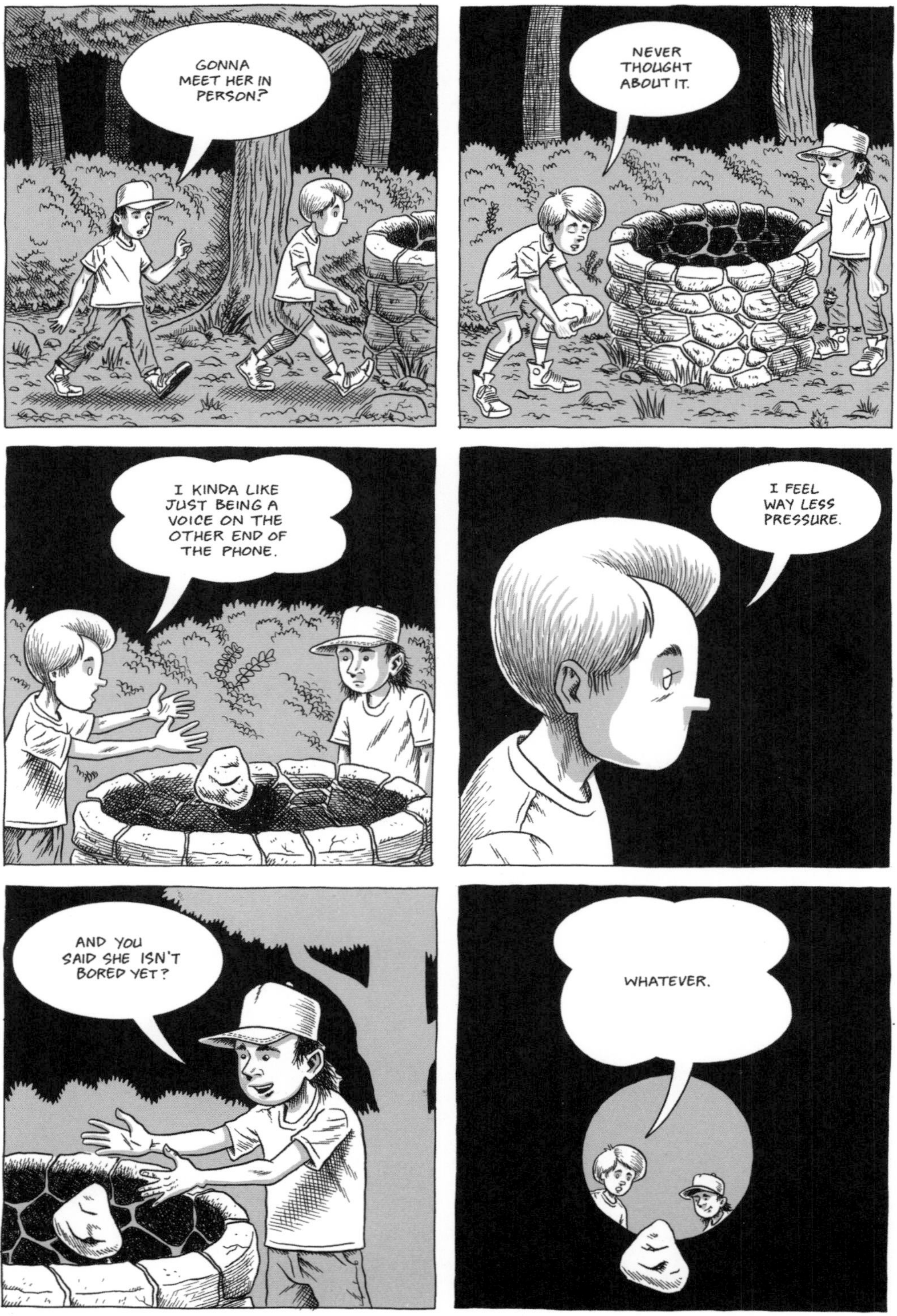
GONNA MEET HER IN PERSON?
NEVER THOUGHT ABOUT IT.
I KINDA LIKE JUST BEING A VOICE ON THE OTHER END OF THE PHONE.
I FEEL WAY LESS PRESSURE.
AND YOU SAID SHE ISN'T BORED YET?
WHATEVER.

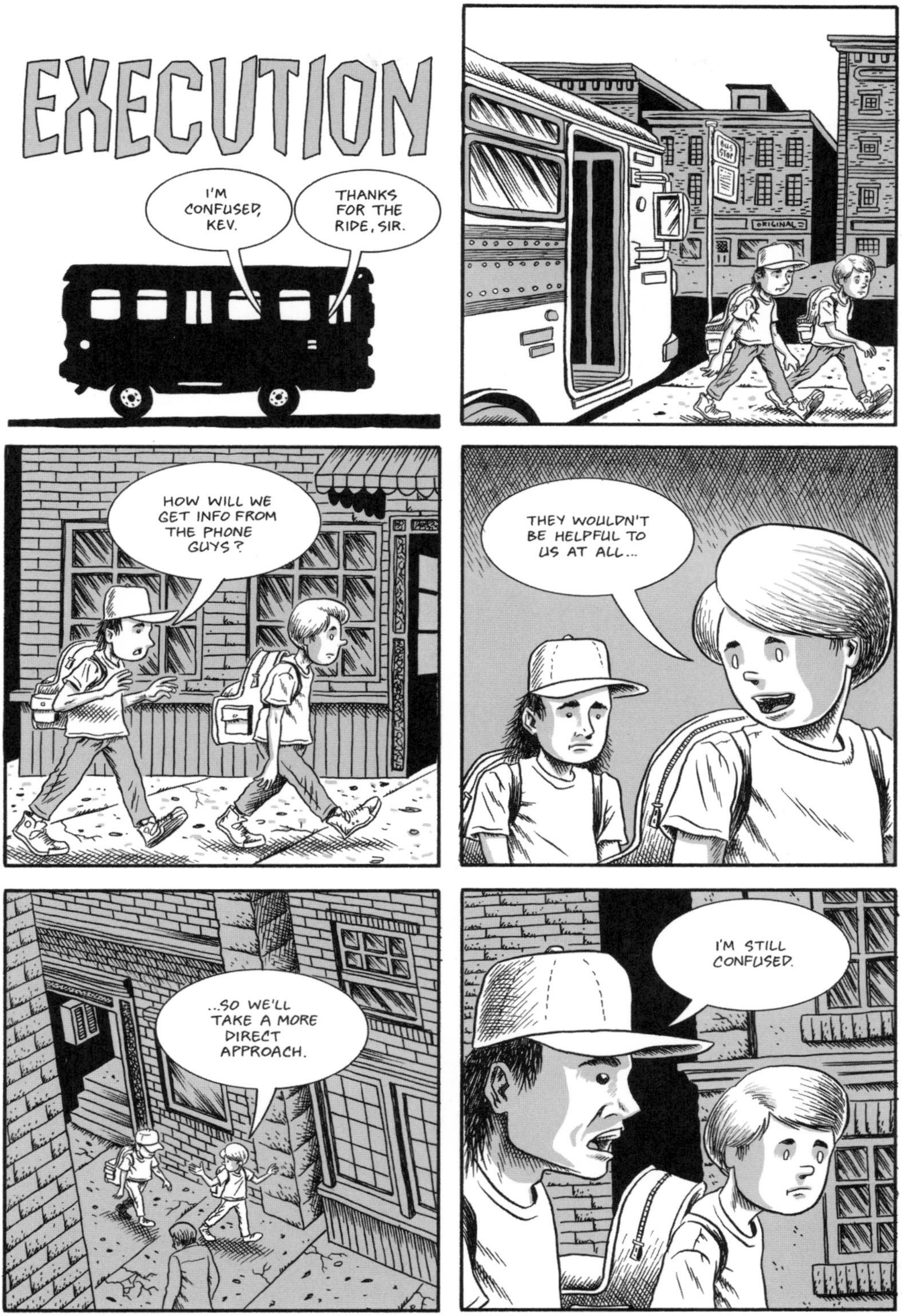
EXECUTION
I'M CONFUSED, KEV.
THANKS FOR THE RIDE, SIR.
HOW WILL WE GET INFO FROM THE PHONE GUYS?
THEY WOULDN'T BE HELPFUL TO US AT ALL...
...SO WE'LL TAKE A MORE DIRECT APPROACH.
I'M STILL CONFUSED.

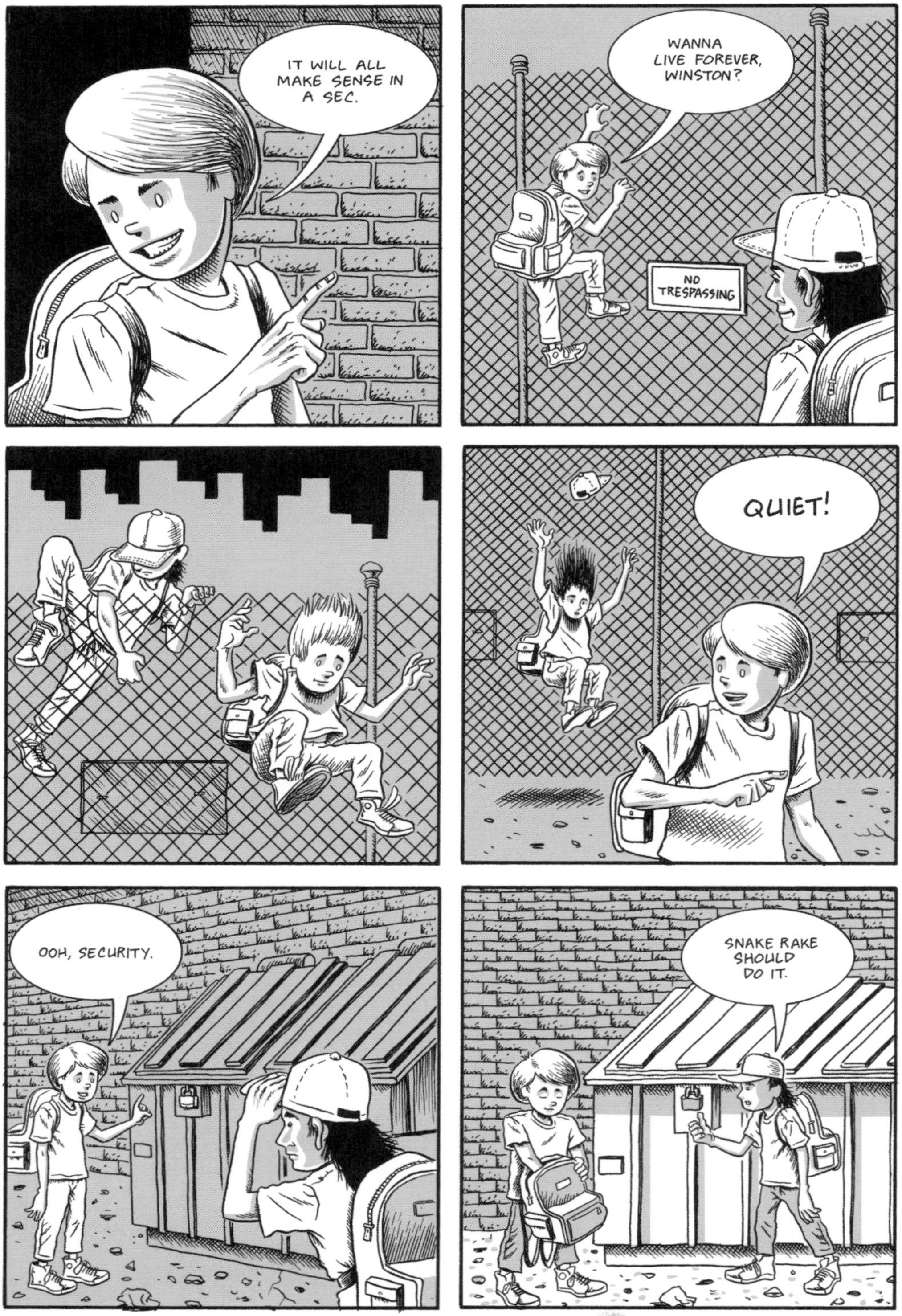
IT WILL ALL MAKE SENSE IN A SEC.
WANNA LIVE FOREVER, WINSTON?
NO TRESPASSING
QUIET!
OOH, SECURITY.
SNAKE RAKE SHOULD DO IT.

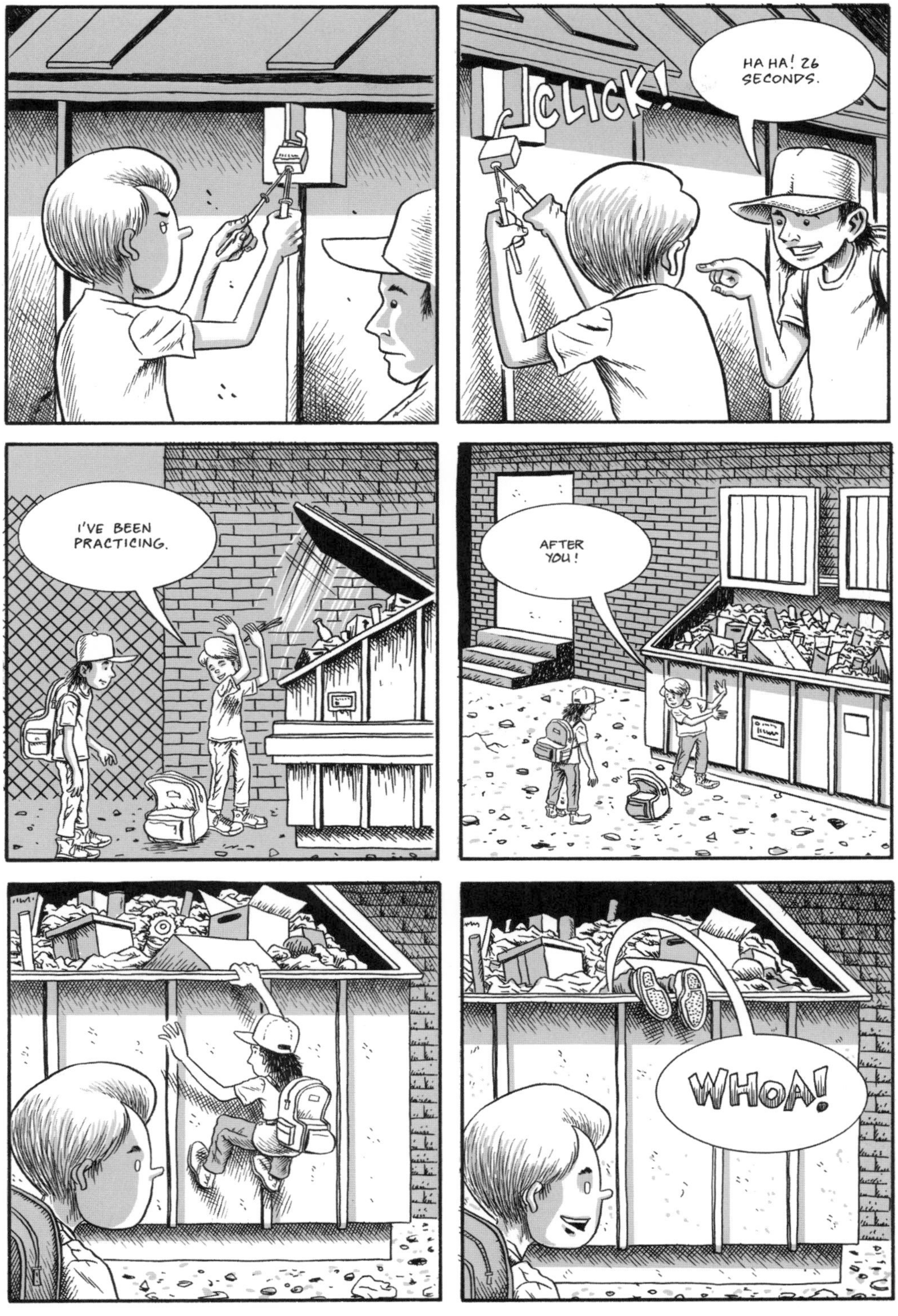
CLICK!
HA HA! 26 SECONDS.
I'VE BEEN PRACTICING.
AFTER YOU!
WHOA!

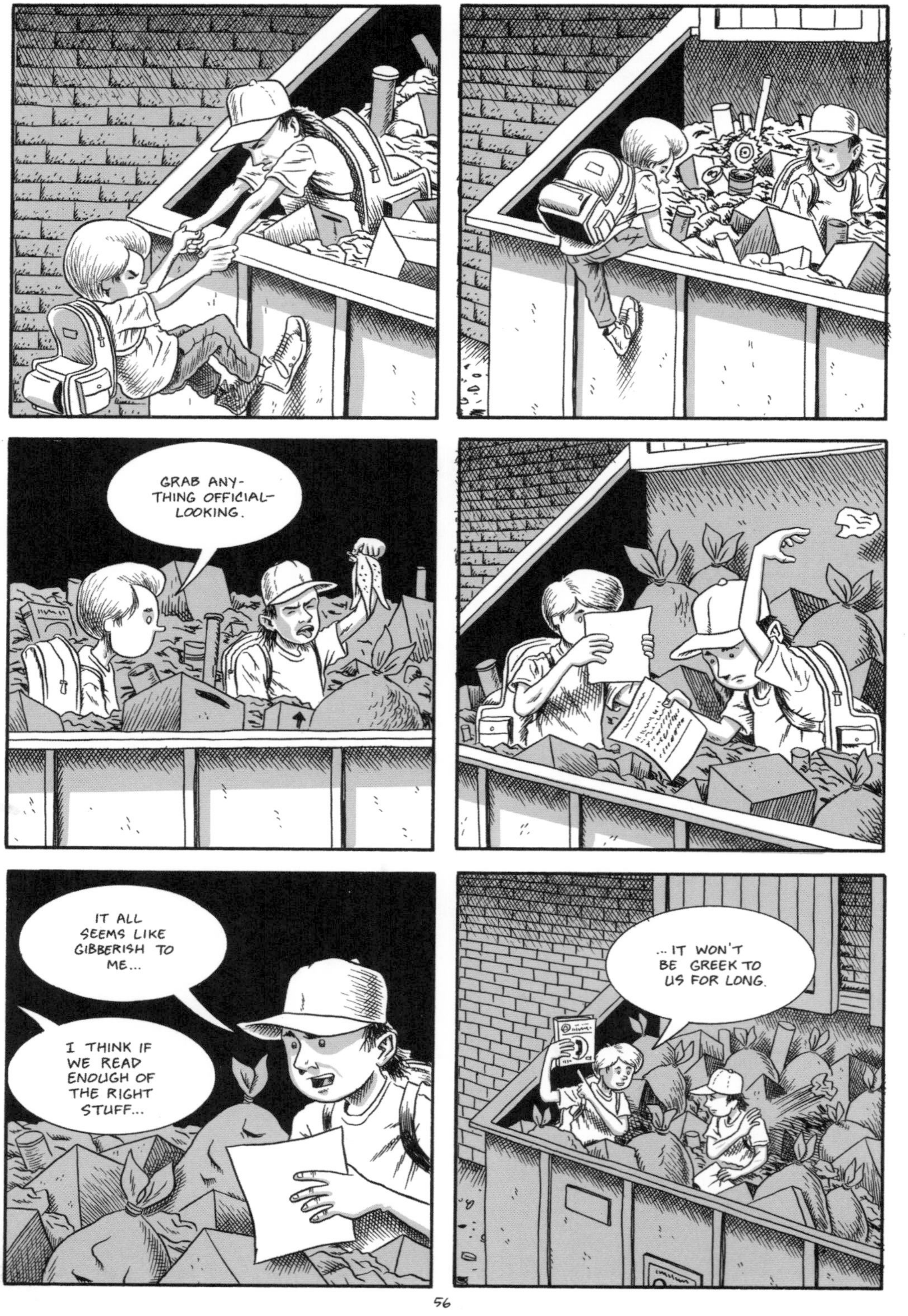
GRAB ANY-THING OFFICIAL-LOOKING.
IT ALL SEEMS LIKE GIBBERISH TO ME...
I THINK IF WE READ ENOUGH OF THE RIGHT STUFF...
...IT WON'T BE GREEK TO US FOR LONG.

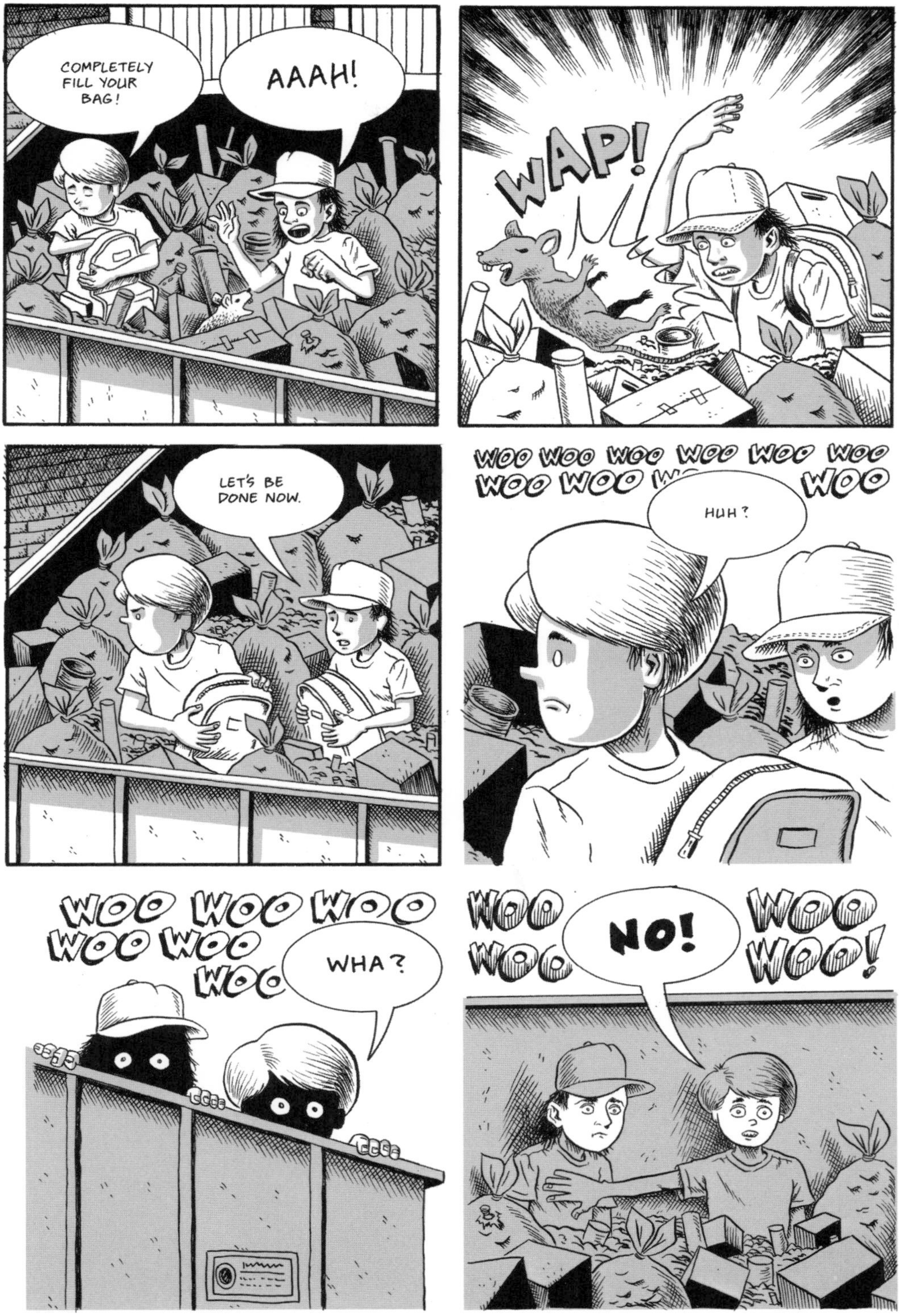
COMPLETELY FILL YOUR BAG!
AAAH!
WAP!
LET'S BE DONE NOW.
WOO WOO WOO WOO WOO WOO
WOO WOO WOO
HUH?
WOO WOO WOO
WOO WOO
WOO
WHA?
WOO
WOO
NO!
WOO
WOO!

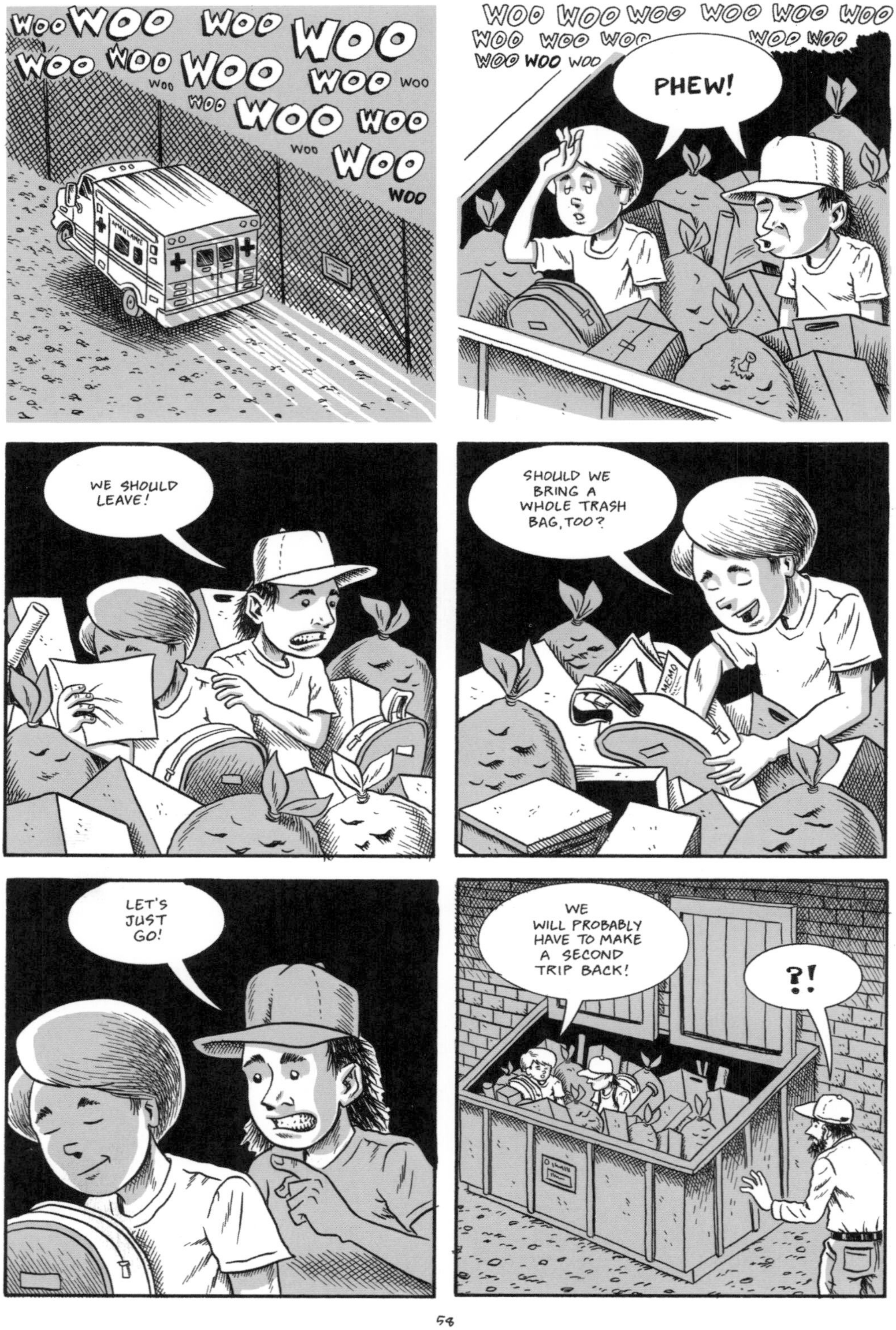
WOO WOO WOO WOO
WOO WOO WOO WOO
WOO WOO WOO WOO
WOO WOO WOO WOO
WOO WOO WOO
WOO WOO WOO WOO WOO WOO
WOO WOO WOO WOO WOO
WOO WOO WOO
PHEW!
WE SHOULD LEAVE!
SHOULD WE BRING A WHOLE TRASH BAG, TOO?
MEMO
LET'S JUST GO!
WE WILL PROBABLY HAVE TO MAKE A SECOND TRIP BACK!
?!

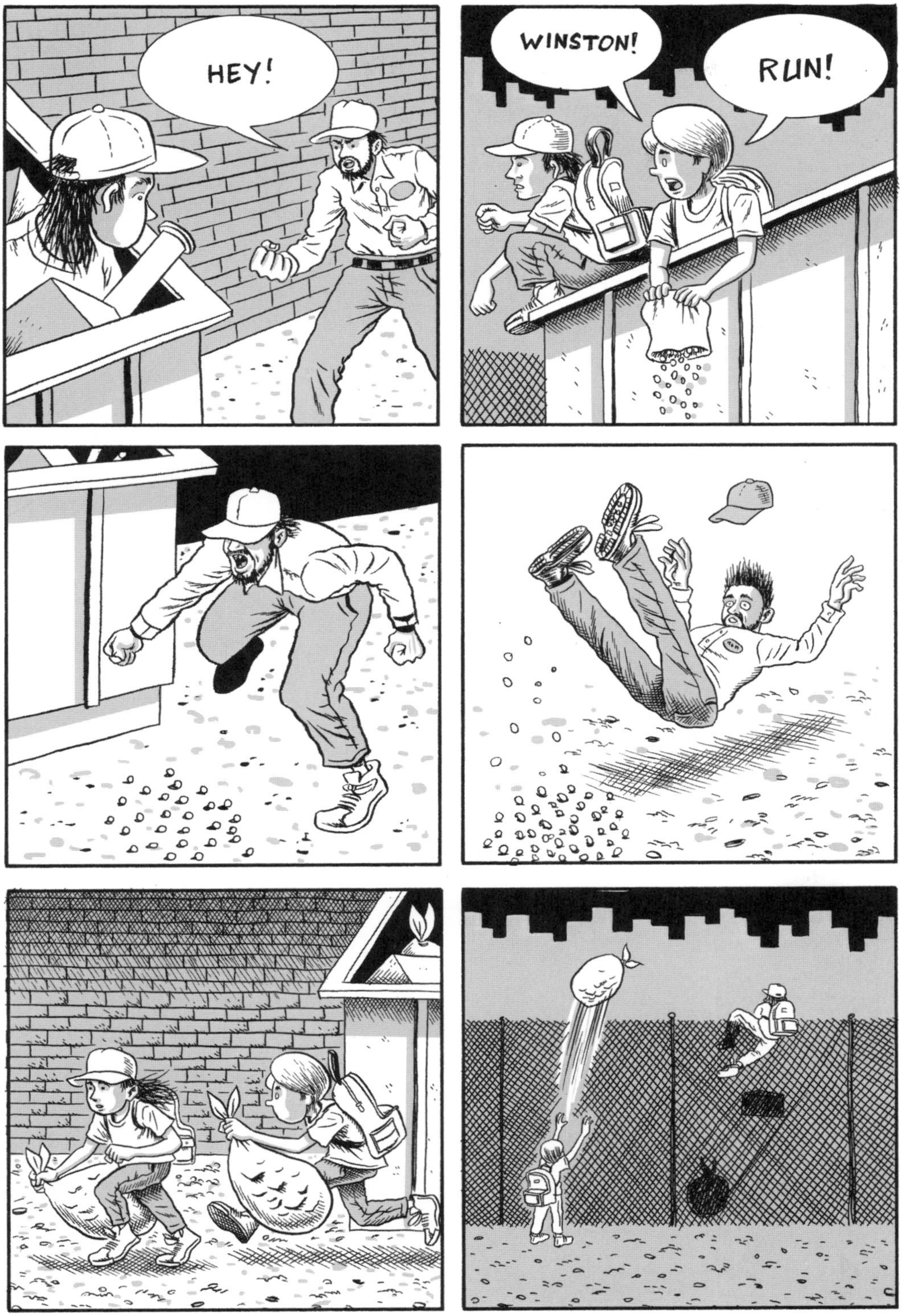
HEY!
WINSTON!
RUN!

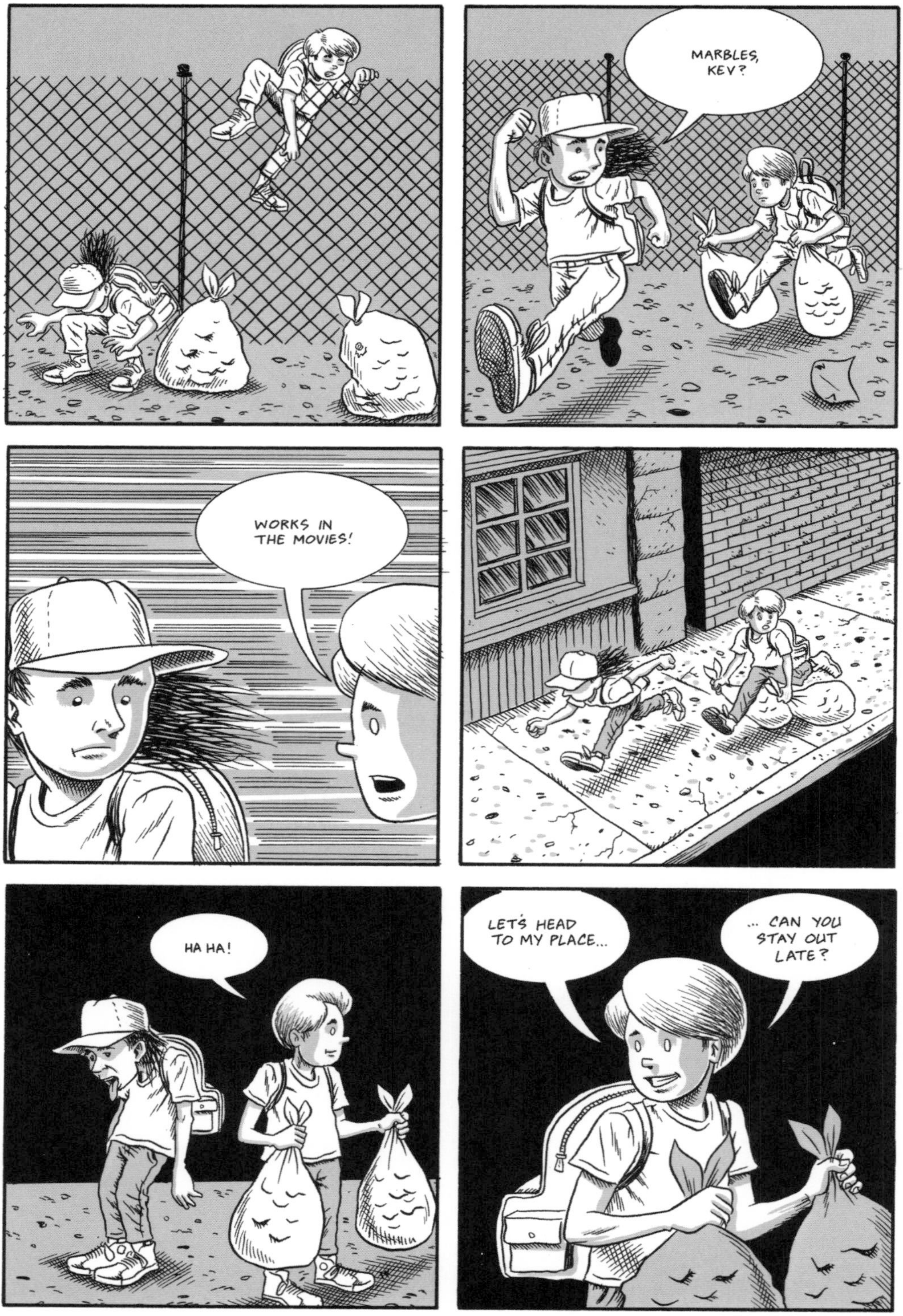
MARBLES, KEV?
WORKS IN THE MOVIES!
HA HA!
LET'S HEAD TO MY PLACE...
... CAN YOU STAY OUT LATE?

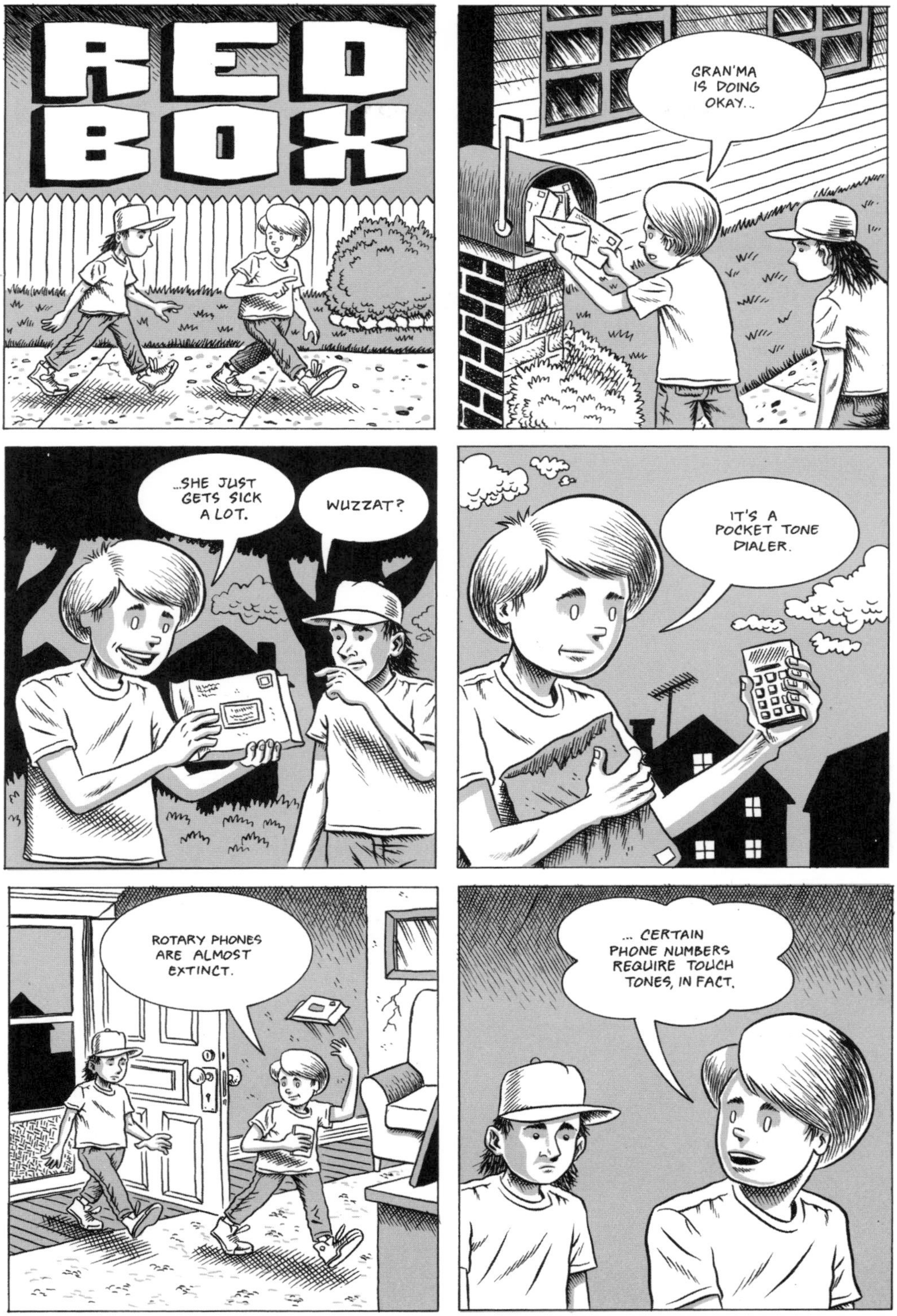
RED BOX
GRAN'MA IS DOING OKAY...
...SHE JUST GETS SICK A LOT.
WUZZAT?
IT'S A POCKET TONE DIALER.
ROTARY PHONES ARE ALMOST EXTINCT.
... CERTAIN PHONE NUMBERS REQUIRE TOUCH TONES, IN FACT.

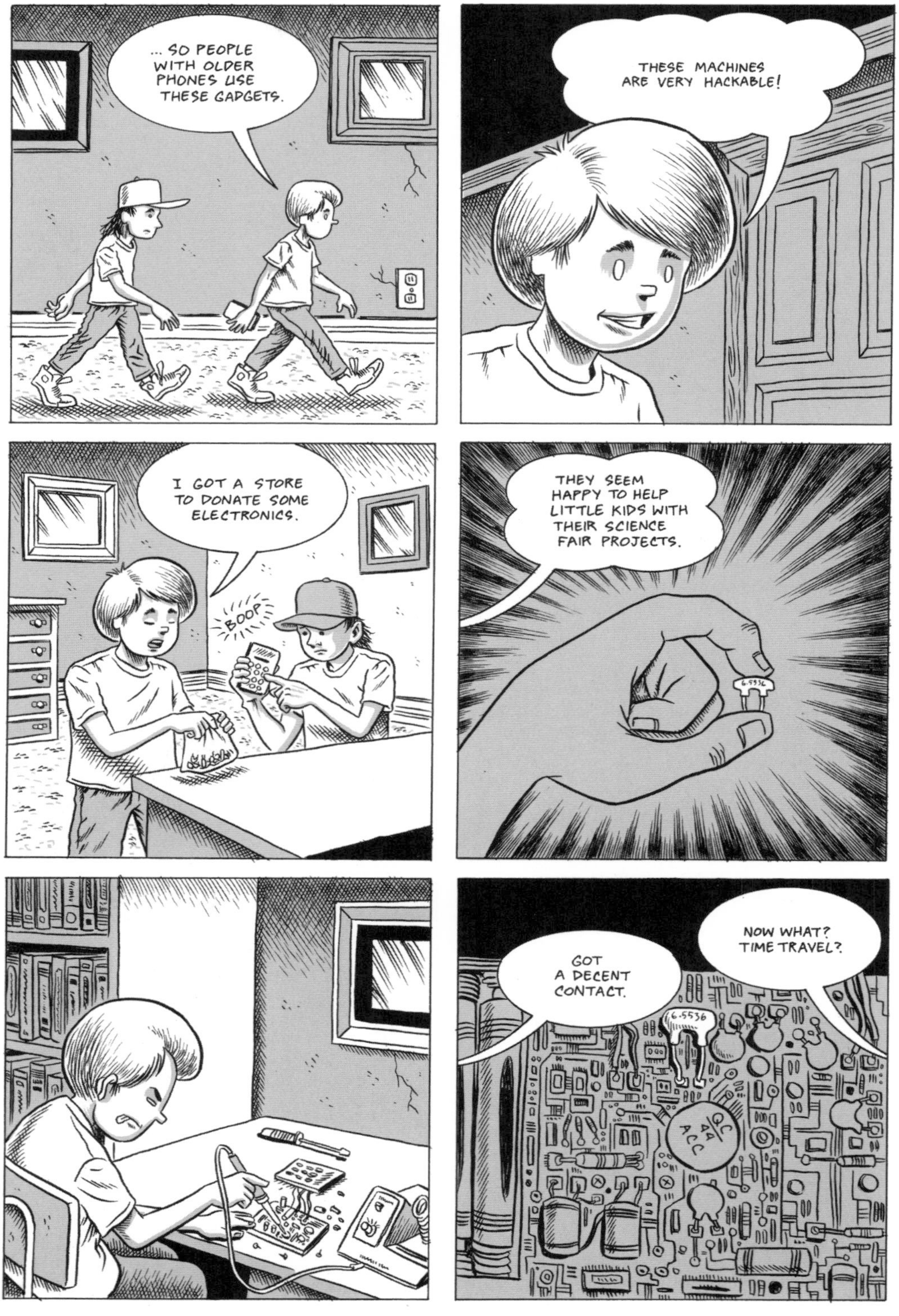
... SO PEOPLE WITH OLDER PHONES USE THESE GADGETS.
THESE MACHINES ARE VERY HACKABLE!
I GOT A STORE TO DONATE SOME ELECTRONICS.
BOOP
THEY SEEM HAPPY TO HELP LITTLE KIDS WITH THEIR SCIENCE FAIR PROJECTS.
6.5536
GOT A DECENT CONTACT.
NOW WHAT? TIME TRAVEL?
6.5536

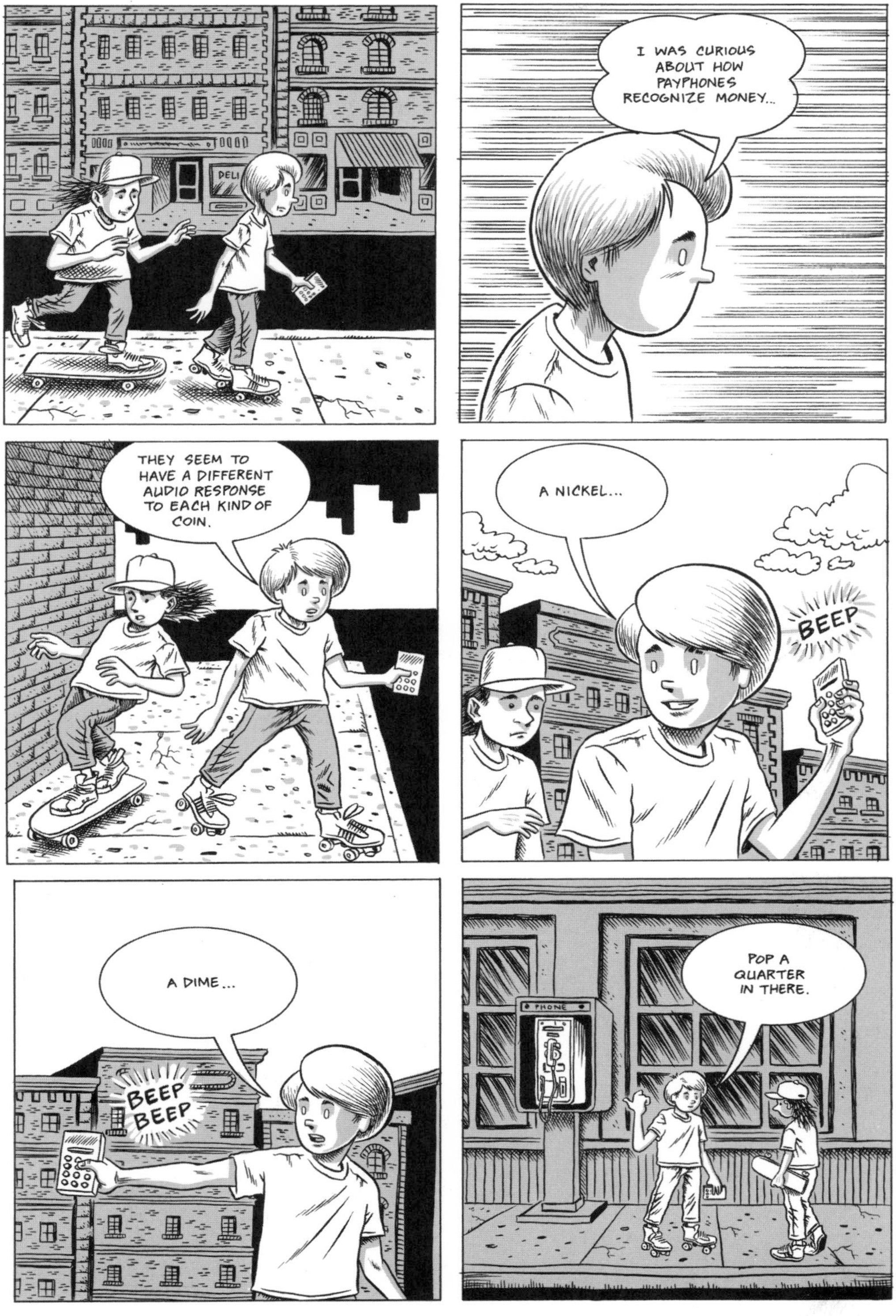
DELI
I WAS CURIOUS ABOUT HOW PAYPHONES RECOGNIZE MONEY...
THEY SEEM TO HAVE A DIFFERENT AUDIO RESPONSE TO EACH KIND OF COIN.
A NICKEL...
BEEP
A DIME...
BEEP BEEP
PHONE
POP A QUARTER IN THERE.

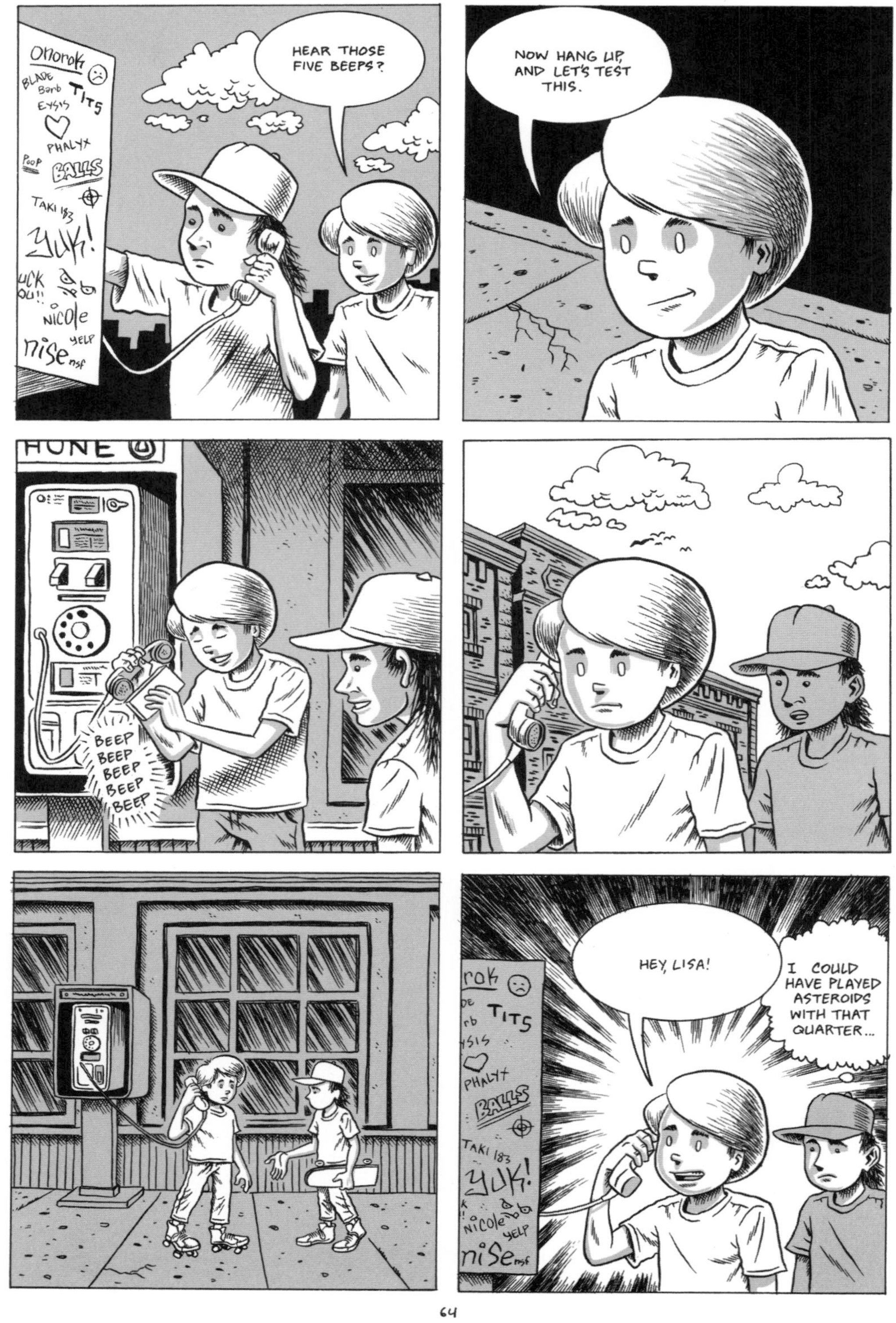
HEAR THOSE FIVE BEEPS?
NOW HANG UP, AND LET'S TEST THIS.
HONE
BEEP BEEP BEEP BEEP BEEP
HEY, LISA!
I COULD HAVE PLAYED ASTEROIDS WITH THAT QUARTER...

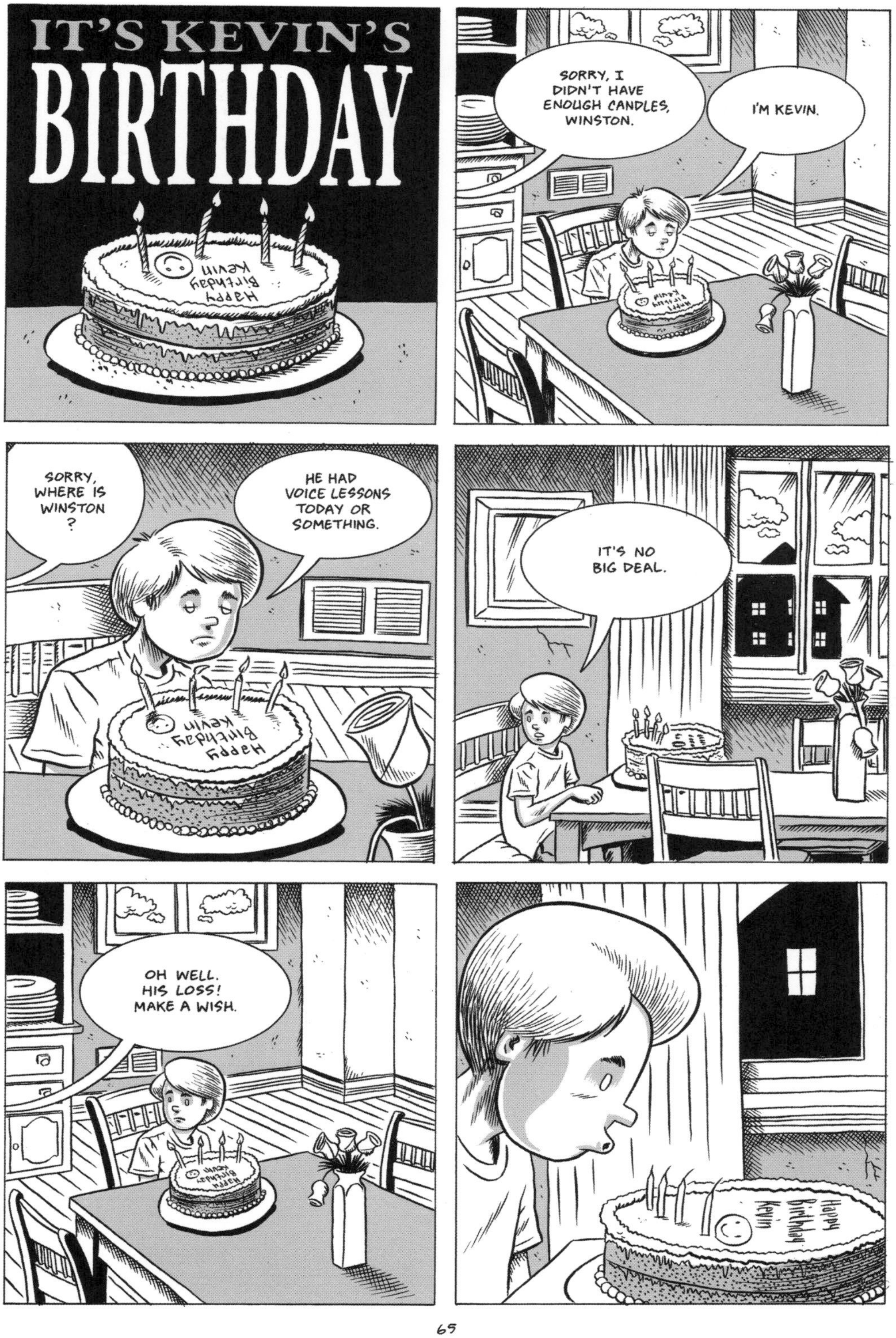
IT'S KEVIN'S
BIRTHDAY
Happy Birthday Kevin
SORRY, I DIDN'T HAVE ENOUGH CANDLES, WINSTON.
I'M KEVIN.
SORRY, WHERE IS WINSTON ?
HE HAD VOICE LESSONS TODAY OR SOMETHING.
IT'S NO BIG DEAL.
OH WELL. HIS LOSS! MAKE A WISH.
Happy Birthday Kevin

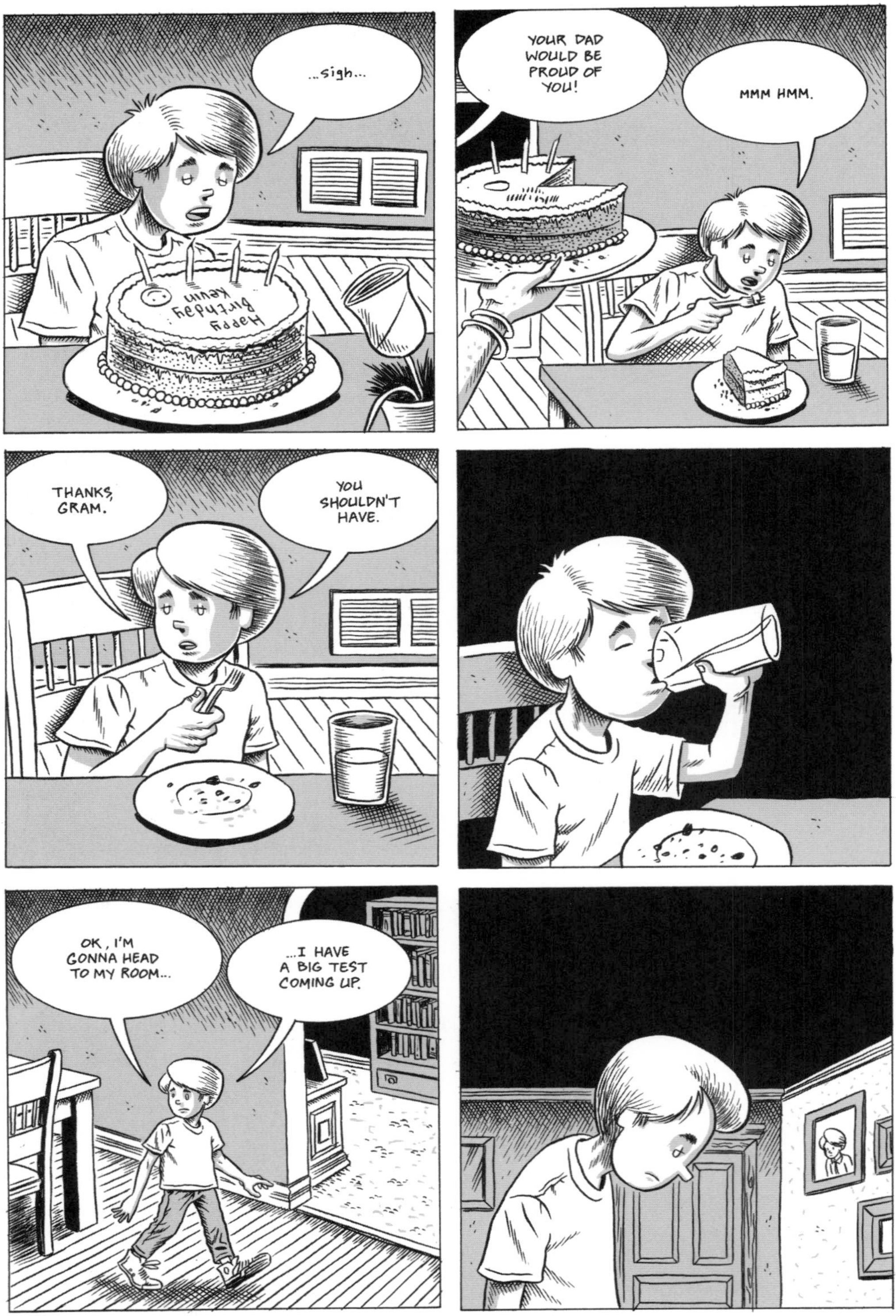
...sigh...
YOUR DAD WOULD BE PROUD OF YOU!
MMM HMM.
THANKS, GRAM.
YOU SHOULDN'T HAVE.
OK, I'M GONNA HEAD TO MY ROOM...
...I HAVE A BIG TEST COMING UP.

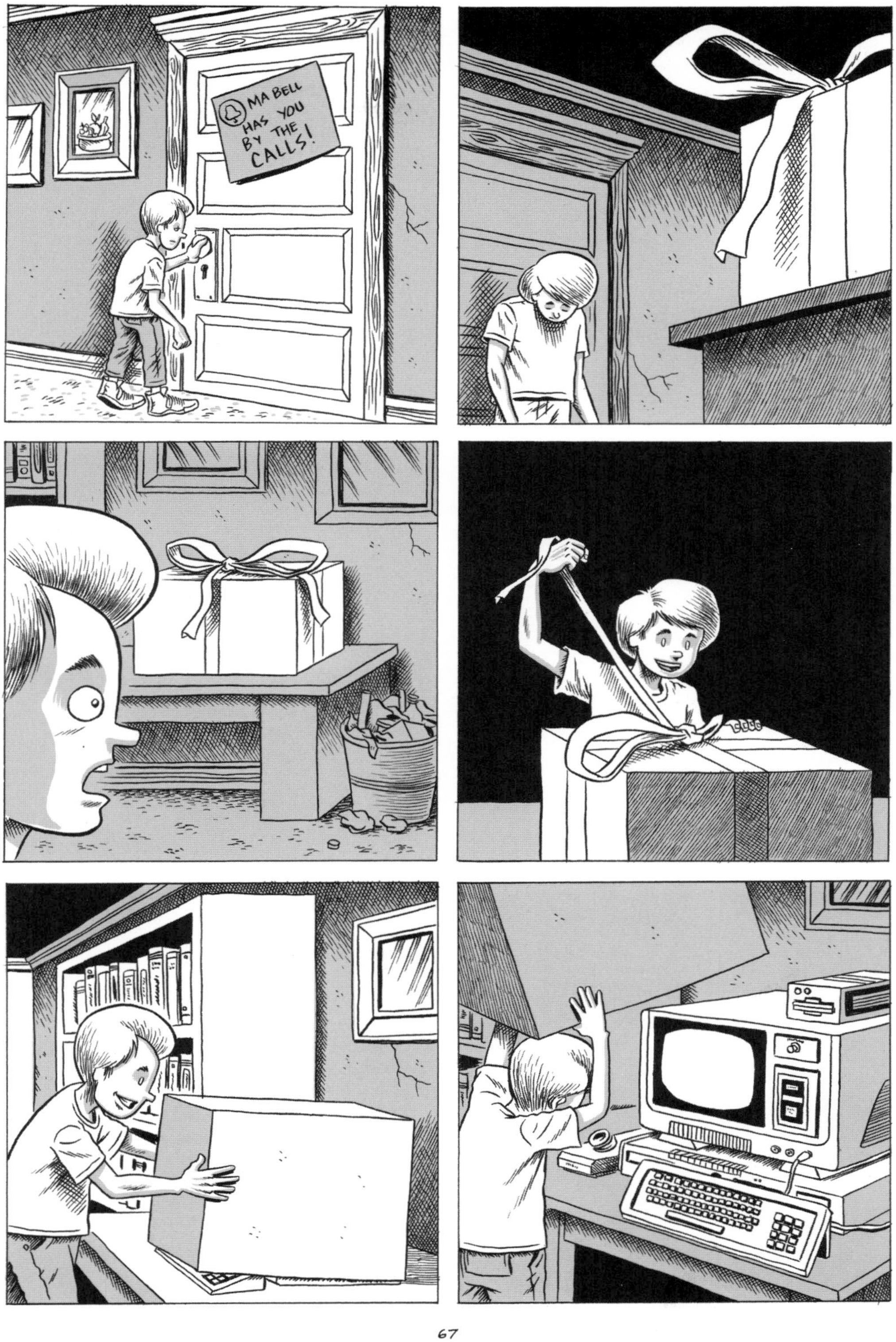
MA BELL
HAS YOU
BY THE
CALLS!

...MY GOSH...

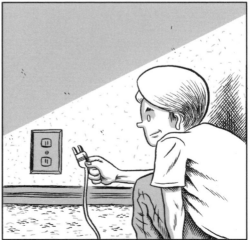

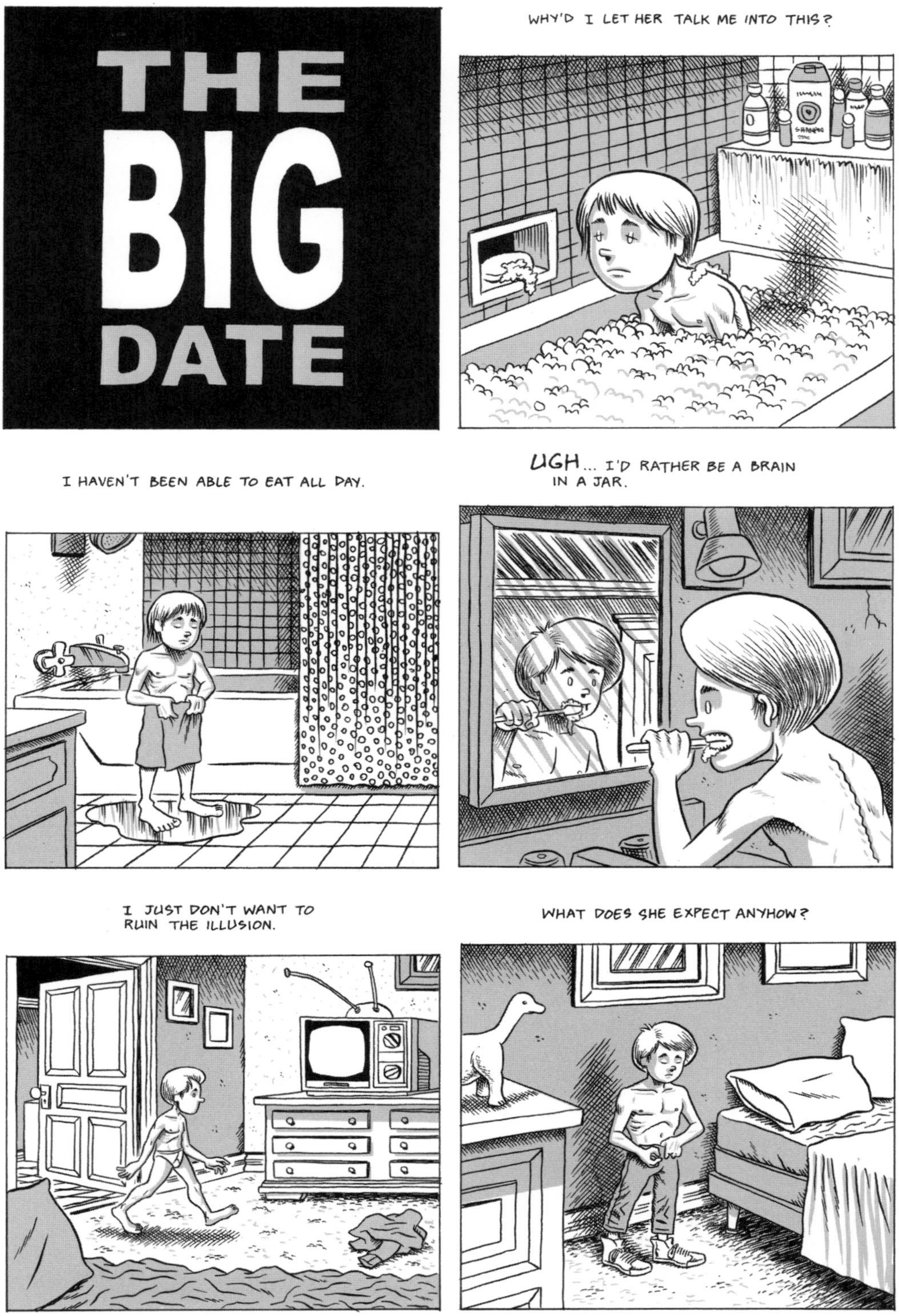
THE BIG DATE
WHY'D I LET HER TALK ME INTO THIS?
I HAVEN'T BEEN ABLE TO EAT ALL DAY.
UGH... I'D RATHER BE A BRAIN IN A JAR.
I JUST DON'T WANT TO RUIN THE ILLUSION.
WHAT DOES SHE EXPECT ANYHOW?

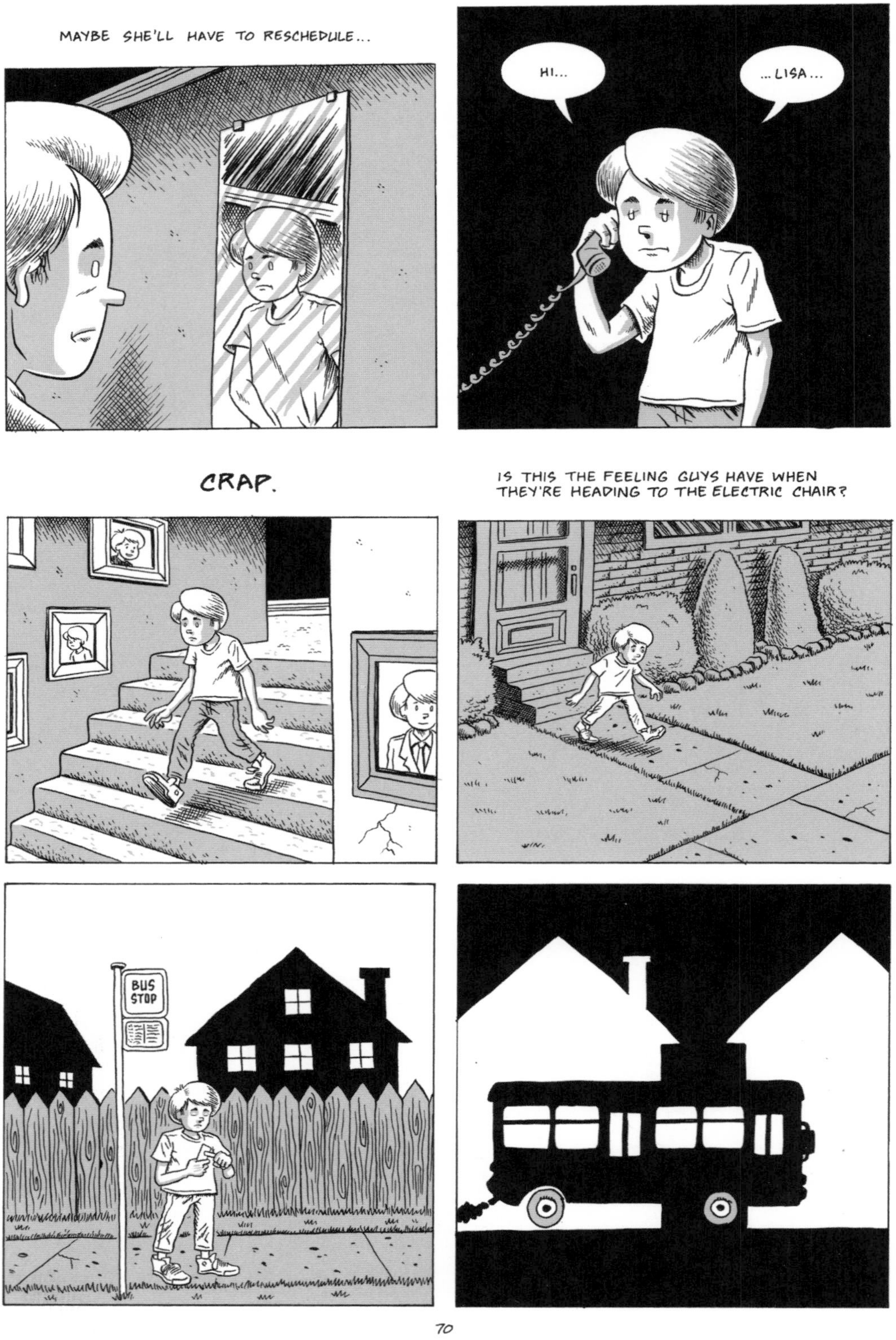
MAYBE SHE'LL HAVE TO RESCHEDULE...
HI...
...LISA...
CRAP.
IS THIS THE FEELING GUYS HAVE WHEN THEY'RE HEADING TO THE ELECTRIC CHAIR?
BUS STOP

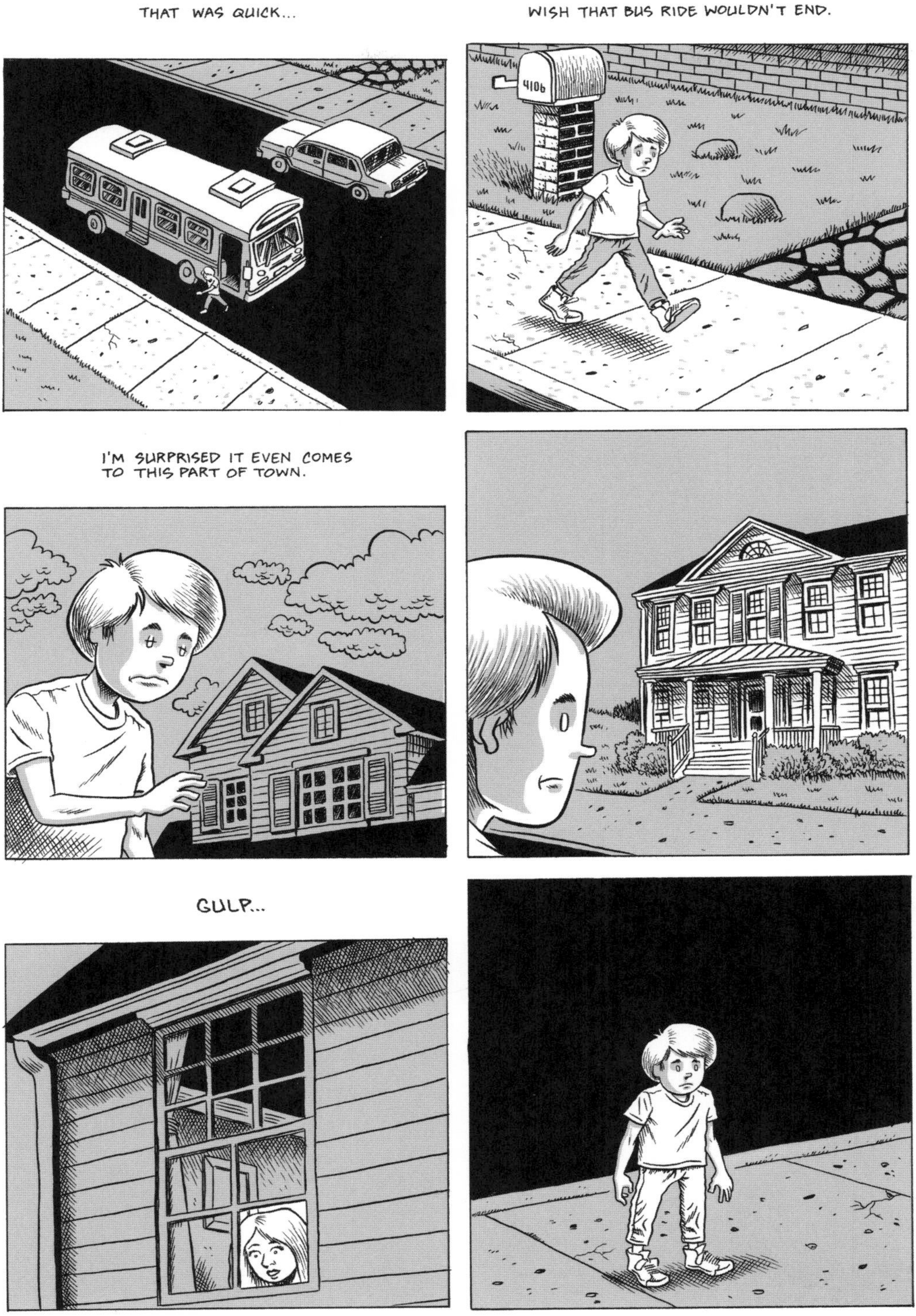
THAT WAS QUICK...
WISH THAT BUS RIDE WOULDN'T END.
4106
I'M SURPRISED IT EVEN COMES TO THIS PART OF TOWN.
GULP...

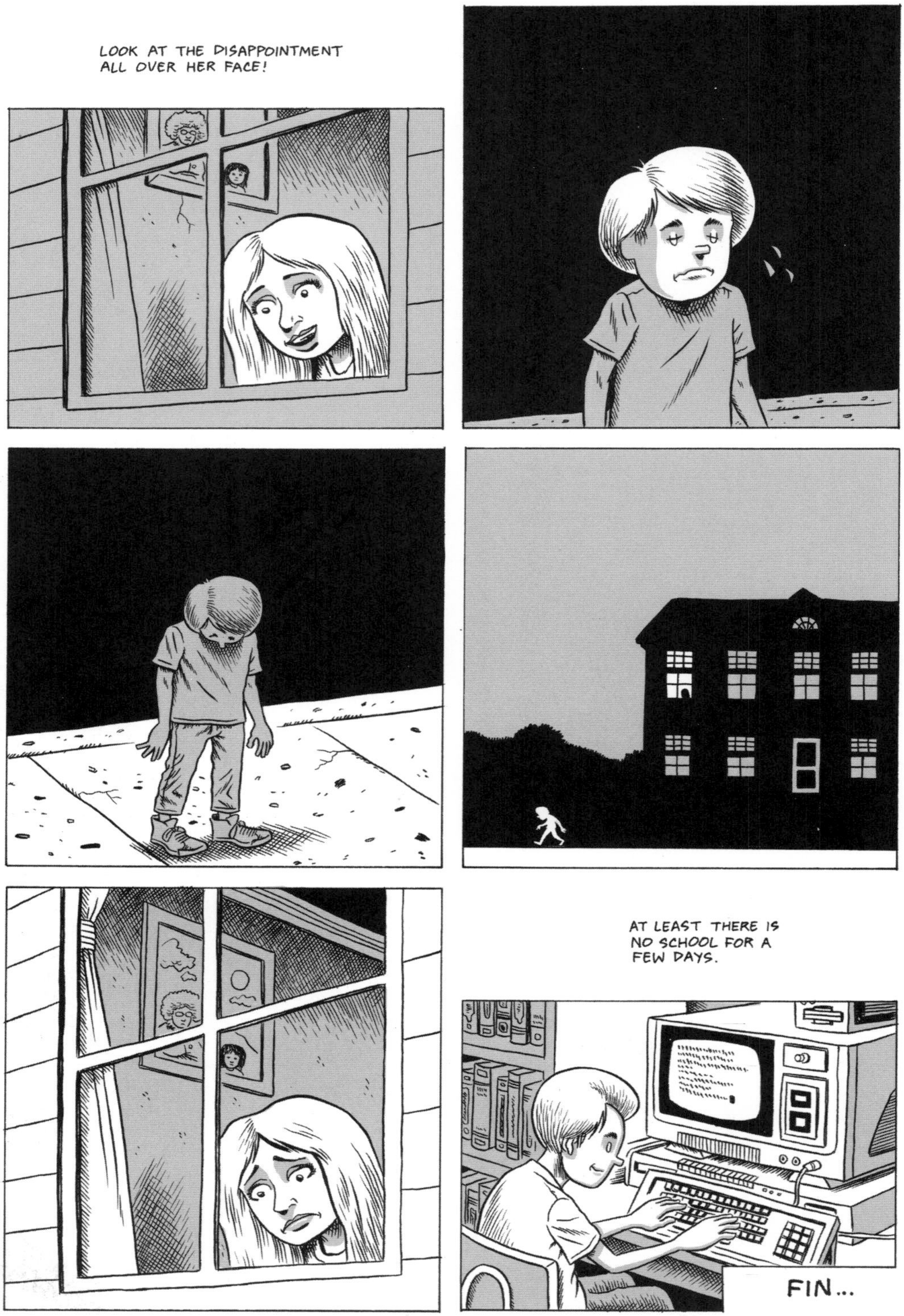
LOOK AT THE DISAPPOINTMENT ALL OVER HER FACE!
AT LEAST THERE IS NO SCHOOL FOR A FEW DAYS.
FIN...

CHAPTER 3

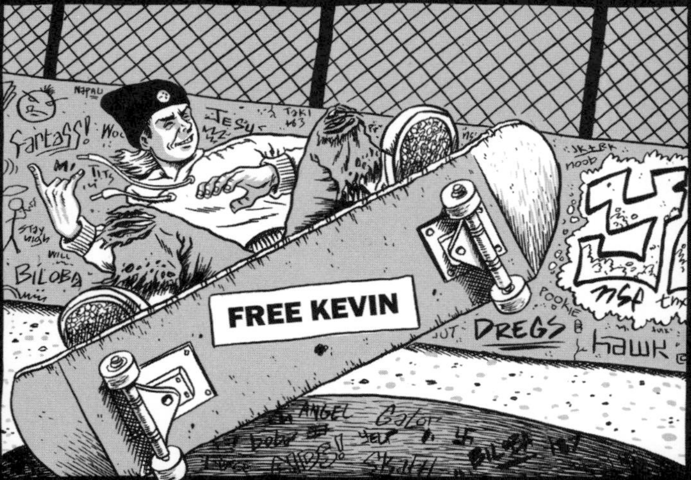
FREE KEVIN
DREGS
BILOBA
hawk
ANGEL

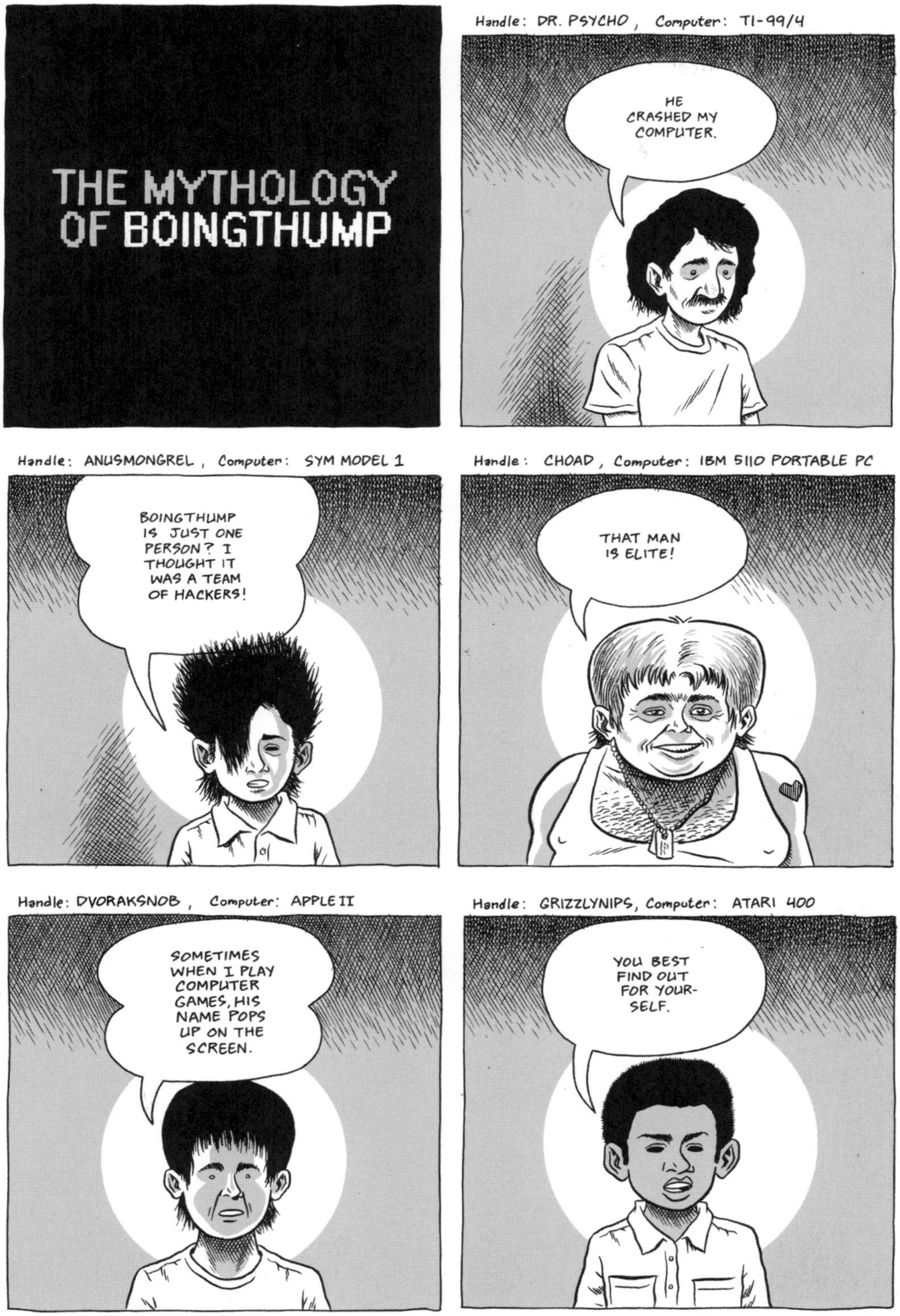
THE MYTHOLOGY OF BOINGTHUMP
Handle: DR. PSYCHO, Computer: TI-99/4
HE CRASHED MY COMPUTER.
Handle: ANUSMONGREL, Computer: SYM MODEL 1
BOINGTHUMP IS JUST ONE PERSON? I THOUGHT IT WAS A TEAM OF HACKERS!
Handle: CHOAD, Computer: IBM 5110 PORTABLE PC
THAT MAN IS ELITE!
Handle: DVORAKSNOB, Computer: APPLE II
SOMETIMES WHEN I PLAY COMPUTER GAMES, HIS NAME POPS UP ON THE SCREEN.
Handle: GRIZZLYNIPS, Computer: ATARI 400
YOU BEST FIND OUT FOR YOUR-SELF.

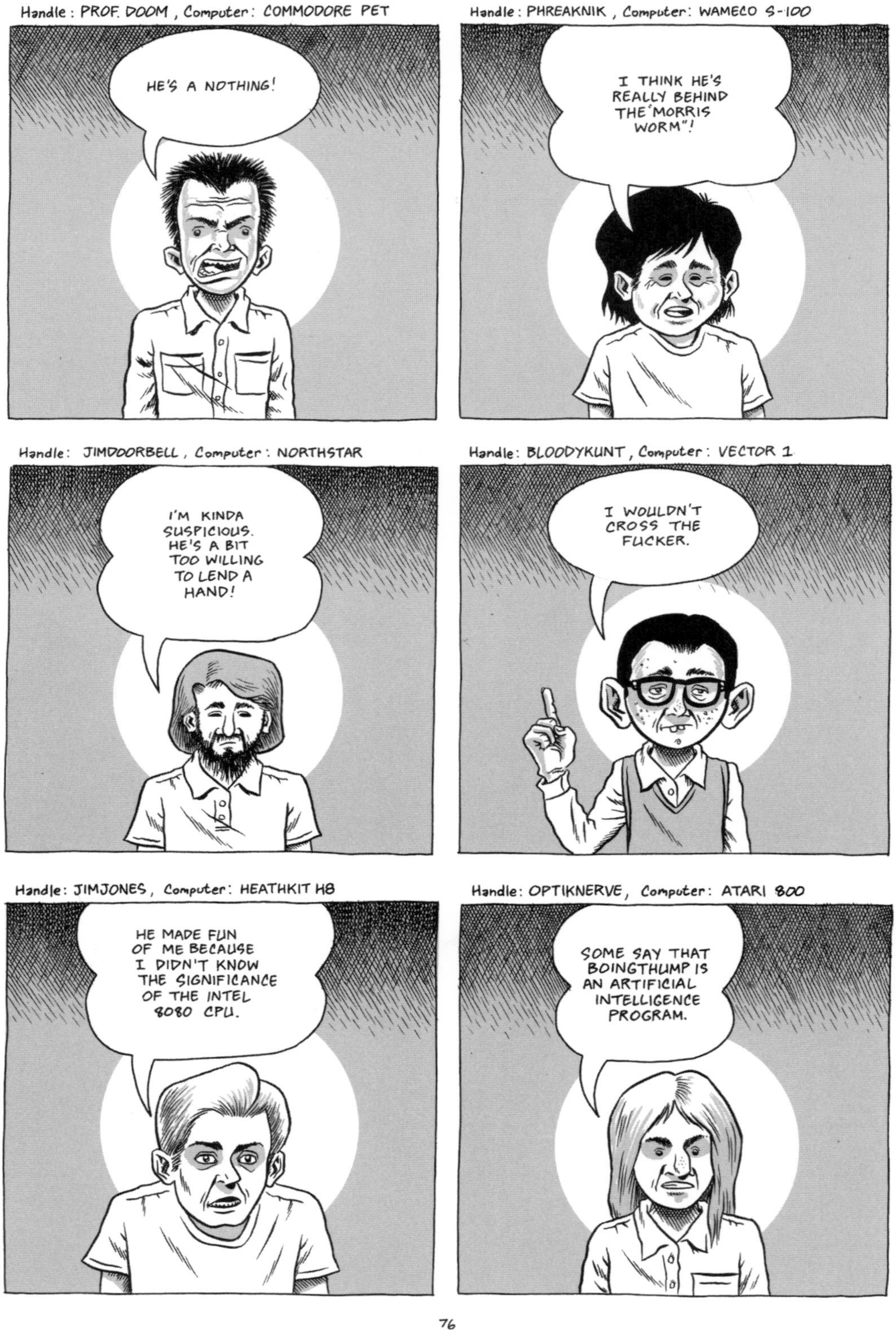
Handle: PROF. DOOM, Computer: COMMODORE PET
HE'S A NOTHING!
Handle: PHREAKNIK, Computer: WAMECO S-100
I THINK HE'S REALLY BEHIND THE "MORRIS WORM"!
Handle: JIMDOORBELL, Computer: NORTHSTAR
I'M KINDA SUSPICIOUS. HE'S A BIT TOO WILLING TO LEND A HAND!
Handle: BLOODYKUNT, Computer: VECTOR 1
I WOULDN'T CROSS THE FUCKER.
Handle: JIMJONES, Computer: HEATHKIT H8
HE MADE FUN OF ME BECAUSE I DIDN'T KNOW THE SIGNIFICANCE OF THE INTEL 8080 CPU.
Handle: OPTIKNERVE, Computer: ATARI 800
SOME SAY THAT BOINGTHUMP IS AN ARTIFICIAL INTELLIGENCE PROGRAM.

OFF THE ROCKER

with your host

WINSTON SMITH

WABCD 108.3 ON YOUR FM DIAL

I UNDERSTAND THAT KEVIN WAS INITIALLY ON THE RUN FOR LIKE FIVE YEARS...

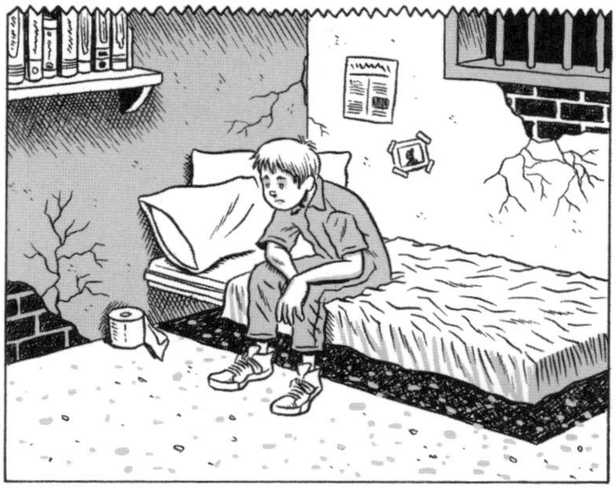

... BUT HE'S BEEN LOCKED UP FOR OVER A YEAR WITH NO TRIAL IN SIGHT...

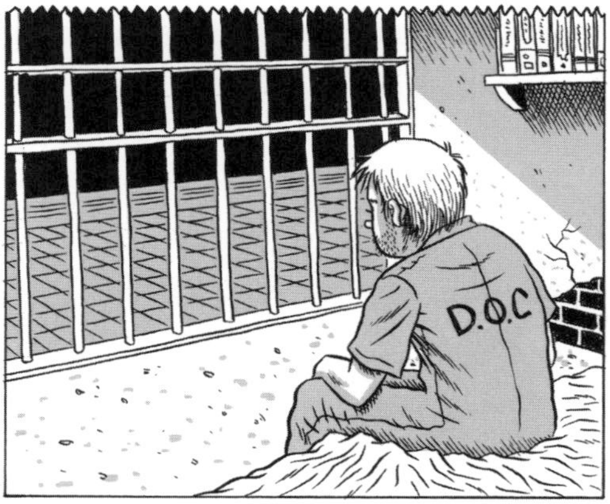
D.O.C

IT'S INEXCUSABLE! AT LEAST NOW WE KNOW SOME OF THE CHARGES AGAINST HIM...

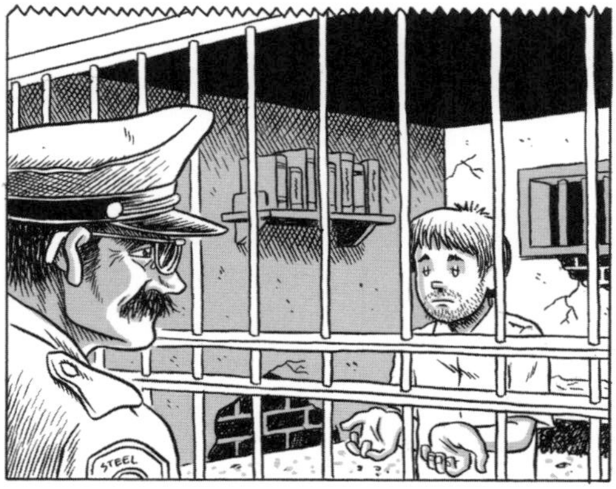
STEEL

... MULTIPLE CHARGES OF MAIL, WIRE, AND COMPUTER FRAUD, POSSESSION OF ACCESS DEVICES, OBSTRUCTION OF JUSTICE, MONEY LAUNDERING, PAROLE VIOLATION...

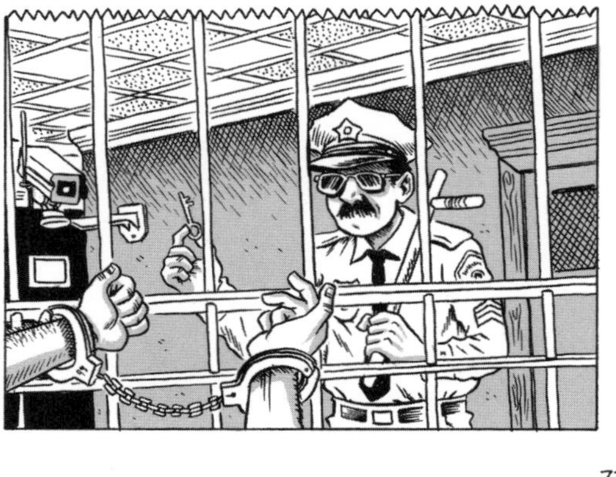

... JUST TO NAME A FEW...

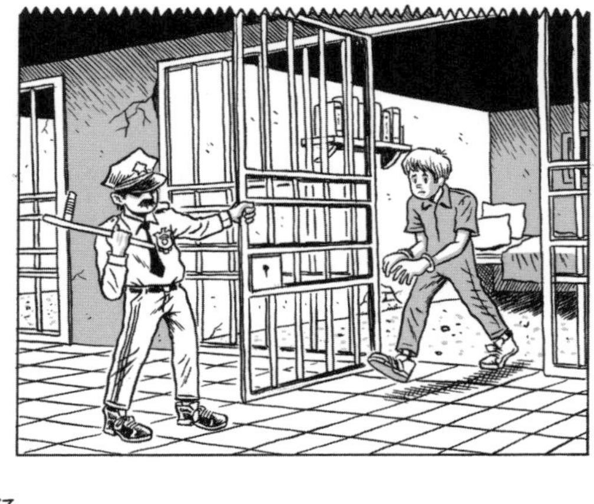

... ALSO, THE AMOUNT OF COST SOME COMPANIES CLAIM TO HAVE LOST DUE TO SECURITY BREACHES ARE NUTS!

THEY'RE ATTACHING WHAT THEY SPENT TO CREATE THE SYSTEMS THAT KEV BROKE INTO FOR THEIR FINAL TOTALS!

THE AUTHORITIES ARE SO AFRAID OF KEVIN THAT THEY WILL KEEP HIM IN THERE FOREVER IF THEY CAN.

AS IT STANDS NOW, IF HE WAS TO DO THE MAX AMOUNT OF TIME FOR THE LISTED CHARGES...

... HE WOULD BE LOCKED UP FOR OVER 100 YEARS!

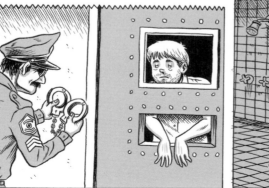

ALL FOR CRIMES WITH NO REAL, HUMAN VICTIMS...

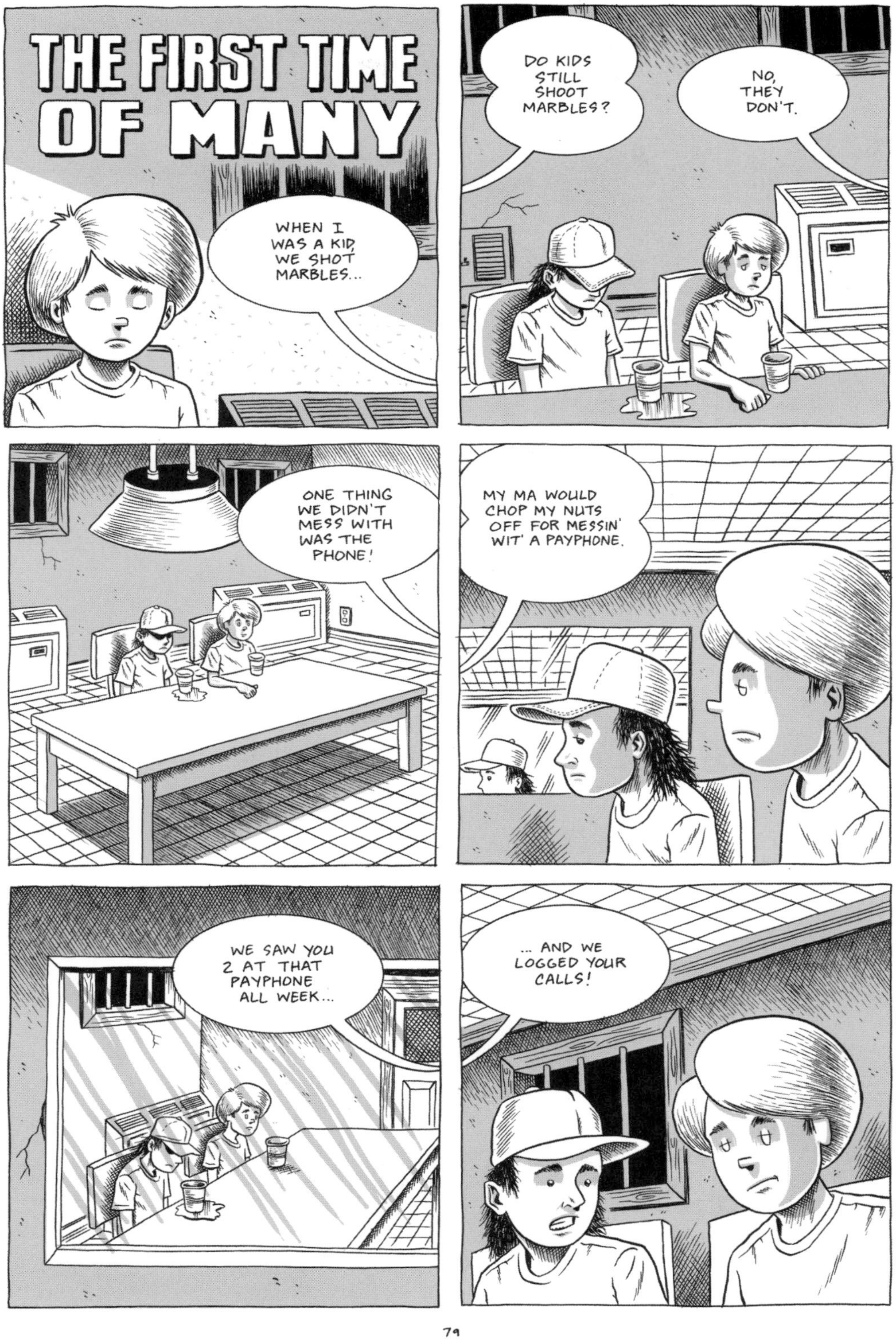
THE FIRST TIME OF MANY
WHEN I WAS A KID, WE SHOT MARBLES...
DO KIDS STILL SHOOT MARBLES?
NO, THEY DON'T.
ONE THING WE DIDN'T MESS WITH WAS THE PHONE!
MY MA WOULD CHOP MY NUTS OFF FOR MESSIN' WIT' A PAYPHONE.
WE SAW YOU 2 AT THAT PAYPHONE ALL WEEK...
... AND WE LOGGED YOUR CALLS!

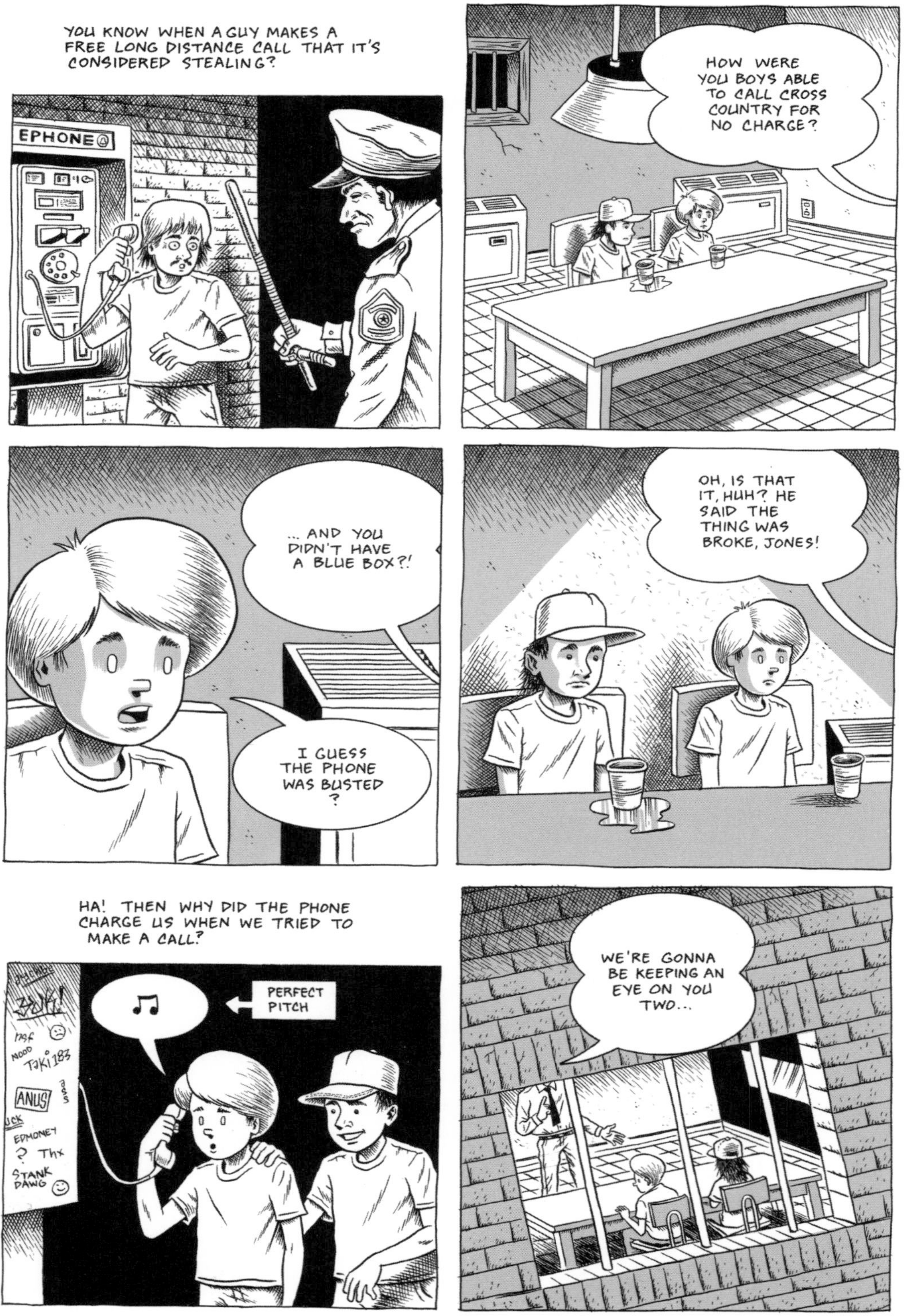
YOU KNOW WHEN A GUY MAKES A FREE LONG DISTANCE CALL THAT IT'S CONSIDERED STEALING?
EPHONE
HOW WERE YOU BOYS ABLE TO CALL CROSS COUNTRY FOR NO CHARGE?
... AND YOU DIDN'T HAVE A BLUE BOX?!
I GUESS THE PHONE WAS BUSTED?
OH, IS THAT IT, HUH? HE SAID THE THING WAS BROKE, JONES!
HA! THEN WHY DID THE PHONE CHARGE US WHEN WE TRIED TO MAKE A CALL?
PERFECT PITCH
TAKI 183
ANUS
EDMONEY
? Thx
STANK DAWG
WE'RE GONNA BE KEEPING AN EYE ON YOU TWO...

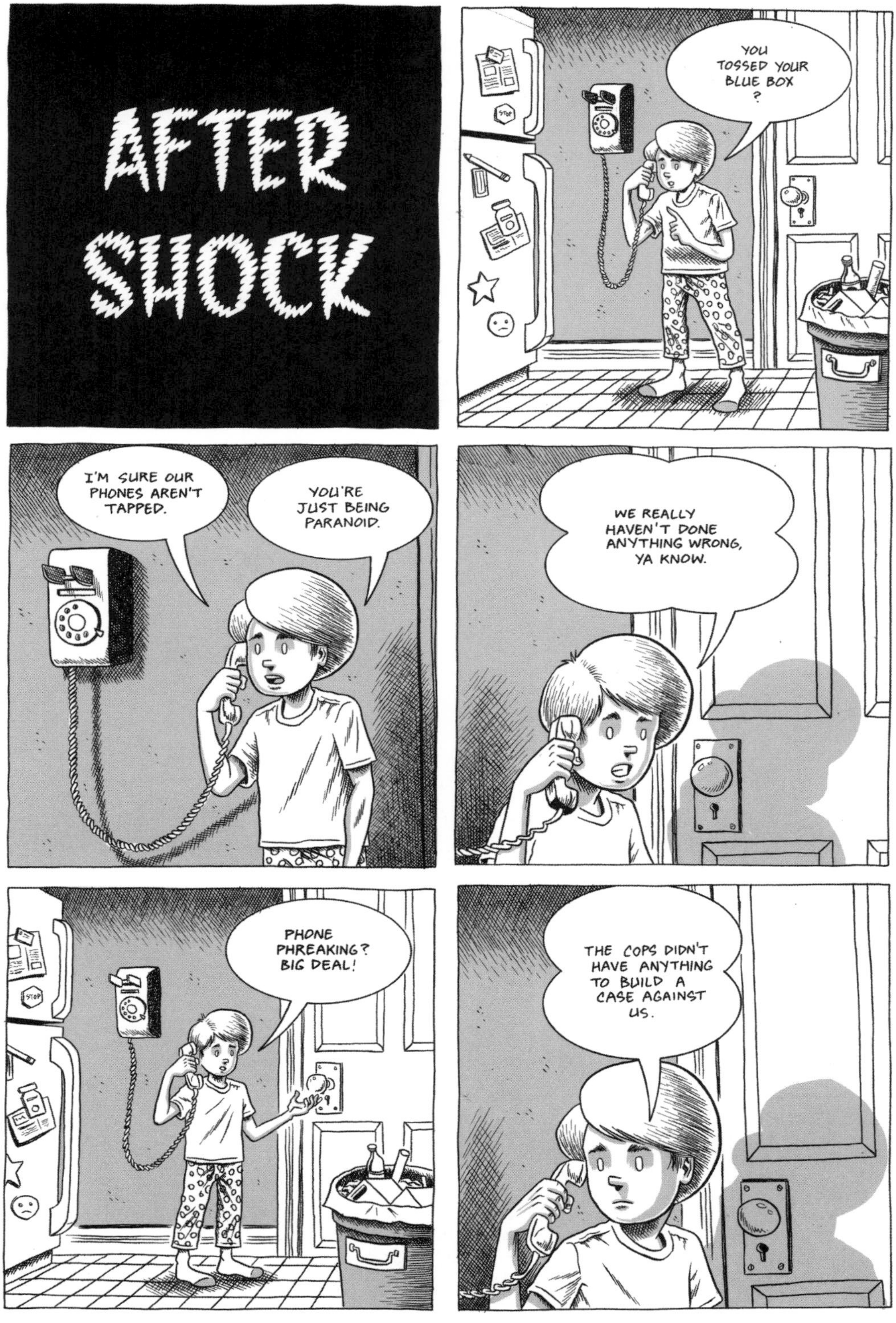
AFTER SHOCK
YOU TOSSED YOUR BLUE BOX ?
STOP
I'M SURE OUR PHONES AREN'T TAPPED.
YOU'RE JUST BEING PARANOID.
WE REALLY HAVEN'T DONE ANYTHING WRONG, YA KNOW.
PHONE PHREAKING? BIG DEAL!
STOP
THE COPS DIDN'T HAVE ANYTHING TO BUILD A CASE AGAINST US.

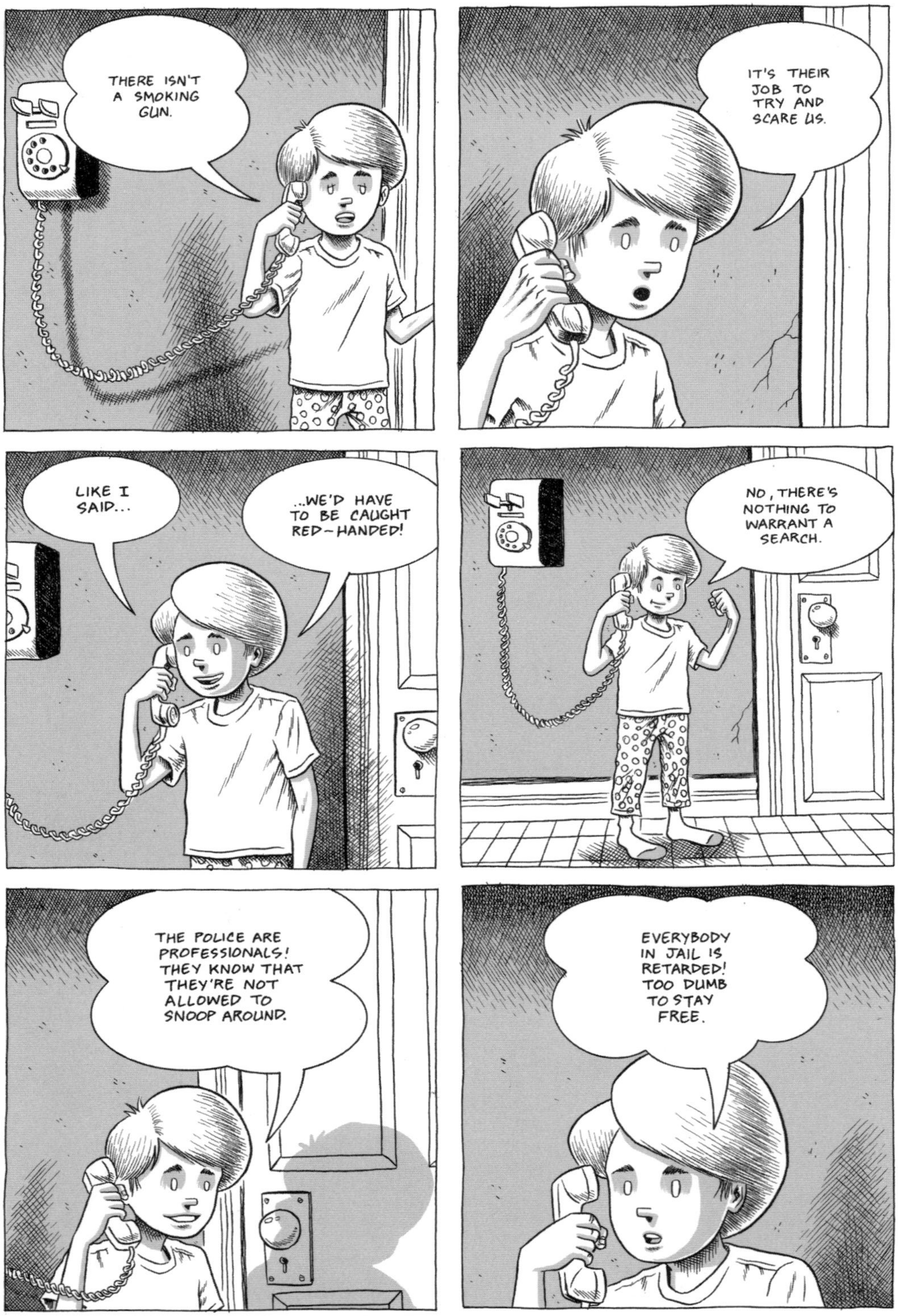
THERE ISN'T A SMOKING GUN.
IT'S THEIR JOB TO TRY AND SCARE US.
LIKE I SAID...
...WE'D HAVE TO BE CAUGHT RED-HANDED!
NO, THERE'S NOTHING TO WARRANT A SEARCH.
THE POLICE ARE PROFESSIONALS! THEY KNOW THAT THEY'RE NOT ALLOWED TO SNOOP AROUND.
EVERYBODY IN JAIL IS RETARDED! TOO DUMB TO STAY FREE.

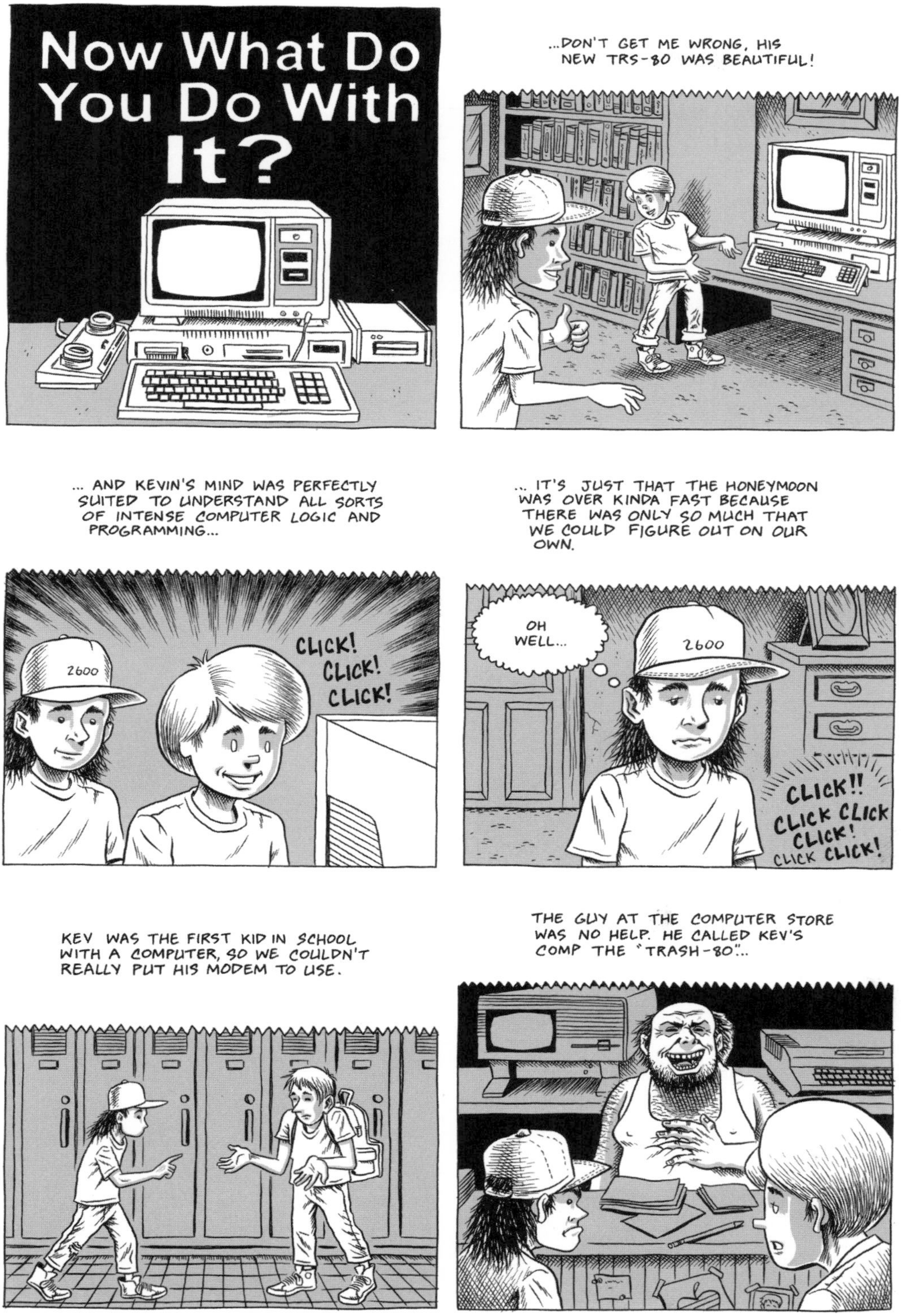
Now What Do You Do With It?
...DON'T GET ME WRONG, HIS NEW TRS-80 WAS BEAUTIFUL!
... AND KEVIN'S MIND WAS PERFECTLY SUITED TO UNDERSTAND ALL SORTS OF INTENSE COMPUTER LOGIC AND PROGRAMMING...
2600
CLICK! CLICK! CLICK!
... IT'S JUST THAT THE HONEYMOON WAS OVER KINDA FAST BECAUSE THERE WAS ONLY SO MUCH THAT WE COULD FIGURE OUT ON OUR OWN.
OH WELL...
2600
CLICK!! CLICK CLICK CLICK! CLICK CLICK!
KEV WAS THE FIRST KID IN SCHOOL WITH A COMPUTER, SO WE COULDN'T REALLY PUT HIS MODEM TO USE.
THE GUY AT THE COMPUTER STORE WAS NO HELP. HE CALLED KEV'S COMP THE "TRASH-80"...

... SOOO ONE OF US DECIDED TO KEEP THE BALL FROM A COMPUTER MOUSE.

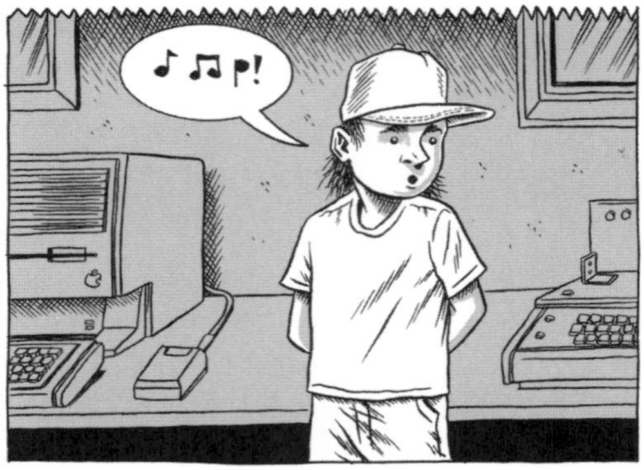

I'LL NEVER FORGET THAT GUY. HE WAS A SUCKER FOR APPLE PRODUCTS.

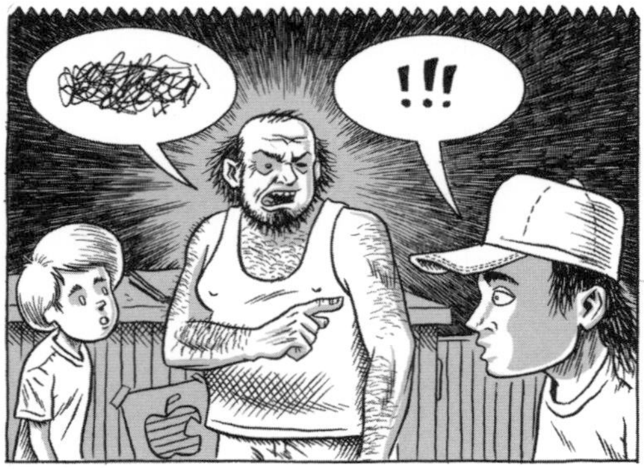
!!!

HE REALLY FLIPPED WHEN I MADE FUN OF THEIR "LEMMINGS" COMMERCIAL.

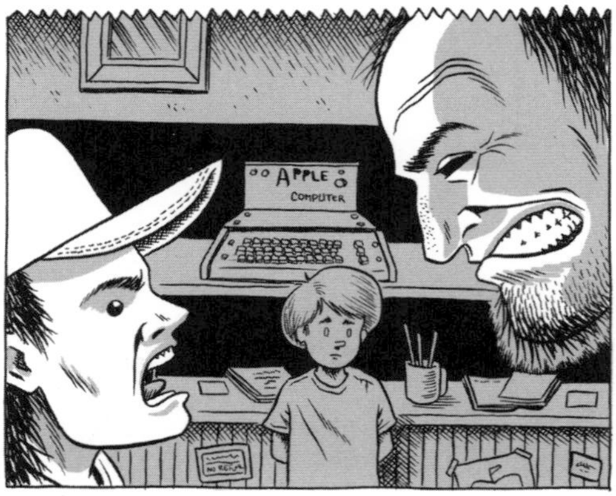
APPLE
COMPUTER

AT THE TIME, I DIDN'T REALIZE I WAS PROVIDING KEV SOME COVER...

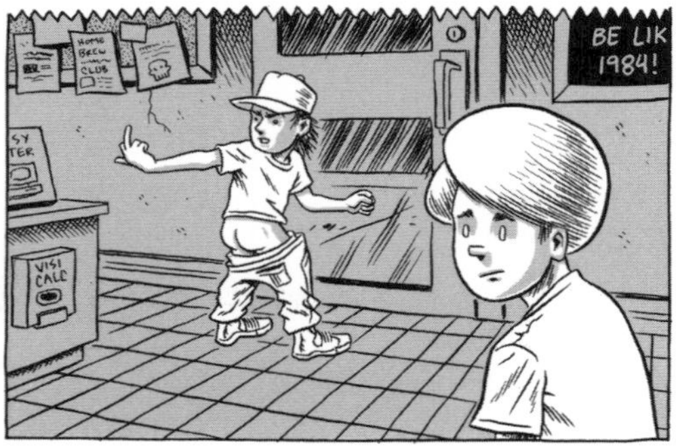
BE LIK
1984!
HOME BREW CLUB
VISI CALC

... BECAUSE HE SWIPED A BUNCH OF COMPUTER BBS NUMBERS FOR US TO CONNECT WITH.

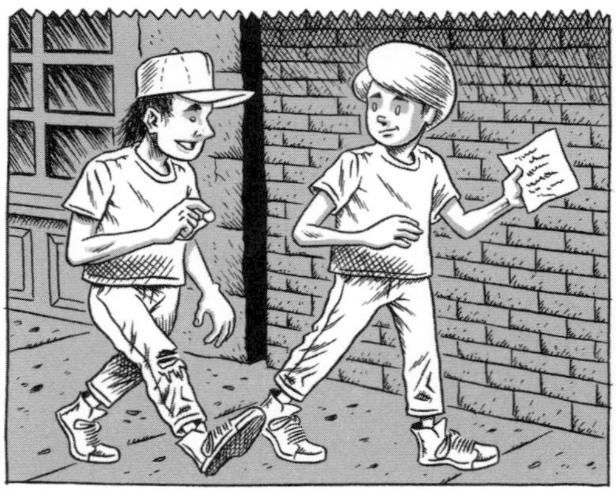

THAT'S WHEN WE GOT THE BALL ROLLING, SO TO SPEAK...

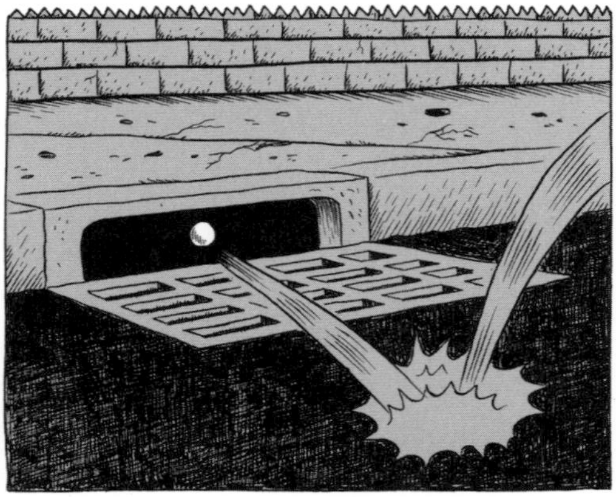

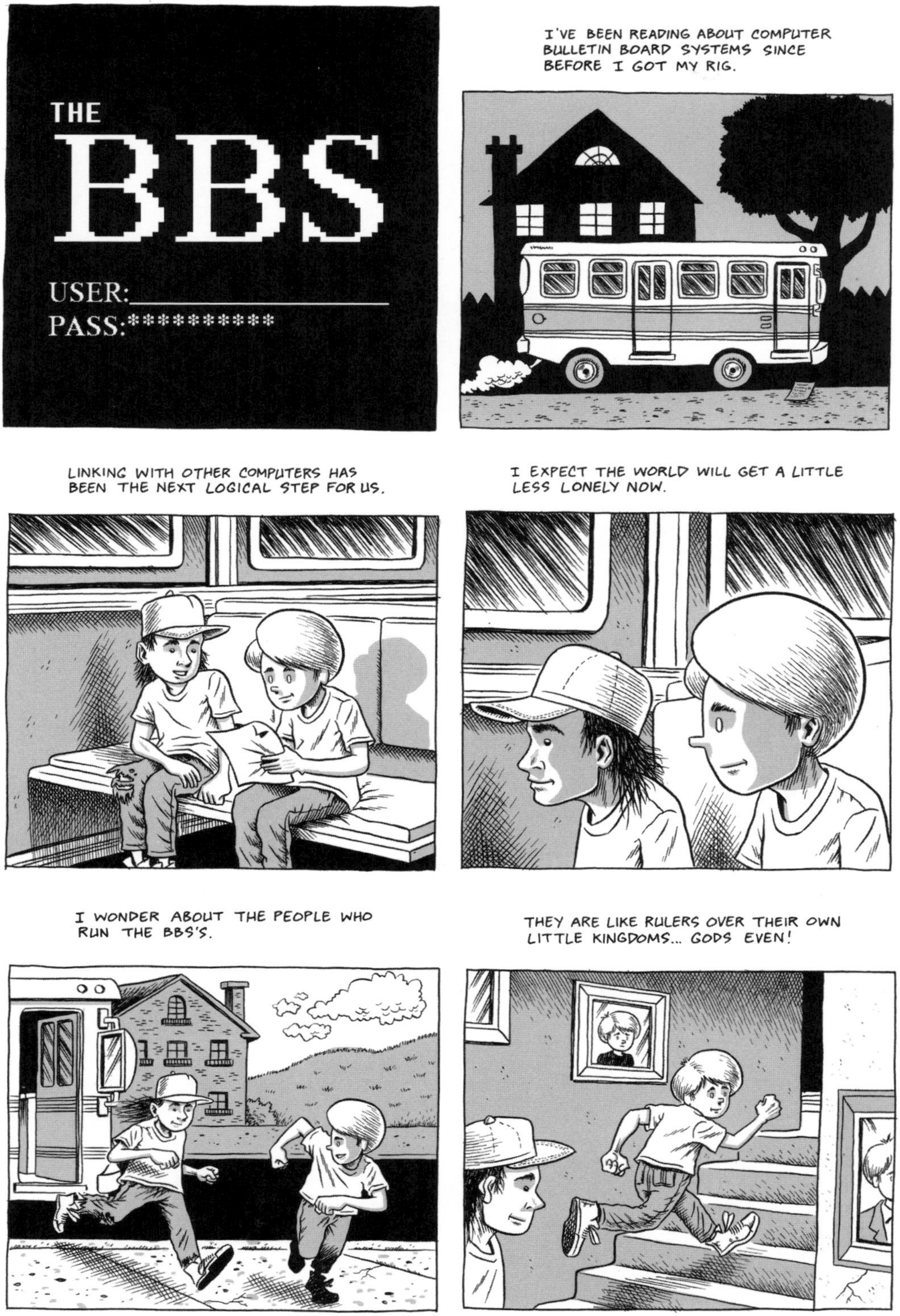
THE BBS
USER:
PASS:**********
I'VE BEEN READING ABOUT COMPUTER BULLETIN BOARD SYSTEMS SINCE BEFORE I GOT MY RIG.
LINKING WITH OTHER COMPUTERS HAS BEEN THE NEXT LOGICAL STEP FOR US.
I EXPECT THE WORLD WILL GET A LITTLE LESS LONELY NOW.
I WONDER ABOUT THE PEOPLE WHO RUN THE BBS'S.
THEY ARE LIKE RULERS OVER THEIR OWN LITTLE KINGDOMS... GODS EVEN!

THERE IS PROBABLY SO MUCH THAT I CAN LEARN FROM THEM.

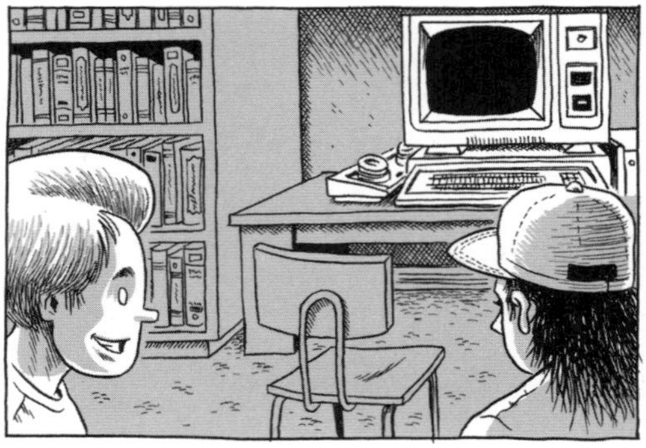

WE WILL PROBABLY BE TREATED WITH GREATER RESPECT TOO, SINCE NO ONE WILL KNOW WE'RE JUST KIDS.

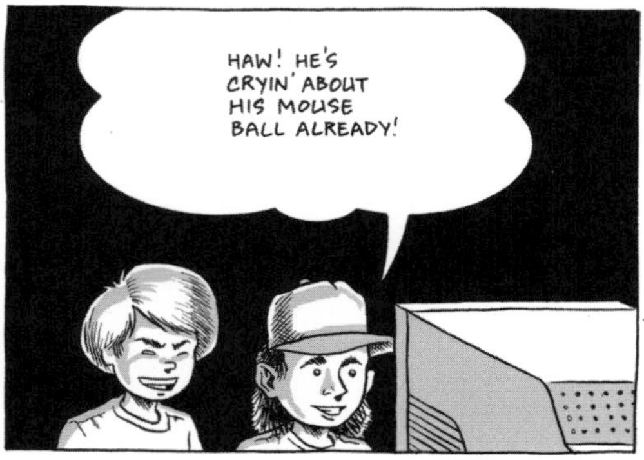
HAW! HE'S CRYIN' ABOUT HIS MOUSE BALL ALREADY!

DAMMIT! EVERY FUN—SOUNDING BOARD IS PASSWORD PROTECTED. I'LL HAVE TO WORK ON THAT.

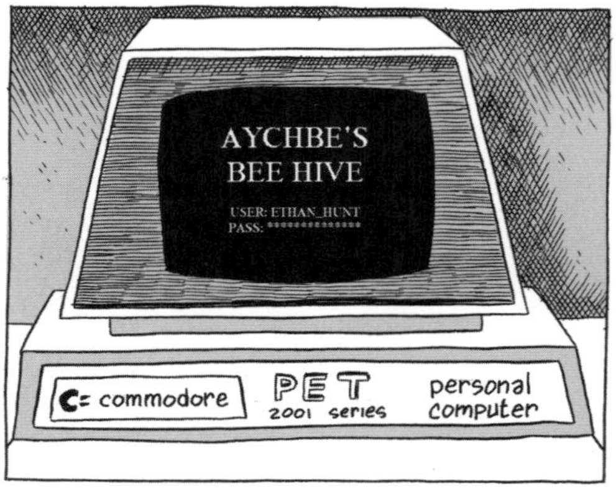
AYCHBE'S
BEE HIVE
USER: ETHAN_HUNT
PASS: **************
commodore
PET
2001 series
personal computer

UGH! MOST OF THESE LOCAL ONES ARE DULL AS HELL.

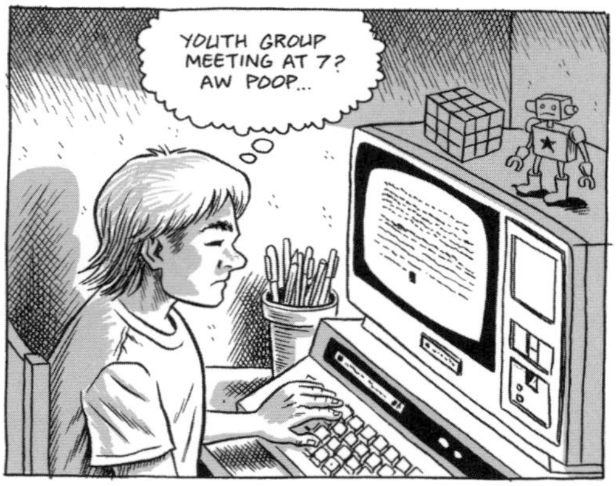
YOUTH GROUP MEETING AT 7? AW POOP...

THERE IS ONE PIRATE BOARD ON THE LIST THOUGH.

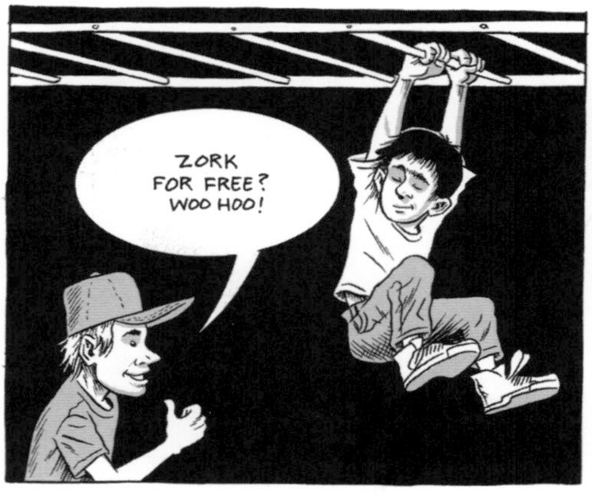
ZORK FOR FREE? WOO HOO!

JUST LIKE REAL LIFE, THERE ARE SOME DARK ALLEYS THAT I FIND IMPRESSIVE.

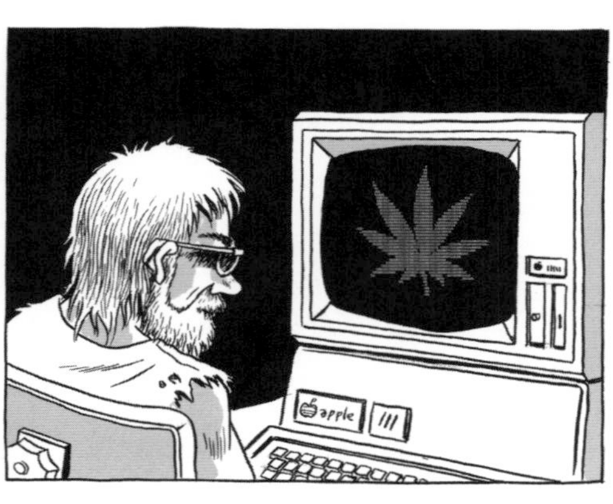
apple
///

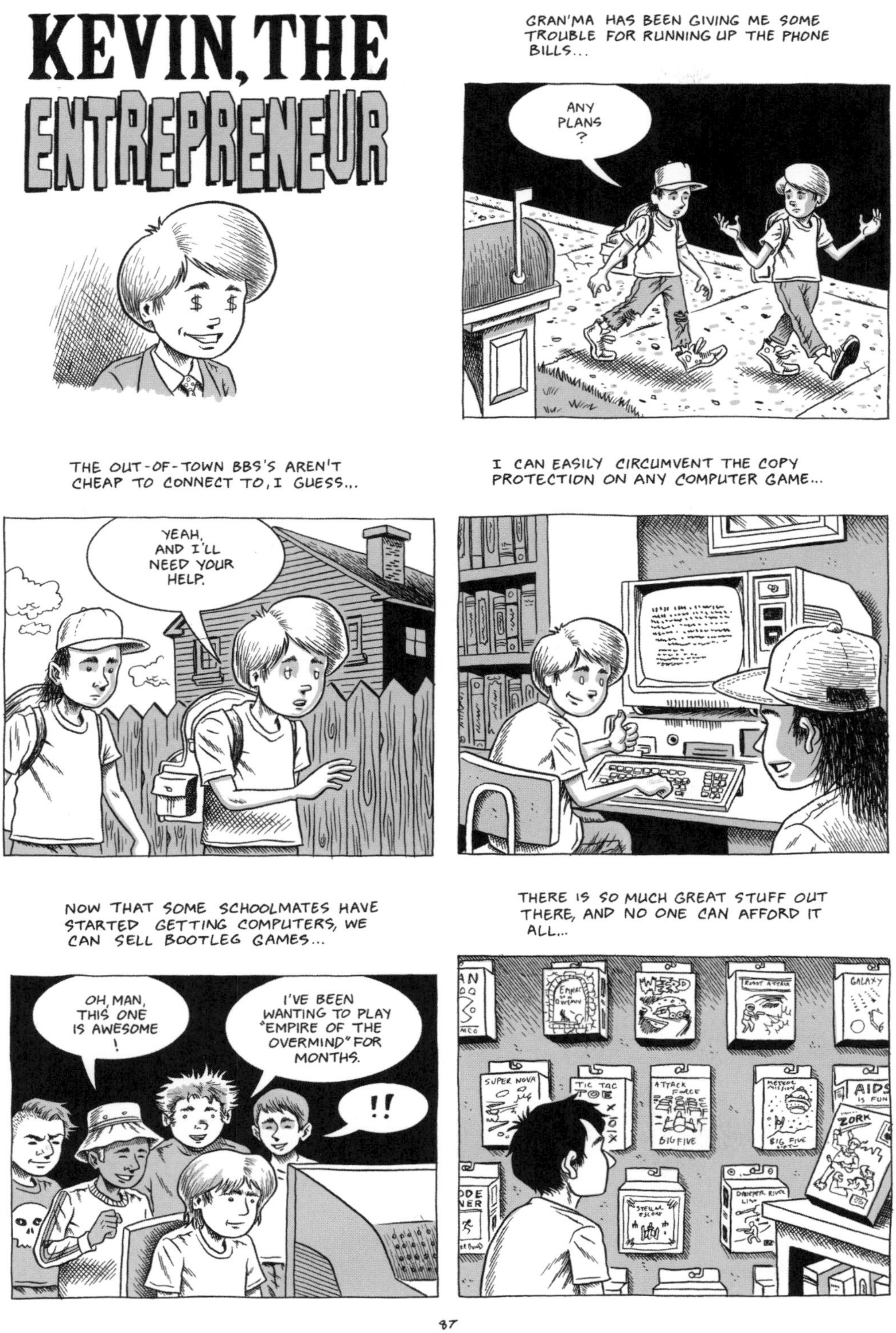
KEVIN, THE ENTREPRENEUR
GRAN'MA HAS BEEN GIVING ME SOME TROUBLE FOR RUNNING UP THE PHONE BILLS...
ANY PLANS ?
THE OUT-OF-TOWN BBS'S AREN'T CHEAP TO CONNECT TO, I GUESS...
YEAH, AND I'LL NEED YOUR HELP.
I CAN EASILY CIRCUMVENT THE COPY PROTECTION ON ANY COMPUTER GAME...
NOW THAT SOME SCHOOLMATES HAVE STARTED GETTING COMPUTERS, WE CAN SELL BOOTLEG GAMES...
OH, MAN, THIS ONE IS AWESOME !
I'VE BEEN WANTING TO PLAY "EMPIRE OF THE OVERMIND" FOR MONTHS.
!!
THERE IS SO MUCH GREAT STUFF OUT THERE, AND NO ONE CAN AFFORD IT ALL...
GALAXY
SUPER NOVA
TIC TAC TOE
ATTACK FORCE
BIG FIVE
AIDS IS FUN
ZORK

WINSTON'S JOB IS TO ASK AROUND AND TAKE ORDERS...

WE BORROW GAMES, RIP THEM, SELL COPIES, AND MAKE A PROFIT. BUT THERE IS A CATCH.

WELL, KEV...

...IT'S GONNA BE A LONG WEEKEND!

HERE'S YOUR COPY OF "PLANET MINERS".

JAZZY!

BECAUSE I CAN'T HELP MYSELF, I DECIDED TO INJECT SOME CODE OF MY OWN INTO THE COPIES.

EVERY 100 PLAYS WILL LOAD A SCREEN WITH MY COMPUTER HANDLE AND A SILLY MESSAGE BEFORE REBOOTING.

THIS IS FANTASTIC!

HA HA!! ha ha HA!! ha HA!!

!!!

HA HA HA HA! !!!

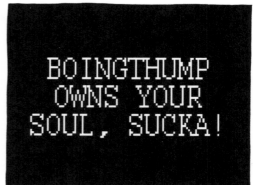

BOINGTHUMP OWNS YOUR SOUL, SUCKA!

WHAT'S THE POINT OF ANYTHING, IF YOU CAN'T HAVE FUN WITH IT?

I BET NO ONE BOOTS ANY DUMB GAME CLOSE TO 100 TIMES ANYHOW.

I CAN EAVESDROP ON CELLULAR PHONE CALLS USING HI-BAND UHF FROM MY TV.

...RIGHT IN MY ASS. OH YEAH.

DA HELL IS THIS BOINGTHUMP SHIT?!

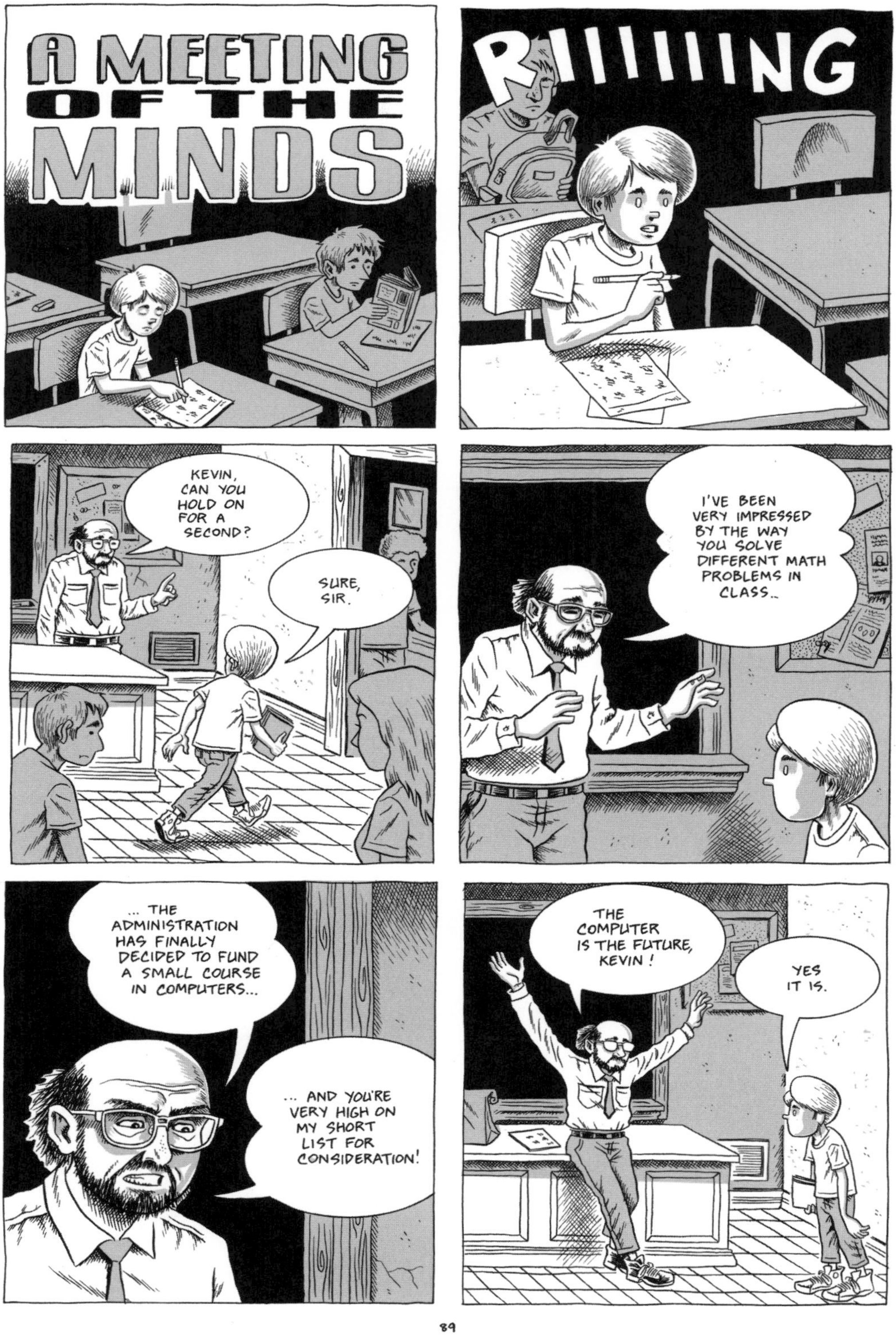
A MEETING OF THE MINDS
RIIIIIING
KEVIN, CAN YOU HOLD ON FOR A SECOND?
SURE, SIR.
I'VE BEEN VERY IMPRESSED BY THE WAY YOU SOLVE DIFFERENT MATH PROBLEMS IN CLASS..
... THE ADMINISTRATION HAS FINALLY DECIDED TO FUND A SMALL COURSE IN COMPUTERS...
... AND YOU'RE VERY HIGH ON MY SHORT LIST FOR CONSIDERATION!
THE COMPUTER IS THE FUTURE, KEVIN!
YES IT IS.

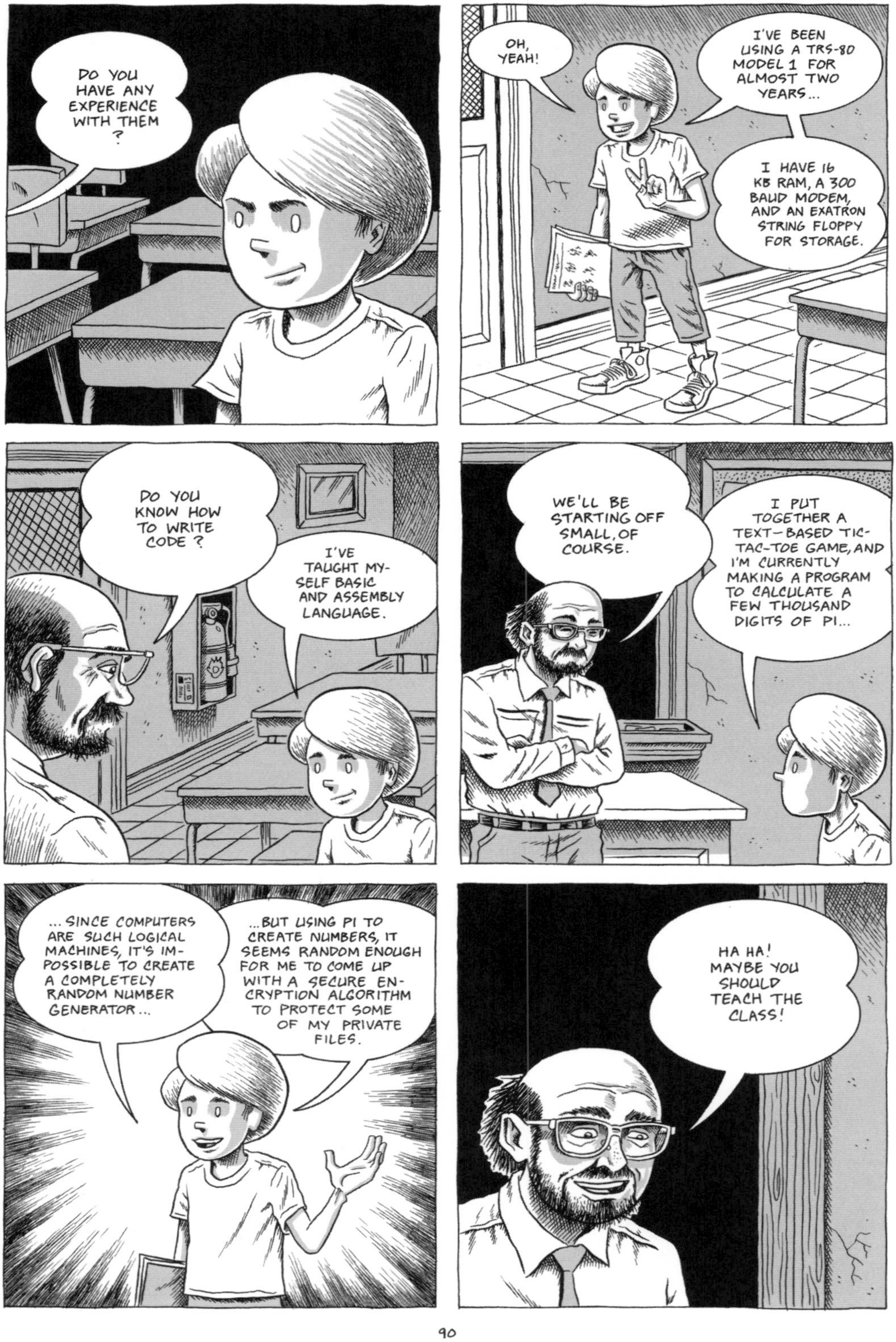
DO YOU HAVE ANY EXPERIENCE WITH THEM ?
OH, YEAH!
I'VE BEEN USING A TRS-80 MODEL 1 FOR ALMOST TWO YEARS...
I HAVE 16 KB RAM, A 300 BAUD MODEM, AND AN EXATRON STRING FLOPPY FOR STORAGE.
DO YOU KNOW HOW TO WRITE CODE ?
I'VE TAUGHT MY-SELF BASIC AND ASSEMBLY LANGUAGE.
WE'LL BE STARTING OFF SMALL, OF COURSE.
I PUT TOGETHER A TEXT-BASED TIC-TAC-TOE GAME, AND I'M CURRENTLY MAKING A PROGRAM TO CALCULATE A FEW THOUSAND DIGITS OF PI...
... SINCE COMPUTERS ARE SUCH LOGICAL MACHINES, IT'S IM-POSSIBLE TO CREATE A COMPLETELY RANDOM NUMBER GENERATOR...
...BUT USING PI TO CREATE NUMBERS, IT SEEMS RANDOM ENOUGH FOR ME TO COME UP WITH A SECURE EN-CRYPTION ALGORITHM TO PROTECT SOME OF MY PRIVATE FILES.
HA HA! MAYBE YOU SHOULD TEACH THE CLASS!

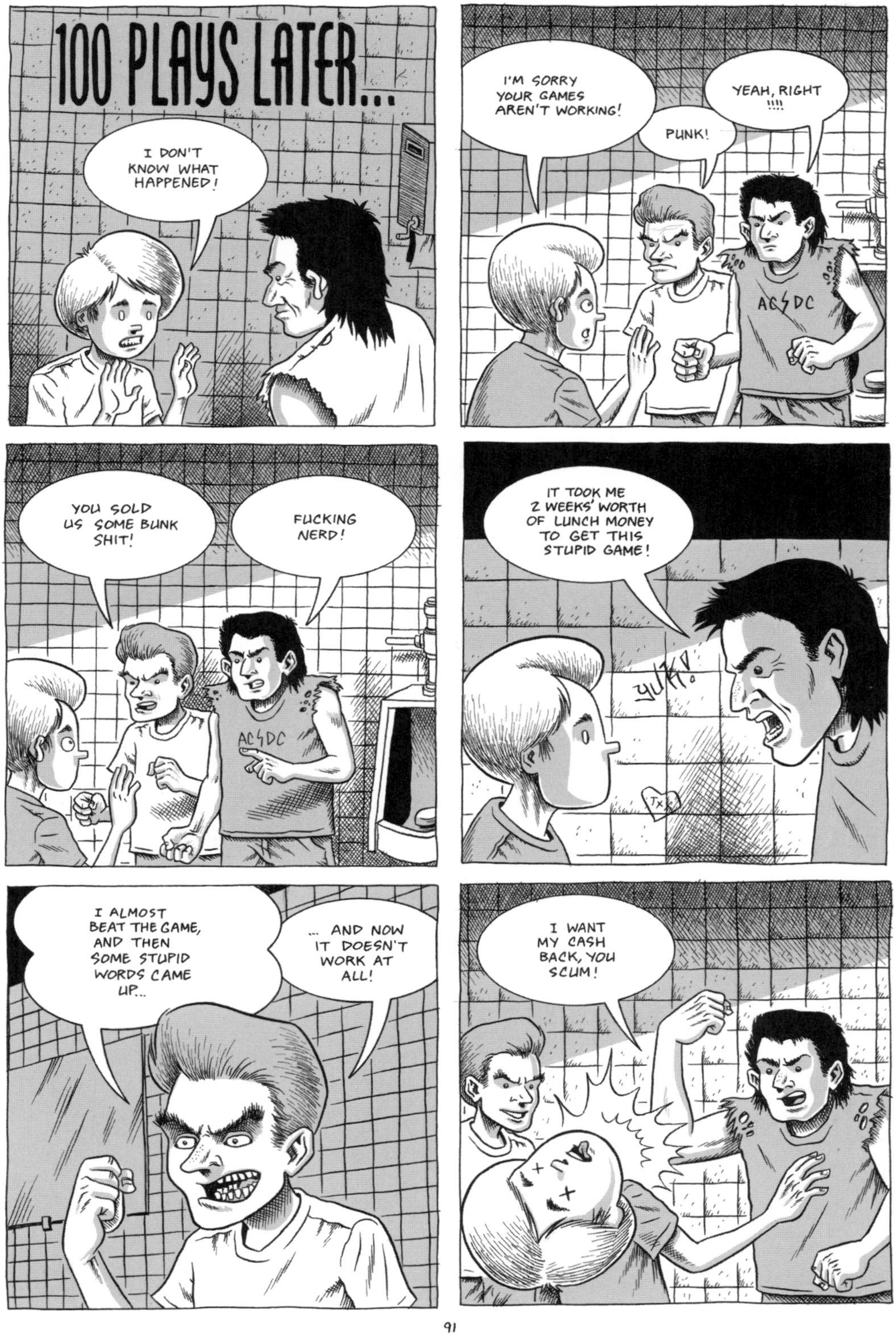

100 PLAYS LATER...
I DON'T KNOW WHAT HAPPENED!
I'M SORRY YOUR GAMES AREN'T WORKING!
PUNK!
YEAH, RIGHT !!!!
YOU SOLD US SOME BUNK SHIT!
FUCKING NERD!
IT TOOK ME 2 WEEKS' WORTH OF LUNCH MONEY TO GET THIS STUPID GAME!
I ALMOST BEAT THE GAME, AND THEN SOME STUPID WORDS CAME UP...
... AND NOW IT DOESN'T WORK AT ALL!
I WANT MY CASH BACK, YOU SCUM!

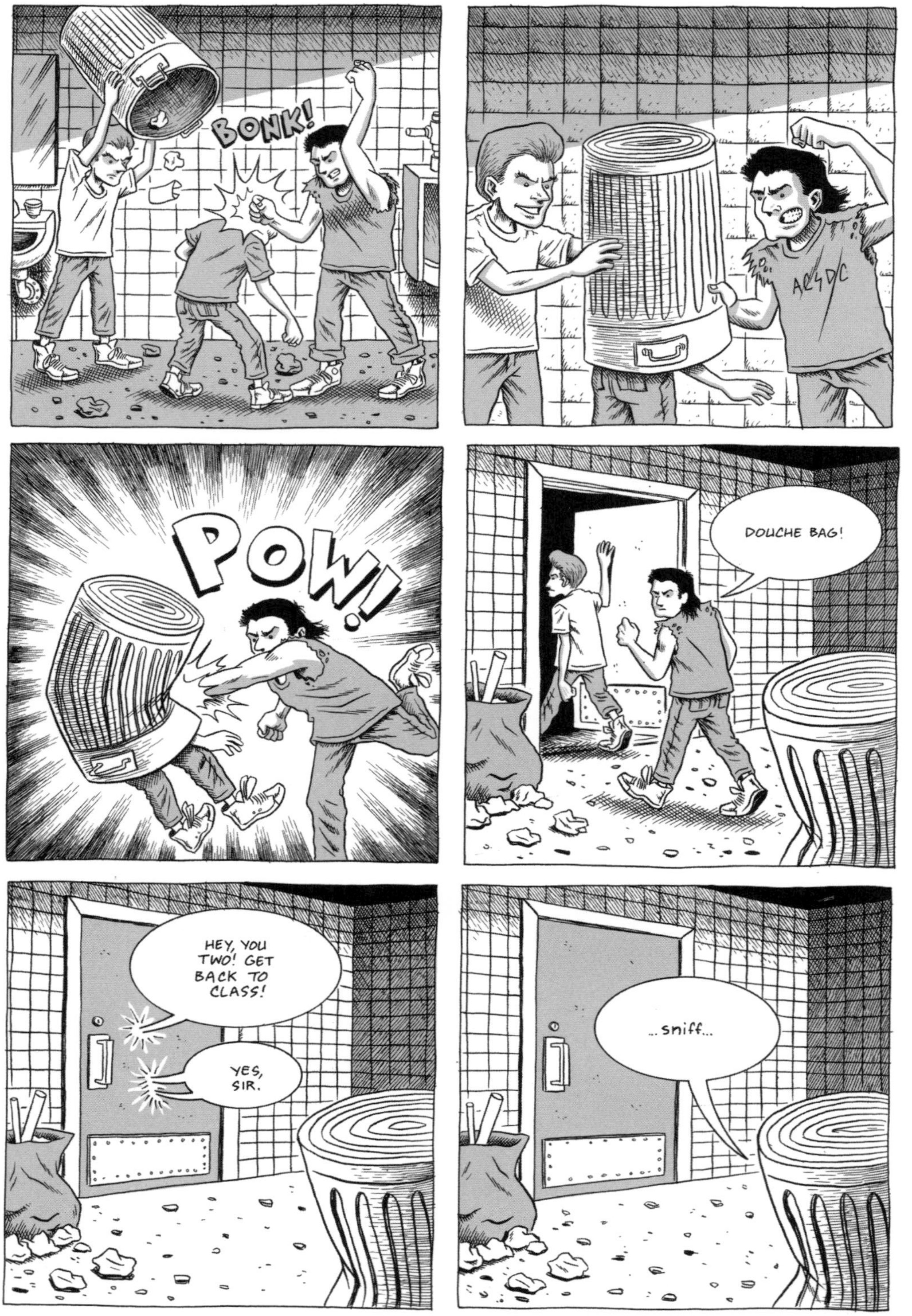
BONK!
AC/DC
POW!
DOUCHE BAG!
HEY, YOU TWO! GET BACK TO CLASS!
YES, SIR.
...sniff...

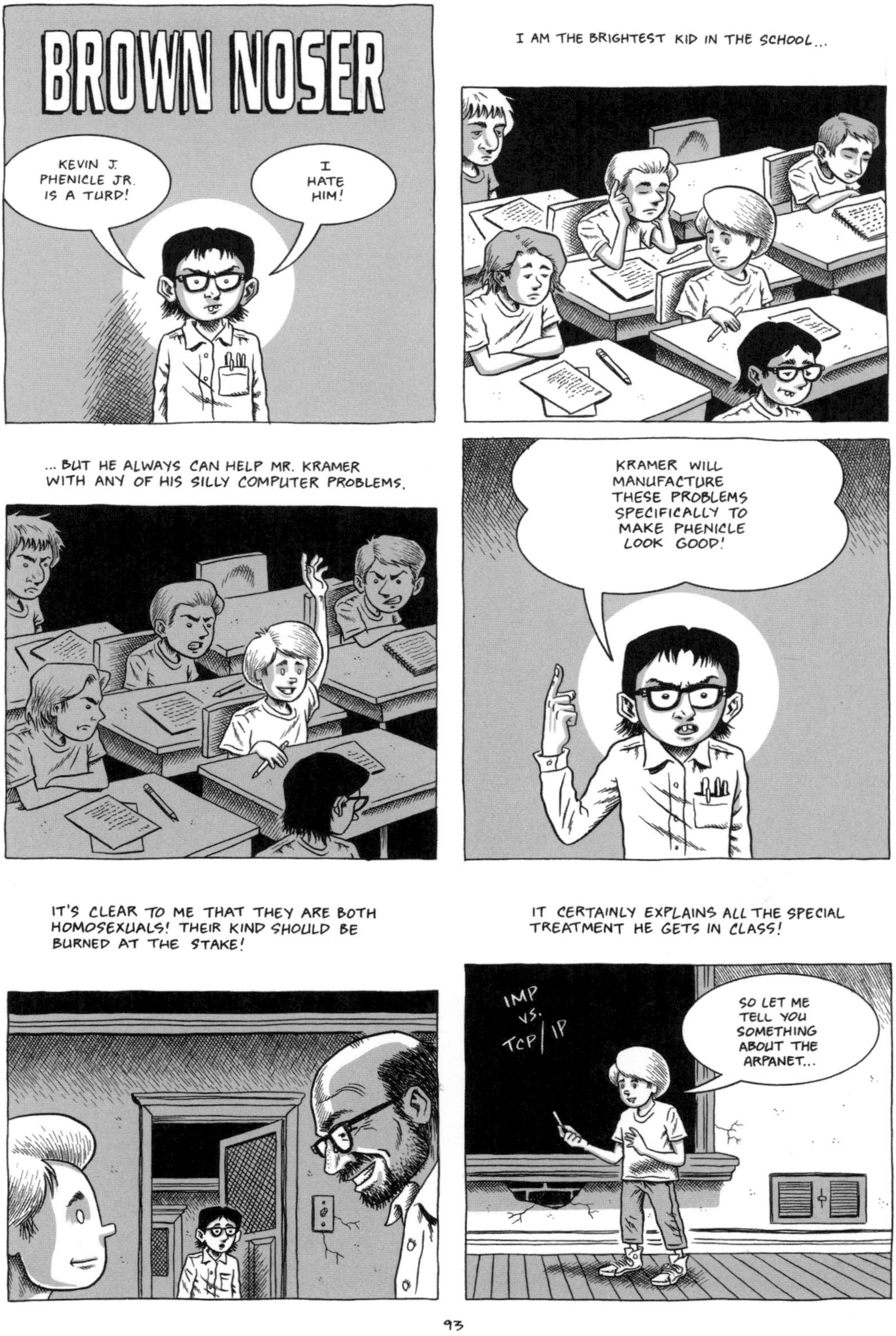
BROWN NOSER
KEVIN J. PHENICLE JR. IS A TURD!
I HATE HIM!
I AM THE BRIGHTEST KID IN THE SCHOOL...
...BUT HE ALWAYS CAN HELP MR. KRAMER WITH ANY OF HIS SILLY COMPUTER PROBLEMS.
KRAMER WILL MANUFACTURE THESE PROBLEMS SPECIFICALLY TO MAKE PHENICLE LOOK GOOD!
IT'S CLEAR TO ME THAT THEY ARE BOTH HOMOSEXUALS! THEIR KIND SHOULD BE BURNED AT THE STAKE!
IT CERTAINLY EXPLAINS ALL THE SPECIAL TREATMENT HE GETS IN CLASS!
IMP VS. TCP/IP
SO LET ME TELL YOU SOMETHING ABOUT THE ARPANET...

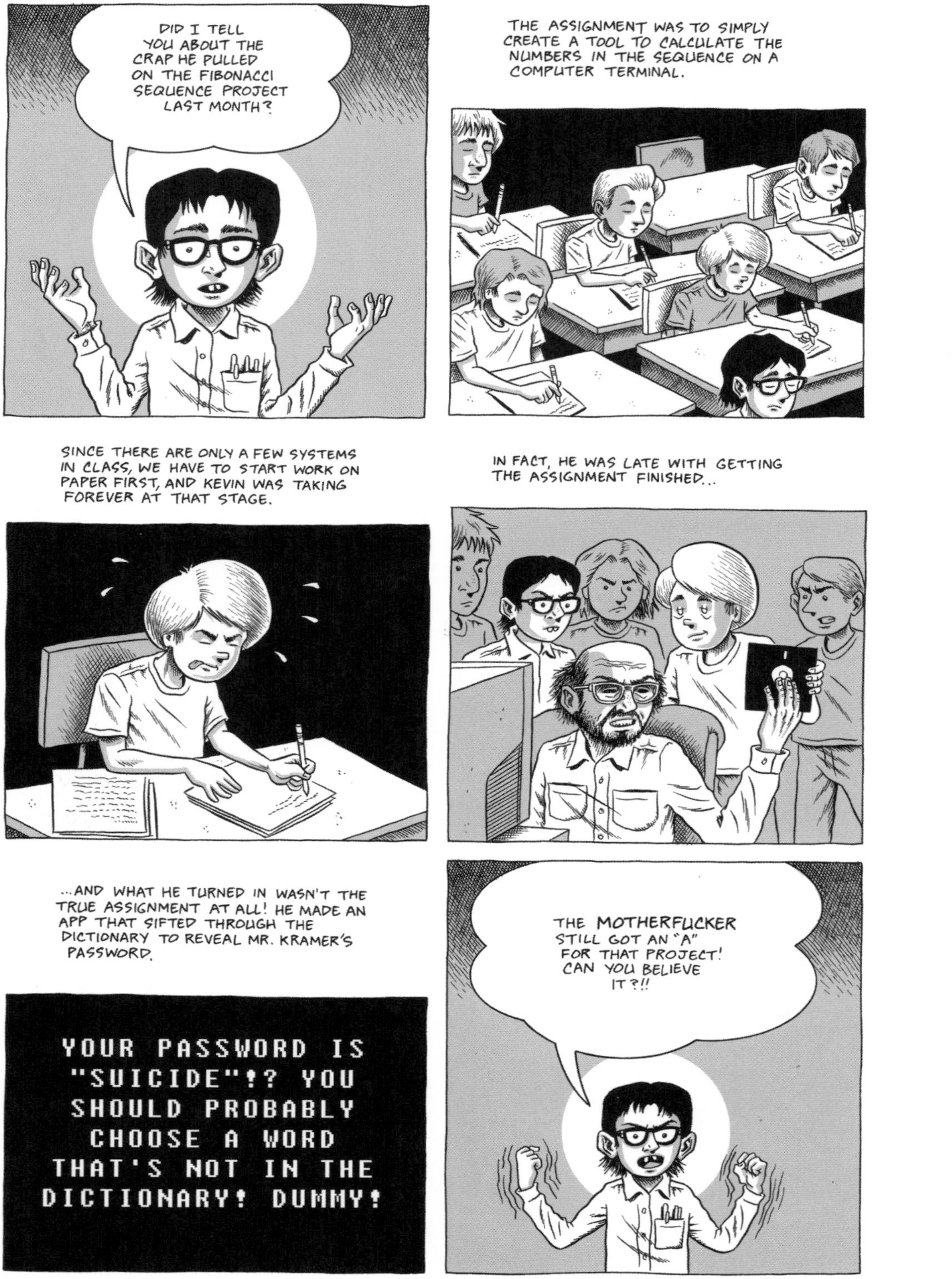
DID I TELL YOU ABOUT THE CRAP HE PULLED ON THE FIBONACCI SEQUENCE PROJECT LAST MONTH?
THE ASSIGNMENT WAS TO SIMPLY CREATE A TOOL TO CALCULATE THE NUMBERS IN THE SEQUENCE ON A COMPUTER TERMINAL.
SINCE THERE ARE ONLY A FEW SYSTEMS IN CLASS, WE HAVE TO START WORK ON PAPER FIRST, AND KEVIN WAS TAKING FOREVER AT THAT STAGE.
IN FACT, HE WAS LATE WITH GETTING THE ASSIGNMENT FINISHED...
...AND WHAT HE TURNED IN WASN'T THE TRUE ASSIGNMENT AT ALL! HE MADE AN APP THAT SIFTED THROUGH THE DICTIONARY TO REVEAL MR. KRAMER'S PASSWORD.
YOUR PASSWORD IS "SUICIDE"!? YOU SHOULD PROBABLY CHOOSE A WORD THAT'S NOT IN THE DICTIONARY! DUMMY!
THE MOTHERFUCKER STILL GOT AN "A" FOR THAT PROJECT! CAN YOU BELIEVE IT?!!

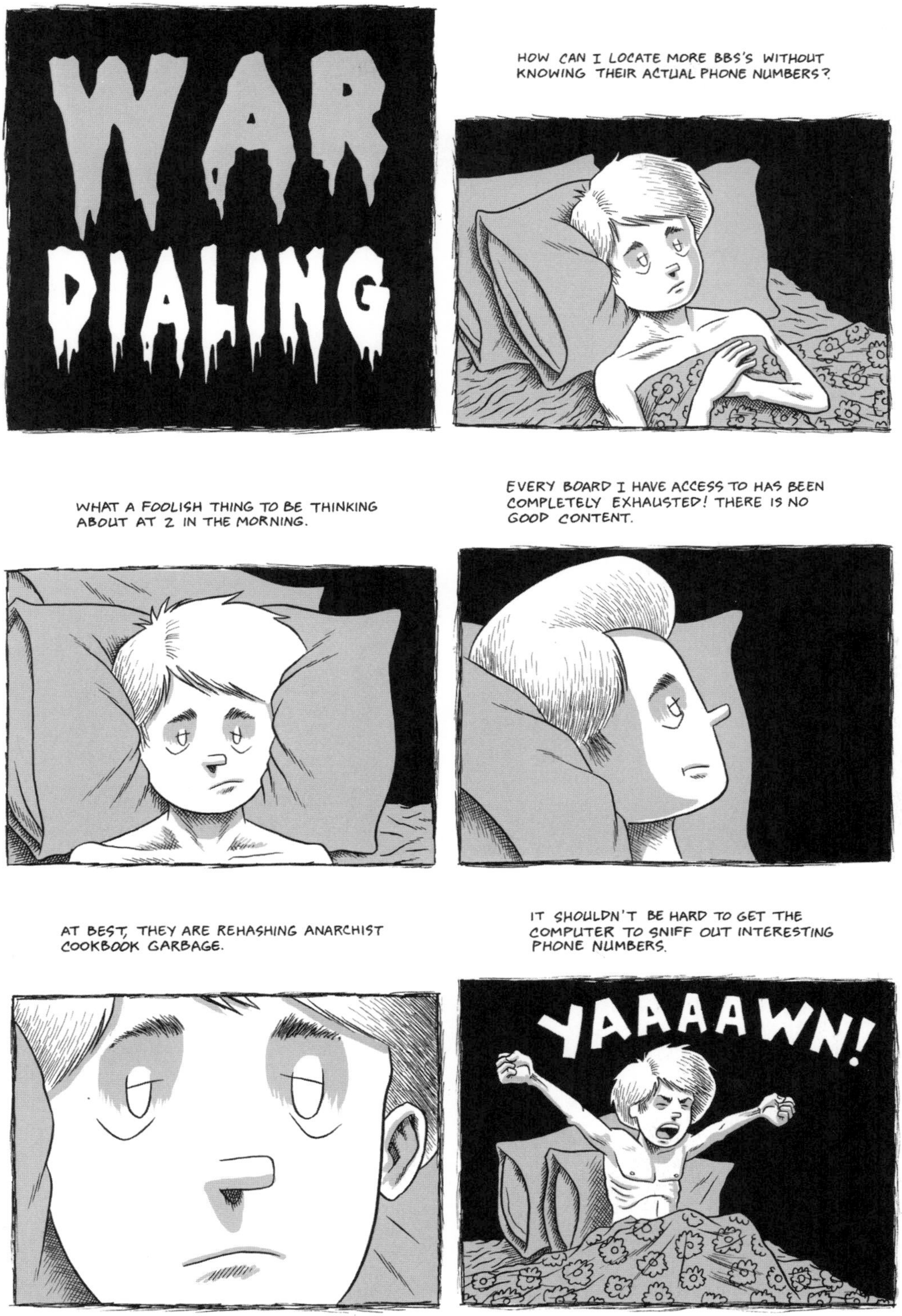
WAR DIALING
HOW CAN I LOCATE MORE BBS'S WITHOUT KNOWING THEIR ACTUAL PHONE NUMBERS?
WHAT A FOOLISH THING TO BE THINKING ABOUT AT 2 IN THE MORNING.
EVERY BOARD I HAVE ACCESS TO HAS BEEN COMPLETELY EXHAUSTED! THERE IS NO GOOD CONTENT.
AT BEST, THEY ARE REHASHING ANARCHIST COOKBOOK GARBAGE.
IT SHOULDN'T BE HARD TO GET THE COMPUTER TO SNIFF OUT INTERESTING PHONE NUMBERS.
YAAAAWN!

I'LL CREATE A SCRIPT TO CALL THROUGH A BLOCK OF PHONE NUMBERS... LIKE EVERYTHING BETWEEN 555-0000 – 555-9999.

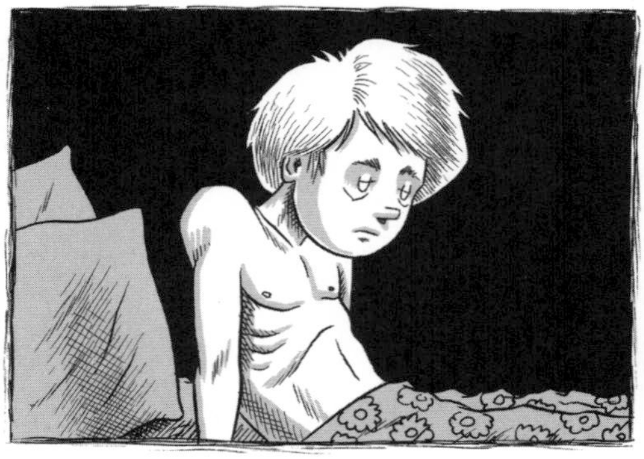

I CAN SET IT TO HANG UP AND TRY A NEW NUMBER IF SOMEONE PICKS UP OR IF IT RINGS.

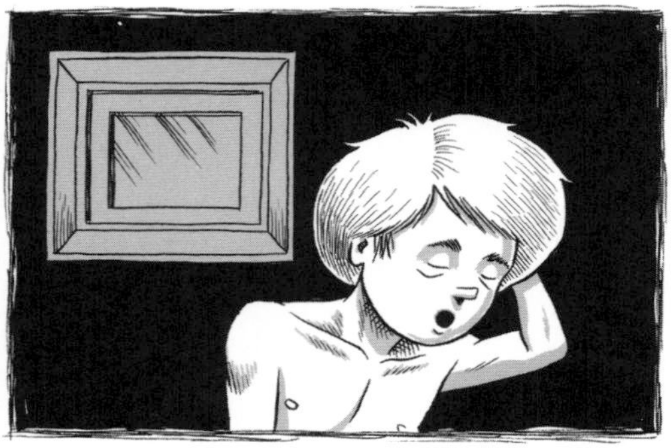

IF THE COMPUTER MAKES A CONNECTION I'LL NEED TO FIGURE OUT HOW TO RECORD THAT NUMBER FOR REVIEW.

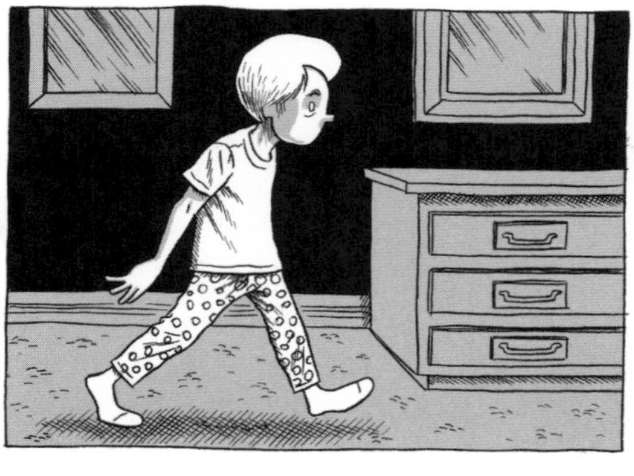

I FEEL CLEAR-HEADED ENOUGH TO SITUATE THESE "IF" AND "THEN" STATEMENTS IN THE CORRECT ORDER.

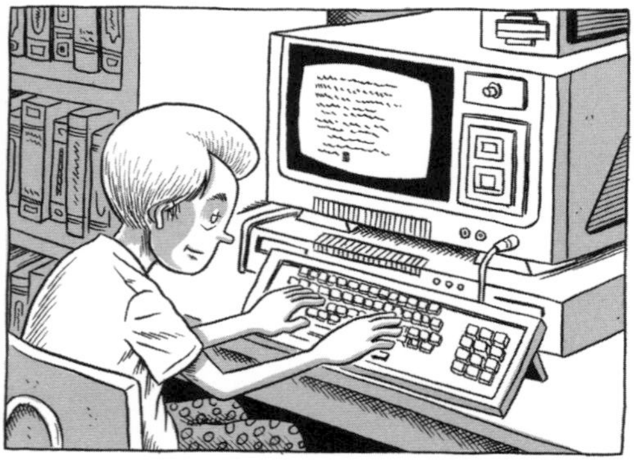

HOLY CRAP! IT'S 6:30 ALREADY. NO CHANCE TO DEBUG!

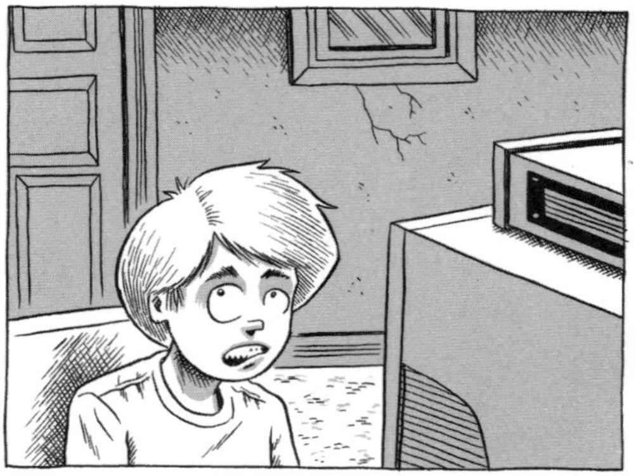

GONNA HAVE TO TEST IT LIVE.

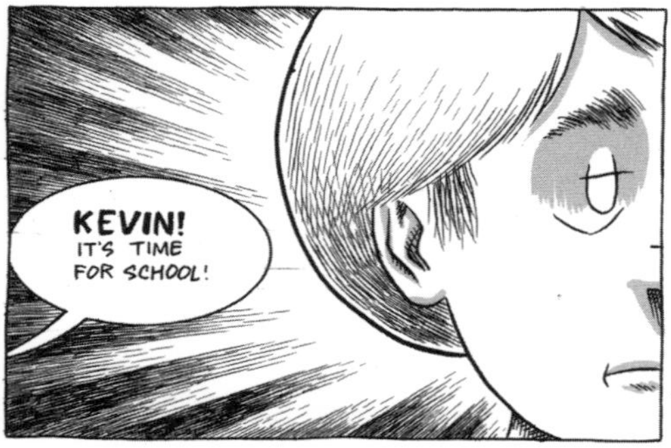
KEVIN! IT'S TIME FOR SCHOOL!

HOPE I COME HOME TO SOME INTERESTING RESULTS.

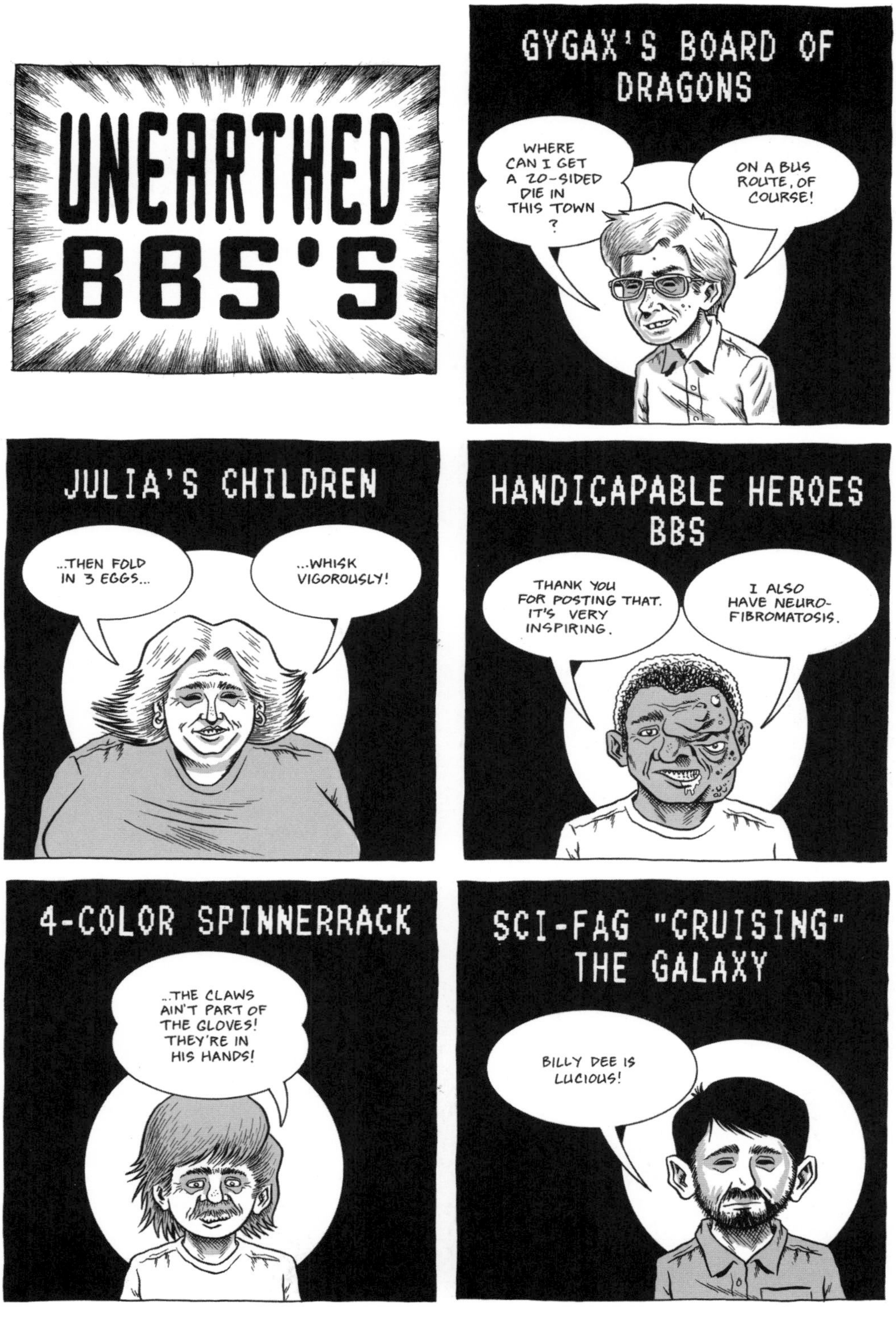
UNEARTHED BBS'S
GYGAX'S BOARD OF DRAGONS
WHERE CAN I GET A 20-SIDED DIE IN THIS TOWN ?
ON A BUS ROUTE, OF COURSE!
JULIA'S CHILDREN
...THEN FOLD IN 3 EGGS...
...WHISK VIGOROUSLY!
HANDICAPABLE HEROES BBS
THANK YOU FOR POSTING THAT. IT'S VERY INSPIRING.
I ALSO HAVE NEURO-FIBROMATOSIS.
4-COLOR SPINNERRACK
...THE CLAWS AIN'T PART OF THE GLOVES! THEY'RE IN HIS HANDS!
SCI-FAG "CRUISING" THE GALAXY
BILLY DEE IS LUCIOUS!

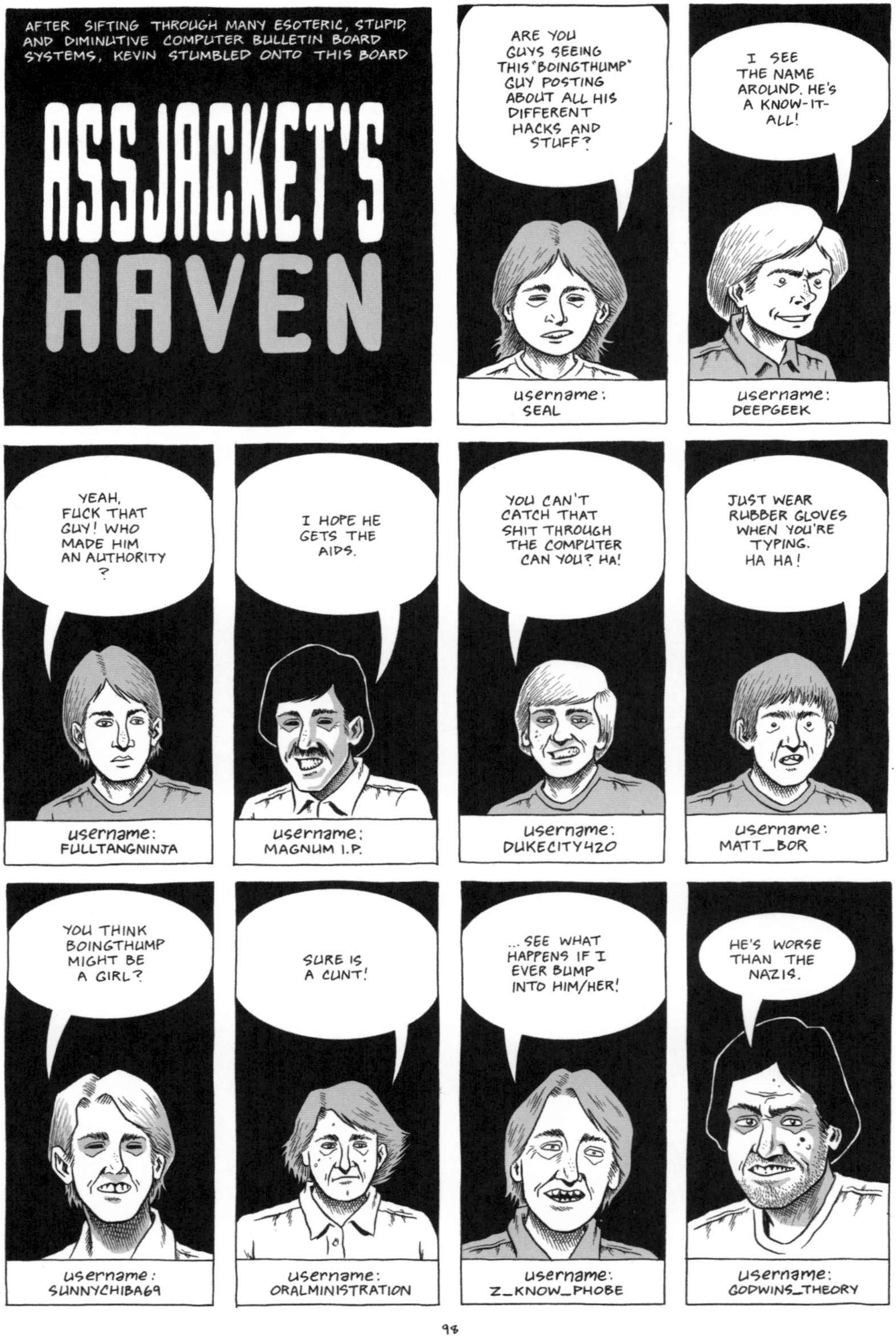
AFTER SIFTING THROUGH MANY ESOTERIC, STUPID, AND DIMINUTIVE COMPUTER BULLETIN BOARD SYSTEMS, KEVIN STUMBLED ONTO THIS BOARD
ASSJACKET'S HAVEN
ARE YOU GUYS SEEING THIS "BOINGTHUMP" GUY POSTING ABOUT ALL HIS DIFFERENT HACKS AND STUFF?
username: SEAL
I SEE THE NAME AROUND. HE'S A KNOW-IT-ALL!
username: DEEPGEEK
YEAH, FUCK THAT GUY! WHO MADE HIM AN AUTHORITY?
username: FULLTANGNINJA
I HOPE HE GETS THE AIDS.
username: MAGNUM I.P.
YOU CAN'T CATCH THAT SHIT THROUGH THE COMPUTER CAN YOU? HA!
username: DUKECITY420
JUST WEAR RUBBER GLOVES WHEN YOU'RE TYPING. HA HA!
username: MATT_BOR
YOU THINK BOINGTHUMP MIGHT BE A GIRL?
username: SUNNYCHIBA69
SURE IS A CUNT!
username: ORALMINISTRATION
...SEE WHAT HAPPENS IF I EVER BUMP INTO HIM/HER!
username: Z_KNOW_PHOBE
HE'S WORSE THAN THE NAZIS.
username: GODWINS_THEORY

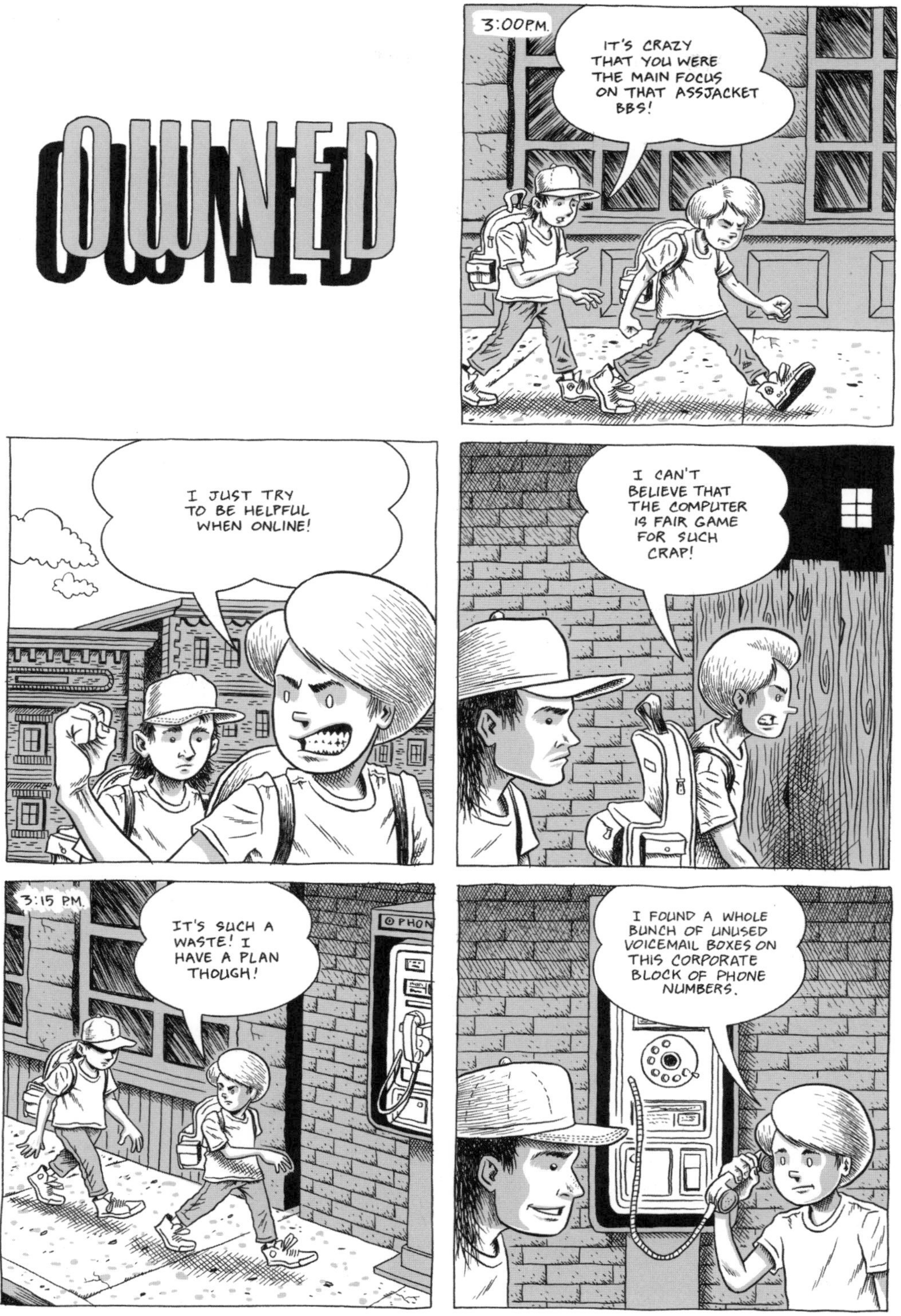
OWNED
3:00 P.M.
IT'S CRAZY THAT YOU WERE THE MAIN FOCUS ON THAT ASSJACKET BBS!
I JUST TRY TO BE HELPFUL WHEN ONLINE!
I CAN'T BELIEVE THAT THE COMPUTER IS FAIR GAME FOR SUCH CRAP!
3:15 P.M.
IT'S SUCH A WASTE! I HAVE A PLAN THOUGH!
I FOUND A WHOLE BUNCH OF UNUSED VOICEMAIL BOXES ON THIS CORPORATE BLOCK OF PHONE NUMBERS.

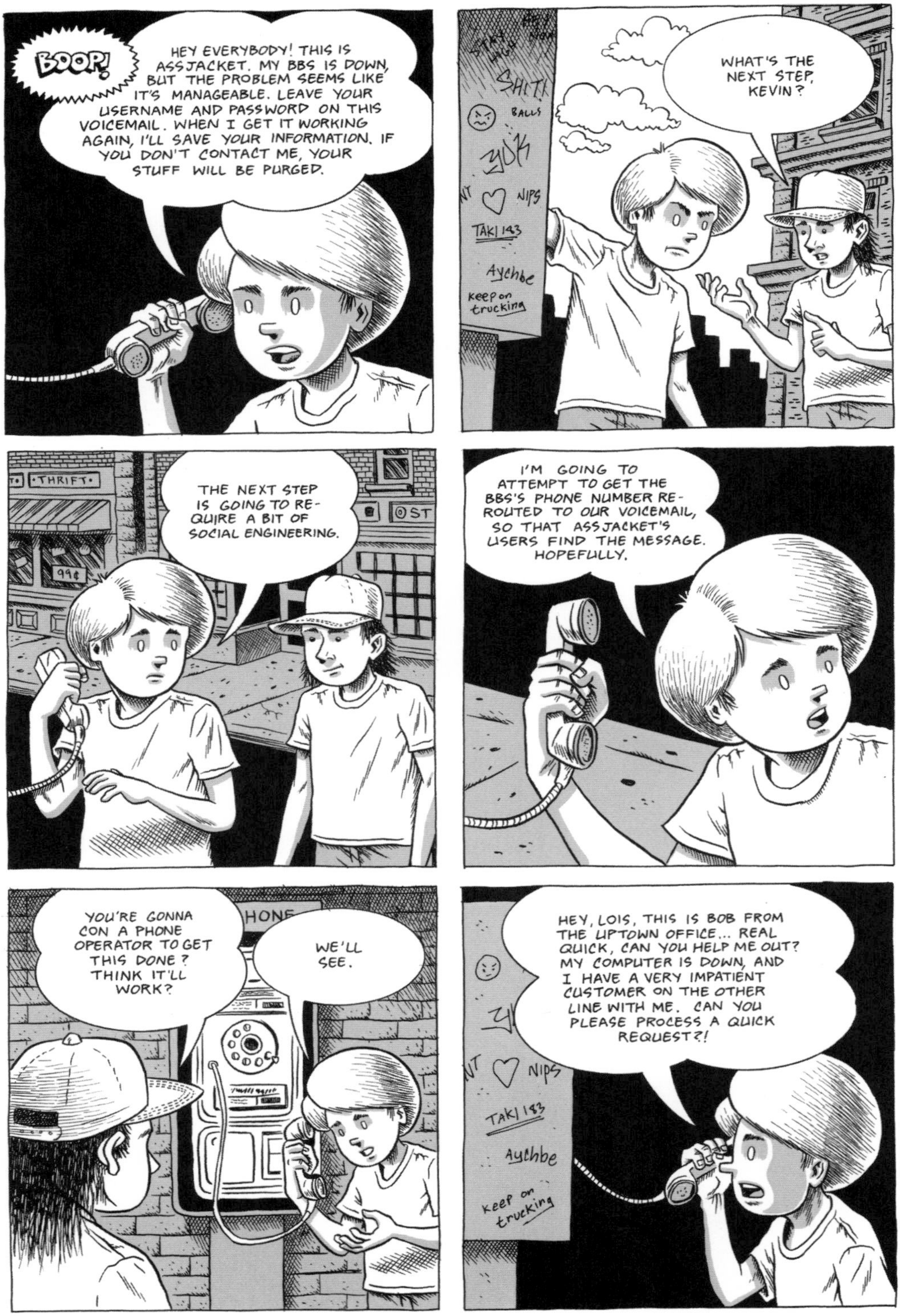
BOOP!
HEY EVERYBODY! THIS IS ASSJACKET. MY BBS IS DOWN, BUT THE PROBLEM SEEMS LIKE IT'S MANAGEABLE. LEAVE YOUR USERNAME AND PASSWORD ON THIS VOICEMAIL. WHEN I GET IT WORKING AGAIN, I'LL SAVE YOUR INFORMATION. IF YOU DON'T CONTACT ME, YOUR STUFF WILL BE PURGED.
SHIT!
BALLS
NIPS
TAKI 183
Aychbe
keep on trucking
WHAT'S THE NEXT STEP, KEVIN?
THRIFT
99¢
THE NEXT STEP IS GOING TO REQUIRE A BIT OF SOCIAL ENGINEERING.
I'M GOING TO ATTEMPT TO GET THE BBS'S PHONE NUMBER RE-ROUTED TO OUR VOICEMAIL, SO THAT ASSJACKET'S USERS FIND THE MESSAGE. HOPEFULLY.
YOU'RE GONNA CON A PHONE OPERATOR TO GET THIS DONE? THINK IT'LL WORK?
WE'LL SEE.
HEY, LOIS, THIS IS BOB FROM THE UPTOWN OFFICE... REAL QUICK, CAN YOU HELP ME OUT? MY COMPUTER IS DOWN, AND I HAVE A VERY IMPATIENT CUSTOMER ON THE OTHER LINE WITH ME. CAN YOU PLEASE PROCESS A QUICK REQUEST?!
NIPS
TAKI 183
Aychbe
Keep on trucking

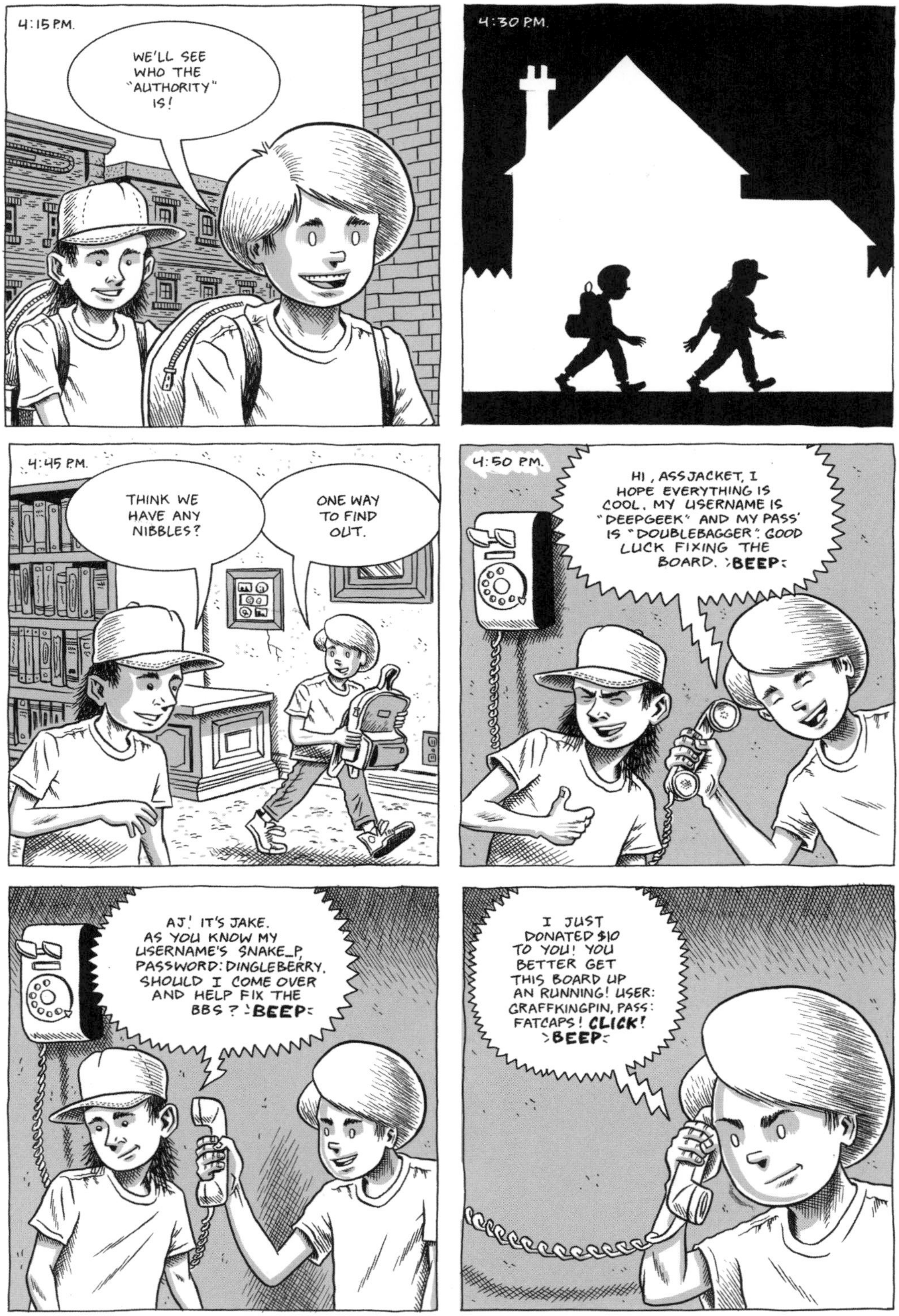
4:15 P.M.
WE'LL SEE WHO THE "AUTHORITY" IS!
4:30 P.M.
4:45 P.M.
THINK WE HAVE ANY NIBBLES?
ONE WAY TO FIND OUT.
4:50 P.M.
HI, ASSJACKET, I HOPE EVERYTHING IS COOL. MY USERNAME IS "DEEPGEEK" AND MY PASS' IS "DOUBLEBAGGER". GOOD LUCK FIXING THE BOARD. -BEEP-
AJ! IT'S JAKE. AS YOU KNOW MY USERNAME'S SNAKE_P, PASSWORD: DINGLEBERRY. SHOULD I COME OVER AND HELP FIX THE BBS? -BEEP-
I JUST DONATED $10 TO YOU! YOU BETTER GET THIS BOARD UP AN RUNNING! USER: GRAFFKINGPIN, PASS: FATCAPS! CLICK! -BEEP-

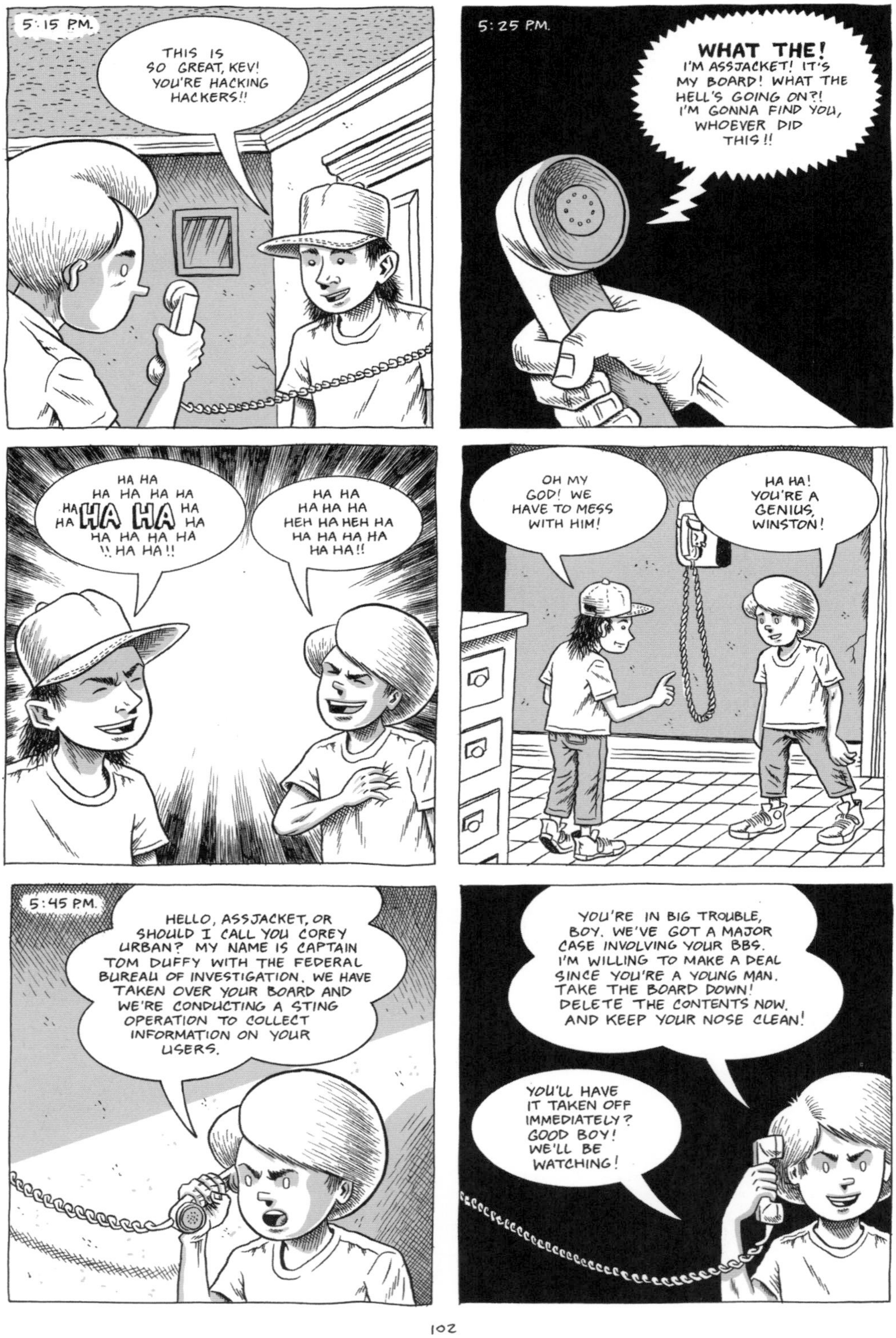
5:15 P.M.
THIS IS SO GREAT, KEV! YOU'RE HACKING HACKERS!!
5:25 P.M.
WHAT THE! I'M ASSJACKET! IT'S MY BOARD! WHAT THE HELL'S GOING ON?! I'M GONNA FIND YOU, WHOEVER DID THIS!!
HA HA HA HA HA HA HA HA HA HA HA HA HA HA HA HA HA HA !! HA HA!!
HA HA HA HA HA HEH HA HEH HA HA HA HA HA HA HA!!
OH MY GOD! WE HAVE TO MESS WITH HIM!
HA HA! YOU'RE A GENIUS, WINSTON!
5:45 P.M.
HELLO, ASSJACKET, OR SHOULD I CALL YOU COREY URBAN? MY NAME IS CAPTAIN TOM DUFFY WITH THE FEDERAL BUREAU OF INVESTIGATION. WE HAVE TAKEN OVER YOUR BOARD AND WE'RE CONDUCTING A STING OPERATION TO COLLECT INFORMATION ON YOUR USERS.
YOU'RE IN BIG TROUBLE, BOY. WE'VE GOT A MAJOR CASE INVOLVING YOUR BBS. I'M WILLING TO MAKE A DEAL SINCE YOU'RE A YOUNG MAN. TAKE THE BOARD DOWN! DELETE THE CONTENTS NOW. AND KEEP YOUR NOSE CLEAN!
YOU'LL HAVE IT TAKEN OFF IMMEDIATELY? GOOD BOY! WE'LL BE WATCHING!

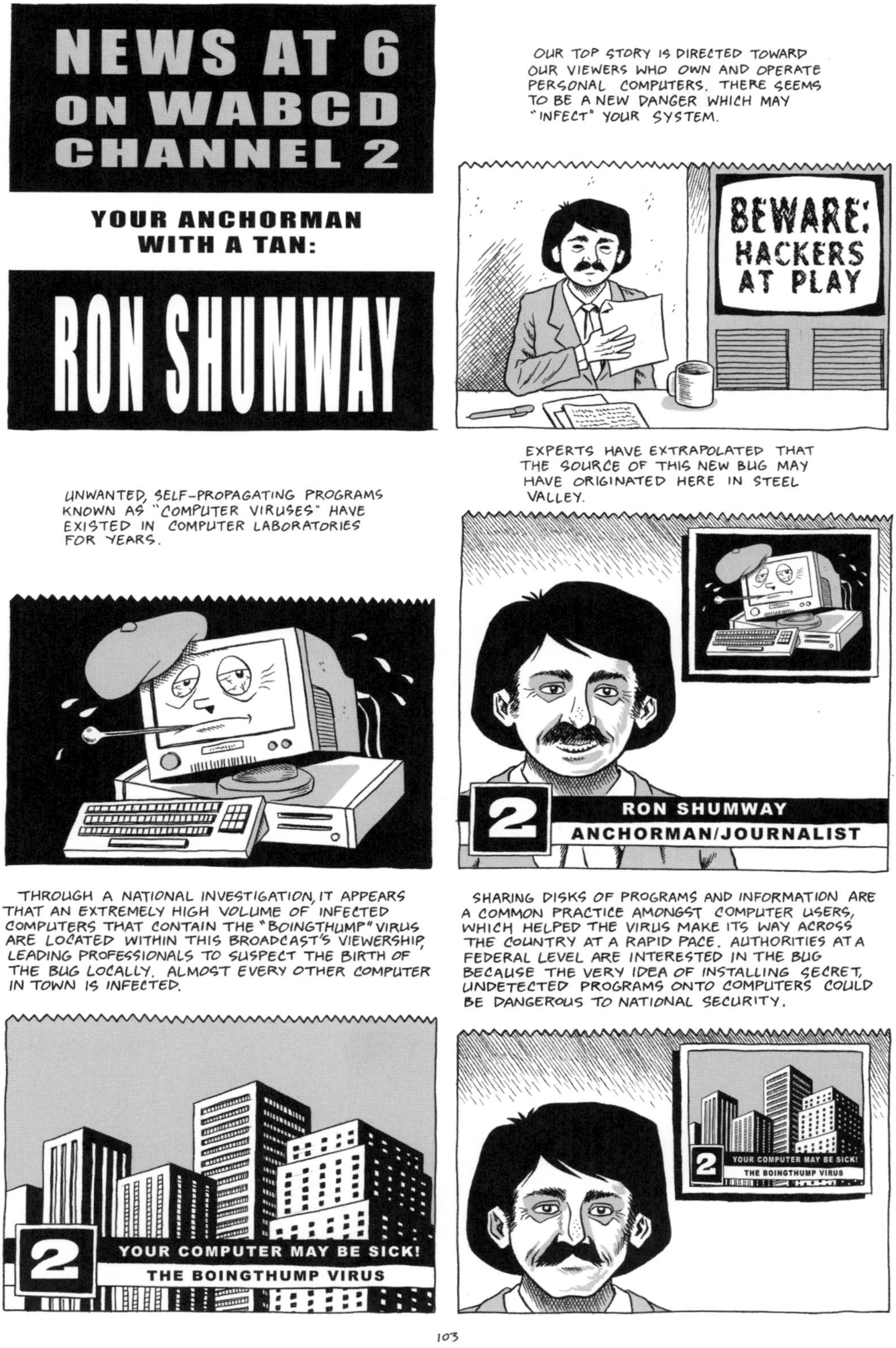
NEWS AT 6 ON WABCD CHANNEL 2
YOUR ANCHORMAN WITH A TAN:
RON SHUMWAY
OUR TOP STORY IS DIRECTED TOWARD OUR VIEWERS WHO OWN AND OPERATE PERSONAL COMPUTERS. THERE SEEMS TO BE A NEW DANGER WHICH MAY "INFECT" YOUR SYSTEM.
BEWARE: HACKERS AT PLAY
UNWANTED, SELF-PROPAGATING PROGRAMS KNOWN AS "COMPUTER VIRUSES" HAVE EXISTED IN COMPUTER LABORATORIES FOR YEARS.
EXPERTS HAVE EXTRAPOLATED THAT THE SOURCE OF THIS NEW BUG MAY HAVE ORIGINATED HERE IN STEEL VALLEY.
2
RON SHUMWAY
ANCHORMAN/JOURNALIST
THROUGH A NATIONAL INVESTIGATION, IT APPEARS THAT AN EXTREMELY HIGH VOLUME OF INFECTED COMPUTERS THAT CONTAIN THE "BOINGTHUMP" VIRUS ARE LOCATED WITHIN THIS BROADCAST'S VIEWERSHIP, LEADING PROFESSIONALS TO SUSPECT THE BIRTH OF THE BUG LOCALLY. ALMOST EVERY OTHER COMPUTER IN TOWN IS INFECTED.
2
YOUR COMPUTER MAY BE SICK!
THE BOINGTHUMP VIRUS
SHARING DISKS OF PROGRAMS AND INFORMATION ARE A COMMON PRACTICE AMONGST COMPUTER USERS, WHICH HELPED THE VIRUS MAKE ITS WAY ACROSS THE COUNTRY AT A RAPID PACE. AUTHORITIES AT A FEDERAL LEVEL ARE INTERESTED IN THE BUG BECAUSE THE VERY IDEA OF INSTALLING SECRET, UNDETECTED PROGRAMS ONTO COMPUTERS COULD BE DANGEROUS TO NATIONAL SECURITY.
2
YOUR COMPUTER MAY BE SICK!
THE BOINGTHUMP VIRUS

THE BOINGTHUMP VIRUS REVEALS ITSELF EVERY 100 TIMES A USER 'BOOTS' HIS COMPUTER. THE SOMEWHAT INSULTING MESSAGE MAKES THE COMPUTER UNUSABLE, BUT CAN SIMPLY BE RESTARTED, MAKING THE VIRUS LIE DORMANT FOR 100 MORE START-UPS. NO OTHER DAMAGE IS INFLICTED AS A RESULT OF THIS BUG.

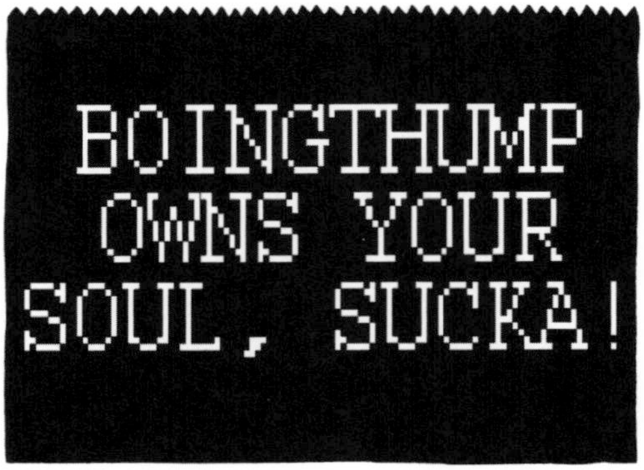
BOINGTHUMP OWNS YOUR SOUL, SUCKA!

THE VIRUS IS KNOWN TO INSTALL ITSELF BY BOOTING AN INFECTED FLOPPY DISK THAT CONTAINS THE PROGRAM. THE BUG ADDS ITSELF TO YOUR SYSTEM AND INFECTS ANY OTHER DISKS THAT ARE INSERTED INTO THE COMPUTER.

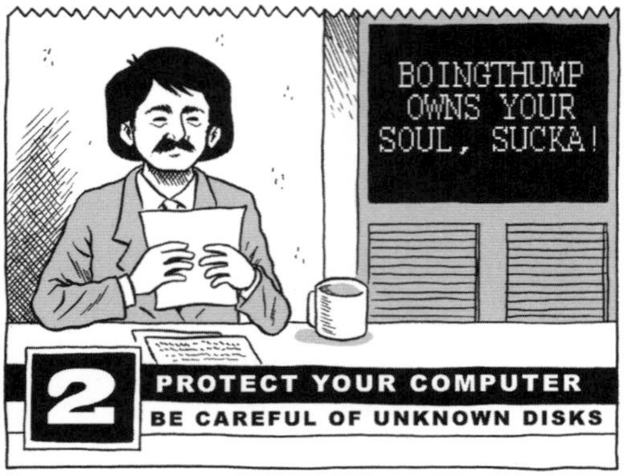
BOINGTHUMP OWNS YOUR SOUL, SUCKA!
2
PROTECT YOUR COMPUTER
BE CAREFUL OF UNKNOWN DISKS

BECAUSE THE VIRUS IS REVEALED AFTER 100 TIMES THE COMPUTER IS TURNED ON, A SYSTEM CAN HOUSE THIS VIRUS MONTHS BEFORE THE OWNER DISCOVERS THE PROBLEM, POTENTIALLY CORRUPTING DISKS ALL THE WHILE. WE SPOKE WITH A LOCAL COMPUTER SCIENTIST WHO HAD THIS TO SAY:

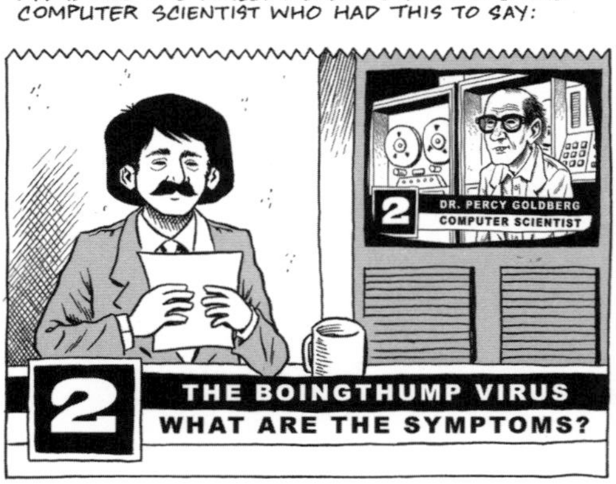
2
DR. PERCY GOLDBERG
COMPUTER SCIENTIST
2
THE BOINGTHUMP VIRUS
WHAT ARE THE SYMPTOMS?

THE VIRUS ITSELF IS A MINOR NUISANCE, THANK GOODNESS, BUT THE IDEA OF A SELF-REPRODUCING APPLICATION IS VERY ALARMING. IMAGINE IF THE CREATOR OF THIS VIRUS WANTED TO DESTROY DATA OR SOMEHOW RENDER YOUR COMPUTER USELESS. WE ARE CURRENTLY WORKING HARD ON SOME TOOLS THAT WILL DETECT SPECIFIC STRANGE BEHAVIORS WHICH MAY INDICATE A VIRUS, BUT IT'S GOING TO TAKE SOME TIME TO WORK THE BUGS OUT.

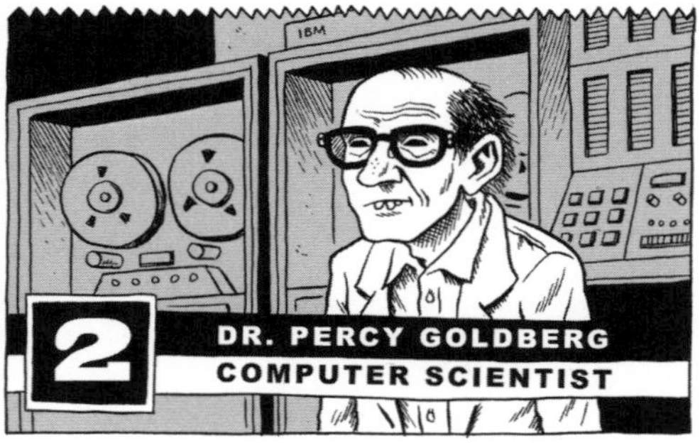
IBM
2
DR. PERCY GOLDBERG
COMPUTER SCIENTIST

MANY QUESTIONS ARE RAISED ABOUT THE AUTHOR OF THE VIRUS. WHAT MOTIVATES HIM? WHAT WAS THE PURPOSE OF UNLEASHING THIS? AUTHORITIES WOULD APPRECIATE ANY LEADS AS TO WHO THIS GRIEFER MAY BE. IN CLOSING, AN FBI AGENT SAID:

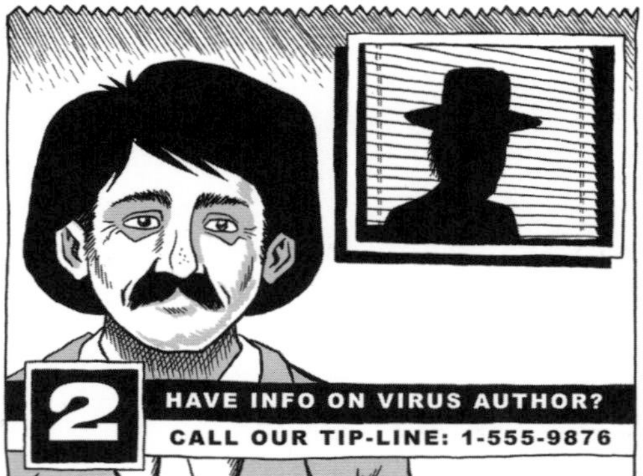
2
HAVE INFO ON VIRUS AUTHOR?
CALL OUR TIP-LINE: 1-555-9876

EVEN THOUGH THERE IS NO LAW ON THE BOOKS FOR COMPUTER VIRUSES, WE ARE GOING TO HAVE TO PREPARE FOR AN ERA WHERE DIGITAL CRIME EXISTS. THIS VIRUS TOOK A LOT OF TIME TO BE DISCOVERED. THOUSANDS OF COMPUTERS CAN BE INFECTED WITH SOMETHING HAZARDOUS RIGHT NOW, AND IT COULD SIT DORMANT LIKE A TIME BOMB WAITING TO GO OFF AT THE MOST INOPPORTUNE TIME.

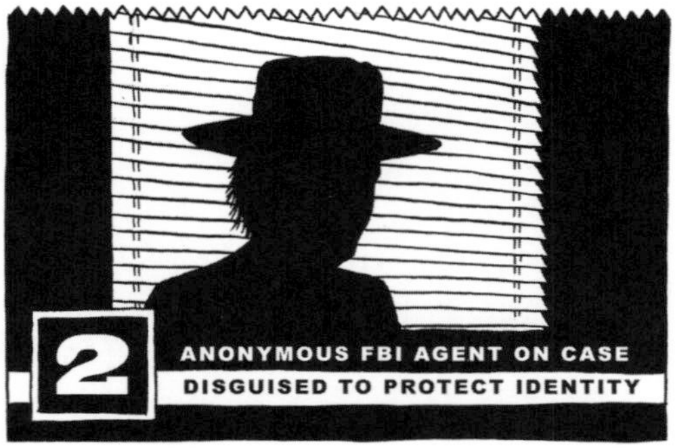
2
ANONYMOUS FBI AGENT ON CASE
DISGUISED TO PROTECT IDENTITY

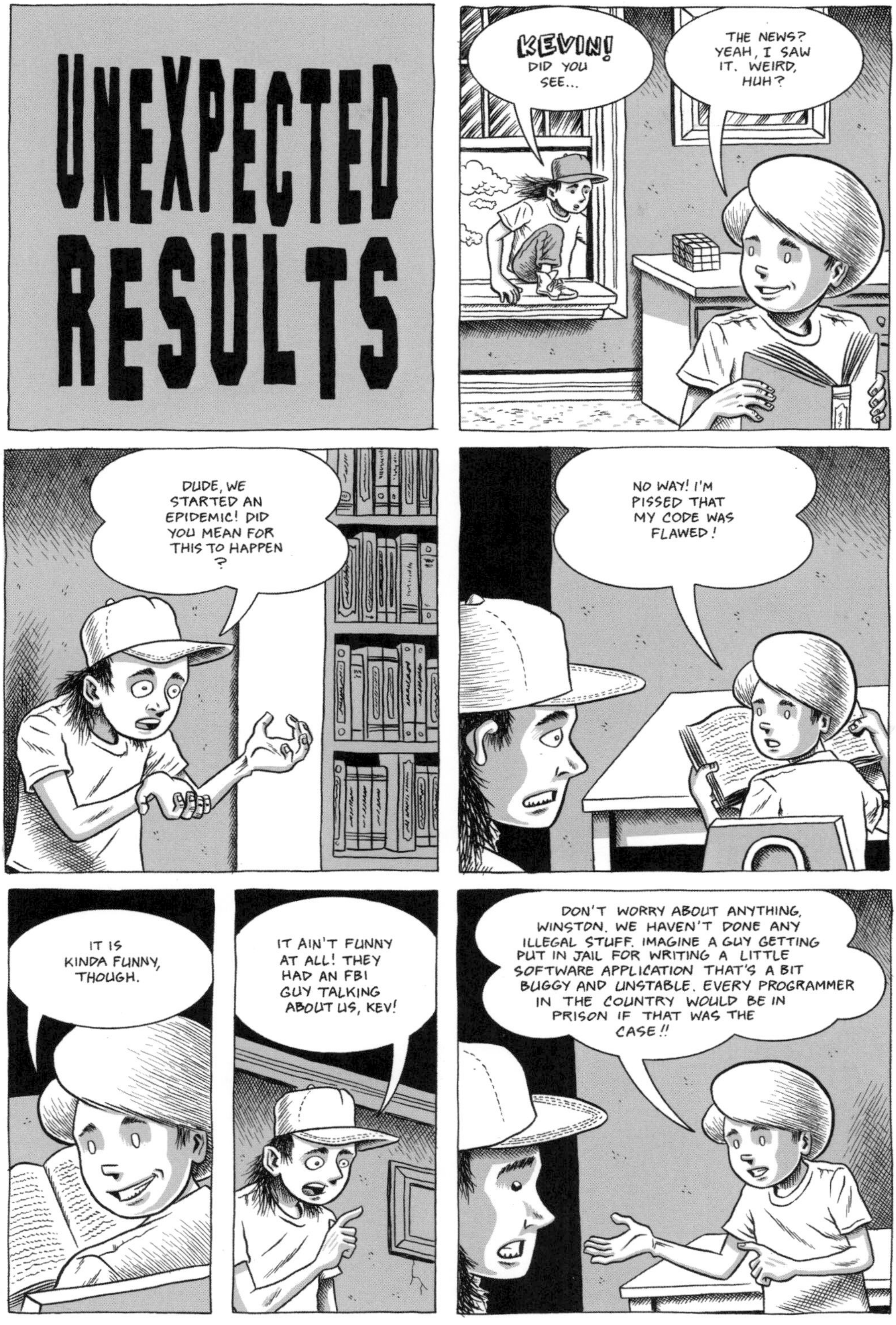
UNEXPECTED RESULTS
KEVIN! DID YOU SEE...
THE NEWS? YEAH, I SAW IT. WEIRD, HUH?
DUDE, WE STARTED AN EPIDEMIC! DID YOU MEAN FOR THIS TO HAPPEN ?
NO WAY! I'M PISSED THAT MY CODE WAS FLAWED!
IT IS KINDA FUNNY, THOUGH.
IT AIN'T FUNNY AT ALL! THEY HAD AN FBI GUY TALKING ABOUT US, KEV!
DON'T WORRY ABOUT ANYTHING, WINSTON. WE HAVEN'T DONE ANY ILLEGAL STUFF. IMAGINE A GUY GETTING PUT IN JAIL FOR WRITING A LITTLE SOFTWARE APPLICATION THAT'S A BIT BUGGY AND UNSTABLE. EVERY PROGRAMMER IN THE COUNTRY WOULD BE IN PRISON IF THAT WAS THE CASE!!

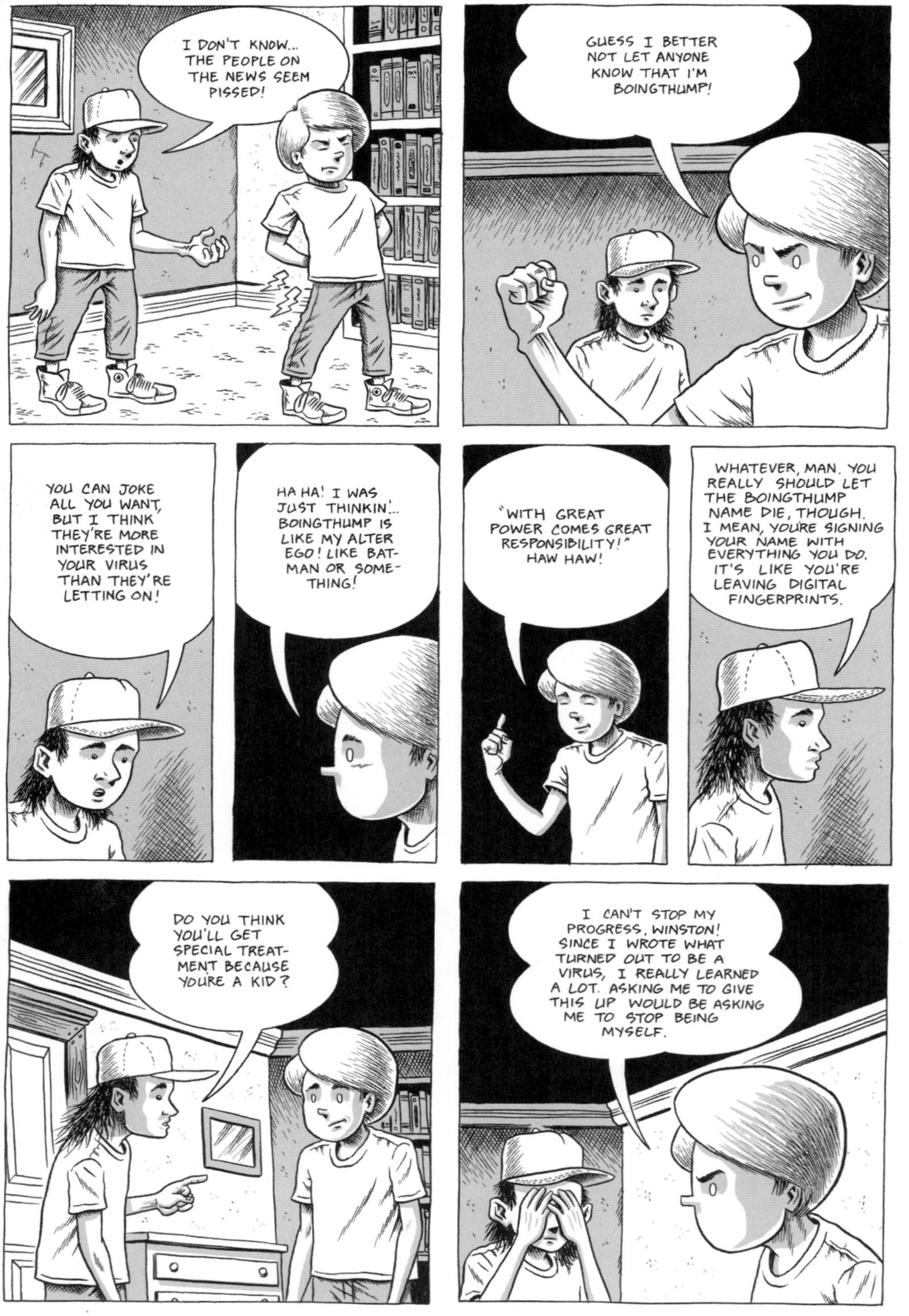
I DON'T KNOW... THE PEOPLE ON THE NEWS SEEM PISSED!
GUESS I BETTER NOT LET ANYONE KNOW THAT I'M BOINGTHUMP!
YOU CAN JOKE ALL YOU WANT, BUT I THINK THEY'RE MORE INTERESTED IN YOUR VIRUS THAN THEY'RE LETTING ON!
HA HA! I WAS JUST THINKIN'... BOINGTHUMP IS LIKE MY ALTER EGO! LIKE BATMAN OR SOMETHING!
"WITH GREAT POWER COMES GREAT RESPONSIBILITY!" HAW HAW!
WHATEVER, MAN. YOU REALLY SHOULD LET THE BOINGTHUMP NAME DIE, THOUGH. I MEAN, YOU'RE SIGNING YOUR NAME WITH EVERYTHING YOU DO. IT'S LIKE YOU'RE LEAVING DIGITAL FINGERPRINTS.
DO YOU THINK YOU'LL GET SPECIAL TREATMENT BECAUSE YOU'RE A KID?
I CAN'T STOP MY PROGRESS, WINSTON! SINCE I WROTE WHAT TURNED OUT TO BE A VIRUS, I REALLY LEARNED A LOT. ASKING ME TO GIVE THIS UP WOULD BE ASKING ME TO STOP BEING MYSELF.

CHAPTER 4

FREE KEVIN!
poop
YUK!
chemist
ANGLO

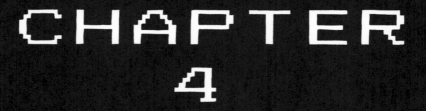

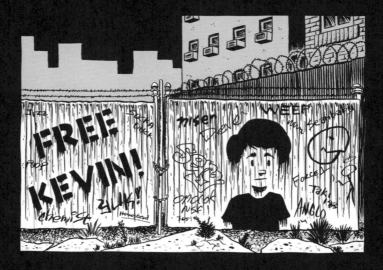

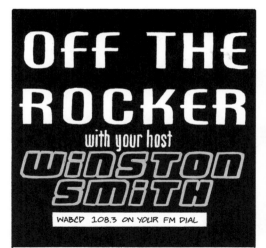

OFF THE ROCKER

with your host
WINSTON SMITH

WABCD 108.3 ON YOUR FM DIAL

...THE END OF THIS CHAPTER HIT ME LIKE A TON OF BRICKS...

I WAS WARDIALING OVER THE WEEKEND, AND I FOUND A VERY EXCITING PHONE NUMBER!

... BUT I WAS EXCITED TO PURSUE MY COMMUNICATIONS DEGREE.

IT BELONGS TO THE PHONE COMPANY BUT THE LOG-IN SCREEN IS PASS-WORD PROTECTED.

KEVIN WASN'T SO SURE ABOUT WHAT HE WANTED TO DO, THOUGH.

I'M HAVING SOME TROUBLE BREAKING IN, THOUGH, BECAUSE MY PASSWORD PROGRAM ONLY WORKS IF A WORD IN THE DICTIONARY IS USED TO GAIN ENTRY. THE PASSWORD IS MORE COMPLICATED THAN THAT, IT SEEMS.

I MEAN, I GUESS HE MAY HAVE HAD SOME VAGUE IDEA...

I'M DETERMINED TO GET IN THERE. I THINK THAT SYSTEM IS IMPORTANT.

... CERTAINLY SOMETHING IN THE TELECOMMUNICATIONS OR THE COMPUTER FIELD.

OK KIDS! IT'S TIME TO START!

UNFORTUNATELY, KEVIN MADE SOME MISTAKES, AND WE'RE STUCK WITH WHAT WE HAVE NOW.

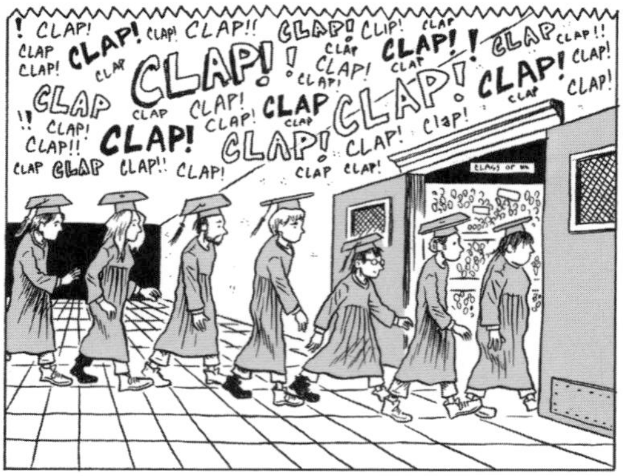
CLAP!
CLAP!
CLAP!!
CLAP!
CLAP!
CLAP!

2 YEARS IN PRISON! 2 YEARS WITH NO TRIAL! IS THIS JUSTICE?!

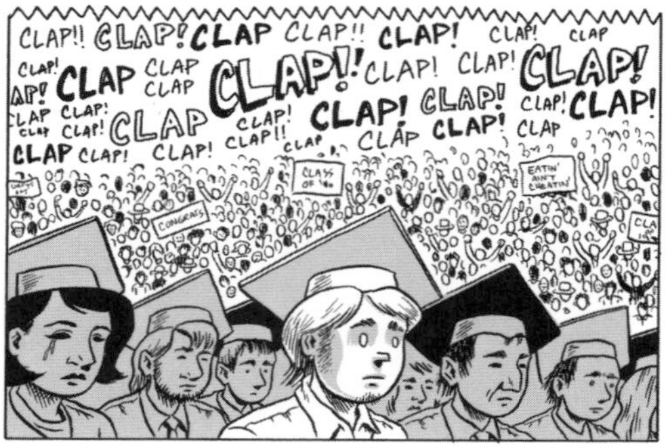
CLAP!! CLAP! CLAP CLAP!! CLAP!
CLAP!! CLAP! CLAP!
CLASS OF '96
CONGRATS

I WAS FORTUNATE ENOUGH TO VISIT HIM LAST WEEK. THE MAN STILL HAS FAITH THAT THE SYSTEM WON'T COMPLETELY RAPE HIM...

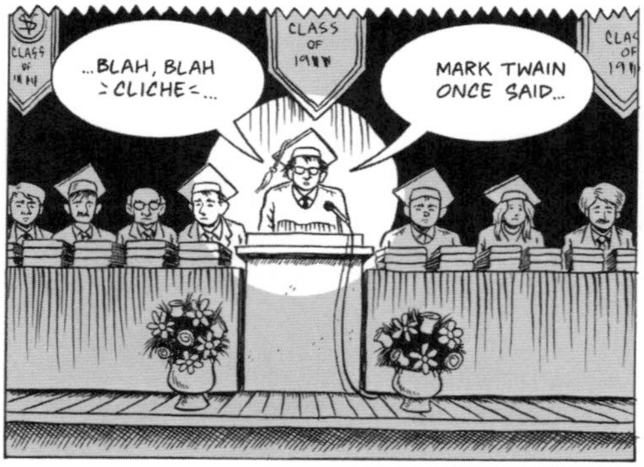
CLASS OF
...BLAH, BLAH >CLICHE<...
MARK TWAIN ONCE SAID...

... EVEN WITH THIS MORE ACCURATE SET OF CHARGES, HE REMAINS OPTIMISTIC.

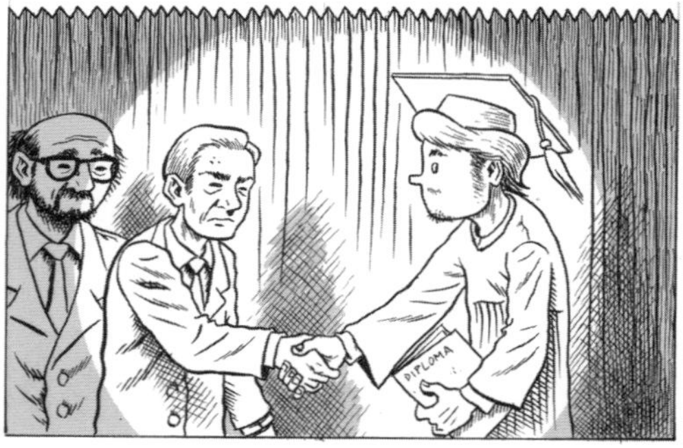
DIPLOMA

4 CHARGES MAIL FRAUD, 5 COUNTS WIRE AND COMPUTER FRAUD, 18 COUNTS OF POSSESSING ILLEGAL ACCESS DEVICES, 3 FOR MONEY LAUNDERING, 11 OBSTRUCTION OF JUSTICE VIOLATIONS, TO NAME A FEW...

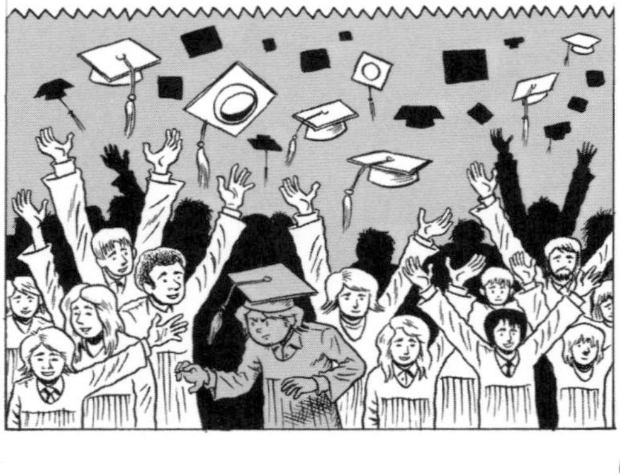

IT'S TIME FOR US TO WRITE OUR ELECTED OFFICIALS! CONGRESSMEN, SENATORS, EVERYBODY!!

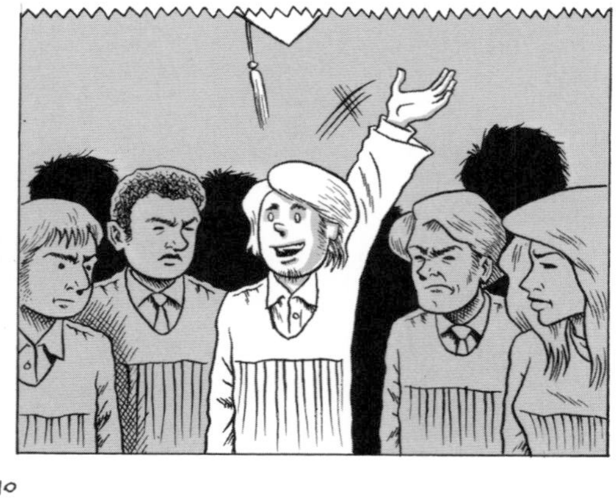

PRELUDE TO THE BREACH

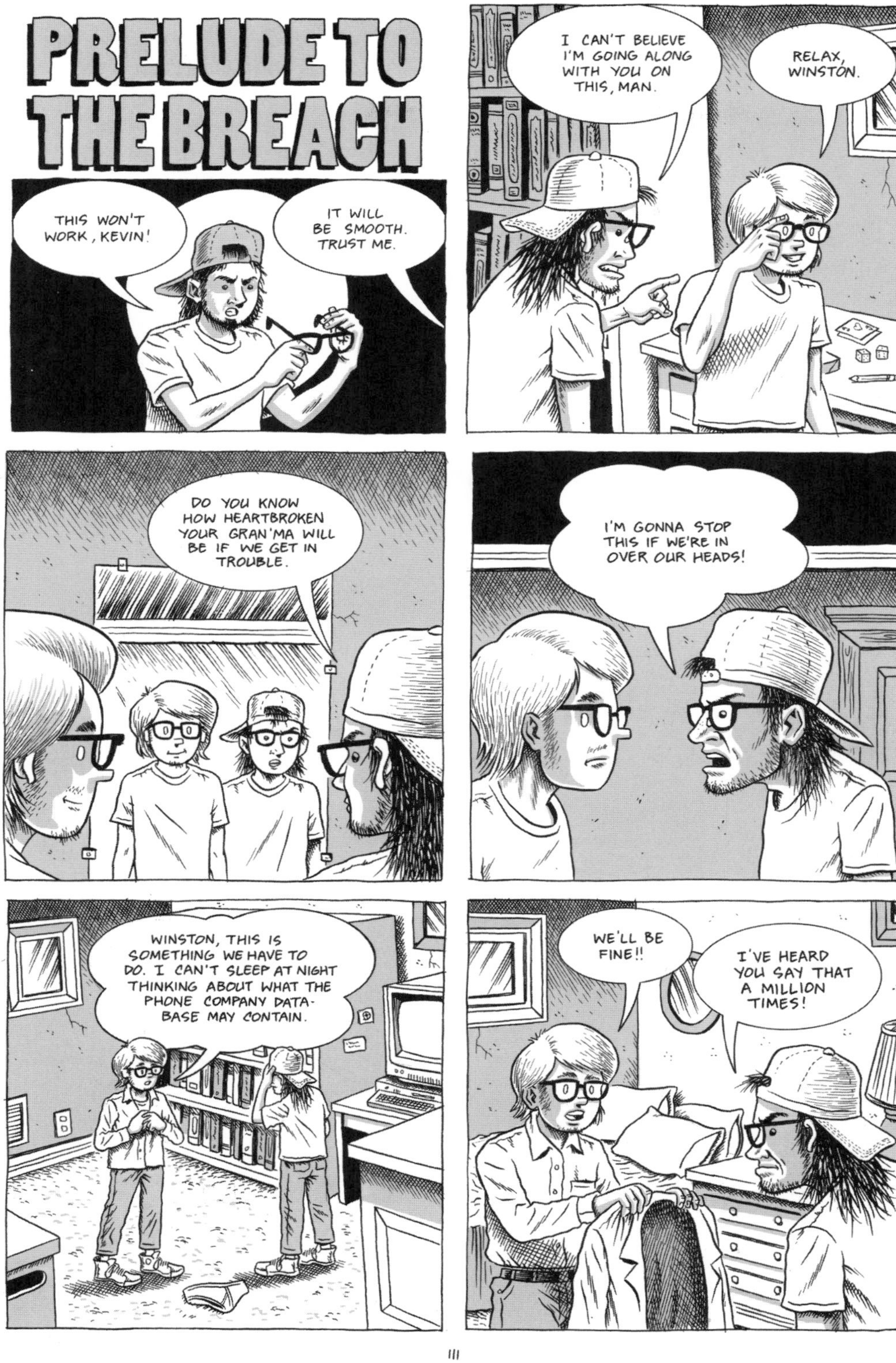
THIS WON'T WORK, KEVIN!
IT WILL BE SMOOTH. TRUST ME.
I CAN'T BELIEVE I'M GOING ALONG WITH YOU ON THIS, MAN.
RELAX, WINSTON.
DO YOU KNOW HOW HEARTBROKEN YOUR GRAN'MA WILL BE IF WE GET IN TROUBLE.
I'M GONNA STOP THIS IF WE'RE IN OVER OUR HEADS!
WINSTON, THIS IS SOMETHING WE HAVE TO DO. I CAN'T SLEEP AT NIGHT THINKING ABOUT WHAT THE PHONE COMPANY DATA-BASE MAY CONTAIN.
WE'LL BE FINE!!
I'VE HEARD YOU SAY THAT A MILLION TIMES!

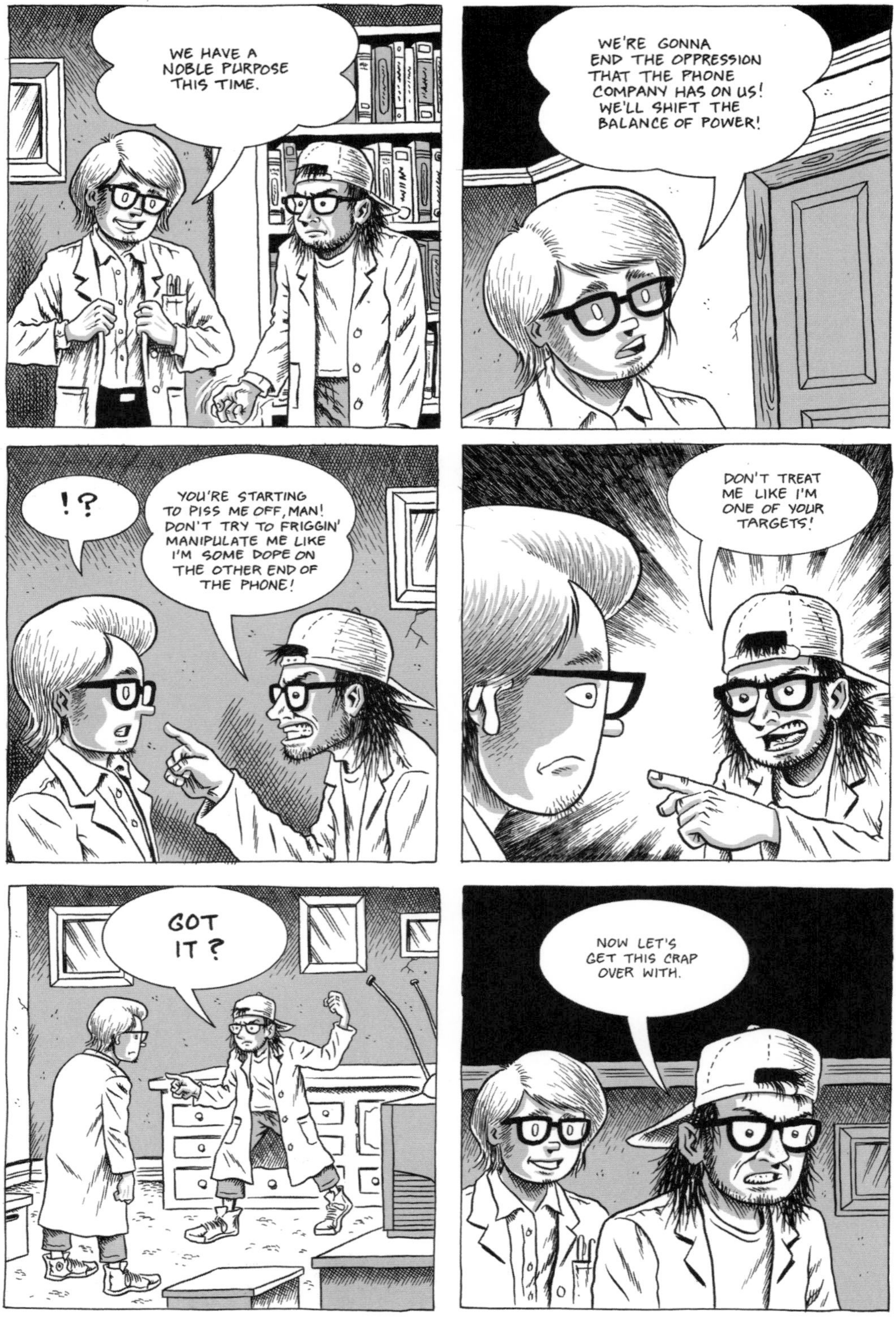
WE HAVE A NOBLE PURPOSE THIS TIME.
WE'RE GONNA END THE OPPRESSION THAT THE PHONE COMPANY HAS ON US! WE'LL SHIFT THE BALANCE OF POWER!
!?
YOU'RE STARTING TO PISS ME OFF, MAN! DON'T TRY TO FRIGGIN' MANIPULATE ME LIKE I'M SOME DOPE ON THE OTHER END OF THE PHONE!
DON'T TREAT ME LIKE I'M ONE OF YOUR TARGETS!
GOT IT?
NOW LET'S GET THIS CRAP OVER WITH.

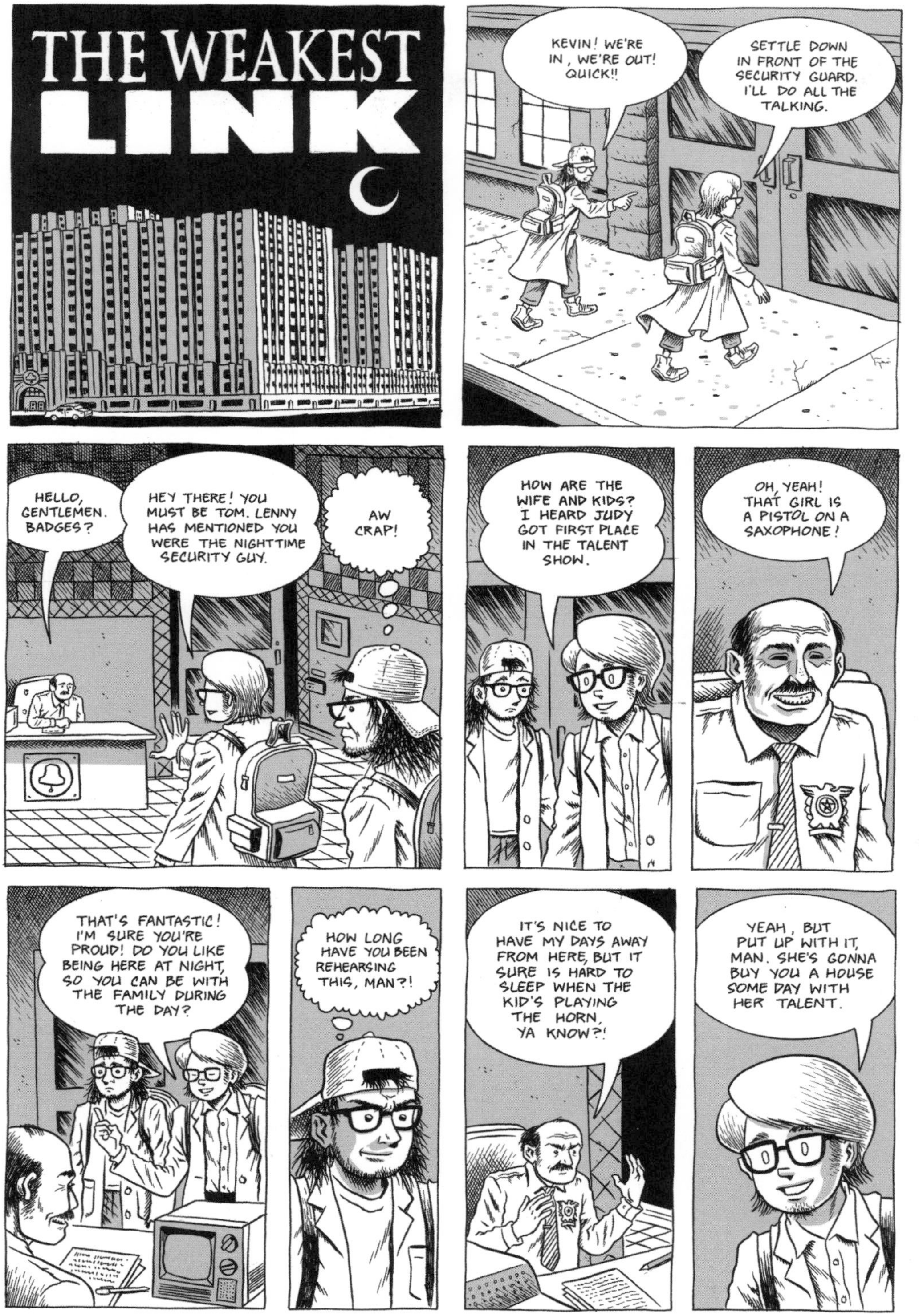
THE WEAKEST
LINK
KEVIN! WE'RE IN, WE'RE OUT! QUICK!!
SETTLE DOWN IN FRONT OF THE SECURITY GUARD. I'LL DO ALL THE TALKING.
HELLO, GENTLEMEN. BADGES?
HEY THERE! YOU MUST BE TOM. LENNY HAS MENTIONED YOU WERE THE NIGHTTIME SECURITY GUY.
AW CRAP!
HOW ARE THE WIFE AND KIDS? I HEARD JUDY GOT FIRST PLACE IN THE TALENT SHOW.
OH, YEAH! THAT GIRL IS A PISTOL ON A SAXOPHONE!
THAT'S FANTASTIC! I'M SURE YOU'RE PROUD! DO YOU LIKE BEING HERE AT NIGHT, SO YOU CAN BE WITH THE FAMILY DURING THE DAY?
HOW LONG HAVE YOU BEEN REHEARSING THIS, MAN?!
IT'S NICE TO HAVE MY DAYS AWAY FROM HERE, BUT IT SURE IS HARD TO SLEEP WHEN THE KID'S PLAYING THE HORN, YA KNOW?!
YEAH, BUT PUT UP WITH IT, MAN. SHE'S GONNA BUY YOU A HOUSE SOME DAY WITH HER TALENT.

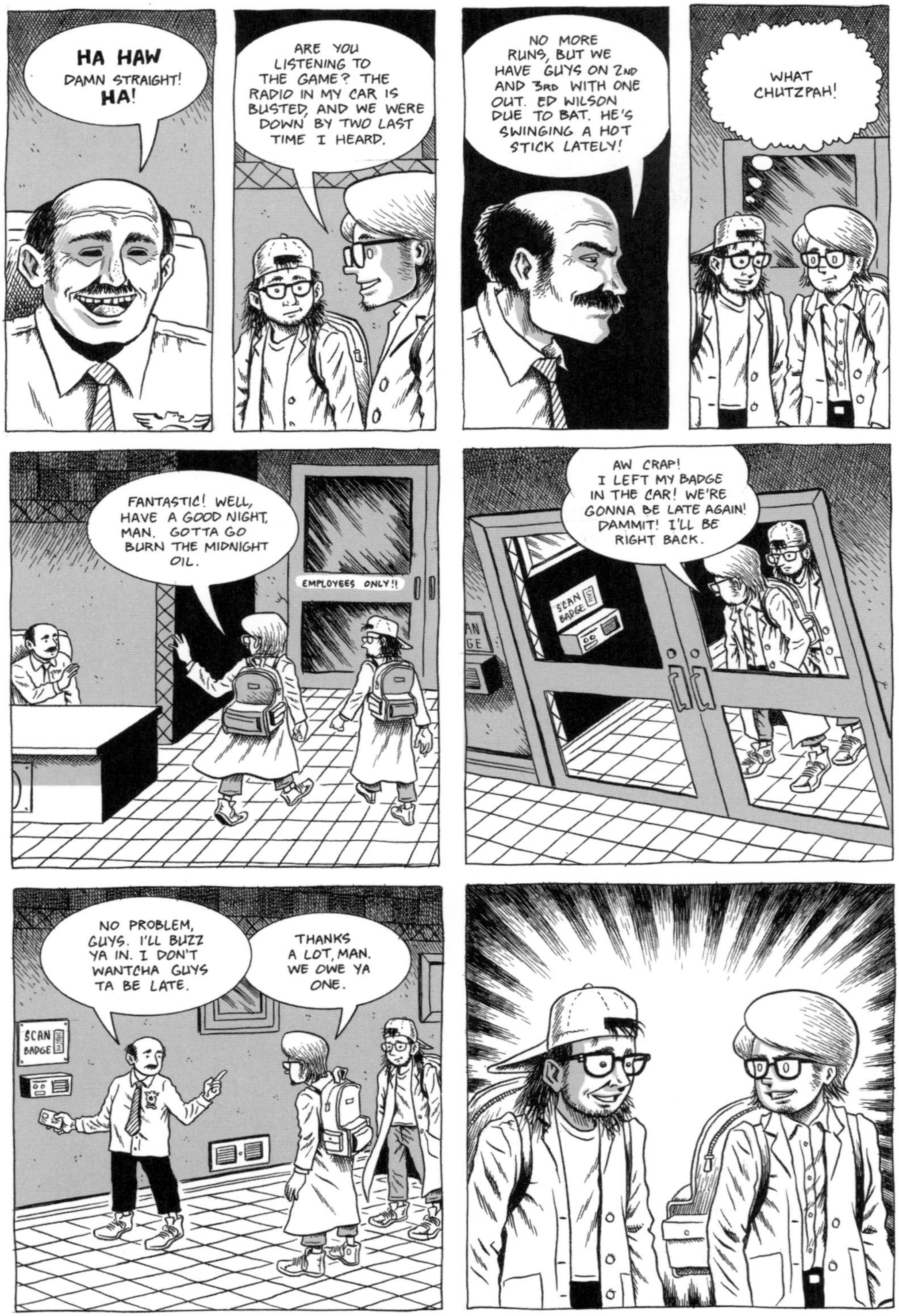

HA HAW
DAMN STRAIGHT!
HA!
ARE YOU LISTENING TO THE GAME? THE RADIO IN MY CAR IS BUSTED, AND WE WERE DOWN BY TWO LAST TIME I HEARD.
NO MORE RUNS, BUT WE HAVE GUYS ON 2ND AND 3RD WITH ONE OUT. ED WILSON DUE TO BAT. HE'S SWINGING A HOT STICK LATELY!
WHAT CHUTZPAH!
FANTASTIC! WELL, HAVE A GOOD NIGHT, MAN. GOTTA GO BURN THE MIDNIGHT OIL.
EMPLOYEES ONLY!!
AW CRAP! I LEFT MY BADGE IN THE CAR! WE'RE GONNA BE LATE AGAIN! DAMMIT! I'LL BE RIGHT BACK.
SCAN BADGE
NO PROBLEM, GUYS. I'LL BUZZ YA IN. I DON'T WANTCHA GUYS TA BE LATE.
THANKS A LOT, MAN. WE OWE YA ONE.
SCAN BADGE

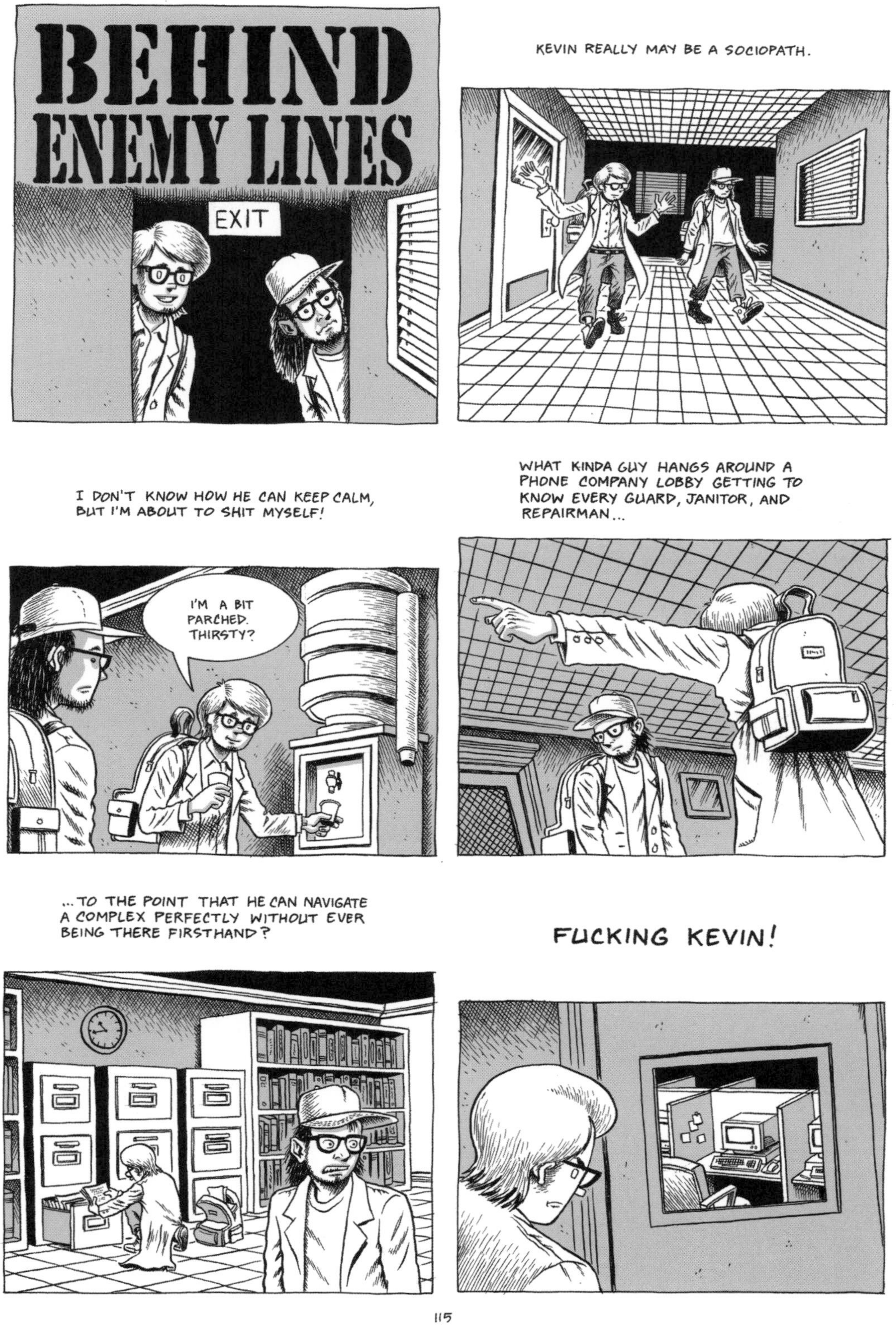
BEHIND ENEMY LINES
EXIT
KEVIN REALLY MAY BE A SOCIOPATH.
I DON'T KNOW HOW HE CAN KEEP CALM, BUT I'M ABOUT TO SHIT MYSELF!
I'M A BIT PARCHED. THIRSTY?
WHAT KINDA GUY HANGS AROUND A PHONE COMPANY LOBBY GETTING TO KNOW EVERY GUARD, JANITOR, AND REPAIRMAN...
...TO THE POINT THAT HE CAN NAVIGATE A COMPLEX PERFECTLY WITHOUT EVER BEING THERE FIRSTHAND?
FUCKING KEVIN!

THE COMPUTER ROOM WAS LOCKED, BUT THE KEY WAS EASILY LOCATED ON A RING IN THE JANITOR'S CLOSET.

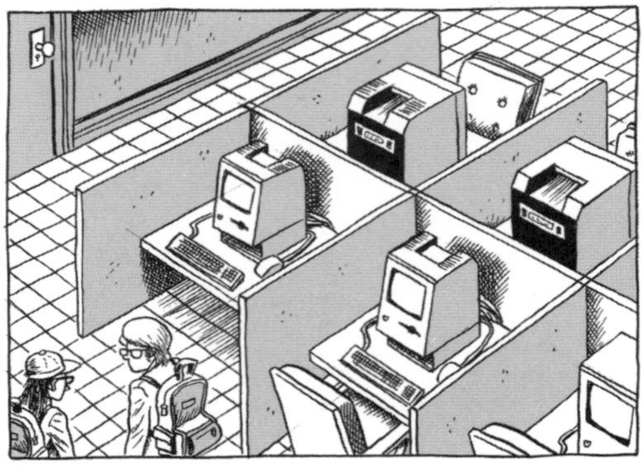

THEY SURE CARE A LOT ABOUT SECURITY IN THIS PLACE.

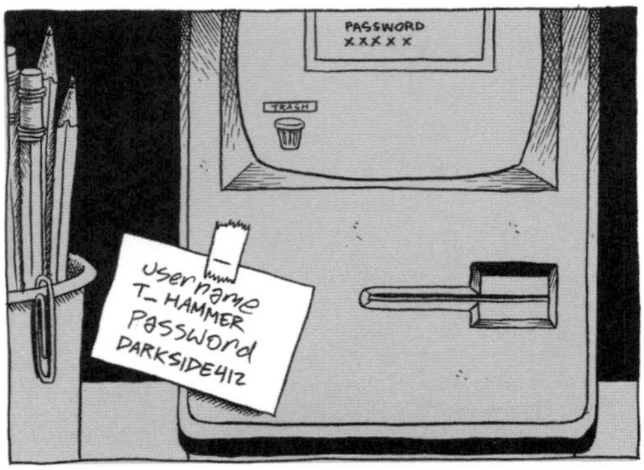
PASSWORD
XXXXX
TRASH
username
T_HAMMER
Password
DARKSIDE412

WE GOT WHAT WE CAME FOR, BUT IT'S HARD TO CONVINCE KEV TO LEAVE.

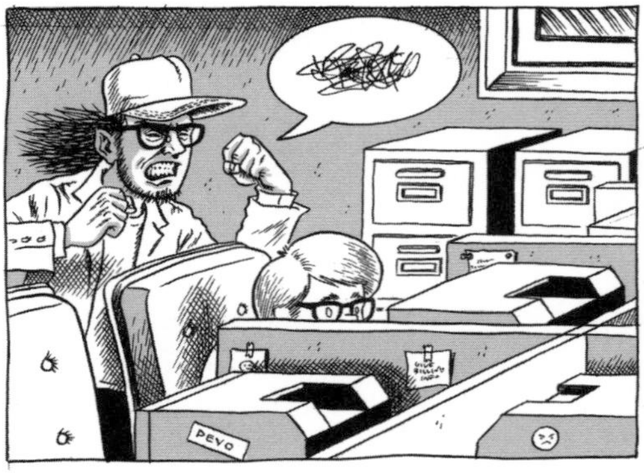
DEVO

HE'S JUST NEVER SATISFIED.

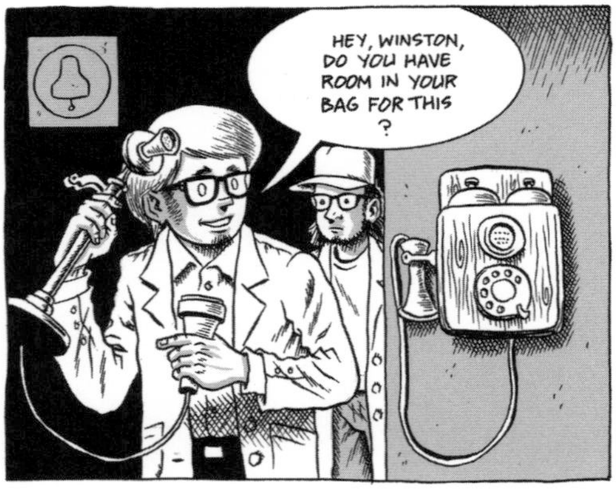
HEY, WINSTON, DO YOU HAVE ROOM IN YOUR BAG FOR THIS ?

HOW DOES THAT SAYING GO? SOMETHING ABOUT FLYING TOO CLOSE TO THE SUN WITH WAX WINGS ?!

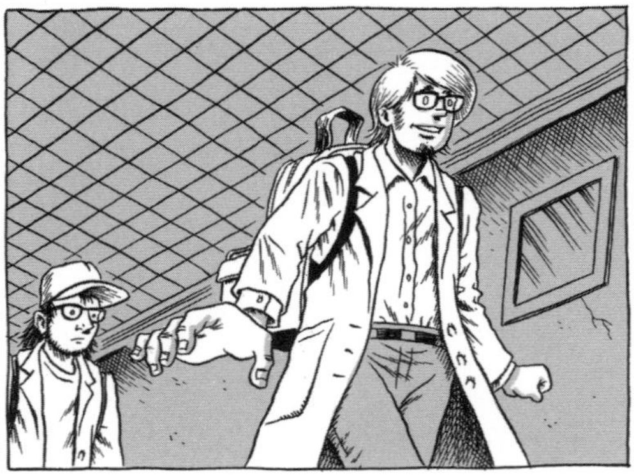

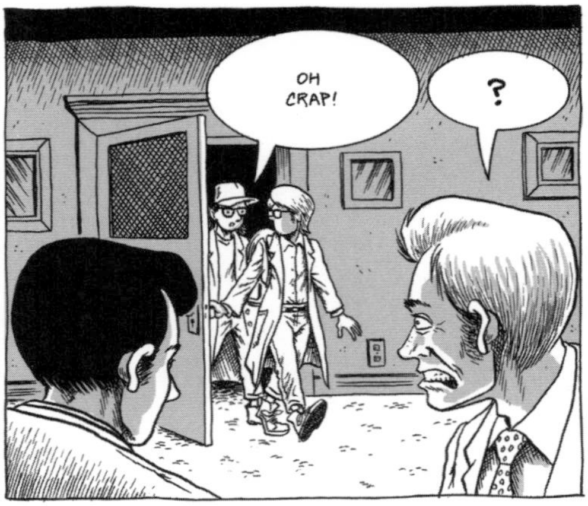
OH CRAP!
?

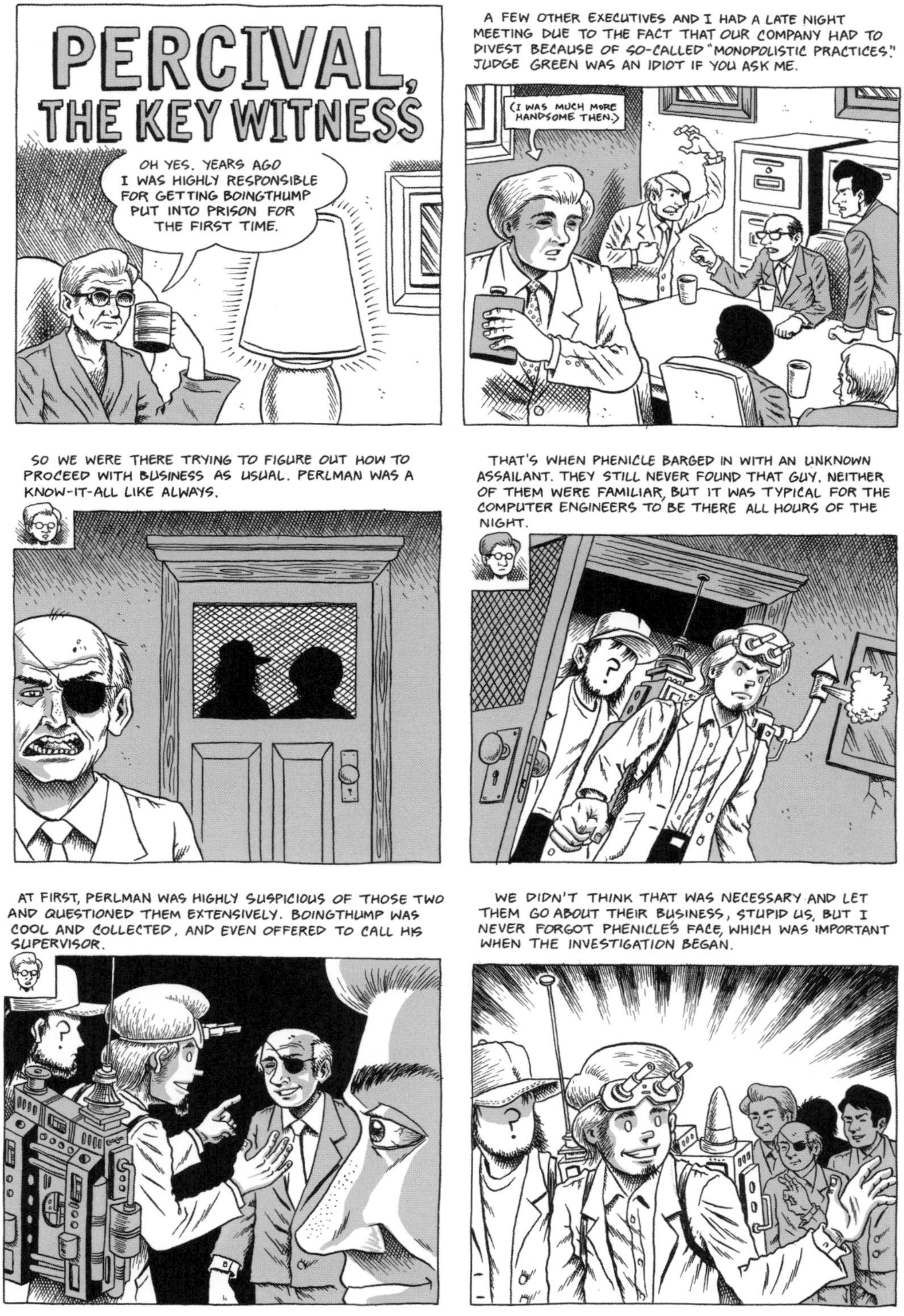
PERCIVAL, THE KEY WITNESS
OH YES. YEARS AGO I WAS HIGHLY RESPONSIBLE FOR GETTING BOINGTHUMP PUT INTO PRISON FOR THE FIRST TIME.
A FEW OTHER EXECUTIVES AND I HAD A LATE NIGHT MEETING DUE TO THE FACT THAT OUR COMPANY HAD TO DIVEST BECAUSE OF SO-CALLED "MONOPOLISTIC PRACTICES." JUDGE GREEN WAS AN IDIOT IF YOU ASK ME.
(I WAS MUCH MORE HANDSOME THEN.)
SO WE WERE THERE TRYING TO FIGURE OUT HOW TO PROCEED WITH BUSINESS AS USUAL. PERLMAN WAS A KNOW-IT-ALL LIKE ALWAYS.
THAT'S WHEN PHENICLE BARGED IN WITH AN UNKNOWN ASSAILANT. THEY STILL NEVER FOUND THAT GUY. NEITHER OF THEM WERE FAMILIAR, BUT IT WAS TYPICAL FOR THE COMPUTER ENGINEERS TO BE THERE ALL HOURS OF THE NIGHT.
AT FIRST, PERLMAN WAS HIGHLY SUSPICIOUS OF THOSE TWO AND QUESTIONED THEM EXTENSIVELY. BOINGTHUMP WAS COOL AND COLLECTED, AND EVEN OFFERED TO CALL HIS SUPERVISOR.
WE DIDN'T THINK THAT WAS NECESSARY AND LET THEM GO ABOUT THEIR BUSINESS, STUPID US, BUT I NEVER FORGOT PHENICLE'S FACE, WHICH WAS IMPORTANT WHEN THE INVESTIGATION BEGAN.

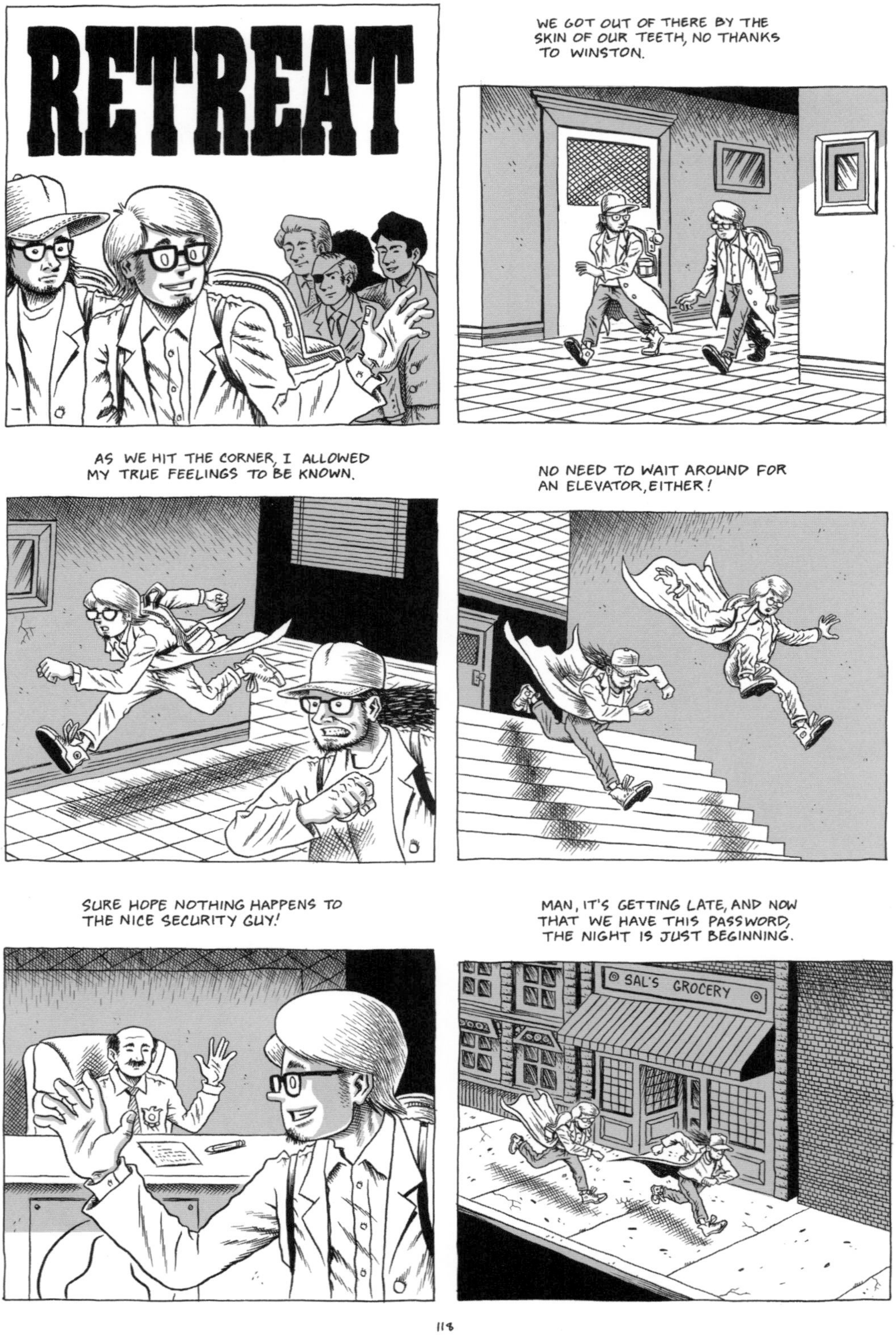
RETREAT
WE GOT OUT OF THERE BY THE SKIN OF OUR TEETH, NO THANKS TO WINSTON.
AS WE HIT THE CORNER, I ALLOWED MY TRUE FEELINGS TO BE KNOWN.
NO NEED TO WAIT AROUND FOR AN ELEVATOR, EITHER!
SURE HOPE NOTHING HAPPENS TO THE NICE SECURITY GUY!
MAN, IT'S GETTING LATE, AND NOW THAT WE HAVE THIS PASSWORD, THE NIGHT IS JUST BEGINNING.
SAL'S GROCERY

30 Days Of Access

DAY 1: KEVIN THOROUGHLY LOOKS THROUGH THE PHONE COMPANY COMPUTER SYSTEM. HE REALIZES THAT WITH THE SPECIAL PERMISSIONS GRANTED BY THE STOLEN PASSWORD HE CAN BASICALLY DO WHATEVER HE WANTS, SO...

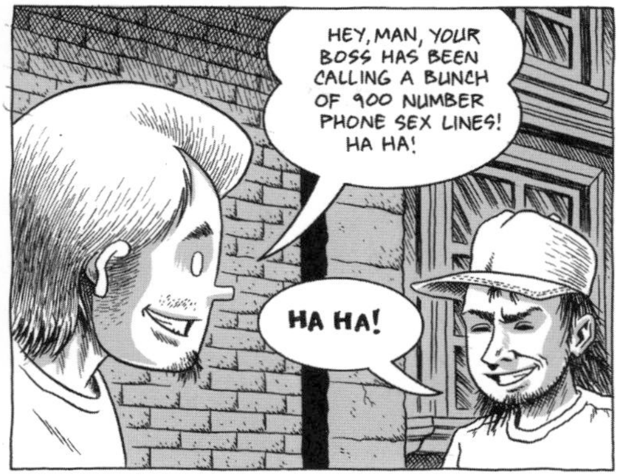
HEY, MAN, YOUR BOSS HAS BEEN CALLING A BUNCH OF 900 NUMBER PHONE SEX LINES! HA HA!
HA HA!

DAY 3: KEVIN CAN NOW CALL ANY LONG DISTANCE PHONE NUMBER AND BBS FROM HOME, WHICH MAKES HIM HAPPY. HE CAN MAKE THOSE RECORDS DISAPPEAR FROM HIS GRANDMOTHER'S PHONE BILL WITH EASE.

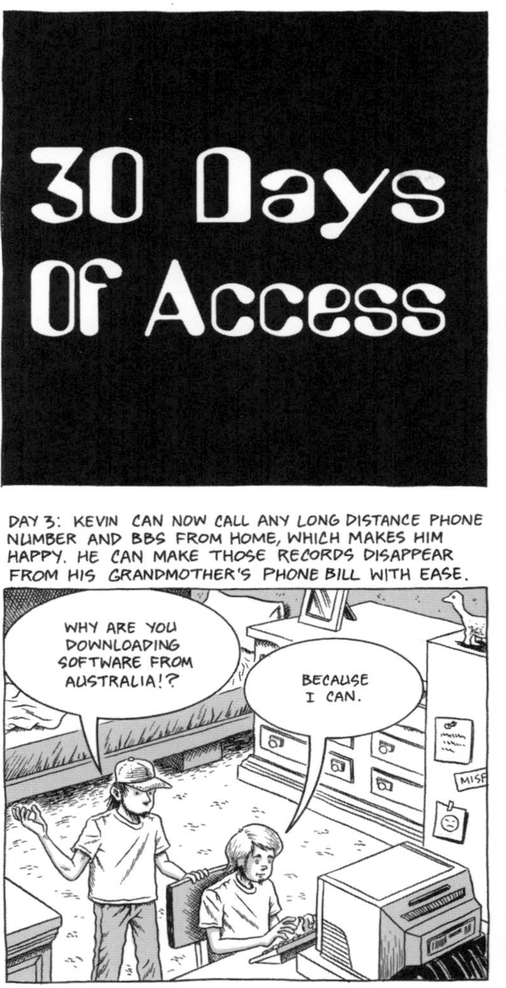
WHY ARE YOU DOWNLOADING SOFTWARE FROM AUSTRALIA!?
BECAUSE I CAN.

DAY 6: KEVIN LEARNS ABOUT A WEIRD, NEW, CREEPY FEATURE CALLED "CALLER I.D." HE WONDERS WHEN THIS WILL BE AVAILABLE TO THE PUBLIC.

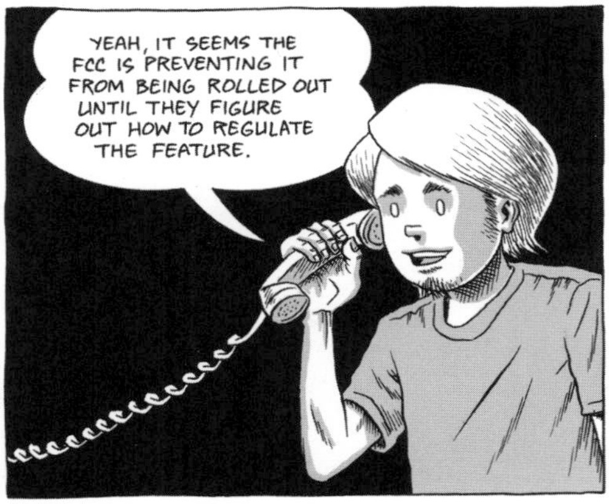
YEAH, IT SEEMS THE FCC IS PREVENTING IT FROM BEING ROLLED OUT UNTIL THEY FIGURE OUT HOW TO REGULATE THE FEATURE.

DAY 7: KEVIN ADDS CALLER ID TO THE PHONE LINE AT HIS HOUSE.

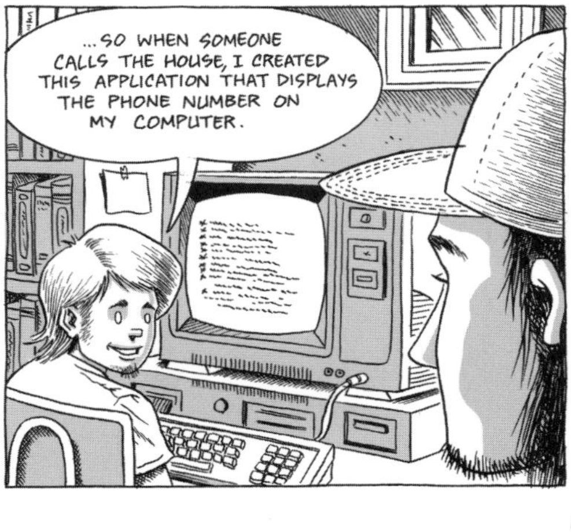
...SO WHEN SOMEONE CALLS THE HOUSE, I CREATED THIS APPLICATION THAT DISPLAYS THE PHONE NUMBER ON MY COMPUTER.

DAY 13: KEVIN THINKS IT WOULD BE A GOOD IDEA TO CHANGE THE INTERNAL CLOCK ON THE DATABASE FROM 3:00 AM TO 3:00 PM. IT WILL TAKE SOME TIME FOR THE PHONE COMPANY TO BECOME AWARE OF THE DISCREPANCY.

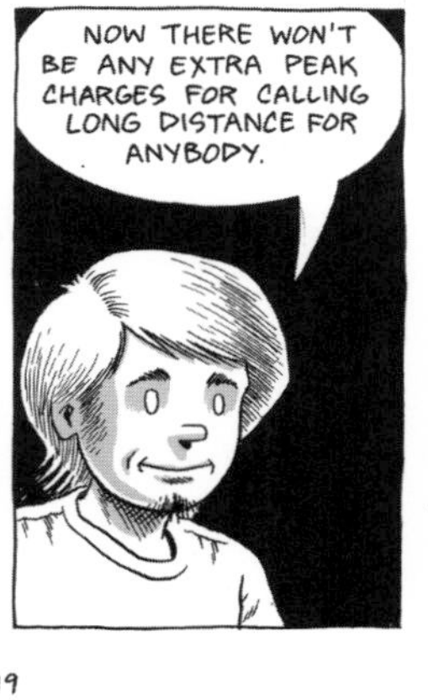
NOW THERE WON'T BE ANY EXTRA PEAK CHARGES FOR CALLING LONG DISTANCE FOR ANYBODY.

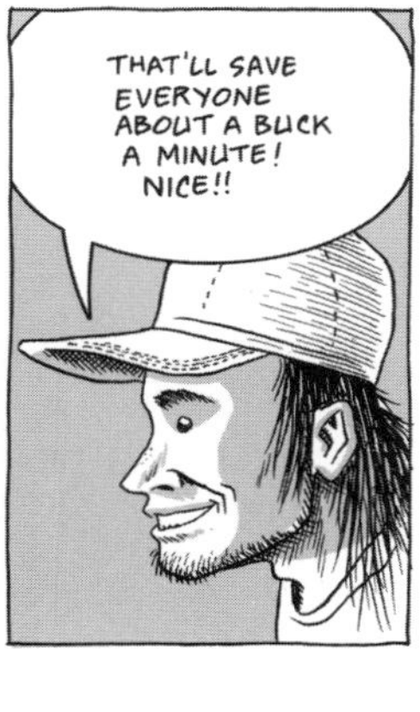
THAT'LL SAVE EVERYONE ABOUT A BUCK A MINUTE! NICE!!

DAY 16: KEVIN SCUFFLES WITH A FEW DRUNK PEOPLE WHO REMEMBERED HIM FROM HIGH SCHOOL. THAT NIGHT, THE INTOXICATED MAN'S PHONE BILL SOMEHOW GOT MIXED UP WITH THE LOCAL HOSPITAL'S $32,000 PHONE BILL.

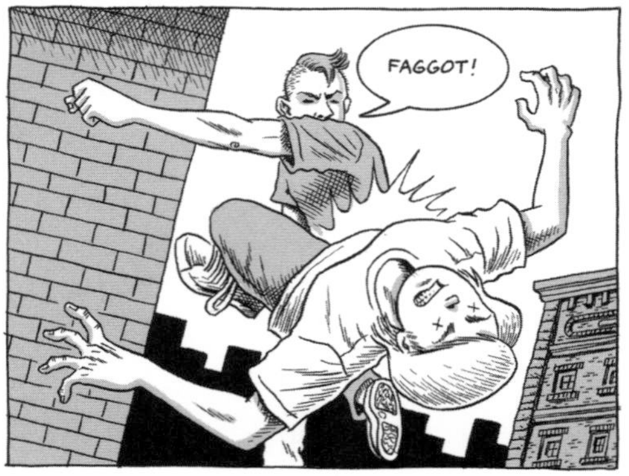
FAGGOT!

DAY 20: KEVIN ACTIVATES A DEAD PHONE LINE IN HIS ROOM WITH JUST A FEW CLICKS OF THE KEYBOARD.

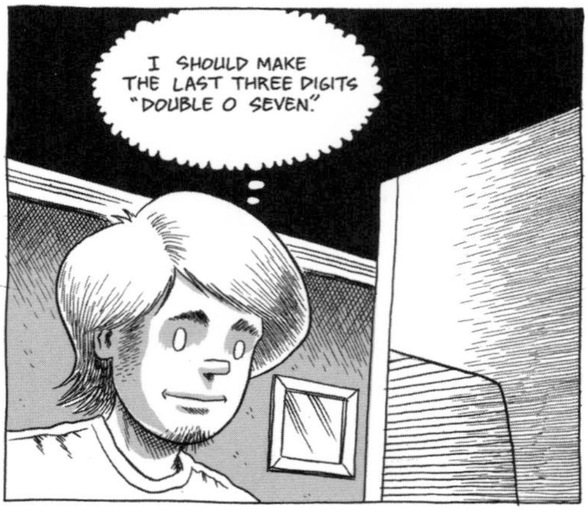
I SHOULD MAKE THE LAST THREE DIGITS "DOUBLE O SEVEN."

DAY 22: KEVIN MAKES A GAME OF COLLECTING THE PHONE NUMBERS AND ADDRESSES OF CELEBRITIES.

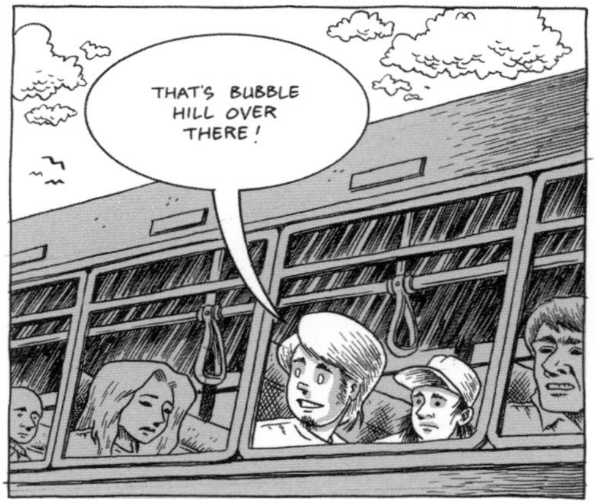
THAT'S BUBBLE HILL OVER THERE!

DAY 25: KEVIN MAKES OUTGOING CALLS FREE-OF-CHARGE AT THE PAYPHONE ON THE CORNER OF 21 AND LEWIS.

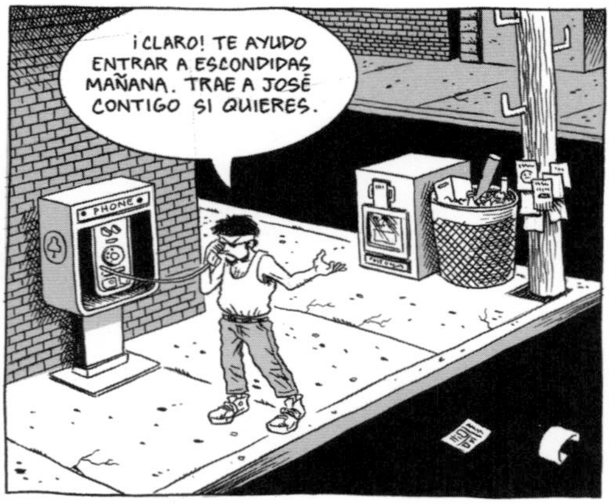
¡CLARO! TE AYUDO ENTRAR A ESCONDIDAS MAÑANA. TRAE A JOSÉ CONTIGO SI QUIERES.
PHONE

DAY 27: KEVIN FINDS A FILE DEEP WITHIN THE DATA-BASE THAT LOGS THE PHONE NUMBER OF EVERY COMPUTER THAT ACCESSES THE SYSTEM, INCLUDING KEVIN'S HOME PHONE NUMBER.

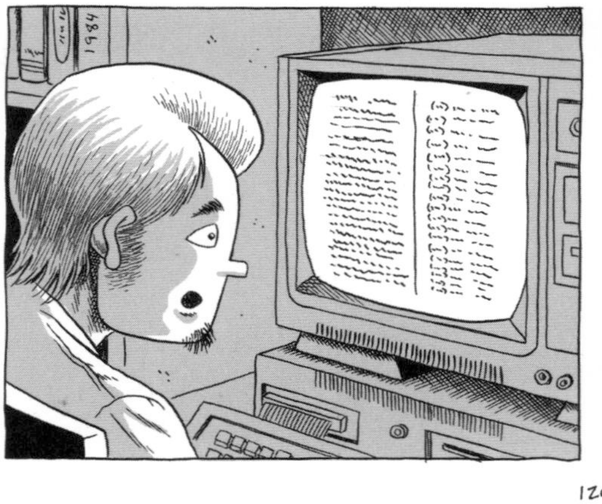
1984

DAY 30: AFTER DAYS OF TRYING TO HIDE HIS TRACKS ON THE COMPUTER, KEVIN HEARS A FEW FIERCE, RAPID KNOCKS ON THE DOOR OF HIS BEDROOM.

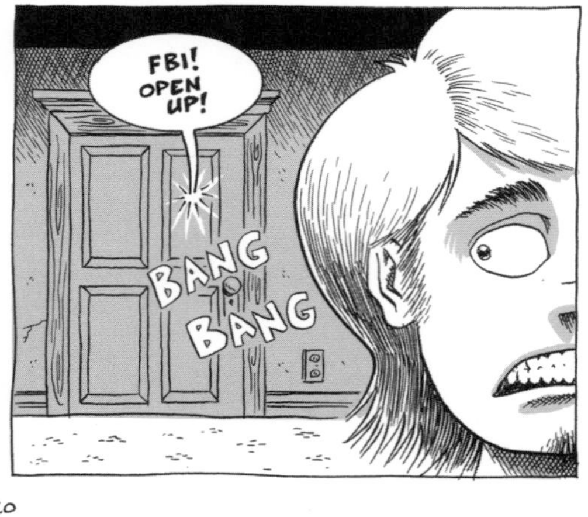
FBI! OPEN UP!
BANG BANG

TRUE CRIME IN STEEL VALLEY

NARRATED BY RON SHUMWAY

LAST JUNE, THE PHONE COMPANY FELL VICTIM TO A PSYCHOTIC INVADER BENT ON USING THEIR TECHNOLOGY AGAINST THEM!

REENACTMENT

KEVIN `BOINGTHUMP' PHENICLE WAS THE MASTERMIND BEHIND THE INTRUSION AND WAS RAPIDLY CAPTURED ONCE THE TELCO REPORTED THE BREACH TO THE FBI.

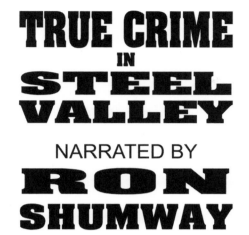

>BEEP< YOU PIGS!

REENACTMENT

AT PHENICLE'S HOME, MANY PIECES OF COMPUTER EQUIPMENT WERE LOCATED ON THE PREMISES. HUNDREDS OF PIECES OF PROPRIETARY TELCO PROPERTY WERE ALSO CONFISCATED AT HIS LAIR.

HOW'D THIS KID GET ALL THIS STUFF?

I DON'T KNOW, AND I DON'T LIKE IT!

REENACTMENT

WHILE IN CUSTODY, THE MAD GENIUS, KEVIN, WAS QUESTIONED FOR DAYS AS THE AUTHORITIES GOT TO KNOW THE EXTENT OF HIS KNOWLEDGE AND COMPUTER INTRUSION TRACK RECORD.

DOC

REENACTMENT

IT TURNED OUT THAT PHENICLE HAD MADE A LIFE OF HACKING, PHONE PHREAKING, AND ESPIONAGE. THE FBI REALIZED QUICKLY THAT THEY HAD A VERY DANGEROUS INDIVIDUAL IN CUSTODY.

C'MERE, PIG! I GOT SUMPTHIN' FOR YA!!

REENACTMENT

HIS PUBLIC DEFENDER HAD A HARD TIME ARGUING THE CHARGES AGAINST HIM!

THE JUDGE HAD LITTLE SYMPATHY FOR THE HEINOUS CRIMES OF PHENICLE AND NOBLY INVOKED THE MAXIMUM SENTENCE POSSIBLE FOR THIS MANIACAL INDIVIDUAL.

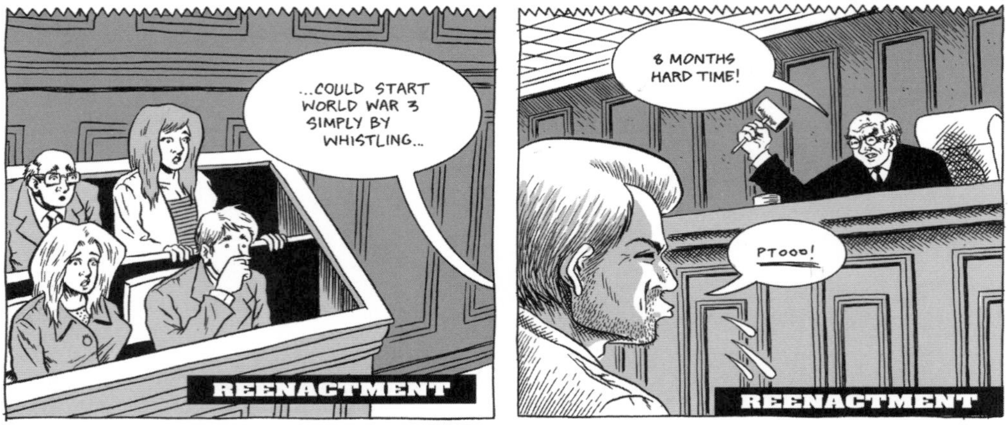
...COULD START WORLD WAR 3 SIMPLY BY WHISTLING...
REENACTMENT
8 MONTHS HARD TIME!
PTOOO!
REENACTMENT

WINSTON'S DILEMMA

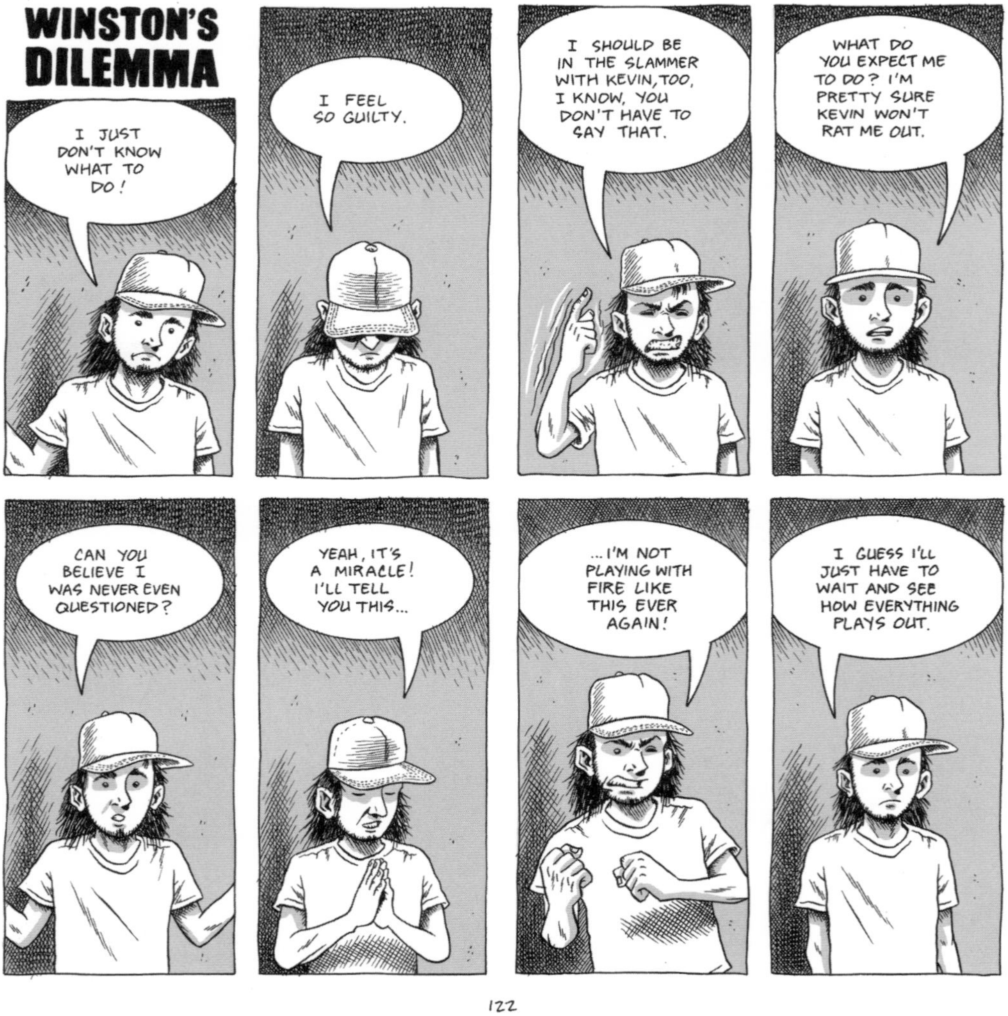
I JUST DON'T KNOW WHAT TO DO!
I FEEL SO GUILTY.
I SHOULD BE IN THE SLAMMER WITH KEVIN, TOO, I KNOW, YOU DON'T HAVE TO SAY THAT.
WHAT DO YOU EXPECT ME TO DO? I'M PRETTY SURE KEVIN WON'T RAT ME OUT.
CAN YOU BELIEVE I WAS NEVER EVEN QUESTIONED?
YEAH, IT'S A MIRACLE! I'LL TELL YOU THIS...
...I'M NOT PLAYING WITH FIRE LIKE THIS EVER AGAIN!
I GUESS I'LL JUST HAVE TO WAIT AND SEE HOW EVERYTHING PLAYS OUT.

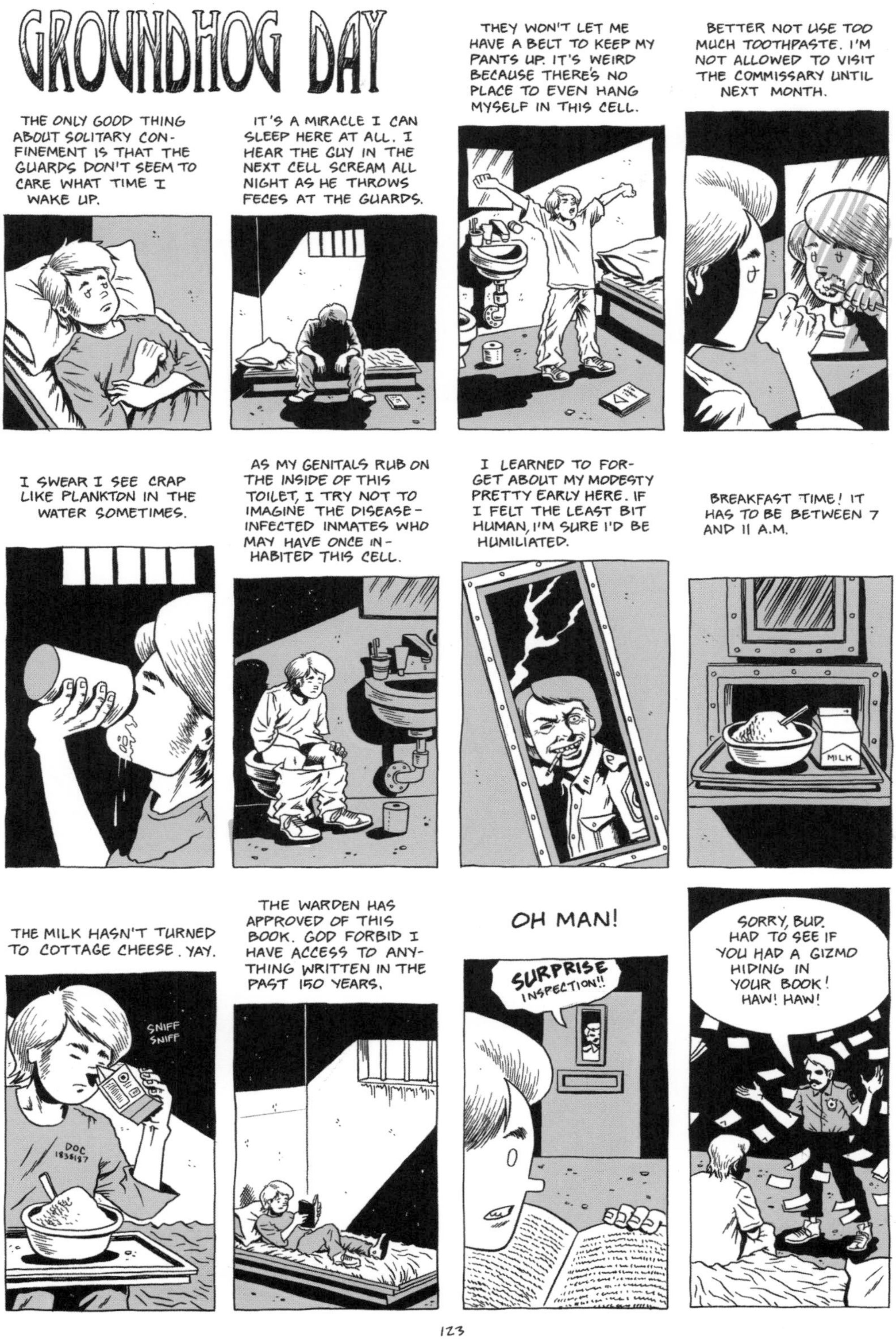
GROUNDHOG DAY
THE ONLY GOOD THING ABOUT SOLITARY CONFINEMENT IS THAT THE GUARDS DON'T SEEM TO CARE WHAT TIME I WAKE UP.
IT'S A MIRACLE I CAN SLEEP HERE AT ALL. I HEAR THE GUY IN THE NEXT CELL SCREAM ALL NIGHT AS HE THROWS FECES AT THE GUARDS.
THEY WON'T LET ME HAVE A BELT TO KEEP MY PANTS UP. IT'S WEIRD BECAUSE THERE'S NO PLACE TO EVEN HANG MYSELF IN THIS CELL.
BETTER NOT USE TOO MUCH TOOTHPASTE. I'M NOT ALLOWED TO VISIT THE COMMISSARY UNTIL NEXT MONTH.
I SWEAR I SEE CRAP LIKE PLANKTON IN THE WATER SOMETIMES.
AS MY GENITALS RUB ON THE INSIDE OF THIS TOILET, I TRY NOT TO IMAGINE THE DISEASE-INFECTED INMATES WHO MAY HAVE ONCE INHABITED THIS CELL.
I LEARNED TO FORGET ABOUT MY MODESTY PRETTY EARLY HERE. IF I FELT THE LEAST BIT HUMAN, I'M SURE I'D BE HUMILIATED.
BREAKFAST TIME! IT HAS TO BE BETWEEN 7 AND 11 A.M.
MILK
THE MILK HASN'T TURNED TO COTTAGE CHEESE. YAY.
SNIFF SNIFF
DOC 1838187
THE WARDEN HAS APPROVED OF THIS BOOK. GOD FORBID I HAVE ACCESS TO ANYTHING WRITTEN IN THE PAST 150 YEARS.
OH MAN!
SURPRISE INSPECTION!!
SORRY, BUD. HAD TO SEE IF YOU HAD A GIZMO HIDING IN YOUR BOOK! HAW! HAW!

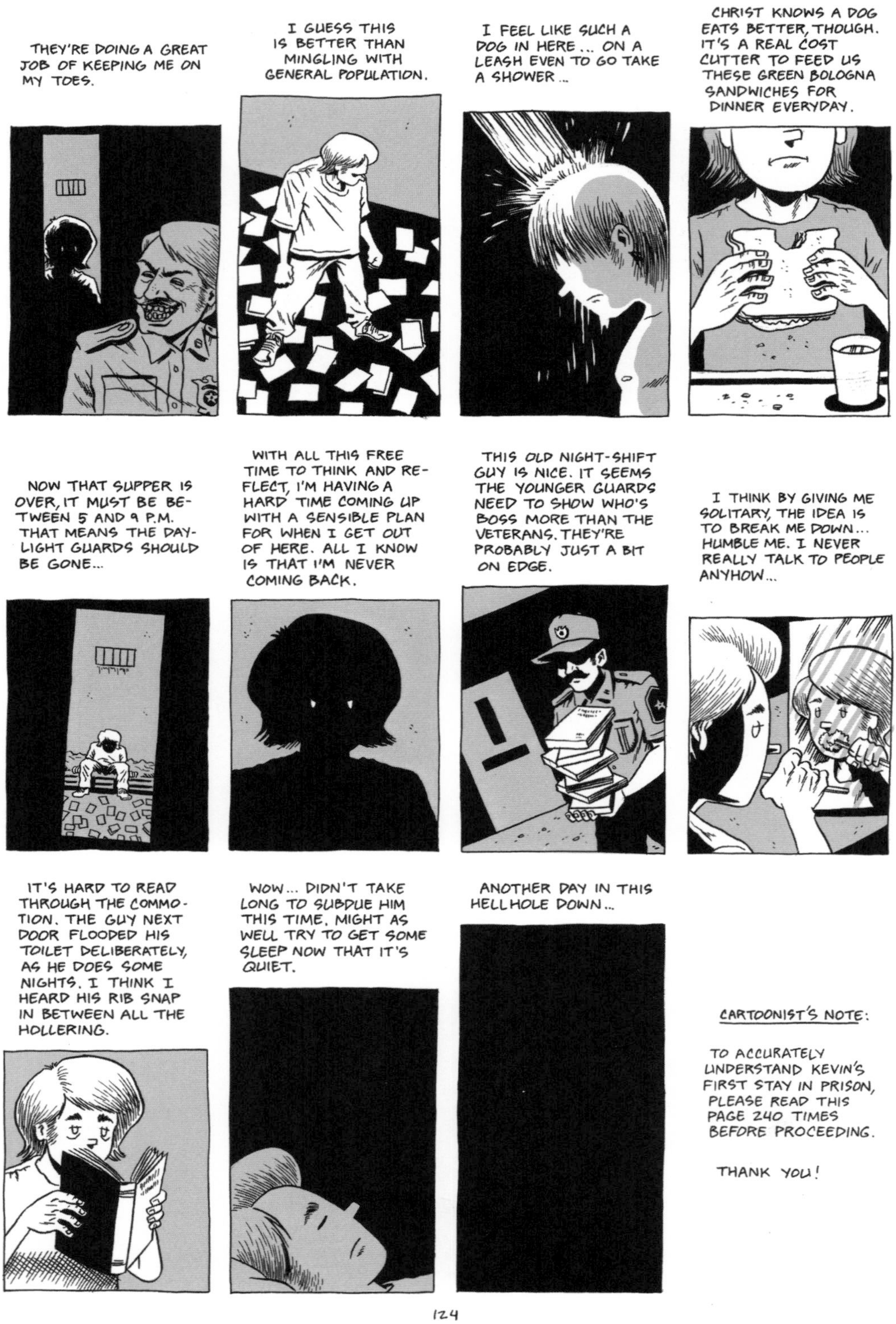
THEY'RE DOING A GREAT JOB OF KEEPING ME ON MY TOES.
I GUESS THIS IS BETTER THAN MINGLING WITH GENERAL POPULATION.
I FEEL LIKE SUCH A DOG IN HERE... ON A LEASH EVEN TO GO TAKE A SHOWER...
CHRIST KNOWS A DOG EATS BETTER, THOUGH. IT'S A REAL COST CUTTER TO FEED US THESE GREEN BOLOGNA SANDWICHES FOR DINNER EVERYDAY.
NOW THAT SUPPER IS OVER, IT MUST BE BETWEEN 5 AND 9 P.M. THAT MEANS THE DAYLIGHT GUARDS SHOULD BE GONE...
WITH ALL THIS FREE TIME TO THINK AND REFLECT, I'M HAVING A HARD TIME COMING UP WITH A SENSIBLE PLAN FOR WHEN I GET OUT OF HERE. ALL I KNOW IS THAT I'M NEVER COMING BACK.
THIS OLD NIGHT-SHIFT GUY IS NICE. IT SEEMS THE YOUNGER GUARDS NEED TO SHOW WHO'S BOSS MORE THAN THE VETERANS. THEY'RE PROBABLY JUST A BIT ON EDGE.
I THINK BY GIVING ME SOLITARY, THE IDEA IS TO BREAK ME DOWN... HUMBLE ME. I NEVER REALLY TALK TO PEOPLE ANYHOW...
IT'S HARD TO READ THROUGH THE COMMOTION. THE GUY NEXT DOOR FLOODED HIS TOILET DELIBERATELY, AS HE DOES SOME NIGHTS. I THINK I HEARD HIS RIB SNAP IN BETWEEN ALL THE HOLLERING.
WOW... DIDN'T TAKE LONG TO SUBDUE HIM THIS TIME. MIGHT AS WELL TRY TO GET SOME SLEEP NOW THAT IT'S QUIET.
ANOTHER DAY IN THIS HELLHOLE DOWN...
CARTOONIST'S NOTE:
TO ACCURATELY UNDERSTAND KEVIN'S FIRST STAY IN PRISON, PLEASE READ THIS PAGE 240 TIMES BEFORE PROCEEDING.
THANK YOU!

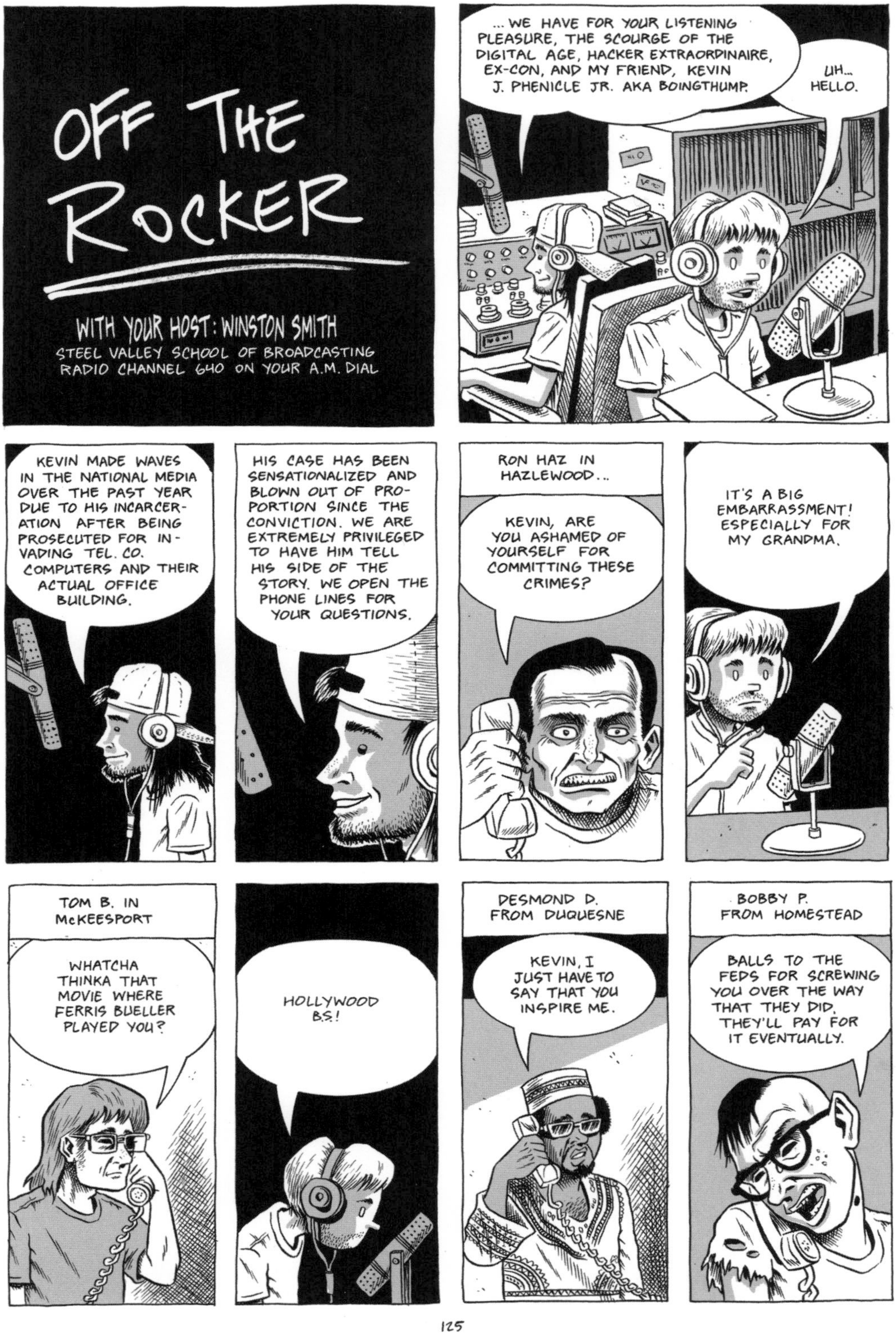
OFF THE ROCKER
WITH YOUR HOST: WINSTON SMITH
STEEL VALLEY SCHOOL OF BROADCASTING
RADIO CHANNEL 640 ON YOUR A.M. DIAL
... WE HAVE FOR YOUR LISTENING PLEASURE, THE SCOURGE OF THE DIGITAL AGE, HACKER EXTRAORDINAIRE, EX-CON, AND MY FRIEND, KEVIN J. PHENICLE JR. AKA BOINGTHUMP.
UH... HELLO.
KEVIN MADE WAVES IN THE NATIONAL MEDIA OVER THE PAST YEAR DUE TO HIS INCARCER-ATION AFTER BEING PROSECUTED FOR IN-VADING TEL. CO. COMPUTERS AND THEIR ACTUAL OFFICE BUILDING.
HIS CASE HAS BEEN SENSATIONALIZED AND BLOWN OUT OF PRO-PORTION SINCE THE CONVICTION. WE ARE EXTREMELY PRIVILEGED TO HAVE HIM TELL HIS SIDE OF THE STORY. WE OPEN THE PHONE LINES FOR YOUR QUESTIONS.
RON HAZ IN HAZLEWOOD...
KEVIN, ARE YOU ASHAMED OF YOURSELF FOR COMMITTING THESE CRIMES?
IT'S A BIG EMBARRASSMENT! ESPECIALLY FOR MY GRANDMA.
TOM B. IN McKEESPORT
WHATCHA THINKA THAT MOVIE WHERE FERRIS BUELLER PLAYED YOU?
HOLLYWOOD B.S.!
DESMOND D. FROM DUQUESNE
KEVIN, I JUST HAVE TO SAY THAT YOU INSPIRE ME.
BOBBY P. FROM HOMESTEAD
BALLS TO THE FEDS FOR SCREWING YOU OVER THE WAY THAT THEY DID, THEY'LL PAY FOR IT EVENTUALLY.

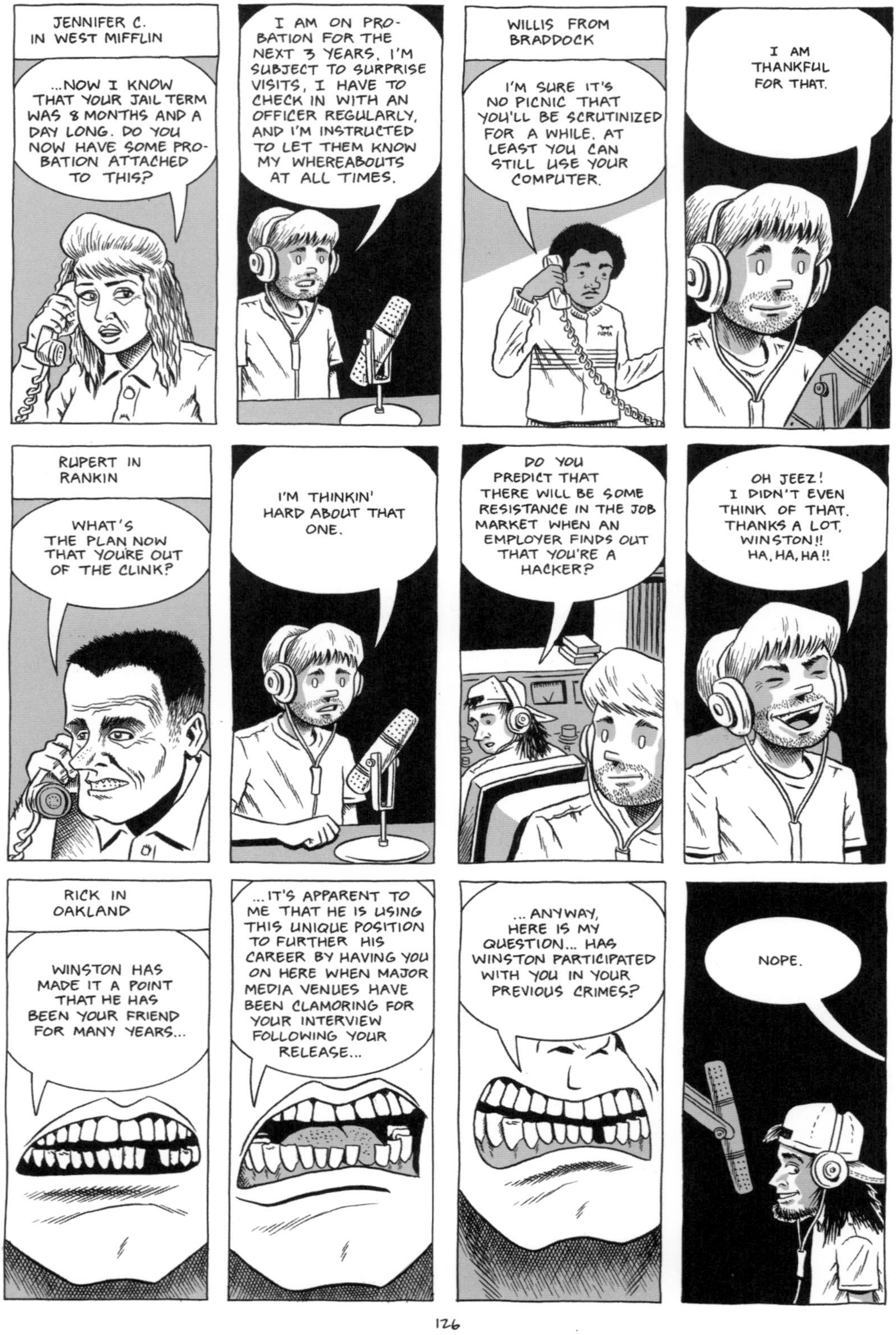
JENNIFER C. IN WEST MIFFLIN
...NOW I KNOW THAT YOUR JAIL TERM WAS 8 MONTHS AND A DAY LONG. DO YOU NOW HAVE SOME PROBATION ATTACHED TO THIS?
I AM ON PROBATION FOR THE NEXT 3 YEARS. I'M SUBJECT TO SURPRISE VISITS, I HAVE TO CHECK IN WITH AN OFFICER REGULARLY, AND I'M INSTRUCTED TO LET THEM KNOW MY WHEREABOUTS AT ALL TIMES.
WILLIS FROM BRADDOCK
I'M SURE IT'S NO PICNIC THAT YOU'LL BE SCRUTINIZED FOR A WHILE. AT LEAST YOU CAN STILL USE YOUR COMPUTER.
I AM THANKFUL FOR THAT.
RUPERT IN RANKIN
WHAT'S THE PLAN NOW THAT YOU'RE OUT OF THE CLINK?
I'M THINKIN' HARD ABOUT THAT ONE.
DO YOU PREDICT THAT THERE WILL BE SOME RESISTANCE IN THE JOB MARKET WHEN AN EMPLOYER FINDS OUT THAT YOU'RE A HACKER?
OH JEEZ! I DIDN'T EVEN THINK OF THAT. THANKS A LOT, WINSTON!! HA, HA, HA!!
RICK IN OAKLAND
WINSTON HAS MADE IT A POINT THAT HE HAS BEEN YOUR FRIEND FOR MANY YEARS...
...IT'S APPARENT TO ME THAT HE IS USING THIS UNIQUE POSITION TO FURTHER HIS CAREER BY HAVING YOU ON HERE WHEN MAJOR MEDIA VENUES HAVE BEEN CLAMORING FOR YOUR INTERVIEW FOLLOWING YOUR RELEASE...
...ANYWAY, HERE IS MY QUESTION... HAS WINSTON PARTICIPATED WITH YOU IN YOUR PREVIOUS CRIMES?
NOPE.

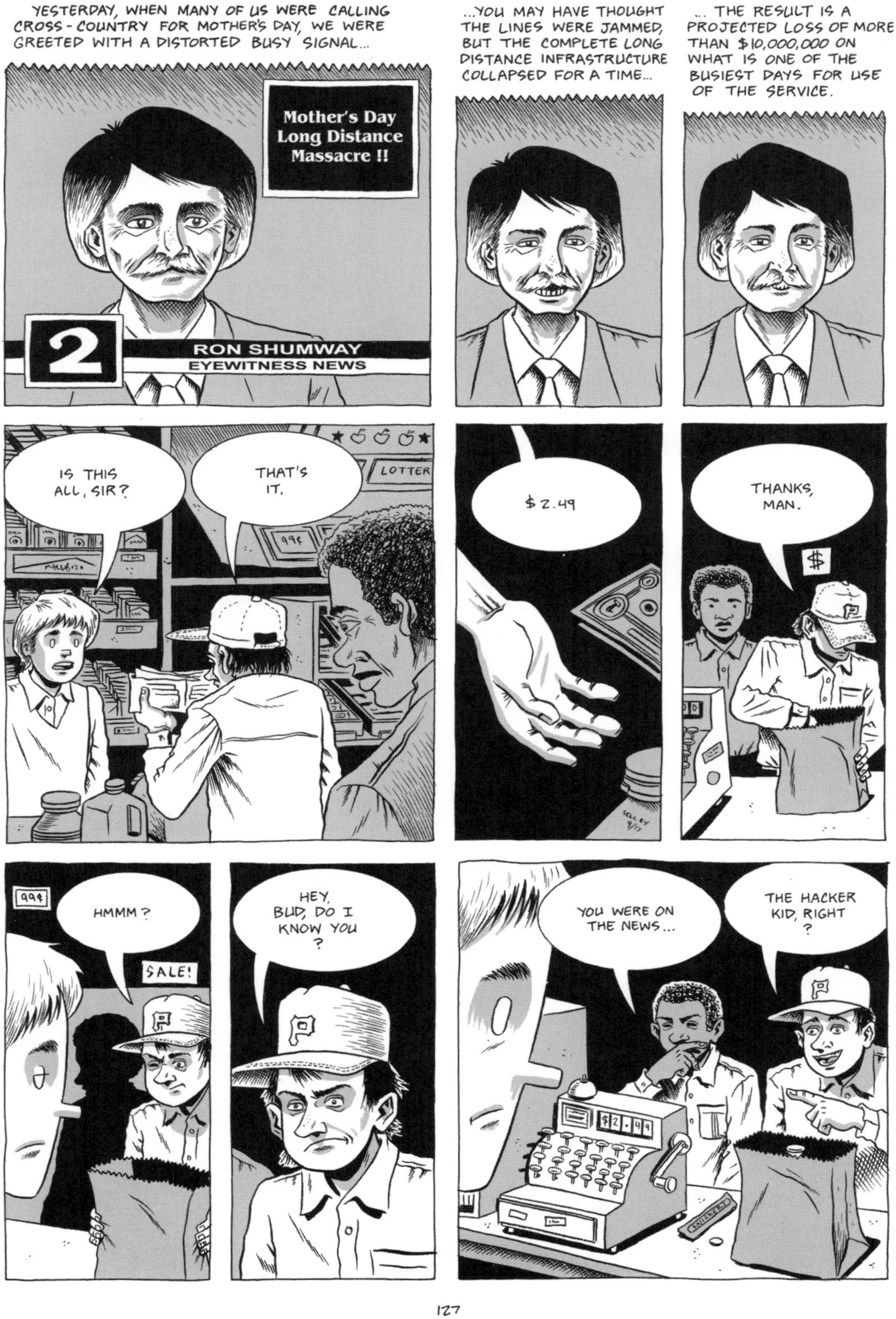
YESTERDAY, WHEN MANY OF US WERE CALLING CROSS-COUNTRY FOR MOTHER'S DAY, WE WERE GREETED WITH A DISTORTED BUSY SIGNAL...
Mother's Day Long Distance Massacre !!
2
RON SHUMWAY
EYEWITNESS NEWS
...YOU MAY HAVE THOUGHT THE LINES WERE JAMMED, BUT THE COMPLETE LONG DISTANCE INFRASTRUCTURE COLLAPSED FOR A TIME...
... THE RESULT IS A PROJECTED LOSS OF MORE THAN $10,000,000 ON WHAT IS ONE OF THE BUSIEST DAYS FOR USE OF THE SERVICE.
LOTTER
IS THIS ALL, SIR?
THAT'S IT.
99¢
$ 2.49
THANKS, MAN.
$
99¢
HMMM?
SALE!
HEY, BUD, DO I KNOW YOU ?
YOU WERE ON THE NEWS...
THE HACKER KID, RIGHT ?

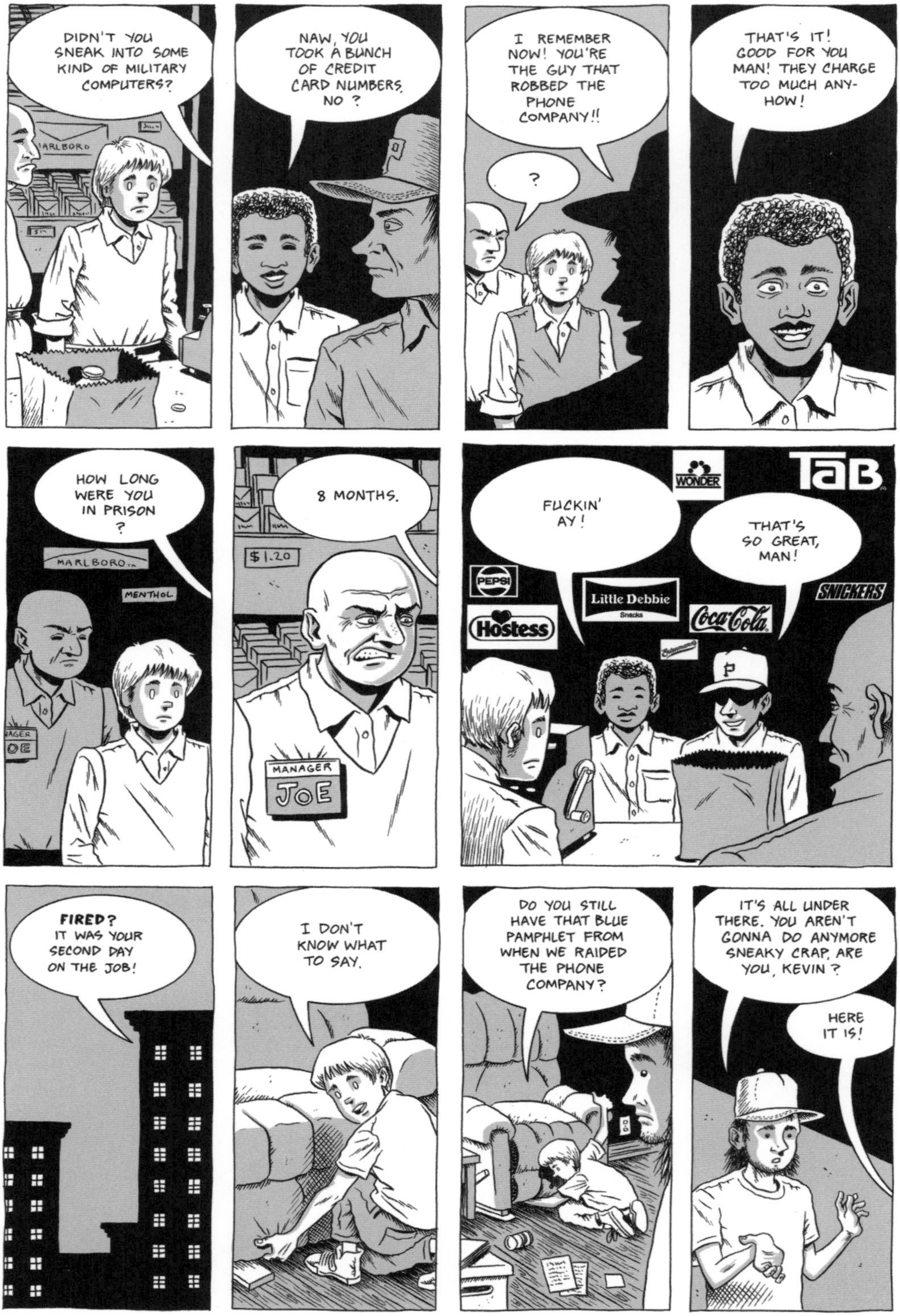
DIDN'T YOU SNEAK INTO SOME KIND OF MILITARY COMPUTERS?
MARLBORO
NAW, YOU TOOK A BUNCH OF CREDIT CARD NUMBERS, NO ?
I REMEMBER NOW! YOU'RE THE GUY THAT ROBBED THE PHONE COMPANY!!
?
THAT'S IT! GOOD FOR YOU MAN! THEY CHARGE TOO MUCH ANY-HOW!
HOW LONG WERE YOU IN PRISON ?
MARLBORO
MENTHOL
8 MONTHS.
$1.20
MANAGER
JOE
WONDER
TAB
FUCKIN' AY!
THAT'S SO GREAT, MAN!
PEPSI
Little Debbie
Snacks
Hostess
Coca-Cola
SNICKERS
FIRED? IT WAS YOUR SECOND DAY ON THE JOB!
I DON'T KNOW WHAT TO SAY.
DO YOU STILL HAVE THAT BLUE PAMPHLET FROM WHEN WE RAIDED THE PHONE COMPANY?
IT'S ALL UNDER THERE. YOU AREN'T GONNA DO ANYMORE SNEAKY CRAP, ARE YOU, KEVIN ?
HERE IT IS!

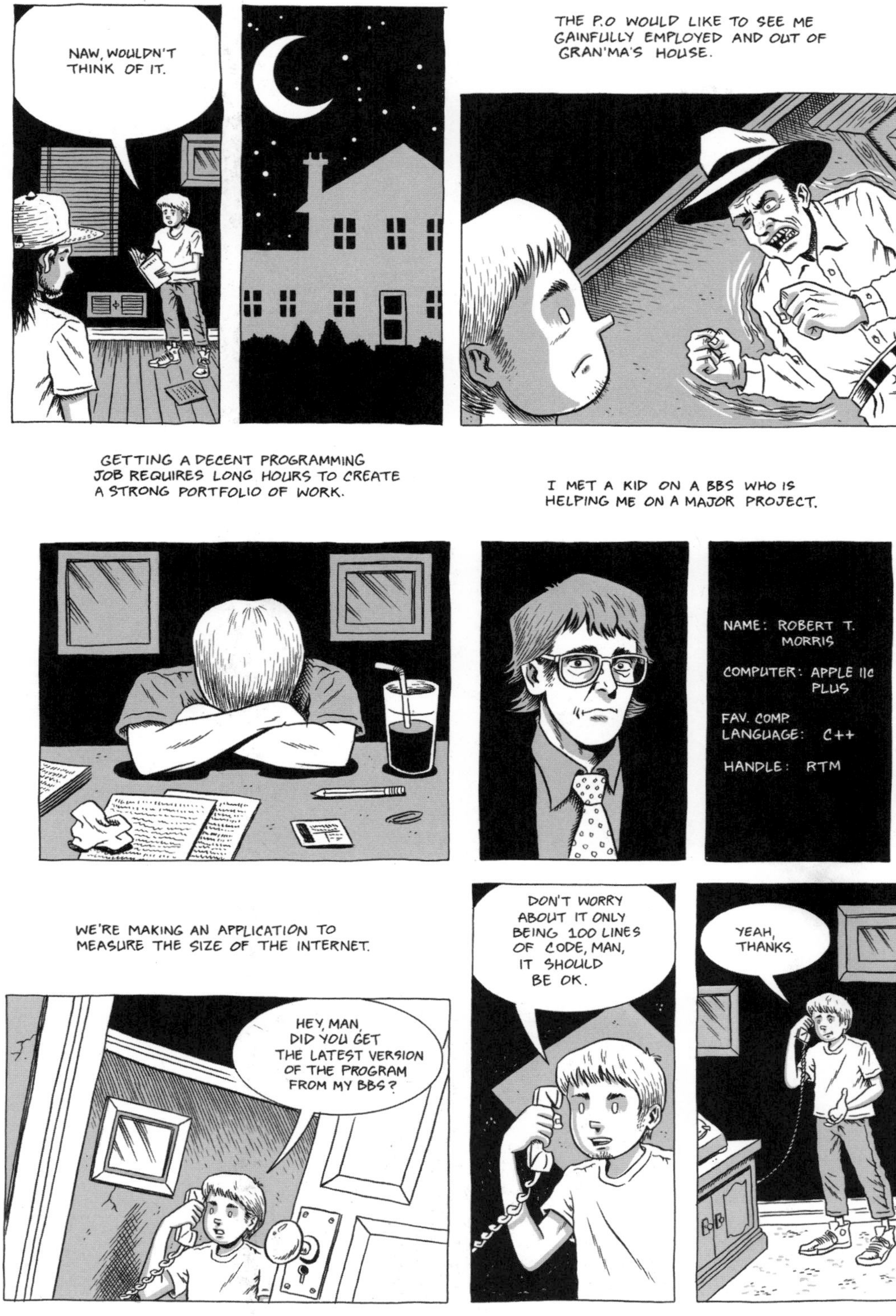
NAW, WOULDN'T THINK OF IT.
THE P.O WOULD LIKE TO SEE ME GAINFULLY EMPLOYED AND OUT OF GRAN'MA'S HOUSE.
GETTING A DECENT PROGRAMMING JOB REQUIRES LONG HOURS TO CREATE A STRONG PORTFOLIO OF WORK.
I MET A KID ON A BBS WHO IS HELPING ME ON A MAJOR PROJECT.
NAME: ROBERT T. MORRIS
COMPUTER: APPLE IIc PLUS
FAV. COMP. LANGUAGE: C++
HANDLE: RTM
WE'RE MAKING AN APPLICATION TO MEASURE THE SIZE OF THE INTERNET.
HEY, MAN, DID YOU GET THE LATEST VERSION OF THE PROGRAM FROM MY BBS?
DON'T WORRY ABOUT IT ONLY BEING 100 LINES OF CODE, MAN, IT SHOULD BE OK.
YEAH, THANKS.

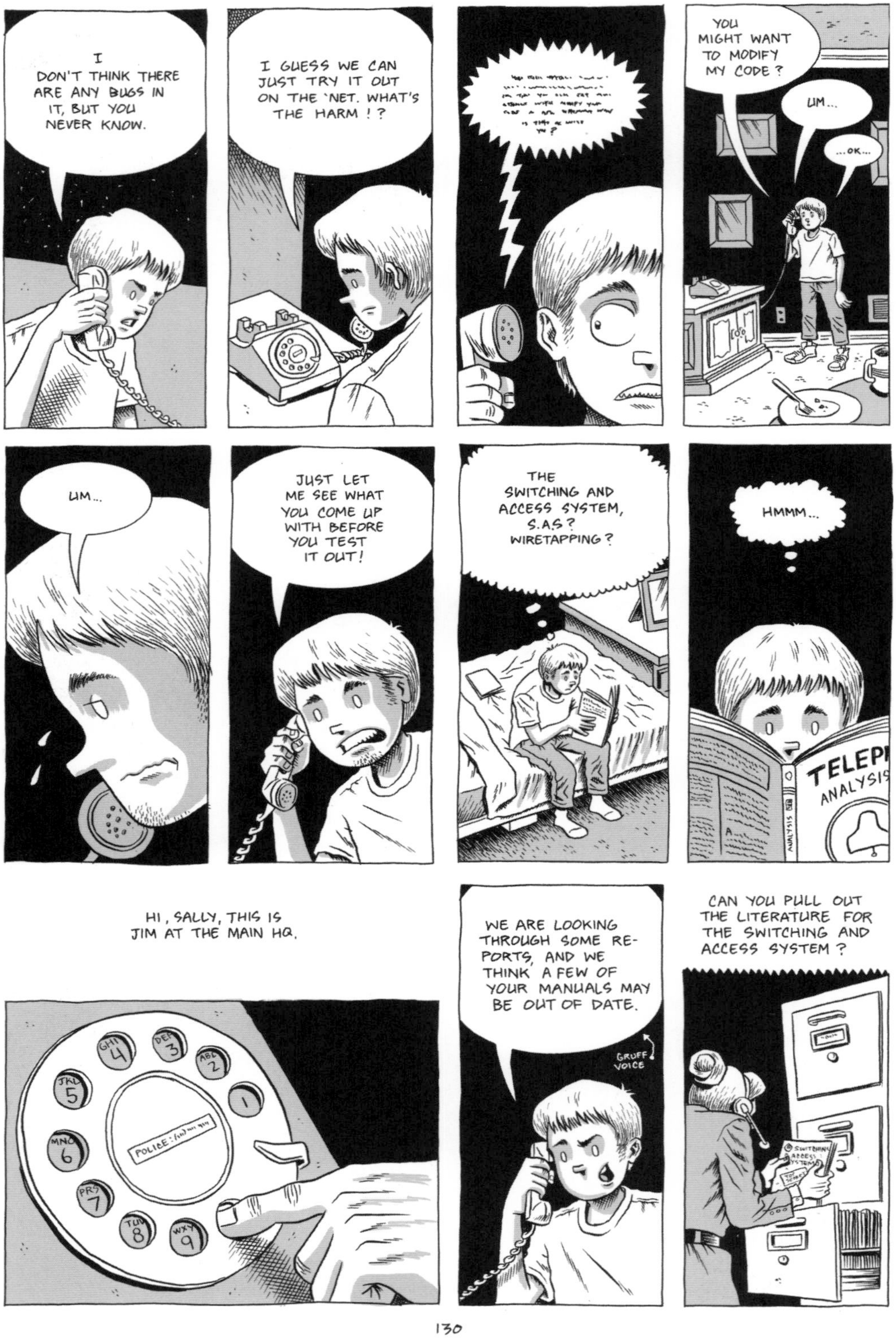
I DON'T THINK THERE ARE ANY BUGS IN IT, BUT YOU NEVER KNOW.
I GUESS WE CAN JUST TRY IT OUT ON THE 'NET. WHAT'S THE HARM !?
YOU MIGHT WANT TO MODIFY MY CODE ?
UM...
...OK...
UM...
JUST LET ME SEE WHAT YOU COME UP WITH BEFORE YOU TEST IT OUT!
THE SWITCHING AND ACCESS SYSTEM, S.A.S? WIRETAPPING?
HMMM...
TELEP
ANALYSIS
HI, SALLY, THIS IS JIM AT THE MAIN HQ.
WE ARE LOOKING THROUGH SOME RE-PORTS, AND WE THINK A FEW OF YOUR MANUALS MAY BE OUT OF DATE.
GRUFF VOICE
CAN YOU PULL OUT THE LITERATURE FOR THE SWITCHING AND ACCESS SYSTEM ?

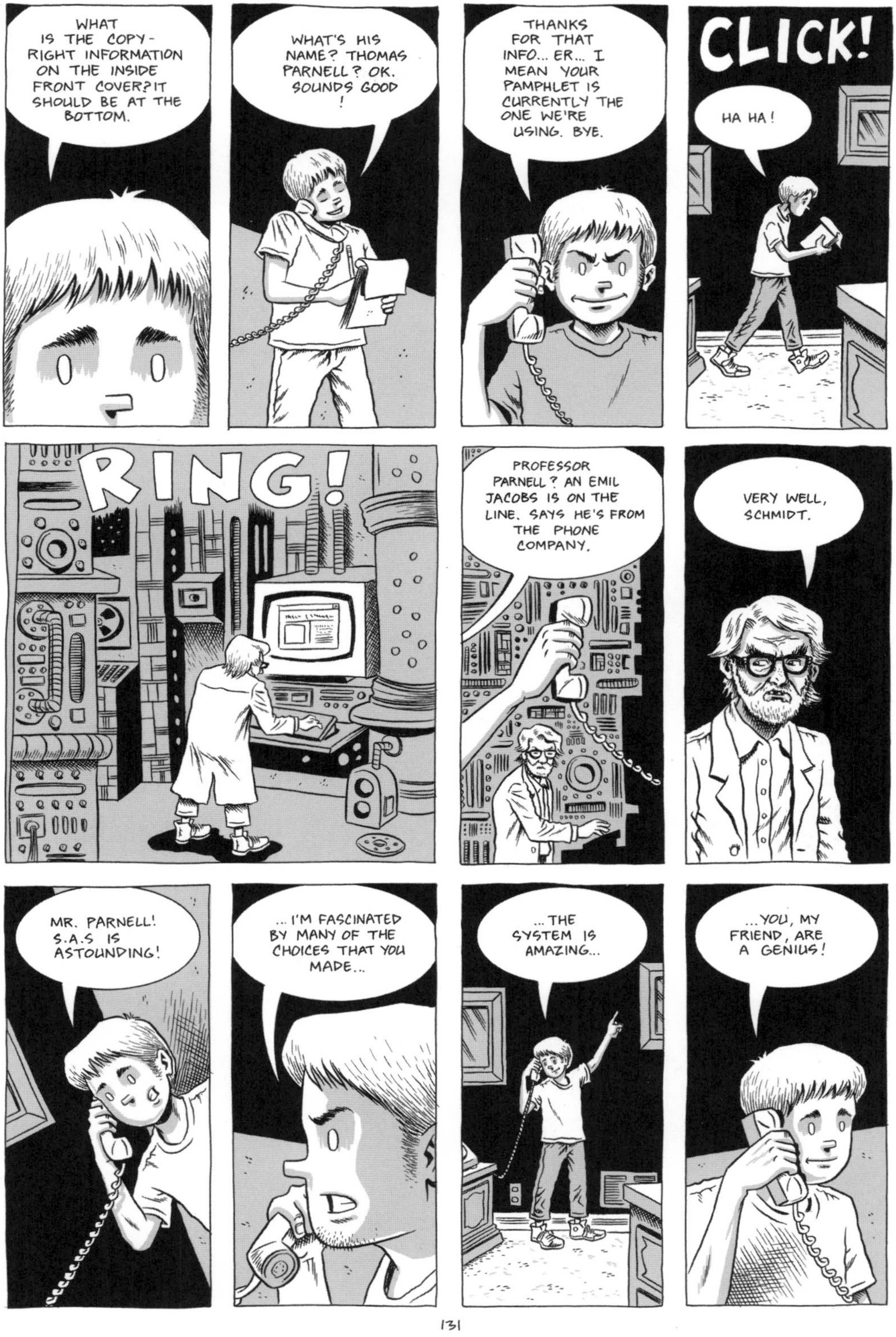
WHAT IS THE COPY-RIGHT INFORMATION ON THE INSIDE FRONT COVER? IT SHOULD BE AT THE BOTTOM.
WHAT'S HIS NAME? THOMAS PARNELL? OK. SOUNDS GOOD!
THANKS FOR THAT INFO... ER... I MEAN YOUR PAMPHLET IS CURRENTLY THE ONE WE'RE USING. BYE.
CLICK!
HA HA!
RING!
PROFESSOR PARNELL? AN EMIL JACOBS IS ON THE LINE. SAYS HE'S FROM THE PHONE COMPANY.
VERY WELL, SCHMIDT.
MR. PARNELL! S.A.S IS ASTOUNDING!
... I'M FASCINATED BY MANY OF THE CHOICES THAT YOU MADE...
... THE SYSTEM IS AMAZING...
... YOU, MY FRIEND, ARE A GENIUS!

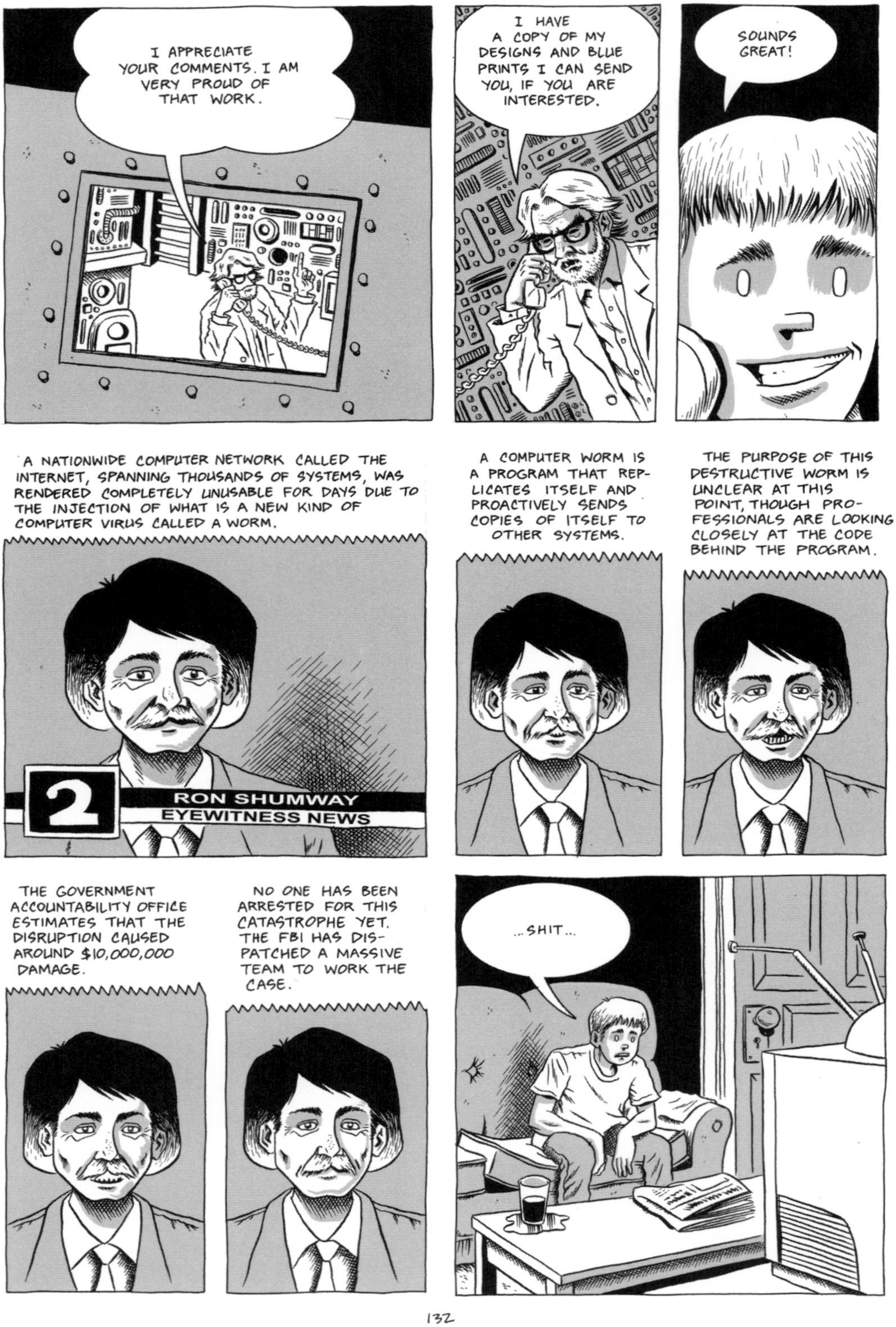
I APPRECIATE YOUR COMMENTS. I AM VERY PROUD OF THAT WORK.
I HAVE A COPY OF MY DESIGNS AND BLUE PRINTS I CAN SEND YOU, IF YOU ARE INTERESTED.
SOUNDS GREAT!
A NATIONWIDE COMPUTER NETWORK CALLED THE INTERNET, SPANNING THOUSANDS OF SYSTEMS, WAS RENDERED COMPLETELY UNUSABLE FOR DAYS DUE TO THE INJECTION OF WHAT IS A NEW KIND OF COMPUTER VIRUS CALLED A WORM.
2
RON SHUMWAY
EYEWITNESS NEWS
A COMPUTER WORM IS A PROGRAM THAT REPLICATES ITSELF AND PROACTIVELY SENDS COPIES OF ITSELF TO OTHER SYSTEMS.
THE PURPOSE OF THIS DESTRUCTIVE WORM IS UNCLEAR AT THIS POINT, THOUGH PROFESSIONALS ARE LOOKING CLOSELY AT THE CODE BEHIND THE PROGRAM.
THE GOVERNMENT ACCOUNTABILITY OFFICE ESTIMATES THAT THE DISRUPTION CAUSED AROUND $10,000,000 DAMAGE.
NO ONE HAS BEEN ARRESTED FOR THIS CATASTROPHE YET. THE FBI HAS DISPATCHED A MASSIVE TEAM TO WORK THE CASE.
...SHIT...

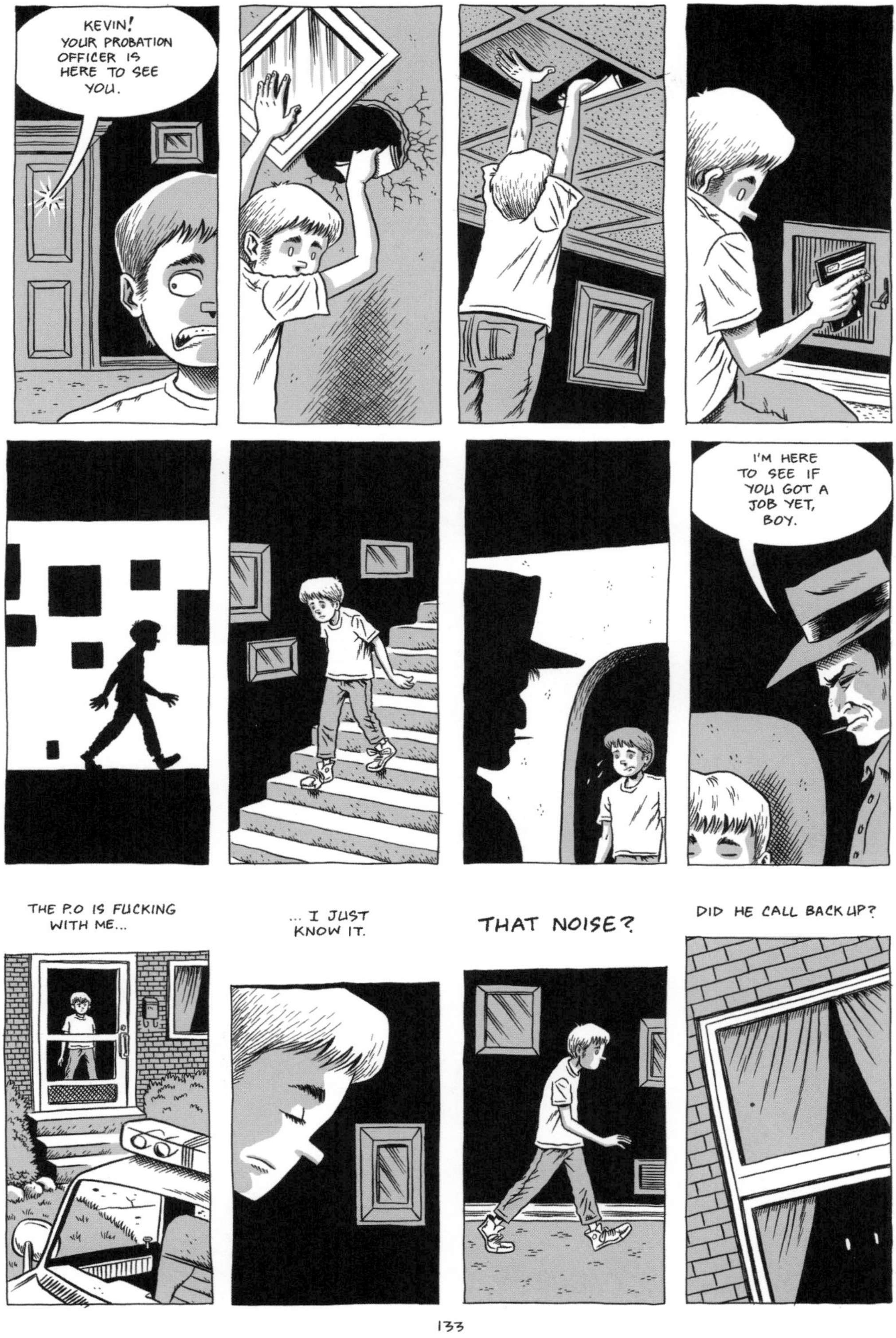
KEVIN! YOUR PROBATION OFFICER IS HERE TO SEE YOU.
I'M HERE TO SEE IF YOU GOT A JOB YET, BOY.
THE P.O IS FUCKING WITH ME...
... I JUST KNOW IT.
THAT NOISE?
DID HE CALL BACK UP?

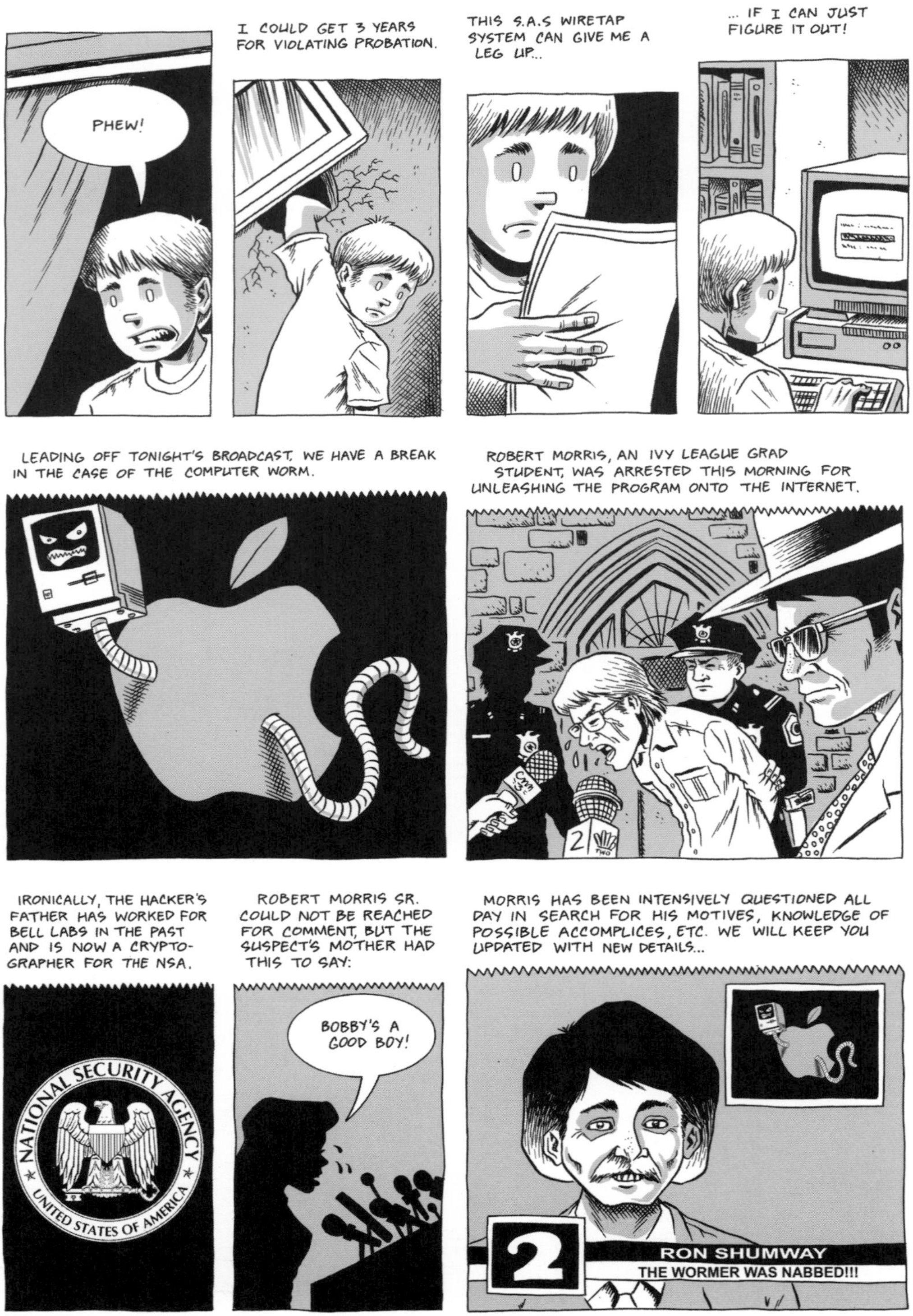
PHEW!
I COULD GET 3 YEARS FOR VIOLATING PROBATION.
THIS S.A.S WIRETAP SYSTEM CAN GIVE ME A LEG UP...
... IF I CAN JUST FIGURE IT OUT!
LEADING OFF TONIGHT'S BROADCAST, WE HAVE A BREAK IN THE CASE OF THE COMPUTER WORM.
ROBERT MORRIS, AN IVY LEAGUE GRAD STUDENT, WAS ARRESTED THIS MORNING FOR UNLEASHING THE PROGRAM ONTO THE INTERNET.
IRONICALLY, THE HACKER'S FATHER HAS WORKED FOR BELL LABS IN THE PAST AND IS NOW A CRYPTOGRAPHER FOR THE NSA.
NATIONAL SECURITY AGENCY
UNITED STATES OF AMERICA
ROBERT MORRIS SR. COULD NOT BE REACHED FOR COMMENT, BUT THE SUSPECT'S MOTHER HAD THIS TO SAY:
BOBBY'S A GOOD BOY!
MORRIS HAS BEEN INTENSIVELY QUESTIONED ALL DAY IN SEARCH FOR HIS MOTIVES, KNOWLEDGE OF POSSIBLE ACCOMPLICES, ETC. WE WILL KEEP YOU UPDATED WITH NEW DETAILS...
2
RON SHUMWAY
THE WORMER WAS NABBED!!!

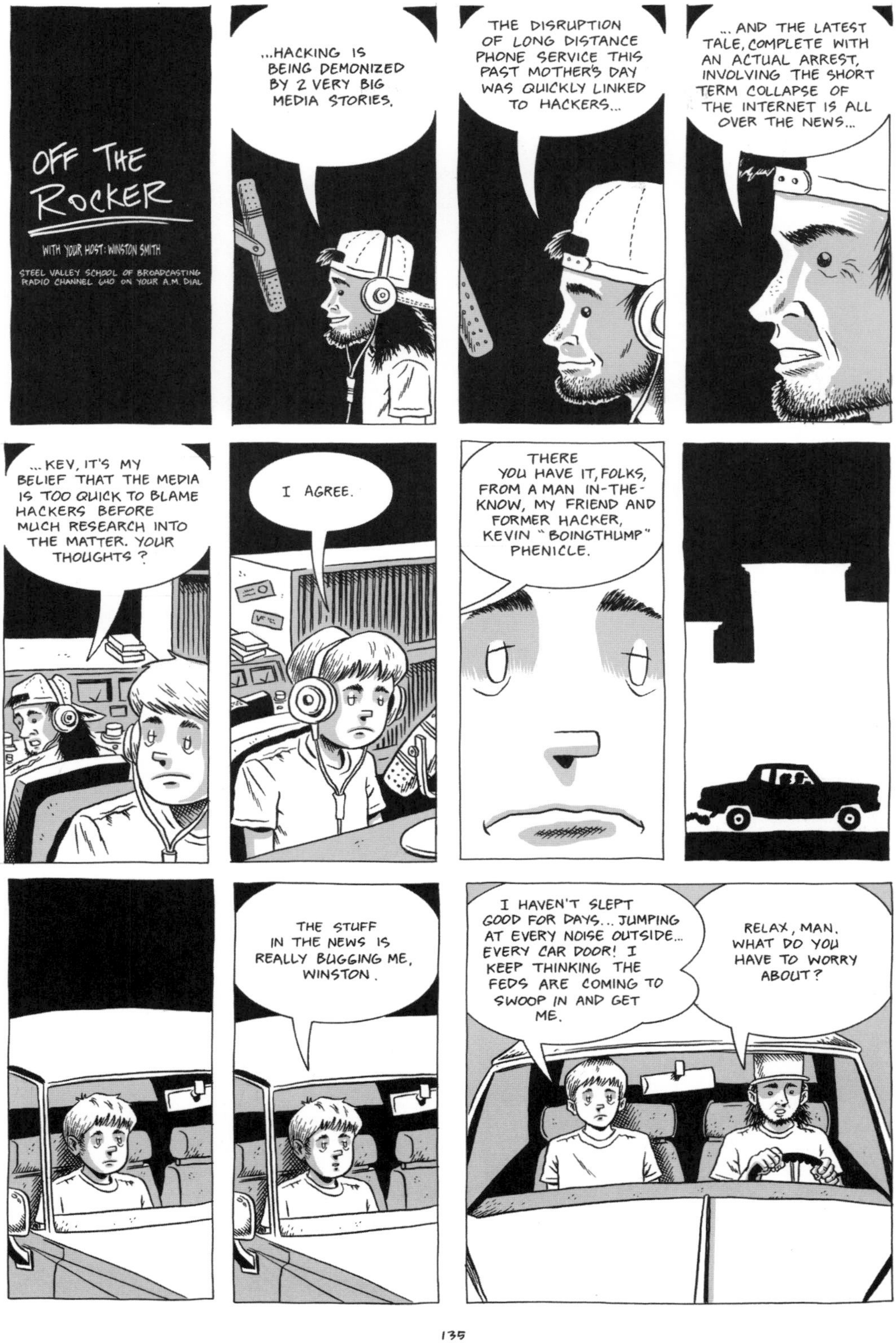
OFF THE ROCKER
WITH YOUR HOST: WINSTON SMITH
STEEL VALLEY SCHOOL OF BROADCASTING RADIO CHANNEL 640 ON YOUR A.M. DIAL
...HACKING IS BEING DEMONIZED BY 2 VERY BIG MEDIA STORIES.
THE DISRUPTION OF LONG DISTANCE PHONE SERVICE THIS PAST MOTHER'S DAY WAS QUICKLY LINKED TO HACKERS...
...AND THE LATEST TALE, COMPLETE WITH AN ACTUAL ARREST, INVOLVING THE SHORT TERM COLLAPSE OF THE INTERNET IS ALL OVER THE NEWS...
...KEV, IT'S MY BELIEF THAT THE MEDIA IS TOO QUICK TO BLAME HACKERS BEFORE MUCH RESEARCH INTO THE MATTER. YOUR THOUGHTS?
I AGREE.
THERE YOU HAVE IT, FOLKS, FROM A MAN IN-THE-KNOW, MY FRIEND AND FORMER HACKER, KEVIN "BOINGTHUMP" PHENICLE.
THE STUFF IN THE NEWS IS REALLY BUGGING ME, WINSTON.
I HAVEN'T SLEPT GOOD FOR DAYS... JUMPING AT EVERY NOISE OUTSIDE... EVERY CAR DOOR! I KEEP THINKING THE FEDS ARE COMING TO SWOOP IN AND GET ME.
RELAX, MAN. WHAT DO YOU HAVE TO WORRY ABOUT?

THRIFT
I... UH...
... MAY ACTUALLY BE A BIT TO BLAME FOR THIS "MORRIS WORM" FIASCO.
WHAT?!
YOU'VE GOTTA BE KIDDING ME!!
WINSTON, I...
NO, KEVIN!
I DON'T WANT TO BE PART OF THIS CRAP, MAN. I CAN'T!
GET OUT, MAN! GET THE HELL OUT!
!

I DON'T BLAME HIM.
STOP
SUICIDE IS AN OPTION...
...BUT I'M A PUSSY.
Computer Networks and the Commercial Sector
an editorial by
Ron Shumway
The internet is becoming a common household appliance.
SPRINGFIELD NEWS
Computer Networks & the Commercial Sector.
With the commodification of this network, many pundits are screaming for regulation.
Those who have worked with the network for years are of an opposite mindset. They want no interference from outside organizations.
BRA SALE!

"Information should be free," they say, but how can we trust this system with our financial identity as commercialism is on the horizon?

Are your children safe on this "Internet?"

I THINK WE CAN ALL AGREE...

...WE KNOW THEY ARE OUT THERE READY TO EXPLOIT US, AND WE WILL HUNT THEM DOWN BEFORE THEY STRIKE.

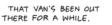
I CAN'T REMEMBER THE LAST TIME I SLEPT.

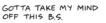
MY JUDGEMENT IS SERIOUSLY CLOUDED. MY STOMACH FEELS LIKE IT'S EATING ITSELF.

I DIDN'T INTEND TO CAUSE ANY DAMAGE, BUT THE AUTHORITIES HAVE NO TOLERANCE FOR IGNORANCE.

I JUST CAN'T LET THEM TAKE ME BACK TO JAIL.

THAT VAN'S BEEN OUT THERE FOR A WHILE.

GOTTA TAKE MY MIND OFF THIS B.S.

WINSTON, I JUST WANTED TO...

CLICK!

DAMMIT, MAN.

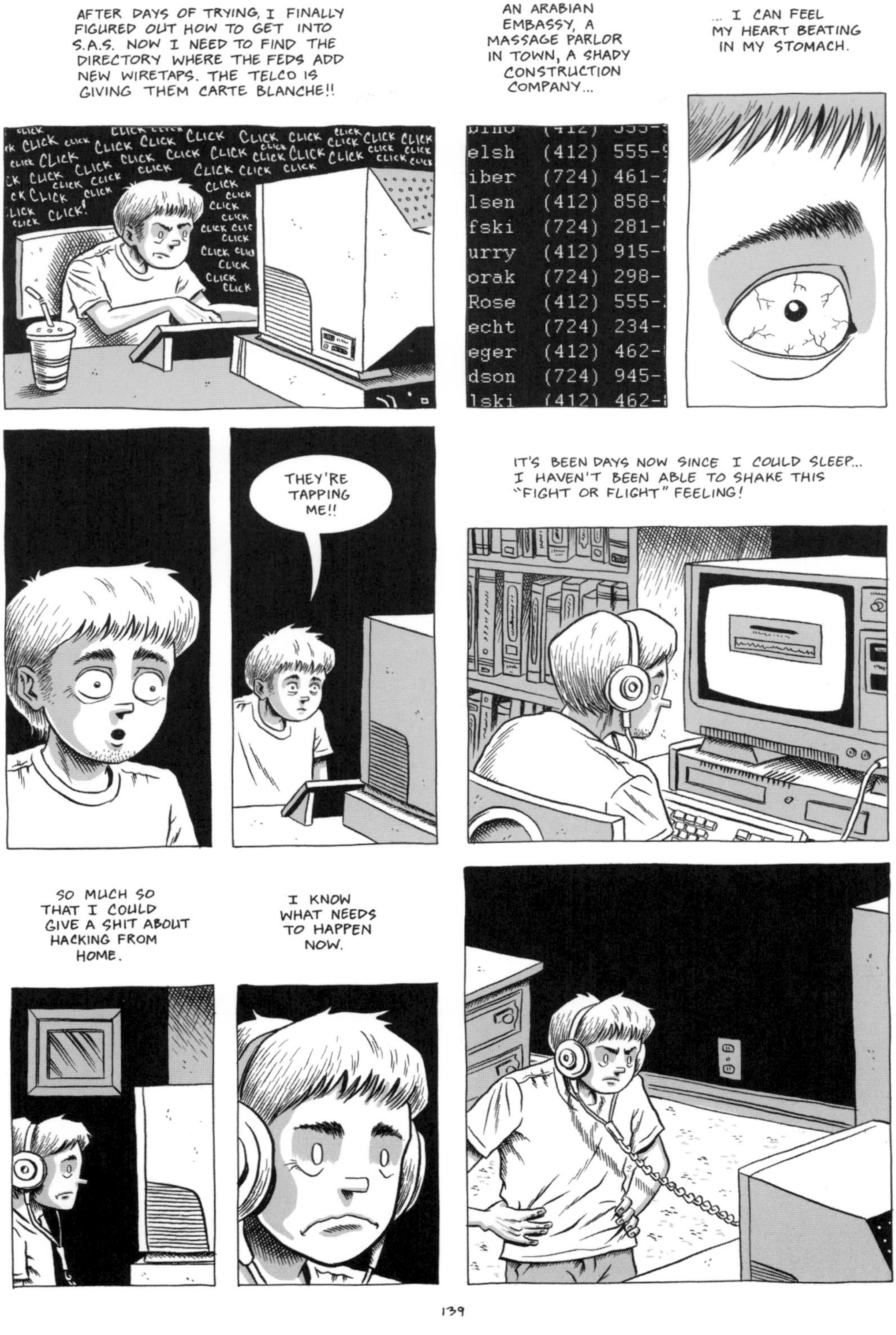

AFTER DAYS OF TRYING, I FINALLY FIGURED OUT HOW TO GET INTO S.A.S. NOW I NEED TO FIND THE DIRECTORY WHERE THE FEDS ADD NEW WIRETAPS. THE TELCO IS GIVING THEM CARTE BLANCHE!!
CLICK CLICK CLICK CLICK CLICK CLICK CLICK CLICK CLICK CLICK CLICK CLICK CLICK!
AN ARABIAN EMBASSY, A MASSAGE PARLOR IN TOWN, A SHADY CONSTRUCTION COMPANY...
elsh (412) 555-
iber (724) 461-
lsen (412) 858-
fski (724) 281-
urry (412) 915-
orak (724) 298-
Rose (412) 555-
echt (724) 234-
eger (412) 462-
dson (724) 945-
lski (412) 462-
... I CAN FEEL MY HEART BEATING IN MY STOMACH.
THEY'RE TAPPING ME!!
IT'S BEEN DAYS NOW SINCE I COULD SLEEP... I HAVEN'T BEEN ABLE TO SHAKE THIS "FIGHT OR FLIGHT" FEELING!
SO MUCH SO THAT I COULD GIVE A SHIT ABOUT HACKING FROM HOME.
I KNOW WHAT NEEDS TO HAPPEN NOW.

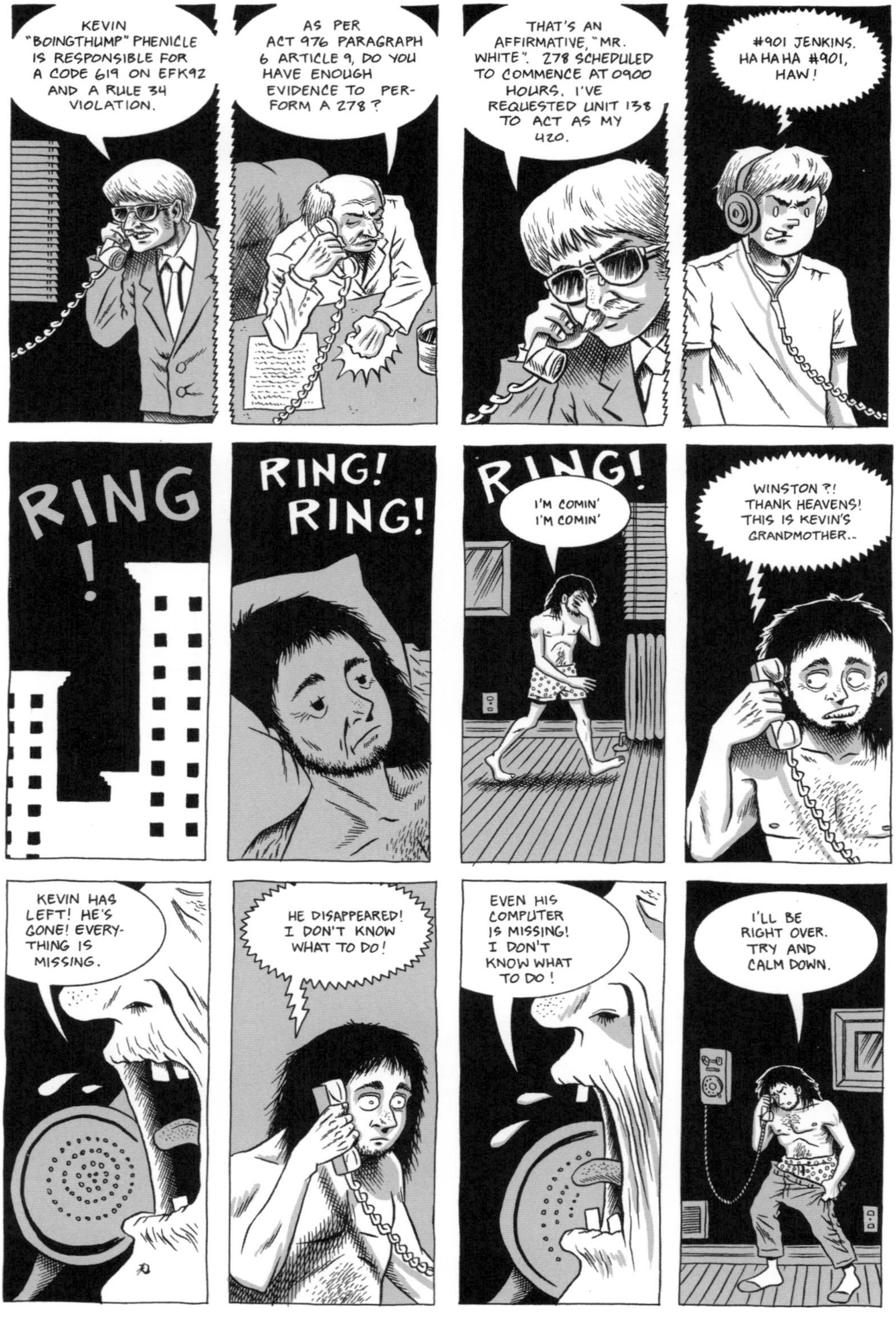

KEVIN "BOINGTHUMP" PHENICLE IS RESPONSIBLE FOR A CODE 619 ON EFK92 AND A RULE 34 VIOLATION.
AS PER ACT 976 PARAGRAPH 6 ARTICLE 9, DO YOU HAVE ENOUGH EVIDENCE TO PERFORM A 278?
THAT'S AN AFFIRMATIVE, "MR. WHITE". 278 SCHEDULED TO COMMENCE AT 0900 HOURS. I'VE REQUESTED UNIT 138 TO ACT AS MY 420.
#901 JENKINS. HA HA HA #901, HAW!
RING!
RING! RING!
RING!
I'M COMIN' I'M COMIN'
WINSTON?! THANK HEAVENS! THIS IS KEVIN'S GRANDMOTHER..
KEVIN HAS LEFT! HE'S GONE! EVERYTHING IS MISSING.
HE DISAPPEARED! I DON'T KNOW WHAT TO DO!
EVEN HIS COMPUTER IS MISSING! I DON'T KNOW WHAT TO DO!
I'LL BE RIGHT OVER. TRY AND CALM DOWN.

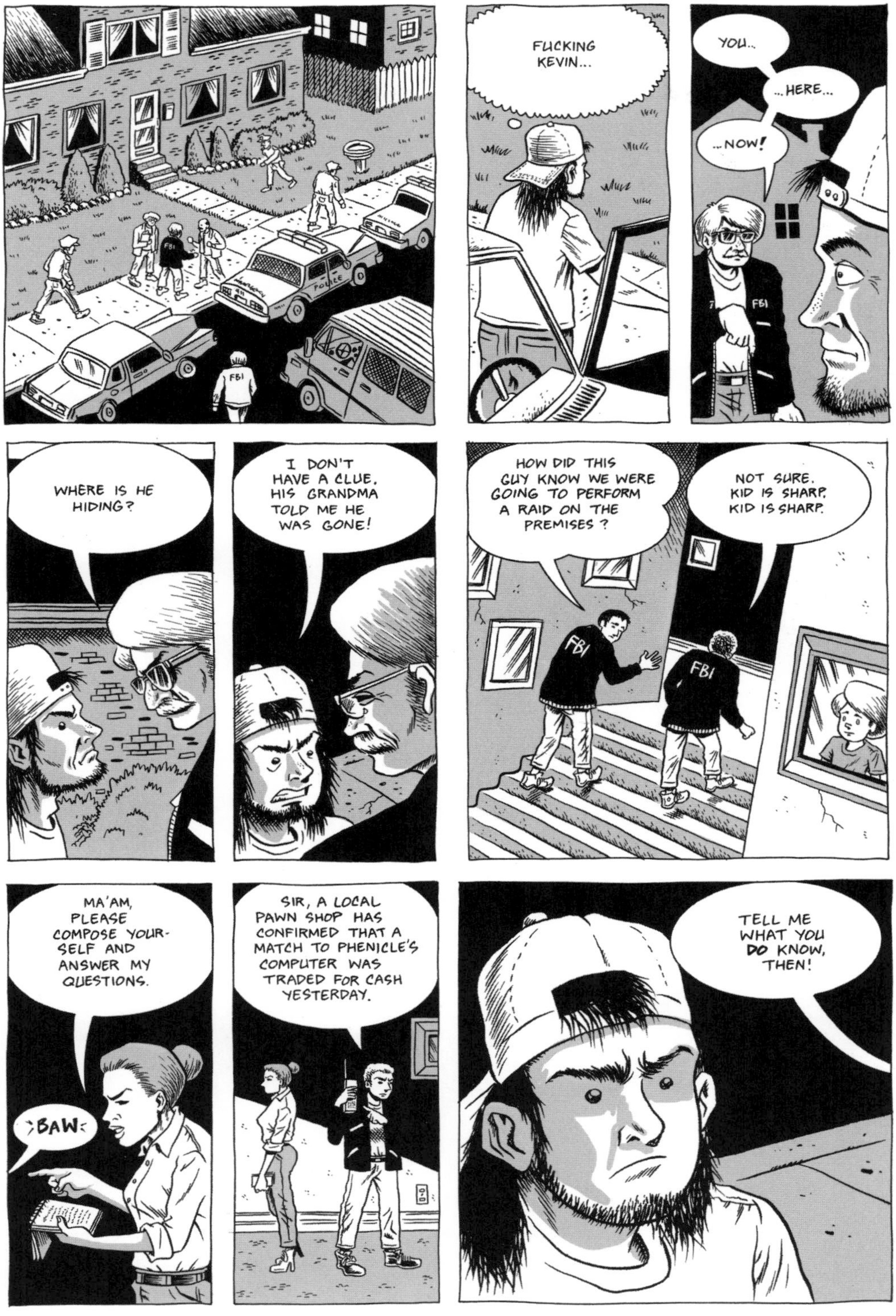
FUCKING KEVIN...
YOU..
...HERE...
...NOW!
WHERE IS HE HIDING?
I DON'T HAVE A CLUE. HIS GRANDMA TOLD ME HE WAS GONE!
HOW DID THIS GUY KNOW WE WERE GOING TO PERFORM A RAID ON THE PREMISES ?
NOT SURE. KID IS SHARP. KID IS SHARP.
MA'AM, PLEASE COMPOSE YOUR-SELF AND ANSWER MY QUESTIONS.
BAW
SIR, A LOCAL PAWN SHOP HAS CONFIRMED THAT A MATCH TO PHENICLE'S COMPUTER WAS TRADED FOR CASH YESTERDAY.
TELL ME WHAT YOU DO KNOW, THEN!

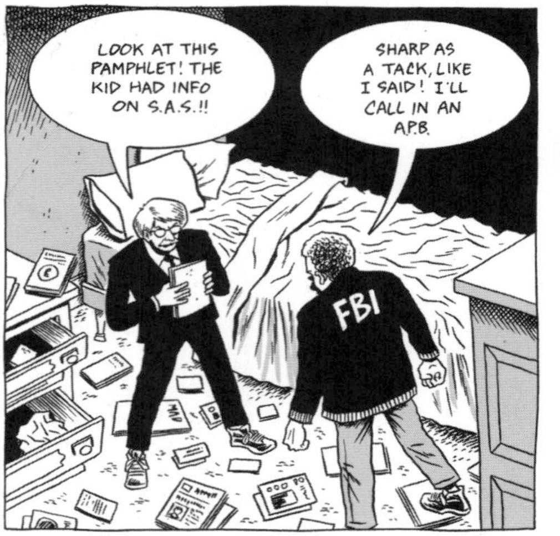
LOOK AT THIS PAMPHLET! THE KID HAD INFO ON S.A.S.!!
SHARP AS A TACK, LIKE I SAID! I'LL CALL IN AN A.P.B.
FBI

SIR, WE'RE CALLING FOR A STATEWIDE 894 ON KEVIN J. PHENICLE JR. CODE 12. HE SHOULD BE CONSIDERED 311 DUE TO A VIOLATION OF PROBATION IN ACCORDANCE WITH ACT 55 ARTICLE 19A.

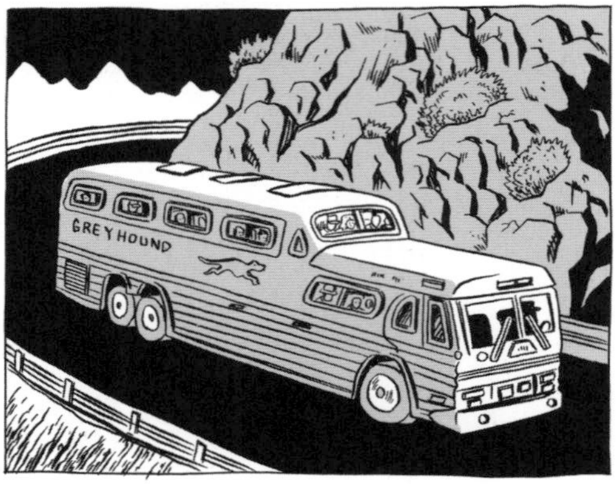
GREYHOUND

SHOULD WE CONTACT THE LOCAL MEDIA AND ALERT THE PUBLIC?

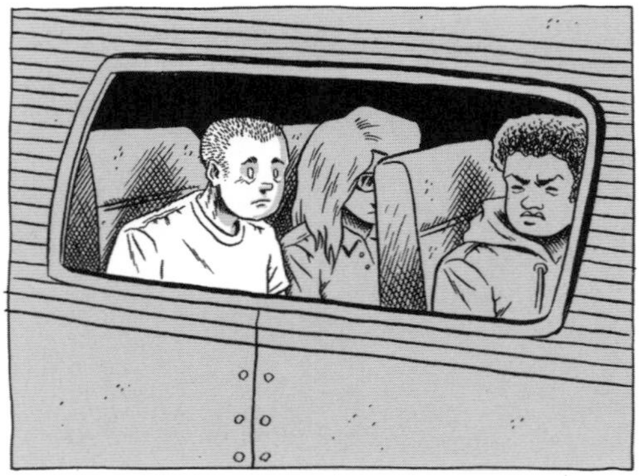

I HAVE A FEELING WE'LL NEED ALL THE HELP WE CAN GET.

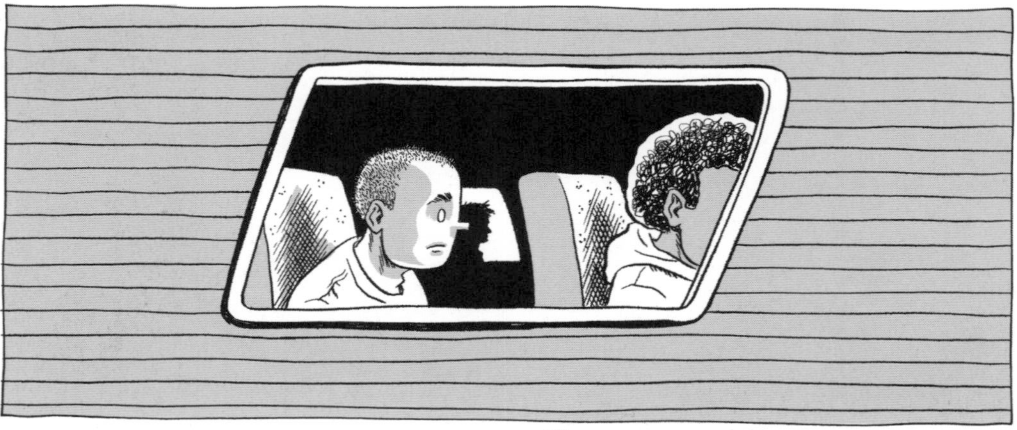

CHAPTER 5

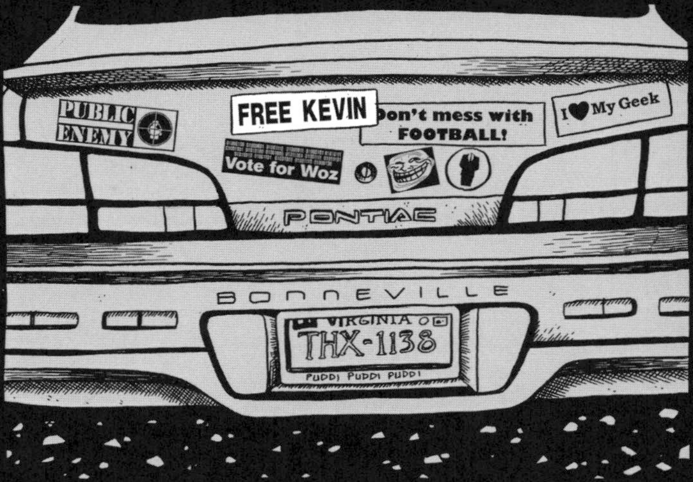
PUBLIC ENEMY
FREE KEVIN
Don't mess with FOOTBALL!
I ♥ My Geek
Vote for Woz
PONTIAC
BONNEVILLE
VIRGINIA
THX-1138
PUDDI PUDDI PUDDI

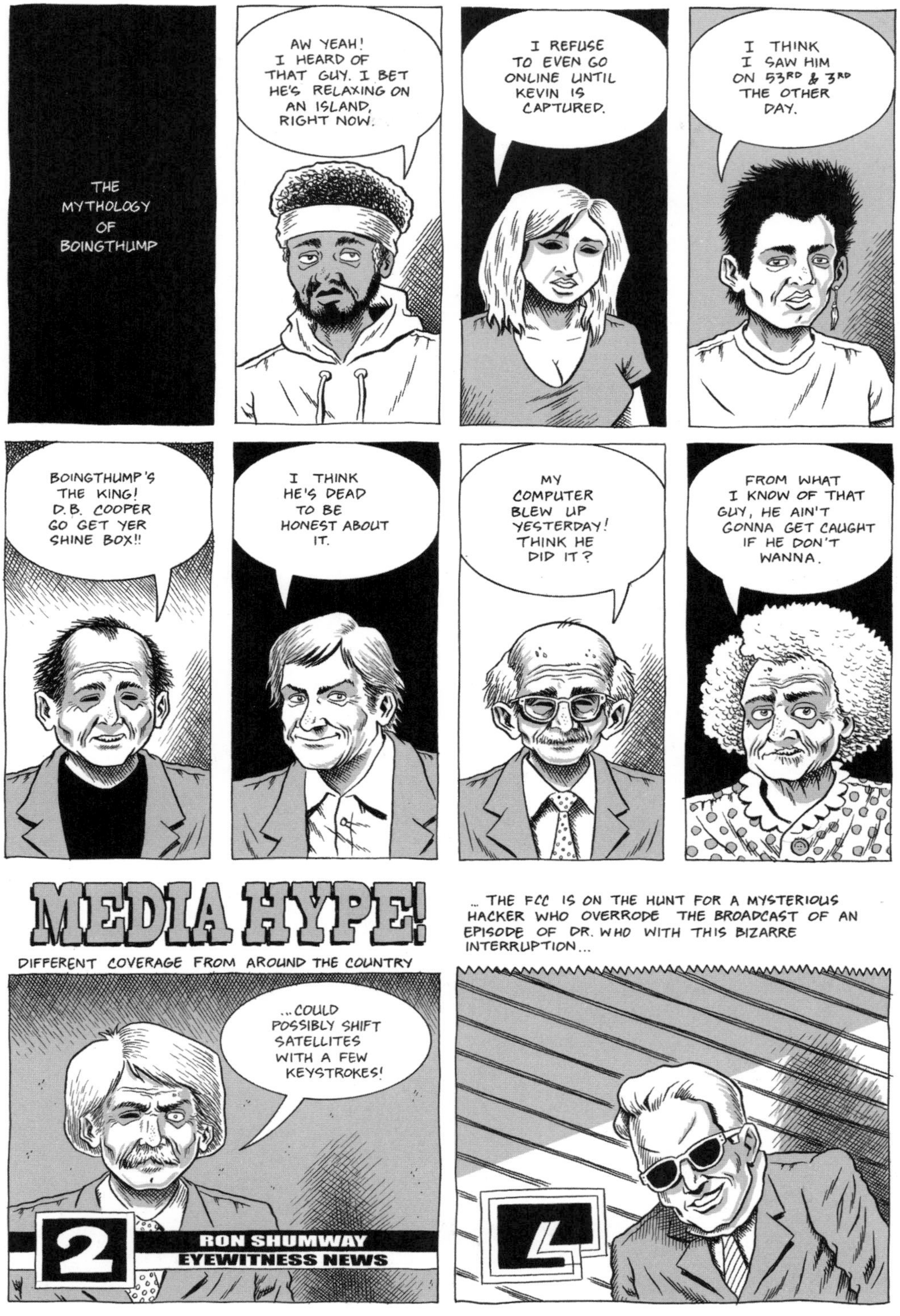
THE MYTHOLOGY OF BOINGTHUMP
AW YEAH! I HEARD OF THAT GUY. I BET HE'S RELAXING ON AN ISLAND, RIGHT NOW.
I REFUSE TO EVEN GO ONLINE UNTIL KEVIN IS CAPTURED.
I THINK I SAW HIM ON 53RD & 3RD THE OTHER DAY.
BOINGTHUMP'S THE KING! D.B. COOPER GO GET YER SHINE BOX!!
I THINK HE'S DEAD TO BE HONEST ABOUT IT.
MY COMPUTER BLEW UP YESTERDAY! THINK HE DID IT?
FROM WHAT I KNOW OF THAT GUY, HE AIN'T GONNA GET CAUGHT IF HE DON'T WANNA.
MEDIA HYPE!
DIFFERENT COVERAGE FROM AROUND THE COUNTRY
... THE FCC IS ON THE HUNT FOR A MYSTERIOUS HACKER WHO OVERRODE THE BROADCAST OF AN EPISODE OF DR. WHO WITH THIS BIZARRE INTERRUPTION...
...COULD POSSIBLY SHIFT SATELLITES WITH A FEW KEYSTROKES!
2
RON SHUMWAY
EYEWITNESS NEWS

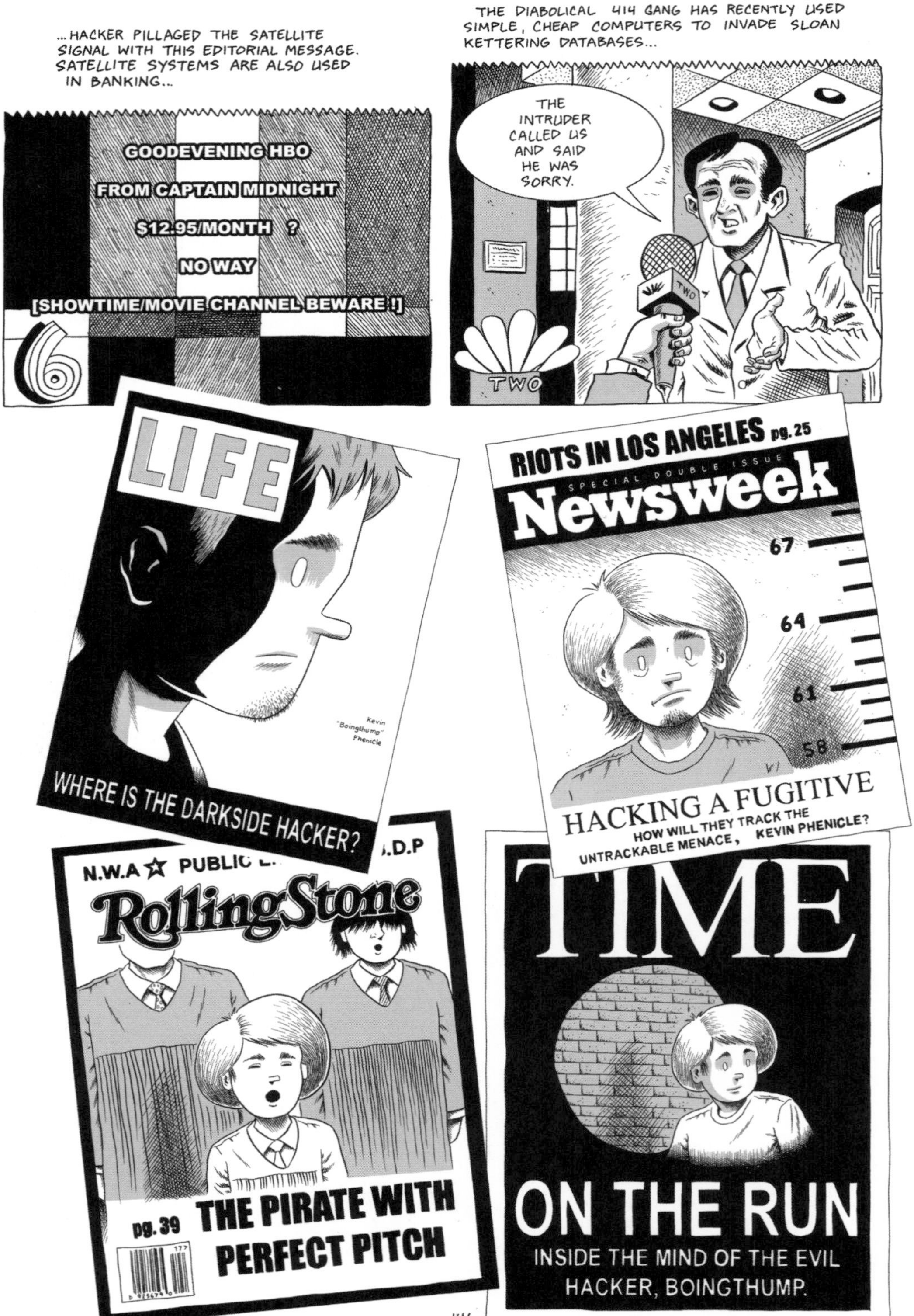
...HACKER PILLAGED THE SATELLITE SIGNAL WITH THIS EDITORIAL MESSAGE. SATELLITE SYSTEMS ARE ALSO USED IN BANKING...
GOODEVENING HBO
FROM CAPTAIN MIDNIGHT
$12.95/MONTH ?
NO WAY
[SHOWTIME/MOVIE CHANNEL BEWARE !]
6
THE DIABOLICAL 414 GANG HAS RECENTLY USED SIMPLE, CHEAP COMPUTERS TO INVADE SLOAN KETTERING DATABASES...
THE INTRUDER CALLED US AND SAID HE WAS SORRY.
TWO
TWO
LIFE
Kevin "Boingthump" Phenicle
WHERE IS THE DARKSIDE HACKER?
RIOTS IN LOS ANGELES pg. 25
SPECIAL DOUBLE ISSUE
Newsweek
67
64
61
58
HACKING A FUGITIVE
HOW WILL THEY TRACK THE UNTRACKABLE MENACE, KEVIN PHENICLE?
N.W.A ☆ PUBLIC
RollingStone
pg. 39
THE PIRATE WITH PERFECT PITCH
TIME
ON THE RUN
INSIDE THE MIND OF THE EVIL HACKER, BOINGTHUMP.

OFF THE ROCKER

with your host

WINSTON SMITH

WABCD 108.3 ON YOUR FM DIAL

... 3 GODDAMN YEARS WITHOUT A TRIAL! OUTRAGEOUS!

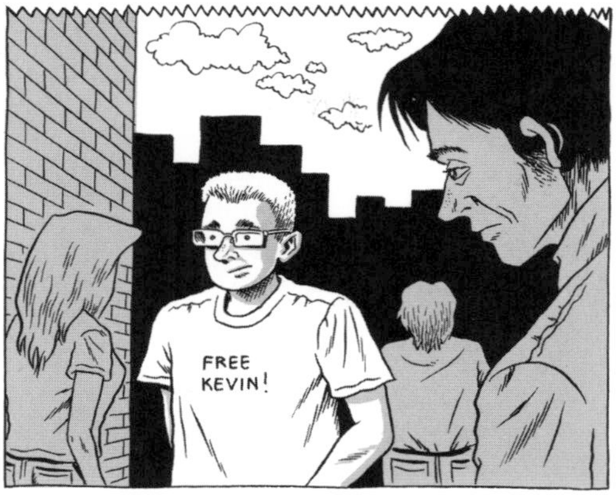
FREE KEVIN!

IF THE AUTHORITIES ARE LISTENING: YOU HAVE MADE YOUR POINT ALREADY!

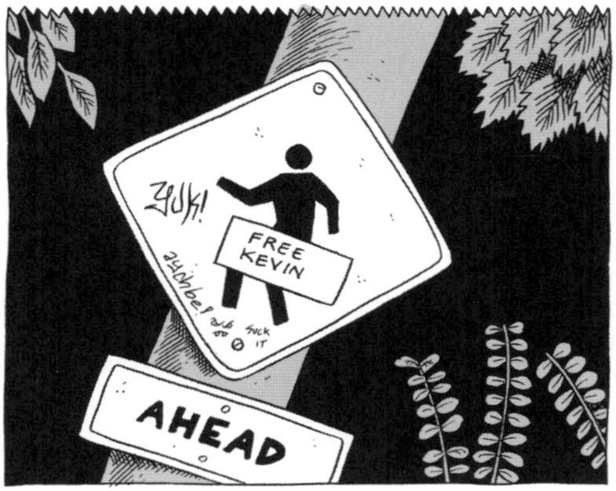
FREE KEVIN
SUCK IT
AHEAD

WHEN KEVIN FINALLY HAS HIS DAY IN COURT, HE BETTER NOT BE SENTENCED ONE DAY MORE THAN 'TIME SERVED.'

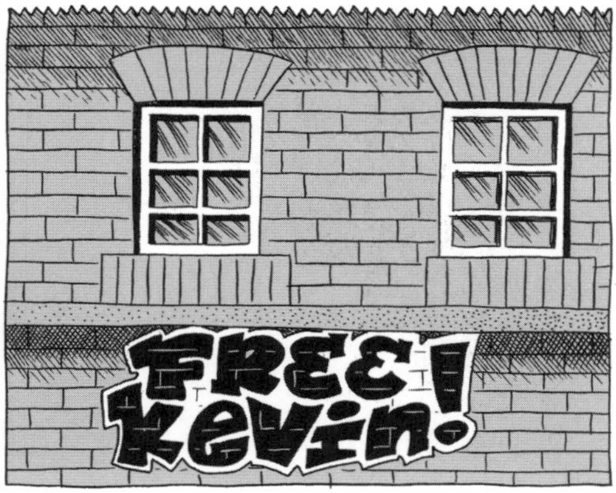
FREE KEVIN!

NOT THAT THERE'S ANYTHING WE CAN DO ABOUT IT, AS I'M FINDING OUT!

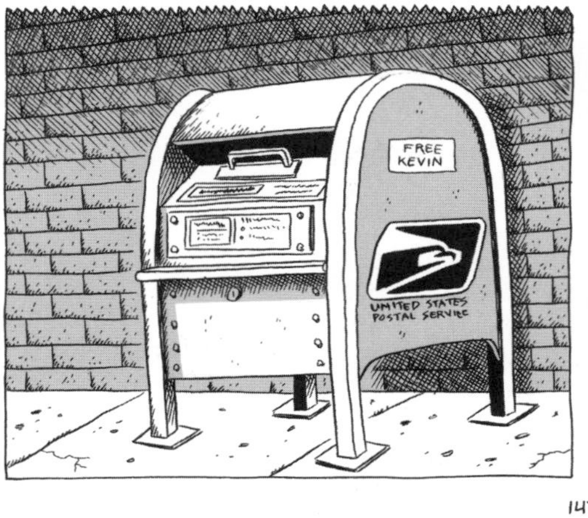
FREE KEVIN
UNITED STATES POSTAL SERVICE

THEY KEEP LEANING ON KEVIN HARD TO COP A PLEA!

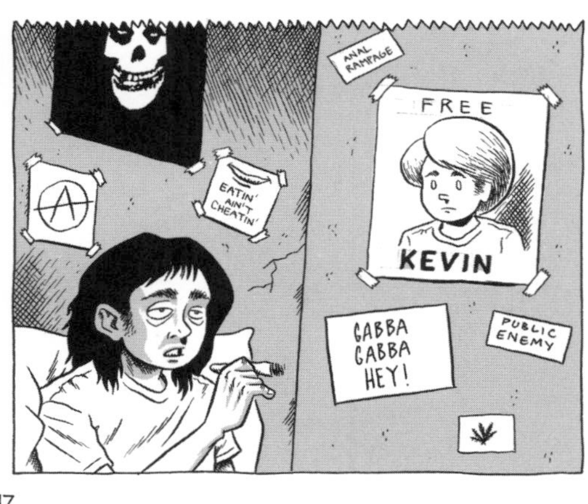
ANAL RAMPAGE
FREE
KEVIN
EATIN' AIN'T CHEATIN'
GABBA GABBA HEY!
PUBLIC ENEMY

CAN YOU IMAGINE ADMITTING TO SOMETHING THAT MAY NOT BE ABLE TO BE PROVEN AGAINST YOU?

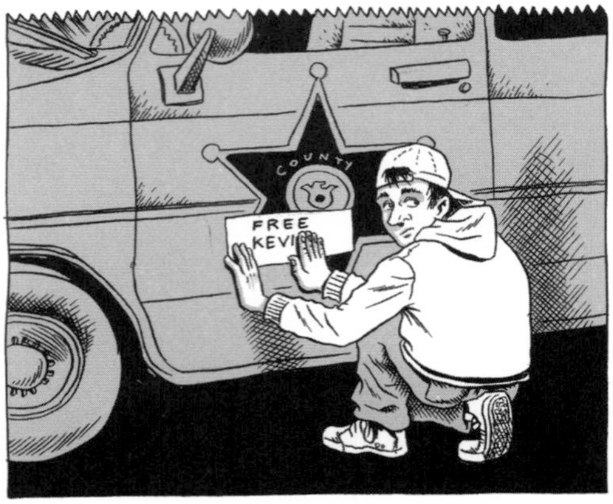
COUNTY
FREE KEVIN

THAT HAS ABSOLUTELY NOTHING TO DO WITH JUSTICE! IT'S ALL ABOUT MONEY.

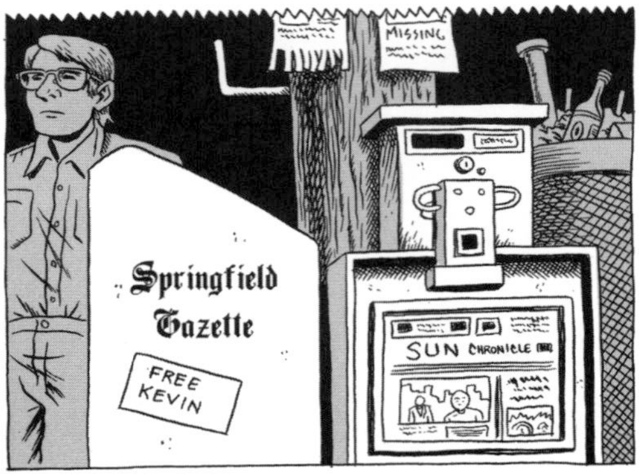
MISSING
Springfield Gazette
FREE KEVIN
SUN CHRONICLE

THANKS TO EVERYBODY FOR CONTRIBUTING TO BOINGTHUMPS DEFENSE!

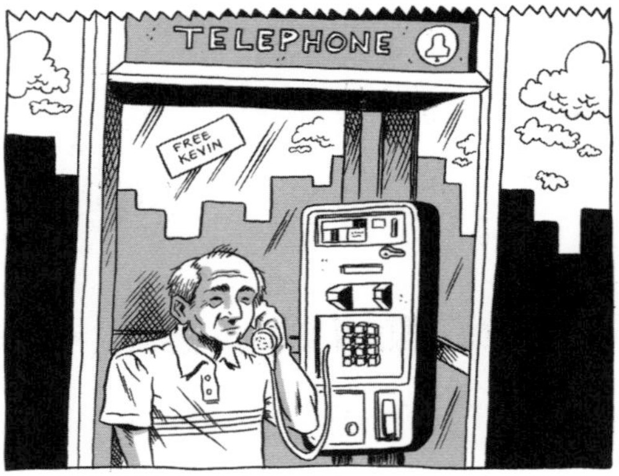
TELEPHONE
FREE KEVIN

THE DEFENSE FUND IS DOING WELL!

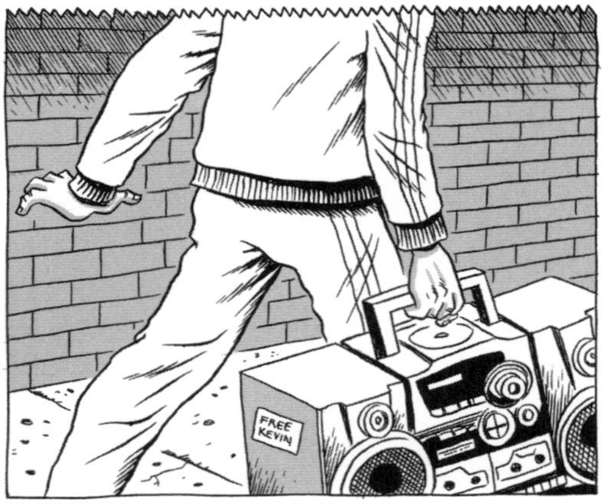
FREE KEVIN

THAT'S THE ONE POSITIVE. BECAUSE YOU BELIEVE IN WHAT'S RIGHT AND YOU PUT YOUR MONEY WHERE YOUR MOUTH IS, KEVIN HAS BEEN ABLE TO FIGHT THIS BATTLE FOR YEARS!!

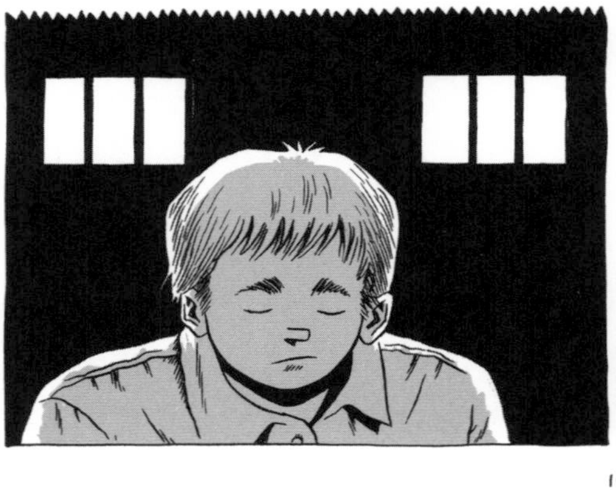

IT SEEMS MOST OF THE PUBLIC AGREES THAT KEVIN NEEDS TO BE CHARGED ALREADY! THE AUTHORITIES SHOULD TAKE HEED!

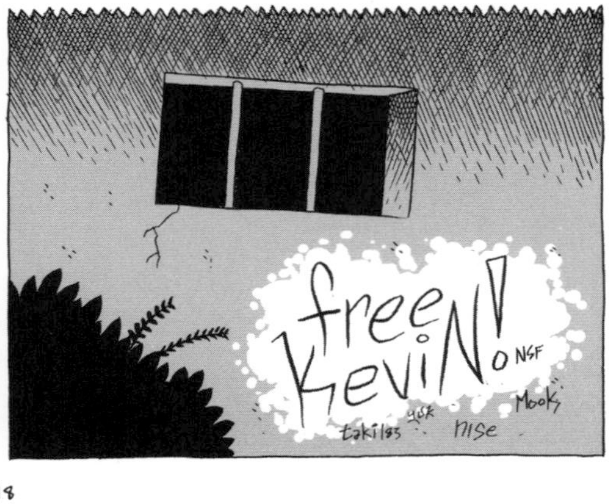
free Kevin!
NSF
Mooks
taki 183
nise

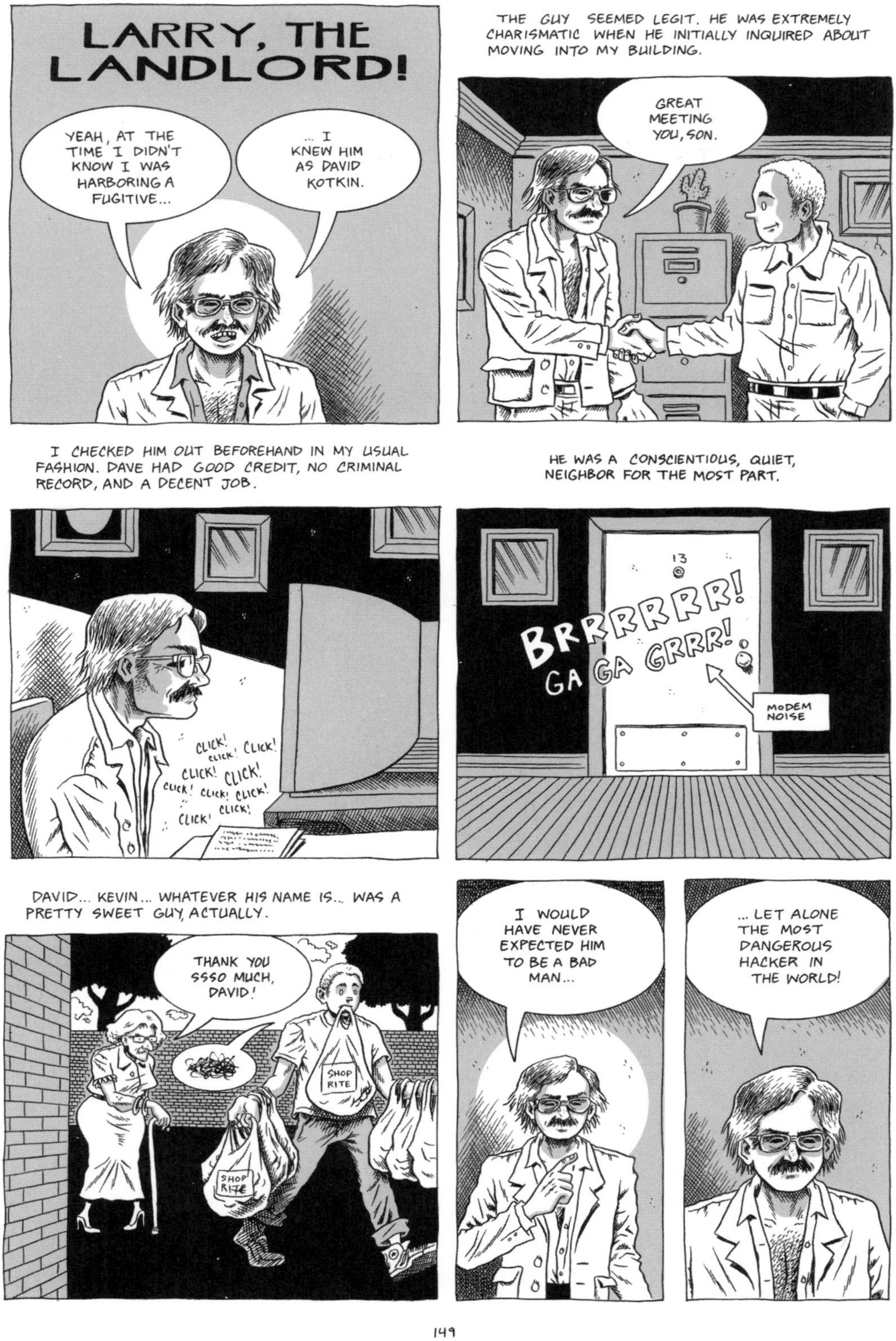
LARRY, THE LANDLORD!
YEAH, AT THE TIME I DIDN'T KNOW I WAS HARBORING A FUGITIVE...
... I KNEW HIM AS DAVID KOTKIN.
THE GUY SEEMED LEGIT. HE WAS EXTREMELY CHARISMATIC WHEN HE INITIALLY INQUIRED ABOUT MOVING INTO MY BUILDING.
GREAT MEETING YOU, SON.
I CHECKED HIM OUT BEFOREHAND IN MY USUAL FASHION. DAVE HAD GOOD CREDIT, NO CRIMINAL RECORD, AND A DECENT JOB.
CLICK! CLICK! CLICK! CLICK! CLICK! CLICK! CLICK! CLICK! CLICK! CLICK!
HE WAS A CONSCIENTIOUS, QUIET, NEIGHBOR FOR THE MOST PART.
13
BRRRRRR! GA GA GRRR!
MODEM NOISE
DAVID... KEVIN... WHATEVER HIS NAME IS... WAS A PRETTY SWEET GUY, ACTUALLY.
THANK YOU SSSO MUCH, DAVID!
SHOP RITE
SHOP RITE
I WOULD HAVE NEVER EXPECTED HIM TO BE A BAD MAN...
... LET ALONE THE MOST DANGEROUS HACKER IN THE WORLD!

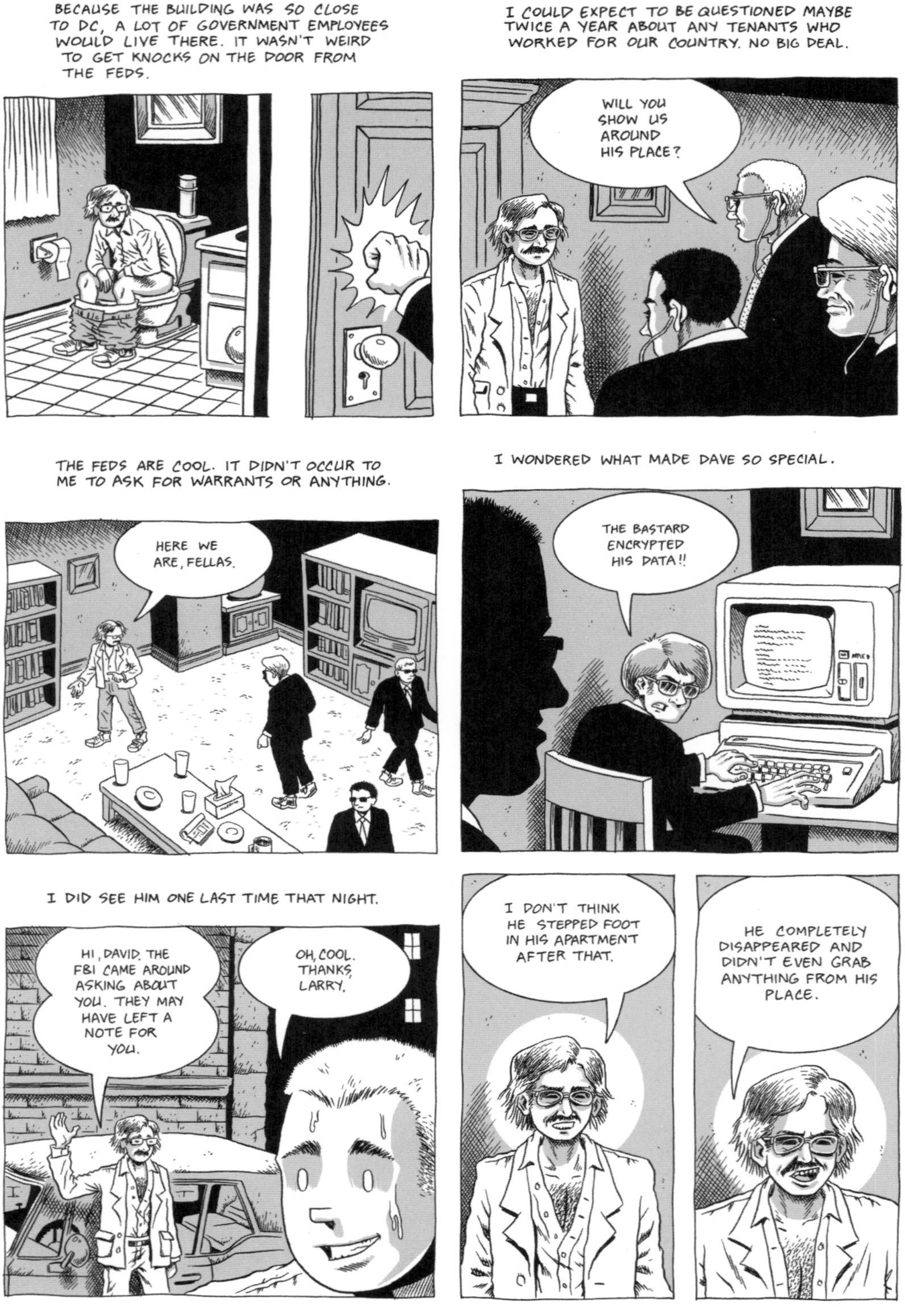
BECAUSE THE BUILDING WAS SO CLOSE TO DC, A LOT OF GOVERNMENT EMPLOYEES WOULD LIVE THERE. IT WASN'T WEIRD TO GET KNOCKS ON THE DOOR FROM THE FEDS.
I COULD EXPECT TO BE QUESTIONED MAYBE TWICE A YEAR ABOUT ANY TENANTS WHO WORKED FOR OUR COUNTRY. NO BIG DEAL.
WILL YOU SHOW US AROUND HIS PLACE?
THE FEDS ARE COOL. IT DIDN'T OCCUR TO ME TO ASK FOR WARRANTS OR ANYTHING.
HERE WE ARE, FELLAS.
I WONDERED WHAT MADE DAVE SO SPECIAL.
THE BASTARD ENCRYPTED HIS DATA!!
I DID SEE HIM ONE LAST TIME THAT NIGHT.
HI, DAVID. THE FBI CAME AROUND ASKING ABOUT YOU. THEY MAY HAVE LEFT A NOTE FOR YOU.
OH, COOL. THANKS, LARRY.
I DON'T THINK HE STEPPED FOOT IN HIS APARTMENT AFTER THAT.
HE COMPLETELY DISAPPEARED AND DIDN'T EVEN GRAB ANYTHING FROM HIS PLACE.

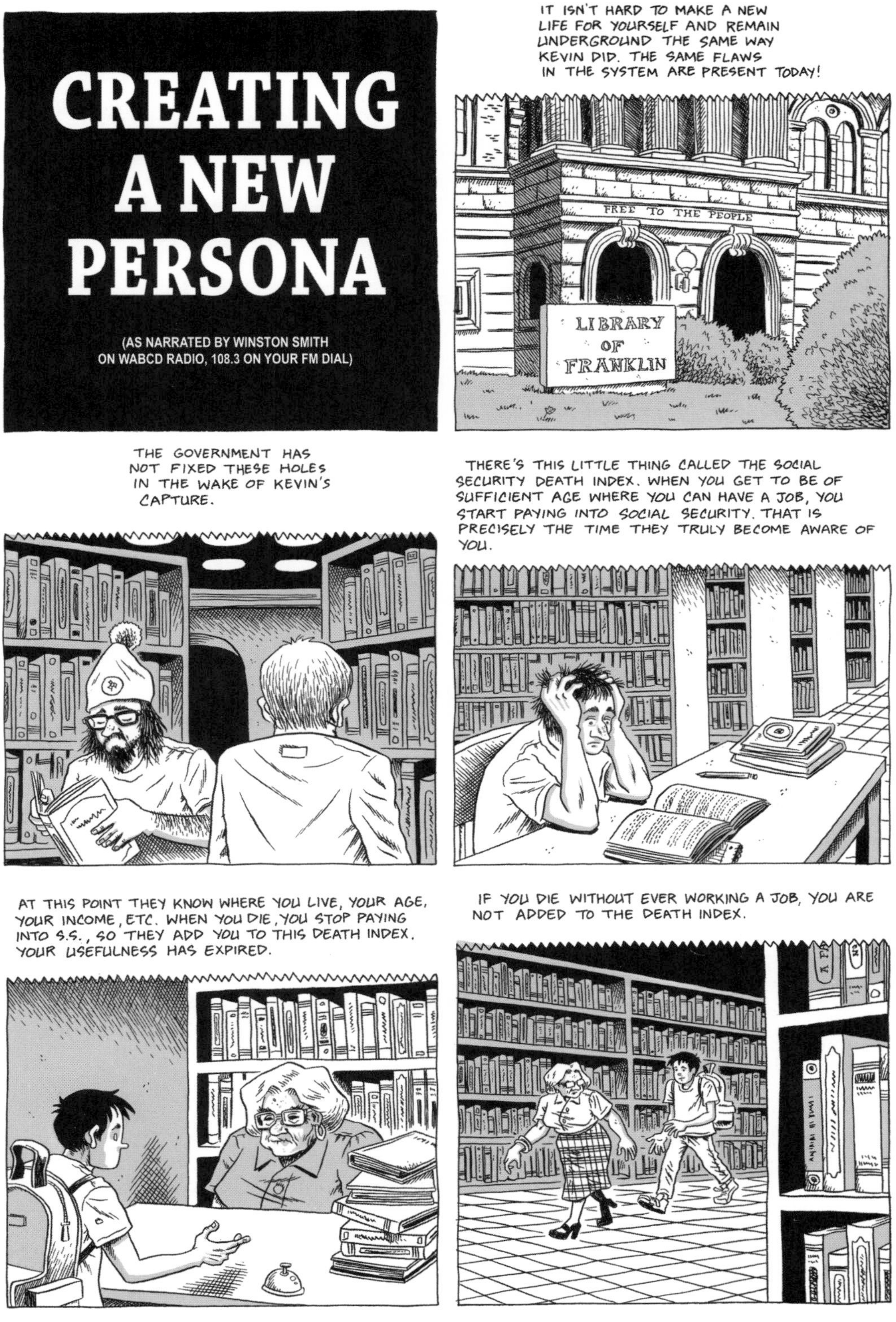
CREATING A NEW PERSONA
(AS NARRATED BY WINSTON SMITH ON WABCD RADIO, 108.3 ON YOUR FM DIAL)
IT ISN'T HARD TO MAKE A NEW LIFE FOR YOURSELF AND REMAIN UNDERGROUND THE SAME WAY KEVIN DID. THE SAME FLAWS IN THE SYSTEM ARE PRESENT TODAY!
FREE TO THE PEOPLE
LIBRARY OF FRANKLIN
THE GOVERNMENT HAS NOT FIXED THESE HOLES IN THE WAKE OF KEVIN'S CAPTURE.
THERE'S THIS LITTLE THING CALLED THE SOCIAL SECURITY DEATH INDEX. WHEN YOU GET TO BE OF SUFFICIENT AGE WHERE YOU CAN HAVE A JOB, YOU START PAYING INTO SOCIAL SECURITY. THAT IS PRECISELY THE TIME THEY TRULY BECOME AWARE OF YOU.
AT THIS POINT THEY KNOW WHERE YOU LIVE, YOUR AGE, YOUR INCOME, ETC. WHEN YOU DIE, YOU STOP PAYING INTO S.S., SO THEY ADD YOU TO THIS DEATH INDEX. YOUR USEFULNESS HAS EXPIRED.
IF YOU DIE WITHOUT EVER WORKING A JOB, YOU ARE NOT ADDED TO THE DEATH INDEX.

NOW THAT I EXPLAINED THE SYSTEM TO YOU, HERE IS HOW THE EXPLOIT WORKS. IT WILL REQUIRE SOME RESEARCH ON YOUR PART.

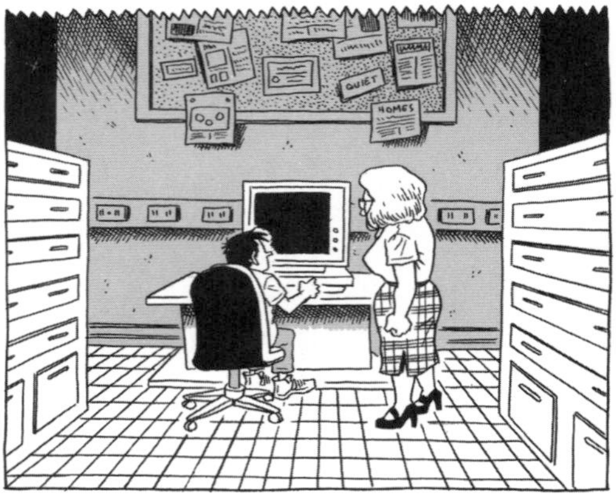
QUIET
HOMES

YOU NEED TO SCOUR OLD NEWSPAPERS AT THE LIBRARY, LOOKING FOR SOMEONE WHO DIED AT A YOUNG AGE, WHO NEVER HAD A JOB, AND WHO WOULD BE AROUND YOUR AGE.

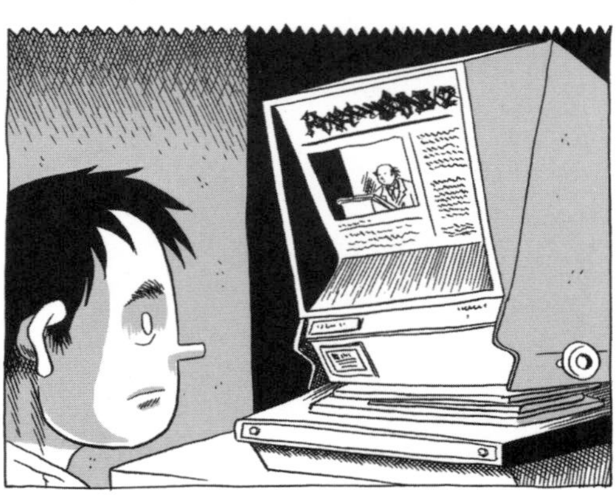

YOU NEED TO MAKE SURE TO MEMORIZE THE SURVIVING KIN FROM THE OBITUARY. YOU MAY BE ASKED QUESTIONS.

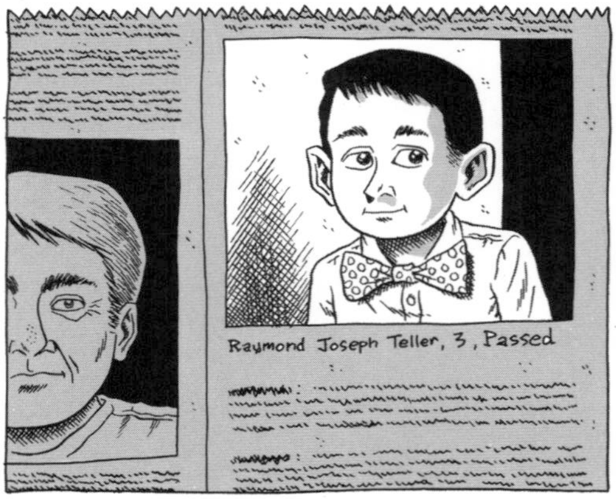
Raymond Joseph Teller, 3, Passed

YOU HAVE TO BE CONFIDENT ON THE PHONE WHEN APPLYING FOR YOUR BIRTH CERTIFICATE. TAKE NOTES IF YOU THINK IT WILL HELP.

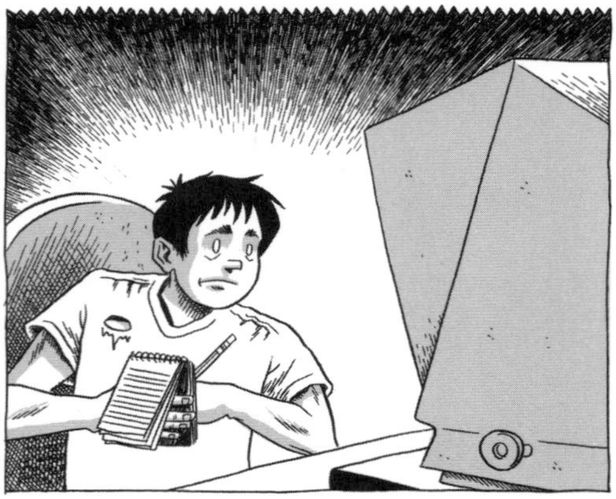

THE BUREAU OF PUBLIC RECORDS WILL RUN A FEW CHECKS TO MAKE SURE YOU WERE EVEN BORN IN THE FIRST PLACE. THEN THEY CHECK THE DEATH INDEX. ONCE THEY ARE SATISFIED THEY WILL SEND YOU A BEAUTIFUL NEW BIRTH CERTIFICATE.

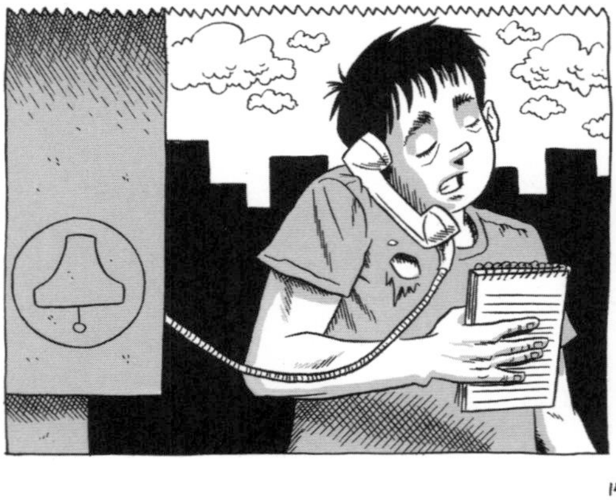

WITH THAT SIMPLE PIECE OF PAPER, YOU CAN THEN APPLY FOR A SOCIAL SECURITY CARD, DRIVERS LICENSE, PASSPORT, WHATEVER. MAKE SURE TO THROW AWAY YOUR REAL I.D. CARRYING AROUND I.D.'S WITH DIFFERENT NAMES IS FOR NOOBS.

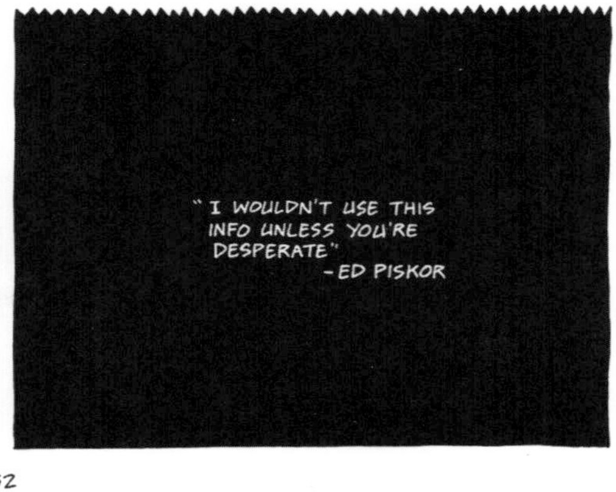
"I WOULDN'T USE THIS INFO UNLESS YOU'RE DESPERATE"
-ED PISKOR

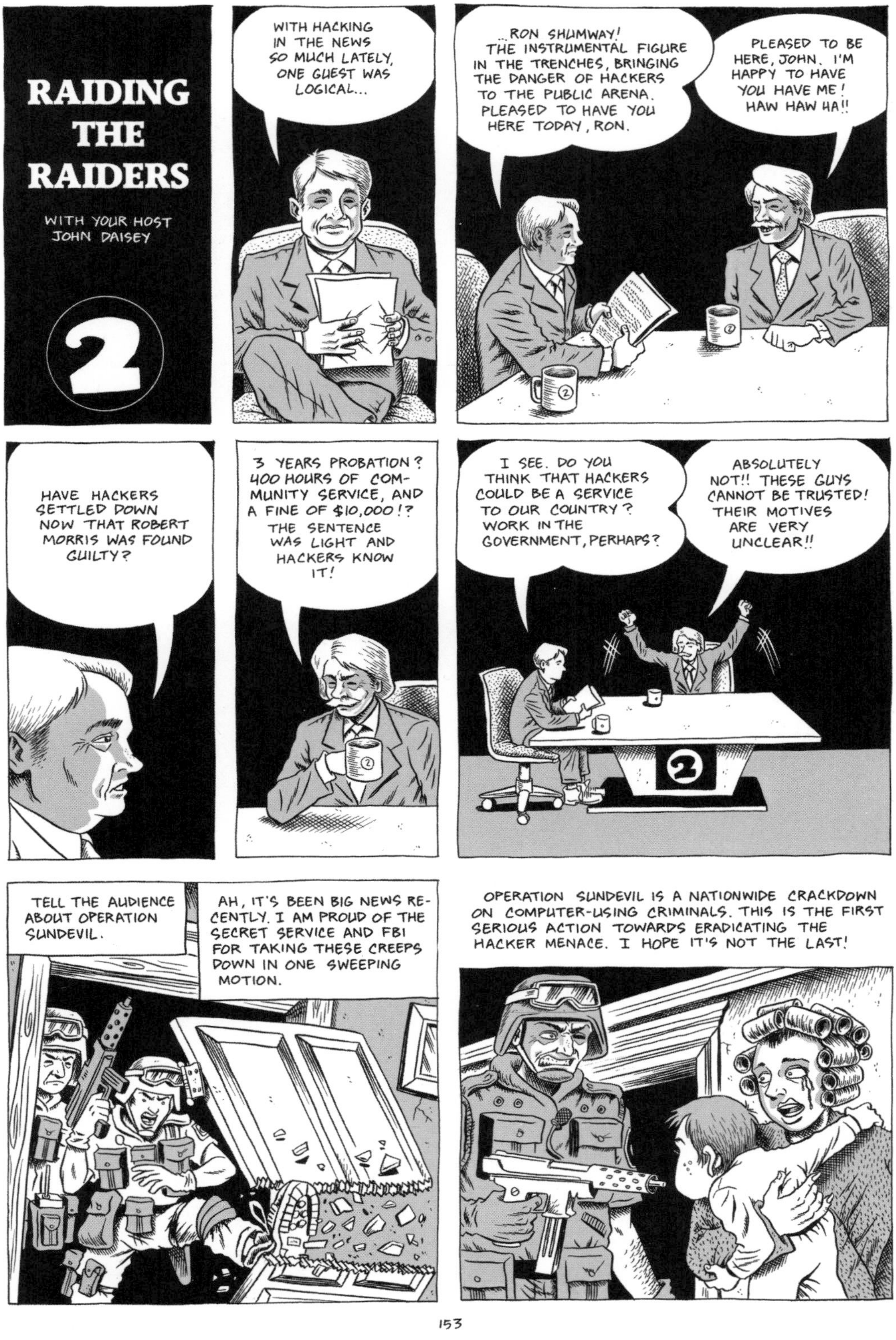
RAIDING THE RAIDERS
WITH YOUR HOST JOHN DAISEY
2
WITH HACKING IN THE NEWS SO MUCH LATELY, ONE GUEST WAS LOGICAL...
...RON SHUMWAY! THE INSTRUMENTAL FIGURE IN THE TRENCHES, BRINGING THE DANGER OF HACKERS TO THE PUBLIC ARENA. PLEASED TO HAVE YOU HERE TODAY, RON.
PLEASED TO BE HERE, JOHN. I'M HAPPY TO HAVE YOU HAVE ME! HAW HAW HA!!
HAVE HACKERS SETTLED DOWN NOW THAT ROBERT MORRIS WAS FOUND GUILTY?
3 YEARS PROBATION? 400 HOURS OF COMMUNITY SERVICE, AND A FINE OF $10,000!? THE SENTENCE WAS LIGHT AND HACKERS KNOW IT!
I SEE. DO YOU THINK THAT HACKERS COULD BE A SERVICE TO OUR COUNTRY? WORK IN THE GOVERNMENT, PERHAPS?
ABSOLUTELY NOT!! THESE GUYS CANNOT BE TRUSTED! THEIR MOTIVES ARE VERY UNCLEAR!!
TELL THE AUDIENCE ABOUT OPERATION SUNDEVIL.
AH, IT'S BEEN BIG NEWS RECENTLY. I AM PROUD OF THE SECRET SERVICE AND FBI FOR TAKING THESE CREEPS DOWN IN ONE SWEEPING MOTION.
OPERATION SUNDEVIL IS A NATIONWIDE CRACKDOWN ON COMPUTER-USING CRIMINALS. THIS IS THE FIRST SERIOUS ACTION TOWARDS ERADICATING THE HACKER MENACE. I HOPE IT'S NOT THE LAST!

RAIDS WERE PERFORMED IN EVERY MAJOR CITY IN THE COUNTRY, SEIZING THE 'TOOLS OF THE TRADE' THAT THESE VILLAINS USED TO PERFORM THEIR HEINOUS WORK.

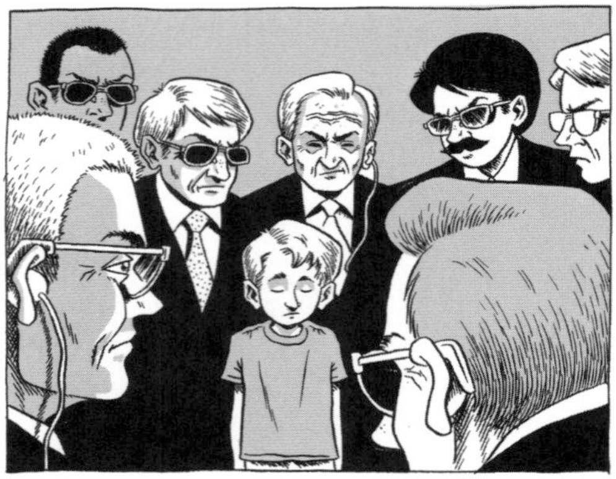

THEY ARE CUNNING INDIVIDUALS, THESE HACKERS!! THEY COULD HIDE DATA ANYWHERE! PAPER, AUDIO TAPES, FLOPPY DISKS— THOUSANDS OF PIECES OF CONTRABAND ARE NOW IN THE POSSESSION OF AUTHORITIES.

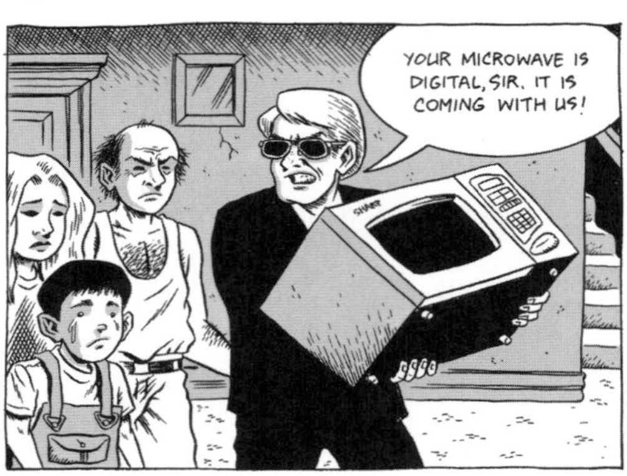
YOUR MICROWAVE IS DIGITAL, SIR. IT IS COMING WITH US!

ONE OF THE MOST DISGUSTING PIECES OF INFORMATION THAT PROMPTED THE OPERATION WAS THE ELECTRONIC DISTRIBUTION OF A PROPRIETARY DOCUMENT USED FOR INTERNAL BUSINESS WITHIN 911 EMERGENCY OFFICES.

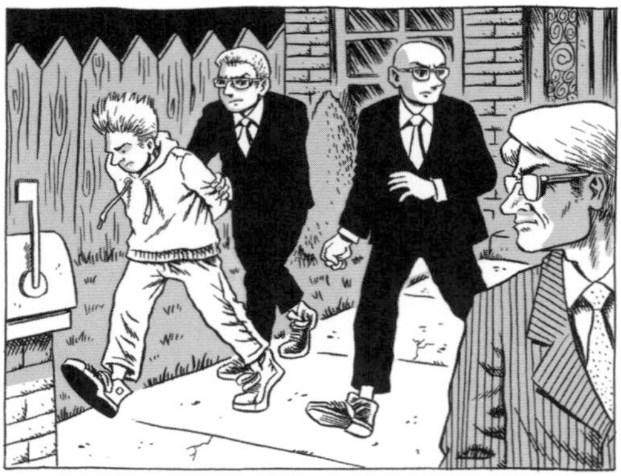

I MEAN, CAN YOU BELIEVE THE AUDACITY OF THAT! IMAGINE THE DAMAGE THEY COULD HAVE CAUSED.

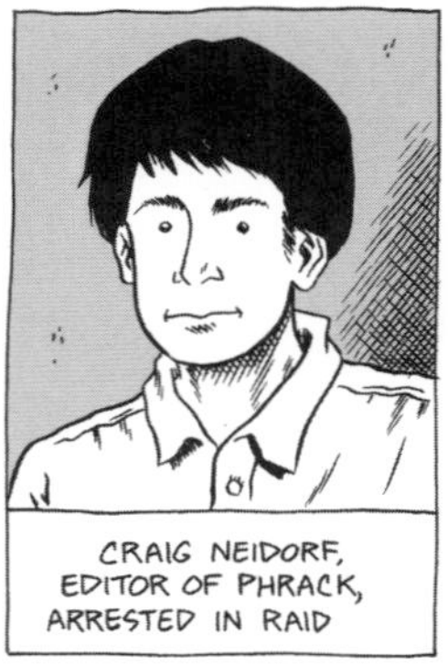
CRAIG NEIDORF, EDITOR OF PHRACK, ARRESTED IN RAID

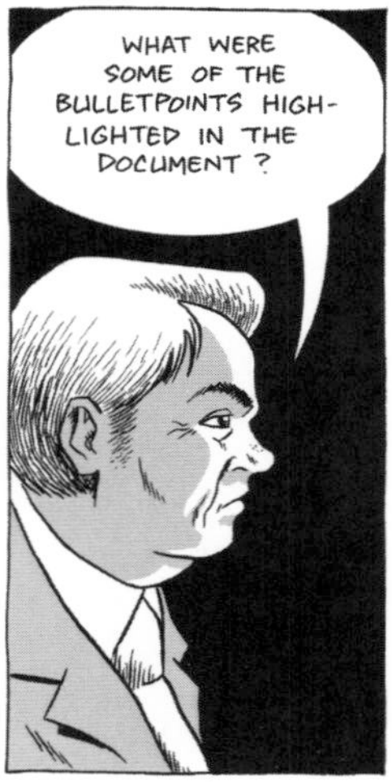
WHAT WERE SOME OF THE BULLETPOINTS HIGHLIGHTED IN THE DOCUMENT ?

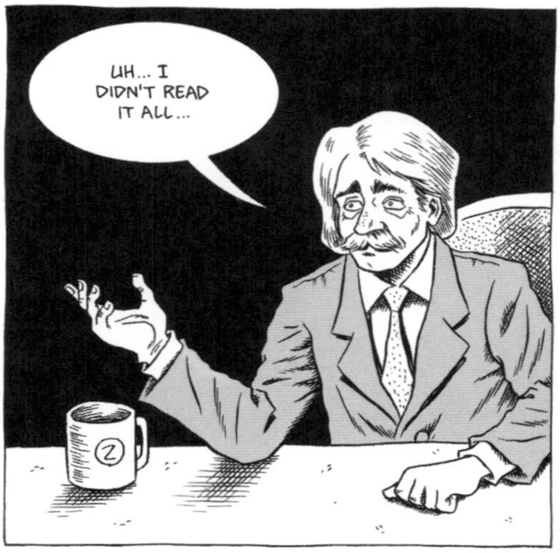
UH... I DIDN'T READ IT ALL...

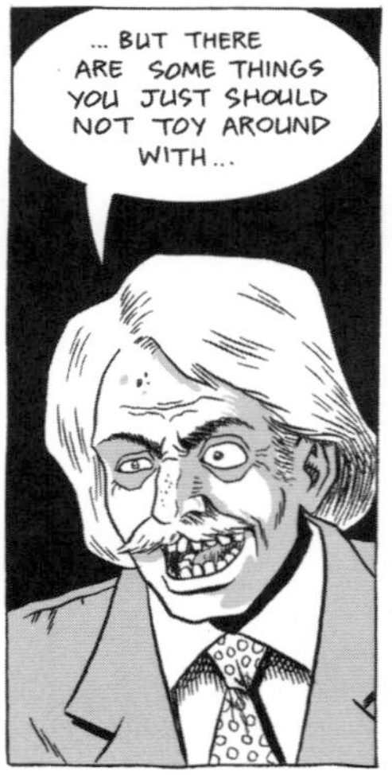
... BUT THERE ARE SOME THINGS YOU JUST SHOULD NOT TOY AROUND WITH...

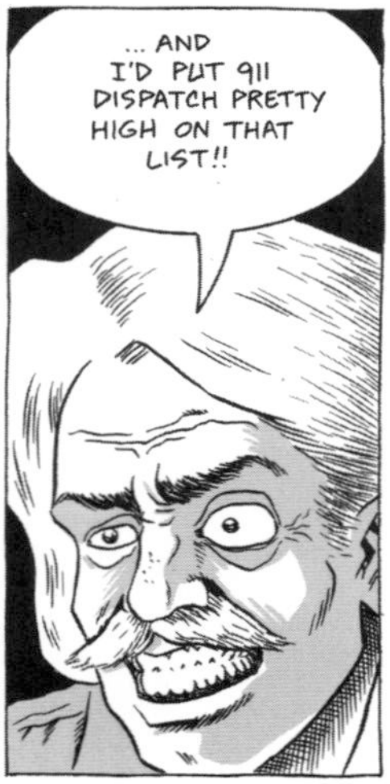
... AND I'D PUT 911 DISPATCH PRETTY HIGH ON THAT LIST!!

ONE OF THE PLACES THAT WAS TARGETED IN THE RAID WAS A ROLEPLAYING GAME COMPANY BASED IN TEXAS. A COMPANY WITH INTIMATE ACCESS TO CHILDREN.

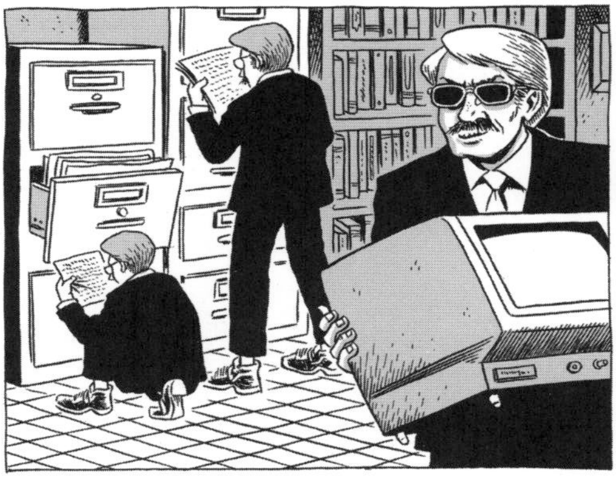

IT IS BELIEVED THAT ONE OF THEIR GAMES REQUIRES A HANDBOOK THAT THEY PUBLISH, AND IT SEEMS THAT IT IS AN ACTUAL GUIDE THAT TEACHES YOU HOW TO HACK!

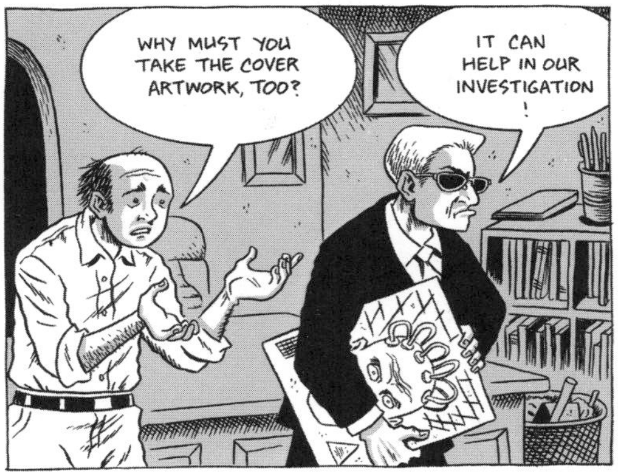
WHY MUST YOU TAKE THE COVER ARTWORK, TOO?
IT CAN HELP IN OUR INVESTIGATION!

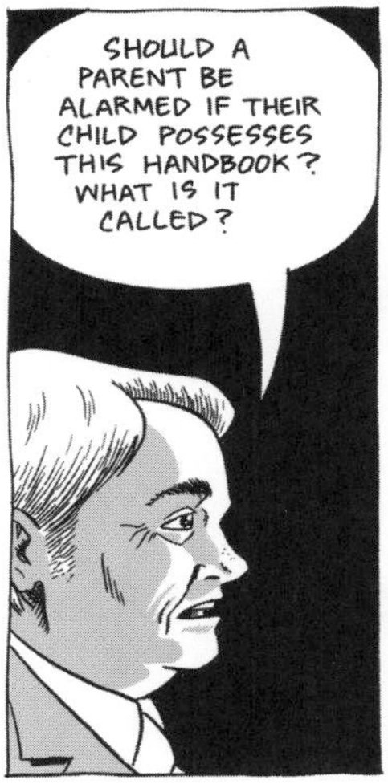
SHOULD A PARENT BE ALARMED IF THEIR CHILD POSSESSES THIS HANDBOOK? WHAT IS IT CALLED?

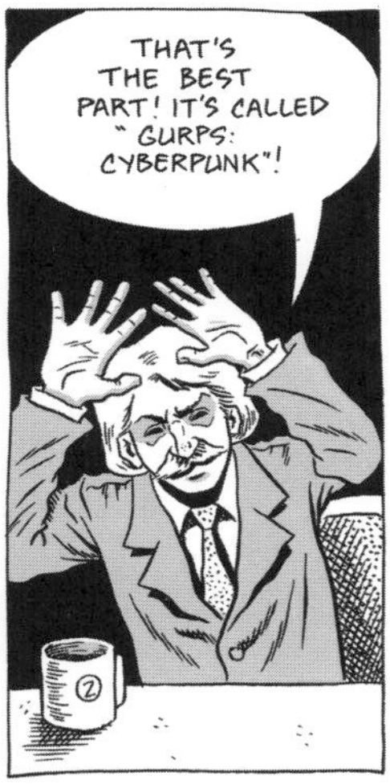
THAT'S THE BEST PART! IT'S CALLED "GURPS: CYBERPUNK"!

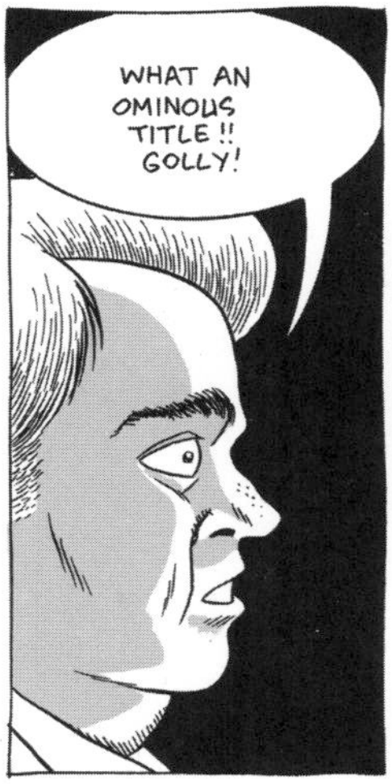
WHAT AN OMINOUS TITLE!! GOLLY!

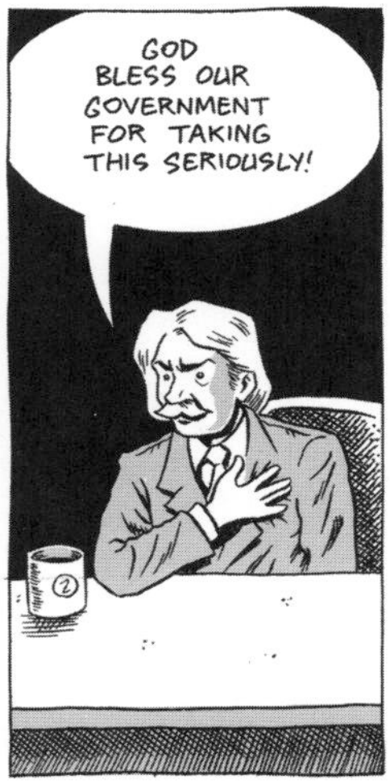
GOD BLESS OUR GOVERNMENT FOR TAKING THIS SERIOUSLY!

THIS RAID SENDS A CLEAR MESSAGE TO THESE CREEPS THAT THEY WILL NO LONGER VICTIMIZE US ANONYMOUSLY.

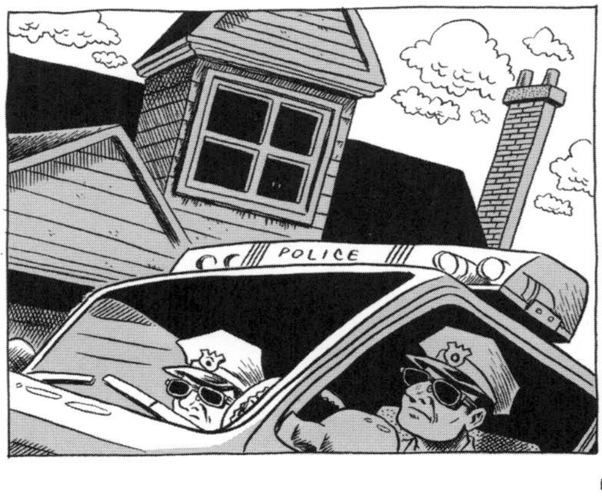
POLICE

SPEAKING OF "CREEPS", IS KEVIN "BOING-THUMP" PHENICLE CLOSER TO BEING APPREHENDED THANKS TO OPERATION SUNDEVIL, RON?

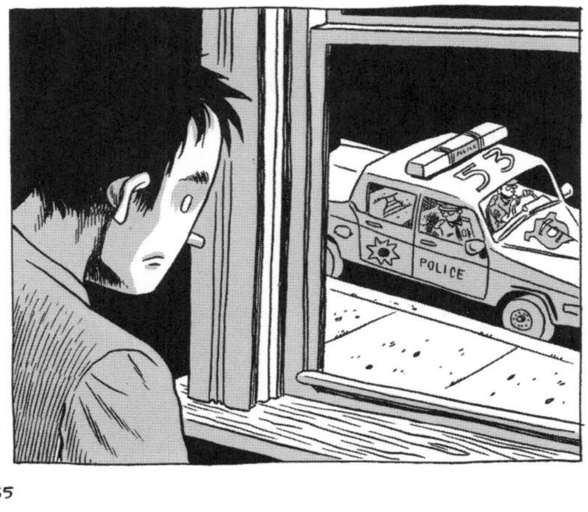
POLICE

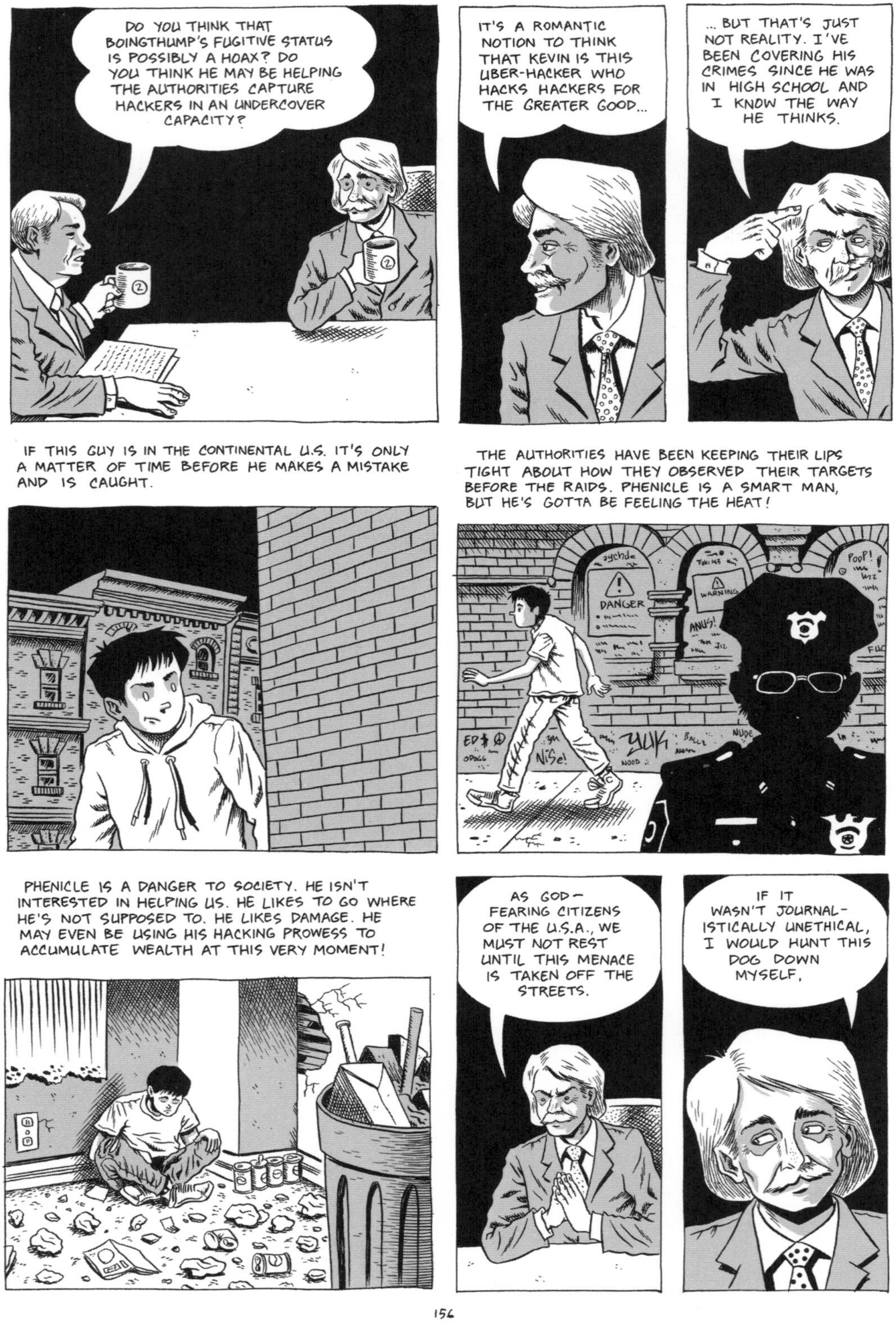
DO YOU THINK THAT BOINGTHUMP'S FUGITIVE STATUS IS POSSIBLY A HOAX? DO YOU THINK HE MAY BE HELPING THE AUTHORITIES CAPTURE HACKERS IN AN UNDERCOVER CAPACITY?
IT'S A ROMANTIC NOTION TO THINK THAT KEVIN IS THIS UBER-HACKER WHO HACKS HACKERS FOR THE GREATER GOOD...
... BUT THAT'S JUST NOT REALITY. I'VE BEEN COVERING HIS CRIMES SINCE HE WAS IN HIGH SCHOOL AND I KNOW THE WAY HE THINKS.
IF THIS GUY IS IN THE CONTINENTAL U.S. IT'S ONLY A MATTER OF TIME BEFORE HE MAKES A MISTAKE AND IS CAUGHT.
THE AUTHORITIES HAVE BEEN KEEPING THEIR LIPS TIGHT ABOUT HOW THEY OBSERVED THEIR TARGETS BEFORE THE RAIDS. PHENICLE IS A SMART MAN, BUT HE'S GOTTA BE FEELING THE HEAT!
DANGER
WARNING
POOP!
ANUS!
NUDE
PHENICLE IS A DANGER TO SOCIETY. HE ISN'T INTERESTED IN HELPING US. HE LIKES TO GO WHERE HE'S NOT SUPPOSED TO. HE LIKES DAMAGE. HE MAY EVEN BE USING HIS HACKING PROWESS TO ACCUMULATE WEALTH AT THIS VERY MOMENT!
AS GOD-FEARING CITIZENS OF THE U.S.A., WE MUST NOT REST UNTIL THIS MENACE IS TAKEN OFF THE STREETS.
IF IT WASN'T JOURNALISTICALLY UNETHICAL, I WOULD HUNT THIS DOG DOWN MYSELF.

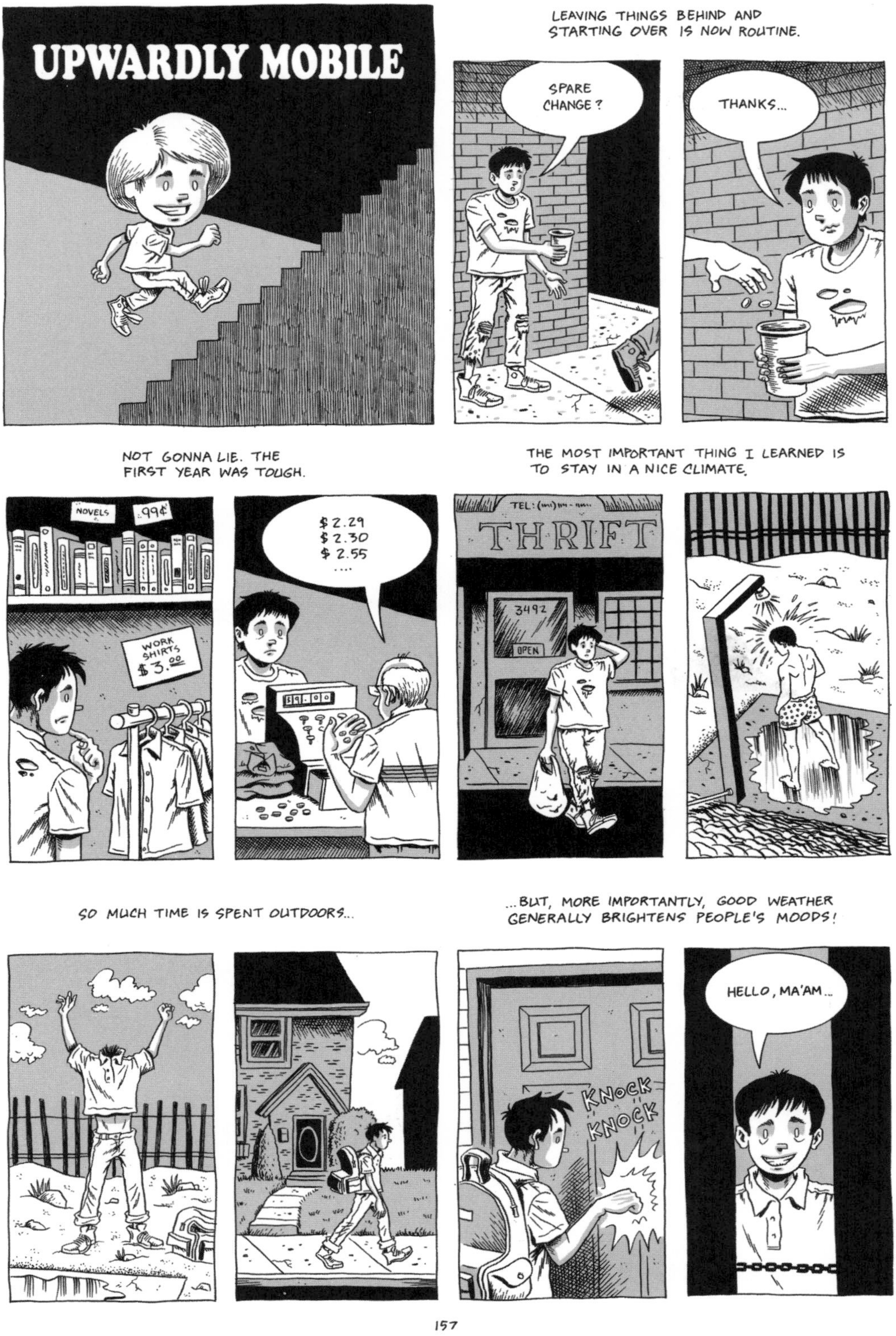
UPWARDLY MOBILE
LEAVING THINGS BEHIND AND STARTING OVER IS NOW ROUTINE.
SPARE CHANGE?
THANKS...
NOT GONNA LIE. THE FIRST YEAR WAS TOUGH.
NOVELS
.99¢
WORK SHIRTS $3.00
$2.29
$2.30
$2.55
....
THE MOST IMPORTANT THING I LEARNED IS TO STAY IN A NICE CLIMATE.
THRIFT
3492
OPEN
SO MUCH TIME IS SPENT OUTDOORS...
...BUT, MORE IMPORTANTLY, GOOD WEATHER GENERALLY BRIGHTENS PEOPLE'S MOODS!
KNOCK KNOCK
HELLO, MA'AM...

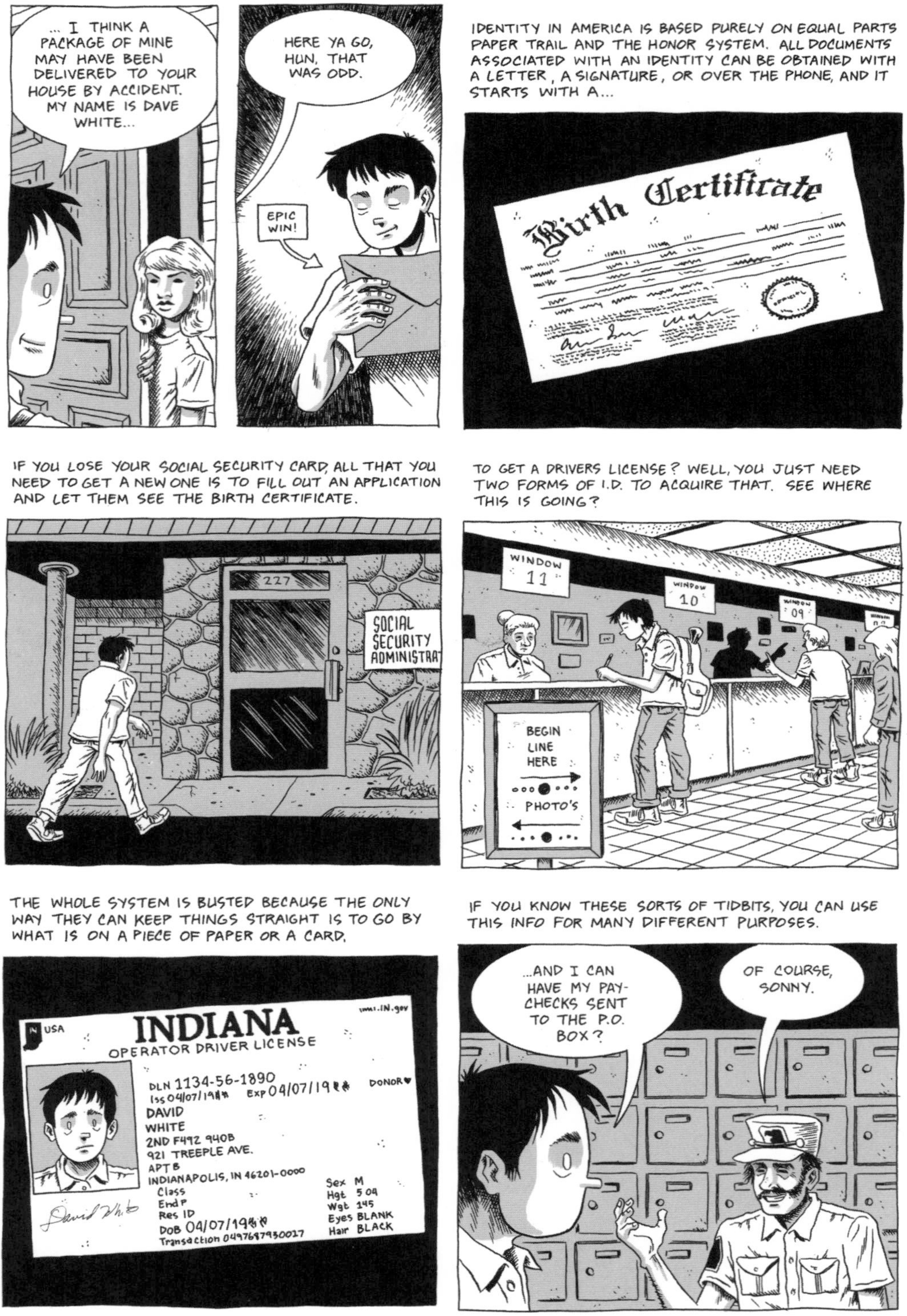
... I THINK A PACKAGE OF MINE MAY HAVE BEEN DELIVERED TO YOUR HOUSE BY ACCIDENT. MY NAME IS DAVE WHITE...
HERE YA GO, HUN, THAT WAS ODD.
EPIC WIN!
IDENTITY IN AMERICA IS BASED PURELY ON EQUAL PARTS PAPER TRAIL AND THE HONOR SYSTEM. ALL DOCUMENTS ASSOCIATED WITH AN IDENTITY CAN BE OBTAINED WITH A LETTER, A SIGNATURE, OR OVER THE PHONE, AND IT STARTS WITH A...
Birth Certificate
IF YOU LOSE YOUR SOCIAL SECURITY CARD, ALL THAT YOU NEED TO GET A NEW ONE IS TO FILL OUT AN APPLICATION AND LET THEM SEE THE BIRTH CERTIFICATE.
227
SOCIAL SECURITY ADMINISTRAT
TO GET A DRIVERS LICENSE? WELL, YOU JUST NEED TWO FORMS OF I.D. TO ACQUIRE THAT. SEE WHERE THIS IS GOING?
WINDOW 11
WINDOW 10
WINDOW 09
BEGIN LINE HERE
PHOTO'S
THE WHOLE SYSTEM IS BUSTED BECAUSE THE ONLY WAY THEY CAN KEEP THINGS STRAIGHT IS TO GO BY WHAT IS ON A PIECE OF PAPER OR A CARD.
USA
INDIANA
OPERATOR DRIVER LICENSE
DLN 1134-56-1890
DONOR
DAVID
WHITE
921 TREEPLE AVE.
APT B
INDIANAPOLIS, IN 46201-0000
Class
Res ID
Sex M
Wgt 145
Eyes BLANK
Hair BLACK
IF YOU KNOW THESE SORTS OF TIDBITS, YOU CAN USE THIS INFO FOR MANY DIFFERENT PURPOSES.
...AND I CAN HAVE MY PAY-CHECKS SENT TO THE P.O. BOX?
OF COURSE, SONNY.

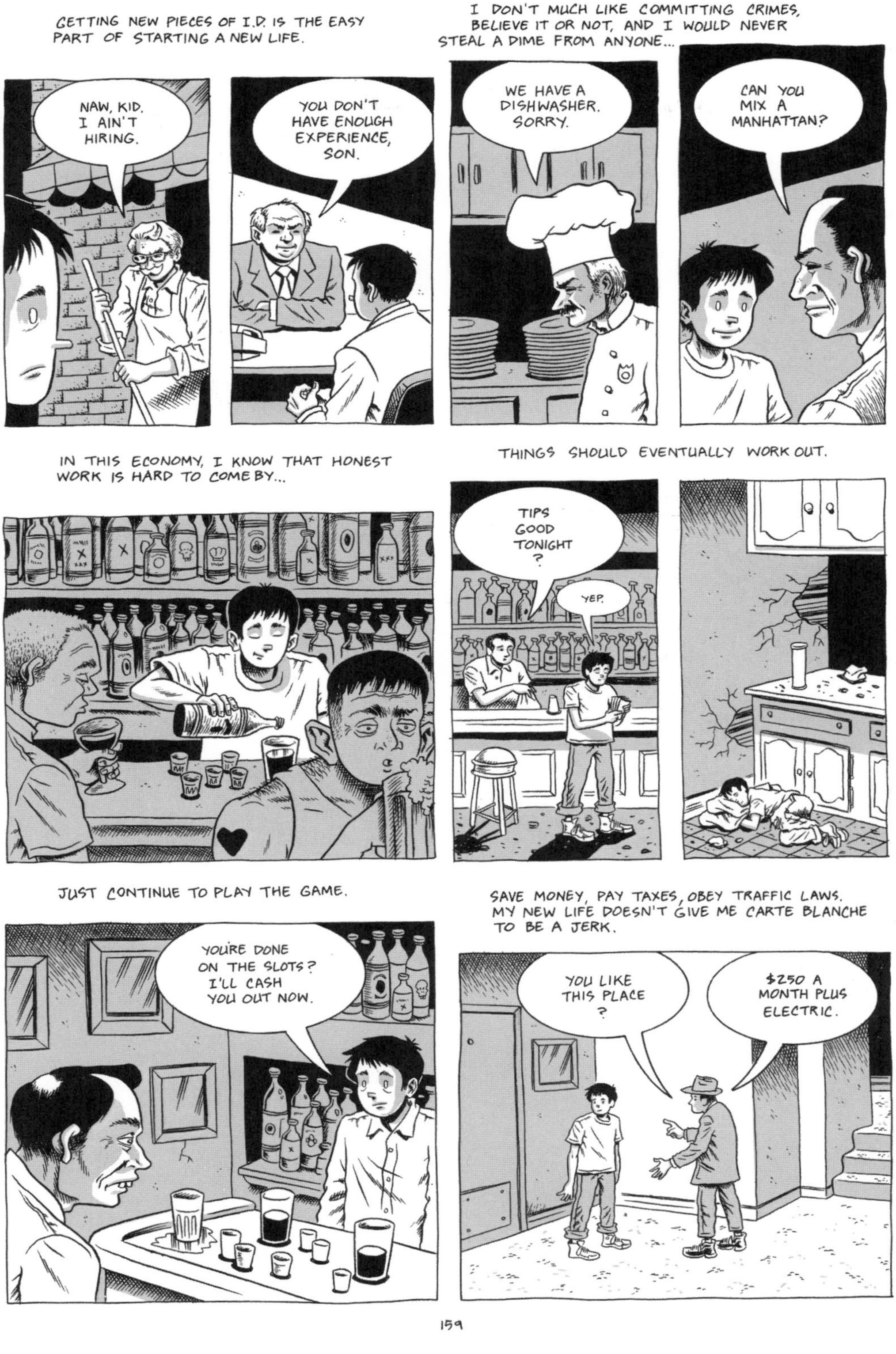
GETTING NEW PIECES OF I.D. IS THE EASY PART OF STARTING A NEW LIFE.
NAW, KID. I AIN'T HIRING.
YOU DON'T HAVE ENOUGH EXPERIENCE, SON.
I DON'T MUCH LIKE COMMITTING CRIMES, BELIEVE IT OR NOT, AND I WOULD NEVER STEAL A DIME FROM ANYONE...
WE HAVE A DISHWASHER. SORRY.
CAN YOU MIX A MANHATTAN?
IN THIS ECONOMY, I KNOW THAT HONEST WORK IS HARD TO COME BY...
THINGS SHOULD EVENTUALLY WORK OUT.
TIPS GOOD TONIGHT ?
YEP.
JUST CONTINUE TO PLAY THE GAME.
YOU'RE DONE ON THE SLOTS? I'LL CASH YOU OUT NOW.
SAVE MONEY, PAY TAXES, OBEY TRAFFIC LAWS. MY NEW LIFE DOESN'T GIVE ME CARTE BLANCHE TO BE A JERK.
YOU LIKE THIS PLACE ?
$250 A MONTH PLUS ELECTRIC.

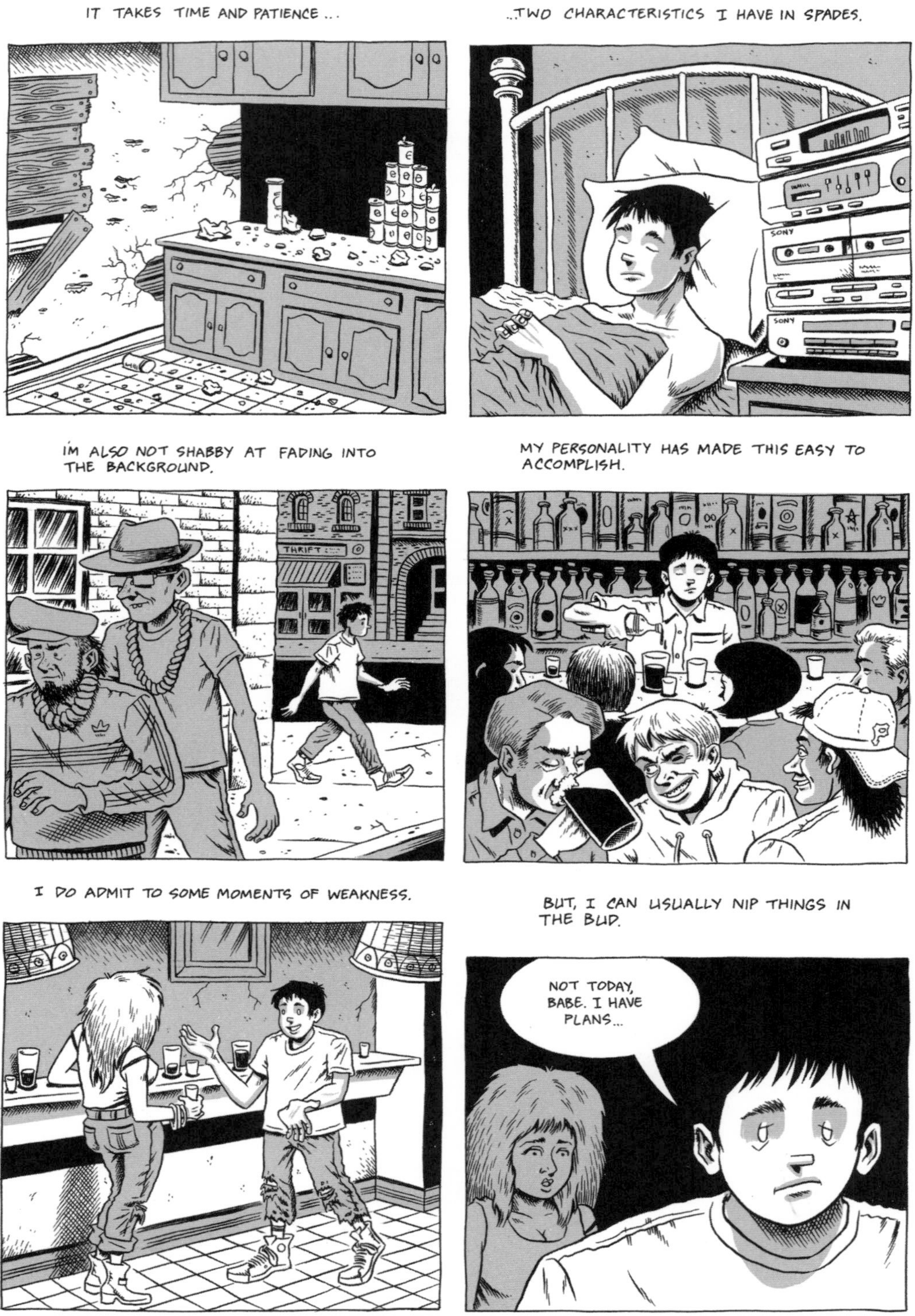
IT TAKES TIME AND PATIENCE...
..TWO CHARACTERISTICS I HAVE IN SPADES.
SONY
SONY
I'M ALSO NOT SHABBY AT FADING INTO THE BACKGROUND.
THRIFT
MY PERSONALITY HAS MADE THIS EASY TO ACCOMPLISH.
I DO ADMIT TO SOME MOMENTS OF WEAKNESS.
BUT, I CAN USUALLY NIP THINGS IN THE BUD.
NOT TODAY, BABE. I HAVE PLANS...

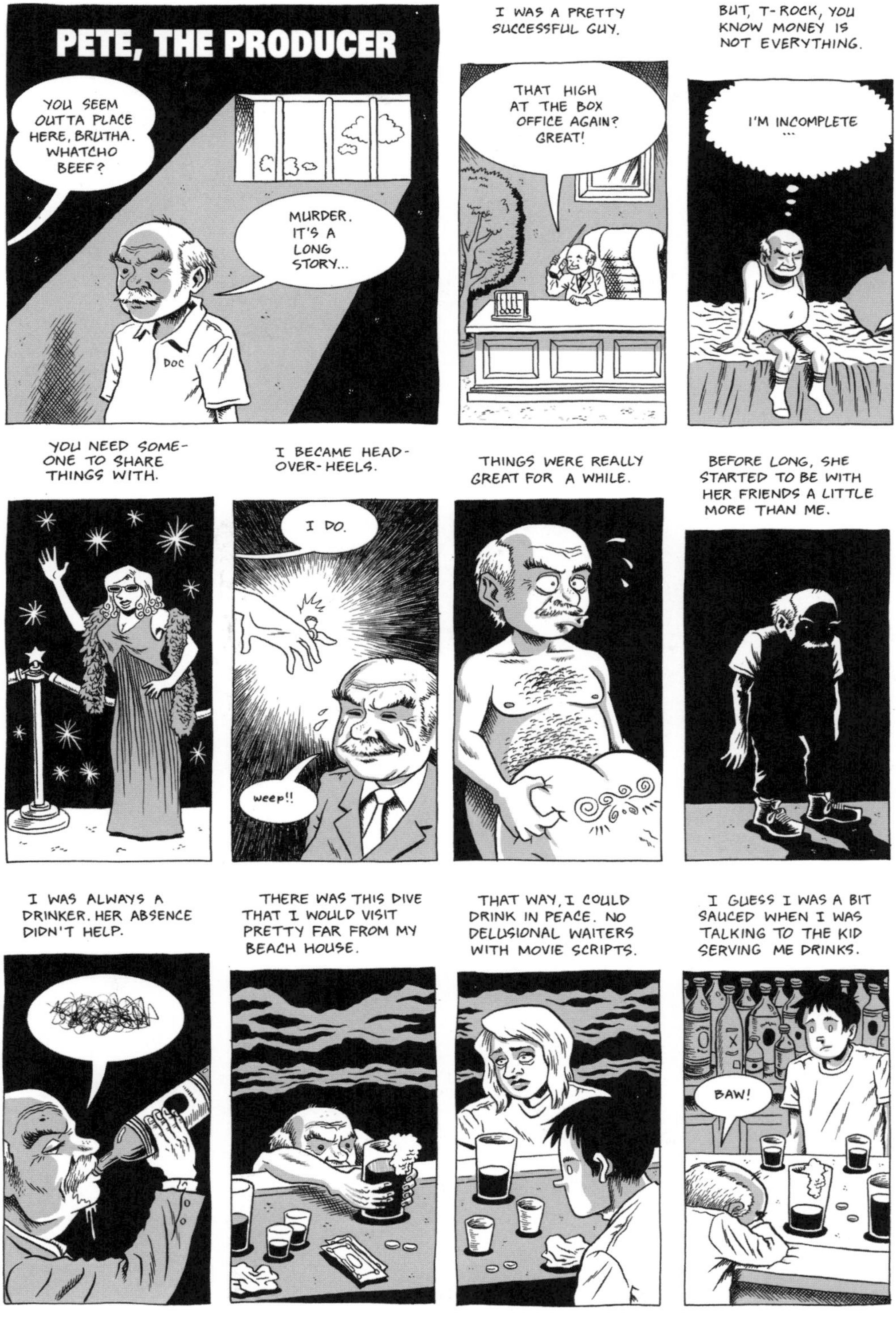
PETE, THE PRODUCER
YOU SEEM OUTTA PLACE HERE, BRUTHA. WHATCHO BEEF?
MURDER. IT'S A LONG STORY...
DOC
I WAS A PRETTY SUCCESSFUL GUY.
THAT HIGH AT THE BOX OFFICE AGAIN? GREAT!
BUT, T-ROCK, YOU KNOW MONEY IS NOT EVERYTHING.
I'M INCOMPLETE ...
YOU NEED SOME-ONE TO SHARE THINGS WITH.
I BECAME HEAD-OVER-HEELS.
I DO.
weep!!
THINGS WERE REALLY GREAT FOR A WHILE.
BEFORE LONG, SHE STARTED TO BE WITH HER FRIENDS A LITTLE MORE THAN ME.
I WAS ALWAYS A DRINKER. HER ABSENCE DIDN'T HELP.
THERE WAS THIS DIVE THAT I WOULD VISIT PRETTY FAR FROM MY BEACH HOUSE.
THAT WAY, I COULD DRINK IN PEACE. NO DELUSIONAL WAITERS WITH MOVIE SCRIPTS.
I GUESS I WAS A BIT SAUCED WHEN I WAS TALKING TO THE KID SERVING ME DRINKS.
BAW!

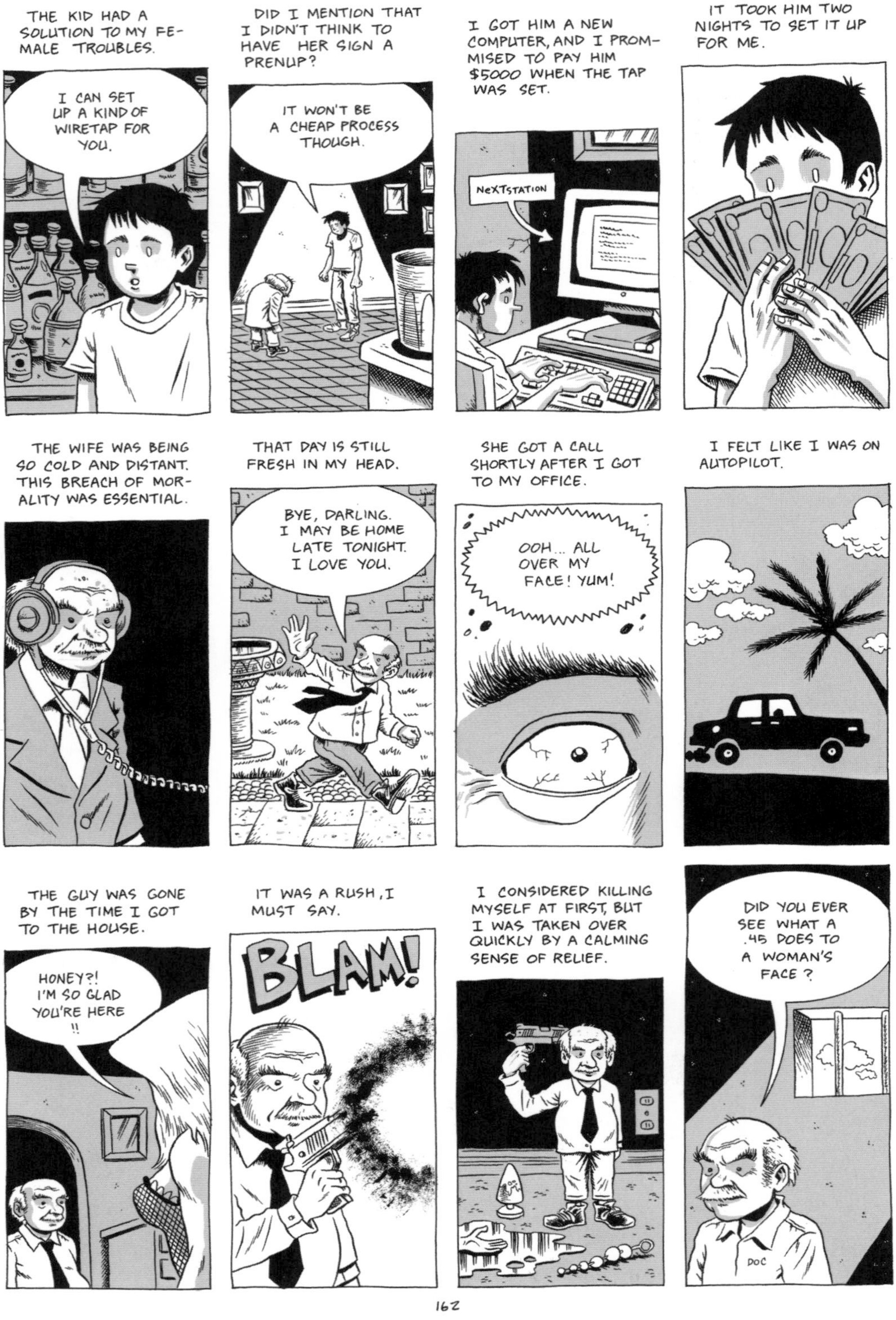
THE KID HAD A SOLUTION TO MY FE-MALE TROUBLES.
I CAN SET UP A KIND OF WIRETAP FOR YOU.
DID I MENTION THAT I DIDN'T THINK TO HAVE HER SIGN A PRENUP?
IT WON'T BE A CHEAP PROCESS THOUGH.
I GOT HIM A NEW COMPUTER, AND I PROM-MISED TO PAY HIM $5000 WHEN THE TAP WAS SET.
NeXTSTATION
IT TOOK HIM TWO NIGHTS TO SET IT UP FOR ME.
THE WIFE WAS BEING SO COLD AND DISTANT. THIS BREACH OF MOR-ALITY WAS ESSENTIAL.
THAT DAY IS STILL FRESH IN MY HEAD.
BYE, DARLING. I MAY BE HOME LATE TONIGHT. I LOVE YOU.
SHE GOT A CALL SHORTLY AFTER I GOT TO MY OFFICE.
OOH... ALL OVER MY FACE! YUM!
I FELT LIKE I WAS ON AUTOPILOT.
THE GUY WAS GONE BY THE TIME I GOT TO THE HOUSE.
HONEY?! I'M SO GLAD YOU'RE HERE !!
IT WAS A RUSH, I MUST SAY.
BLAM!
I CONSIDERED KILLING MYSELF AT FIRST, BUT I WAS TAKEN OVER QUICKLY BY A CALMING SENSE OF RELIEF.
DID YOU EVER SEE WHAT A .45 DOES TO A WOMAN'S FACE ?
DOC

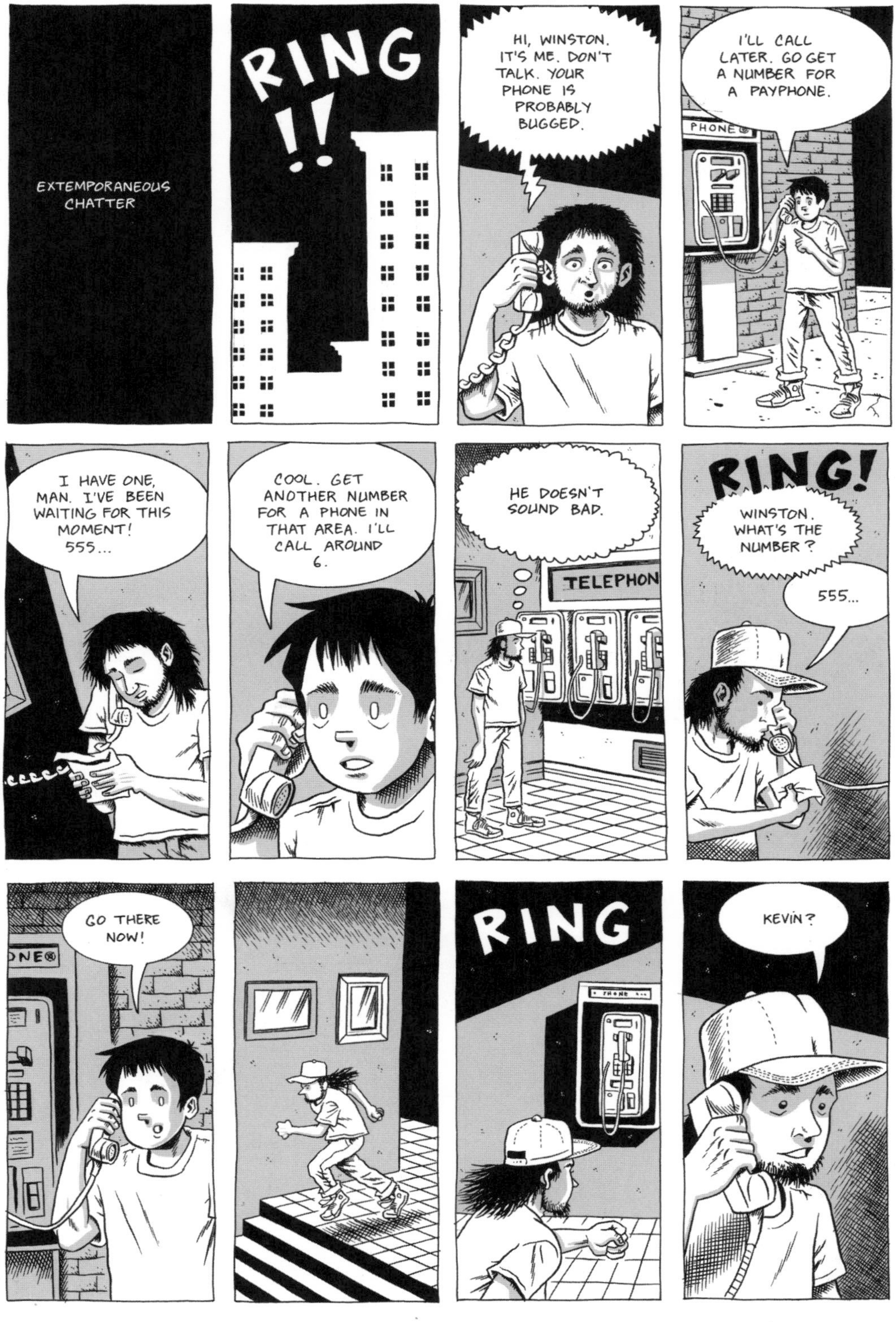
EXTEMPORANEOUS CHATTER
RING !!
HI, WINSTON. IT'S ME. DON'T TALK. YOUR PHONE IS PROBABLY BUGGED.
I'LL CALL LATER. GO GET A NUMBER FOR A PAYPHONE.
PHONE
I HAVE ONE, MAN. I'VE BEEN WAITING FOR THIS MOMENT! 555...
COOL. GET ANOTHER NUMBER FOR A PHONE IN THAT AREA. I'LL CALL AROUND 6.
HE DOESN'T SOUND BAD.
TELEPHON
RING!
WINSTON. WHAT'S THE NUMBER?
555...
GO THERE NOW!
ONE
RING
KEVIN?

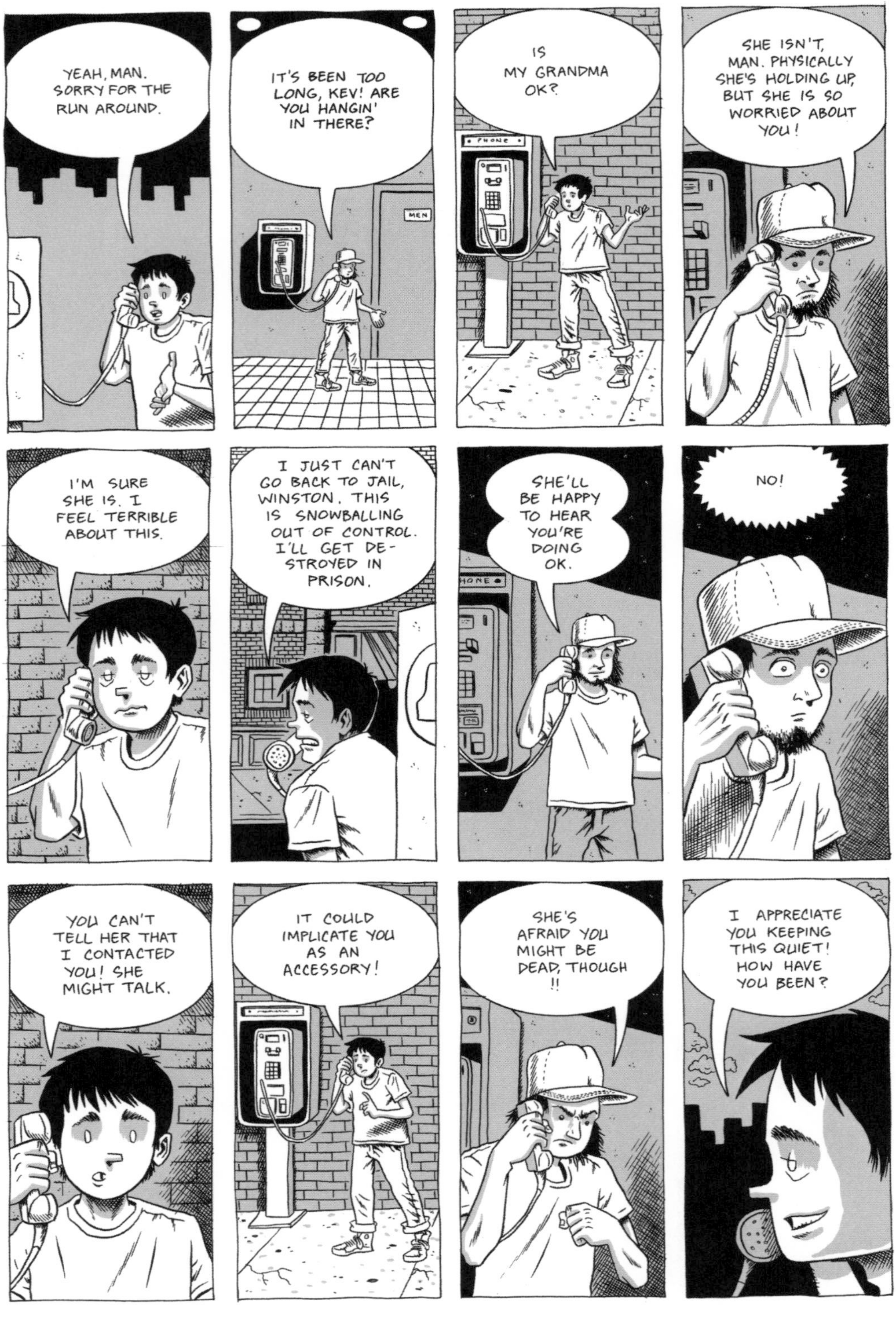
YEAH, MAN. SORRY FOR THE RUN AROUND.
IT'S BEEN TOO LONG, KEV! ARE YOU HANGIN' IN THERE?
MEN
IS MY GRANDMA OK?
PHONE
SHE ISN'T, MAN. PHYSICALLY SHE'S HOLDING UP, BUT SHE IS SO WORRIED ABOUT YOU!
I'M SURE SHE IS. I FEEL TERRIBLE ABOUT THIS.
I JUST CAN'T GO BACK TO JAIL, WINSTON. THIS IS SNOWBALLING OUT OF CONTROL. I'LL GET DE-STROYED IN PRISON.
SHE'LL BE HAPPY TO HEAR YOU'RE DOING OK.
NO!
YOU CAN'T TELL HER THAT I CONTACTED YOU! SHE MIGHT TALK.
IT COULD IMPLICATE YOU AS AN ACCESSORY!
SHE'S AFRAID YOU MIGHT BE DEAD, THOUGH !!
I APPRECIATE YOU KEEPING THIS QUIET! HOW HAVE YOU BEEN?

PARNELL, THE PIMP

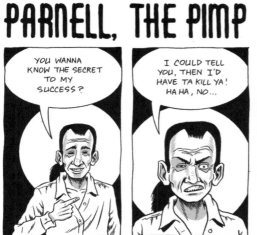

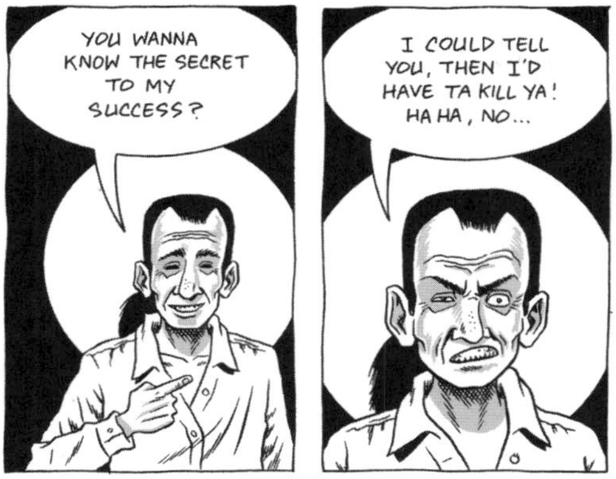
YOU WANNA KNOW THE SECRET TO MY SUCCESS?
I COULD TELL YOU, THEN I'D HAVE TA KILL YA! HA HA, NO...

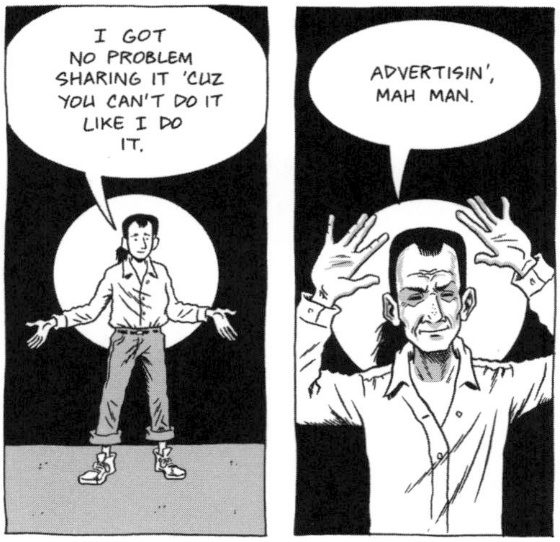
I GOT NO PROBLEM SHARING IT 'CUZ YOU CAN'T DO IT LIKE I DO IT.
ADVERTISIN', MAH MAN.

NOW YOUR RUN-A-THE-MILL ESCORTS, JACK-SHACKS, AND ALL THAT HAVE THEIR ADS IN THOSE WEEKLY PAPERS AROUND TOWN. THIS AIN'T NUTHIN' NEW.

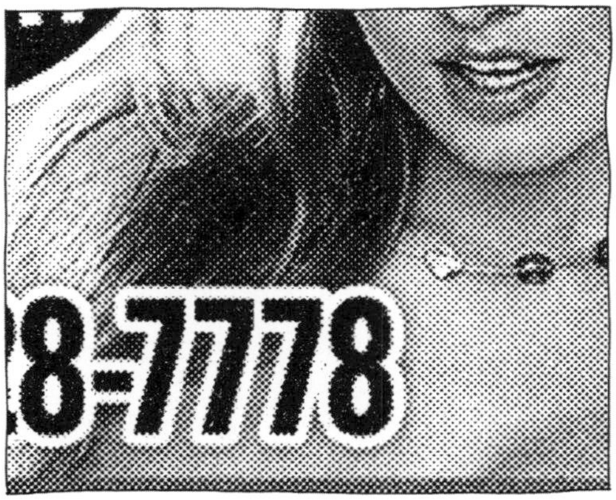
8-7778

THE PROBLEM IS: YOU SPEND ALL THIS CASH, UP FRONT, TO GET YOUR BUSINESS NUMBER IN THE PAPERS. AS QUICK AS YO' DIGITS APPEAR IN THE RAG IS AS QUICK AS THE NUMBER GETS TAKEN DOWN.

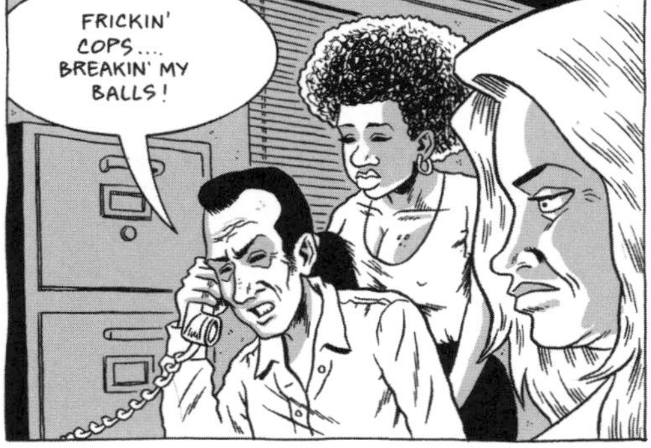
FRICKIN' COPS.... BREAKIN' MY BALLS!

MY MAIN BITCH USED TO PICK UP TRICKS AT THIS BAR OUTSIDE THE CITY LIMITS. BITCH HAD A BIG MOUTH AND MUSTA TALKED ABOUT THIS PROBLEM OF OURS WHILE SHE WAS ON THE TRACK.

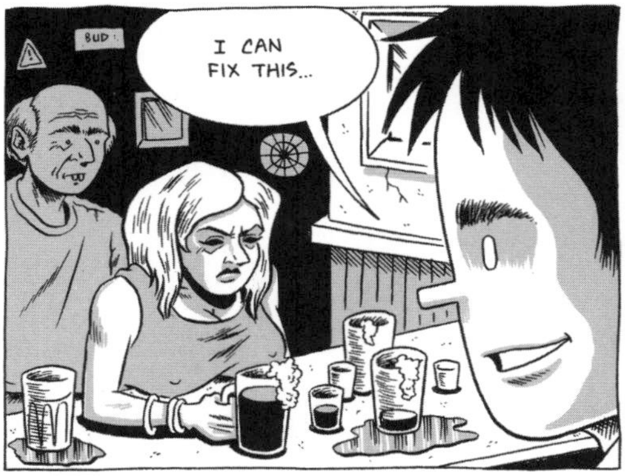
BUD
I CAN FIX THIS...

I MET WITH THE KID FIRST. HAD TO MAKE SURE HE WAS ON THE UP-N-UP.

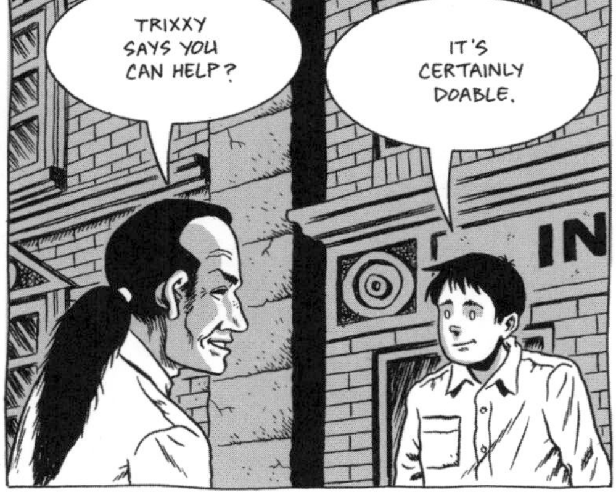
TRIXXY SAYS YOU CAN HELP?
IT'S CERTAINLY DOABLE.
IN

YOU CAN'T HAVE HIS NUMBER. I DON'T EVEN HAVE IT. HE'S PRETTY SECRETIVE WHEN WE MAKE CONTACT. THE KID HAS THE CHARISMA OF DOLEMITE, MAN.

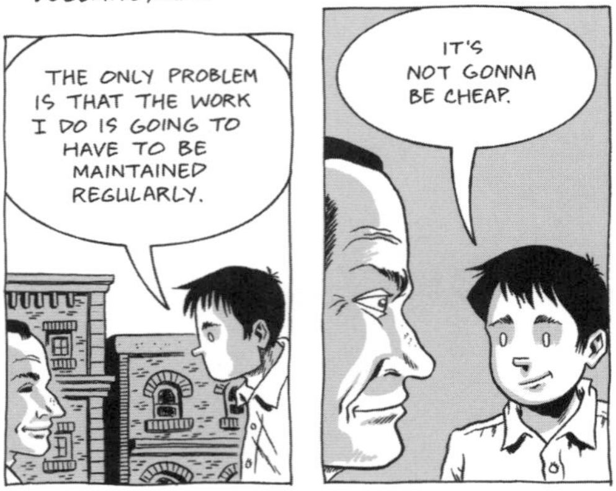
THE ONLY PROBLEM IS THAT THE WORK I DO IS GOING TO HAVE TO BE MAINTAINED REGULARLY.
IT'S NOT GONNA BE CHEAP.

WITH THE AMOUNT OF CASH I MAKE WHEN THE PHONES ARE ACTIVE, HIS PROPOSITION MADE SENSE.

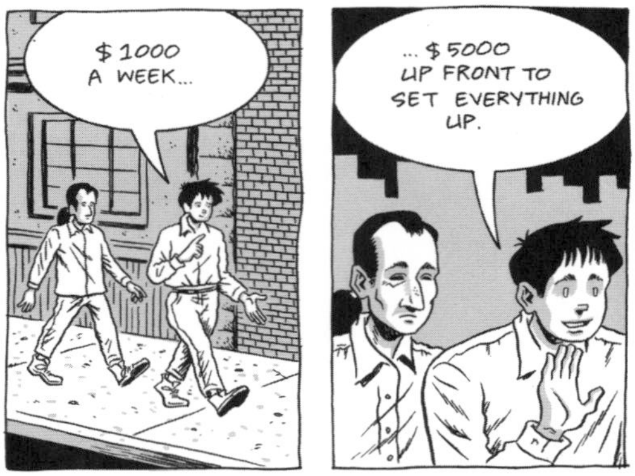
$1000 A WEEK...
... $5000 UP FRONT TO SET EVERYTHING UP.

IT DID TAKE SOME TIME FOR HIM TO SET THINGS UP.

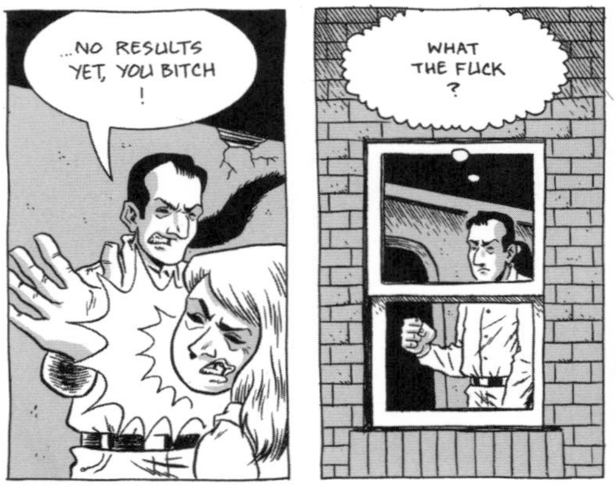
...NO RESULTS YET, YOU BITCH !
WHAT THE FUCK ?

I HAVE NO PROBLEM TALKIN' ABOUT THIS BECAUSE THE BOY IS ONE OF A KIND. YOU AIN'T GONNA FIND HIM AN' I BET HE'S THE ONLY ONE SHARP ENOUGH TO HOOK THIS UP.

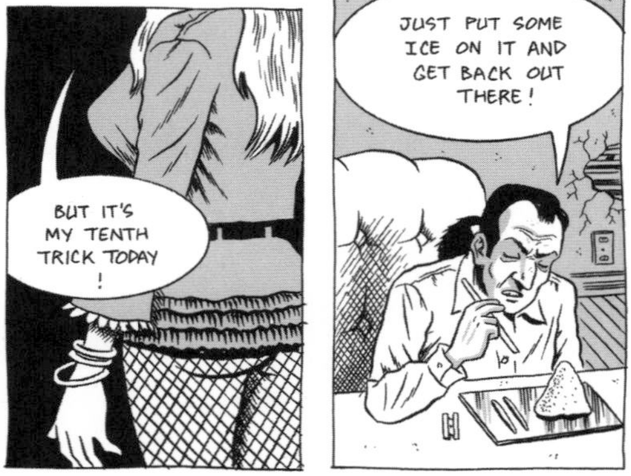
BUT IT'S MY TENTH TRICK TODAY !
JUST PUT SOME ICE ON IT AND GET BACK OUT THERE !

ONCE HE GOT HIS STUFF TOGETHER, IT WAS SO RELIABLE. THE PHONES WOULD ONLY BE DOWN A FEW HOURS A DAY, TOPS.

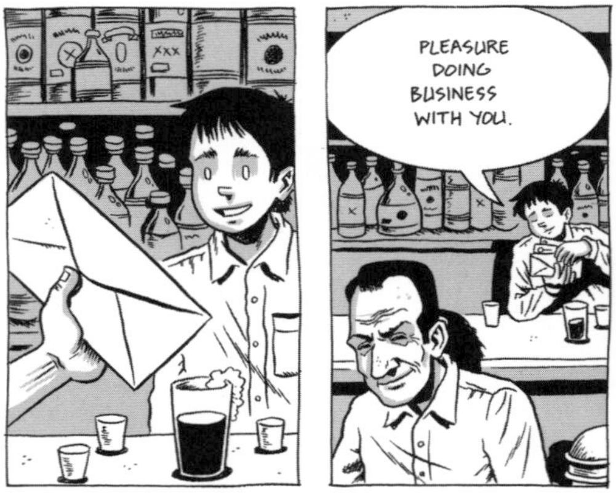
PLEASURE DOING BUSINESS WITH YOU.

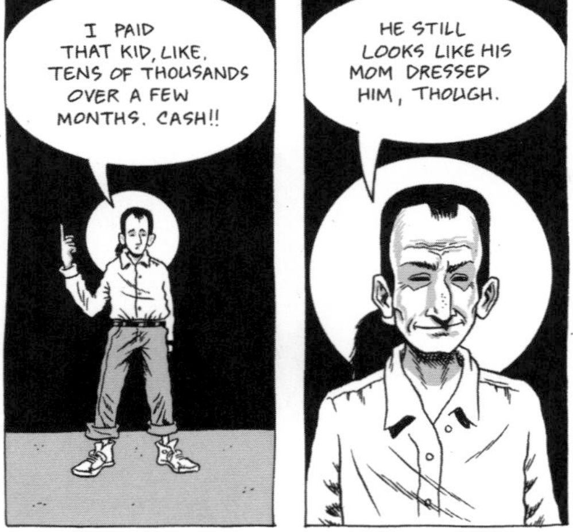
I PAID THAT KID, LIKE, TENS OF THOUSANDS OVER A FEW MONTHS. CASH!!
HE STILL LOOKS LIKE HIS MOM DRESSED HIM, THOUGH.

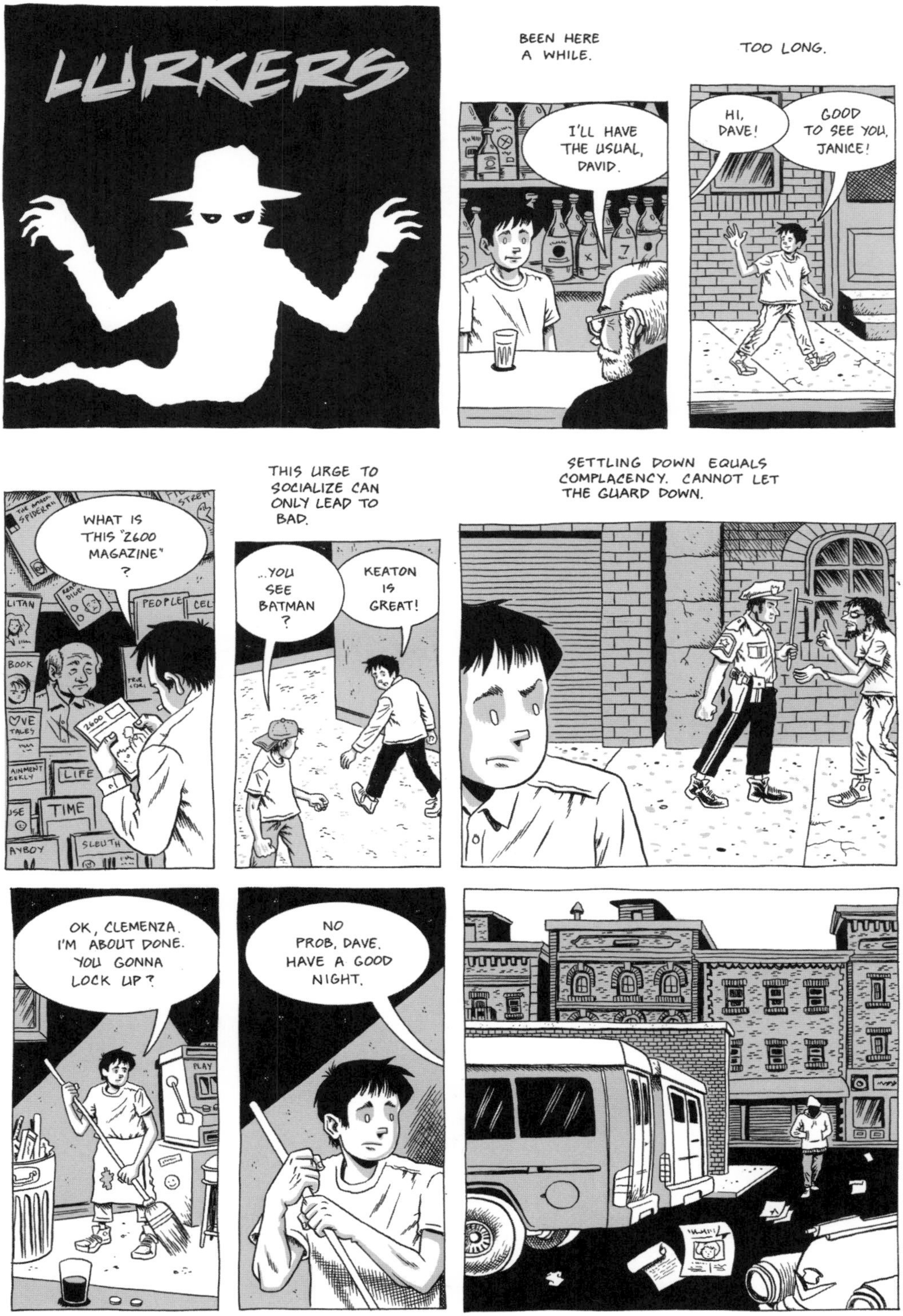
LURKERS
BEEN HERE A WHILE.
I'LL HAVE THE USUAL, DAVID.
TOO LONG.
HI, DAVE!
GOOD TO SEE YOU, JANICE!
WHAT IS THIS "2600 MAGAZINE" ?
THIS URGE TO SOCIALIZE CAN ONLY LEAD TO BAD.
...YOU SEE BATMAN ?
KEATON IS GREAT!
SETTLING DOWN EQUALS COMPLACENCY. CANNOT LET THE GUARD DOWN.
OK, CLEMENZA. I'M ABOUT DONE. YOU GONNA LOCK UP ?
NO PROB, DAVE. HAVE A GOOD NIGHT.

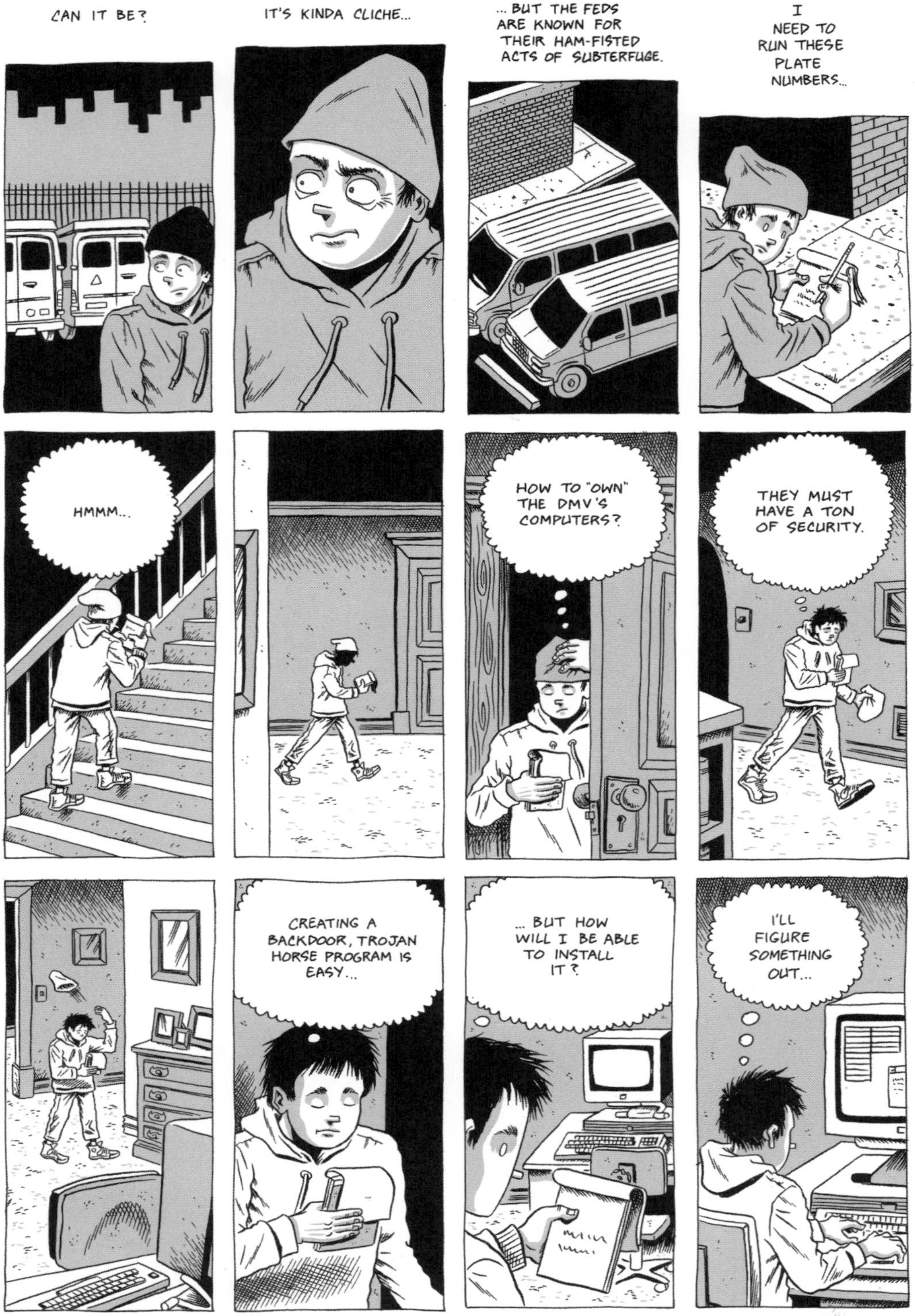
CAN IT BE?
IT'S KINDA CLICHE...
... BUT THE FEDS ARE KNOWN FOR THEIR HAM-FISTED ACTS OF SUBTERFUGE.
I NEED TO RUN THESE PLATE NUMBERS...
HMMM...
HOW TO "OWN" THE DMV'S COMPUTERS?
THEY MUST HAVE A TON OF SECURITY.
CREATING A BACKDOOR, TROJAN HORSE PROGRAM IS EASY...
... BUT HOW WILL I BE ABLE TO INSTALL IT?
I'LL FIGURE SOMETHING OUT...

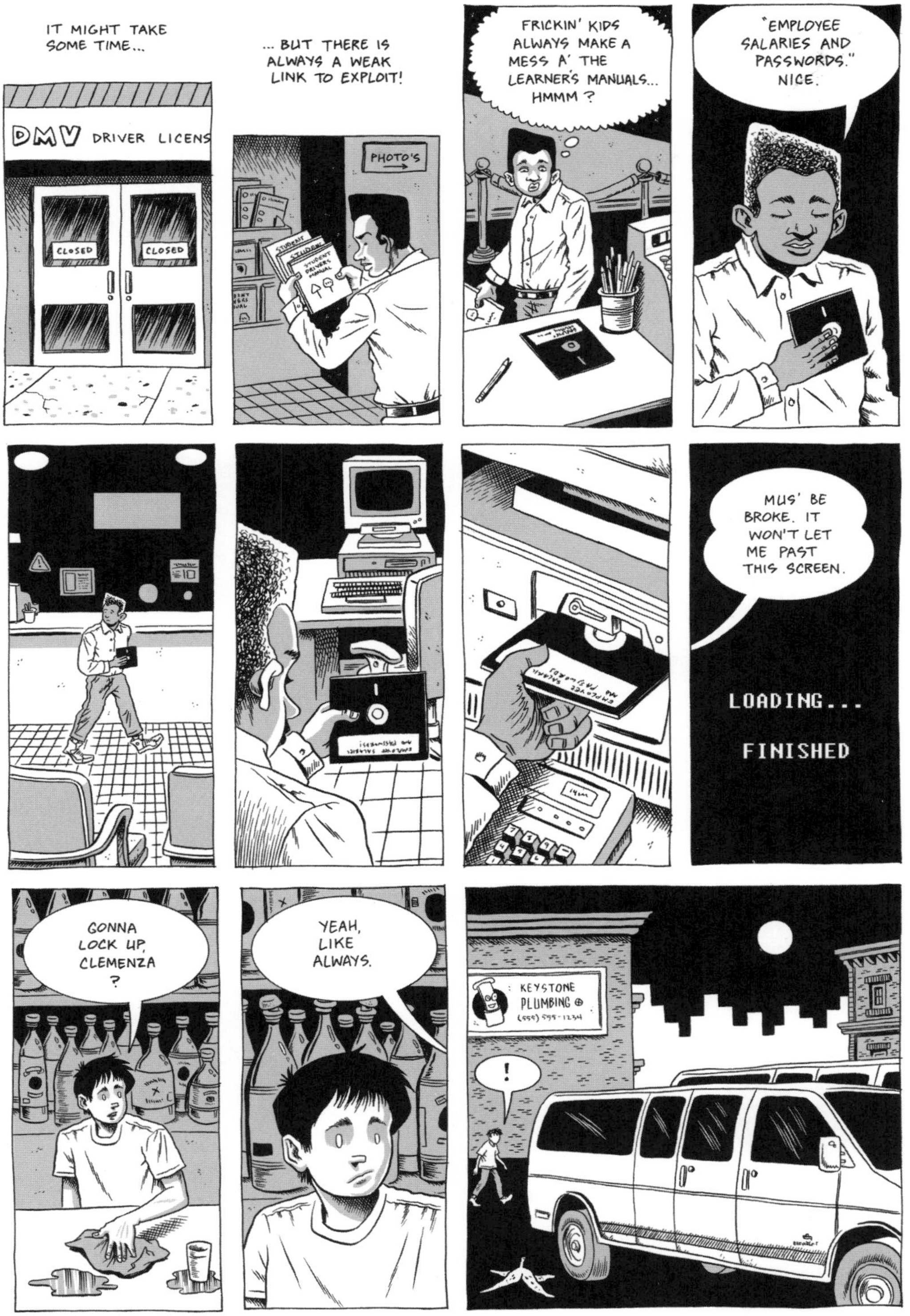
IT MIGHT TAKE SOME TIME...
DMV DRIVER LICENS
CLOSED
CLOSED
... BUT THERE IS ALWAYS A WEAK LINK TO EXPLOIT!
PHOTO'S
STUDENT DRIVERS MANUAL
FRICKIN' KIDS ALWAYS MAKE A MESS A' THE LEARNER'S MANUALS... HMMM ?
"EMPLOYEE SALARIES AND PASSWORDS." NICE.
MUS' BE BROKE. IT WON'T LET ME PAST THIS SCREEN.
LOADING...
FINISHED
GONNA LOCK UP, CLEMENZA ?
YEAH, LIKE ALWAYS.
KEYSTONE PLUMBING
(555) 555-1234
!

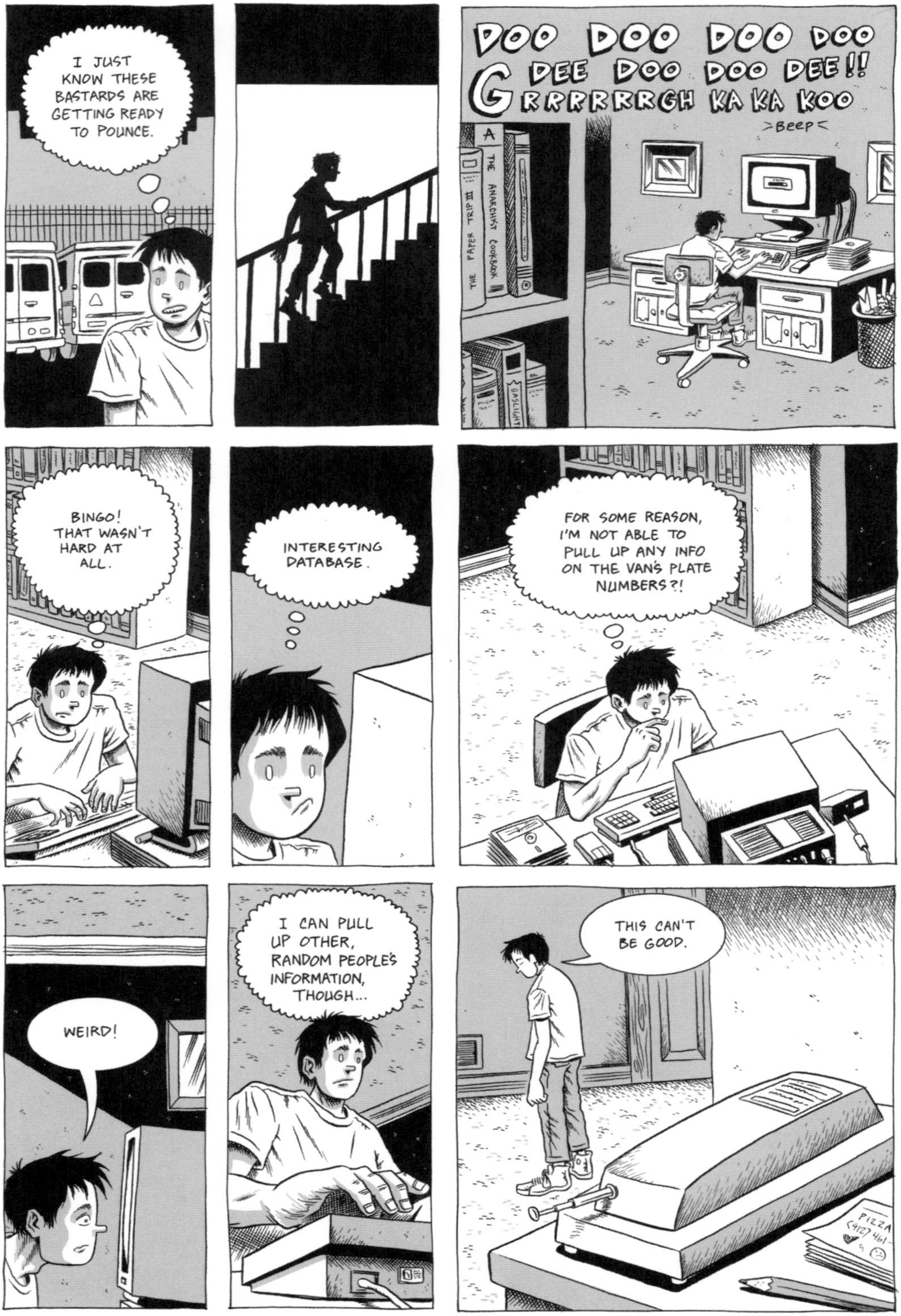
I JUST KNOW THESE BASTARDS ARE GETTING READY TO POUNCE.
DOO DOO DOO DOO DEE DOO DOO DEE!!
GRRRRRRGH KA KA KOO
>BEEP<
A THE ANARCHIST COOKBOOK
THE PAPER TRIP III
GASLIGHT
BINGO! THAT WASN'T HARD AT ALL.
INTERESTING DATABASE.
FOR SOME REASON, I'M NOT ABLE TO PULL UP ANY INFO ON THE VAN'S PLATE NUMBERS?!
WEIRD!
I CAN PULL UP OTHER, RANDOM PEOPLE'S INFORMATION, THOUGH...
THIS CAN'T BE GOOD.
PIZZA (412) 461-

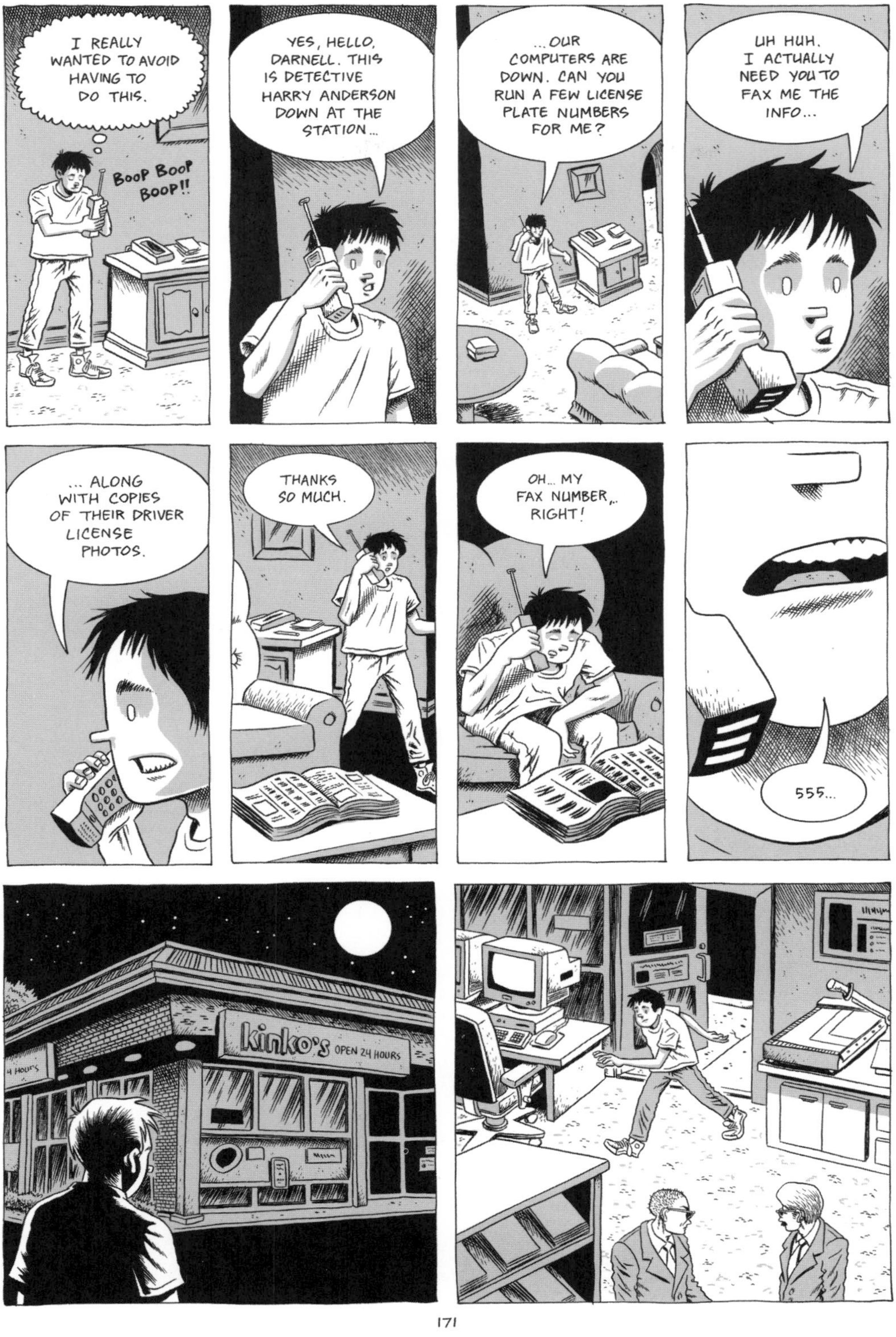
I REALLY WANTED TO AVOID HAVING TO DO THIS.
BOOP BOOP BOOP!!
YES, HELLO, DARNELL. THIS IS DETECTIVE HARRY ANDERSON DOWN AT THE STATION...
...OUR COMPUTERS ARE DOWN. CAN YOU RUN A FEW LICENSE PLATE NUMBERS FOR ME?
UH HUH. I ACTUALLY NEED YOU TO FAX ME THE INFO...
... ALONG WITH COPIES OF THEIR DRIVER LICENSE PHOTOS.
THANKS SO MUCH.
OH... MY FAX NUMBER... RIGHT!
555...
kinko's OPEN 24 HOURS

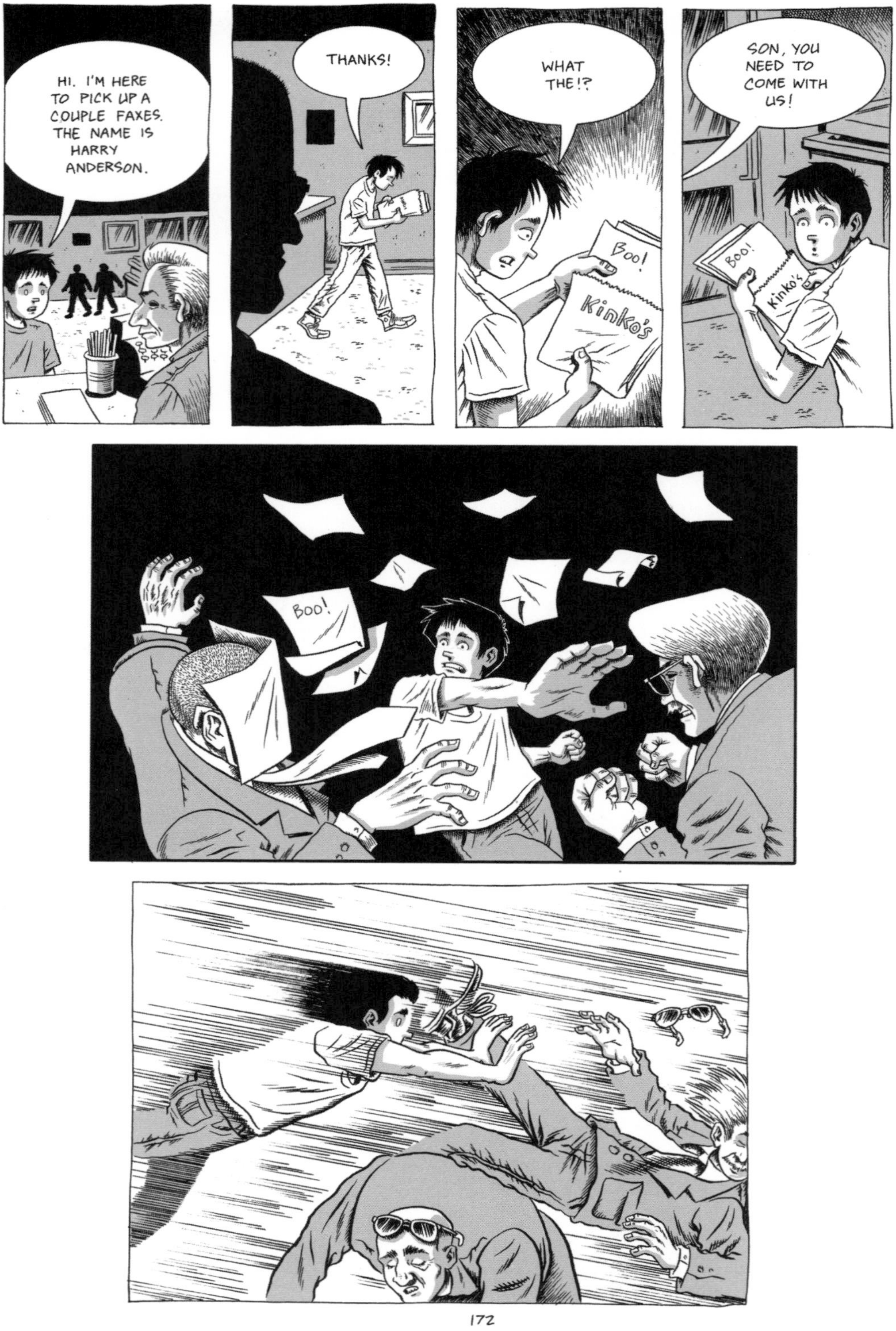
HI. I'M HERE TO PICK UP A COUPLE FAXES. THE NAME IS HARRY ANDERSON.
THANKS!
WHAT THE!?
Boo!
Kinko's
SON, YOU NEED TO COME WITH US!
Boo!
Kinko's
Boo!

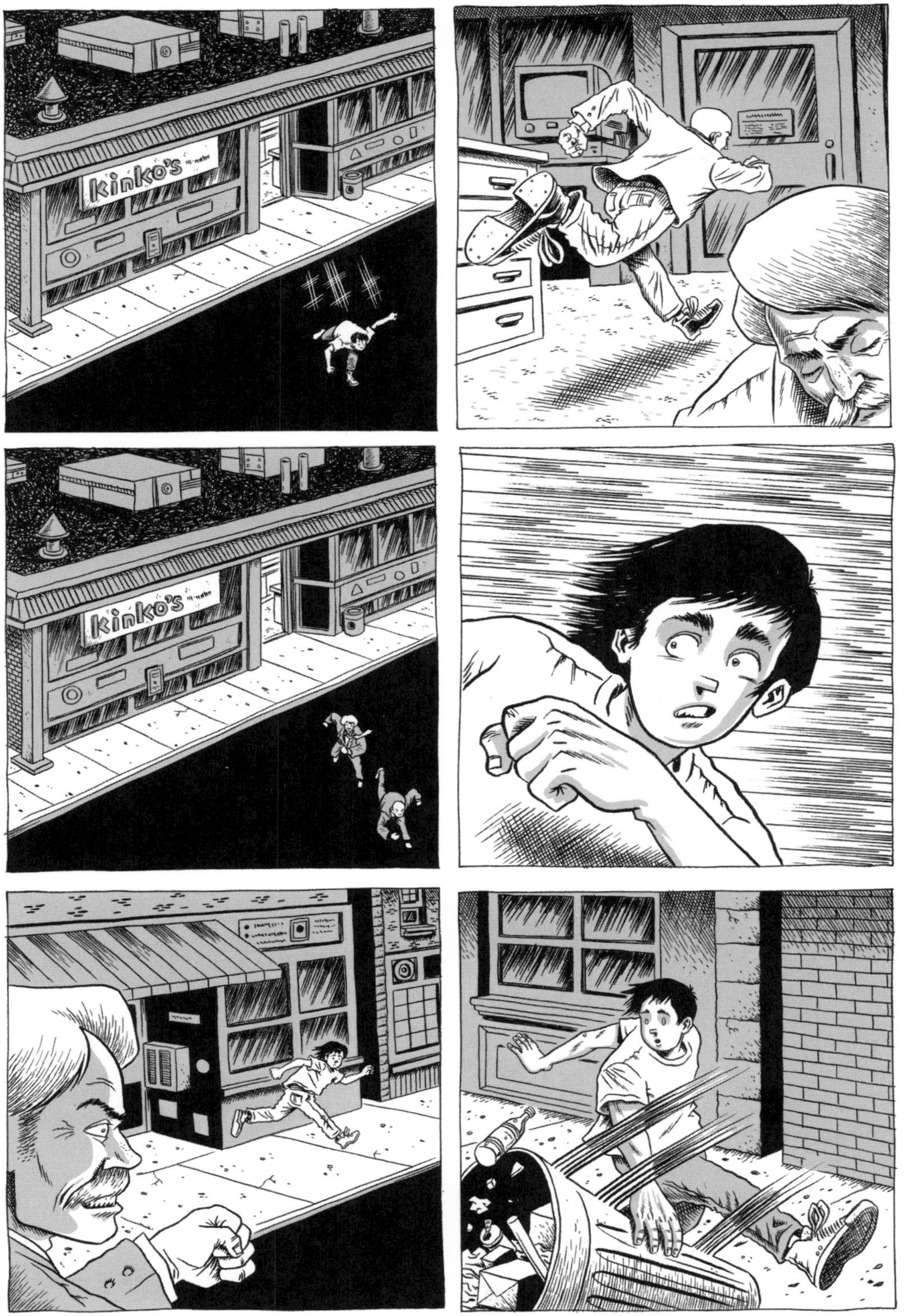
kinko's
kinko's

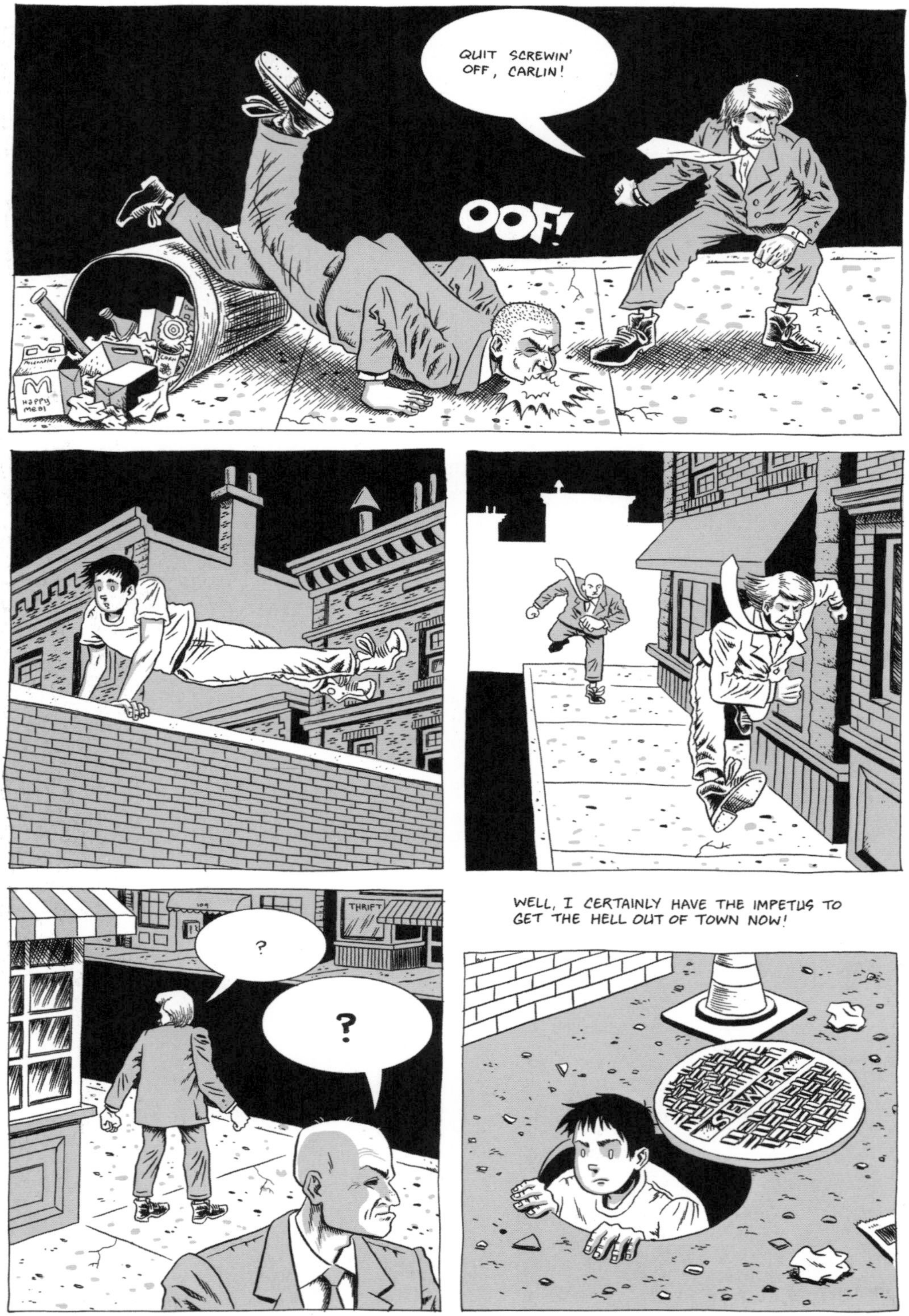
QUIT SCREWIN' OFF, CARLIN!
OOF!
Happy Meal
THRIFT
?
?
WELL, I CERTAINLY HAVE THE IMPETUS TO GET THE HELL OUT OF TOWN NOW!
SEWER

CHAPTER 6

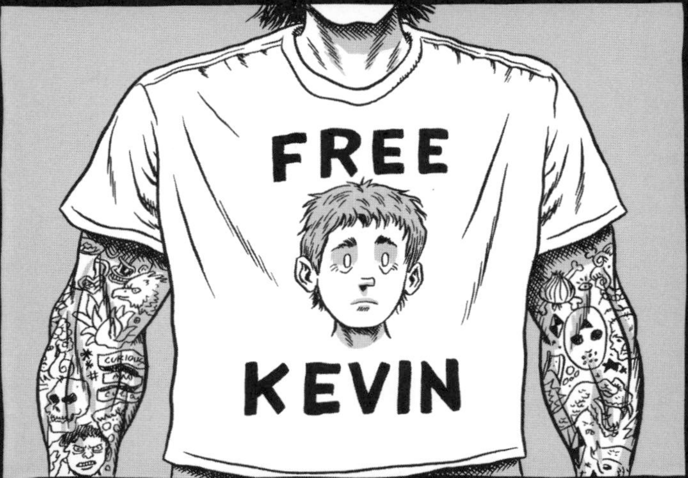
FREE
KEVIN

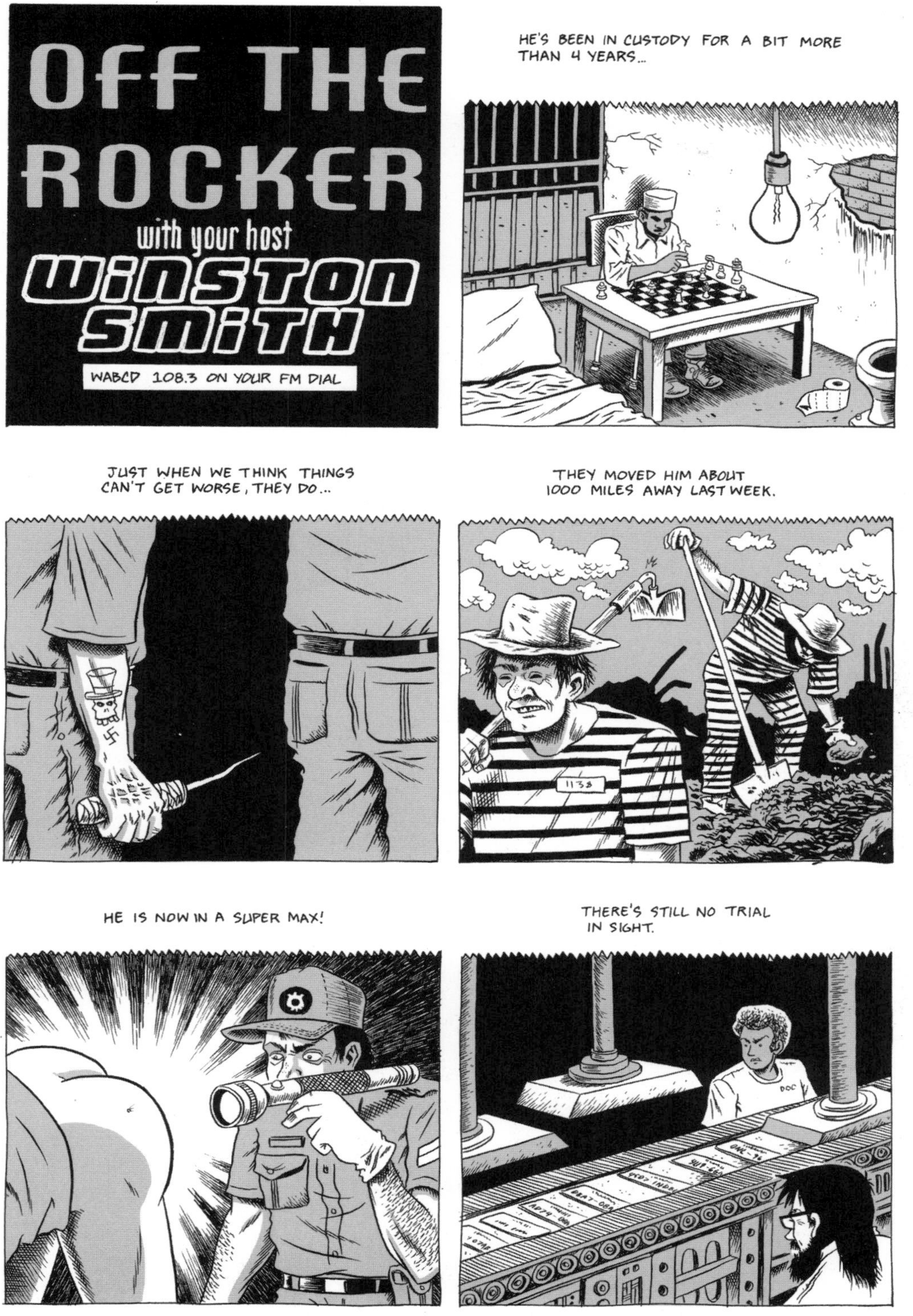
OFF THE ROCKER
with your host
WINSTON SMITH
WABCD 108.3 ON YOUR FM DIAL
HE'S BEEN IN CUSTODY FOR A BIT MORE THAN 4 YEARS...
JUST WHEN WE THINK THINGS CAN'T GET WORSE, THEY DO...
THEY MOVED HIM ABOUT 1000 MILES AWAY LAST WEEK.
1138
HE IS NOW IN A SUPER MAX!
THERE'S STILL NO TRIAL IN SIGHT.
DOC

HIS GRANDMOTHER CANNOT TRAVEL SUCH A DISTANCE TO SEE HIM.

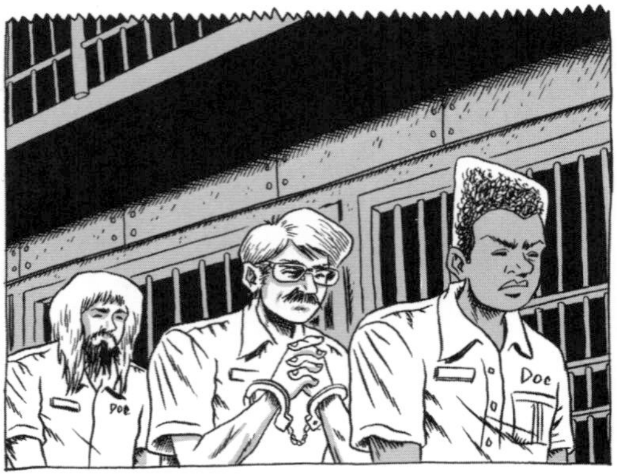
Doc

THEY HAVE OFFICIALLY SEVERED ALL OUTSIDE HUMAN CONTACT FOR KEVIN.

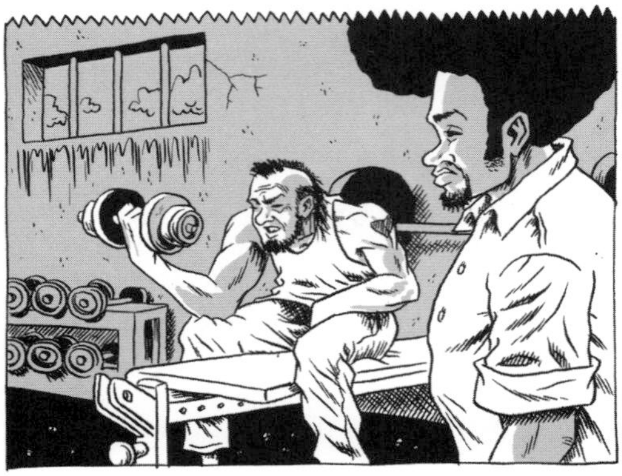

THEY'LL DO ANYTHING TO GET HIM TO CONFESS...

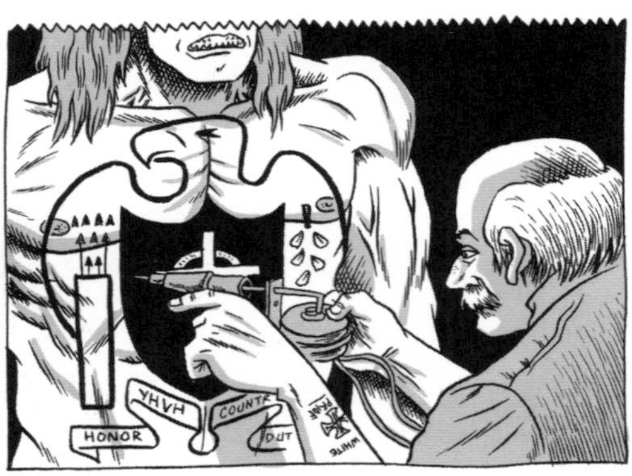
YHVH
HONOR

... BUT THEY CAN'T QUANTIFY WHAT HE IS GUILTY OF...

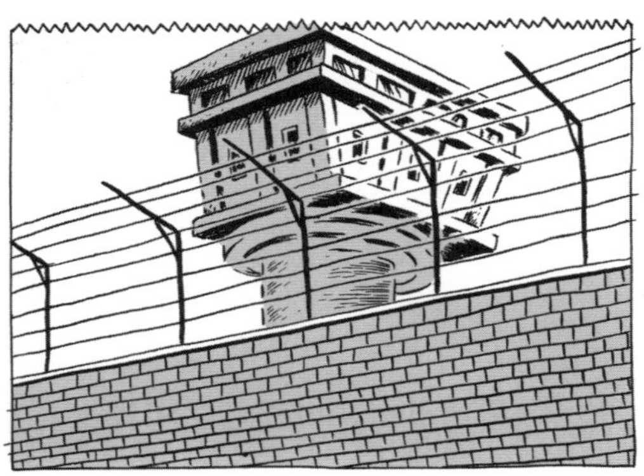

... HIS FORTITUDE AND WILLPOWER REMAIN STRONG.

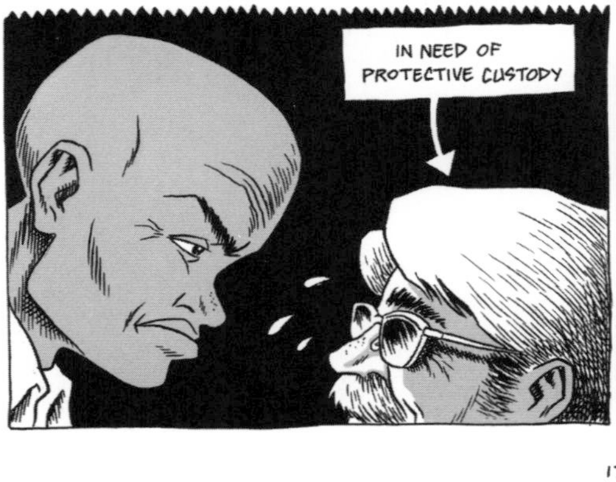
IN NEED OF PROTECTIVE CUSTODY

WHEN IS ENOUGH, ENOUGH ?

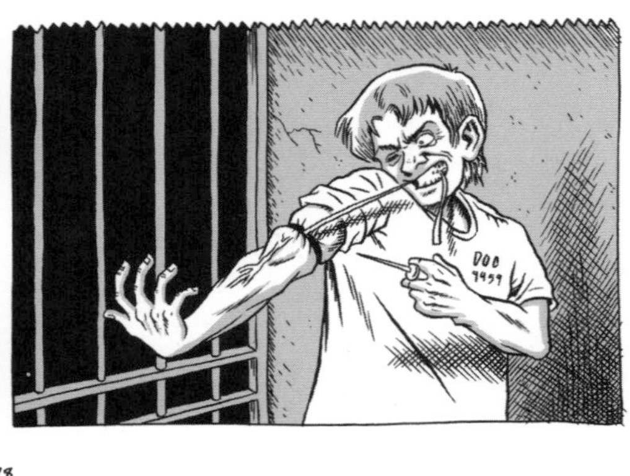

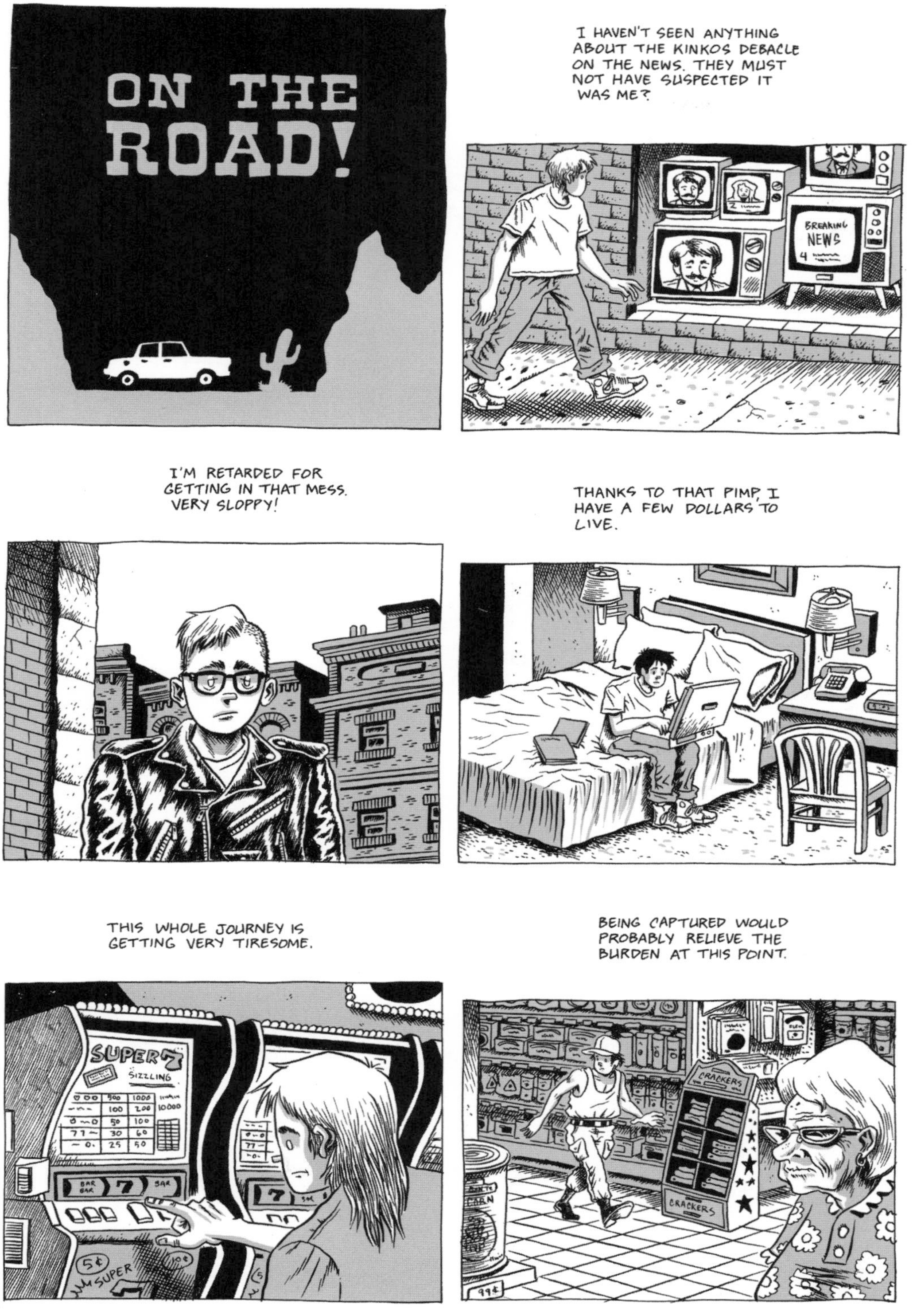
ON THE ROAD!
I HAVEN'T SEEN ANYTHING ABOUT THE KINKOS DEBACLE ON THE NEWS. THEY MUST NOT HAVE SUSPECTED IT WAS ME?
BREAKING NEWS
I'M RETARDED FOR GETTING IN THAT MESS. VERY SLOPPY!
THANKS TO THAT PIMP, I HAVE A FEW DOLLARS TO LIVE.
THIS WHOLE JOURNEY IS GETTING VERY TIRESOME.
SUPER 7
SIZZLING
5¢
SUPER
BEING CAPTURED WOULD PROBABLY RELIEVE THE BURDEN AT THIS POINT.
CRACKERS
CORN
CRACKERS
99¢

... BUT SOMETHING INSIDE WON'T LET ME QUIT.

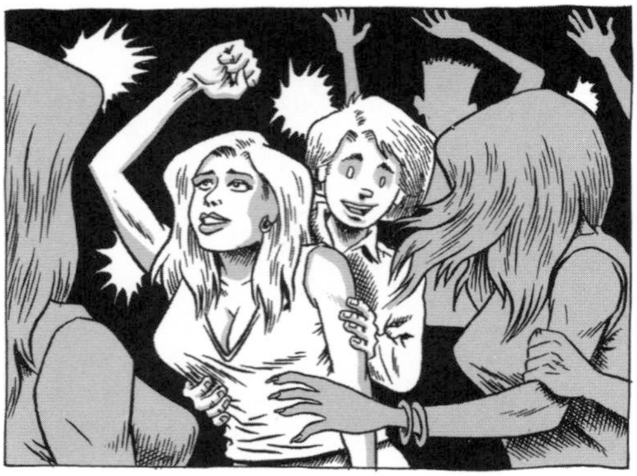

MIGHT AS WELL CONTINUE UNTIL I COMPLETELY RUN OUT OF STEAM.

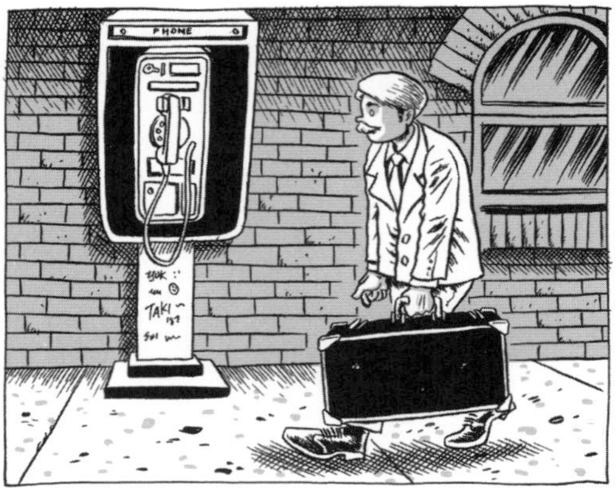
PHONE
TAKI

I'LL NEVER FORGET THAT TIME IN SOLITARY CONFINEMENT.

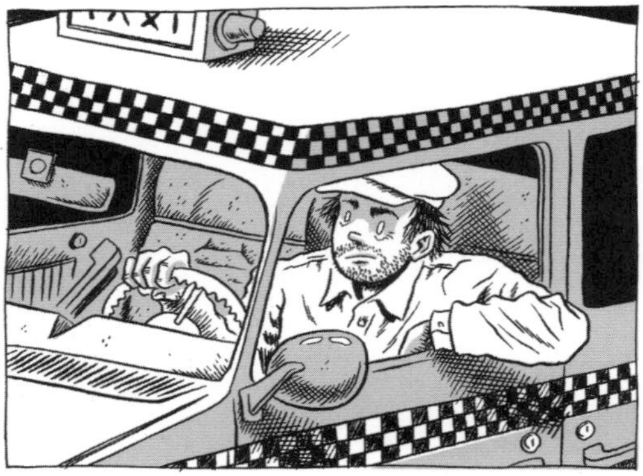

I DO KINDA MISS GRAN'MA THOUGH...

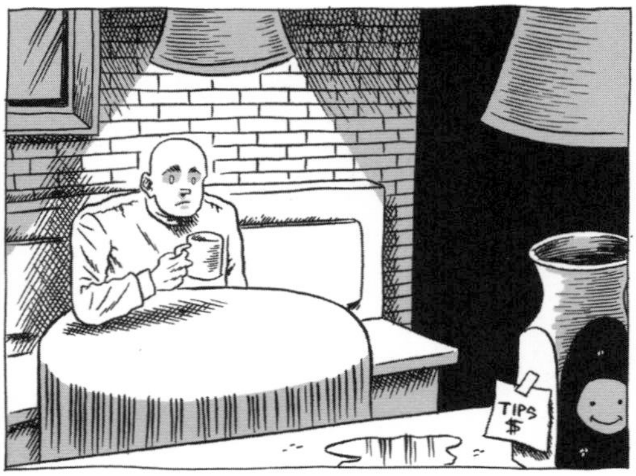
TIPS
$

GUESS I'M TOO NARCISSISTIC TO GIVE UP!

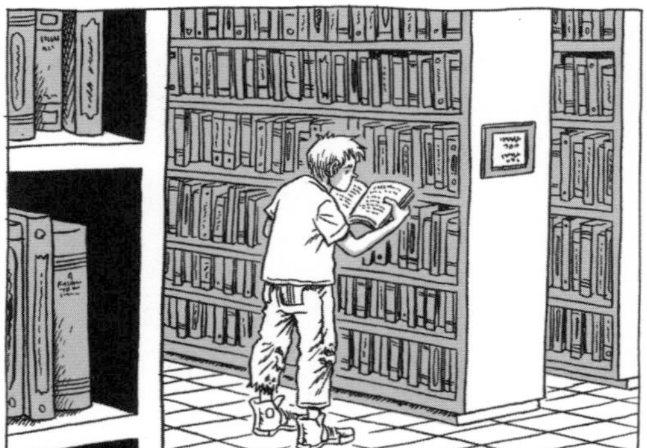

THIS IS A KIND OF PRISON IN ITSELF.

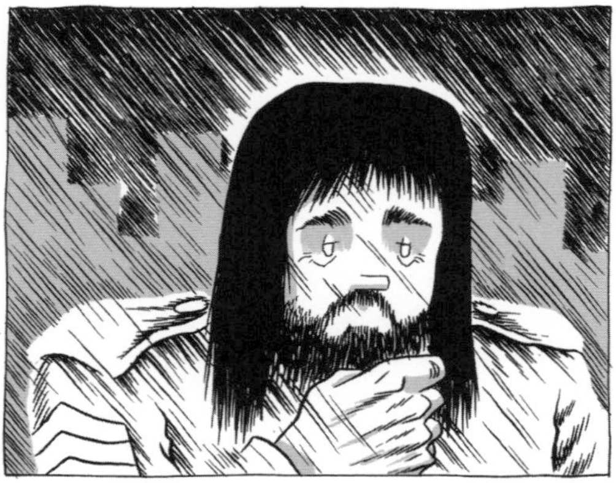

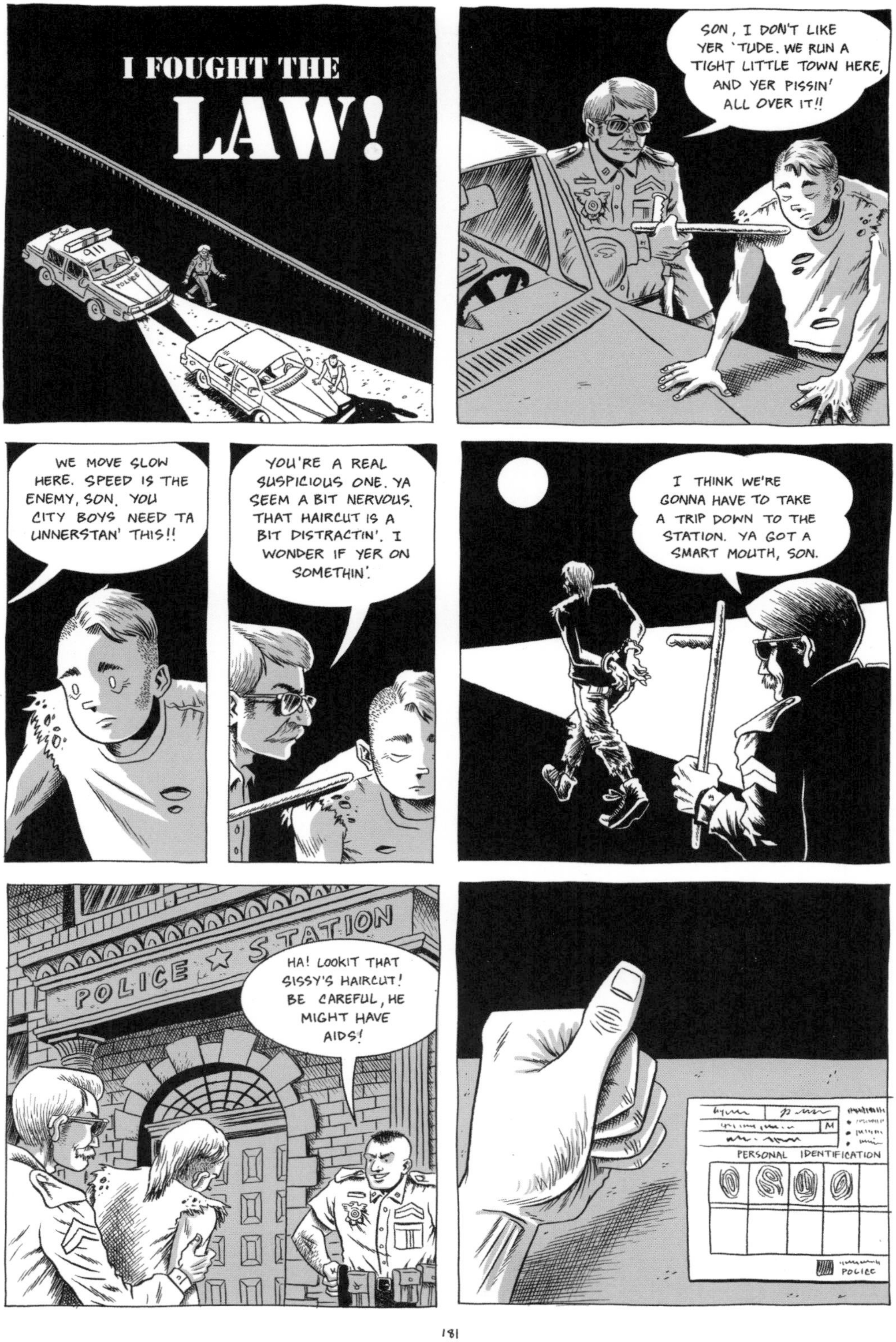
I FOUGHT THE LAW!
SON, I DON'T LIKE YER 'TUDE. WE RUN A TIGHT LITTLE TOWN HERE, AND YER PISSIN' ALL OVER IT!!
WE MOVE SLOW HERE. SPEED IS THE ENEMY, SON. YOU CITY BOYS NEED TA UNNERSTAN' THIS!!
YOU'RE A REAL SUSPICIOUS ONE. YA SEEM A BIT NERVOUS. THAT HAIRCUT IS A BIT DISTRACTIN'. I WONDER IF YER ON SOMETHIN'.
I THINK WE'RE GONNA HAVE TO TAKE A TRIP DOWN TO THE STATION. YA GOT A SMART MOUTH, SON.
POLICE ☆ STATION
HA! LOOKIT THAT SISSY'S HAIRCUT! BE CAREFUL, HE MIGHT HAVE AIDS!
PERSONAL IDENTIFICATION
POLICE

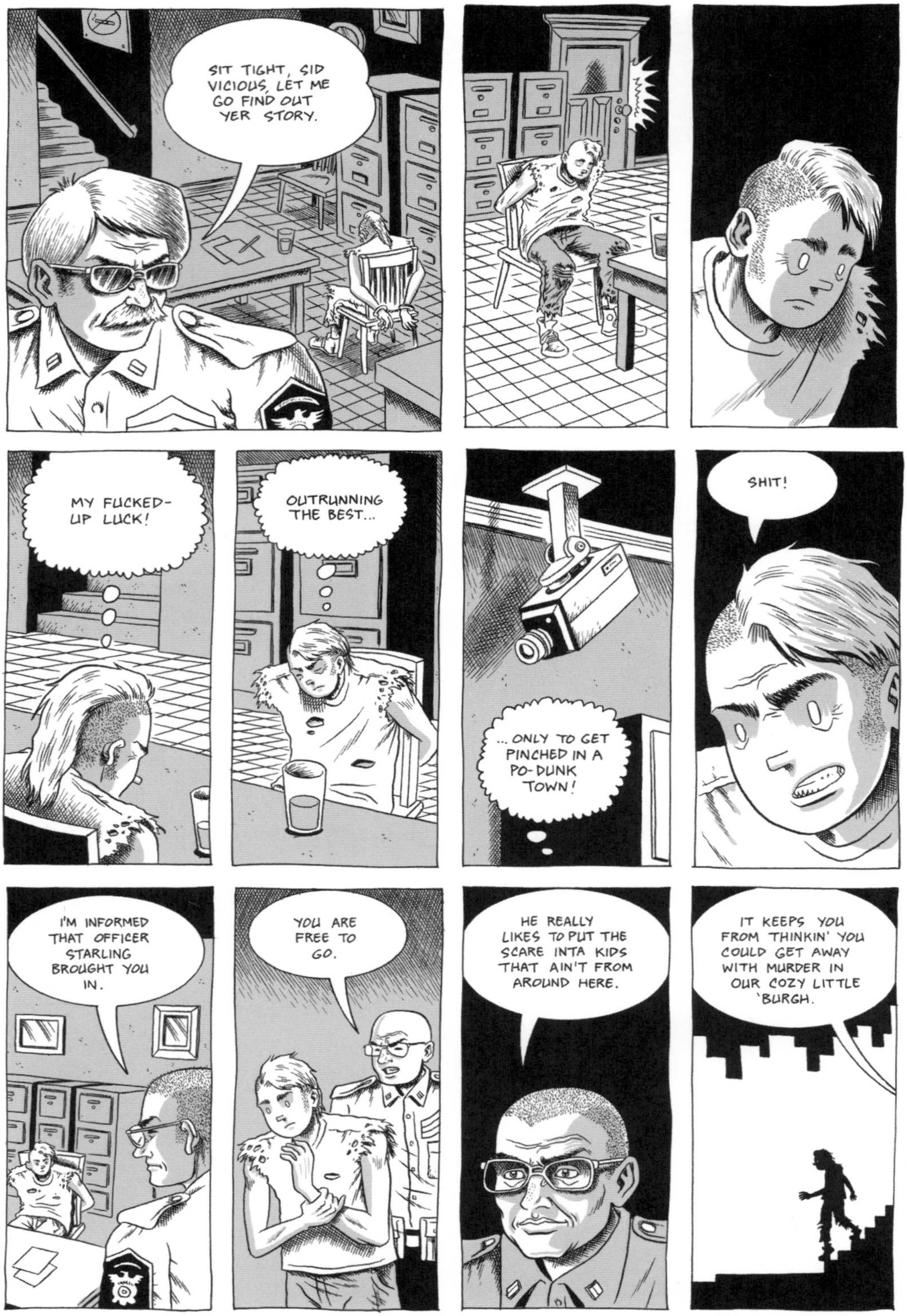
SIT TIGHT, SID VICIOUS, LET ME GO FIND OUT YER STORY.
MY FUCKED-UP LUCK!
OUTRUNNING THE BEST...
...ONLY TO GET PINCHED IN A PO-DUNK TOWN!
SHIT!
I'M INFORMED THAT OFFICER STARLING BROUGHT YOU IN.
YOU ARE FREE TO GO.
HE REALLY LIKES TO PUT THE SCARE INTA KIDS THAT AIN'T FROM AROUND HERE.
IT KEEPS YOU FROM THINKIN' YOU COULD GET AWAY WITH MURDER IN OUR COZY LITTLE 'BURGH.

Temporary Employment

UGH! I DON'T KNOW HOW PEOPLE DO THIS EVERY DAY!

GUESS I DO WAKE UP A TAD EARLIER THAN MOST.

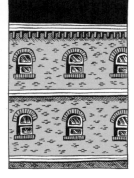

I SHOULDN'T COMPLAIN...

... I'M AT A VERY ADVANTAGEOUS POSITION.

VERY LITTLE HUMAN INTERACTION...

..A STEADY PAYCHECK...

... AND A REVOLVING DOOR OF EMPLOYEES WHO GIVE THE BOSSES NO REAL INCENTIVE TO LEARN ANYONE'S NAME.

MAKES ME CRINGE TO THINK PEOPLE SPEND MOST OF THEIR LIVES LIKE THIS.

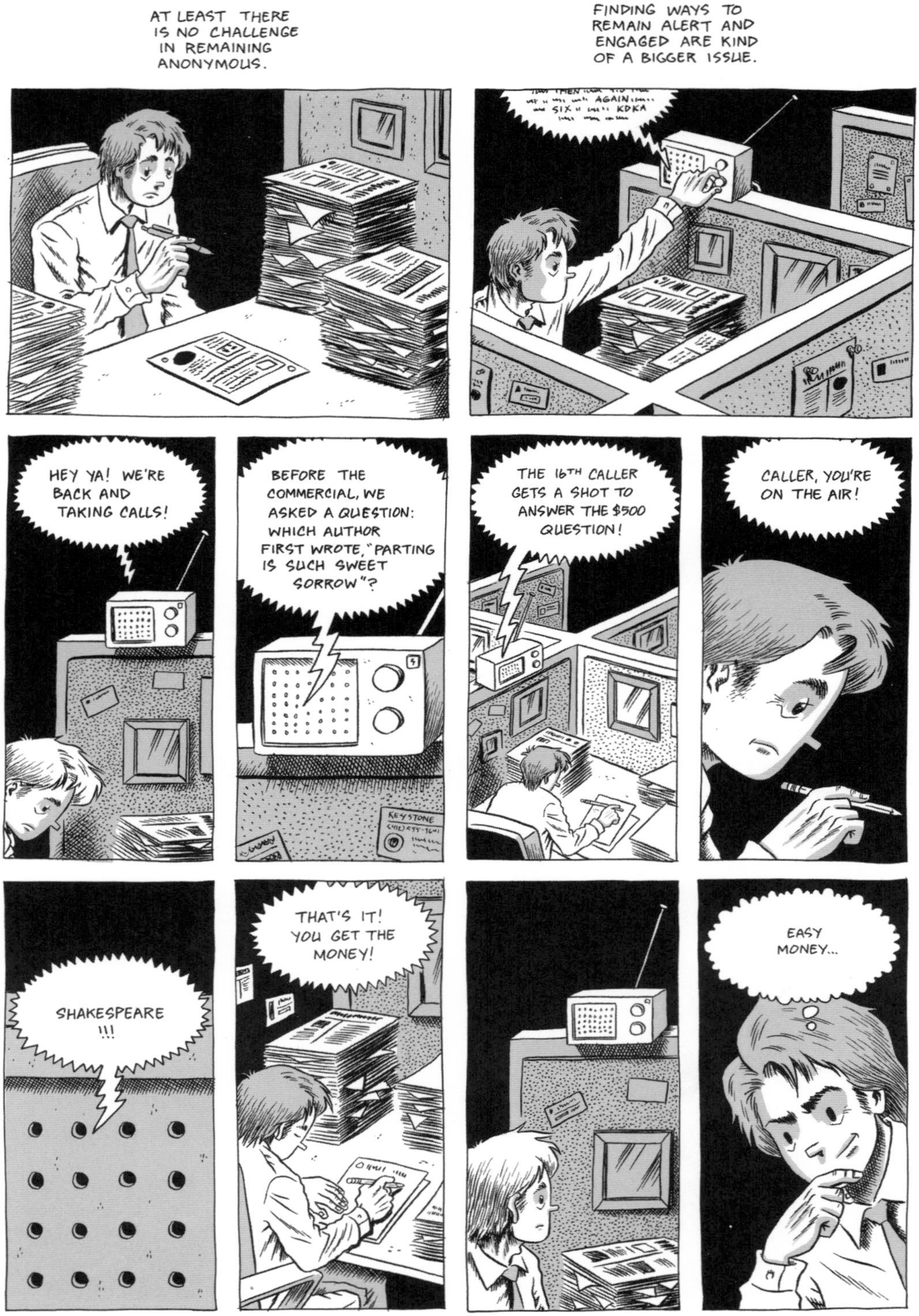
AT LEAST THERE IS NO CHALLENGE IN REMAINING ANONYMOUS.
FINDING WAYS TO REMAIN ALERT AND ENGAGED ARE KIND OF A BIGGER ISSUE.
HEY YA! WE'RE BACK AND TAKING CALLS!
BEFORE THE COMMERCIAL, WE ASKED A QUESTION: WHICH AUTHOR FIRST WROTE, "PARTING IS SUCH SWEET SORROW"?
KEYSTONE
THE 16TH CALLER GETS A SHOT TO ANSWER THE $500 QUESTION!
CALLER, YOU'RE ON THE AIR!
SHAKESPEARE !!!
THAT'S IT! YOU GET THE MONEY!
EASY MONEY...

YET ANOTHER MASTER PLAN

OR

HOW TO RIG RADIO CONTESTS FOR FUN AND PROFIT.

1. IT'S A FAIRLY SIMPLE PROCESS. TRY TO FOLLOW ALONG. IT REQUIRES MULTIPLE PHONE LINES...

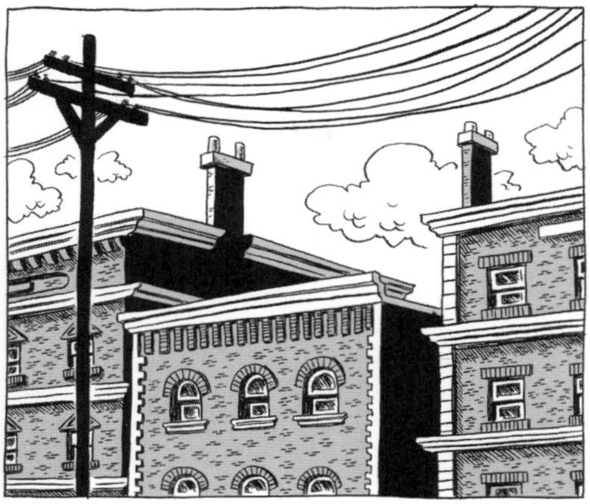

2. WITHIN ALL APARTMENT BUILDINGS THERE IS A TRUNK SOMEWHERE FULL OF THE RESIDENT'S PHONE LINES. MANY ARE UNCONNECTED. RIG THEM UP FOR YOUR OWN USE.

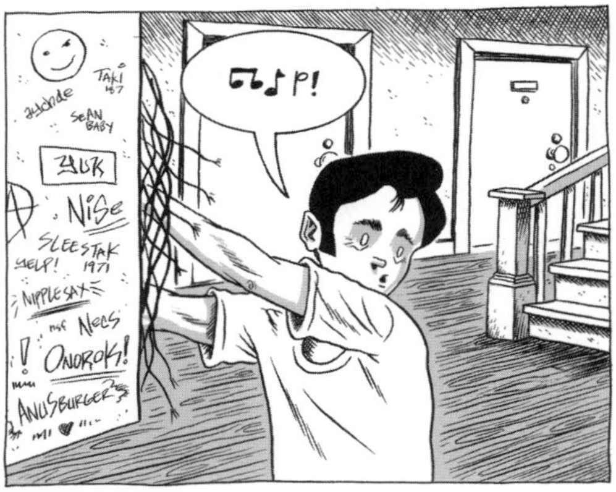
SEAN BABY
YUK
SLEESTAK
NIPPLESAX
ONOROK!
ANUSBURGER

3. HACKING INTO THE PHONE COMPANY DATABASE IN ONE CITY IS THE SAME AS ANY OTHER. GETTING INTO THEIR COMPUTERS IS ESSENTIAL.

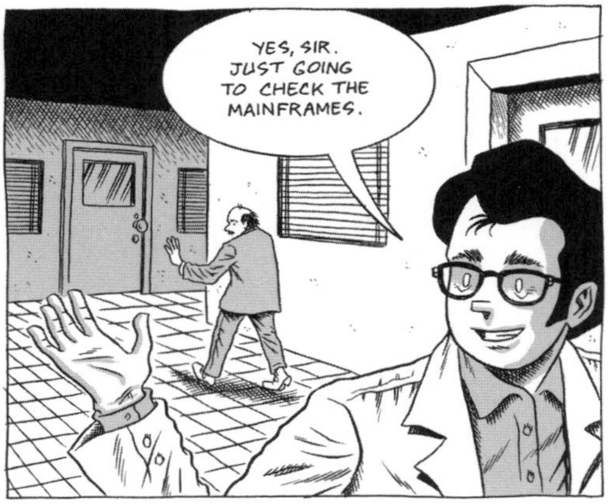
YES, SIR. JUST GOING TO CHECK THE MAINFRAMES.

4. CREATE A LOOP BY DIVERTING THE PHONE LINES AT THE RADIO STATION TO YOUR NEWLY ACTIVATED PHONES.

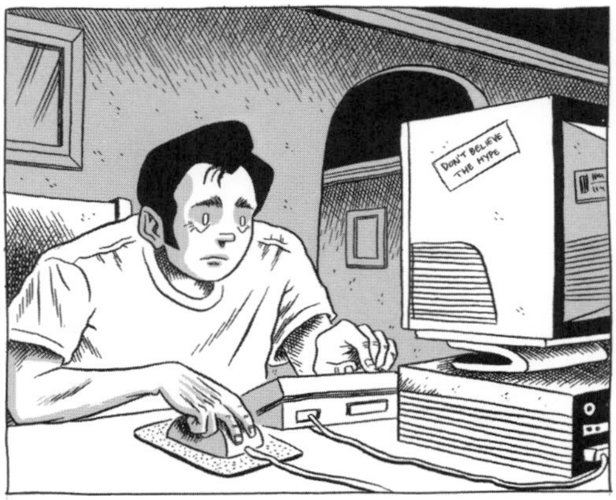
DON'T BELIEVE THE HYPE

5. ADD CALL FORWARDING(*72) ONTO YOUR PHONES AND SEND THE CALLS BACK TO THE RADIO STATION.

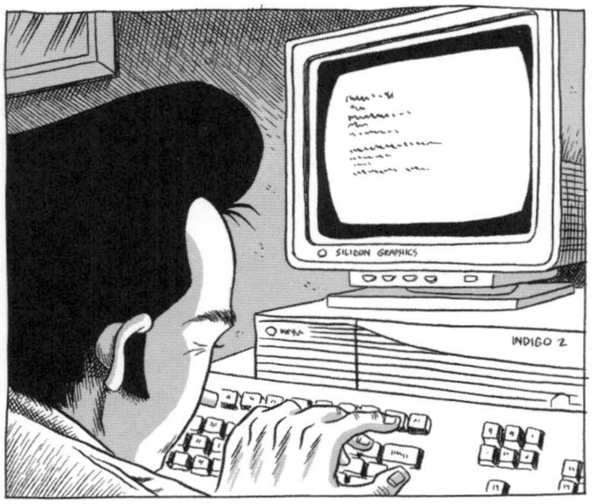
SILICON GRAPHICS
INDIGO 2

6. THIS WAY THE CALLS STILL GET BACK TO THE RADIO DJ THROUGH YOUR CONNECTION, AND THEY'RE NONE THE WISER.

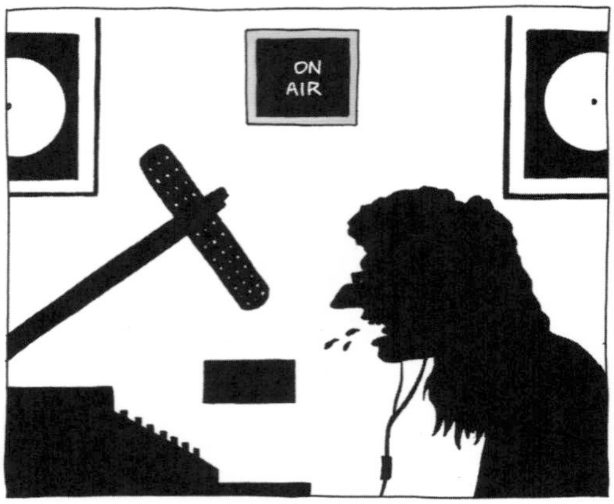
ON AIR

7. EVERY TIME SOMEONE CALLS THE STATION, YOU WILL HEAR A SINGLE RING ON YOUR PHONE INDICATING THAT THE CALL IS BEING FORWARDED.

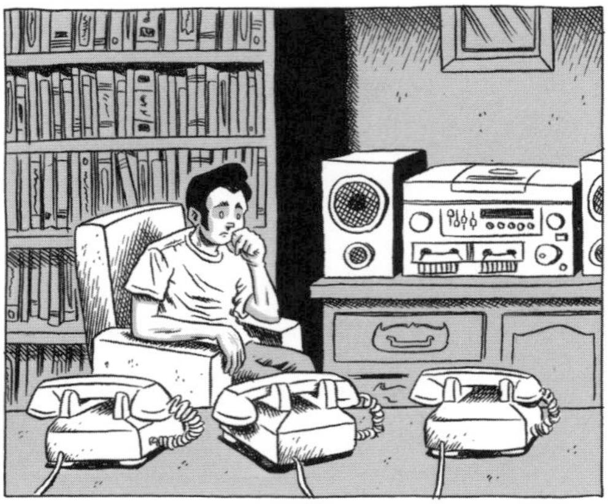

8. THIS IS EXTREMELY HELPFUL WHEN PARTICIPATING IN A RADIO CALL-IN CONTEST THAT REQUIRES PICKING UP THE 75TH CALLER FOR INSTANCE.

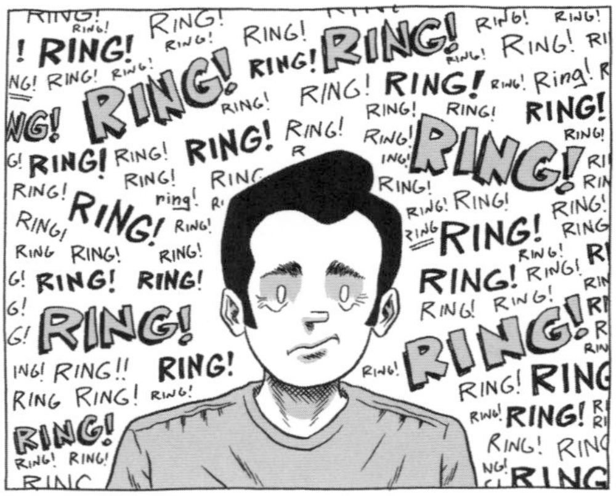
RING!
RING!
RING!
RING!
RING!

9. WHEN YOU HEAR ENOUGH RINGS AS THE WINNING CALL APPROACHES, HIT *72 TO STOP CALL FORWARDING, AND YOU WILL ROUTE ALL CALLERS BACK TO YOUR PHONE LINES.

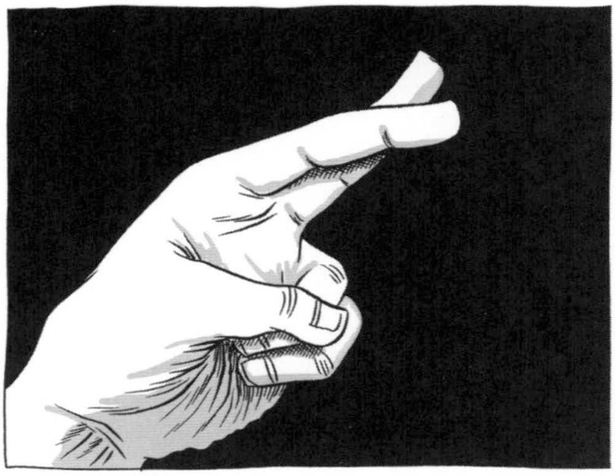

10. YOU'LL HAVE TO MAKE A FEW CALLS TO THE STATION USING DIFFERENT VOICES IF YOU TURNED OFF FORWARDING A BIT EARLY, BUT YOU WILL CERTAINLY BE THE WINNING CALLER IF YOU FOLLOW EVERY STEP PROPERLY.

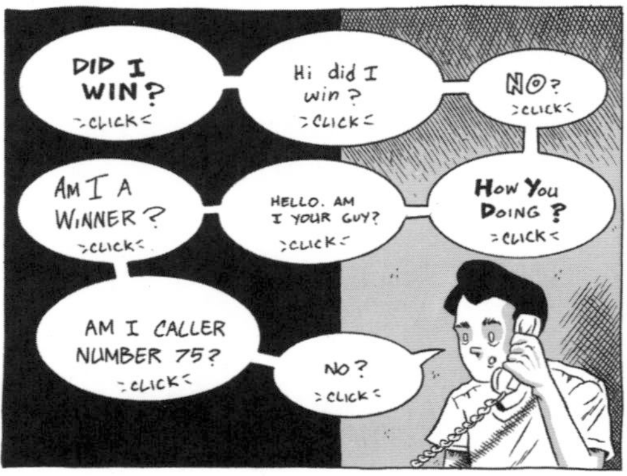
DID I WIN? >CLICK<
Hi did I win? >CLICK<
NO? >CLICK<
HOW YOU DOING? >CLICK<
HELLO. AM I YOUR GUY? >CLICK<
AM I A WINNER? >CLICK<
AM I CALLER NUMBER 75? >CLICK<
NO? >CLICK<

11. THE CHECKS/PRIZES SHOULD ARRIVE WITHIN A WEEK OR SO.

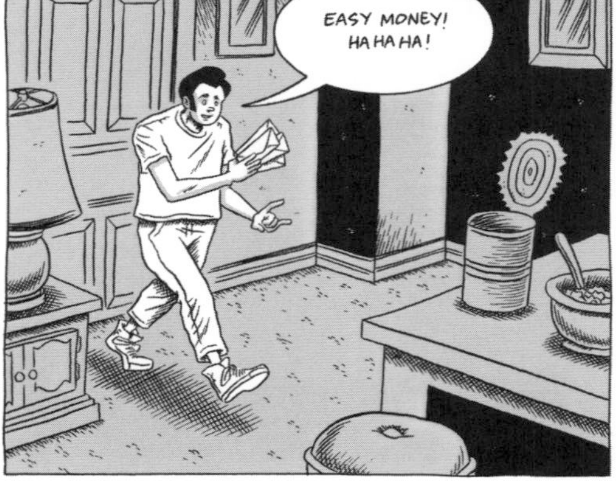
EASY MONEY! HA HA HA!

DOLLY, THE DRUNK...

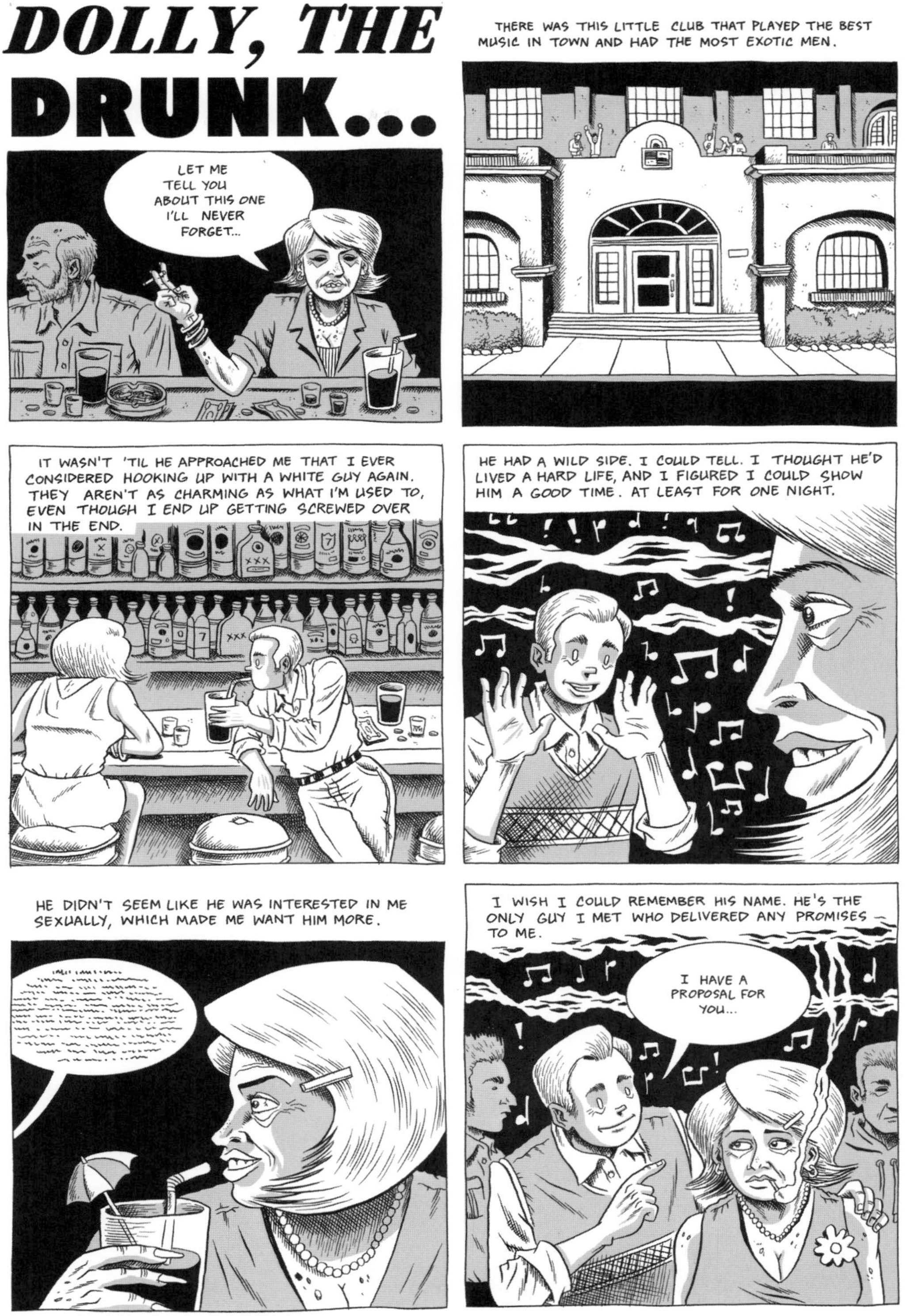
THERE WAS THIS LITTLE CLUB THAT PLAYED THE BEST MUSIC IN TOWN AND HAD THE MOST EXOTIC MEN.
LET ME TELL YOU ABOUT THIS ONE I'LL NEVER FORGET...
IT WASN'T 'TIL HE APPROACHED ME THAT I EVER CONSIDERED HOOKING UP WITH A WHITE GUY AGAIN. THEY AREN'T AS CHARMING AS WHAT I'M USED TO, EVEN THOUGH I END UP GETTING SCREWED OVER IN THE END.
HE HAD A WILD SIDE. I COULD TELL. I THOUGHT HE'D LIVED A HARD LIFE, AND I FIGURED I COULD SHOW HIM A GOOD TIME. AT LEAST FOR ONE NIGHT.
HE DIDN'T SEEM LIKE HE WAS INTERESTED IN ME SEXUALLY, WHICH MADE ME WANT HIM MORE.
I WISH I COULD REMEMBER HIS NAME. HE'S THE ONLY GUY I MET WHO DELIVERED ANY PROMISES TO ME.
I HAVE A PROPOSAL FOR YOU...

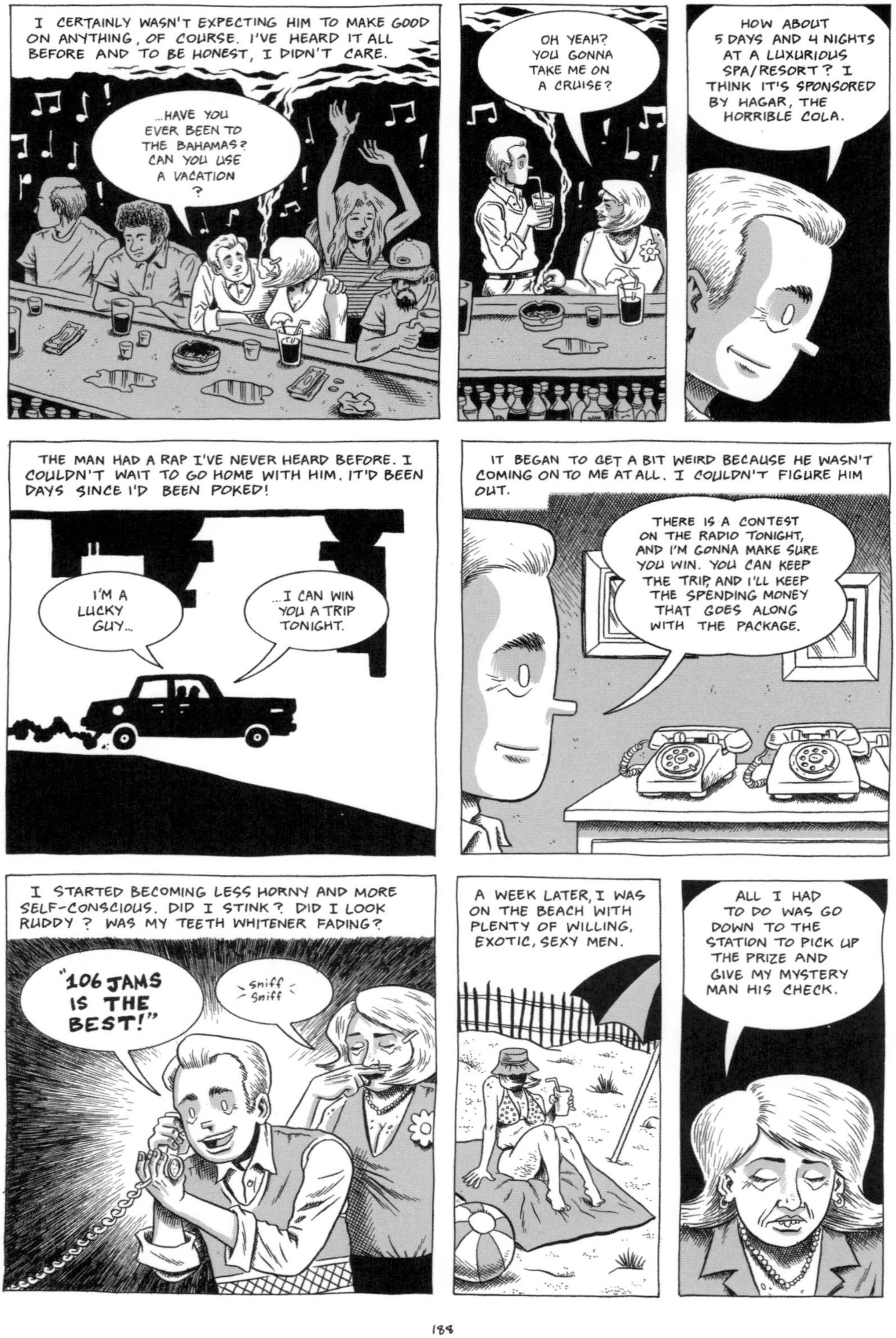
I CERTAINLY WASN'T EXPECTING HIM TO MAKE GOOD ON ANYTHING, OF COURSE. I'VE HEARD IT ALL BEFORE AND TO BE HONEST, I DIDN'T CARE.
...HAVE YOU EVER BEEN TO THE BAHAMAS? CAN YOU USE A VACATION ?
OH YEAH? YOU GONNA TAKE ME ON A CRUISE?
HOW ABOUT 5 DAYS AND 4 NIGHTS AT A LUXURIOUS SPA/RESORT? I THINK IT'S SPONSORED BY HAGAR, THE HORRIBLE COLA.
THE MAN HAD A RAP I'VE NEVER HEARD BEFORE. I COULDN'T WAIT TO GO HOME WITH HIM. IT'D BEEN DAYS SINCE I'D BEEN POKED!
I'M A LUCKY GUY...
...I CAN WIN YOU A TRIP TONIGHT.
IT BEGAN TO GET A BIT WEIRD BECAUSE HE WASN'T COMING ON TO ME AT ALL. I COULDN'T FIGURE HIM OUT.
THERE IS A CONTEST ON THE RADIO TONIGHT, AND I'M GONNA MAKE SURE YOU WIN. YOU CAN KEEP THE TRIP, AND I'LL KEEP THE SPENDING MONEY THAT GOES ALONG WITH THE PACKAGE.
I STARTED BECOMING LESS HORNY AND MORE SELF-CONSCIOUS. DID I STINK? DID I LOOK RUDDY? WAS MY TEETH WHITENER FADING?
"106 JAMS IS THE BEST!"
Sniff Sniff
A WEEK LATER, I WAS ON THE BEACH WITH PLENTY OF WILLING, EXOTIC, SEXY MEN.
ALL I HAD TO DO WAS GO DOWN TO THE STATION TO PICK UP THE PRIZE AND GIVE MY MYSTERY MAN HIS CHECK.

MORE
HAPPY
WINNERS

NAME: JENNY BLUMPKIN
PRIZE: A TRIP TO CANCUN & SPENDING CASH
KEV'S CUT: $3000

> OUR MAGIC ANSWER WAS "STANLEY KIRK BURRELL!"

JENNY'S VICE: OPIATES

NAME: SANDRA McGEE
HER TAKE: A SHOPPING SPREE AT THE MALL.
KEVIN'S CUT: A NEO-GEO GAME CONSOLE AND
      $500 WORTH OF SOFTWARE

> HE WON THE PRIZE BY BEING THE 25TH CALLER.

SANDRA'S VICE: PROMISCUITY

NAME: JANE JACOBS
SHE GOT: 2 TICKETS TO THE BALL GAME
KEVIN EARNED: $1000 WORTH OF OTHER GIFTS

> I KNEW THE ANSWER TO THIS ONE...

> ...ERIC CLAPTON, JEFF BECK, AND JIMMY PAGE!

JANE'S PROBLEM: SEVERE CO-DEPENDENCY

NAME: ANGEL BRIDGES
WON: BBQ RIBS AND MONSTER TRUCK TICKETS
KEV'S CUT: $200

> "BOB CHANDLER" WAS THE ANSWER THAT GOT ME SOME FRONT-ROW SEATS.

ANGEL'S ADDICTION: CHOCOLATE & CRYSTAL METH.

NAME: JESSICA WILSON
HER PART: A TRIP TO THE GRAND CANYON
KEVIN'S PART: $2000

> HE WAS JUST A CERTAIN CALLER # OR SUMPTHIN'...

> ...I GUESS.

JESSICA HAS BEEN DIAGNOSED BI POLAR

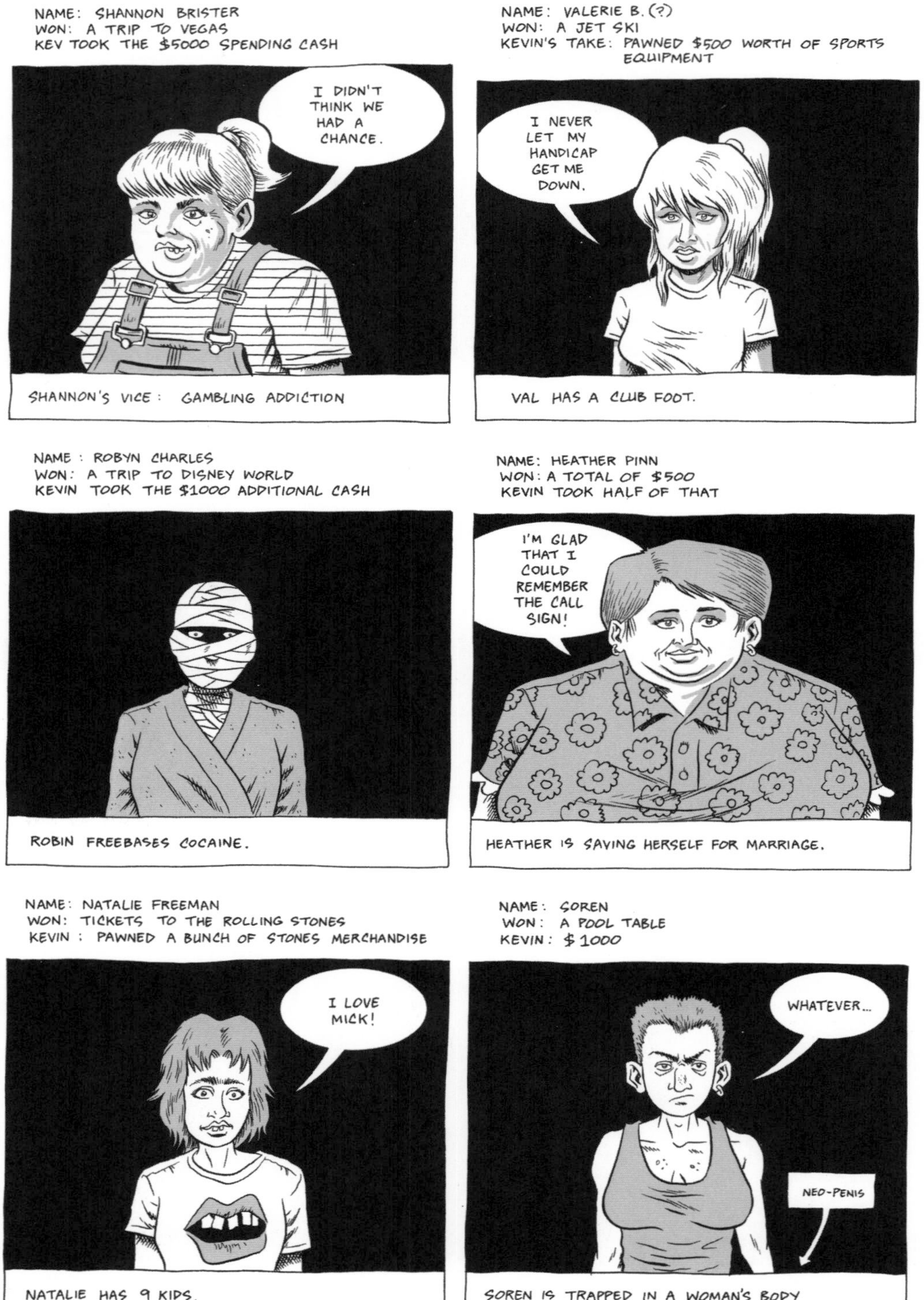
NAME: SHANNON BRISTER
WON: A TRIP TO VEGAS
KEV TOOK THE $5000 SPENDING CASH
I DIDN'T THINK WE HAD A CHANCE.
SHANNON'S VICE: GAMBLING ADDICTION
NAME: VALERIE B. (?)
WON: A JET SKI
KEVIN'S TAKE: PAWNED $500 WORTH OF SPORTS EQUIPMENT
I NEVER LET MY HANDICAP GET ME DOWN.
VAL HAS A CLUB FOOT.
NAME: ROBYN CHARLES
WON: A TRIP TO DISNEY WORLD
KEVIN TOOK THE $1000 ADDITIONAL CASH
ROBIN FREEBASES COCAINE.
NAME: HEATHER PINN
WON: A TOTAL OF $500
KEVIN TOOK HALF OF THAT
I'M GLAD THAT I COULD REMEMBER THE CALL SIGN!
HEATHER IS SAVING HERSELF FOR MARRIAGE.
NAME: NATALIE FREEMAN
WON: TICKETS TO THE ROLLING STONES
KEVIN: PAWNED A BUNCH OF STONES MERCHANDISE
I LOVE MICK!
NATALIE HAS 9 KIDS.
NAME: SOREN
WON: A POOL TABLE
KEVIN: $1000
WHATEVER...
NEO-PENIS
SOREN IS TRAPPED IN A WOMAN'S BODY

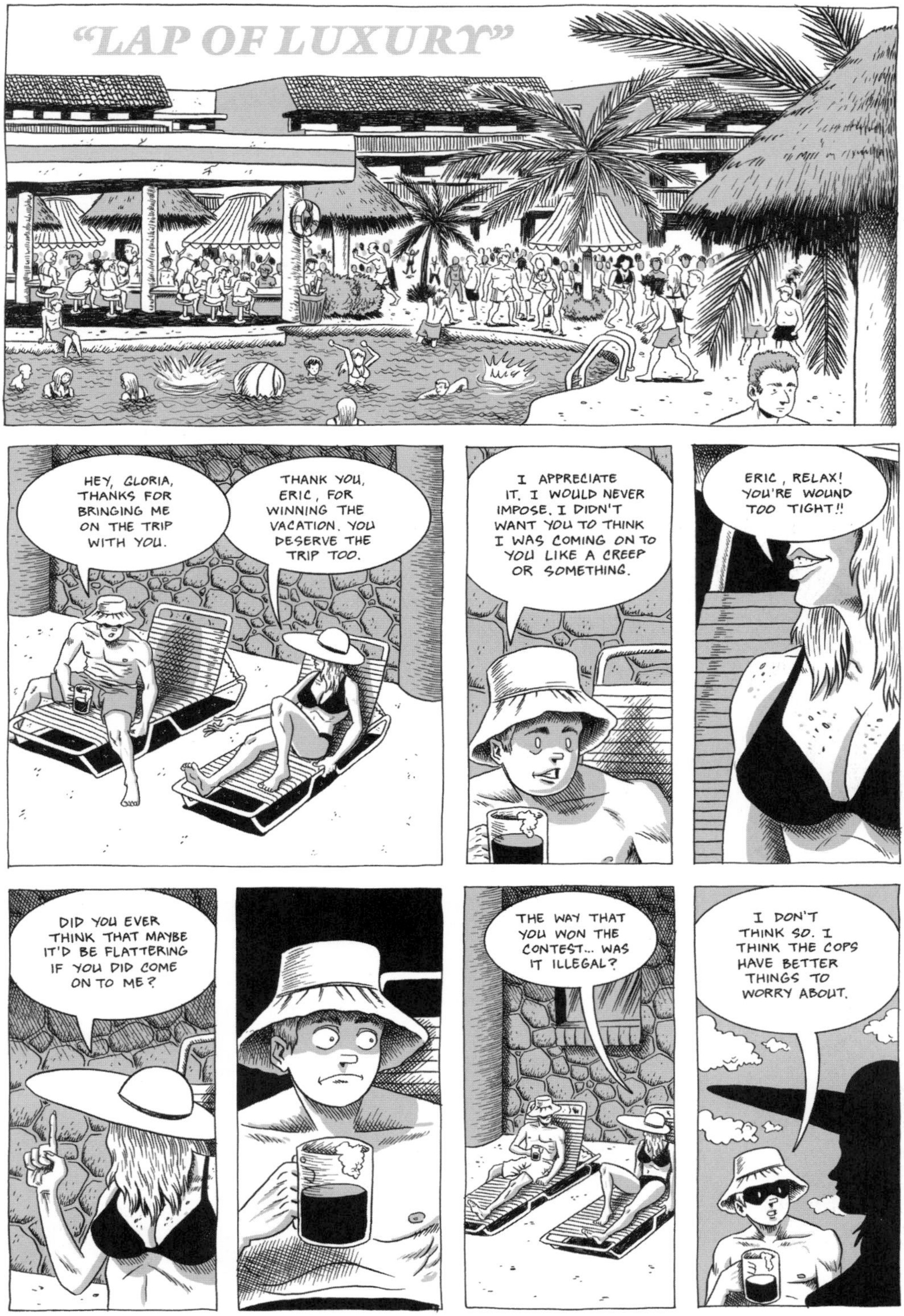
"LAP OF LUXURY"
HEY, GLORIA, THANKS FOR BRINGING ME ON THE TRIP WITH YOU.
THANK YOU, ERIC, FOR WINNING THE VACATION. YOU DESERVE THE TRIP TOO.
I APPRECIATE IT. I WOULD NEVER IMPOSE. I DIDN'T WANT YOU TO THINK I WAS COMING ON TO YOU LIKE A CREEP OR SOMETHING.
ERIC, RELAX! YOU'RE WOUND TOO TIGHT!!
DID YOU EVER THINK THAT MAYBE IT'D BE FLATTERING IF YOU DID COME ON TO ME?
THE WAY THAT YOU WON THE CONTEST... WAS IT ILLEGAL?
I DON'T THINK SO. I THINK THE COPS HAVE BETTER THINGS TO WORRY ABOUT.

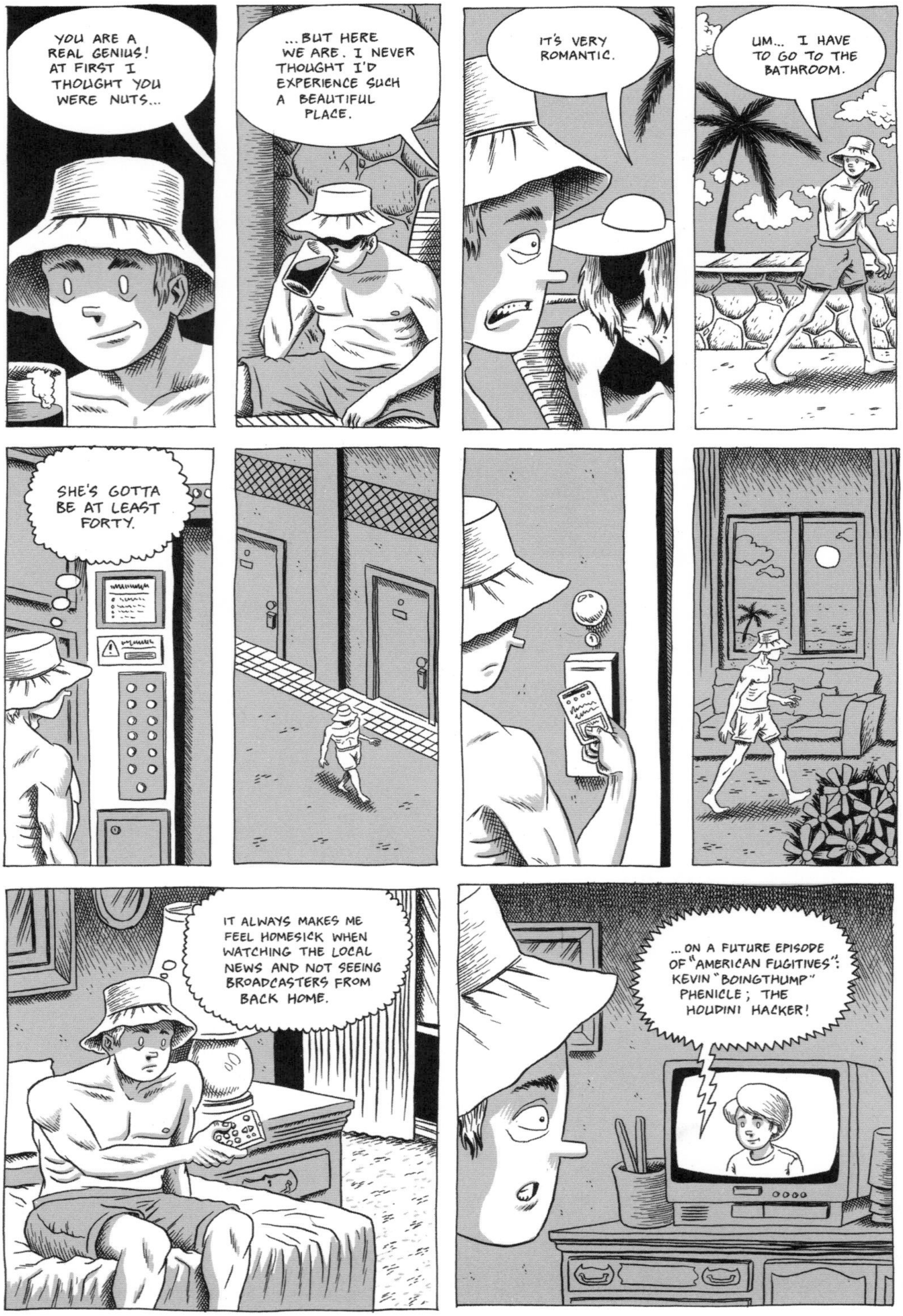
YOU ARE A REAL GENIUS! AT FIRST I THOUGHT YOU WERE NUTS...
...BUT HERE WE ARE. I NEVER THOUGHT I'D EXPERIENCE SUCH A BEAUTIFUL PLACE.
IT'S VERY ROMANTIC.
UM... I HAVE TO GO TO THE BATHROOM.
SHE'S GOTTA BE AT LEAST FORTY.
IT ALWAYS MAKES ME FEEL HOMESICK WHEN WATCHING THE LOCAL NEWS AND NOT SEEING BROADCASTERS FROM BACK HOME.
...ON A FUTURE EPISODE OF "AMERICAN FUGITIVES": KEVIN "BOINGTHUMP" PHENICLE; THE HOUDINI HACKER!

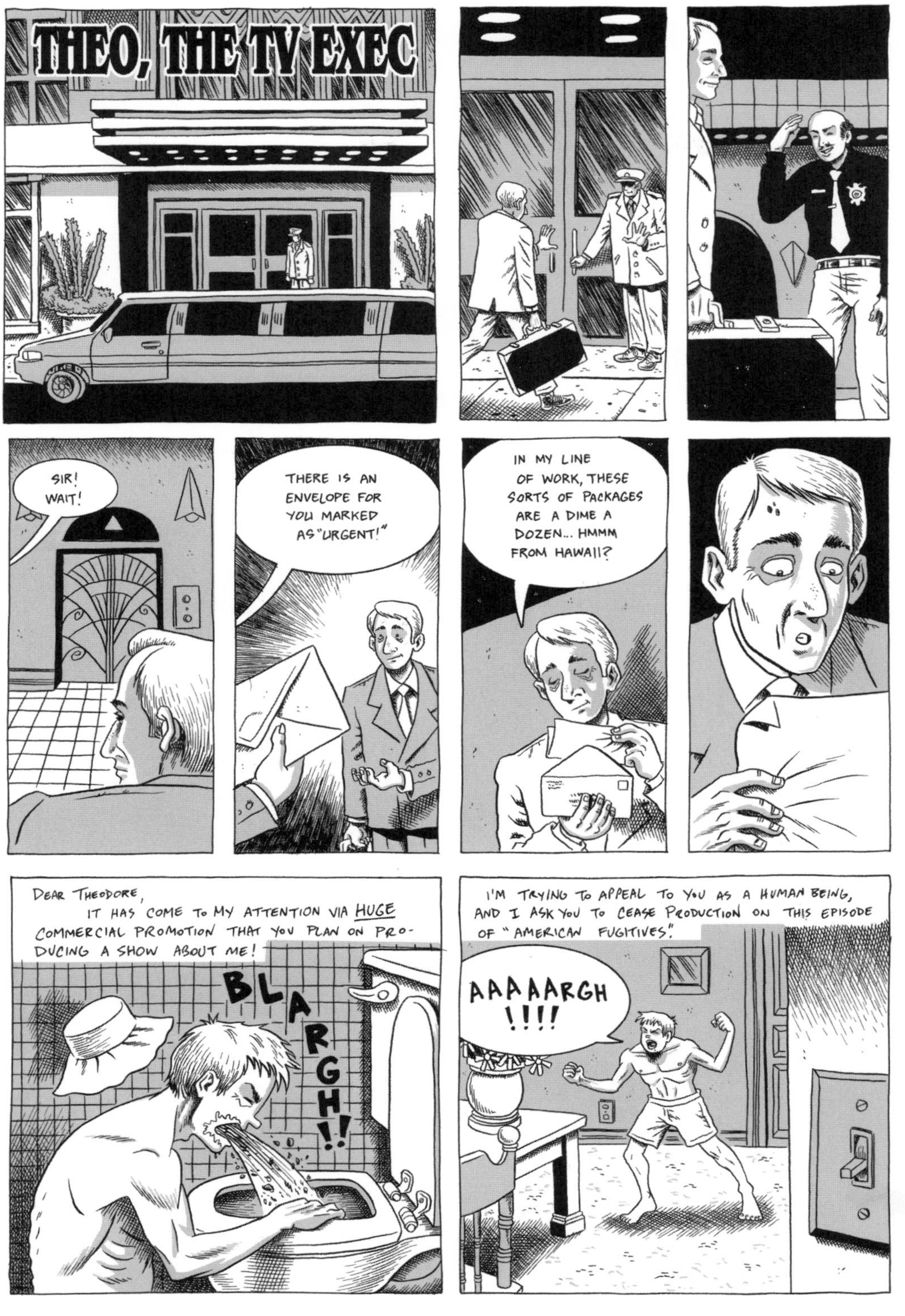
THEO, THE TV EXEC
SIR! WAIT!
THERE IS AN ENVELOPE FOR YOU MARKED AS "URGENT!"
IN MY LINE OF WORK, THESE SORTS OF PACKAGES ARE A DIME A DOZEN... HMMM FROM HAWAII?
DEAR THEODORE, IT HAS COME TO MY ATTENTION VIA HUGE COMMERCIAL PROMOTION THAT YOU PLAN ON PRODUCING A SHOW ABOUT ME!
BLARGH!!
I'M TRYING TO APPEAL TO YOU AS A HUMAN BEING, AND I ASK YOU TO CEASE PRODUCTION ON THIS EPISODE OF "AMERICAN FUGITIVES."
AAAAARGH !!!!

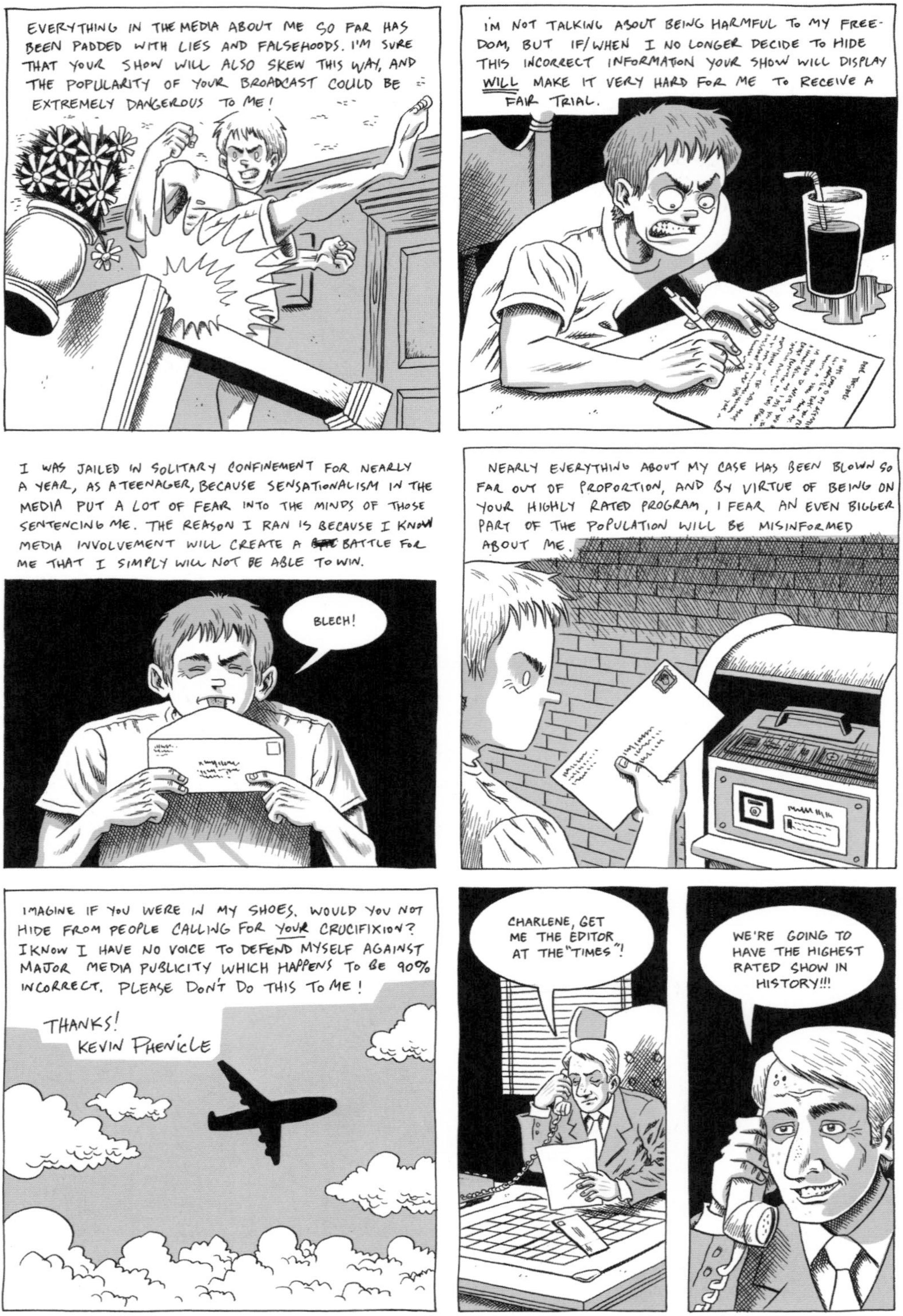
EVERYTHING IN THE MEDIA ABOUT ME SO FAR HAS BEEN PADDED WITH LIES AND FALSEHOODS. I'M SURE THAT YOUR SHOW WILL ALSO SKEW THIS WAY, AND THE POPULARITY OF YOUR BROADCAST COULD BE EXTREMELY DANGEROUS TO ME!
I'M NOT TALKING ABOUT BEING HARMFUL TO MY FREEDOM, BUT IF/WHEN I NO LONGER DECIDE TO HIDE THIS INCORRECT INFORMATION YOUR SHOW WILL DISPLAY WILL MAKE IT VERY HARD FOR ME TO RECEIVE A FAIR TRIAL.
I WAS JAILED IN SOLITARY CONFINEMENT FOR NEARLY A YEAR, AS A TEENAGER, BECAUSE SENSATIONALISM IN THE MEDIA PUT A LOT OF FEAR INTO THE MINDS OF THOSE SENTENCING ME. THE REASON I RAN IS BECAUSE I KNOW MEDIA INVOLVEMENT WILL CREATE A BATTLE FOR ME THAT I SIMPLY WILL NOT BE ABLE TO WIN.
BLECH!
NEARLY EVERYTHING ABOUT MY CASE HAS BEEN BLOWN SO FAR OUT OF PROPORTION, AND BY VIRTUE OF BEING ON YOUR HIGHLY RATED PROGRAM, I FEAR AN EVEN BIGGER PART OF THE POPULATION WILL BE MISINFORMED ABOUT ME.
IMAGINE IF YOU WERE IN MY SHOES. WOULD YOU NOT HIDE FROM PEOPLE CALLING FOR YOUR CRUCIFIXION? I KNOW I HAVE NO VOICE TO DEFEND MYSELF AGAINST MAJOR MEDIA PUBLICITY WHICH HAPPENS TO BE 90% INCORRECT. PLEASE DON'T DO THIS TO ME!
THANKS! KEVIN PHENICLE
CHARLENE, GET ME THE EDITOR AT THE "TIMES"!
WE'RE GOING TO HAVE THE HIGHEST RATED SHOW IN HISTORY!!!

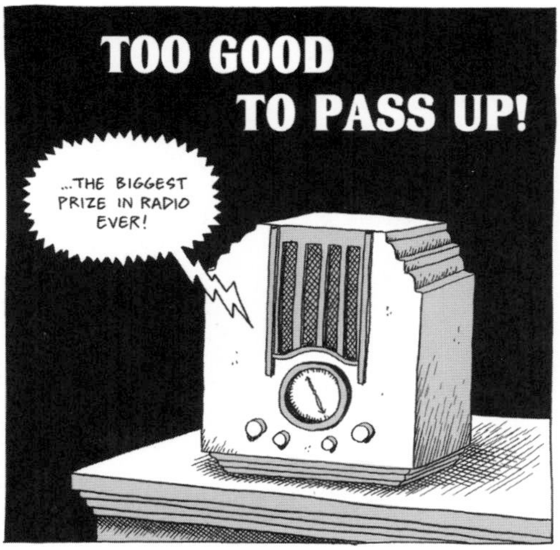
TOO GOOD TO PASS UP!
...THE BIGGEST PRIZE IN RADIO EVER!

...ALL YOU HAVE TO DO IS LISTEN TO 101.6 ON YOUR FM DIAL AND GIVE US A CALL AT THE RIGHT TIME.

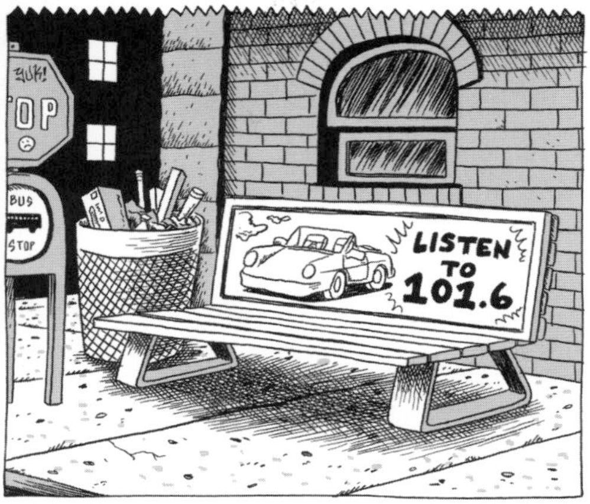
YUK!
BUS STOP
LISTEN TO 101.6

THE CONTEST TAKES PLACE NEXT WEEK, AND YOUR CUE TO CALL WILL BE THE 3RD DOG BARK IN A SINGLE HOUR.

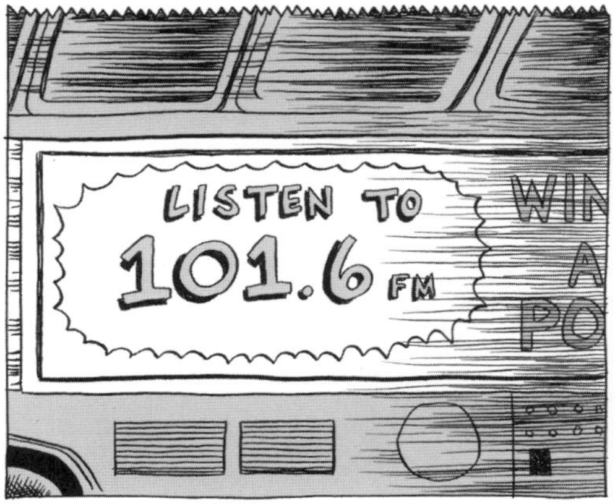
LISTEN TO 101.6 FM

THAT'S ALL IT TAKES TO GET YOUR HANDS ON A BRAND SPANKIN' NEW PORSCHE 911! CAN YA BELIEVE IT, FOLKS!?

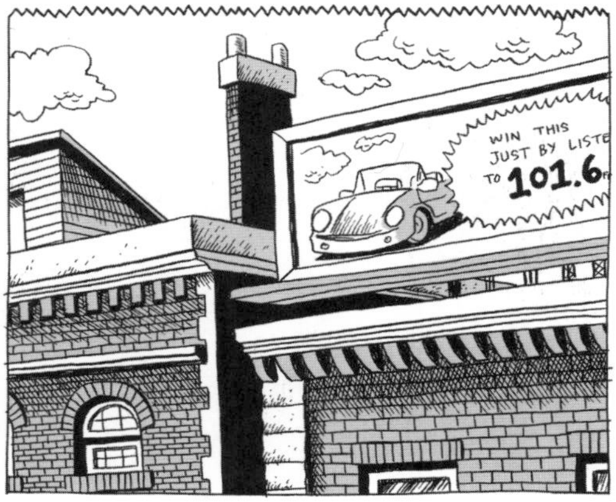
WIN THIS
TO 101.6

DON'T EVER SAY GOOD OL' JIMMY NIGHTTRAIN DOESN'T TAKE CARE OF HIS AUDIENCE! HYUK HYUK!

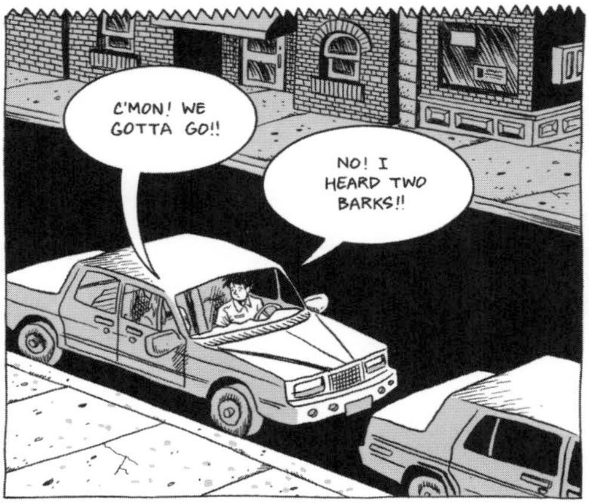
C'MON! WE GOTTA GO!!
NO! I HEARD TWO BARKS!!

YOU WON'T WANT TO MISS OUT ON THIS ONE-OF-A-KIND OPPORTUNITY.

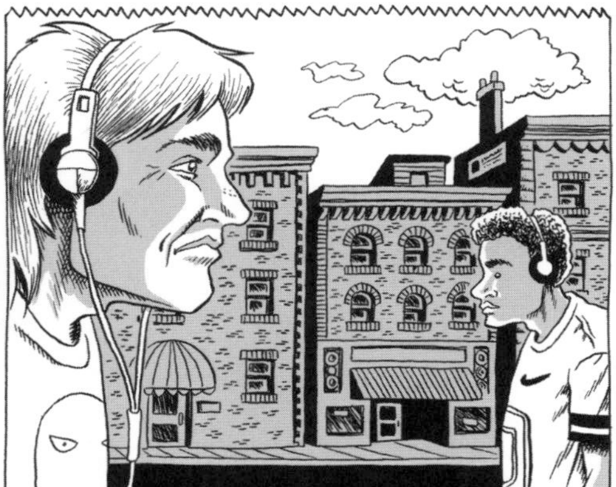

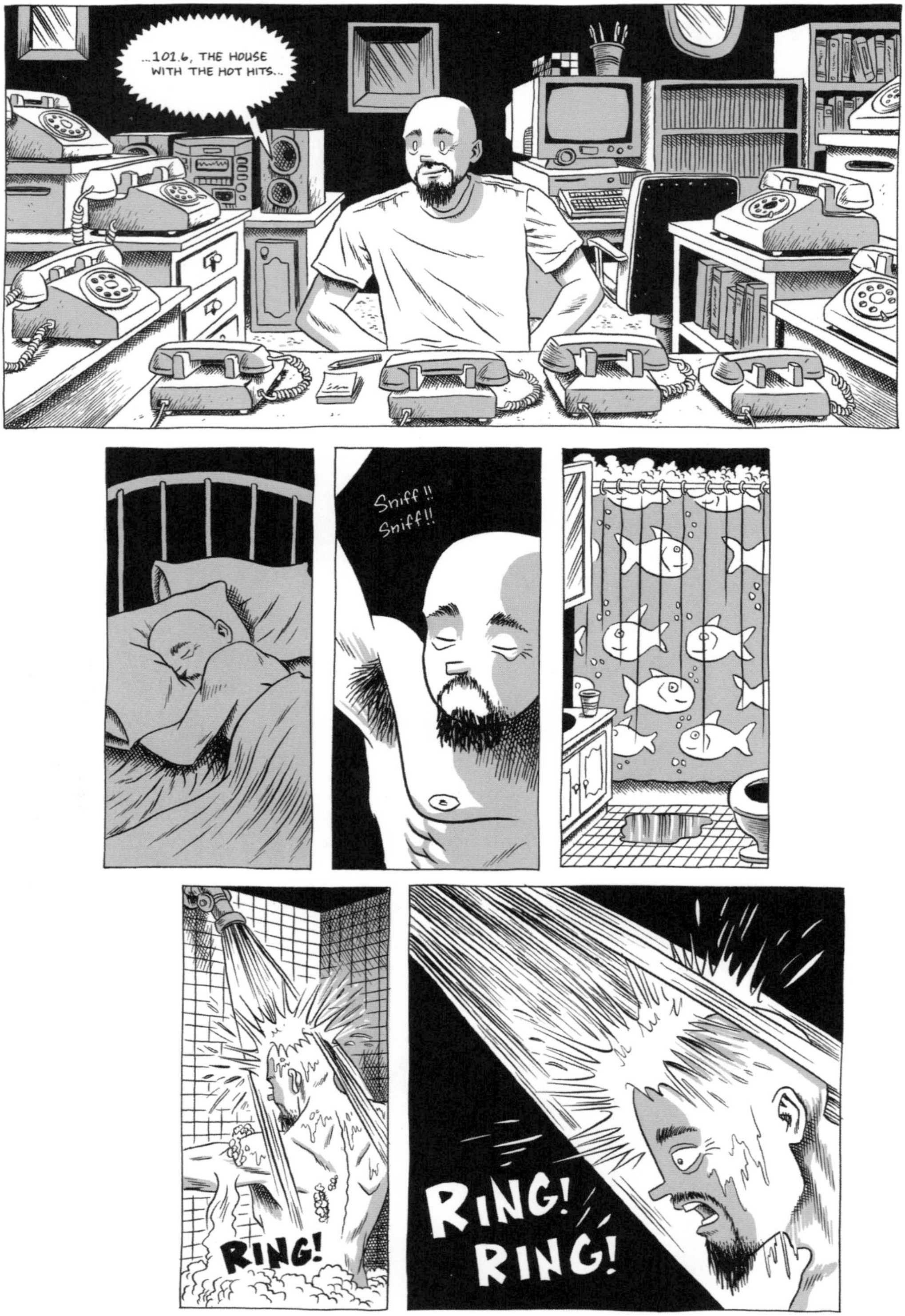
...101.6, THE HOUSE WITH THE HOT HITS...
Sniff!! Sniff!!
RING!
RING! RING!

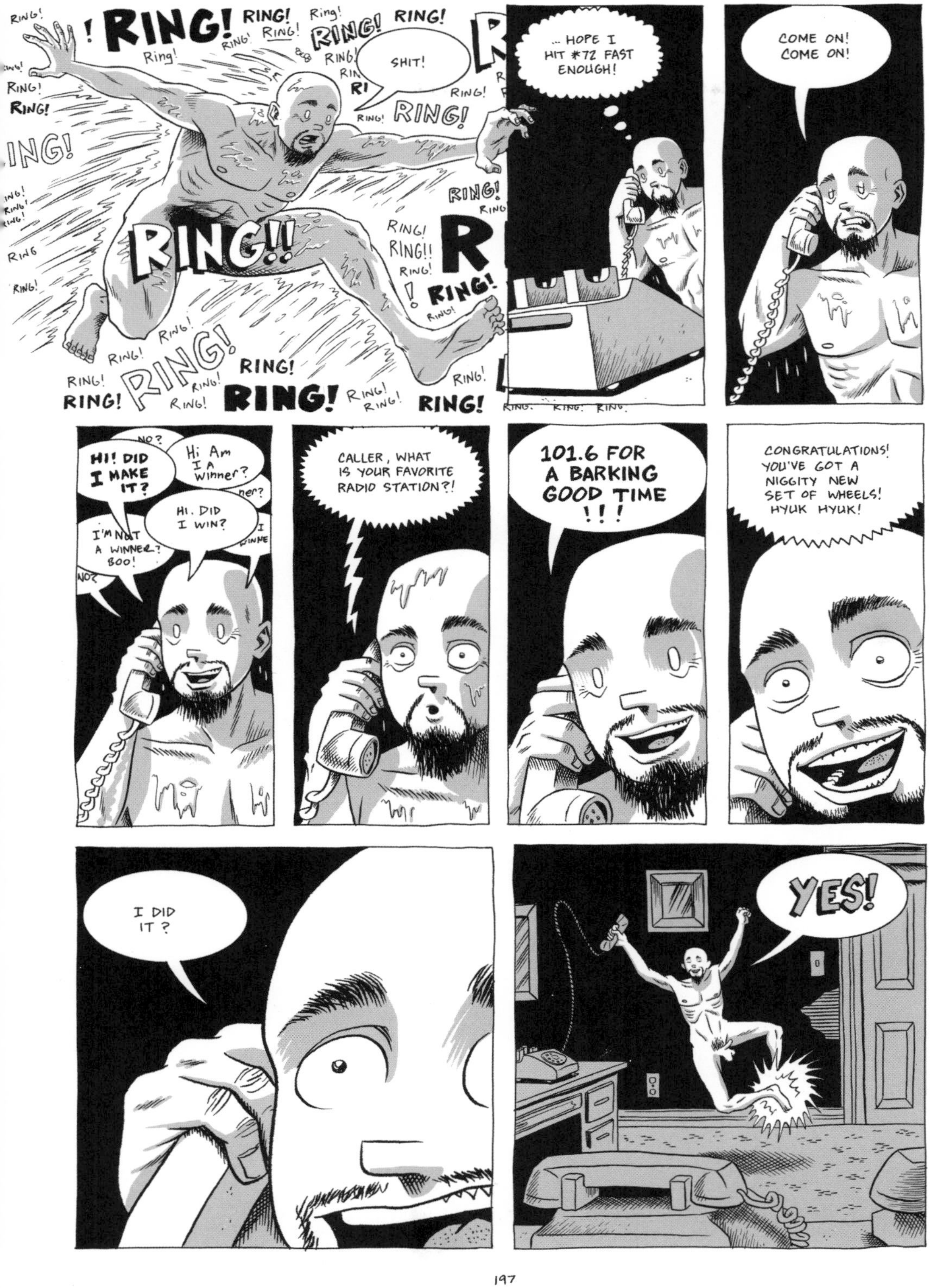
RING!
RING!
RING!
Ring!
RING!
SHIT!
RING!
RING!!
... HOPE I HIT *72 FAST ENOUGH!
COME ON! COME ON!
HI! DID I MAKE IT?
Hi Am I A winner?
HI. DID I WIN?
I'M NOT A WINNER? BOO!
NO?
CALLER, WHAT IS YOUR FAVORITE RADIO STATION?!
101.6 FOR A BARKING GOOD TIME !!!
CONGRATULATIONS! YOU'VE GOT A NIGGITY NEW SET OF WHEELS! HYUK HYUK!
I DID IT?
YES!

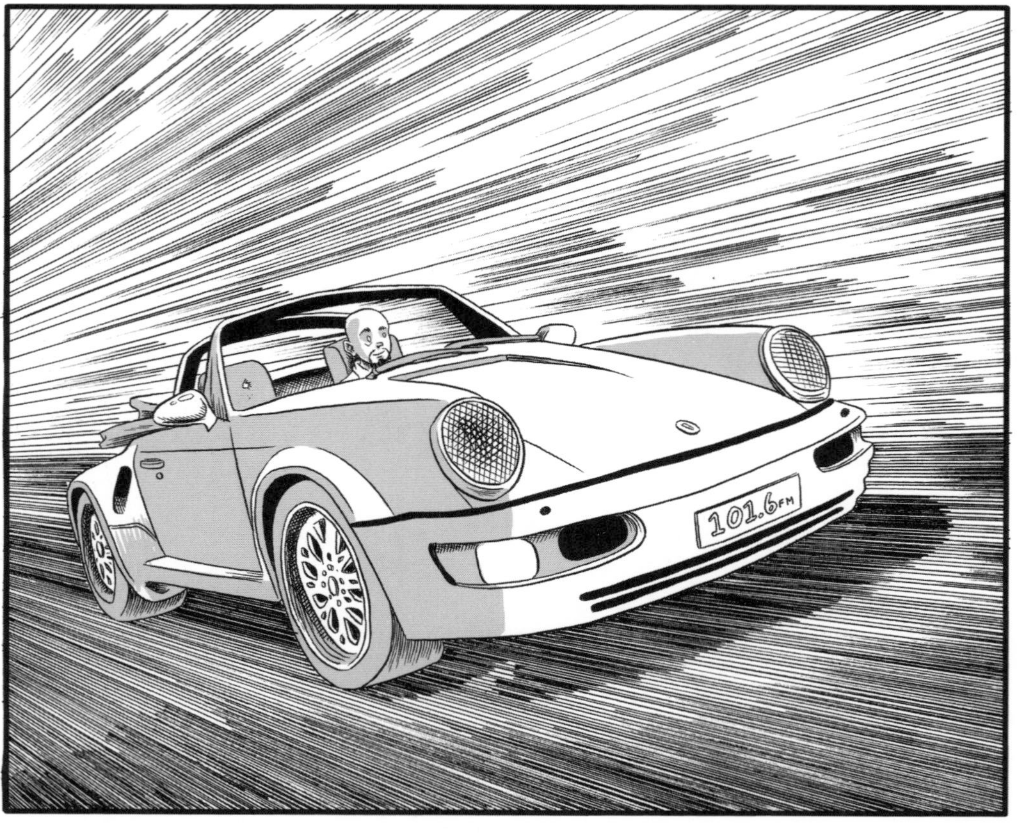
101.6FM

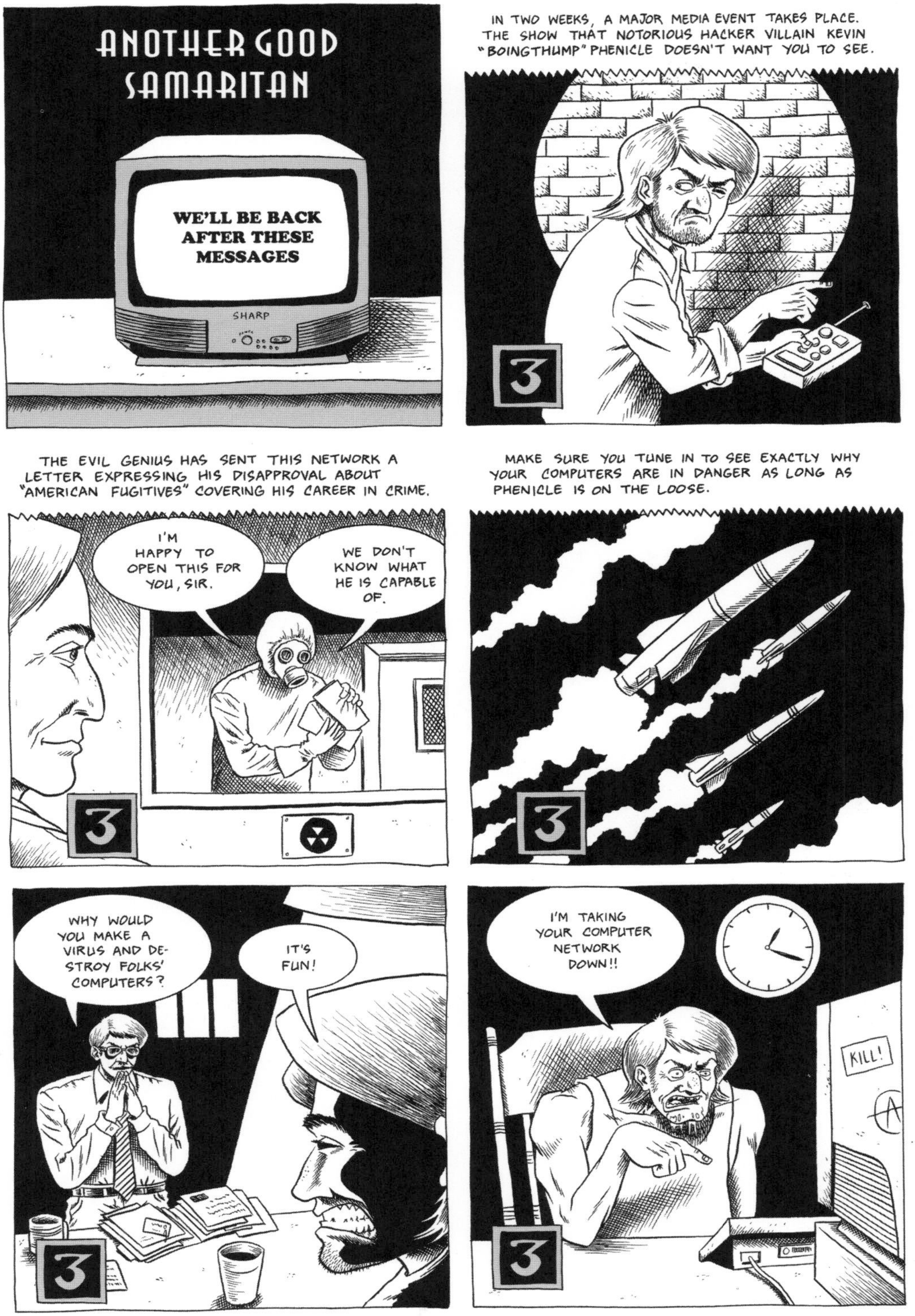
ANOTHER GOOD SAMARITAN
WE'LL BE BACK AFTER THESE MESSAGES
SHARP
IN TWO WEEKS, A MAJOR MEDIA EVENT TAKES PLACE. THE SHOW THAT NOTORIOUS HACKER VILLAIN KEVIN "BOINGTHUMP" PHENICLE DOESN'T WANT YOU TO SEE.
3
THE EVIL GENIUS HAS SENT THIS NETWORK A LETTER EXPRESSING HIS DISAPPROVAL ABOUT "AMERICAN FUGITIVES" COVERING HIS CAREER IN CRIME.
I'M HAPPY TO OPEN THIS FOR YOU, SIR.
WE DON'T KNOW WHAT HE IS CAPABLE OF.
3
MAKE SURE YOU TUNE IN TO SEE EXACTLY WHY YOUR COMPUTERS ARE IN DANGER AS LONG AS PHENICLE IS ON THE LOOSE.
3
WHY WOULD YOU MAKE A VIRUS AND DESTROY FOLKS' COMPUTERS?
IT'S FUN!
3
I'M TAKING YOUR COMPUTER NETWORK DOWN!!
KILL!
3

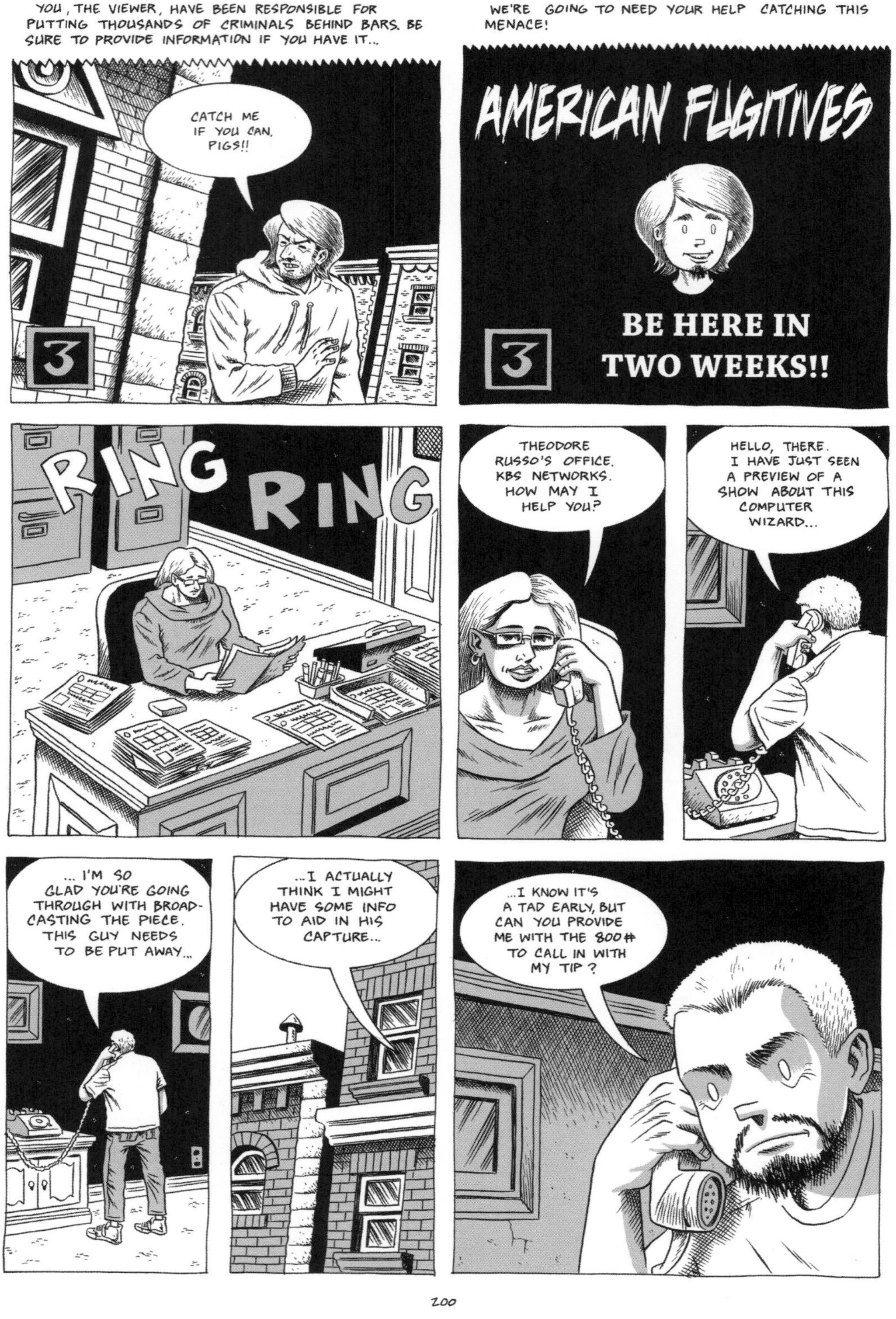
YOU, THE VIEWER, HAVE BEEN RESPONSIBLE FOR PUTTING THOUSANDS OF CRIMINALS BEHIND BARS. BE SURE TO PROVIDE INFORMATION IF YOU HAVE IT...
CATCH ME IF YOU CAN, PIGS!!
3
WE'RE GOING TO NEED YOUR HELP CATCHING THIS MENACE!
AMERICAN FUGITIVES
BE HERE IN TWO WEEKS!!
3
RING RING
THEODORE RUSSO'S OFFICE. KBS NETWORKS. HOW MAY I HELP YOU?
HELLO, THERE. I HAVE JUST SEEN A PREVIEW OF A SHOW ABOUT THIS COMPUTER WIZARD...
... I'M SO GLAD YOU'RE GOING THROUGH WITH BROAD-CASTING THE PIECE. THIS GUY NEEDS TO BE PUT AWAY...
...I ACTUALLY THINK I MIGHT HAVE SOME INFO TO AID IN HIS CAPTURE...
...I KNOW IT'S A TAD EARLY, BUT CAN YOU PROVIDE ME WITH THE 800# TO CALL IN WITH MY TIP?

DEEPER UNDERGROUND

WHAT A STUPID MOVE SENDING THAT LETTER! THE PROMOTION SURROUNDING THAT UPCOMING SHOW IS STAGGERING. EVERY COMMERCIAL BREAK MENTIONS THE EPISODE...

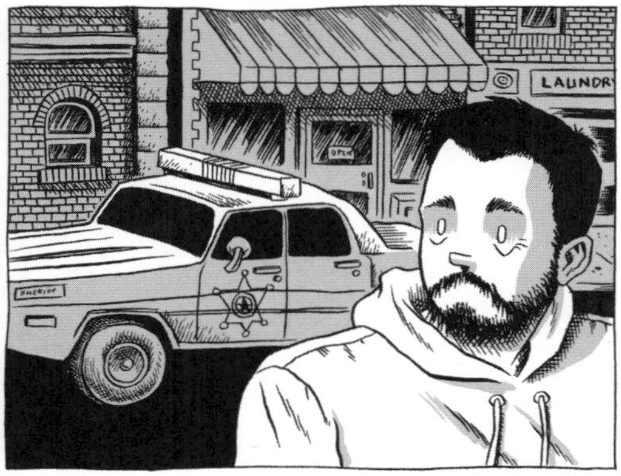
LAUNDRY

ONE COULD HOPE THAT THE CONSTANT BOMBARDMENT OF HYPE WILL CREATE A KIND OF 'WHITE NOISE' EFFECT IN WHICH THE VIEWER WILL JUST TUNE OUT AT THE MERE MENTION OF MY NAME. YEAH, RIGHT!

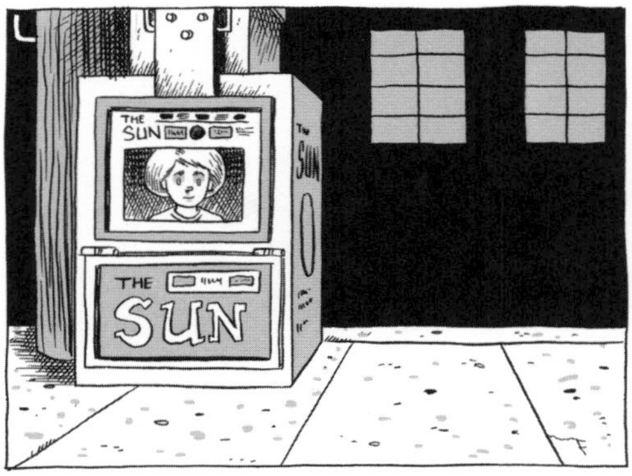
THE SUN
THE SUN

THANKFULLY, THERE IS STILL TIME TO PREPARE BEFORE THIS TREMENDOUS PIECE OF NEGATIVITY AIRS.

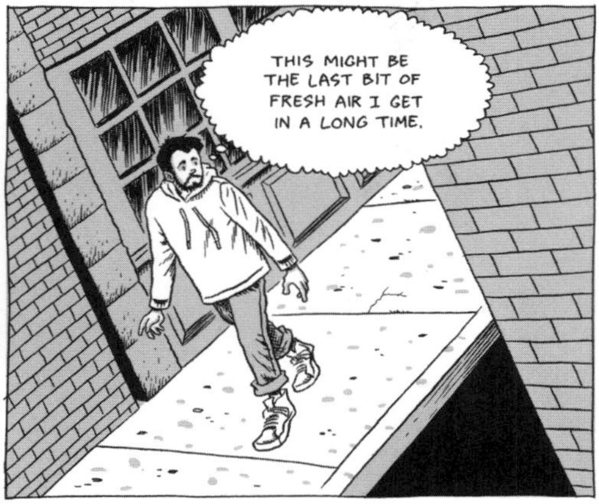
THIS MIGHT BE THE LAST BIT OF FRESH AIR I GET IN A LONG TIME.

IT WASN'T VERY HARD FINDING A HOTEL THAT MEETS MY NEEDS. THE JOINT IS OUT OF THE WAY, THEY ACCEPT CASH, THE ROOM HAS A STOVE, AND NOT MANY QUESTIONS ARE ASKED.

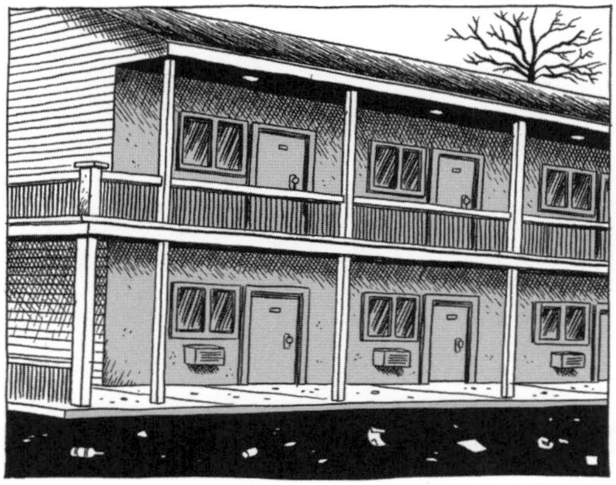

IT WILL BE ESSENTIAL TO KEEP THE MIND BUSY WHILE IN HIDING. NO MORE GOING NUTS AND FALLING INTO A DEEP DEPRESSION BECAUSE CONDITIONS ARE OUT OF MY CONTROL.

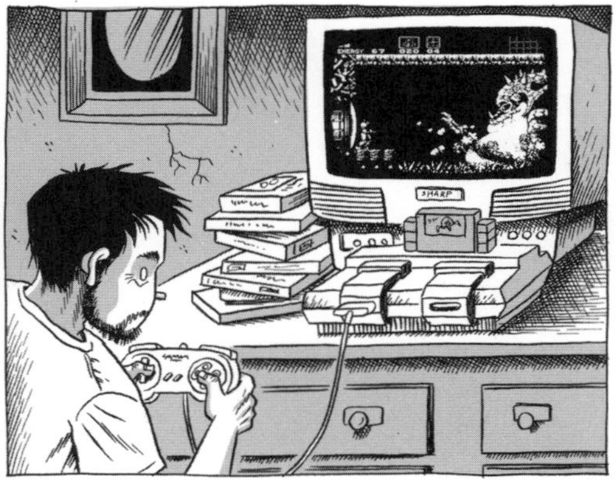
SHARP

THIS COULD PROBABLY BE MY HOME FOR THE NEXT FEW MONTHS.

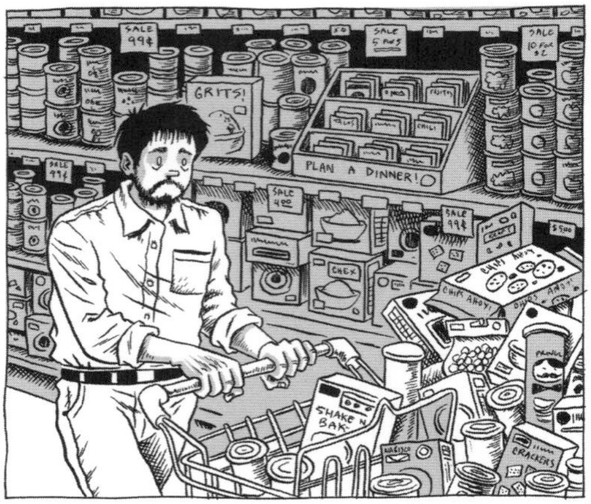
GRITS!
PLAN A DINNER!
CHEX
CRACKERS

MY LAST BIT OF ONLINE ACTIVITY IS DONE FROM A VACANT HOTEL ROOM. THE TOLL-FREE TIP LINE GETS ROUTED TO A PHONE SEX NUMBER.

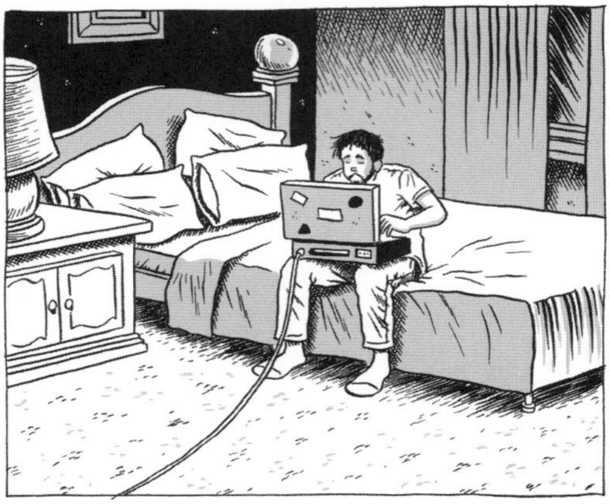

THE SHOW IS GOING TO BROADCAST IN A FEW HOURS. IT IS LOOKING TO BE THE #1 SHOW OF THE NIGHT, AND I'M EXPECTING A PUBLIC FRENZY OF FEARFUL CITIZENS CALLING FOR THE HEAD OF A DERANGED HACKER ON THE LOOSE.

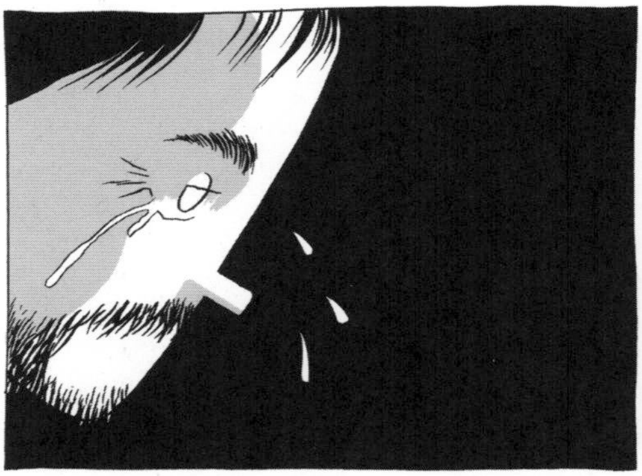

I'VE BEEN AT THIS HOTEL LONG ENOUGH TO HAVE BEEN SPOTTED AT LEAST A FEW TIMES. THE LOCK ON THE BASEMENT DOOR IS A FAIRLY WEAK OBSTACLE IN THE PATH OF MY NEXT PRE-CAUTIONARY MEASURE.

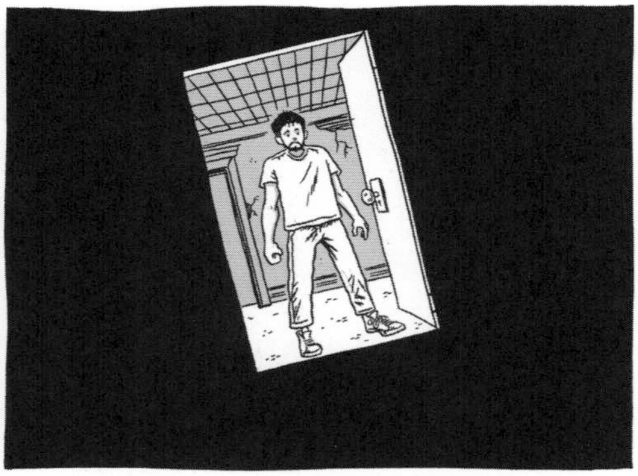

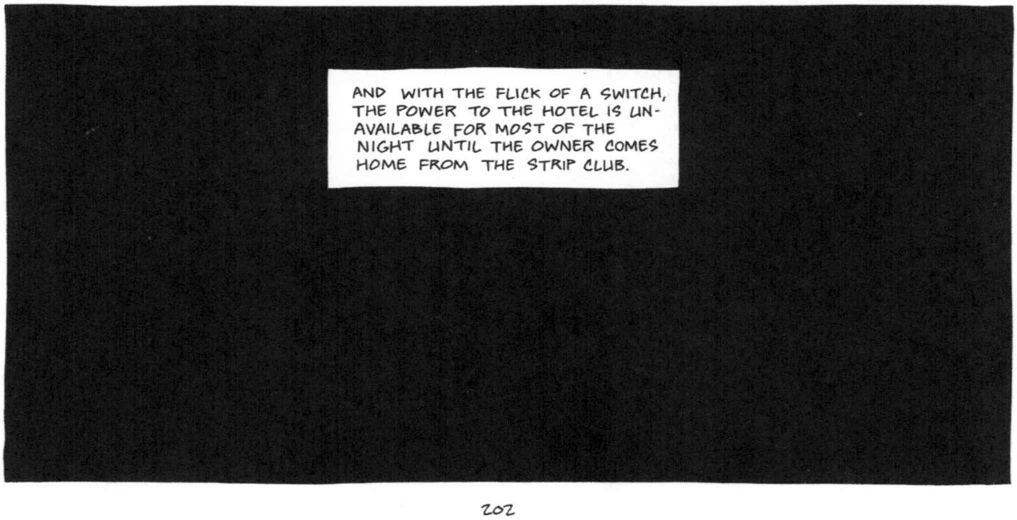
AND WITH THE FLICK OF A SWITCH, THE POWER TO THE HOTEL IS UN-AVAILABLE FOR MOST OF THE NIGHT UNTIL THE OWNER COMES HOME FROM THE STRIP CLUB.

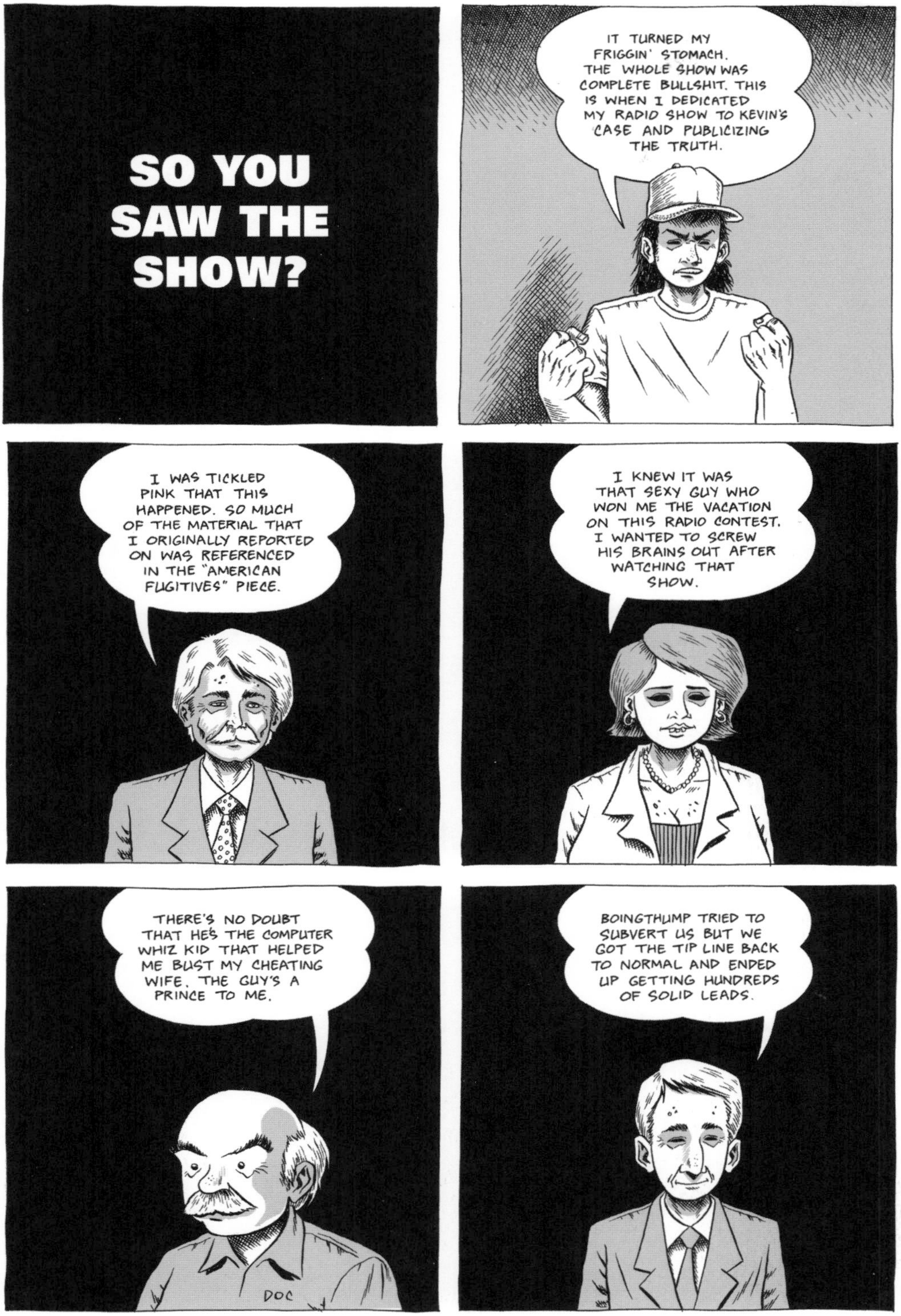

SO YOU SAW THE SHOW?
IT TURNED MY FRIGGIN' STOMACH. THE WHOLE SHOW WAS COMPLETE BULLSHIT. THIS IS WHEN I DEDICATED MY RADIO SHOW TO KEVIN'S CASE AND PUBLICIZING THE TRUTH.
I WAS TICKLED PINK THAT THIS HAPPENED. SO MUCH OF THE MATERIAL THAT I ORIGINALLY REPORTED ON WAS REFERENCED IN THE "AMERICAN FUGITIVES" PIECE.
I KNEW IT WAS THAT SEXY GUY WHO WON ME THE VACATION ON THIS RADIO CONTEST. I WANTED TO SCREW HIS BRAINS OUT AFTER WATCHING THAT SHOW.
THERE'S NO DOUBT THAT HE'S THE COMPUTER WHIZ KID THAT HELPED ME BUST MY CHEATING WIFE. THE GUY'S A PRINCE TO ME.
DOC
BOINGTHUMP TRIED TO SUBVERT US BUT WE GOT THE TIP LINE BACK TO NORMAL AND ENDED UP GETTING HUNDREDS OF SOLID LEADS.

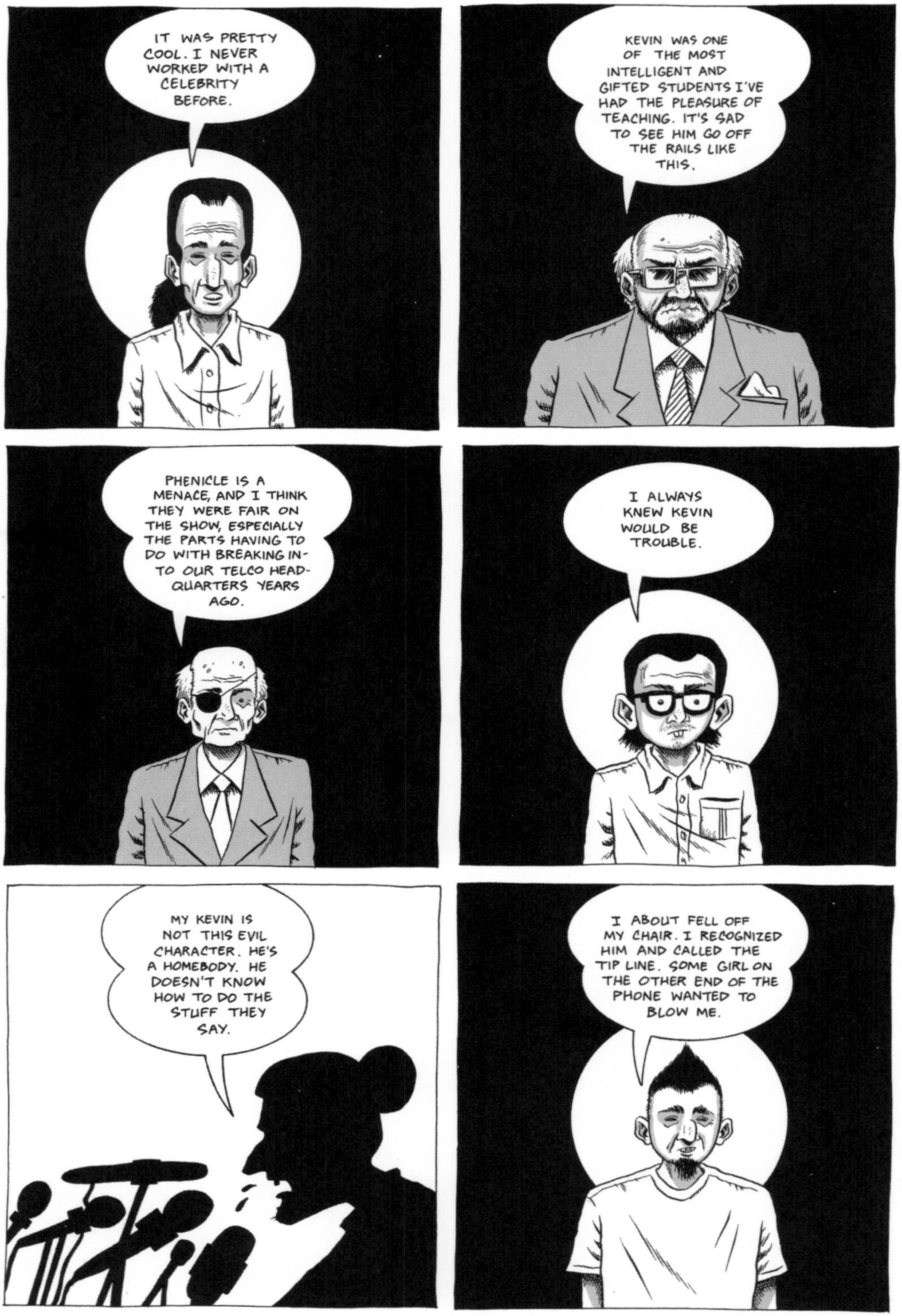
IT WAS PRETTY COOL. I NEVER WORKED WITH A CELEBRITY BEFORE.
KEVIN WAS ONE OF THE MOST INTELLIGENT AND GIFTED STUDENTS I'VE HAD THE PLEASURE OF TEACHING. IT'S SAD TO SEE HIM GO OFF THE RAILS LIKE THIS.
PHENICLE IS A MENACE, AND I THINK THEY WERE FAIR ON THE SHOW, ESPECIALLY THE PARTS HAVING TO DO WITH BREAKING INTO OUR TELCO HEADQUARTERS YEARS AGO.
I ALWAYS KNEW KEVIN WOULD BE TROUBLE.
MY KEVIN IS NOT THIS EVIL CHARACTER. HE'S A HOMEBODY. HE DOESN'T KNOW HOW TO DO THE STUFF THEY SAY.
I ABOUT FELL OFF MY CHAIR. I RECOGNIZED HIM AND CALLED THE TIP LINE. SOME GIRL ON THE OTHER END OF THE PHONE WANTED TO BLOW ME.

ALL GOOD THINGS...

THE MAIN REASON I KEPT THE CAR FOR MYSELF WAS SO THAT I'D HAVE AN ASSET OF SOME VALUE THAT I COULD GET RID OF IN A PINCH.

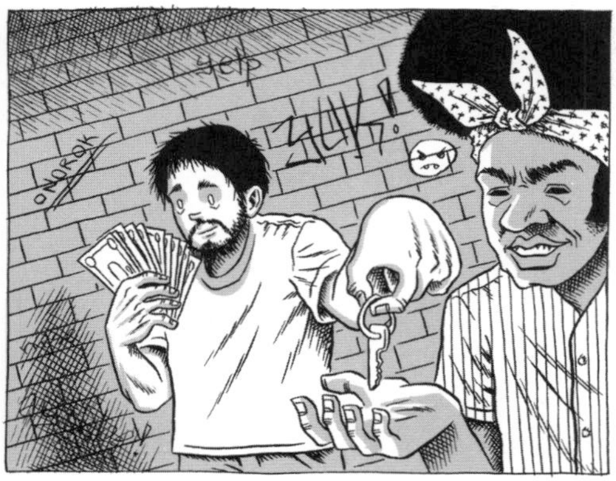

THERE ARE MORE COST-EFFECTIVE WAYS TO MOVE ABOUT THE COUNTRY.

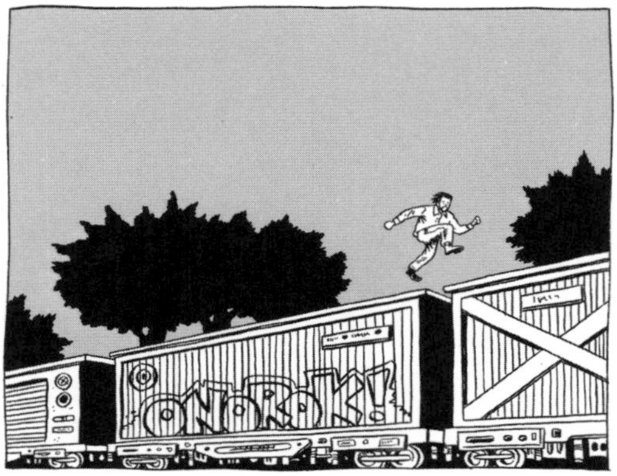

STILL, THE MONEY DOESN'T LAST FOREVER.

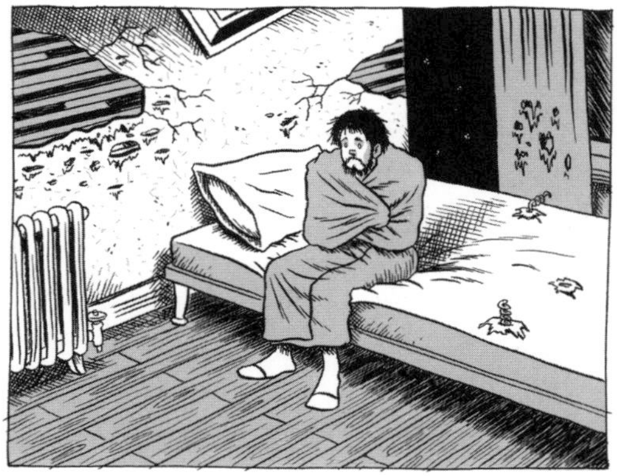

NOT MUCH WORK AVAILABLE IN THE MIDDLE OF NOWHERE.

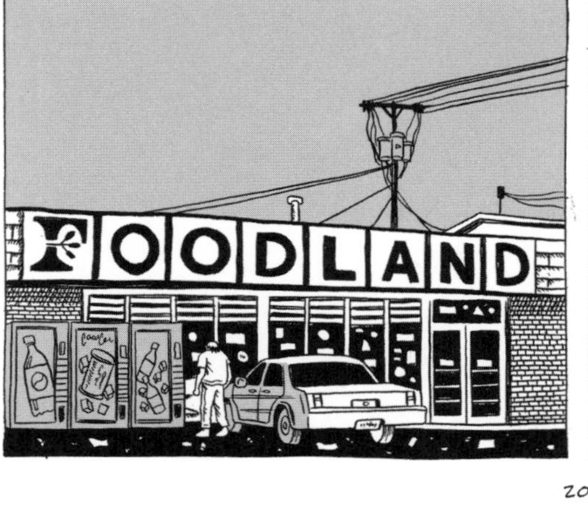
FOODLAND

I HAVE TO AGREE TO TAKE THE SAME WAGE AS THE MEXICANS HE HIRES.

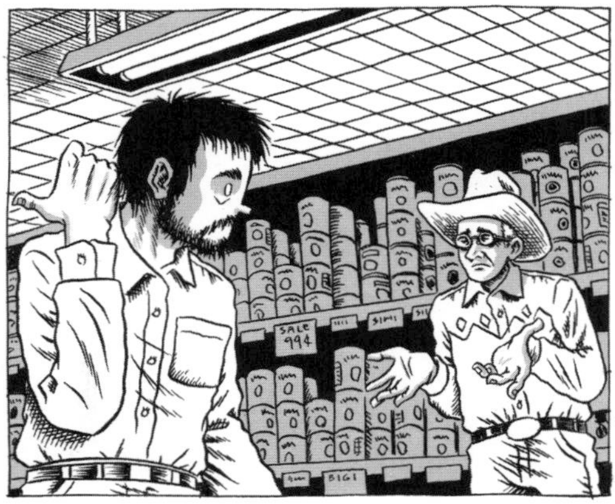

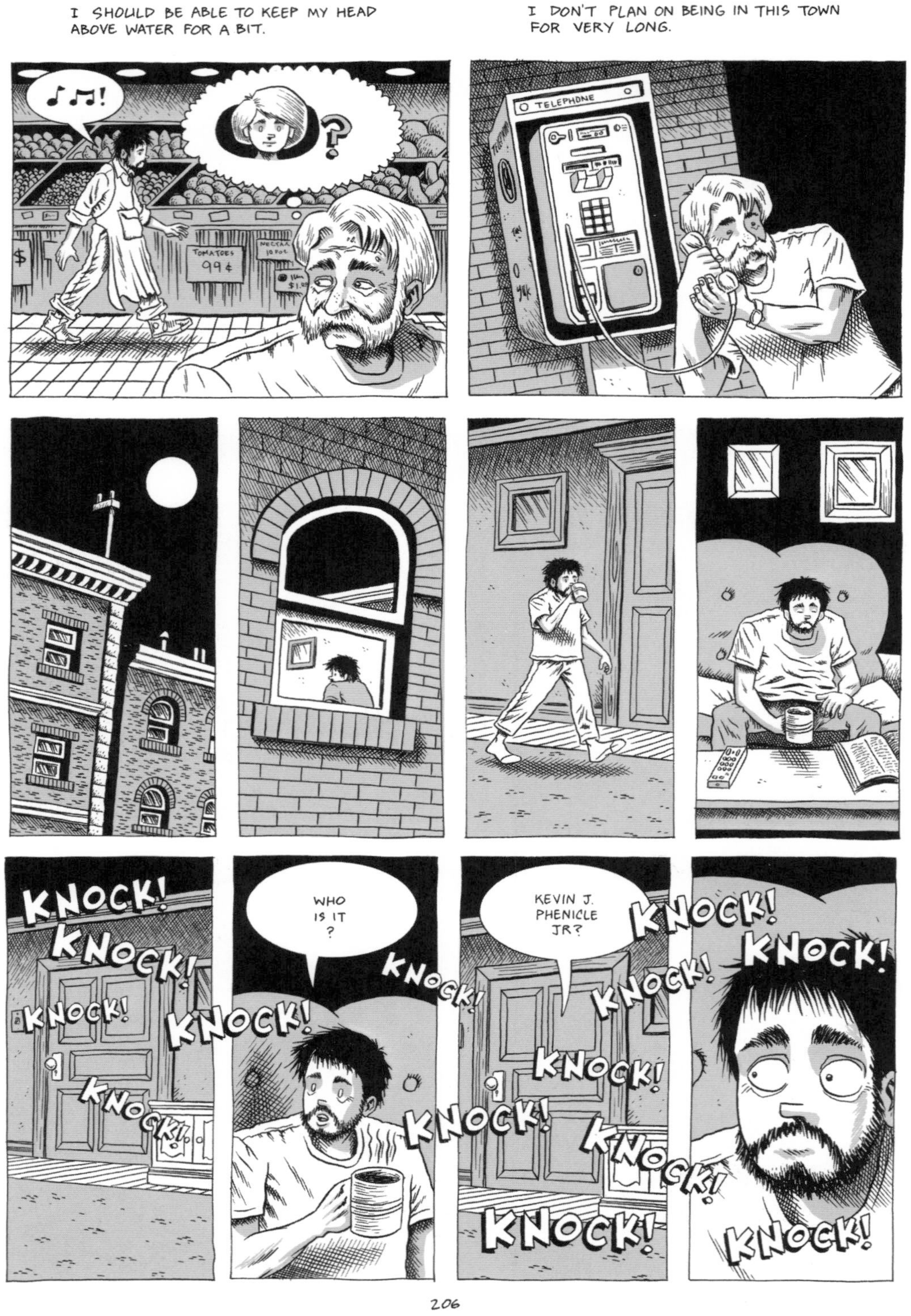
I SHOULD BE ABLE TO KEEP MY HEAD ABOVE WATER FOR A BIT.
I DON'T PLAN ON BEING IN THIS TOWN FOR VERY LONG.
♪♫!
?
$
TOMATOES 99¢
TELEPHONE
KNOCK!
KNOCK!
KNOCK!
KNOCK!
KNOCK!
WHO IS IT ?
KNOCK!
KNOCK!
KEVIN J. PHENICLE JR?
KNOCK!
KNOCK!
KNOCK!
KNOCK!
KNOCK!
KNOCK!
KNOCK!

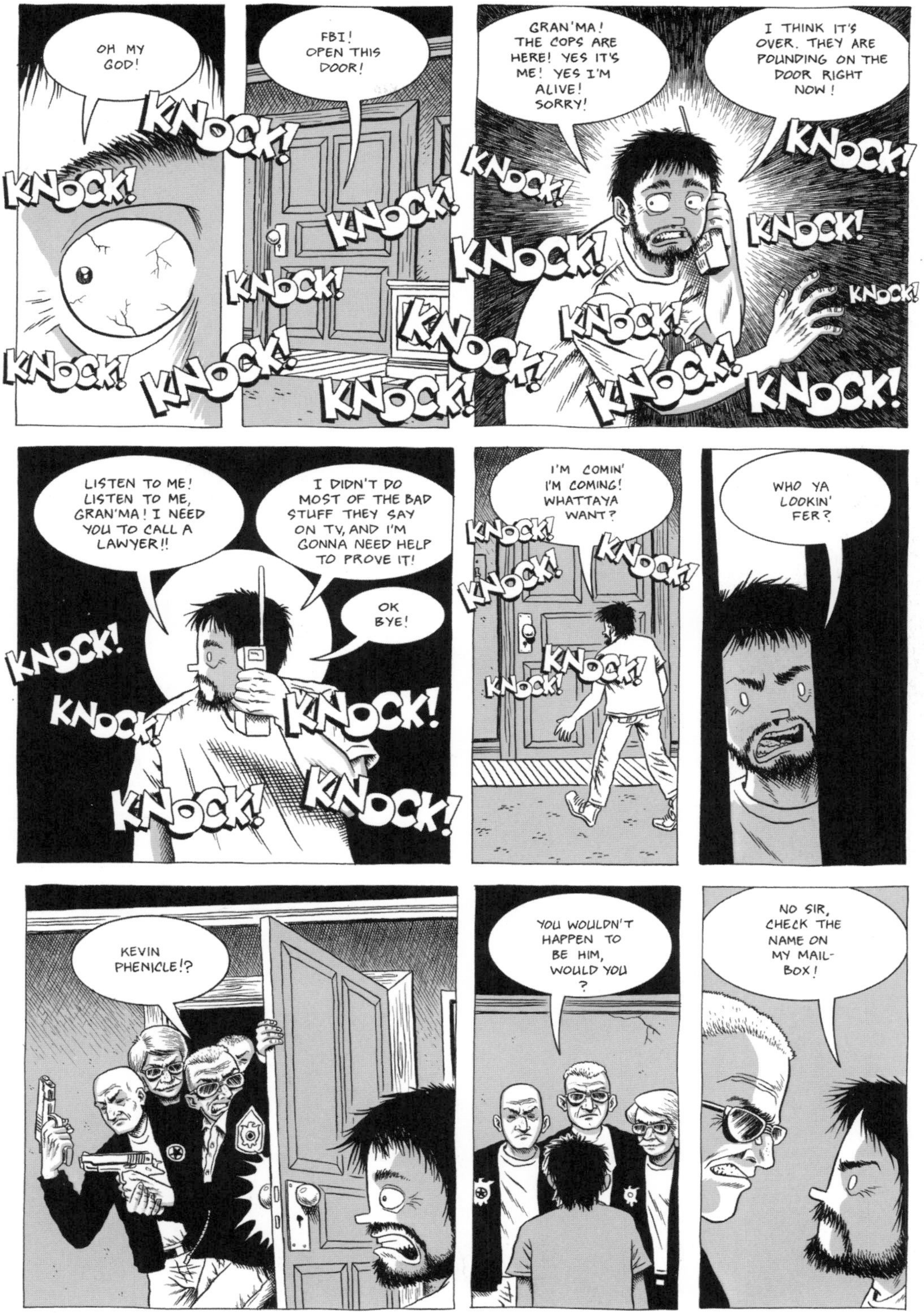
OH MY GOD!
KNOCK! KNOCK! KNOCK!
FBI! OPEN THIS DOOR!
KNOCK! KNOCK! KNOCK! KNOCK!
GRAN'MA! THE COPS ARE HERE! YES IT'S ME! YES I'M ALIVE! SORRY!
I THINK IT'S OVER. THEY ARE POUNDING ON THE DOOR RIGHT NOW!
KNOCK! KNOCK! KNOCK! KNOCK! KNOCK! KNOCK! KNOCK! KNOCK!
LISTEN TO ME! LISTEN TO ME, GRAN'MA! I NEED YOU TO CALL A LAWYER!!
I DIDN'T DO MOST OF THE BAD STUFF THEY SAY ON TV, AND I'M GONNA NEED HELP TO PROVE IT!
OK BYE!
KNOCK! KNOCK! KNOCK! KNOCK! KNOCK!
I'M COMIN' I'M COMING! WHATTAYA WANT?
KNOCK! KNOCK! KNOCK! KNOCK! KNOCK!
WHO YA LOOKIN' FER?
KEVIN PHENICLE!?
YOU WOULDN'T HAPPEN TO BE HIM, WOULD YOU?
NO SIR, CHECK THE NAME ON MY MAIL-BOX!

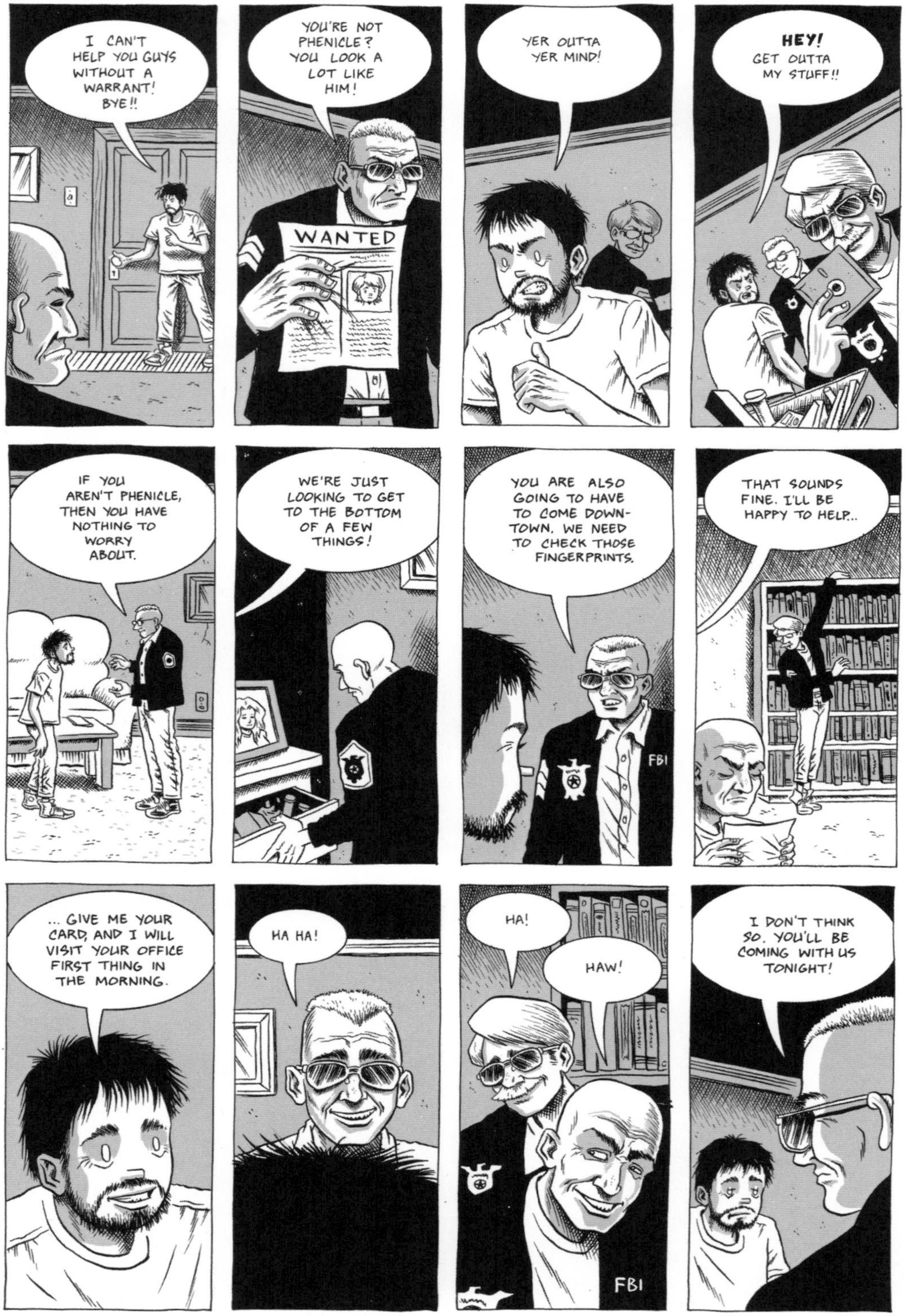
I CAN'T HELP YOU GUYS WITHOUT A WARRANT! BYE!!
YOU'RE NOT PHENICLE? YOU LOOK A LOT LIKE HIM!
WANTED
YER OUTTA YER MIND!
HEY! GET OUTTA MY STUFF!!
IF YOU AREN'T PHENICLE, THEN YOU HAVE NOTHING TO WORRY ABOUT.
WE'RE JUST LOOKING TO GET TO THE BOTTOM OF A FEW THINGS!
YOU ARE ALSO GOING TO HAVE TO COME DOWN-TOWN. WE NEED TO CHECK THOSE FINGERPRINTS.
FBI
THAT SOUNDS FINE. I'LL BE HAPPY TO HELP...
... GIVE ME YOUR CARD, AND I WILL VISIT YOUR OFFICE FIRST THING IN THE MORNING.
HA HA!
HA!
HAW!
FBI
I DON'T THINK SO. YOU'LL BE COMING WITH US TONIGHT!

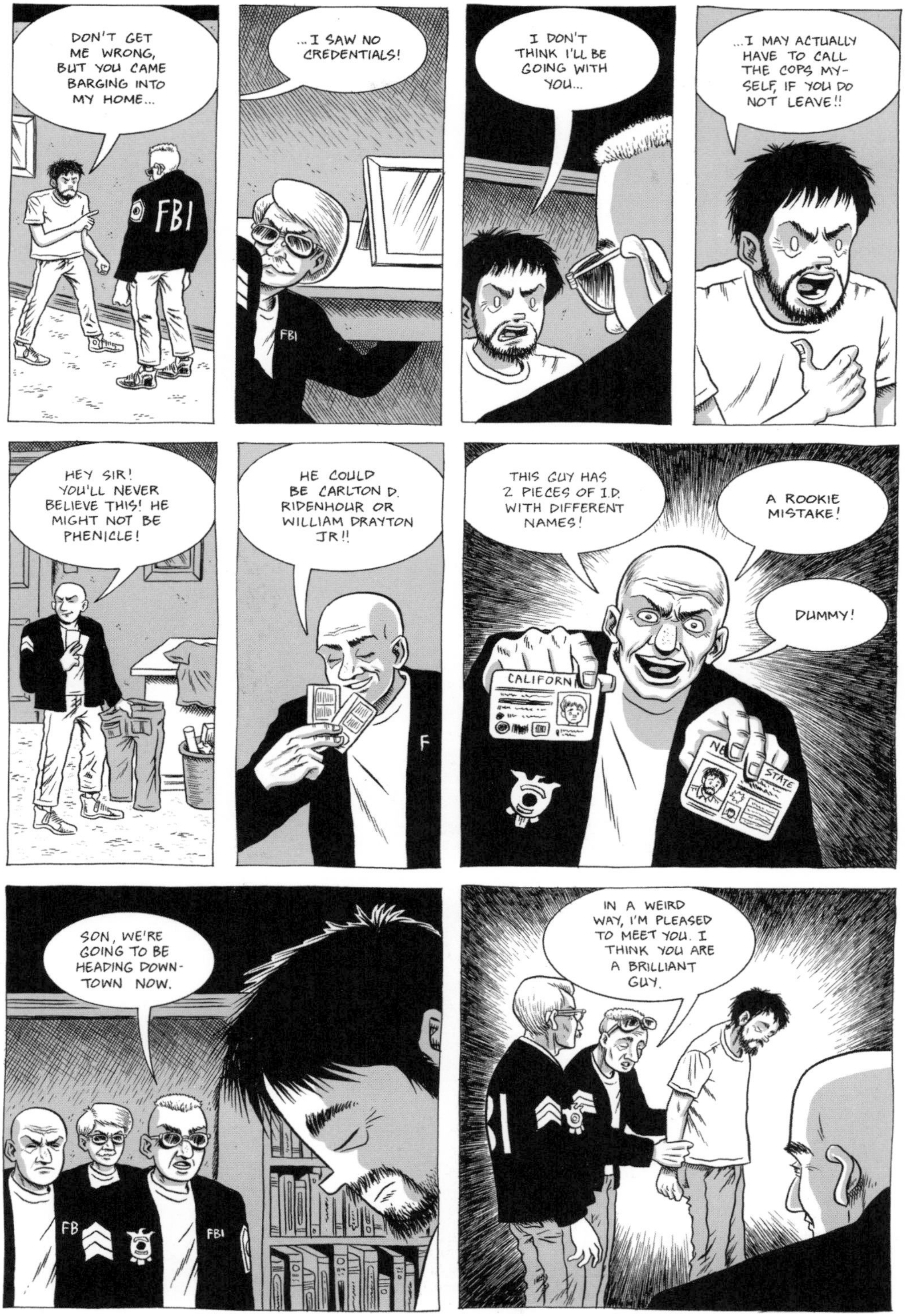
DON'T GET ME WRONG, BUT YOU CAME BARGING INTO MY HOME...
...I SAW NO CREDENTIALS!
I DON'T THINK I'LL BE GOING WITH YOU...
...I MAY ACTUALLY HAVE TO CALL THE COPS MY-SELF, IF YOU DO NOT LEAVE!!
FBI
HEY SIR! YOU'LL NEVER BELIEVE THIS! HE MIGHT NOT BE PHENICLE!
HE COULD BE CARLTON D. RIDENHOUR OR WILLIAM DRAYTON JR!!
THIS GUY HAS 2 PIECES OF I.D. WITH DIFFERENT NAMES!
A ROOKIE MISTAKE!
DUMMY!
CALIFORN
STATE
SON, WE'RE GOING TO BE HEADING DOWN-TOWN NOW.
IN A WEIRD WAY, I'M PLEASED TO MEET YOU. I THINK YOU ARE A BRILLIANT GUY.

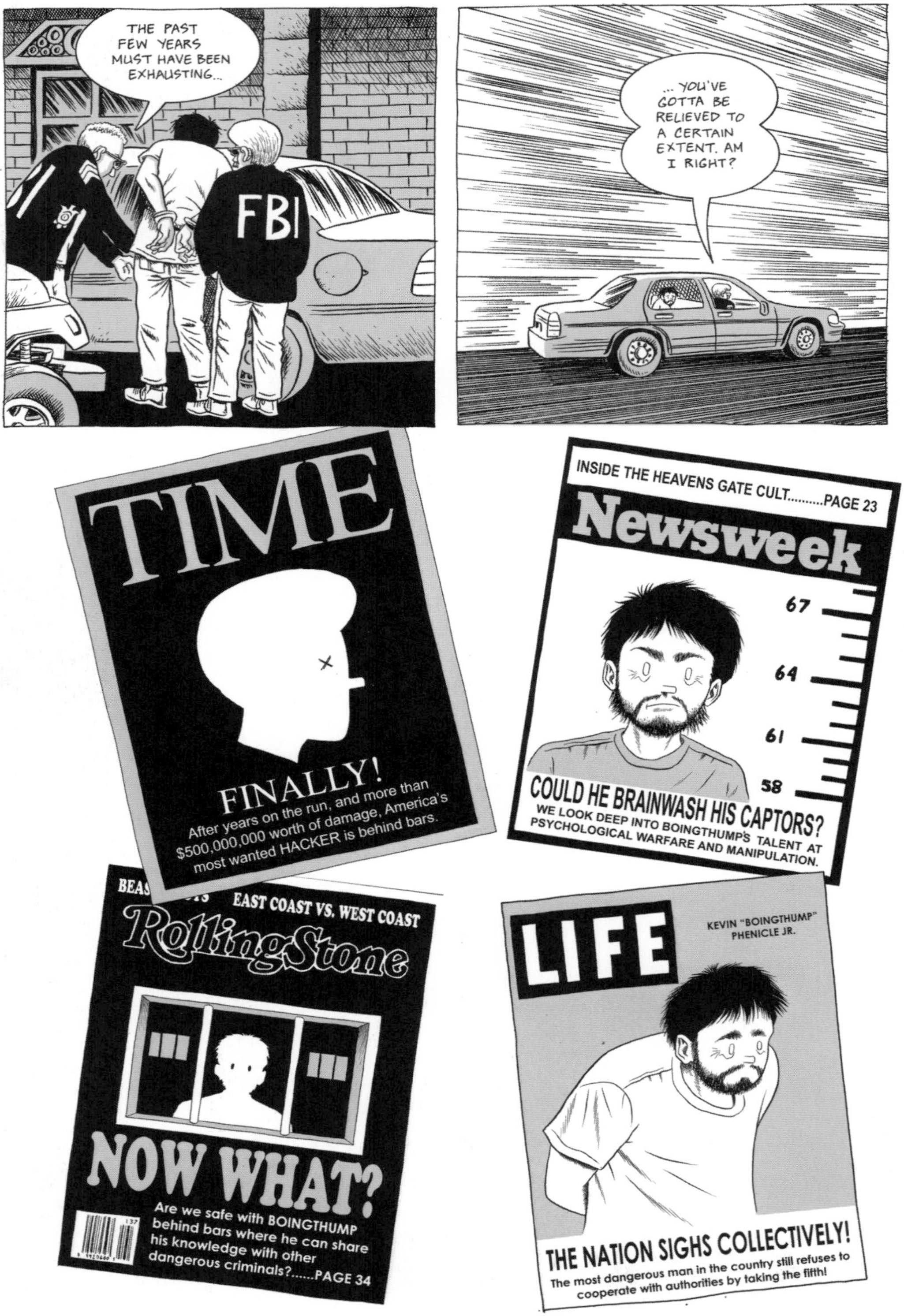
THE PAST FEW YEARS MUST HAVE BEEN EXHAUSTING...
FBI
... YOU'VE GOTTA BE RELIEVED TO A CERTAIN EXTENT. AM I RIGHT?
TIME
FINALLY!
After years on the run, and more than $500,000,000 worth of damage, America's most wanted HACKER is behind bars.
INSIDE THE HEAVENS GATE CULT..........PAGE 23
Newsweek
67
64
61
58
COULD HE BRAINWASH HIS CAPTORS?
WE LOOK DEEP INTO BOINGTHUMP'S TALENT AT PSYCHOLOGICAL WARFARE AND MANIPULATION.
EAST COAST VS. WEST COAST
RollingStone
NOW WHAT?
Are we safe with BOINGTHUMP behind bars where he can share his knowledge with other dangerous criminals?......PAGE 34
LIFE
KEVIN "BOINGTHUMP" PHENICLE JR.
THE NATION SIGHS COLLECTIVELY!
The most dangerous man in the country still refuses to cooperate with authorities by taking the fifth!

CHAPTER 7

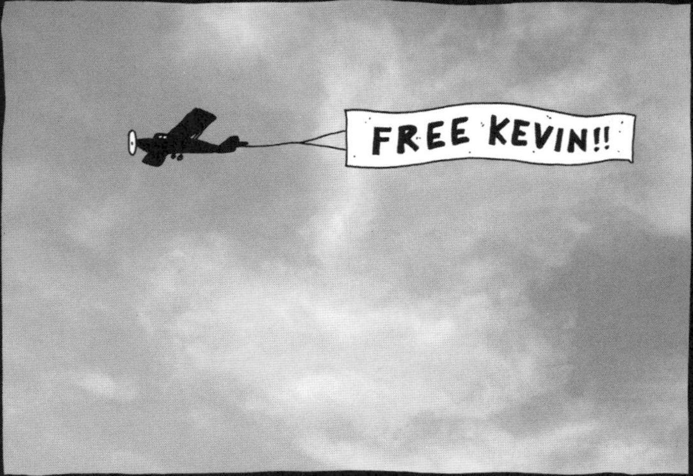
FREE KEVIN!!

TODAY'S GOOD MORNING EARLY SHOW

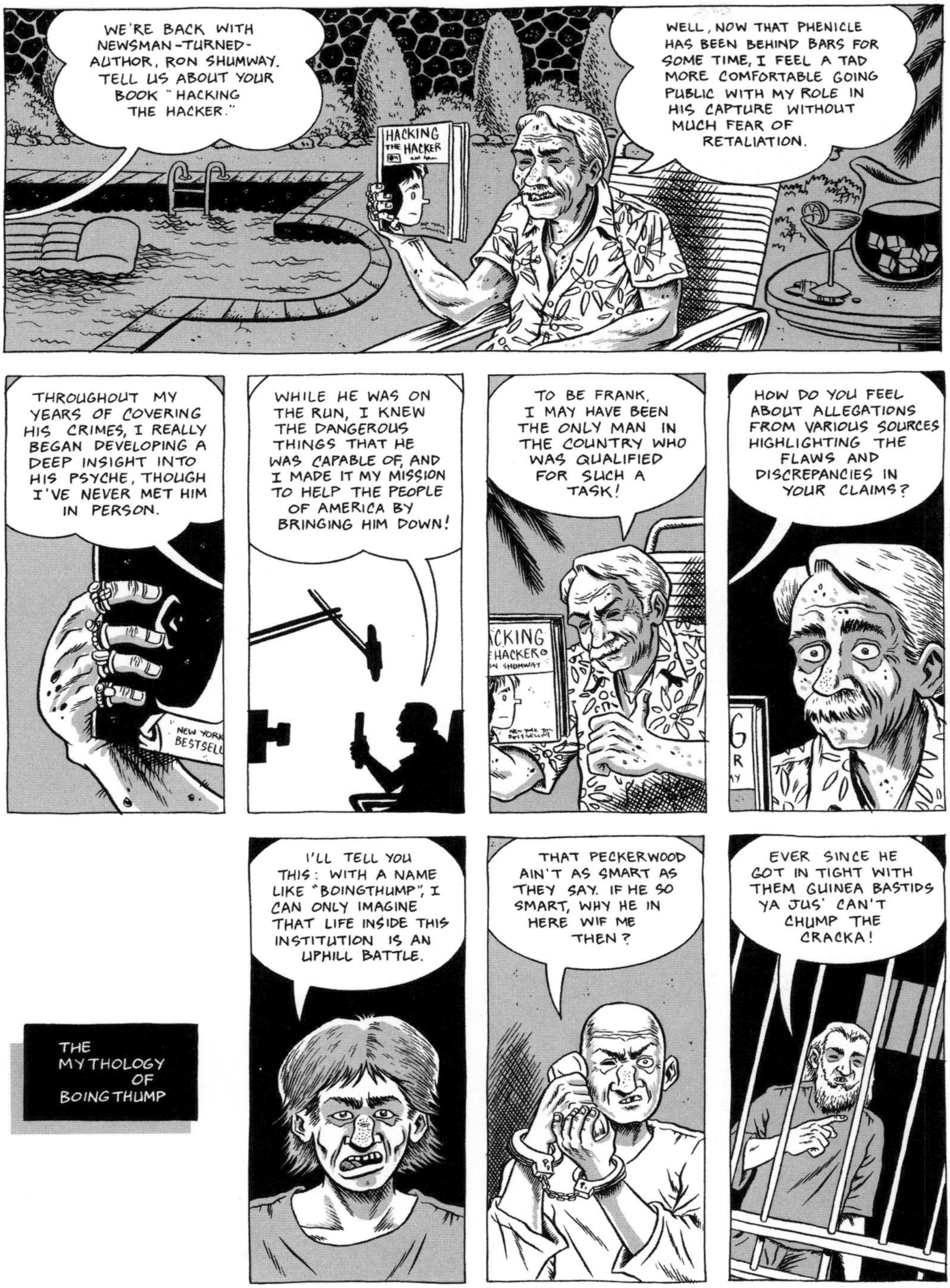
WE'RE BACK WITH NEWSMAN-TURNED-AUTHOR, RON SHUMWAY. TELL US ABOUT YOUR BOOK "HACKING THE HACKER."
HACKING THE HACKER
WELL, NOW THAT PHENICLE HAS BEEN BEHIND BARS FOR SOME TIME, I FEEL A TAD MORE COMFORTABLE GOING PUBLIC WITH MY ROLE IN HIS CAPTURE WITHOUT MUCH FEAR OF RETALIATION.
THROUGHOUT MY YEARS OF COVERING HIS CRIMES, I REALLY BEGAN DEVELOPING A DEEP INSIGHT INTO HIS PSYCHE, THOUGH I'VE NEVER MET HIM IN PERSON.
NEW YORK BESTSELL
WHILE HE WAS ON THE RUN, I KNEW THE DANGEROUS THINGS THAT HE WAS CAPABLE OF, AND I MADE IT MY MISSION TO HELP THE PEOPLE OF AMERICA BY BRINGING HIM DOWN!
TO BE FRANK, I MAY HAVE BEEN THE ONLY MAN IN THE COUNTRY WHO WAS QUALIFIED FOR SUCH A TASK!
ACKING HE HACKER ON SHUMWAY
HOW DO YOU FEEL ABOUT ALLEGATIONS FROM VARIOUS SOURCES HIGHLIGHTING THE FLAWS AND DISCREPANCIES IN YOUR CLAIMS?
I'LL TELL YOU THIS: WITH A NAME LIKE "BOINGTHUMP", I CAN ONLY IMAGINE THAT LIFE INSIDE THIS INSTITUTION IS AN UPHILL BATTLE.
THAT PECKERWOOD AIN'T AS SMART AS THEY SAY. IF HE SO SMART, WHY HE IN HERE WIF ME THEN?
EVER SINCE HE GOT IN TIGHT WITH THEM GUINEA BASTIDS YA JUS' CAN'T CHUMP THE CRACKA!

THE MYTHOLOGY OF BOINGTHUMP

THEY AIN'T FOOLIN' ME. I KNOW HE'S HERE TO RE-PORT ON WHAT'S GOING ON IN GENERAL POP. DON'T TRUS' 'IM.

HE'S GOT HIS ESCAPE PLANNED. HE'LL BE OUT OF HERE IN NO TIME.

I LOST A BET. I VERY MUCH EXPECTED HIM TO CRY HIS FIRST NIGHT IN HERE.

FUCK THAT MOTHERFUCKER !!!

OFF THE ROCKER
with your host WINSTON SMITH
WABCD 108.3 ON YOUR FM DIAL

IT'S BEEN A HANDFUL OF YEARS SINCE MY GOOD FRIEND, KEVIN "BOINGTHUMP"PHENICLE, HAS BEEN IN FEDERAL CUSTODY, AND THIS PAST WEEK WAS HIS MOST PAINFUL. I HAD TO LET HIM KNOW THAT HIS GRANDMOTHER HAD PASSED.

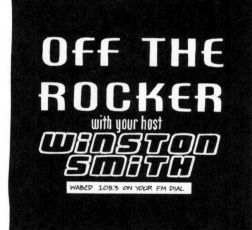

G'NIGHT GRAM...

GREAT MARKS, KEVIN!

REPORT CARD
SUBJECT

THE HARDEST PART OF THIS WAS NOT BEING ABLE TO EVEN PUT A HAND ON HIS SHOULDER AS HE BEGAN TO LOSE IT. FOR VARIOUS REASONS HE HAS BEEN DENIED VISITATION, AND IT TURNS OUT HIS GRANDMA DID NOT LET HIM KNOW HOW SICK SHE WAS.

OH, KEVIN, I MISS YOUR MOM AND DADDY TOO...

DON'T WORRY IF YOU CAN'T GET THE LID OFF FOR ME. THEY PUT THEM ON WITH MACHINES.

I FEEL LIKE I'M OPERATING THIS SHOW WITHIN A VACUUM! THROUGH THIS PUBLICITY I THOUGHT WE'D BE ABLE TO HELP GET KEVIN A TRIAL BY NOW! IT'S BEEN 5 YEARS, AND THEY ARE JUST LETTING HIM ROT IN PURGATORY. I NOW ADMIT THAT MY WORDS HAVE FAILED. IT IS TIME FOR ACTION!

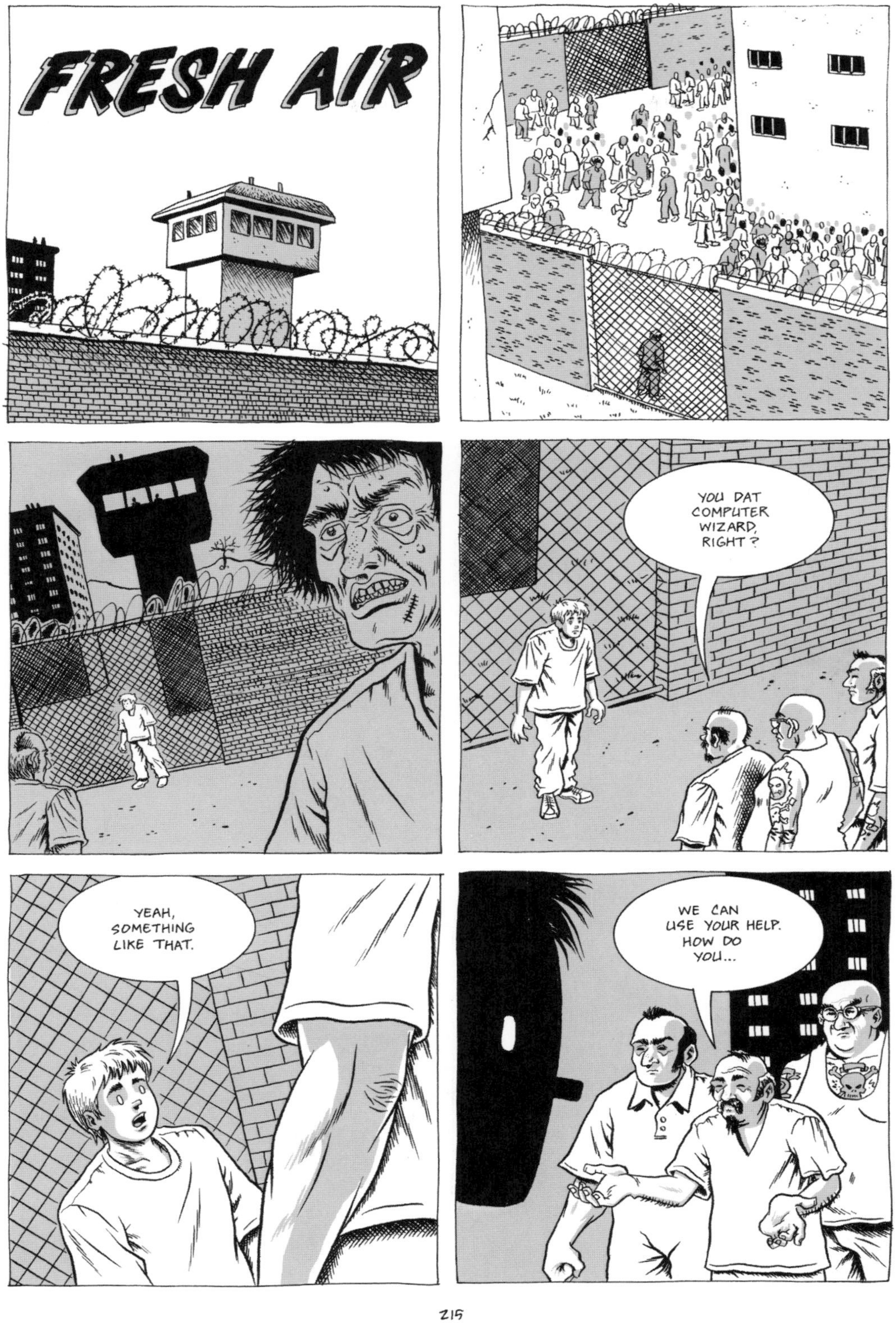
FRESH AIR
YOU DAT COMPUTER WIZARD, RIGHT?
YEAH, SOMETHING LIKE THAT.
WE CAN USE YOUR HELP. HOW DO YOU...

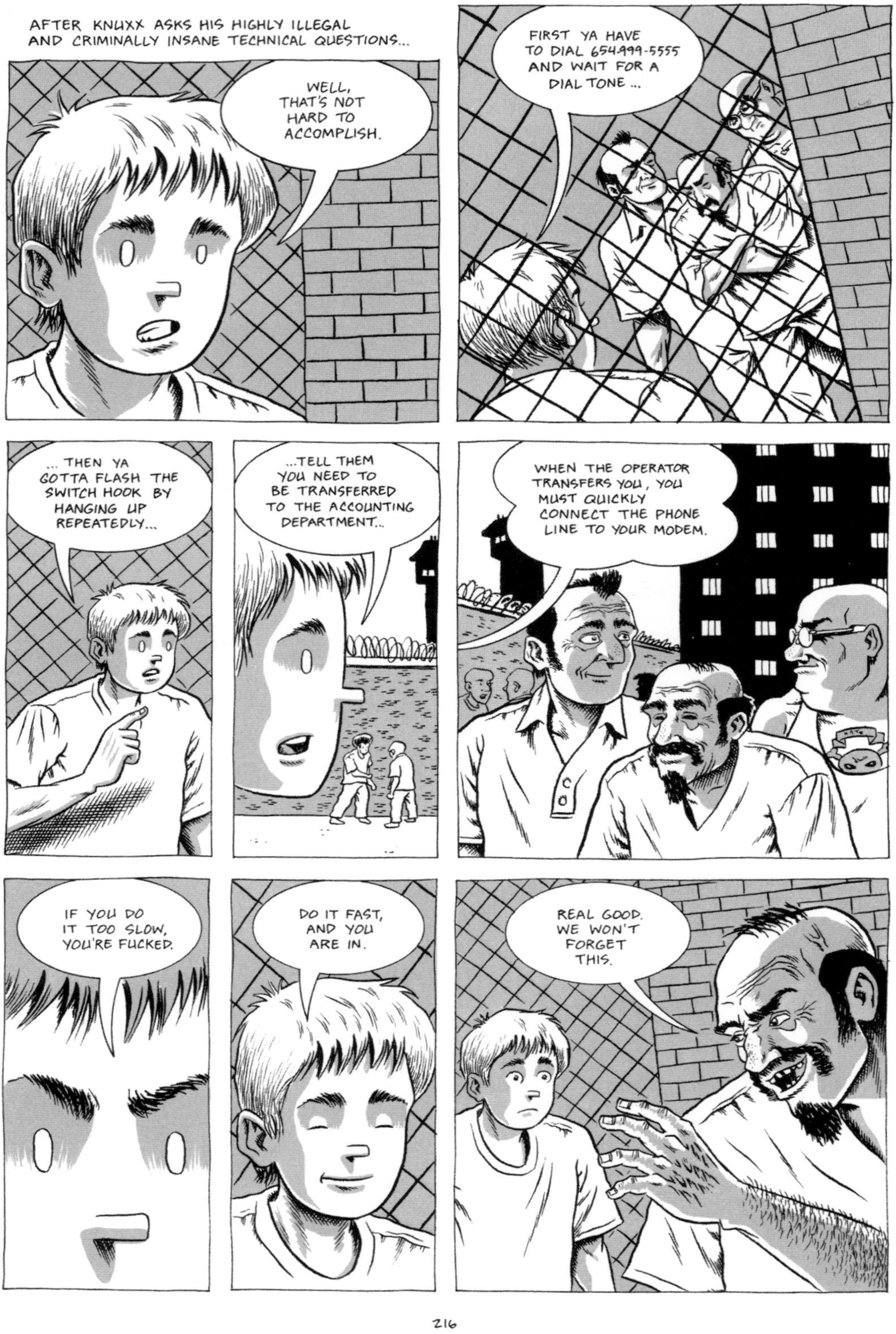
AFTER KNUXX ASKS HIS HIGHLY ILLEGAL AND CRIMINALLY INSANE TECHNICAL QUESTIONS...
WELL, THAT'S NOT HARD TO ACCOMPLISH.
FIRST YA HAVE TO DIAL 654-999-5555 AND WAIT FOR A DIAL TONE ...
... THEN YA GOTTA FLASH THE SWITCH HOOK BY HANGING UP REPEATEDLY...
...TELL THEM YOU NEED TO BE TRANSFERRED TO THE ACCOUNTING DEPARTMENT...
WHEN THE OPERATOR TRANSFERS YOU, YOU MUST QUICKLY CONNECT THE PHONE LINE TO YOUR MODEM.
IF YOU DO IT TOO SLOW, YOU'RE FUCKED.
DO IT FAST, AND YOU ARE IN.
REAL GOOD. WE WON'T FORGET THIS.

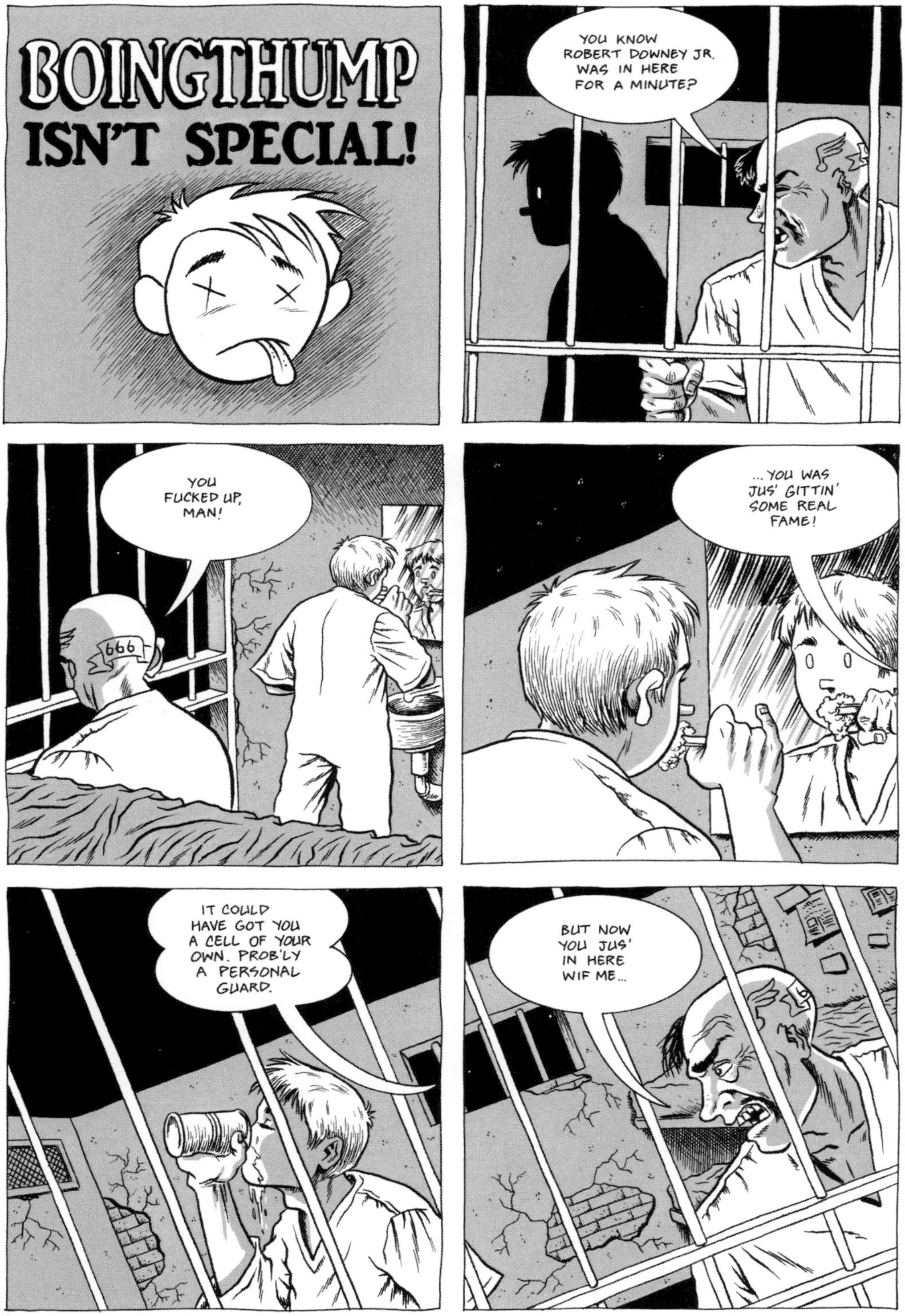
BOINGTHUMP ISN'T SPECIAL!
YOU KNOW ROBERT DOWNEY JR. WAS IN HERE FOR A MINUTE?
YOU FUCKED UP, MAN!
666
...YOU WAS JUS' GITTIN' SOME REAL FAME!
IT COULD HAVE GOT YOU A CELL OF YOUR OWN. PROB'LY A PERSONAL GUARD.
BUT NOW YOU JUS' IN HERE WIF ME...

JUST A FEW OF MY PET PEEVES

THE JERKS GAVE ME A PILLOW CASE, BUT NO PILLOW... FOR MONTHS!

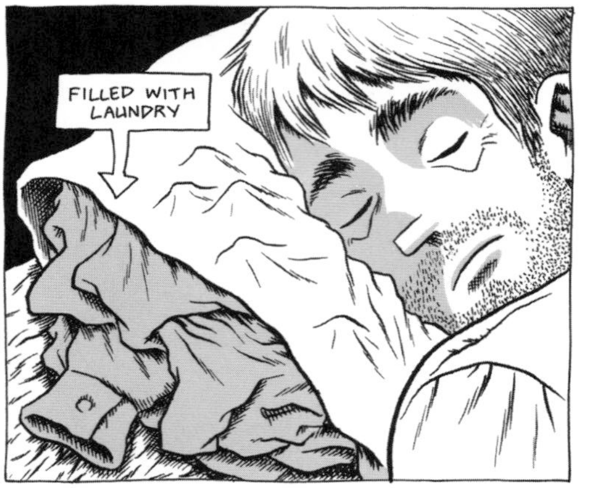
FILLED WITH LAUNDRY

NOTHING BUT SPORTS ON TV IN THE REC ROOM... UNLESS THE ITALIANS KNOW A GANGSTER MOVIE IS ON.

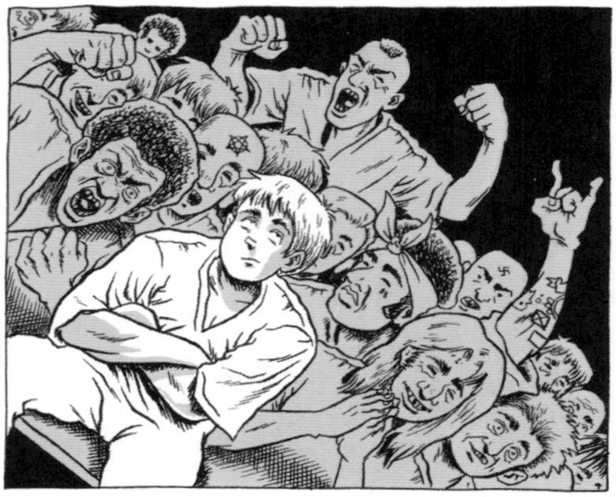

I KEEP PUTTING IN FOR A JOB AT THE LIBRARY TO NO AVAIL.

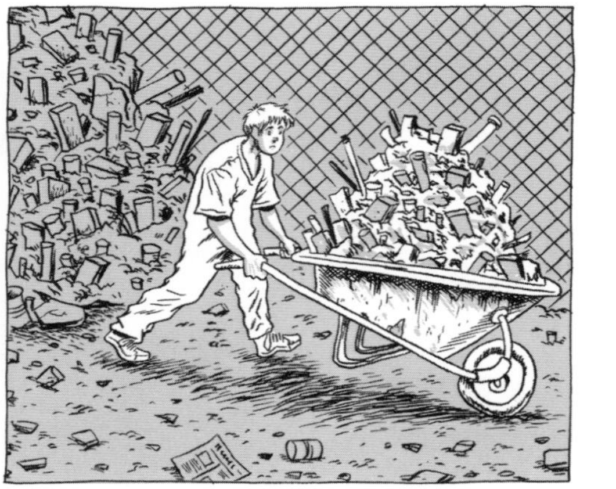

LOTS OF HOMOPHOBIC AND RACIAL EXPLETIVES ON A CONSTANT BASIS.

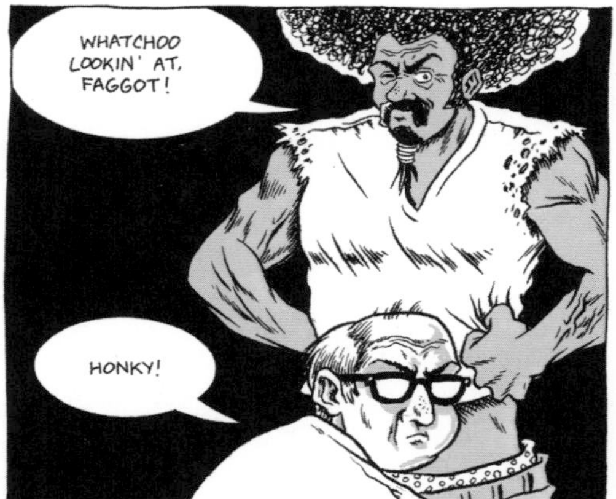
WHATCHOO LOOKIN' AT, FAGGOT!
HONKY!

I LEARNED QUICKLY THAT IT IS FUTILE TO MEDIATE.

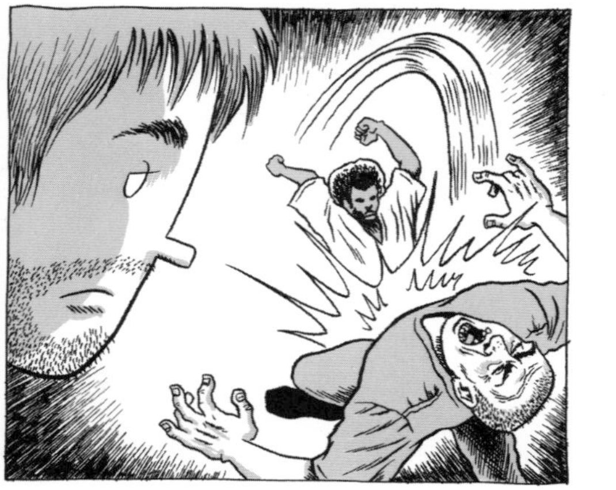

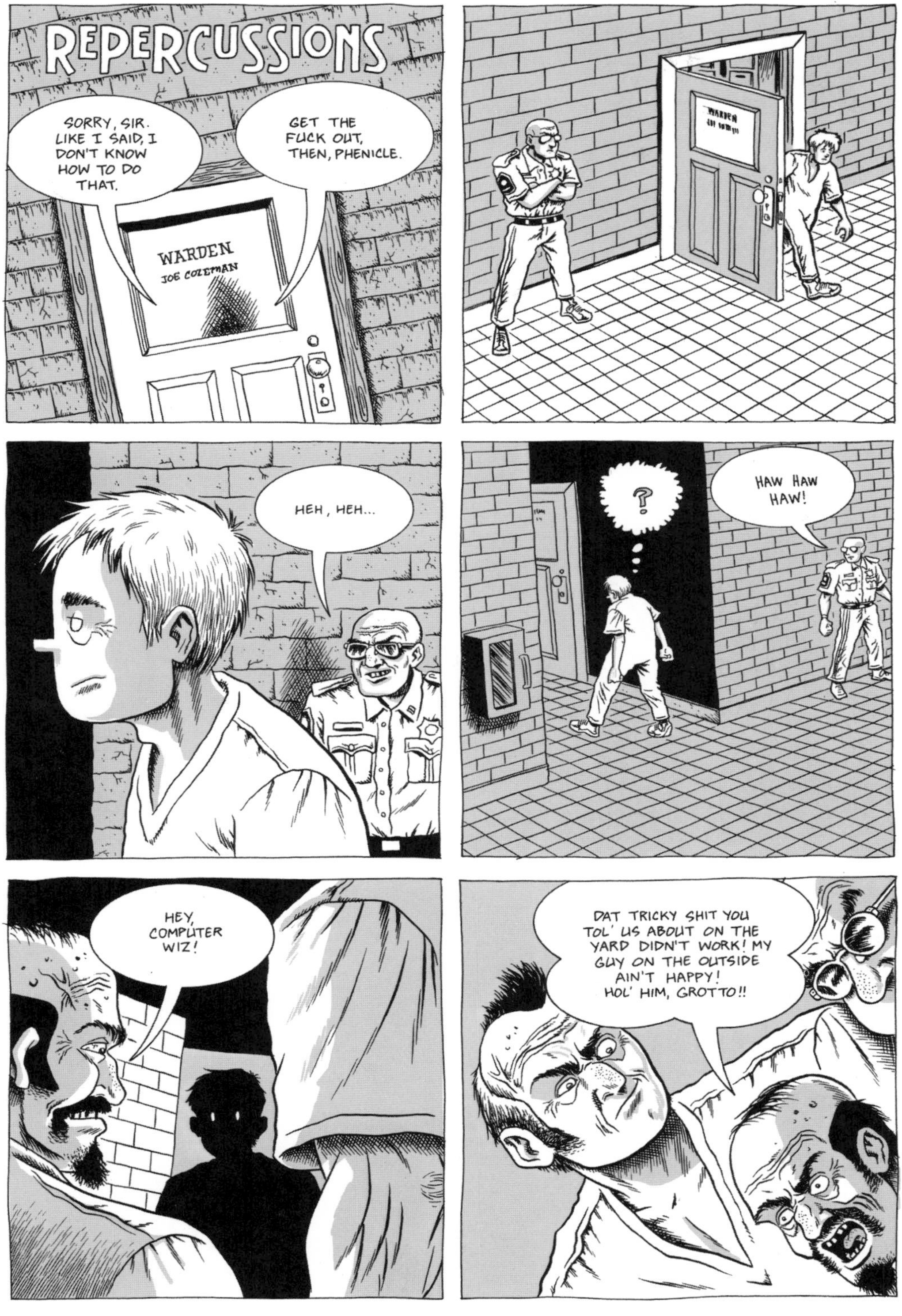
REPERCUSSIONS
SORRY, SIR. LIKE I SAID, I DON'T KNOW HOW TO DO THAT.
GET THE FUCK OUT, THEN, PHENICLE.
WARDEN
JOE COLEMAN
HEH, HEH...
?
HAW HAW HAW!
HEY, COMPUTER WIZ!
DAT TRICKY SHIT YOU TOL' US ABOUT ON THE YARD DIDN'T WORK! MY GUY ON THE OUTSIDE AIN'T HAPPY! HOL' HIM, GROTTO!!

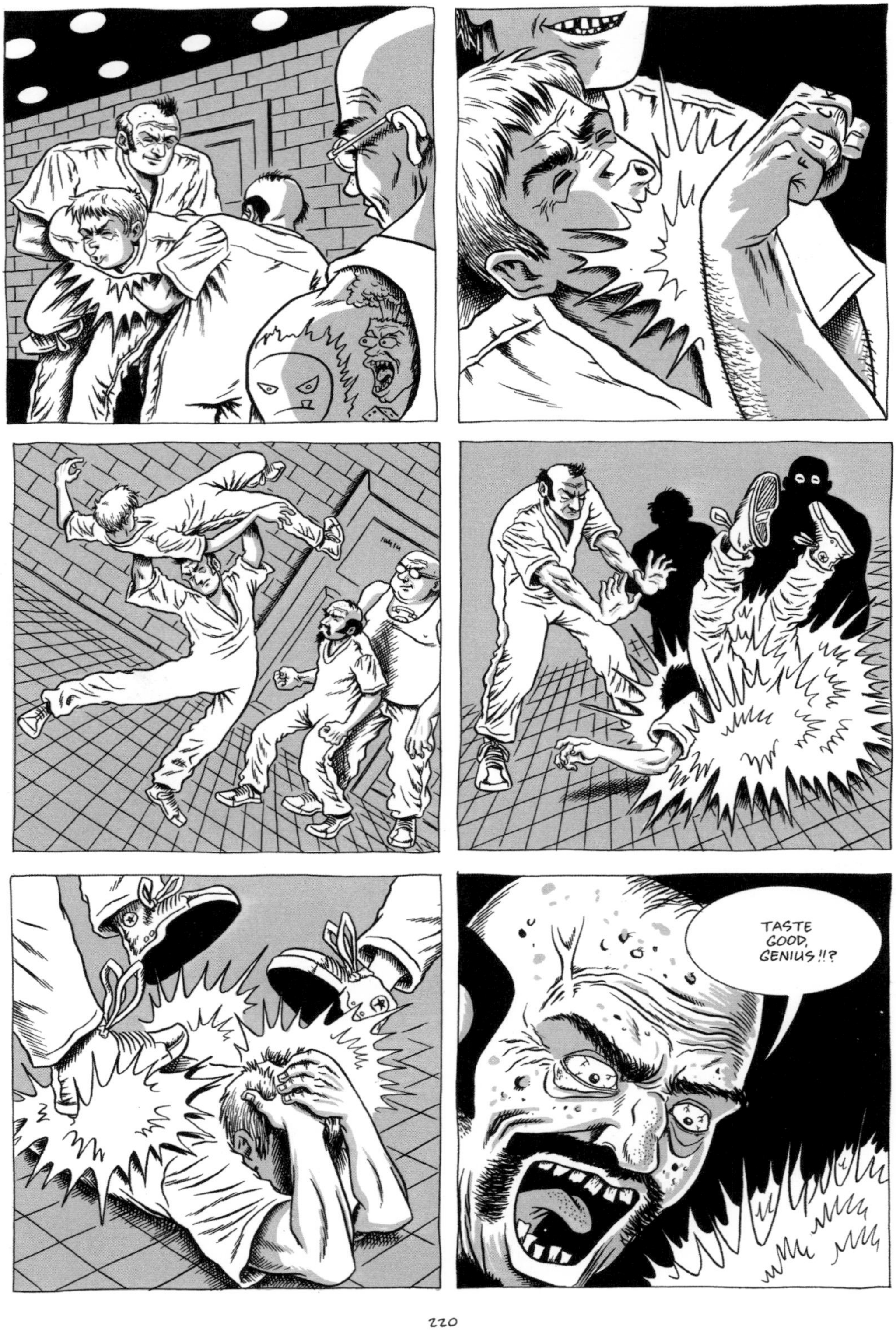
TASTE GOOD, GENIUS !!?

THE CHEESE STANDS ALONE

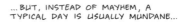
PRISON IS INTERESTING FROM AN ANTHROPOLOGICAL POINT OF VIEW.

OBVIOUSLY, THE WORST OF SOCIETY IS LOCKED UP TOGETHER...

...BUT, INSTEAD OF MAYHEM, A TYPICAL DAY IS USUALLY MUNDANE...

INMATES TREAT EACH OTHER WITH SUCH INTENSE RESPECT MOST OF THE TIME, UNLESS YOU ALLOW YOURSELF TO BE A TARGET.

THE JOINT IS SUCH A PRESSURE—COOKER TYPE OF SITUATION. EVERYONE IS ON EDGE 24/7.

THIS CREATES A SENSITIVE ENVIRONMENT WHERE GUYS MAY GET EASILY OFFENDED AND VIOLENT IF THEY FEEL DISRESPECTED.

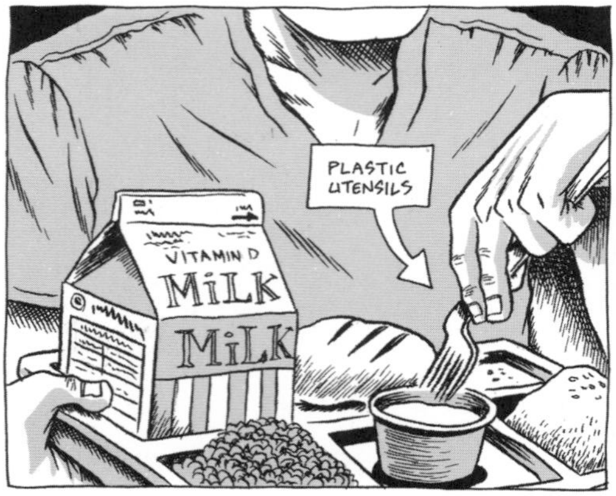
PLASTIC UTENSILS
VITAMIN D
MILK
MILK

IT'S EASY TO SURVIVE AS LONG AS YOU OBSERVE THE CULTURE THAT EXISTS. FOR INSTANCE, IF YOU GET JUMPED BY 3 GUYS WHILE A GUARD IS LAUGHING, YOU BEST KEEP YOUR MOUTH SHUT.

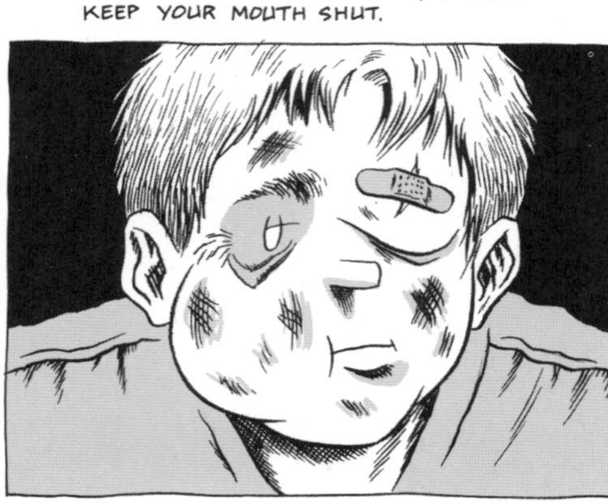

BEING A SNITCH IS AN EASY WAY TO LEAVE HERE IN A BOX.

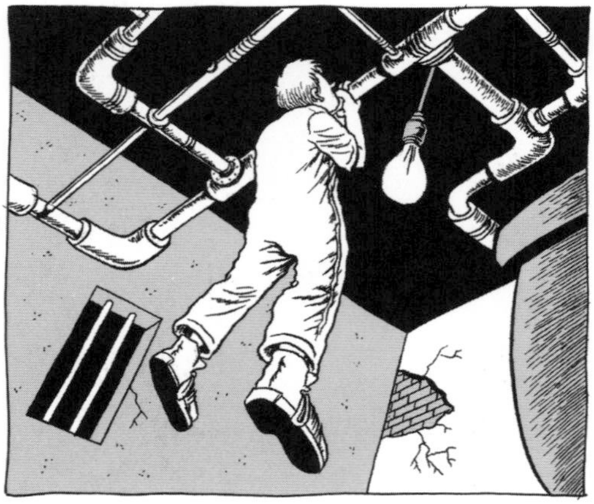

EVEN IF YOU'RE THE ONLY ONE TO TAKE THE FALL, YOU HAVE TO CUT YOUR LOSSES.

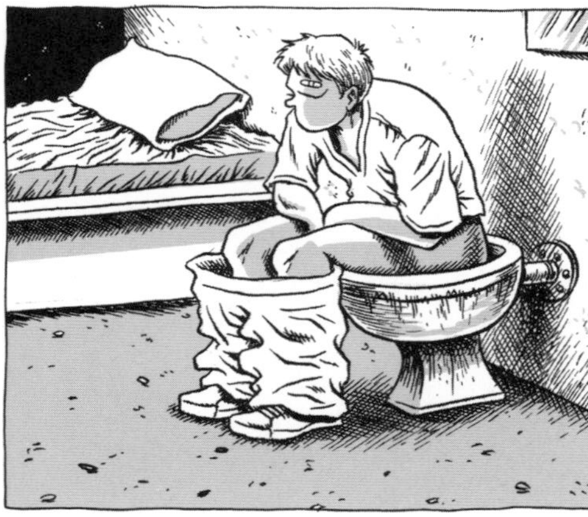

A MONTH OF SOLITARY CONFINEMENT IS NOT THE WORST THAT CAN HAPPEN TO A GUY...

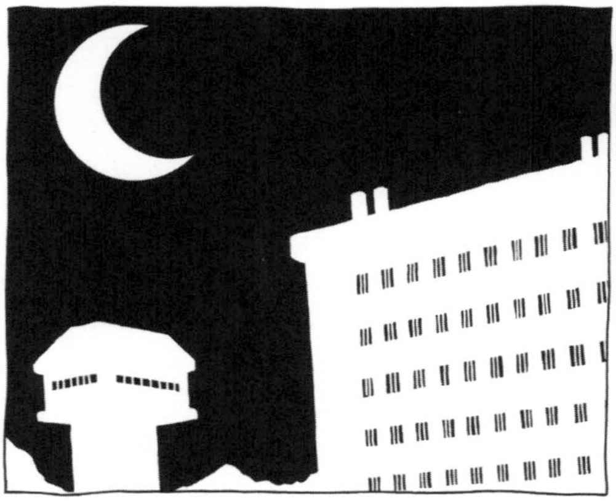

THAT'S, AT LEAST, WHAT I TELL MYSELF WHENEVER I GET INTO A SCRAPE.

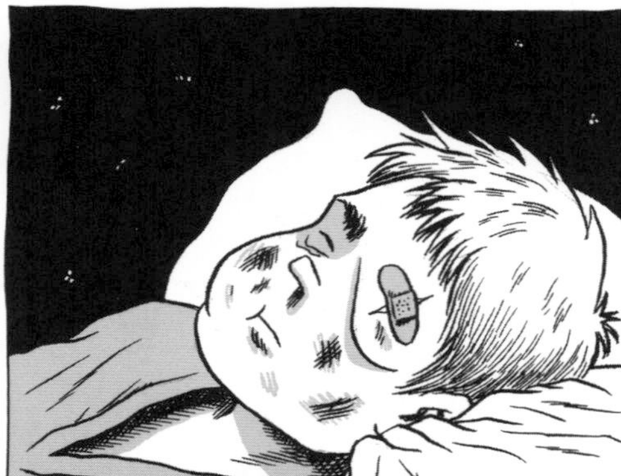

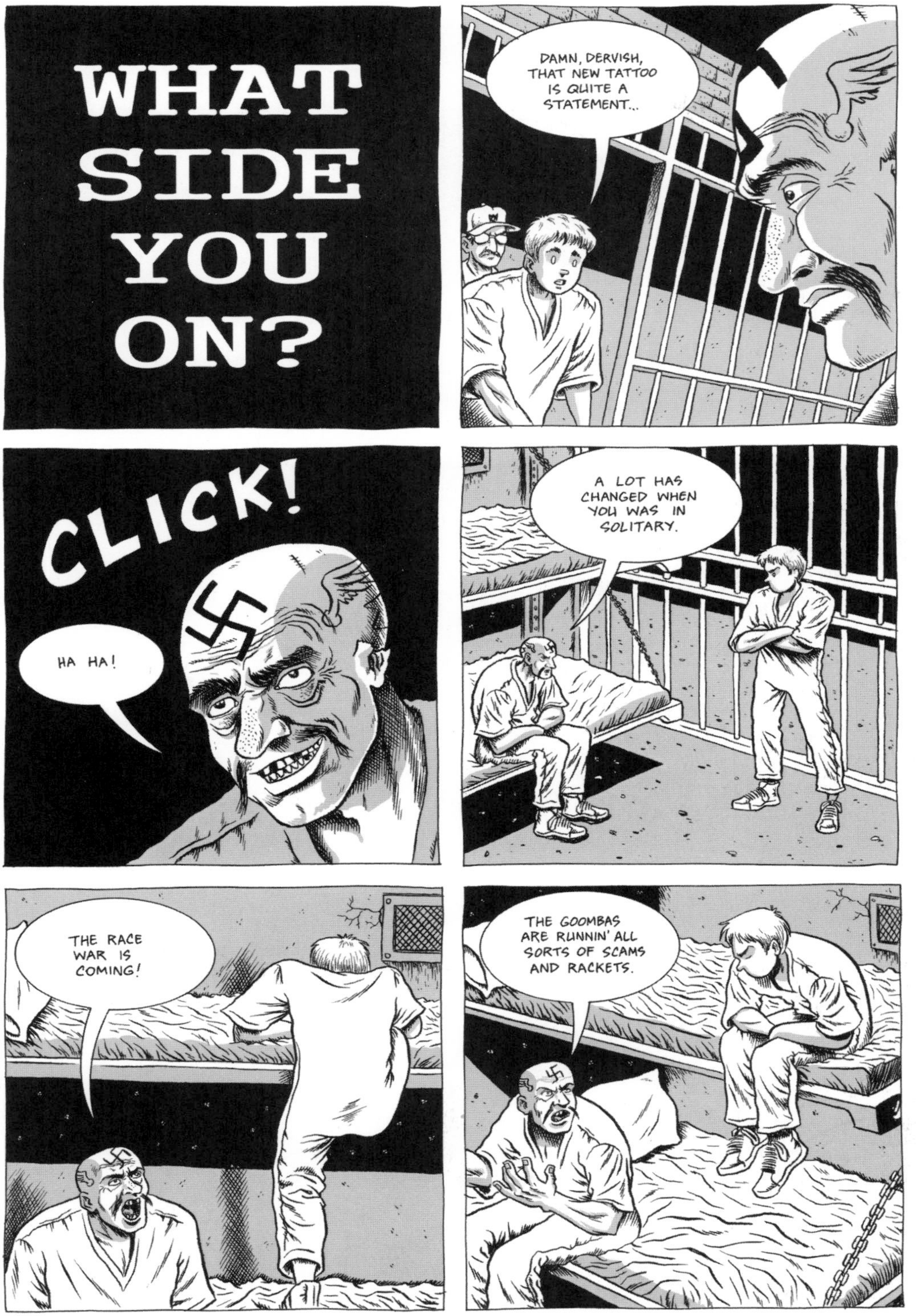
WHAT SIDE YOU ON?
DAMN, DERVISH, THAT NEW TATTOO IS QUITE A STATEMENT...
CLICK!
HA HA!
A LOT HAS CHANGED WHEN YOU WAS IN SOLITARY.
THE RACE WAR IS COMING!
THE GOOMBAS ARE RUNNIN' ALL SORTS OF SCAMS AND RACKETS.

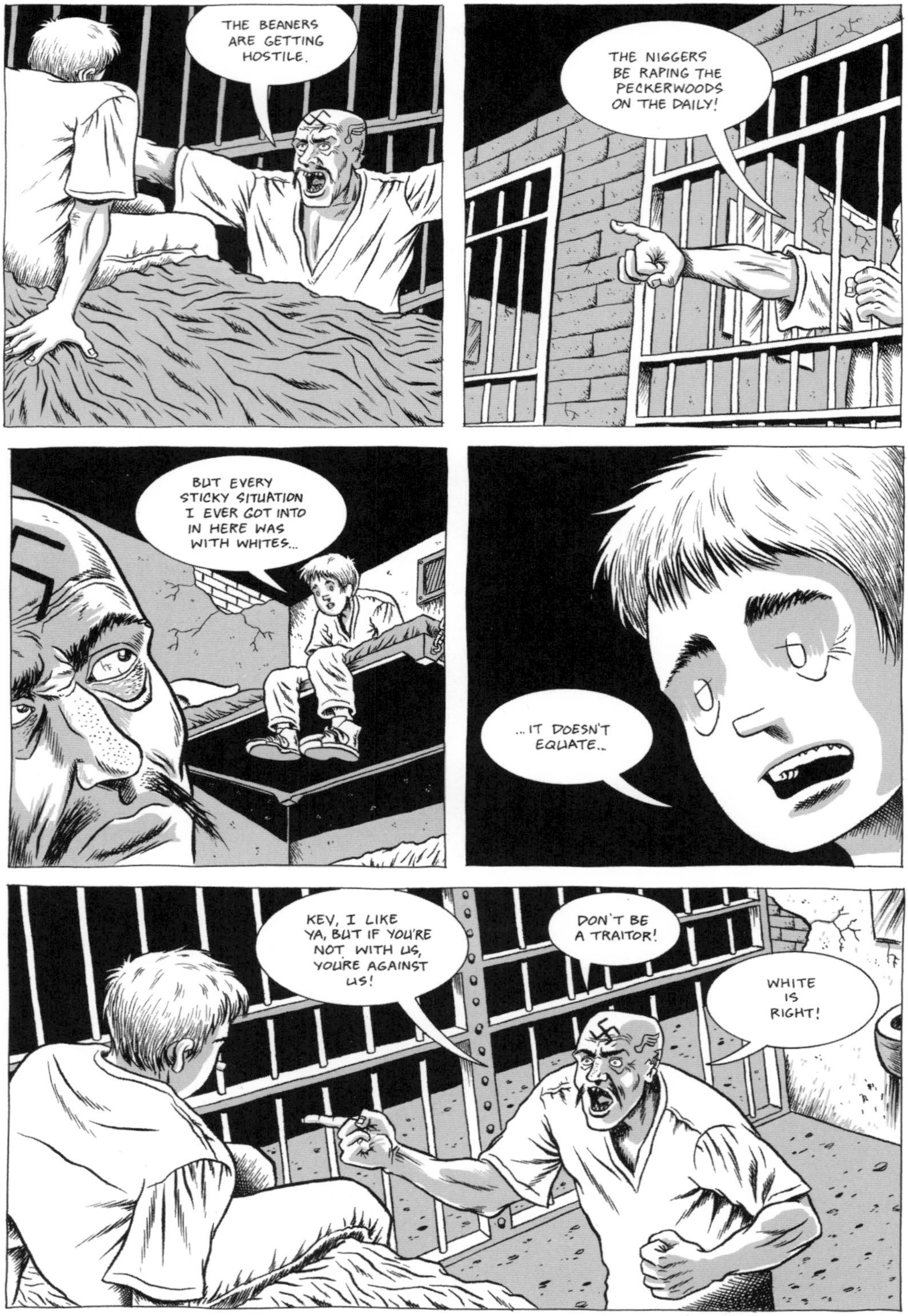
THE BEANERS ARE GETTING HOSTILE.
THE NIGGERS BE RAPING THE PECKERWOODS ON THE DAILY!
BUT EVERY STICKY SITUATION I EVER GOT INTO IN HERE WAS WITH WHITES...
... IT DOESN'T EQUATE..
KEV, I LIKE YA, BUT IF YOU'RE NOT WITH US, YOU'RE AGAINST US!
DON'T BE A TRAITOR!
WHITE IS RIGHT!

AN UNFORTUNATE INCIDENT

BOBBY BANINI IS THE LEADER OF THE BANINI CRIME FAMILY. HE HAS IT EASY IN THE BIG HOUSE.

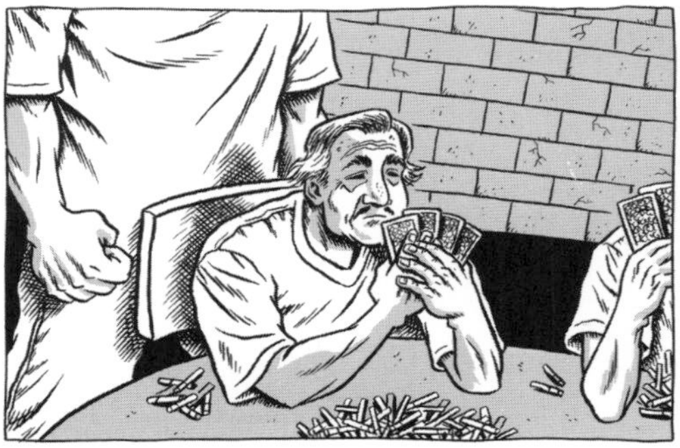

KEVIN SPENDS HIS TIME TRYING TO BE AS INVISIBLE AS POSSIBLE.

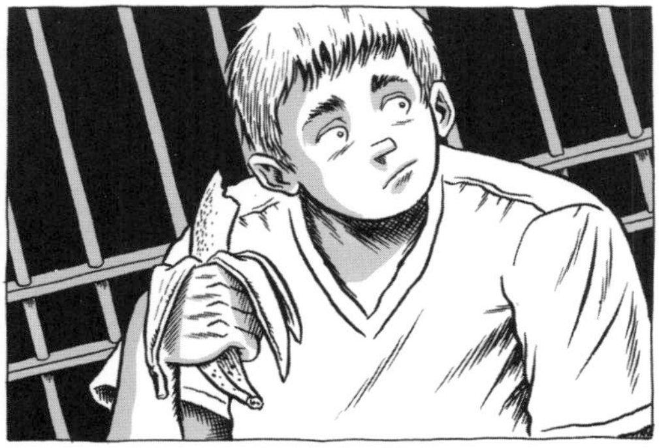

BANINI HAS A LOT OF CLOUT AMONGST THE INMATES AND GUARDS ALIKE. HE ALSO CAN DO PRETTY MUCH WHAT HE WANTS.

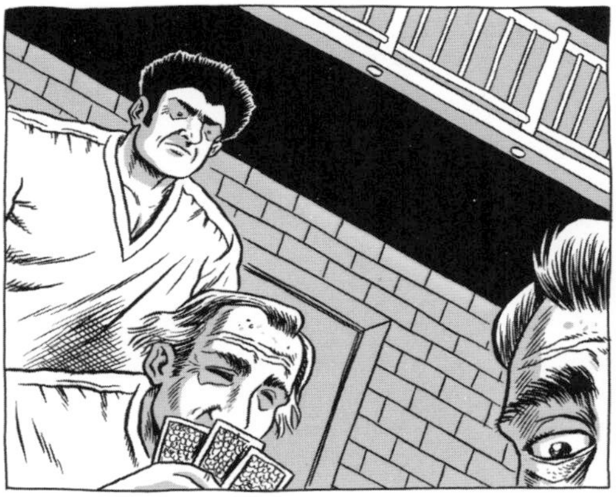

THE GUARDS WATCH KEVIN WITH A CLOSE EYE, MAKING SURE HE DOES THINGS BY THE BOOK.

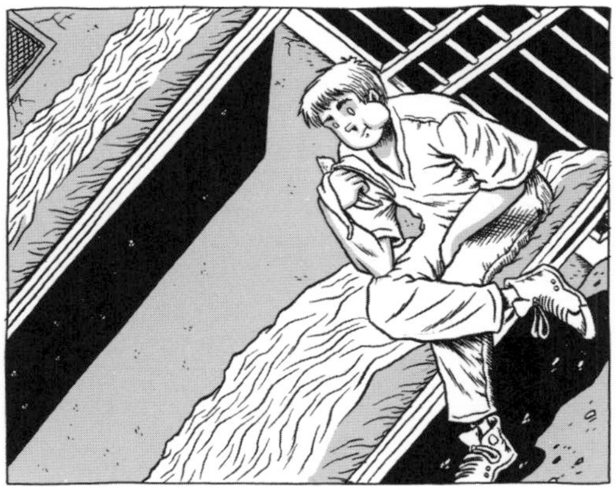

TO SAY THAT BANINI HAS FEW WORRIES IN THE SLAMMER IS PROBABLY AN UNDERSTATEMENT.

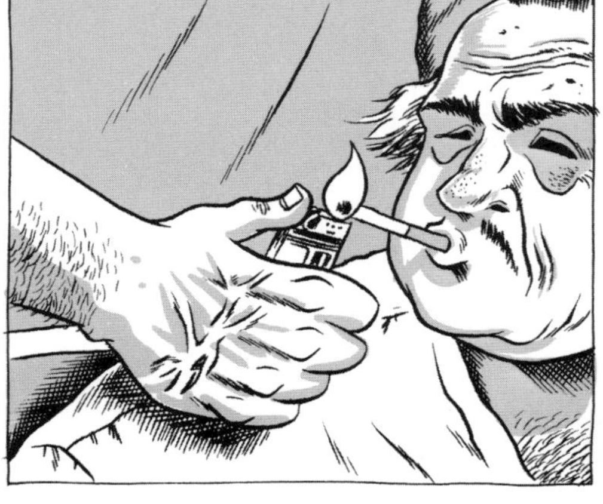

ONE OF KEVIN'S BIGGEST CONCERNS IS TO KEEP HIS CELL CONTRABAND-FREE. THIS INCLUDES FOOD SMUGGLED IN FROM THE OUTSIDE.

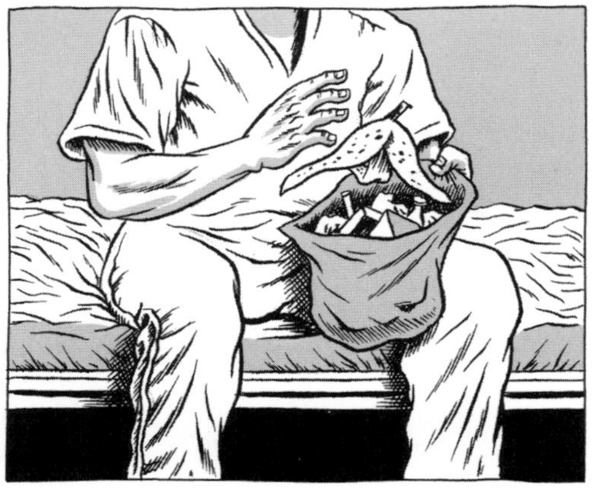

BANINI COULD EVEN BE CONSIDERED COMPLACENT.

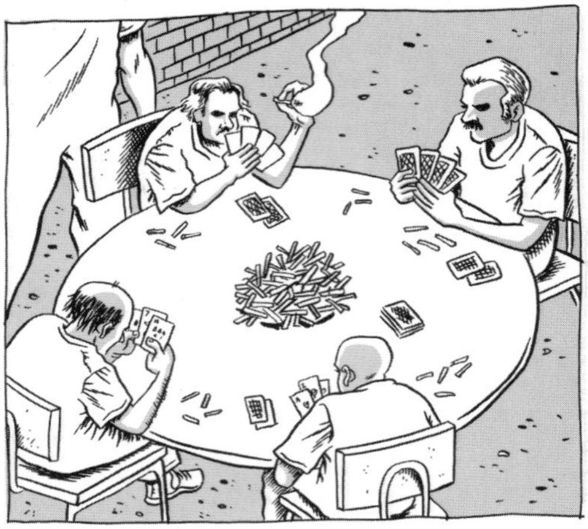

KEVIN IS METICULOUS IN HIS EFFORTS.

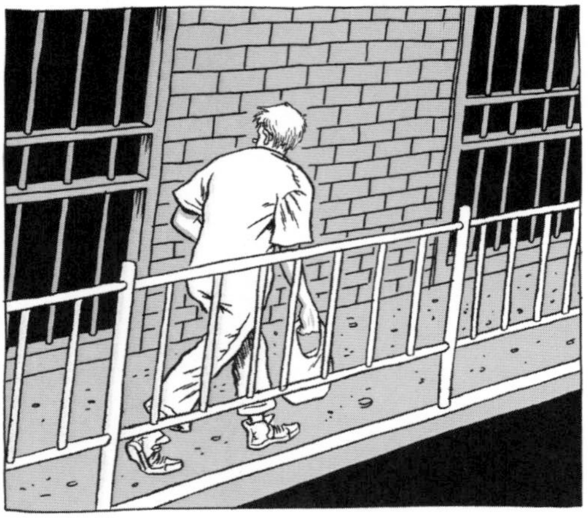

BANINI IS COMPLETELY UNAWARE OF KEVIN'S EXISTENCE.

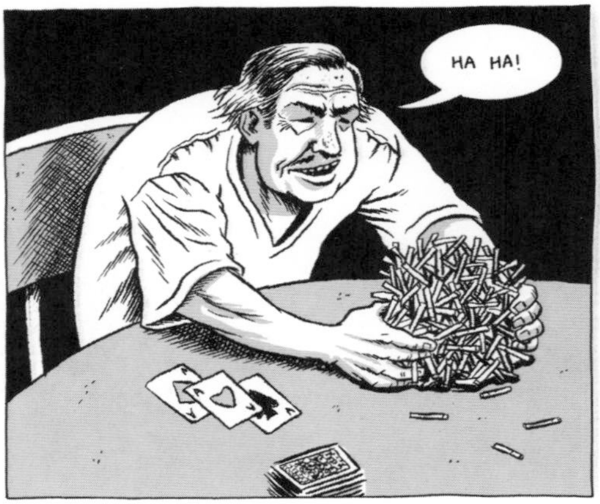
HA HA!

KEVIN IS TOO CLUMSY TO KEEP IT THAT WAY.

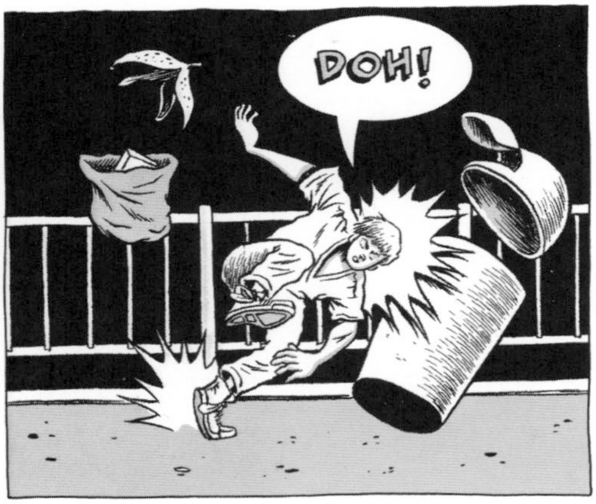
DOH!

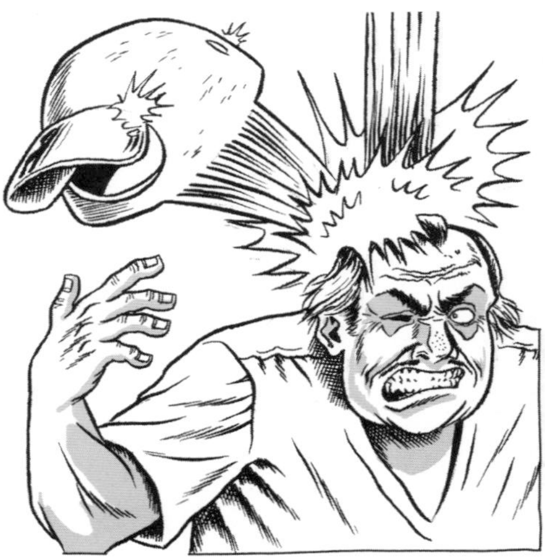

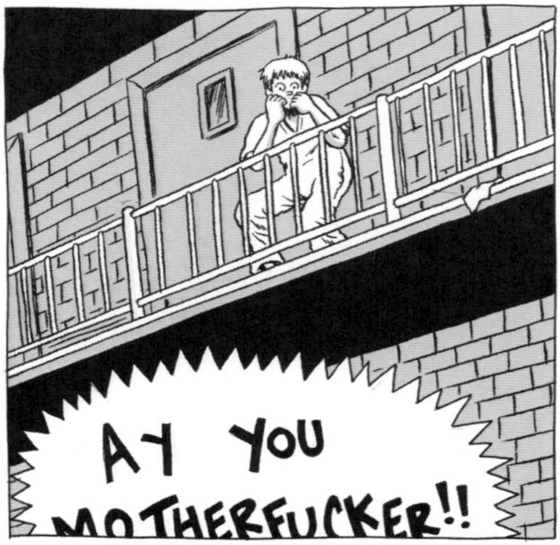
AY YOU MOTHERFUCKER!!

STRANGE BEDFELLOWS

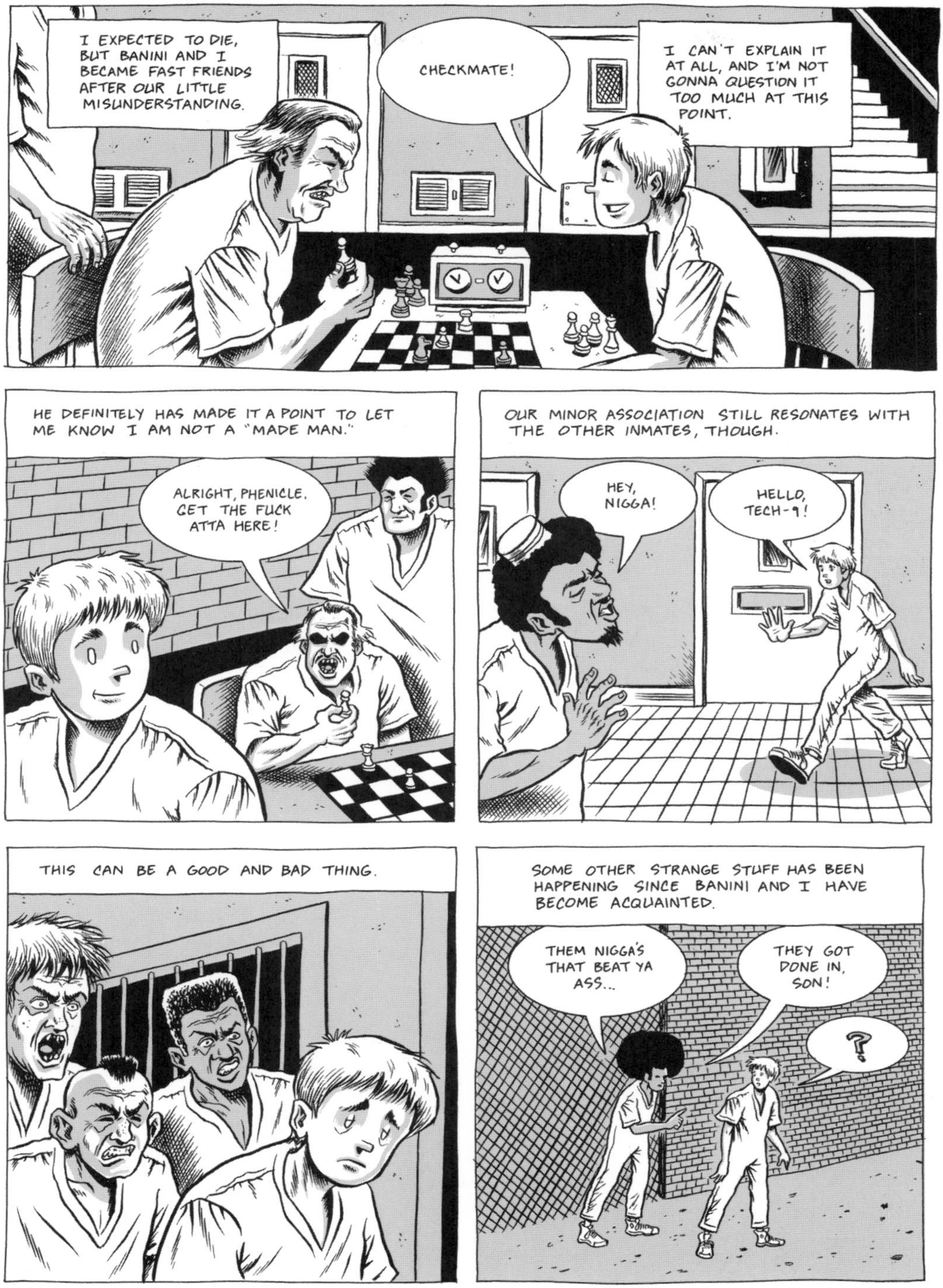
I EXPECTED TO DIE, BUT BANINI AND I BECAME FAST FRIENDS AFTER OUR LITTLE MISUNDERSTANDING.
CHECKMATE!
I CAN'T EXPLAIN IT AT ALL, AND I'M NOT GONNA QUESTION IT TOO MUCH AT THIS POINT.
HE DEFINITELY HAS MADE IT A POINT TO LET ME KNOW I AM NOT A "MADE MAN."
ALRIGHT, PHENICLE. GET THE FUCK ATTA HERE!
OUR MINOR ASSOCIATION STILL RESONATES WITH THE OTHER INMATES, THOUGH.
HEY, NIGGA!
HELLO, TECH-9!
THIS CAN BE A GOOD AND BAD THING.
SOME OTHER STRANGE STUFF HAS BEEN HAPPENING SINCE BANINI AND I HAVE BECOME ACQUAINTED.
THEM NIGGA'S THAT BEAT YA ASS...
THEY GOT DONE IN, SON!
?

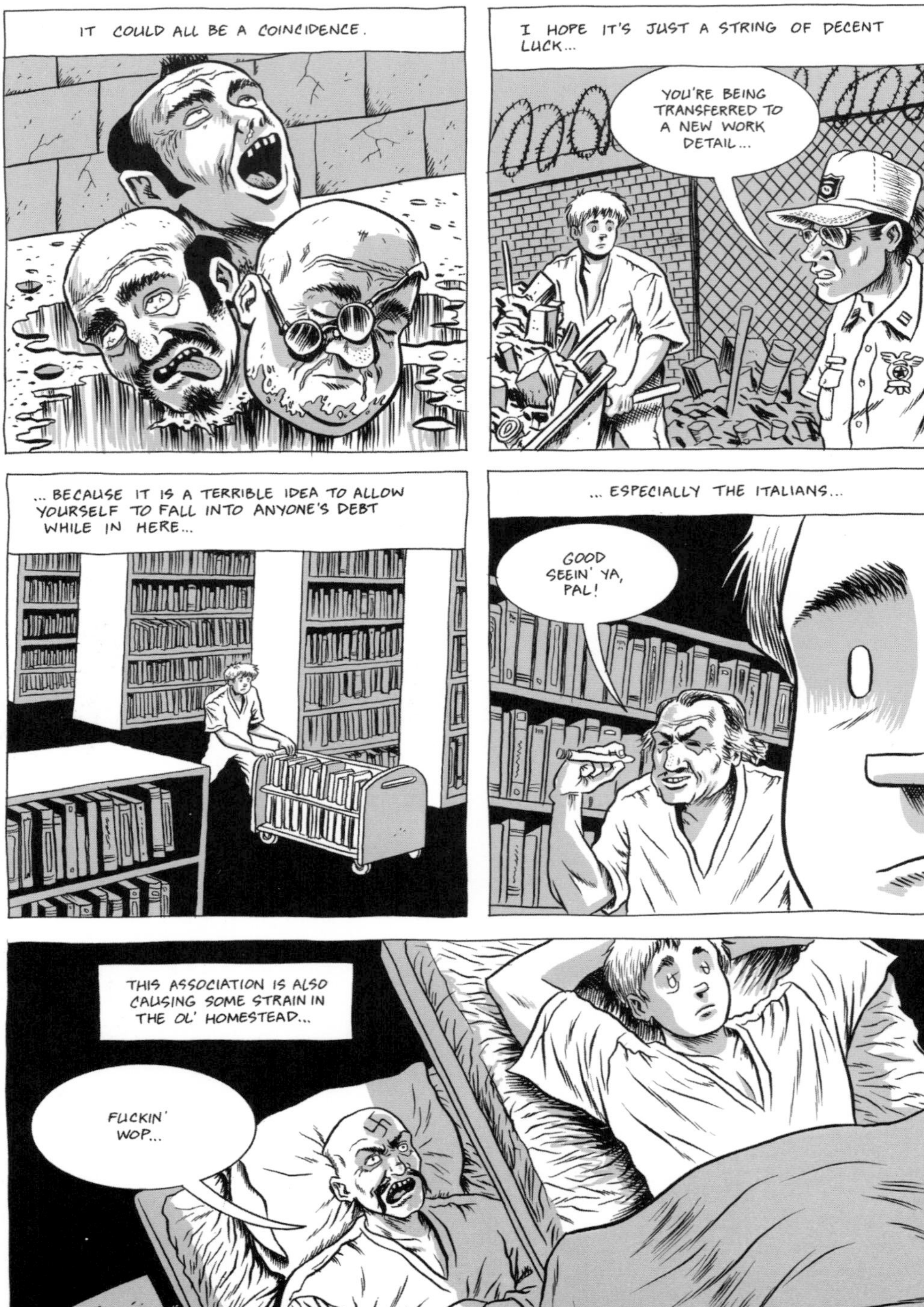
IT COULD ALL BE A COINCIDENCE.
I HOPE IT'S JUST A STRING OF DECENT LUCK...
YOU'RE BEING TRANSFERRED TO A NEW WORK DETAIL...
... BECAUSE IT IS A TERRIBLE IDEA TO ALLOW YOURSELF TO FALL INTO ANYONE'S DEBT WHILE IN HERE...
... ESPECIALLY THE ITALIANS...
GOOD SEEIN' YA, PAL!
THIS ASSOCIATION IS ALSO CAUSING SOME STRAIN IN THE OL' HOMESTEAD...
FUCKIN' WOP...

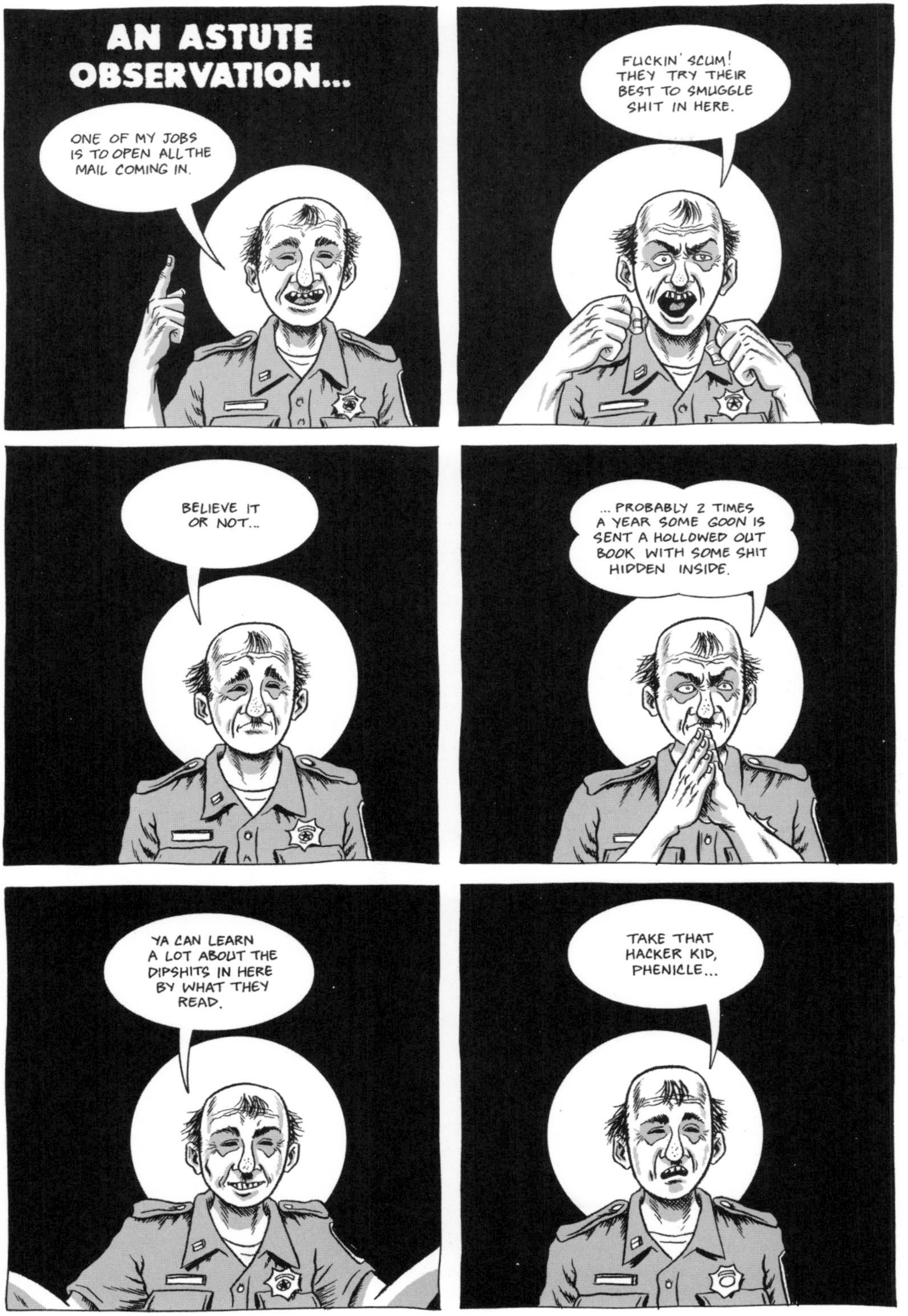
AN ASTUTE OBSERVATION...
ONE OF MY JOBS IS TO OPEN ALL THE MAIL COMING IN.
FUCKIN' SCUM! THEY TRY THEIR BEST TO SMUGGLE SHIT IN HERE.
BELIEVE IT OR NOT...
...PROBABLY 2 TIMES A YEAR SOME GOON IS SENT A HOLLOWED OUT BOOK WITH SOME SHIT HIDDEN INSIDE.
YA CAN LEARN A LOT ABOUT THE DIPSHITS IN HERE BY WHAT THEY READ.
TAKE THAT HACKER KID, PHENICLE...

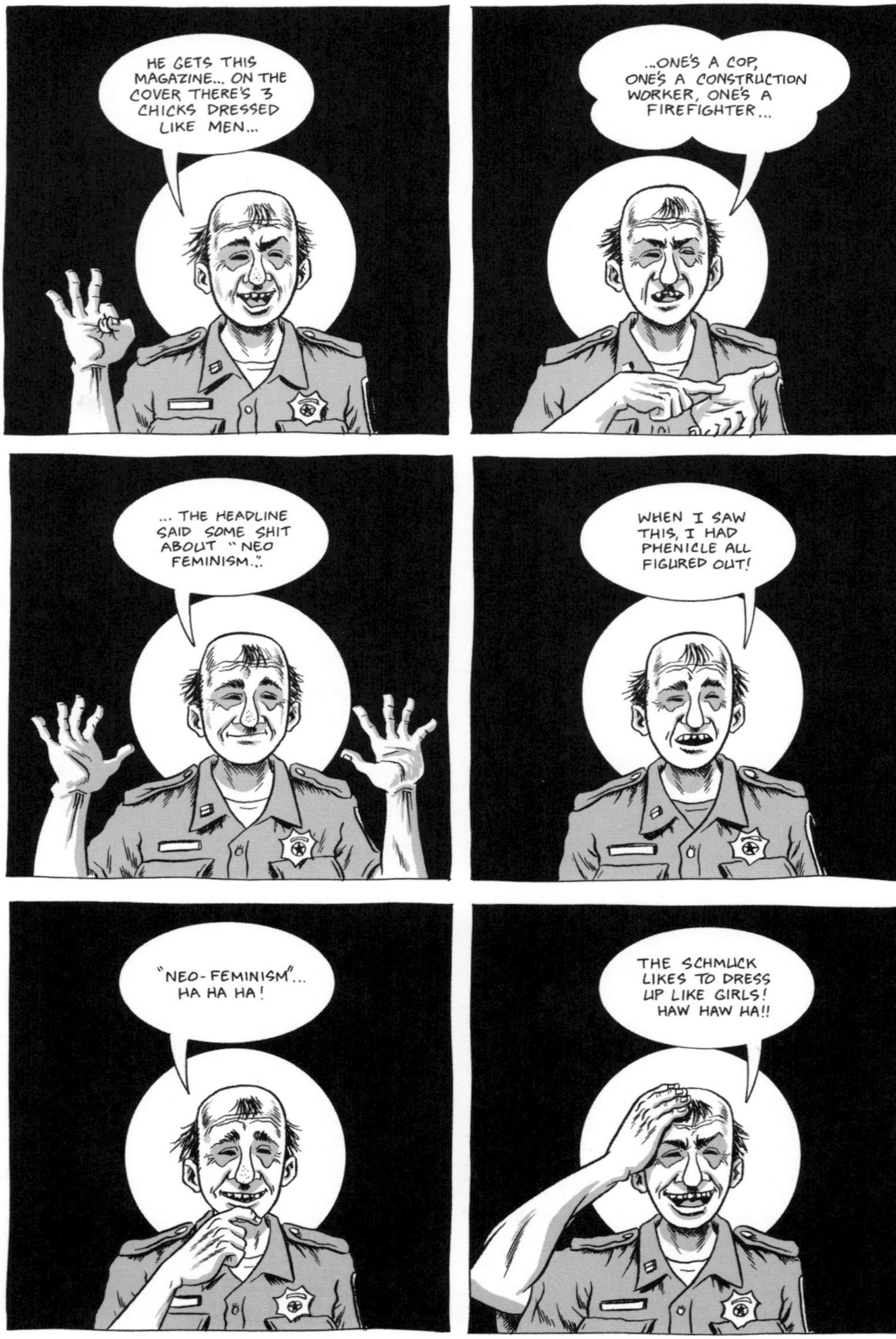
HE GETS THIS MAGAZINE... ON THE COVER THERE'S 3 CHICKS DRESSED LIKE MEN...
...ONE'S A COP, ONE'S A CONSTRUCTION WORKER, ONE'S A FIREFIGHTER...
... THE HEADLINE SAID SOME SHIT ABOUT "NEO FEMINISM..."
WHEN I SAW THIS, I HAD PHENICLE ALL FIGURED OUT!
"NEO-FEMINISM"... HA HA HA!
THE SCHMUCK LIKES TO DRESS UP LIKE GIRLS! HAW HAW HA!!

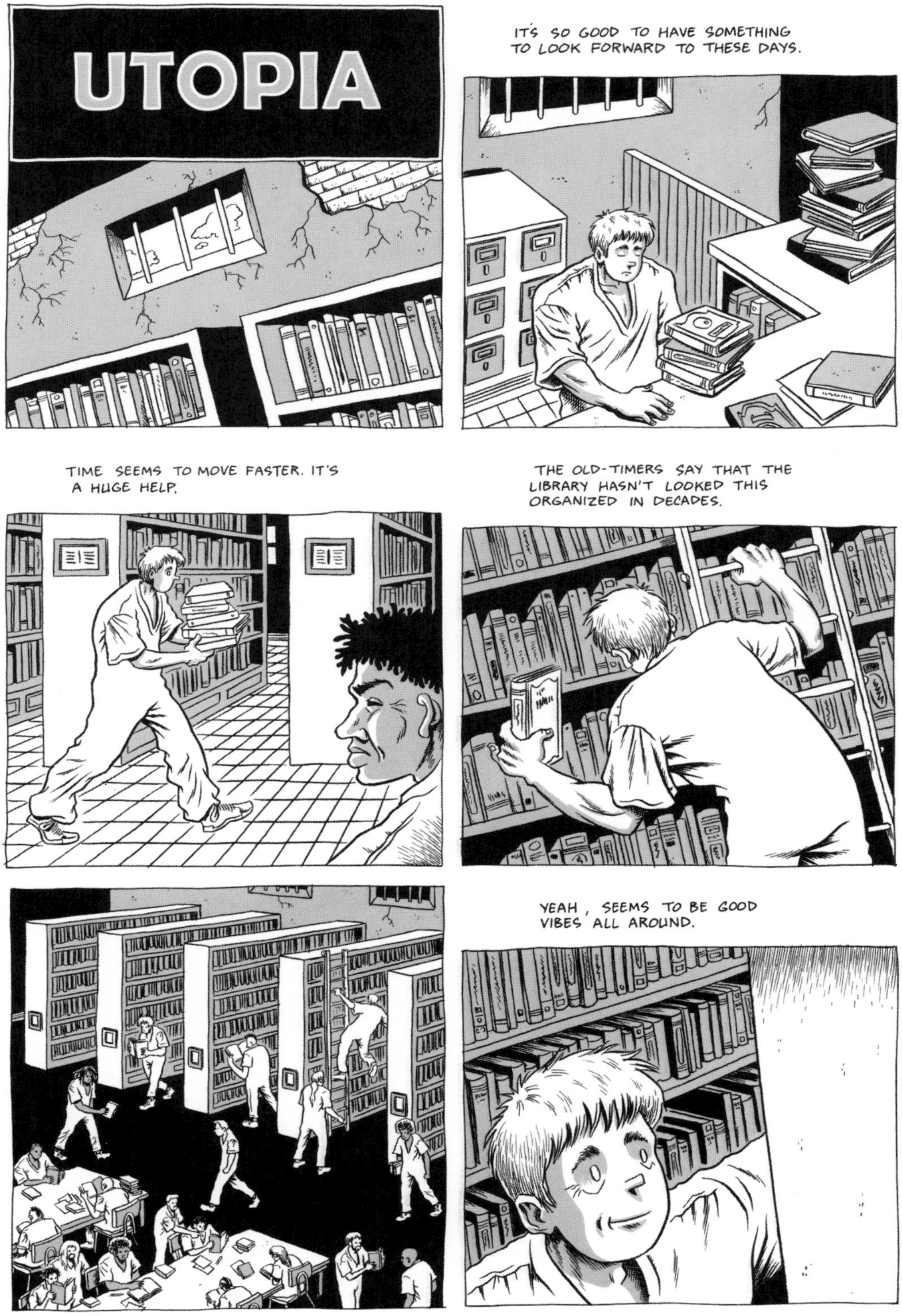
UTOPIA
IT'S SO GOOD TO HAVE SOMETHING TO LOOK FORWARD TO THESE DAYS.
TIME SEEMS TO MOVE FASTER. IT'S A HUGE HELP.
THE OLD-TIMERS SAY THAT THE LIBRARY HASN'T LOOKED THIS ORGANIZED IN DECADES.
YEAH, SEEMS TO BE GOOD VIBES ALL AROUND.

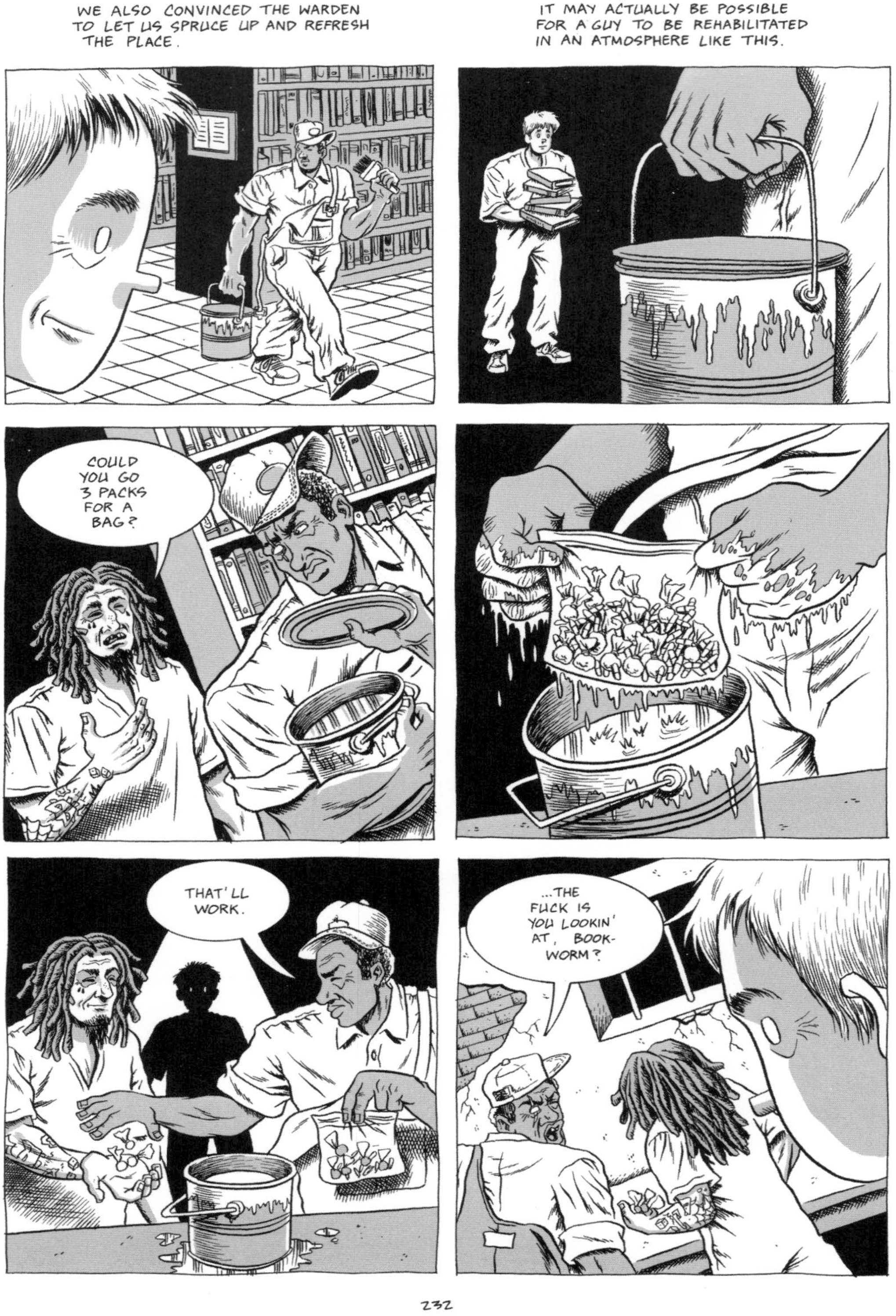
WE ALSO CONVINCED THE WARDEN TO LET US SPRUCE UP AND REFRESH THE PLACE.
IT MAY ACTUALLY BE POSSIBLE FOR A GUY TO BE REHABILITATED IN AN ATMOSPHERE LIKE THIS.
COULD YOU GO 3 PACKS FOR A BAG?
THAT'LL WORK.
...THE FUCK IS YOU LOOKIN' AT, BOOK-WORM?

SUBVERSION...

WINSTON'S RADIO SHOW HAS BEEN GAINING A LOT OF MAINSTREAM MEDIA ATTENTION BECAUSE OF MY STORY.

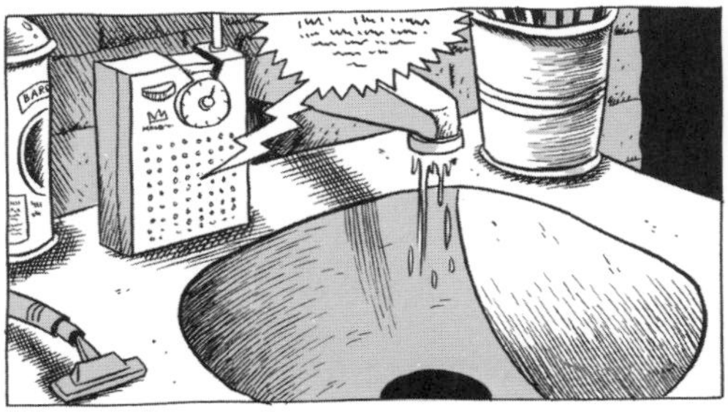

HE'S GOING TO GET A CHANCE TO BE ON A HUGE, NATIONAL, TELEVISION NEWS PROGRAM...

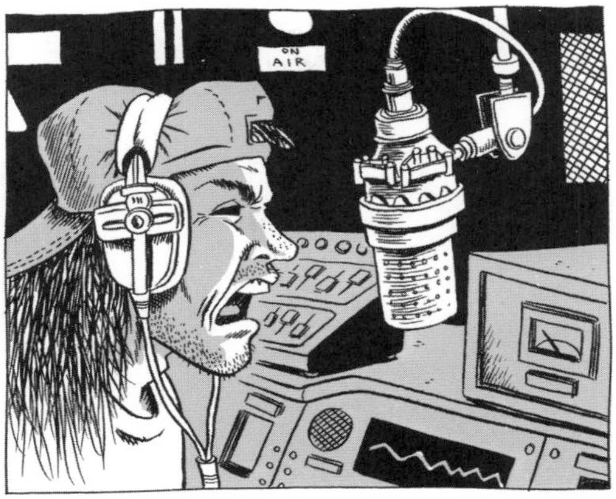
ON AIR

... AND I HAVE A PLAN TO WATCH IT, DESPITE THE MONOPOLY THAT THE GANGS HAVE ON THE REC ROOM.

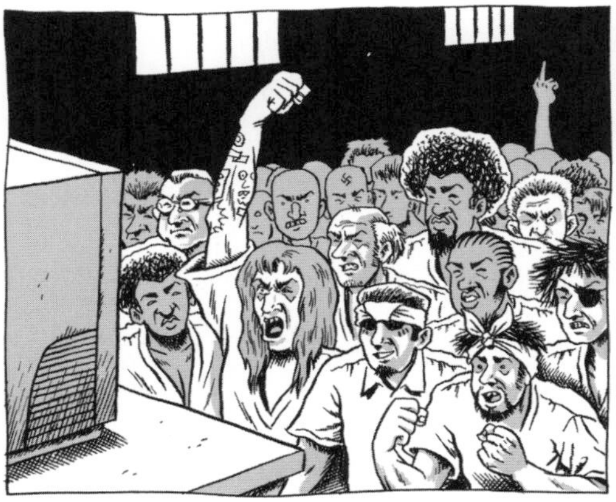

I RECENTLY GOT AHOLD OF SOME OFFICIAL PRISON STATIONARY.

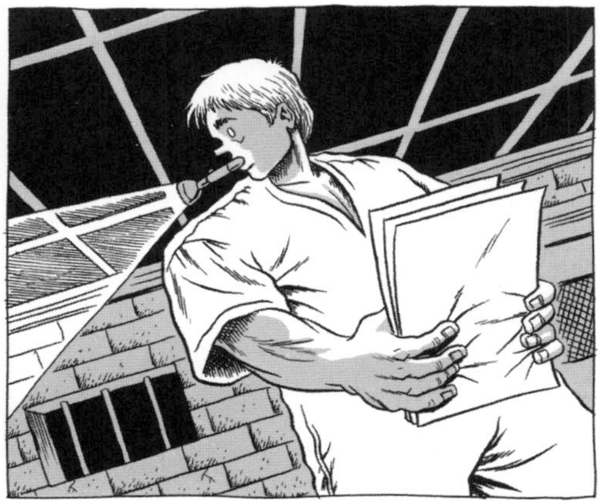

I'M FORBIDDEN FROM TOUCHING ANY COMPUTERS IN HERE, BUT I'M ALLOWED TO USE A TYPEWRITER FOR CORRESPONDENCE WITH MY LAWYER.

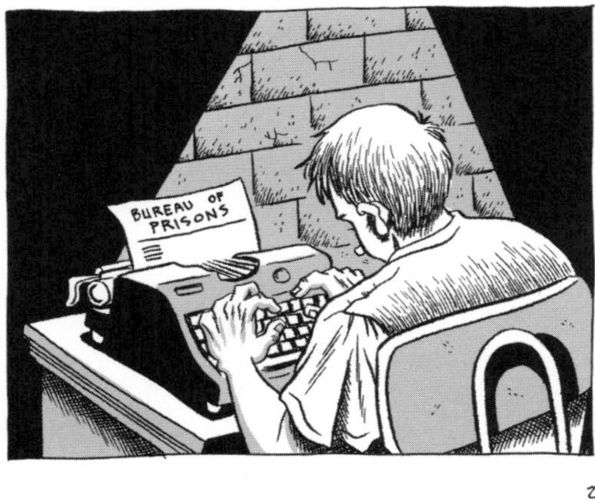
BUREAU OF PRISONS

CONJUGAL VISITS AREN'T ALLOWED IN FEDERAL PRISON, WHICH IS A REAL SADNESS FOR THE CONVICTS HERE.

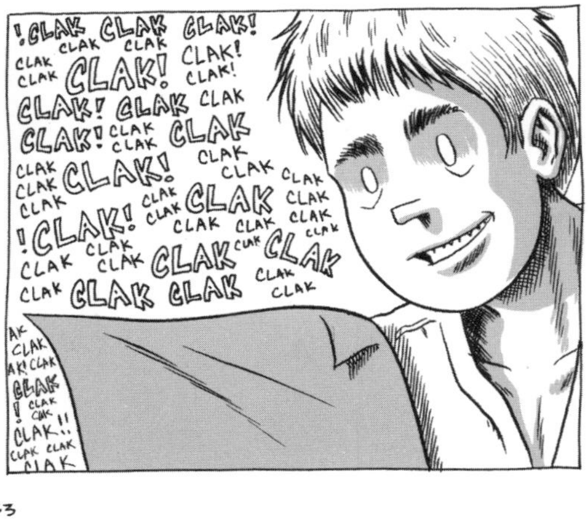
!CLAK CLAK CLAK!
CLAK CLAK CLAK CLAK CLAK! CLAK! CLAK!
CLAK! CLAK CLAK
CLAK! CLAK CLAK CLAK
CLAK CLAK CLAK! CLAK CLAK CLAK
!CLAK! CLAK CLAK CLAK CLAK CLAK CLAK
CLAK CLAK CLAK CLAK CLAK CLAK
CLAK CLAK CLAK CLAK CLAK
AK CLAK AK! CLAK CLAK ! CLAK CLAK CLAK!! CLAK CLAK CLAK

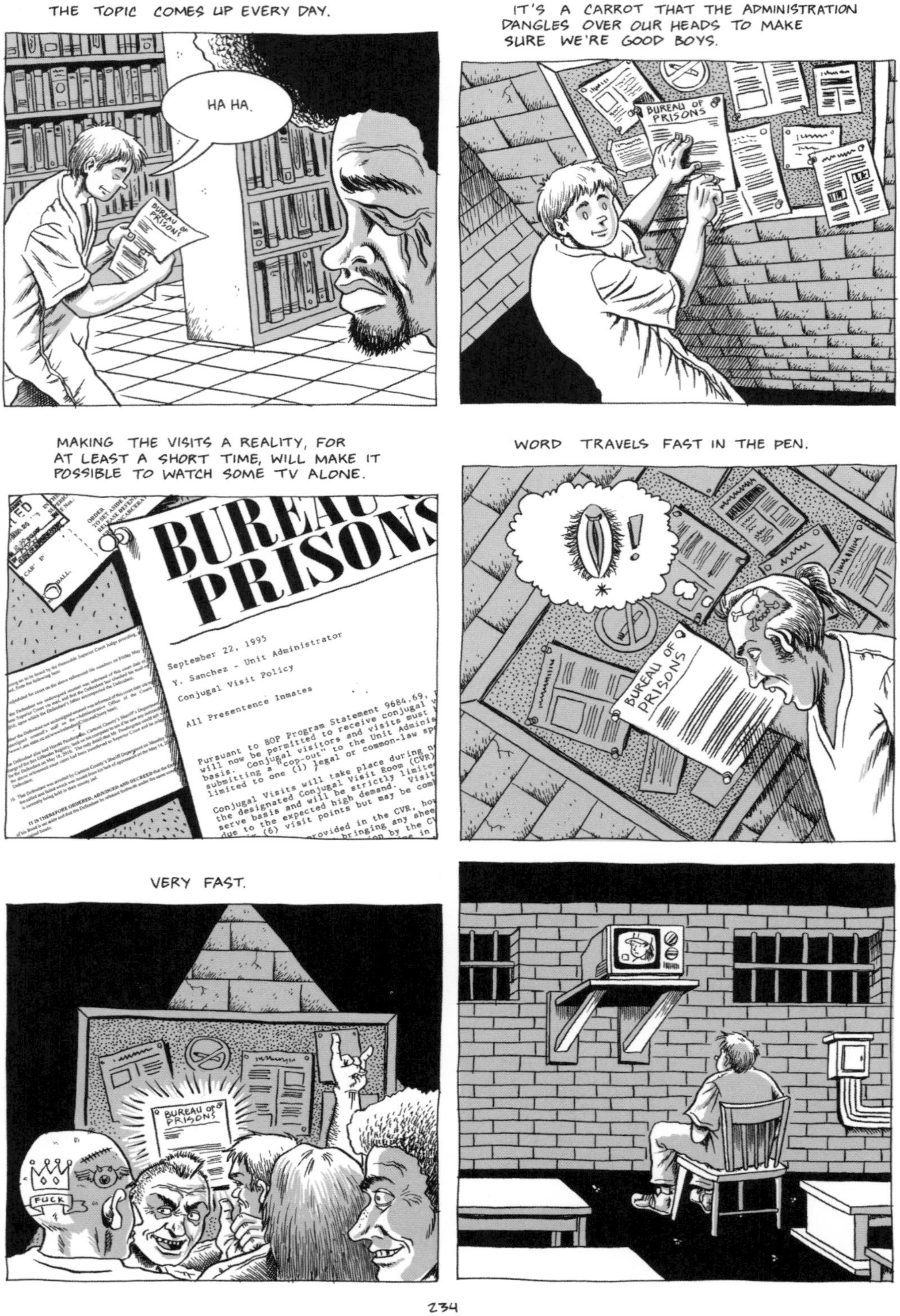
THE TOPIC COMES UP EVERY DAY.
HA HA.
BUREAU OF PRISONS
IT'S A CARROT THAT THE ADMINISTRATION DANGLES OVER OUR HEADS TO MAKE SURE WE'RE GOOD BOYS.
BUREAU OF PRISONS
MAKING THE VISITS A REALITY, FOR AT LEAST A SHORT TIME, WILL MAKE IT POSSIBLE TO WATCH SOME TV ALONE.
PRISONS
September 22, 1995
Y. Sanchez - Unit Administrator
Conjugal Visit Policy
All Presentence Inmates
WORD TRAVELS FAST IN THE PEN.
!
BUREAU OF PRISONS
VERY FAST.
BUREAU OF PRISONS
FUCK

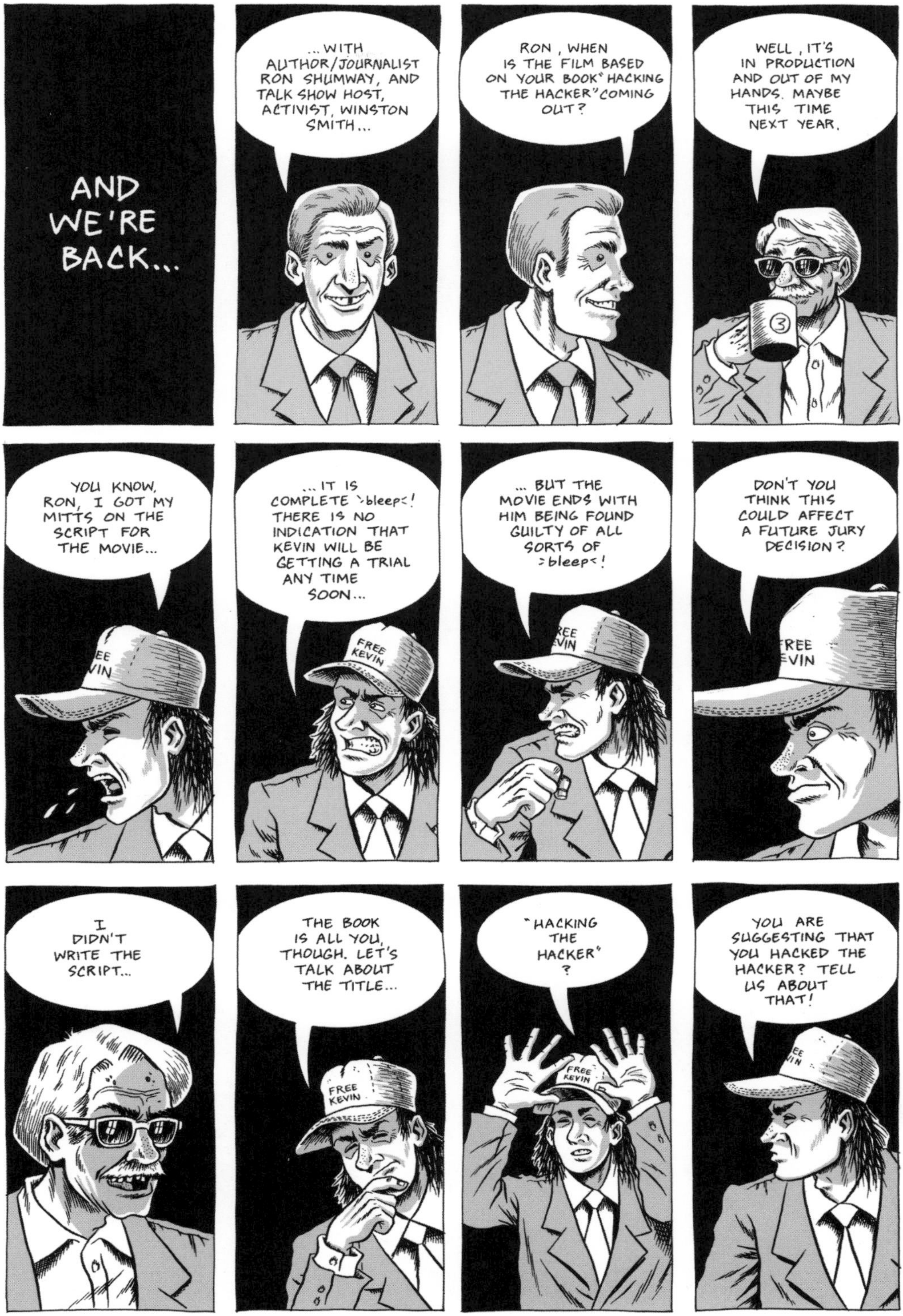
AND WE'RE BACK...
...WITH AUTHOR/JOURNALIST RON SHUMWAY, AND TALK SHOW HOST, ACTIVIST, WINSTON SMITH...
RON, WHEN IS THE FILM BASED ON YOUR BOOK "HACKING THE HACKER" COMING OUT?
WELL, IT'S IN PRODUCTION AND OUT OF MY HANDS. MAYBE THIS TIME NEXT YEAR.
3
YOU KNOW, RON, I GOT MY MITTS ON THE SCRIPT FOR THE MOVIE...
FREE KEVIN
...IT IS COMPLETE >bleep<! THERE IS NO INDICATION THAT KEVIN WILL BE GETTING A TRIAL ANY TIME SOON...
FREE KEVIN
...BUT THE MOVIE ENDS WITH HIM BEING FOUND GUILTY OF ALL SORTS OF >bleep<!
FREE KEVIN
DON'T YOU THINK THIS COULD AFFECT A FUTURE JURY DECISION?
FREE KEVIN
I DIDN'T WRITE THE SCRIPT...
THE BOOK IS ALL YOU, THOUGH. LET'S TALK ABOUT THE TITLE...
FREE KEVIN
"HACKING THE HACKER"?
FREE KEVIN
YOU ARE SUGGESTING THAT YOU HACKED THE HACKER? TELL US ABOUT THAT!

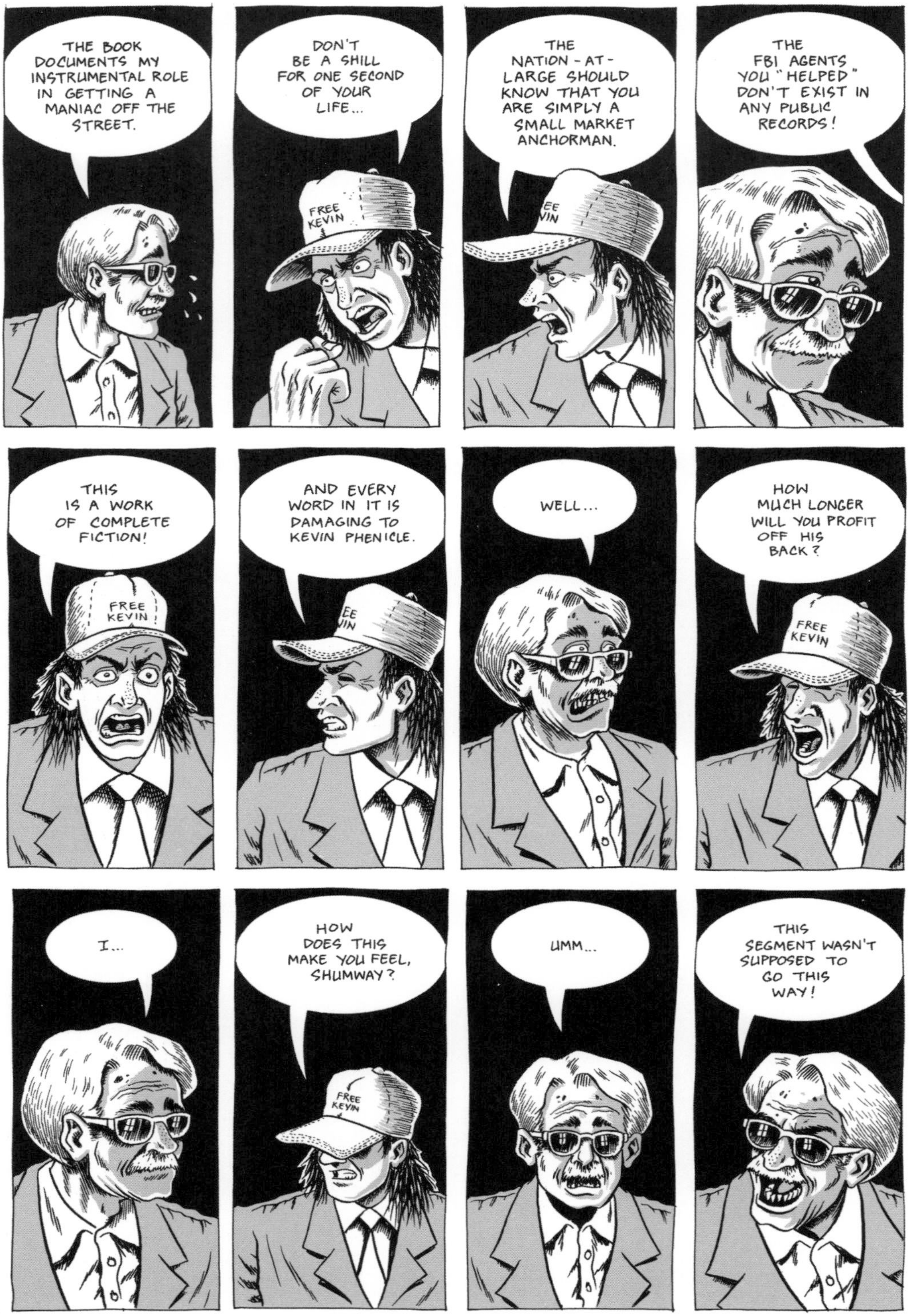
THE BOOK DOCUMENTS MY INSTRUMENTAL ROLE IN GETTING A MANIAC OFF THE STREET.
DON'T BE A SHILL FOR ONE SECOND OF YOUR LIFE...
FREE KEVIN
THE NATION-AT-LARGE SHOULD KNOW THAT YOU ARE SIMPLY A SMALL MARKET ANCHORMAN.
THE FBI AGENTS YOU "HELPED" DON'T EXIST IN ANY PUBLIC RECORDS!
THIS IS A WORK OF COMPLETE FICTION!
FREE KEVIN
AND EVERY WORD IN IT IS DAMAGING TO KEVIN PHENICLE.
WELL...
HOW MUCH LONGER WILL YOU PROFIT OFF HIS BACK?
FREE KEVIN
I...
HOW DOES THIS MAKE YOU FEEL, SHUMWAY?
FREE KEVIN
UMM...
THIS SEGMENT WASN'T SUPPOSED TO GO THIS WAY!

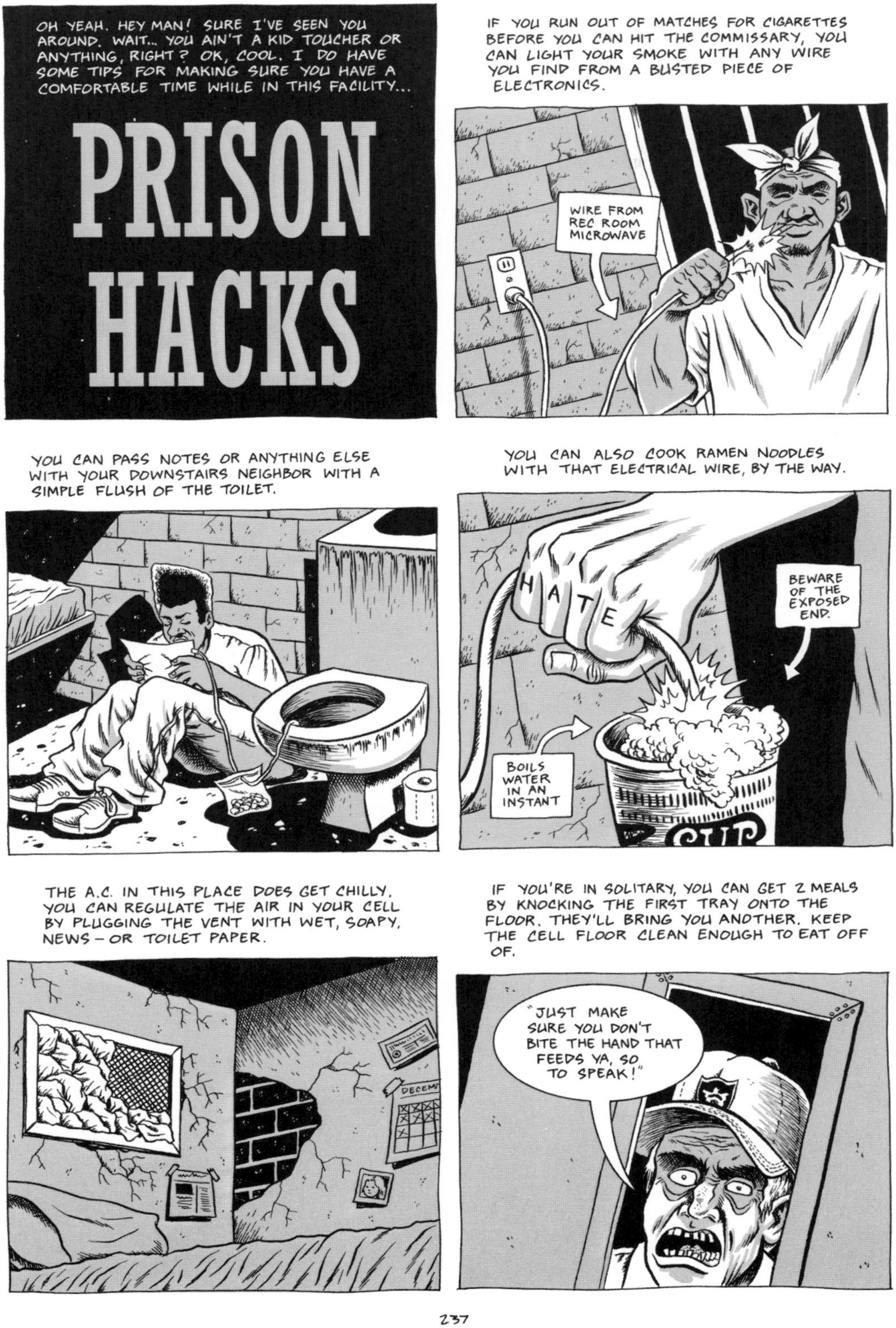

OH YEAH. HEY MAN! SURE I'VE SEEN YOU AROUND. WAIT... YOU AIN'T A KID TOUCHER OR ANYTHING, RIGHT? OK, COOL. I DO HAVE SOME TIPS FOR MAKING SURE YOU HAVE A COMFORTABLE TIME WHILE IN THIS FACILITY...
PRISON HACKS
IF YOU RUN OUT OF MATCHES FOR CIGARETTES BEFORE YOU CAN HIT THE COMMISSARY, YOU CAN LIGHT YOUR SMOKE WITH ANY WIRE YOU FIND FROM A BUSTED PIECE OF ELECTRONICS.
WIRE FROM REC ROOM MICROWAVE
YOU CAN PASS NOTES OR ANYTHING ELSE WITH YOUR DOWNSTAIRS NEIGHBOR WITH A SIMPLE FLUSH OF THE TOILET.
YOU CAN ALSO COOK RAMEN NOODLES WITH THAT ELECTRICAL WIRE, BY THE WAY.
HATE
BEWARE OF THE EXPOSED END.
BOILS WATER IN AN INSTANT
CUP
THE A.C. IN THIS PLACE DOES GET CHILLY. YOU CAN REGULATE THE AIR IN YOUR CELL BY PLUGGING THE VENT WITH WET, SOAPY, NEWS— OR TOILET PAPER.
IF YOU'RE IN SOLITARY, YOU CAN GET 2 MEALS BY KNOCKING THE FIRST TRAY ONTO THE FLOOR. THEY'LL BRING YOU ANOTHER. KEEP THE CELL FLOOR CLEAN ENOUGH TO EAT OFF OF.
"JUST MAKE SURE YOU DON'T BITE THE HAND THAT FEEDS YA, SO TO SPEAK!"

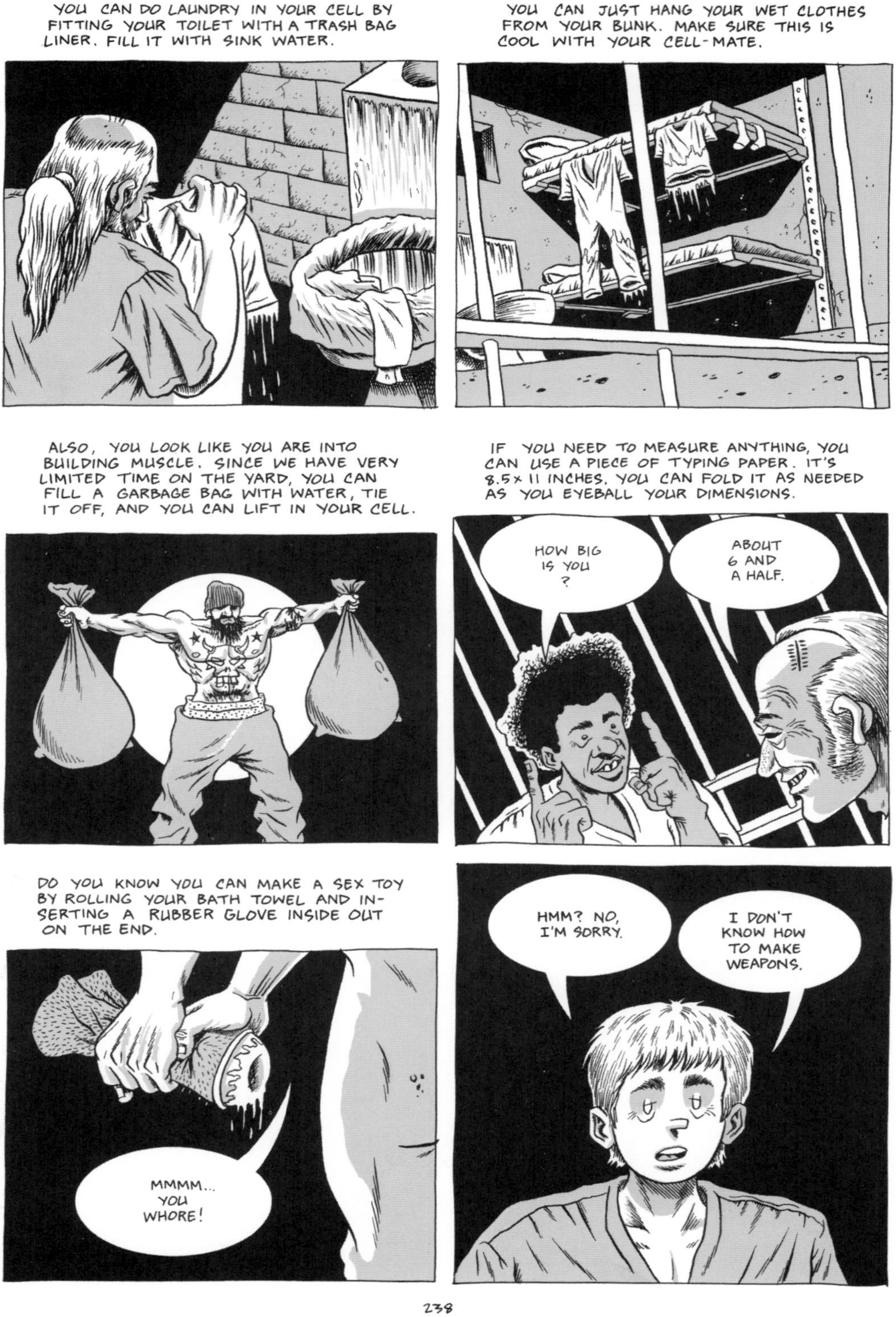
YOU CAN DO LAUNDRY IN YOUR CELL BY FITTING YOUR TOILET WITH A TRASH BAG LINER. FILL IT WITH SINK WATER.
YOU CAN JUST HANG YOUR WET CLOTHES FROM YOUR BUNK. MAKE SURE THIS IS COOL WITH YOUR CELL-MATE.
ALSO, YOU LOOK LIKE YOU ARE INTO BUILDING MUSCLE. SINCE WE HAVE VERY LIMITED TIME ON THE YARD, YOU CAN FILL A GARBAGE BAG WITH WATER, TIE IT OFF, AND YOU CAN LIFT IN YOUR CELL.
IF YOU NEED TO MEASURE ANYTHING, YOU CAN USE A PIECE OF TYPING PAPER. IT'S 8.5×11 INCHES. YOU CAN FOLD IT AS NEEDED AS YOU EYEBALL YOUR DIMENSIONS.
HOW BIG IS YOU ?
ABOUT 6 AND A HALF.
DO YOU KNOW YOU CAN MAKE A SEX TOY BY ROLLING YOUR BATH TOWEL AND IN-SERTING A RUBBER GLOVE INSIDE OUT ON THE END.
MMMM... YOU WHORE!
HMM? NO, I'M SORRY.
I DON'T KNOW HOW TO MAKE WEAPONS.

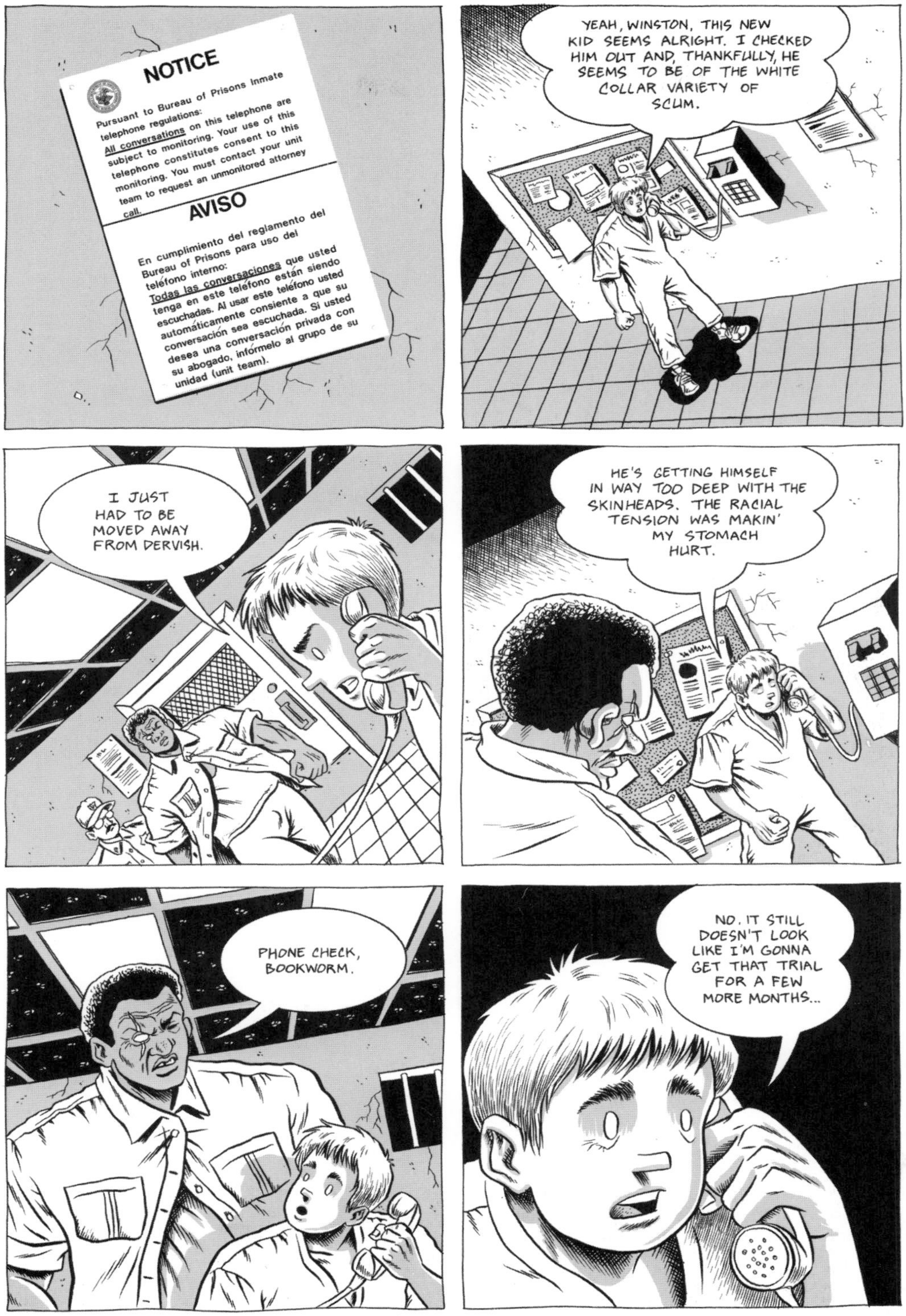
NOTICE
Pursuant to Bureau of Prisons Inmate telephone regulations: All conversations on this telephone are subject to monitoring. Your use of this telephone constitutes consent to this monitoring. You must contact your unit team to request an unmonitored attorney call.
AVISO
En cumplimiento del reglamento del Bureau of Prisons para uso del teléfono interno: Todas las conversaciones que usted tenga en este teléfono están siendo escuchadas. Al usar este teléfono usted automáticamente consiente a que su conversación sea escuchada. Si usted desea una conversación privada con su abogado, infórmelo al grupo de su unidad (unit team).
YEAH, WINSTON, THIS NEW KID SEEMS ALRIGHT. I CHECKED HIM OUT AND, THANKFULLY, HE SEEMS TO BE OF THE WHITE COLLAR VARIETY OF SCUM.
I JUST HAD TO BE MOVED AWAY FROM DERVISH.
HE'S GETTING HIMSELF IN WAY TOO DEEP WITH THE SKINHEADS. THE RACIAL TENSION WAS MAKIN' MY STOMACH HURT.
PHONE CHECK, BOOKWORM.
NO. IT STILL DOESN'T LOOK LIKE I'M GONNA GET THAT TRIAL FOR A FEW MORE MONTHS...

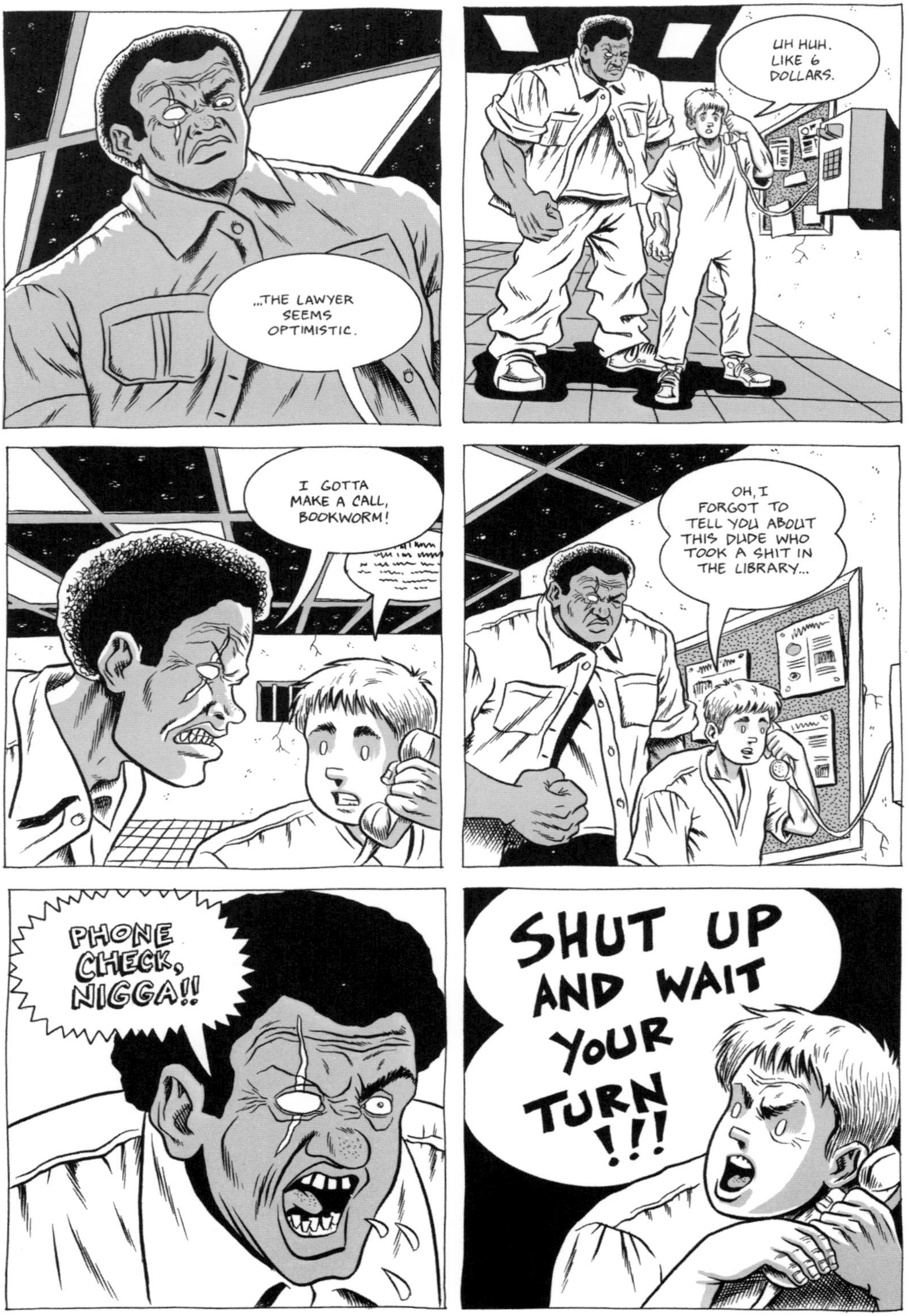
...THE LAWYER SEEMS OPTIMISTIC.
UH HUH. LIKE 6 DOLLARS.
I GOTTA MAKE A CALL, BOOKWORM!
OH, I FORGOT TO TELL YOU ABOUT THIS DUDE WHO TOOK A SHIT IN THE LIBRARY...
PHONE CHECK, NIGGA!!
SHUT UP AND WAIT YOUR TURN !!!

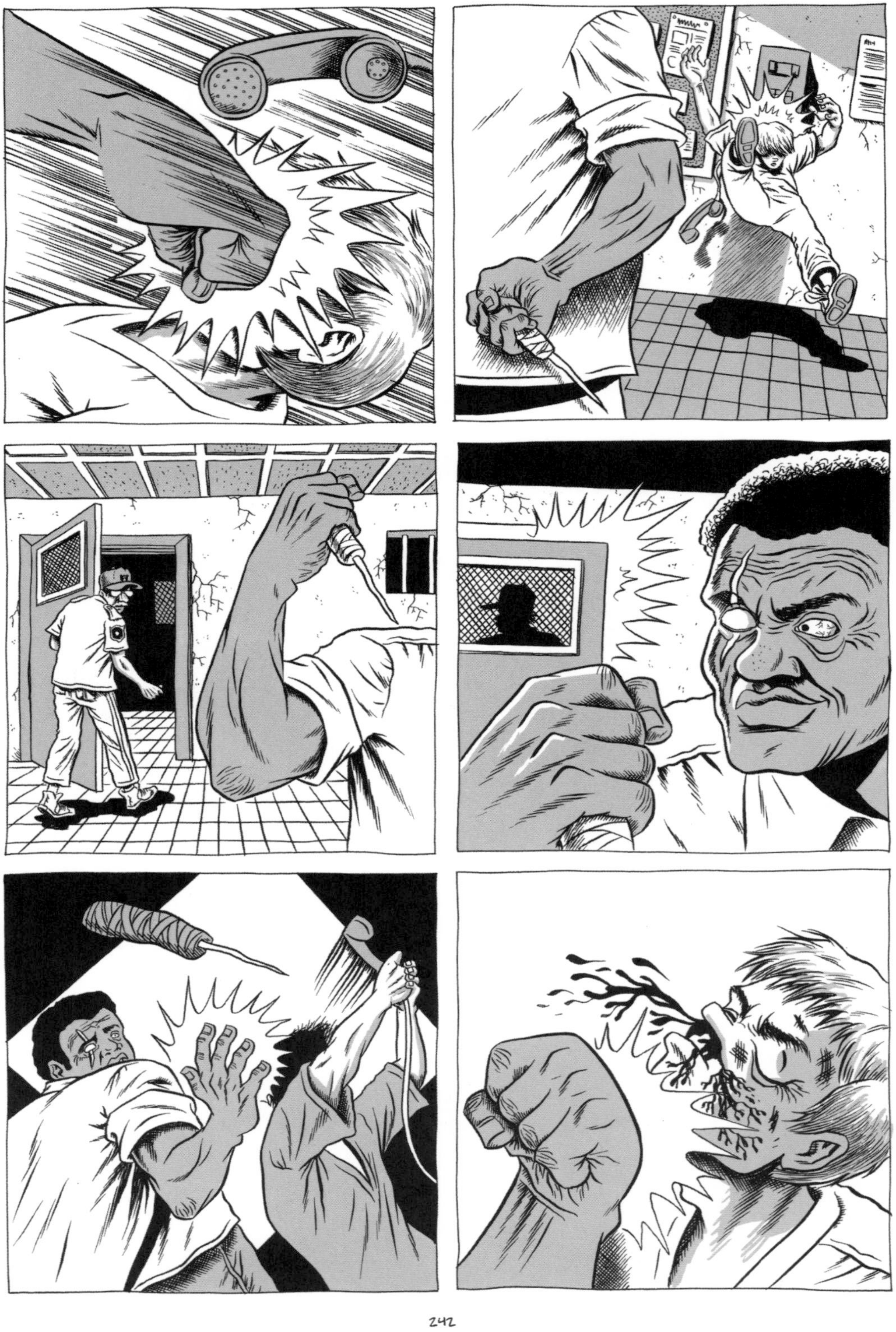

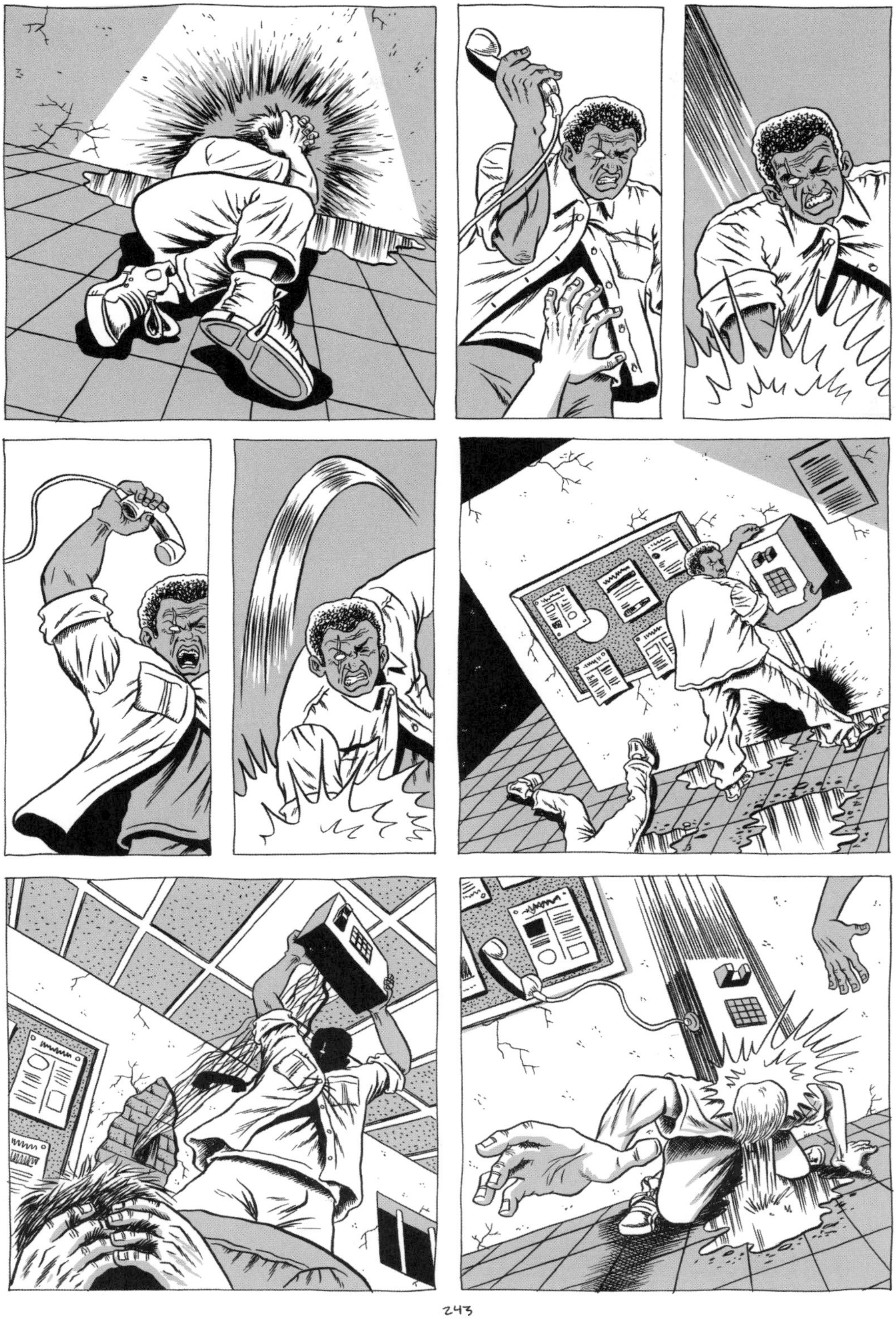

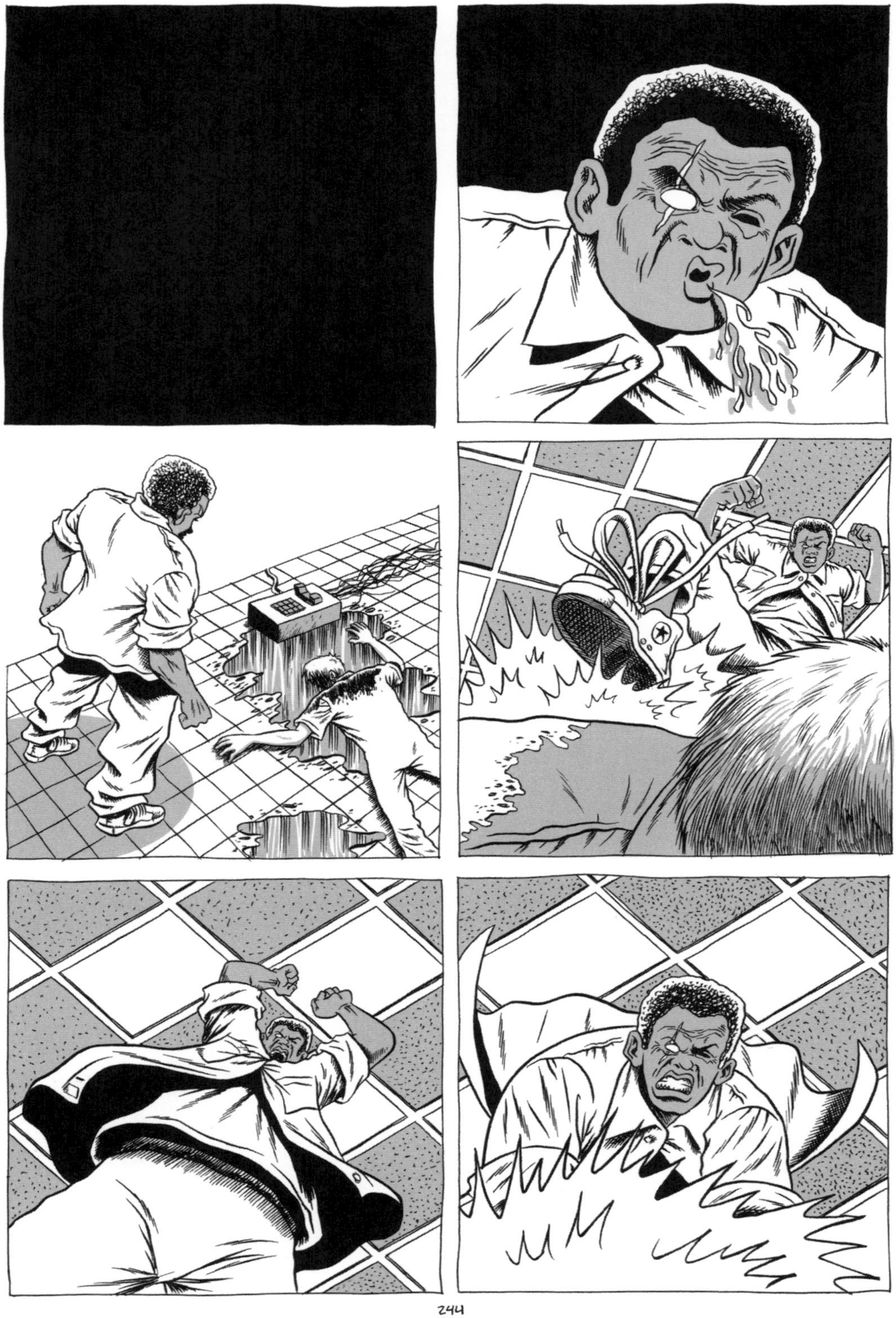

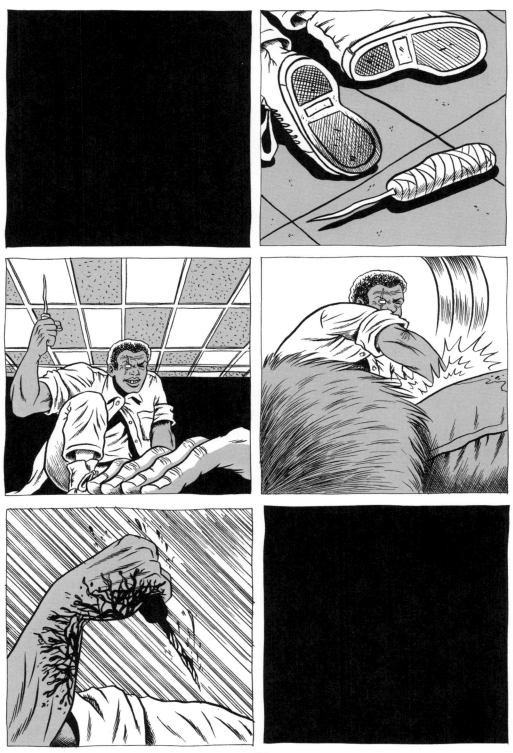

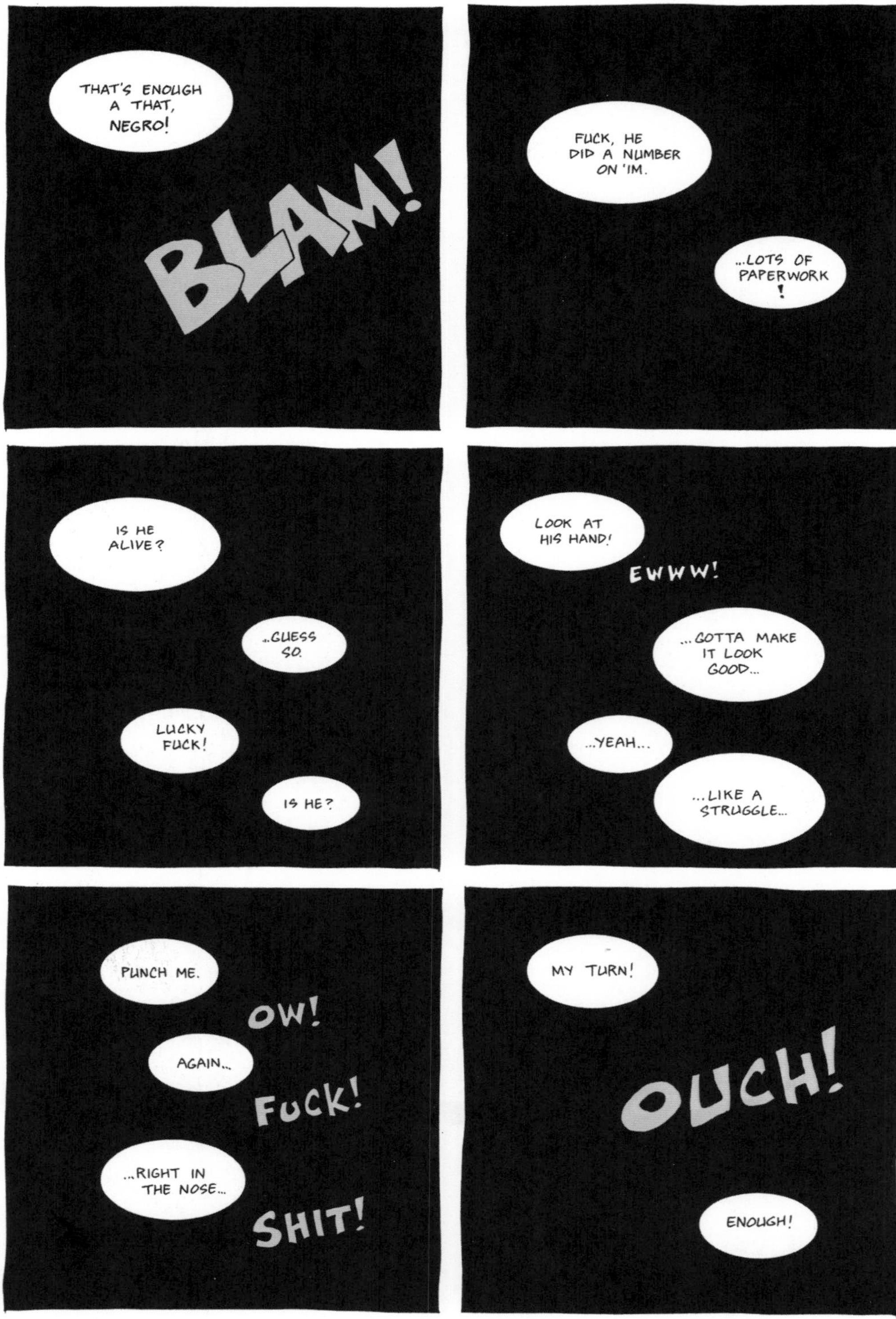
THAT'S ENOUGH A THAT, NEGRO!
BLAM!
FUCK, HE DID A NUMBER ON 'IM.
...LOTS OF PAPERWORK!
IS HE ALIVE?
..GUESS SO.
LUCKY FUCK!
IS HE?
LOOK AT HIS HAND!
EWWW!
...GOTTA MAKE IT LOOK GOOD...
...YEAH...
...LIKE A STRUGGLE...
PUNCH ME.
OW!
AGAIN...
FUCK!
...RIGHT IN THE NOSE...
SHIT!
MY TURN!
OUCH!
ENOUGH!

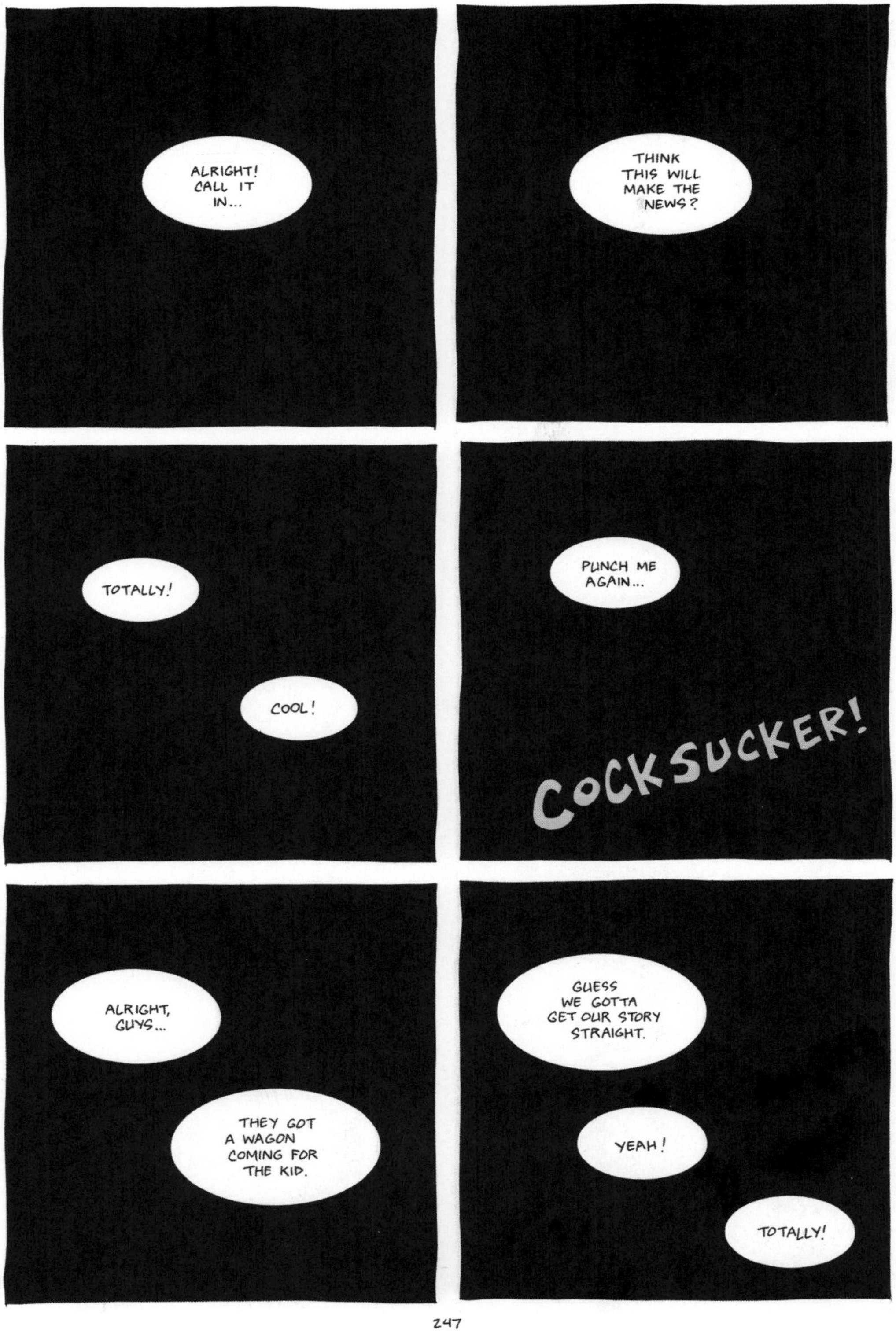
ALRIGHT! CALL IT IN...
THINK THIS WILL MAKE THE NEWS?
TOTALLY!
COOL!
PUNCH ME AGAIN...
COCKSUCKER!
ALRIGHT, GUYS...
THEY GOT A WAGON COMING FOR THE KID.
GUESS WE GOTTA GET OUR STORY STRAIGHT.
YEAH!
TOTALLY!

CHAPTER 8

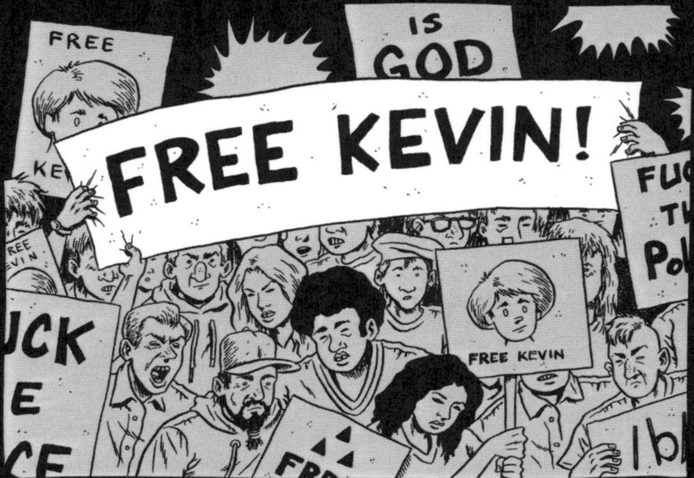
FREE
IS
GOD
FREE KEVIN!
FREE KEVIN

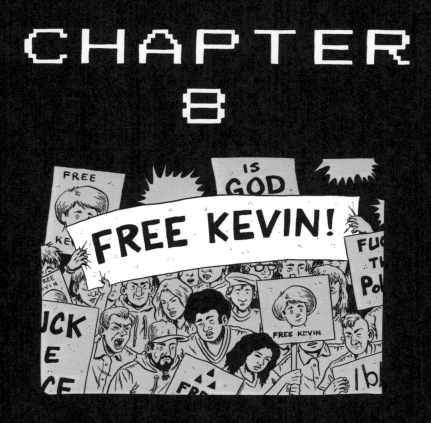

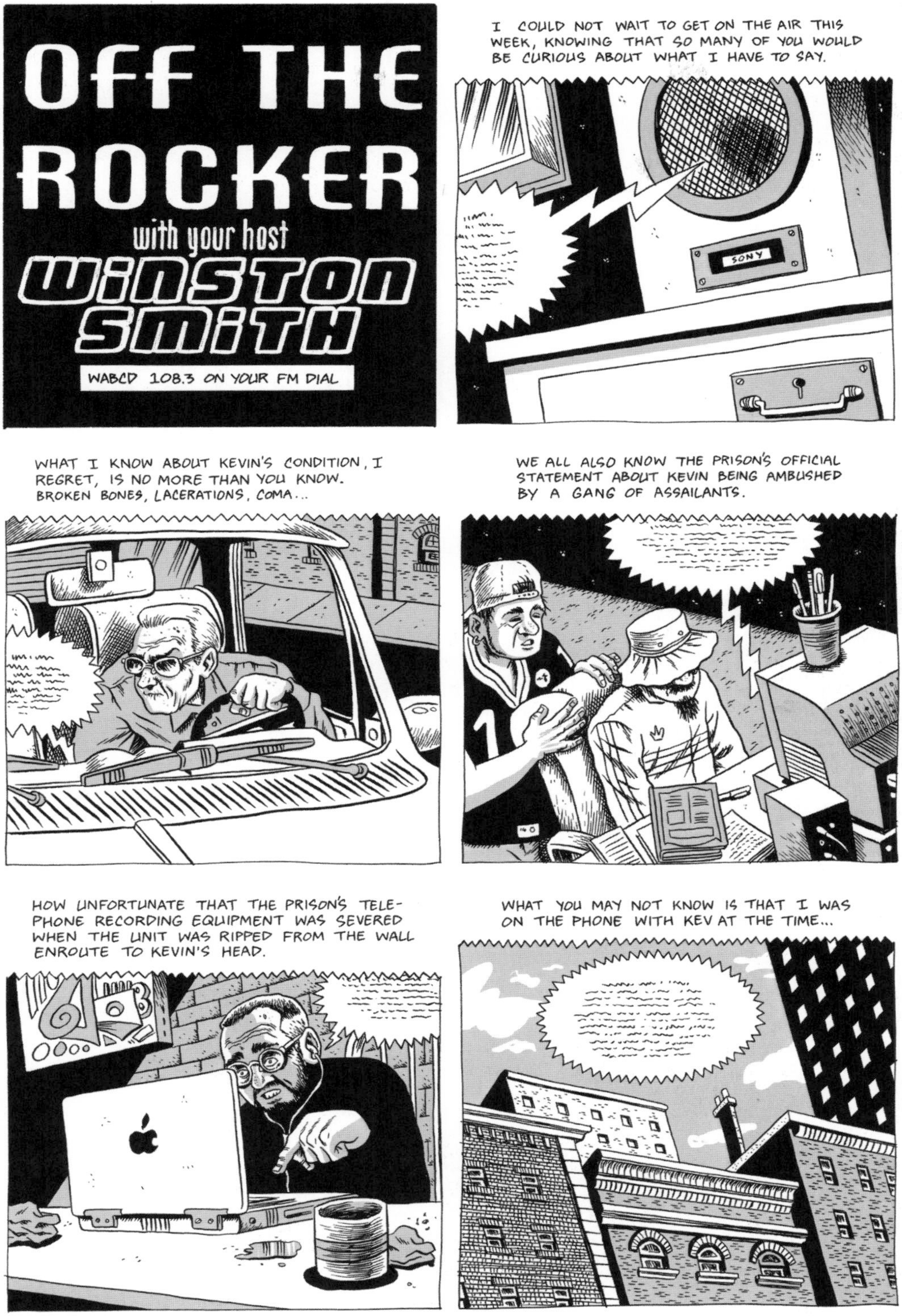
OFF THE ROCKER
with your host
WINSTON SMITH
WABCD 108.3 ON YOUR FM DIAL
I COULD NOT WAIT TO GET ON THE AIR THIS WEEK, KNOWING THAT SO MANY OF YOU WOULD BE CURIOUS ABOUT WHAT I HAVE TO SAY.
SONY
WHAT I KNOW ABOUT KEVIN'S CONDITION, I REGRET, IS NO MORE THAN YOU KNOW. BROKEN BONES, LACERATIONS, COMA...
WE ALL ALSO KNOW THE PRISON'S OFFICIAL STATEMENT ABOUT KEVIN BEING AMBUSHED BY A GANG OF ASSAILANTS.
HOW UNFORTUNATE THAT THE PRISON'S TELEPHONE RECORDING EQUIPMENT WAS SEVERED WHEN THE UNIT WAS RIPPED FROM THE WALL ENROUTE TO KEVIN'S HEAD.
WHAT YOU MAY NOT KNOW IS THAT I WAS ON THE PHONE WITH KEV AT THE TIME...

... AND THE BASIC PHONE CONNECTION STAYED IN TACT. I COULD HEAR EVERYTHING GOING ON!

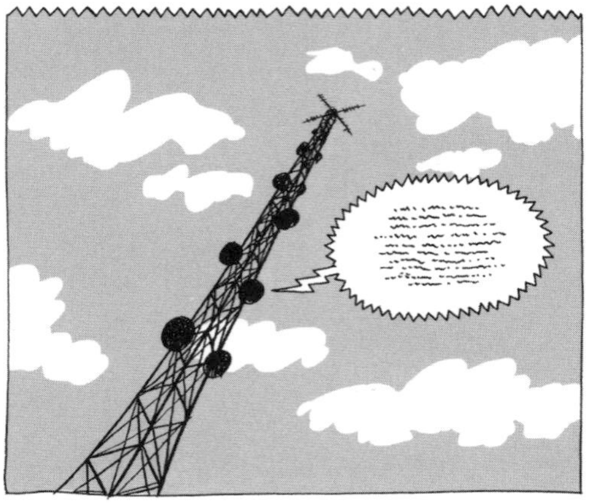

WHAT EVERYONE ALSO DOESN'T KNOW IS THAT I RECORDED EVERY CONVERSATION I HAD WITH PHENICLE ON MY END.

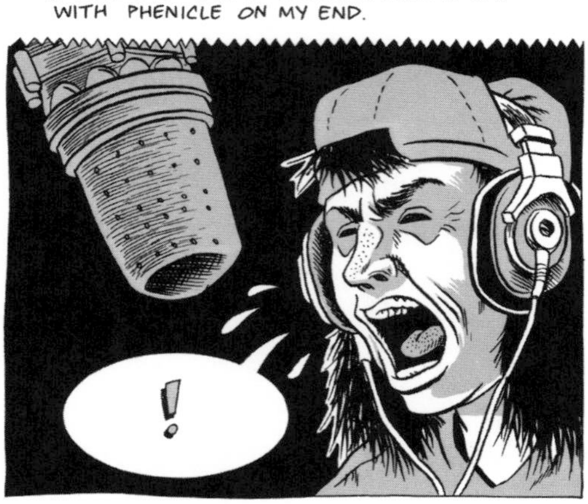
!

SINCE WE LIVE IN A "ONE PARTY STATE", THIS RECORDING IS COMPLETELY LEGAL TO BROADCAST.

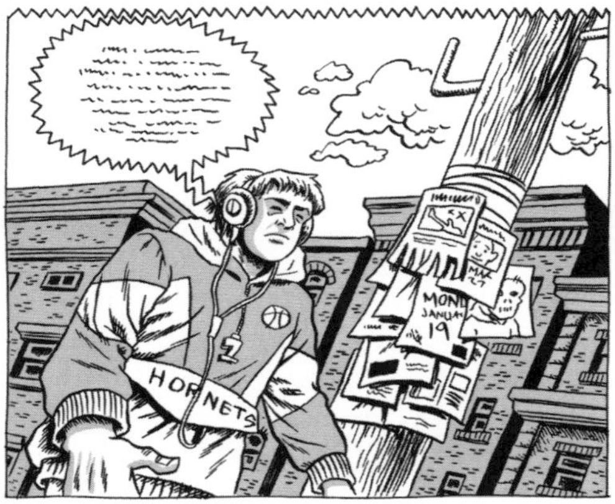
HORNETS

I'D LIKE YOU ALL TO DO ME A FAVOR...

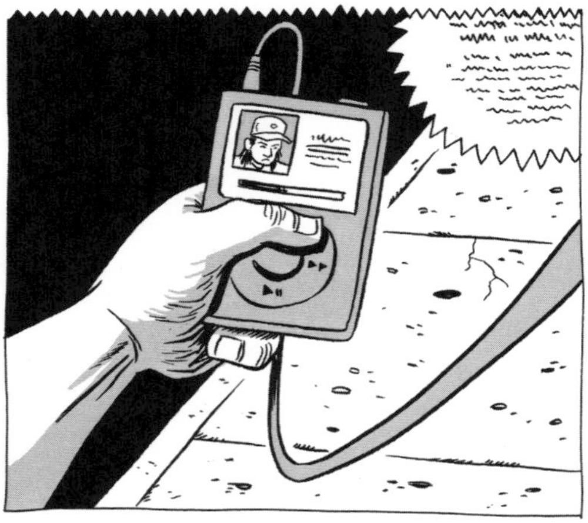

LISTEN TO THIS WITH A CLOSE EAR...

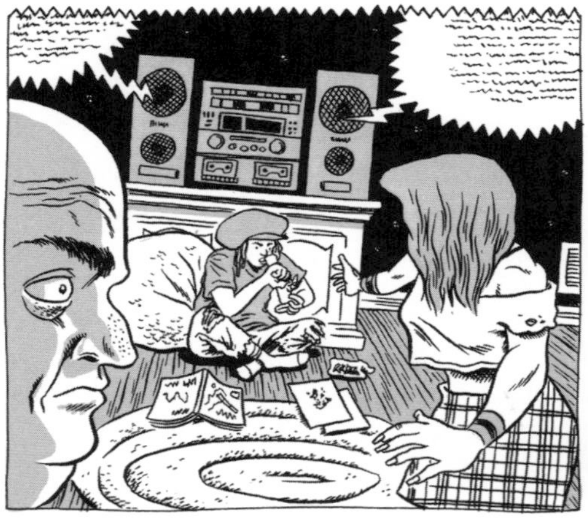

JUDGE FOR YOURSELF IF THE OFFICIAL PRISON STATEMENT MATCHES UP WITH YOUR INTERPRETATION OF WHAT YOU'RE ABOUT TO HEAR...

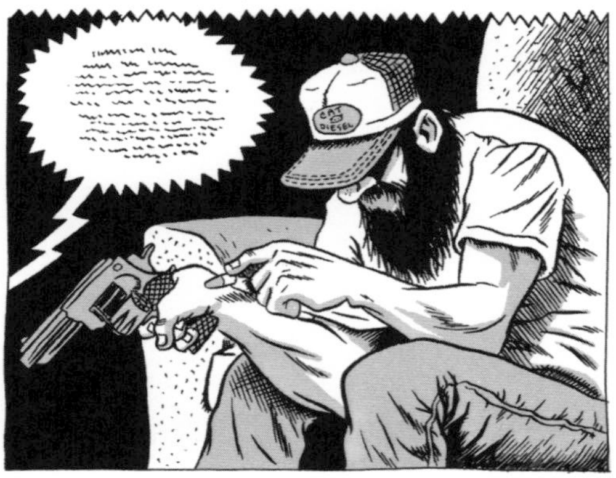

ENOUGH IS ENOUGH...

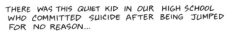

THERE WAS THIS QUIET KID IN OUR HIGH SCHOOL WHO COMMITTED SUICIDE AFTER BEING JUMPED FOR NO REASON...

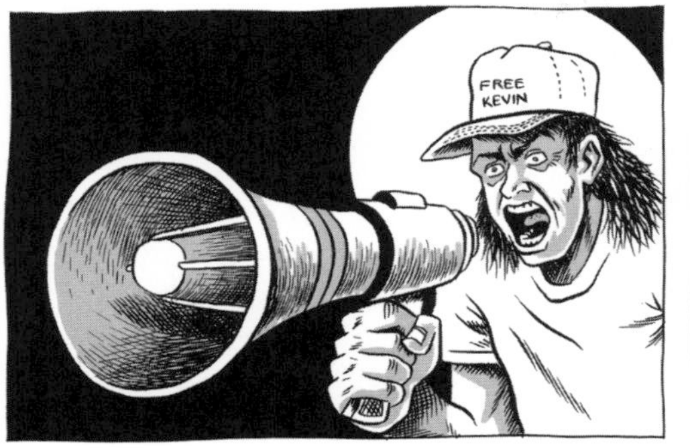
FREE KEVIN

THE FUNERAL WAS ATTENDED BY ALMOST EVERYBODY IN SCHOOL. EVEN THE MOST POPULAR KIDS SHOWED UP.

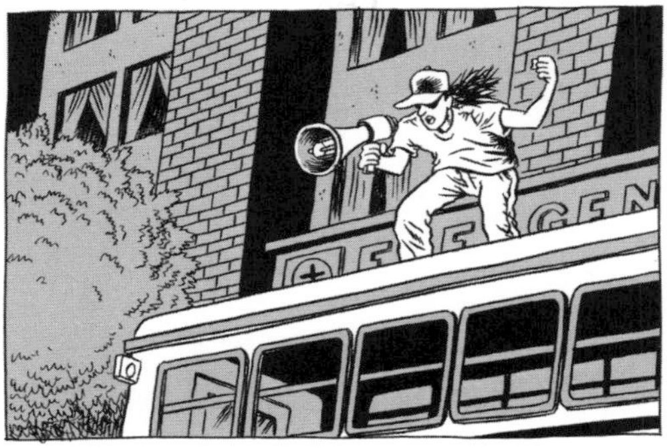

IF YOU ARE LESS CYNICAL THAN KEVIN AND MYSELF, YOU MAY SAY THAT THE COMMUNITY WAS BROUGHT TOGETHER BY TRAGEDY ...

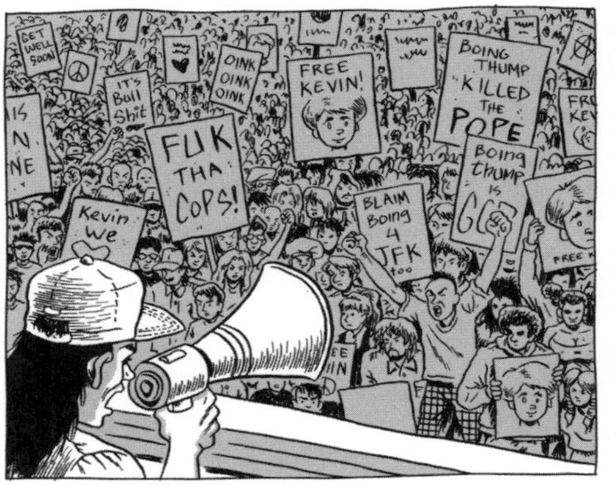
GET WELL SOON
IT'S Bull Shit
OINK OINK OINK
FREE KEVIN!
BOING THUMP KILLED THE POPE
FUK THA COPS!
BLAIM Boing 4 JFK too

... BUT IT REALLY WAS SIMPLY JUST THE SOCIAL EVENT OF THE SCHOOL YEAR.

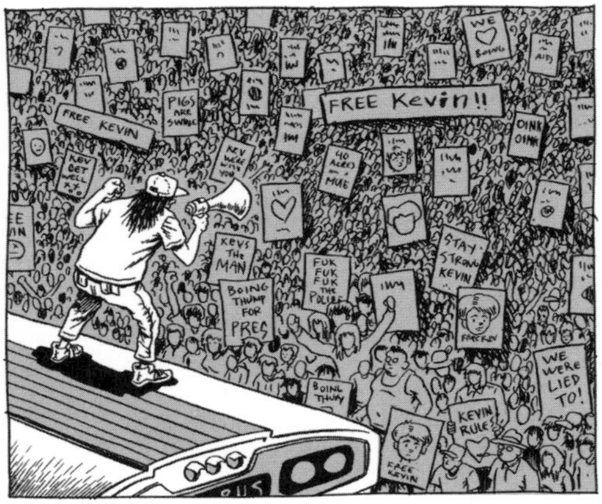
FREE Kevin!!
FREE KEVIN
PIGS ARE SWINE
OINK OINK
KEVS THE MAN
BOING THUMP FOR PRES
STAY STRONG KEVIN
WE WERE LIED TO!
KEVIN RULE

PEOPLE WERE COMMENTING ON EACH OTHER'S OUTFITS THE NEXT DAY. I ALSO REMEMBER THAT THE GENERAL CONSENSUS WAS THAT THE DEAD KID'S PARENTS DIDN'T CRY ENOUGH.

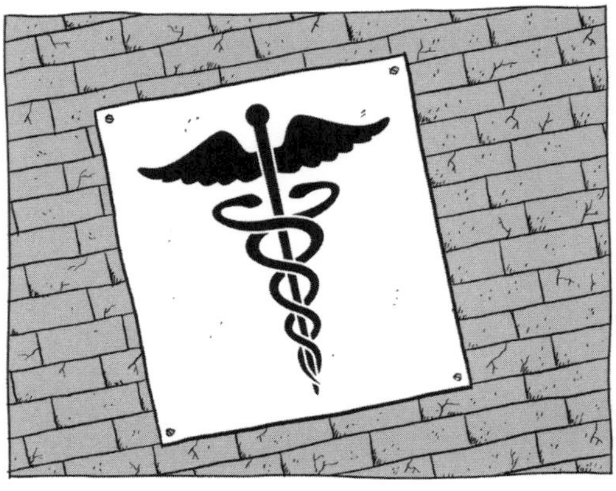

NOW THIS? THIS IS DIFFERENT. EVERYONE HERE IS INSANE WITH RAGE ABOUT WHAT HAPPENED, THANKS TO MY RECORDING.

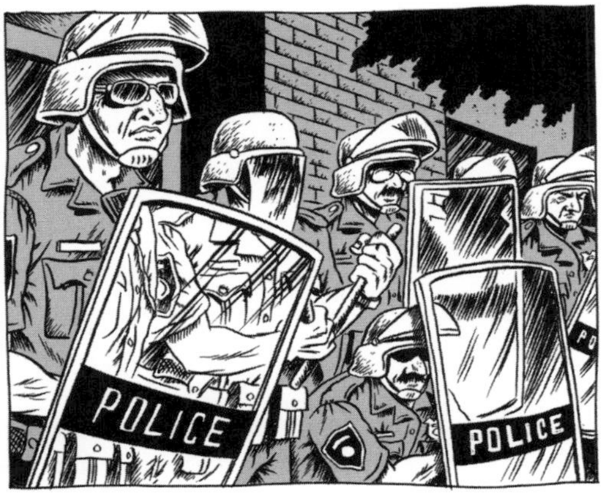
POLICE
POLICE

THEY MAY BE MORE DISGUSTED BY BEING LIED TO BY PRISON OFFICIALS THAN WHAT HAPPENED TO KEVIN...

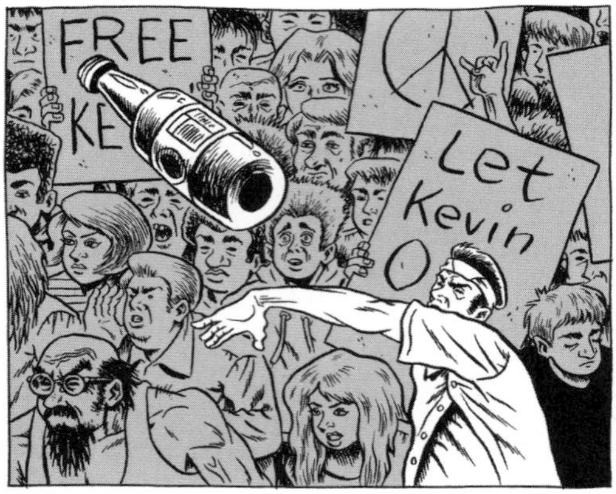
FREE
KE
Let Kevin

... BUT, THEY ALL SHOWED UP, NONETHELESS.

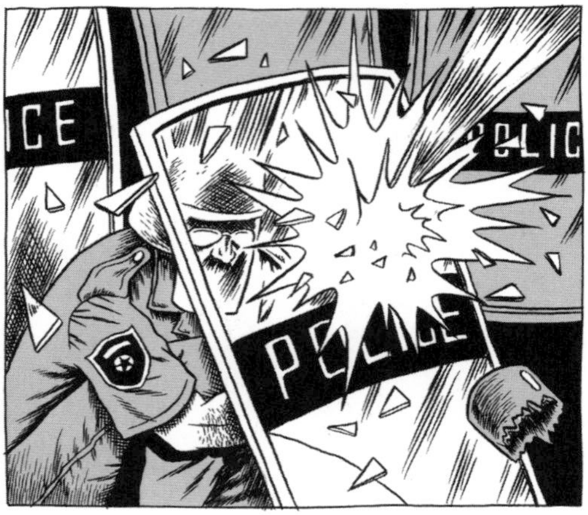
ICE
POLIC

OKAY, I ADMIT, WE DON'T HAVE A STRUCTURE AS TIGHT AS I SAW IT IN MY HEAD...

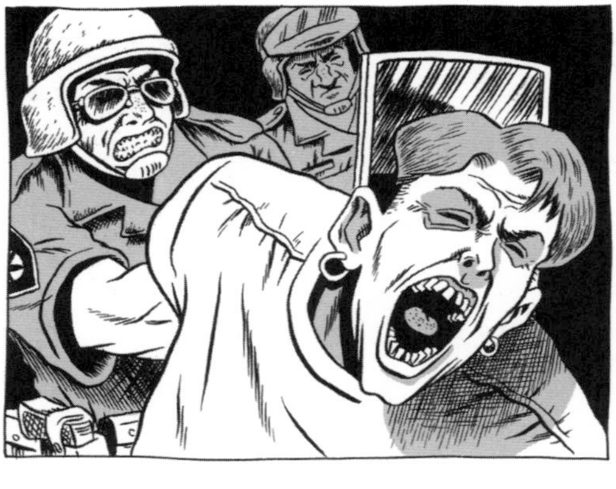

... BUT THE POLITICIANS ARE SCRAMBLING AROUND WITH WEIRD STATEMENTS, NOT KNOWING HOW TO HANDLE THINGS... THE HOSPITAL HAS ZERO FUCKING EXPERIENCE WITH WHAT IS HAPPENING... IT'S A WAR ZONE!

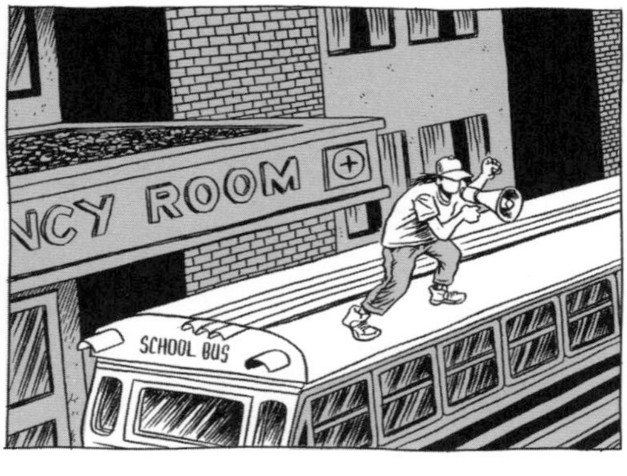
NCY ROOM
SCHOOL BUS

THE ENTIRE INSTITUTION OF LAW, THE COPS, AND PRISON SYSTEM HAVE NEVER LOOKED WORSE THAN THEY DO NOW.

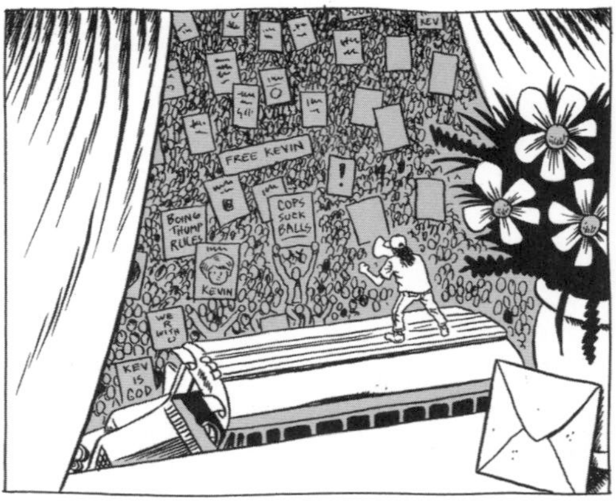
FREE KEVIN
COPS SUCK BALLS
KEVIN
KEV IS GOD

KEV, I WISH YOU COULD SEE THIS RIGHT NOW.

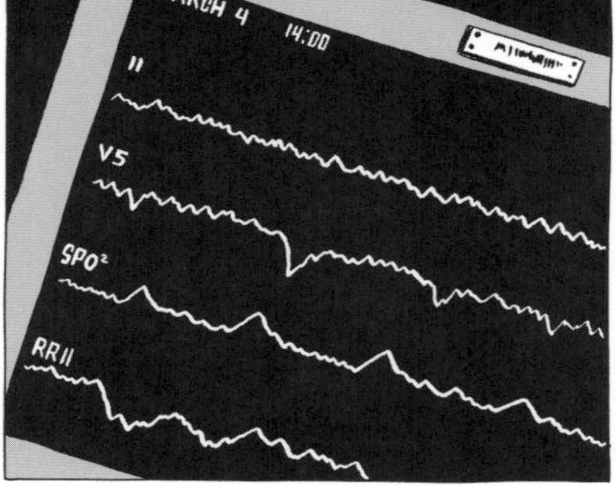
MARCH 4 14:00
II
V5
SPO²
RRII

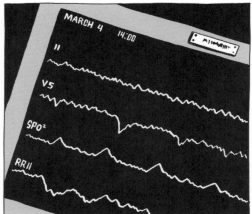

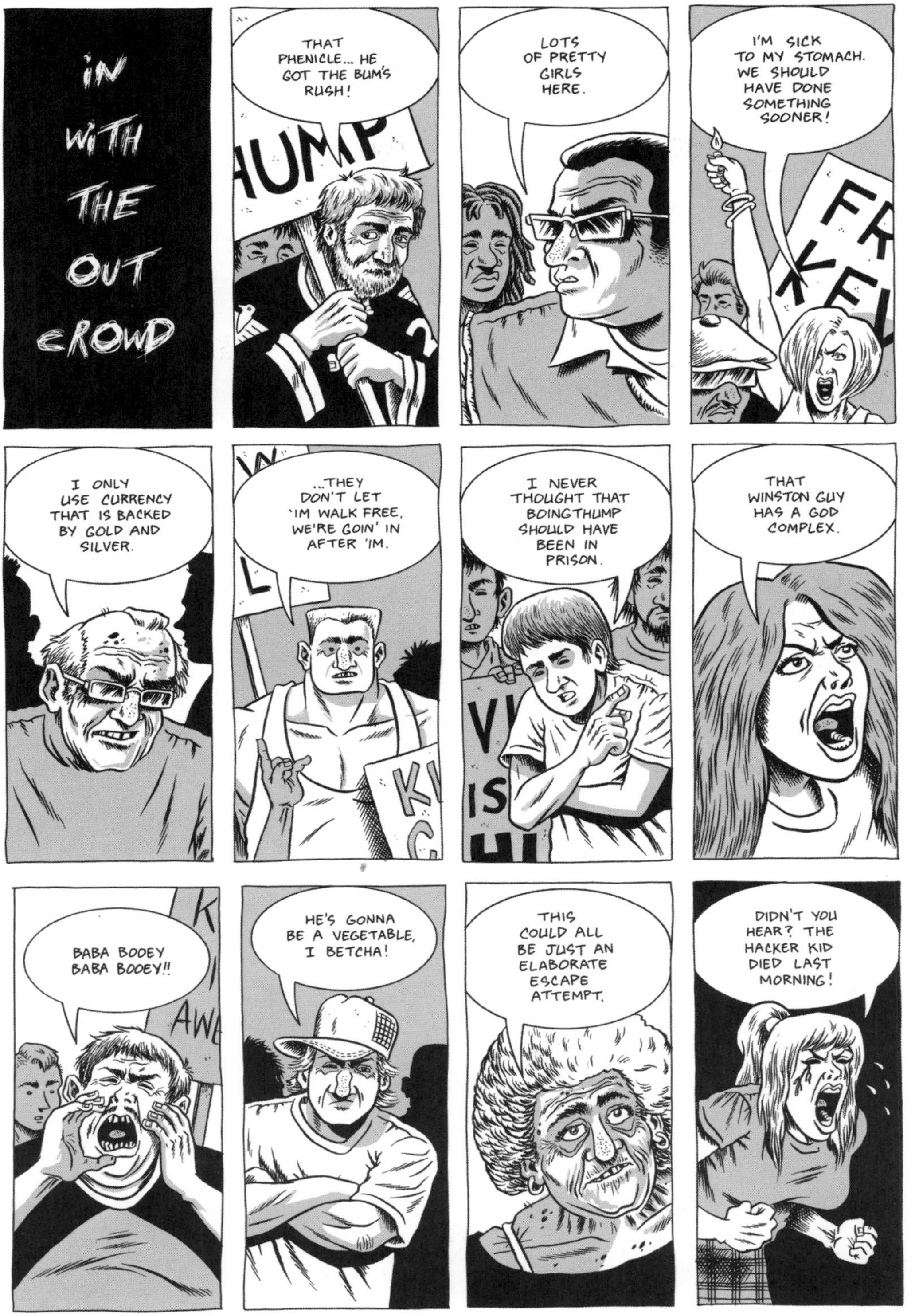
IN WITH THE OUT CROWD
THAT PHENICLE... HE GOT THE BUM'S RUSH!
LOTS OF PRETTY GIRLS HERE.
I'M SICK TO MY STOMACH. WE SHOULD HAVE DONE SOMETHING SOONER!
I ONLY USE CURRENCY THAT IS BACKED BY GOLD AND SILVER.
...THEY DON'T LET 'IM WALK FREE, WE'RE GOIN' IN AFTER 'IM.
I NEVER THOUGHT THAT BOINGTHUMP SHOULD HAVE BEEN IN PRISON.
THAT WINSTON GUY HAS A GOD COMPLEX.
BABA BOOEY BABA BOOEY!!
HE'S GONNA BE A VEGETABLE, I BETCHA!
THIS COULD ALL BE JUST AN ELABORATE ESCAPE ATTEMPT.
DIDN'T YOU HEAR? THE HACKER KID DIED LAST MORNING!

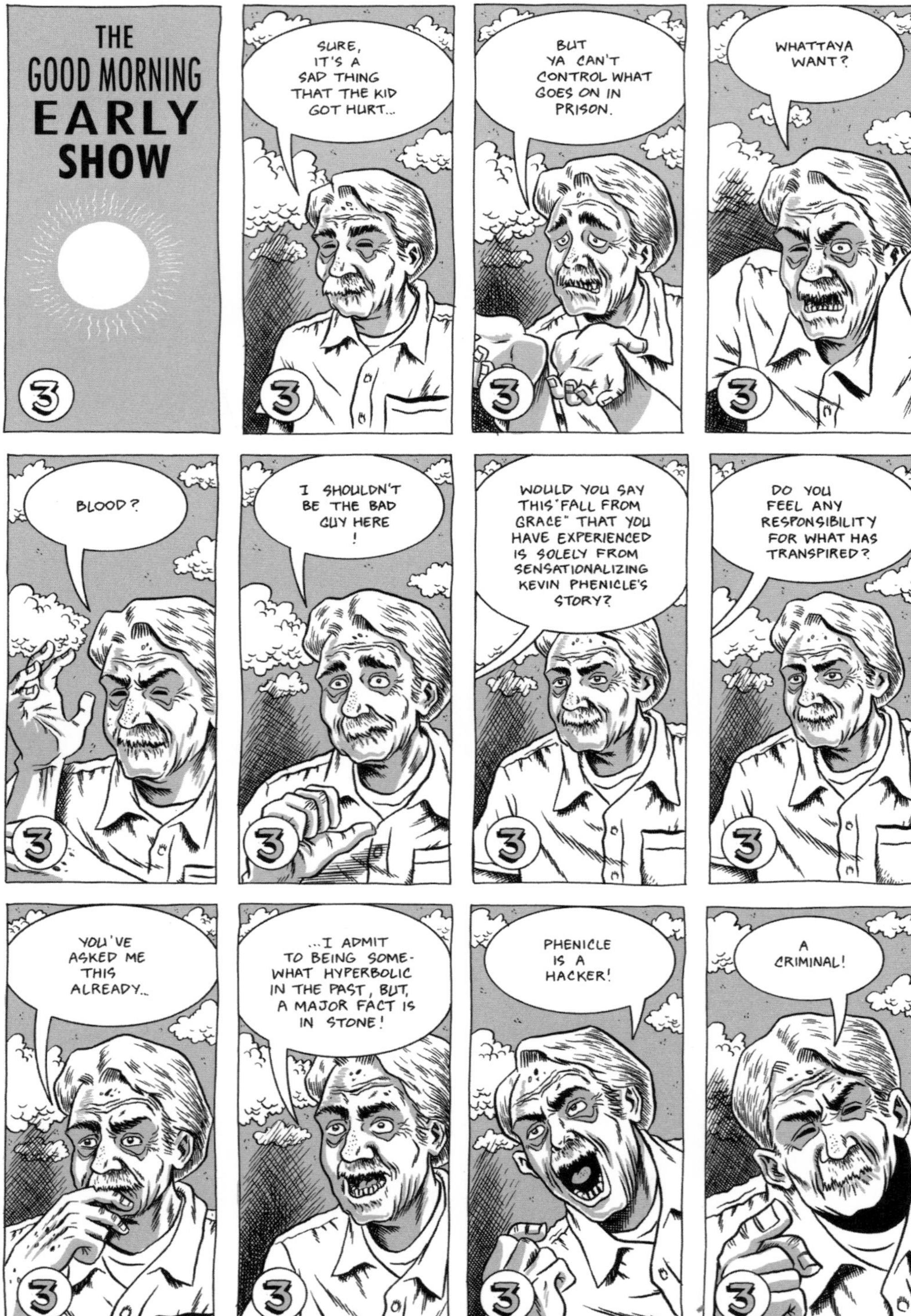
THE GOOD MORNING EARLY SHOW
3
SURE, IT'S A SAD THING THAT THE KID GOT HURT...
BUT YA CAN'T CONTROL WHAT GOES ON IN PRISON.
WHATTAYA WANT?
BLOOD?
I SHOULDN'T BE THE BAD GUY HERE!
WOULD YOU SAY THIS "FALL FROM GRACE" THAT YOU HAVE EXPERIENCED IS SOLELY FROM SENSATIONALIZING KEVIN PHENICLE'S STORY?
DO YOU FEEL ANY RESPONSIBILITY FOR WHAT HAS TRANSPIRED?
YOU'VE ASKED ME THIS ALREADY...
...I ADMIT TO BEING SOMEWHAT HYPERBOLIC IN THE PAST, BUT, A MAJOR FACT IS IN STONE!
PHENICLE IS A HACKER!
A CRIMINAL!

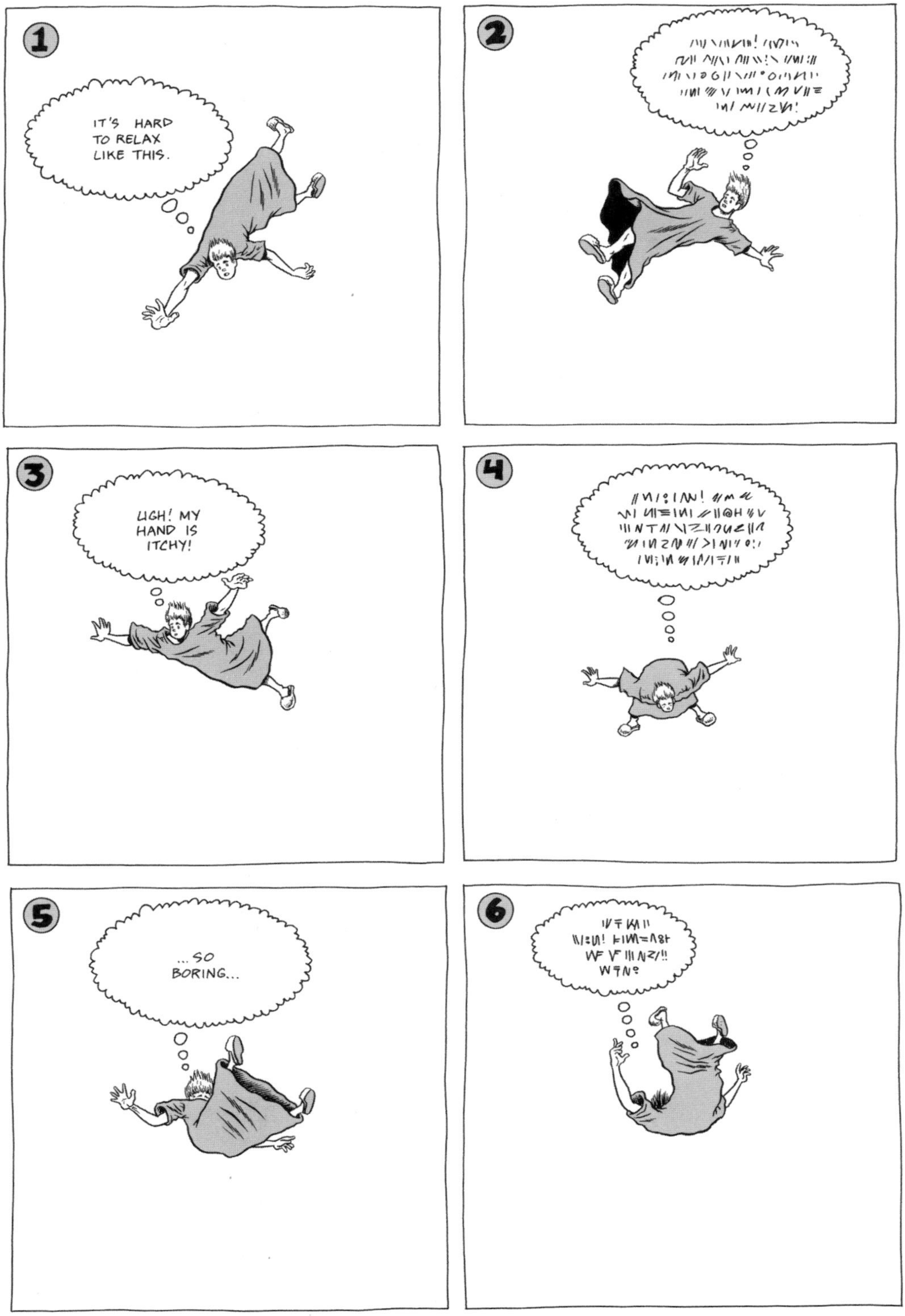
IT'S HARD TO RELAX LIKE THIS.
UGH! MY HAND IS ITCHY!
...SO BORING...

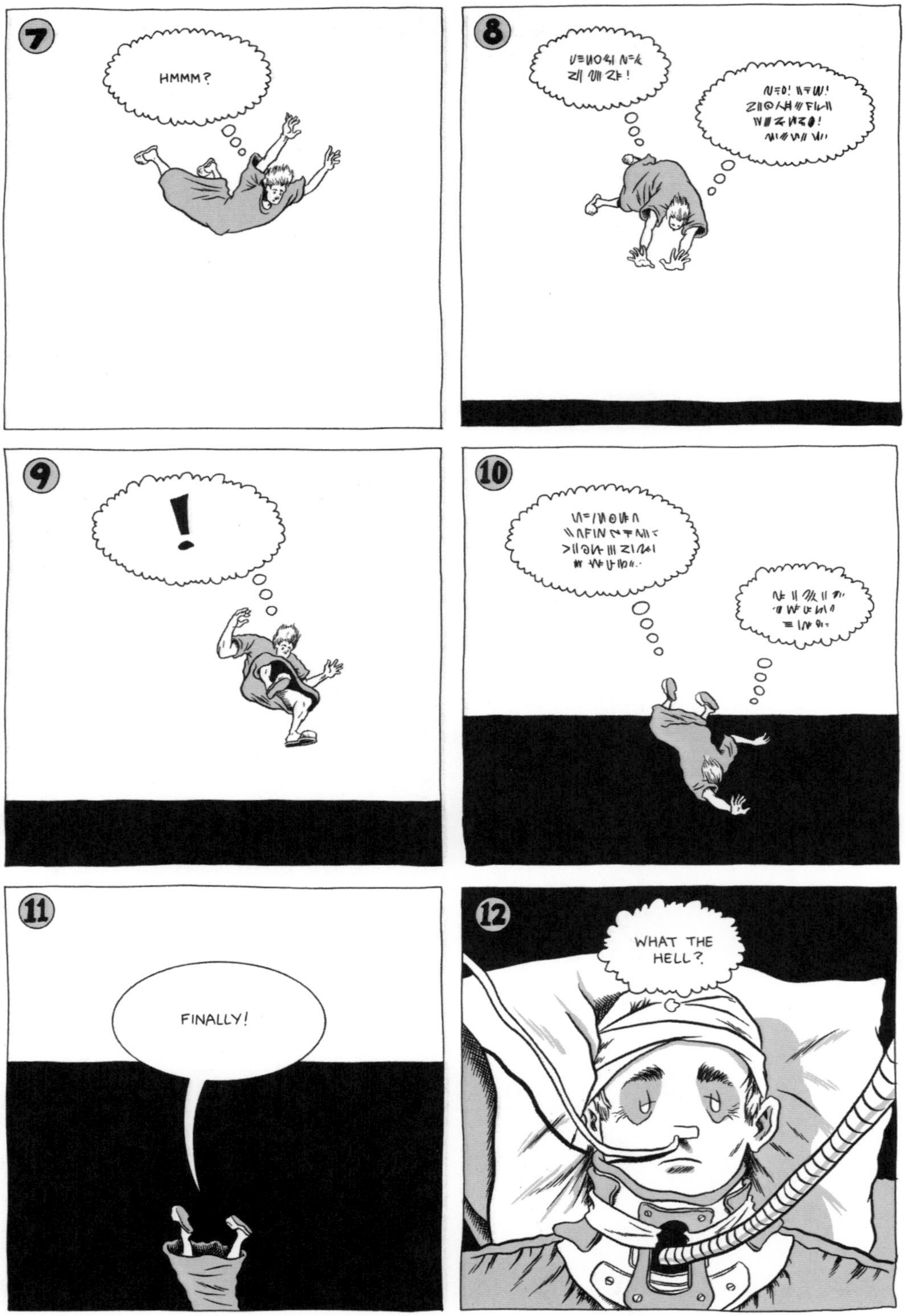
7
HMMM?
8
9
!
10
11
FINALLY!
12
WHAT THE HELL?

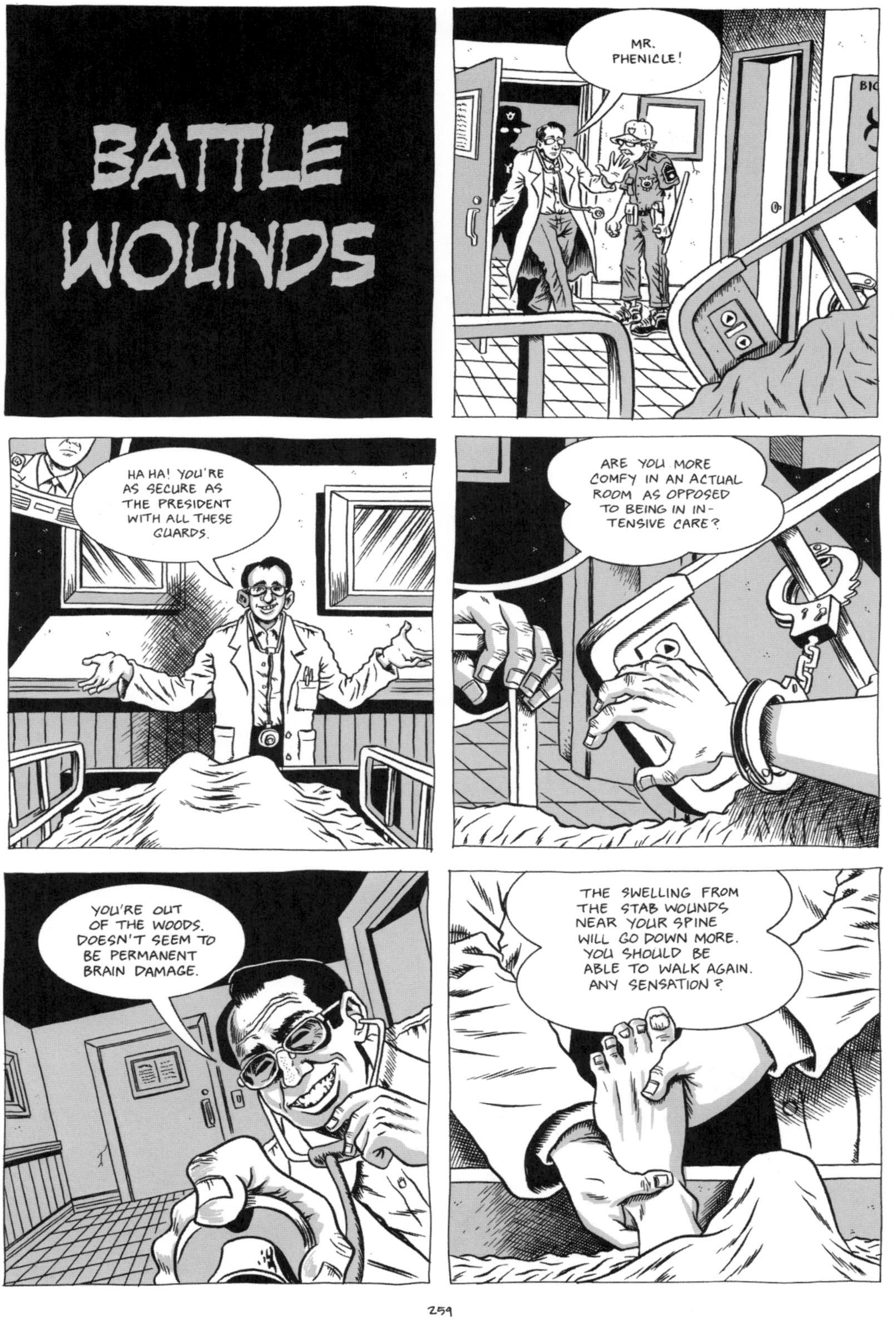
BATTLE WOUNDS
MR. PHENICLE!
BIO
HA HA! YOU'RE AS SECURE AS THE PRESIDENT WITH ALL THESE GUARDS.
ARE YOU MORE COMFY IN AN ACTUAL ROOM AS OPPOSED TO BEING IN INTENSIVE CARE?
YOU'RE OUT OF THE WOODS. DOESN'T SEEM TO BE PERMANENT BRAIN DAMAGE.
THE SWELLING FROM THE STAB WOUNDS NEAR YOUR SPINE WILL GO DOWN MORE. YOU SHOULD BE ABLE TO WALK AGAIN. ANY SENSATION?

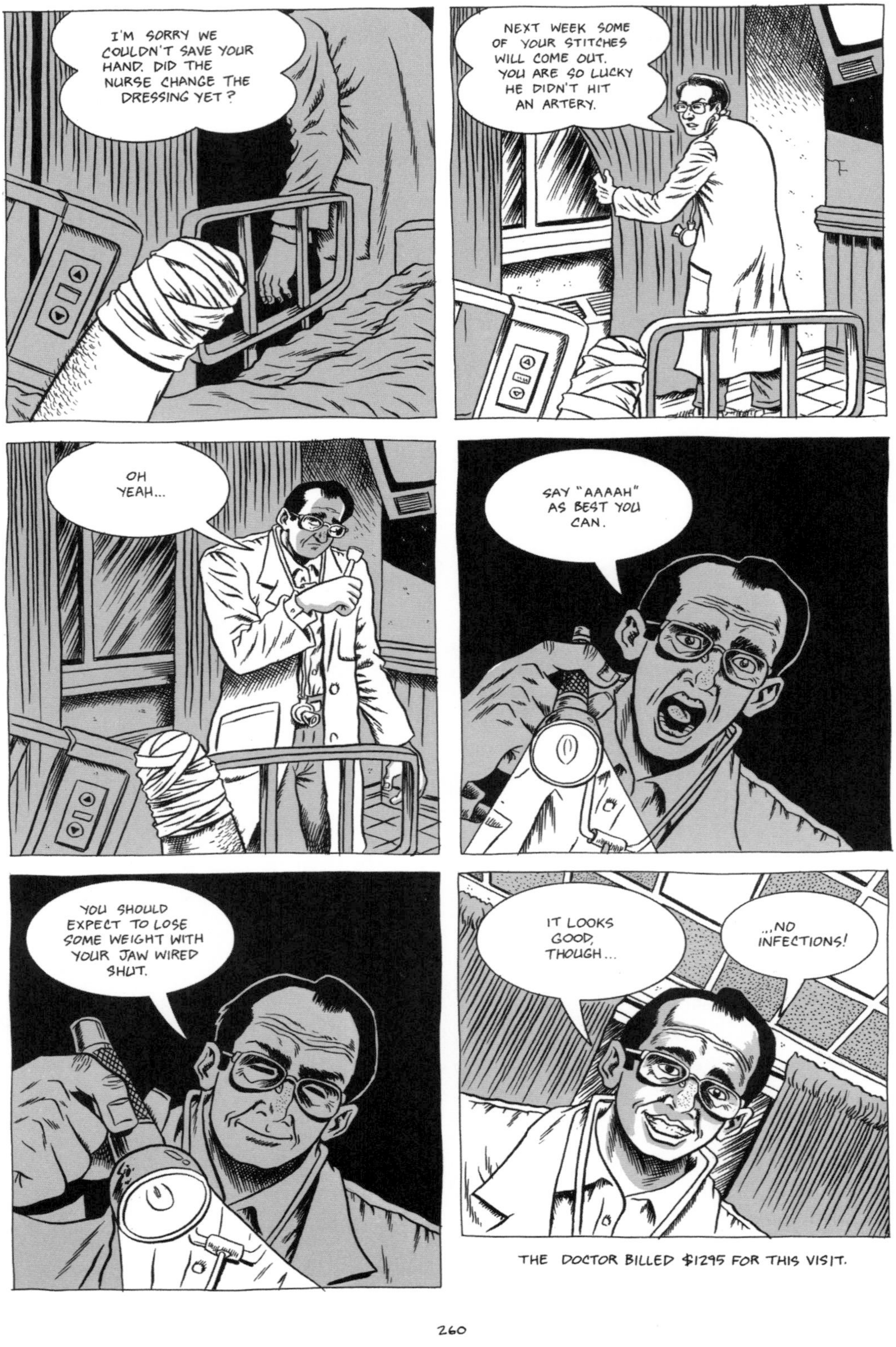
I'M SORRY WE COULDN'T SAVE YOUR HAND. DID THE NURSE CHANGE THE DRESSING YET?
NEXT WEEK SOME OF YOUR STITCHES WILL COME OUT. YOU ARE SO LUCKY HE DIDN'T HIT AN ARTERY.
OH YEAH...
SAY "AAAAH" AS BEST YOU CAN.
YOU SHOULD EXPECT TO LOSE SOME WEIGHT WITH YOUR JAW WIRED SHUT.
IT LOOKS GOOD, THOUGH...
...NO INFECTIONS!

THE DOCTOR BILLED $1295 FOR THIS VISIT.

HELPLESS

THE SCARIEST POTENTIAL ISSUE WITH A WIRED JAW IS EITHER CHOKING OR NAUSEA.

GOTTA DRINK AS MUCH AS POSSIBLE TO TRY AND GET SOME KIND OF NUTRITION. SOME SORT OF CALORIC INTAKE.

TO DIE CHOKING ON VOMIT IS NOT AN INTERESTING WAY TO GO OUT, FOR ME.

THE DOCTOR SUPPLIED ME WITH WIRE-CUTTERS IN THE EVENT THAT THERE IS A PROBLEM.

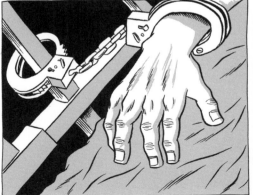

THE COPS DEEMED THE DEVICE TO BE CONTRABAND AND IT WAS TAKEN FROM ME.

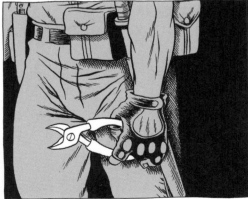

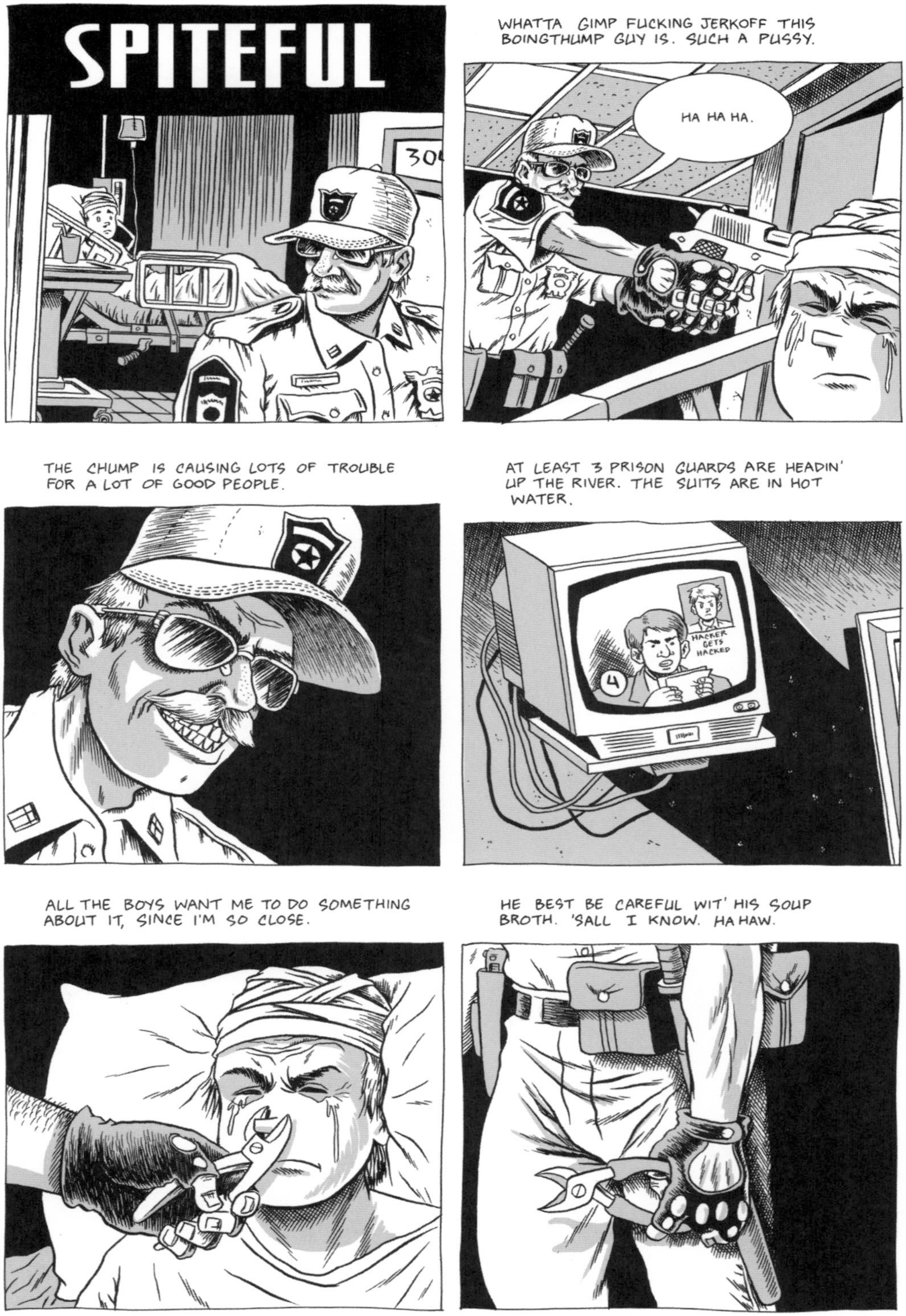
SPITEFUL
WHATTA GIMP FUCKING JERKOFF THIS BOINGTHUMP GUY IS. SUCH A PUSSY.
HA HA HA.
THE CHUMP IS CAUSING LOTS OF TROUBLE FOR A LOT OF GOOD PEOPLE.
AT LEAST 3 PRISON GUARDS ARE HEADIN' UP THE RIVER. THE SUITS ARE IN HOT WATER.
HACKER GETS HACKED
ALL THE BOYS WANT ME TO DO SOMETHING ABOUT IT, SINCE I'M SO CLOSE.
HE BEST BE CAREFUL WIT' HIS SOUP BROTH. 'SALL I KNOW. HA HAW.

NEWS AT NINE, ON 9

THE GRIPPING STORY OF KEVIN "BOINGTHUMP" PHENICLE HAS TAKEN AN EVEN MORE BIZARRE TURN.

LESS THAN A MONTH AFTER RADIO DJ WINSTON SMITH PLAYED THOSE NOTORIOUS RECORDINGS THAT SPARKED NATIONAL OUTRAGE...

... THE 3 CORRECTIONS OFFICERS CAUGHT ON TAPE WERE FOUND DEAD IN THEIR CELLS THIS MORNING. POSSIBLY SELF—INFLICTED INJURIES.

A PRESS CONFERENCE IS EXPECTED TO BE HELD LATER AT 12:00 WITH PRISON OFFICIALS, THE MAYOR, AND THE GOVERNOR.

EXPECT TODAY'S EPISODE OF "YOUNG AND THE RESTLESS" TO BE PREEMPTED.

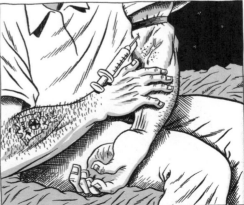

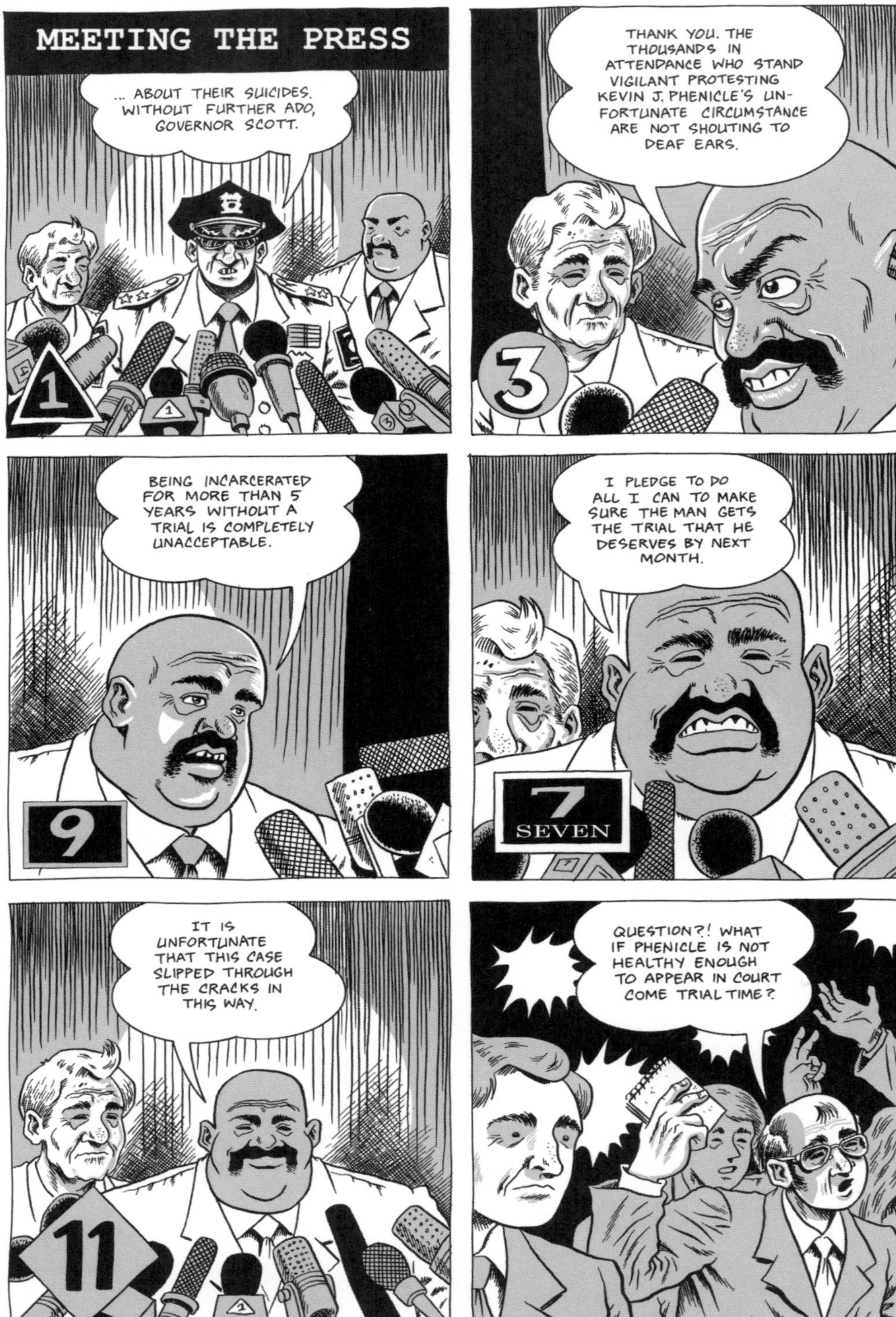
MEETING THE PRESS
... ABOUT THEIR SUICIDES. WITHOUT FURTHER ADO, GOVERNOR SCOTT.
1
THANK YOU. THE THOUSANDS IN ATTENDANCE WHO STAND VIGILANT PROTESTING KEVIN J. PHENICLE'S UNFORTUNATE CIRCUMSTANCE ARE NOT SHOUTING TO DEAF EARS.
3
BEING INCARCERATED FOR MORE THAN 5 YEARS WITHOUT A TRIAL IS COMPLETELY UNACCEPTABLE.
9
I PLEDGE TO DO ALL I CAN TO MAKE SURE THE MAN GETS THE TRIAL THAT HE DESERVES BY NEXT MONTH.
7 SEVEN
IT IS UNFORTUNATE THAT THIS CASE SLIPPED THROUGH THE CRACKS IN THIS WAY.
11
QUESTION?! WHAT IF PHENICLE IS NOT HEALTHY ENOUGH TO APPEAR IN COURT COME TRIAL TIME?

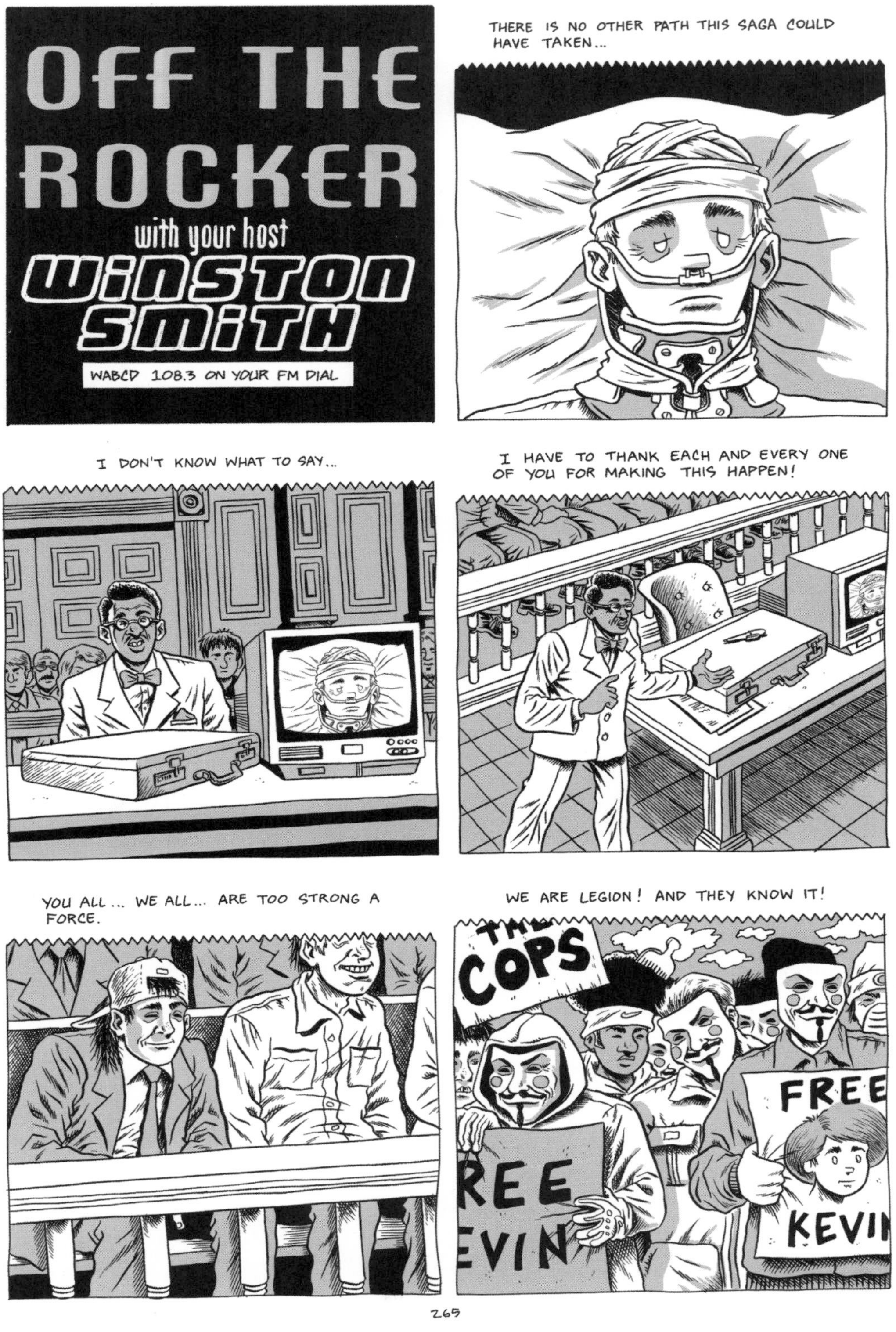
OFF THE ROCKER
with your host
WINSTON SMITH
WABCD 108.3 ON YOUR FM DIAL
THERE IS NO OTHER PATH THIS SAGA COULD HAVE TAKEN...
I DON'T KNOW WHAT TO SAY...
I HAVE TO THANK EACH AND EVERY ONE OF YOU FOR MAKING THIS HAPPEN!
YOU ALL... WE ALL... ARE TOO STRONG A FORCE.
WE ARE LEGION! AND THEY KNOW IT!
COPS
REE
EVIN
FREE
KEVI

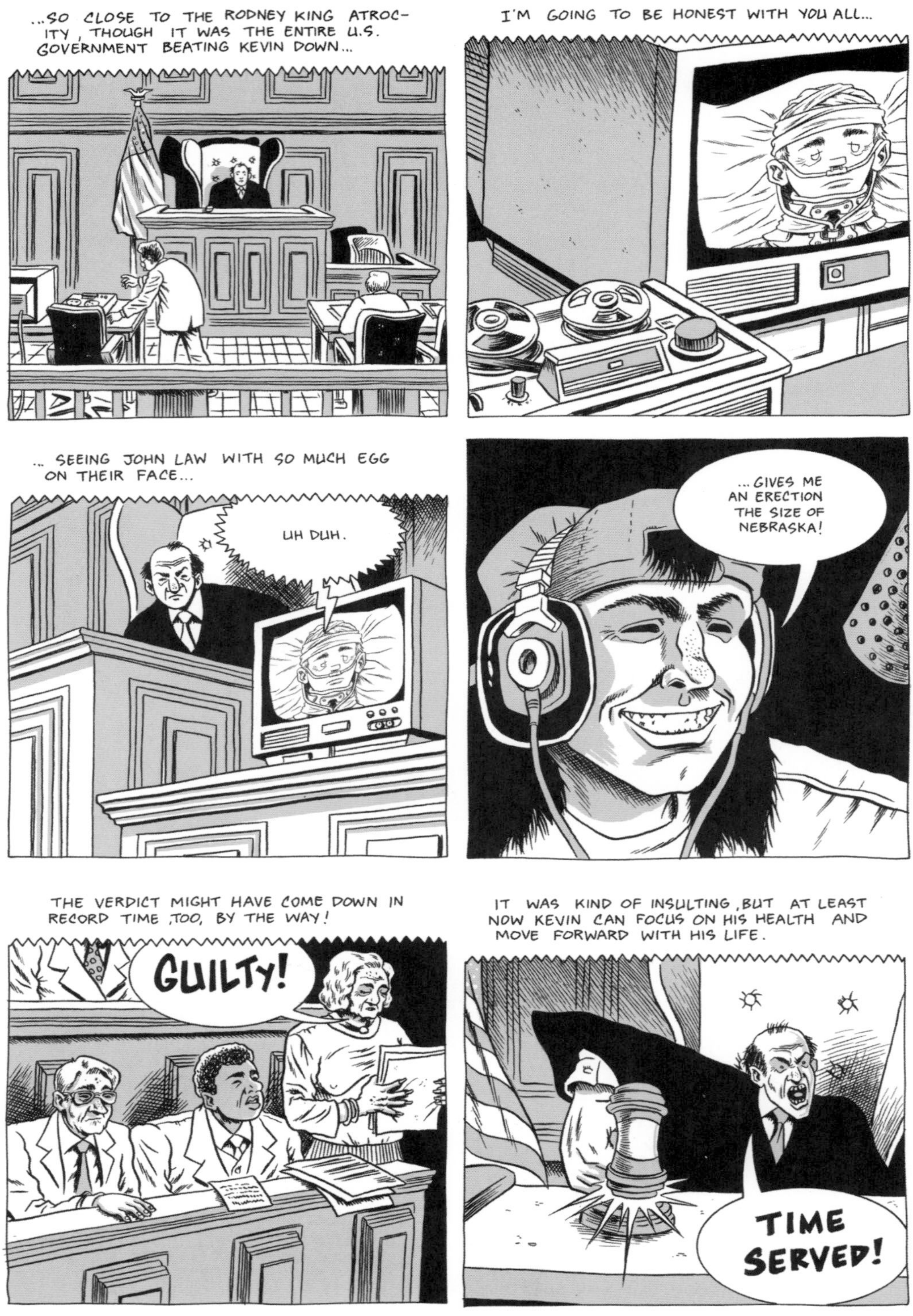
...SO CLOSE TO THE RODNEY KING ATROCITY, THOUGH IT WAS THE ENTIRE U.S. GOVERNMENT BEATING KEVIN DOWN...
I'M GOING TO BE HONEST WITH YOU ALL...
... SEEING JOHN LAW WITH SO MUCH EGG ON THEIR FACE...
UH DUH.
...GIVES ME AN ERECTION THE SIZE OF NEBRASKA!
THE VERDICT MIGHT HAVE COME DOWN IN RECORD TIME, TOO, BY THE WAY!
GUILTY!
IT WAS KIND OF INSULTING, BUT AT LEAST NOW KEVIN CAN FOCUS ON HIS HEALTH AND MOVE FORWARD WITH HIS LIFE.
TIME SERVED!

FIRST THINGS FIRST

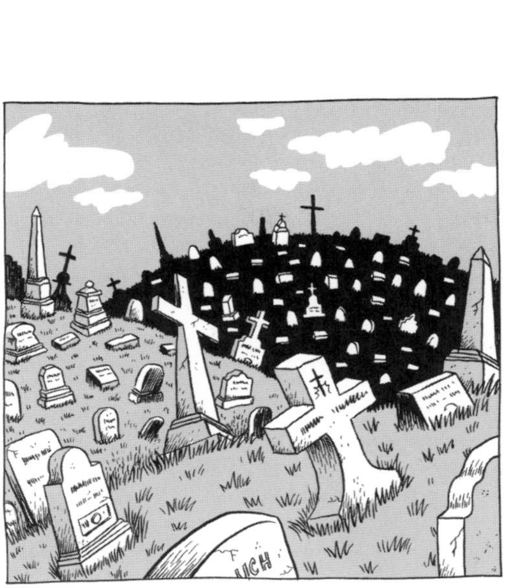
UCH

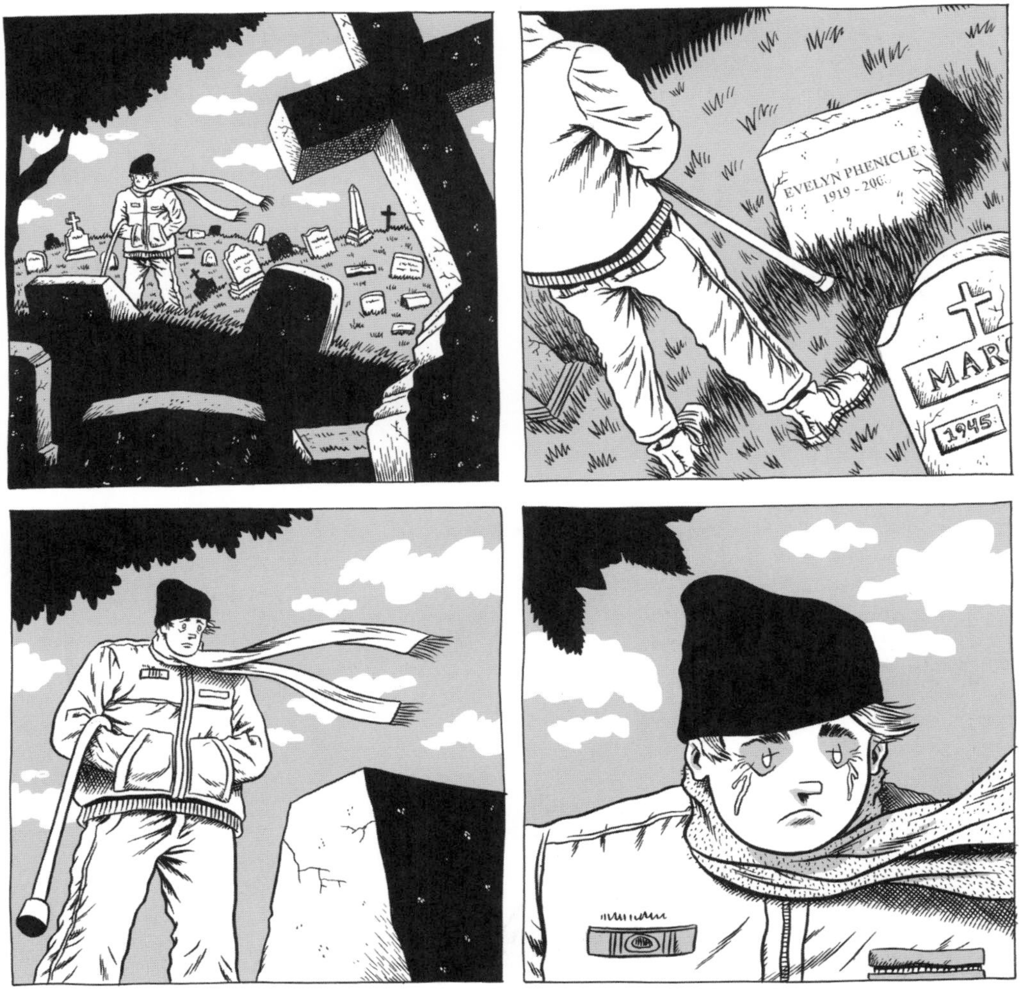
EVELYN PHENICLE
MAR
1945

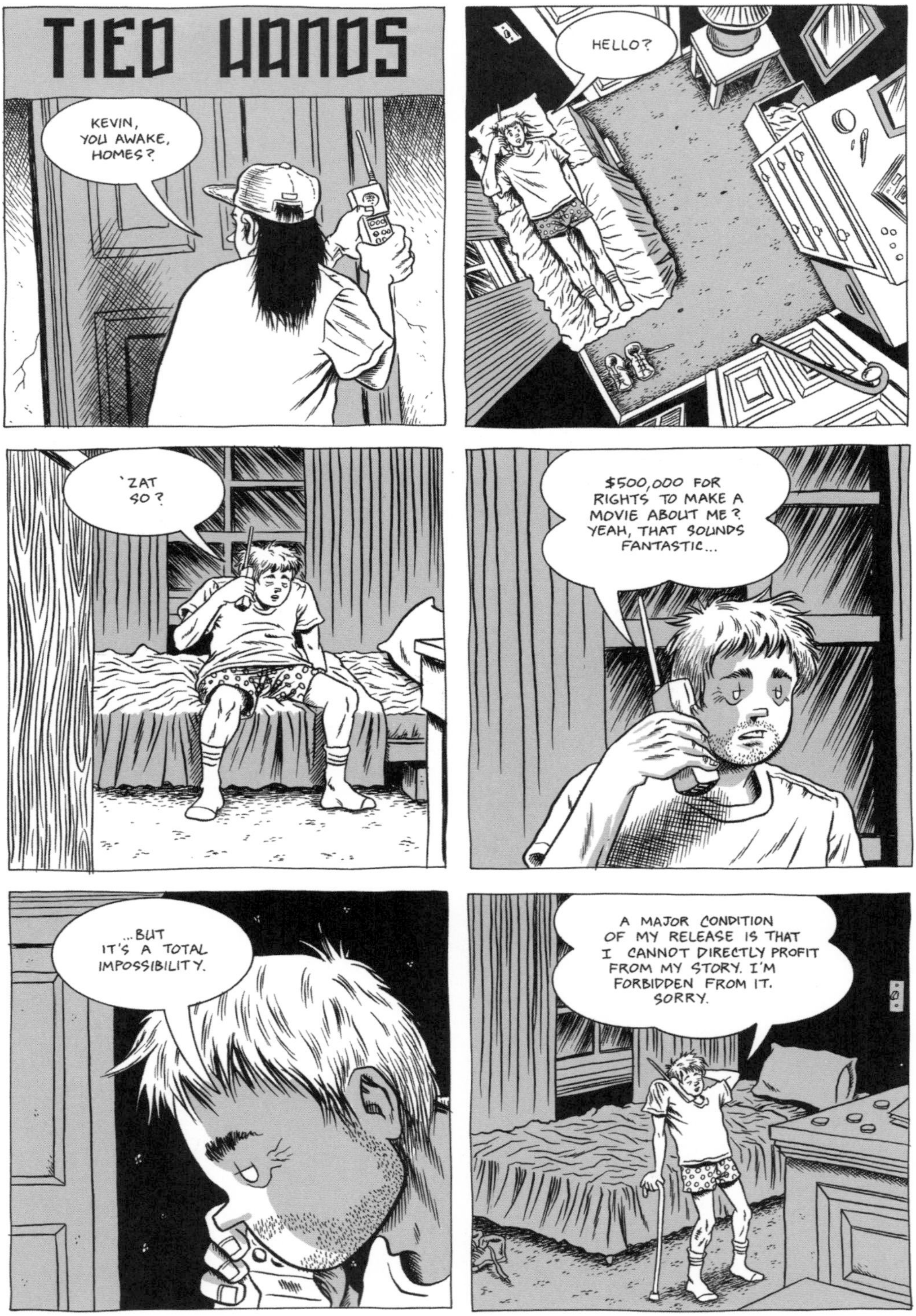
TIED HANDS
KEVIN, YOU AWAKE, HOMES?
HELLO?
`ZAT SO?
$500,000 FOR RIGHTS TO MAKE A MOVIE ABOUT ME? YEAH, THAT SOUNDS FANTASTIC...
...BUT IT'S A TOTAL IMPOSSIBILITY.
A MAJOR CONDITION OF MY RELEASE IS THAT I CANNOT DIRECTLY PROFIT FROM MY STORY. I'M FORBIDDEN FROM IT. SORRY.

The Gauntlet

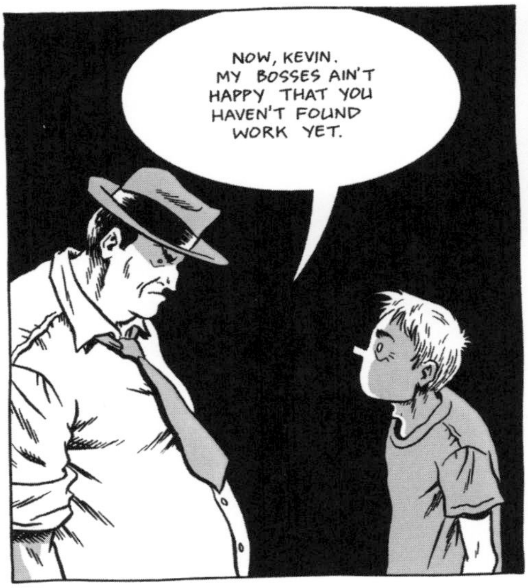
NOW, KEVIN. MY BOSSES AIN'T HAPPY THAT YOU HAVEN'T FOUND WORK YET.

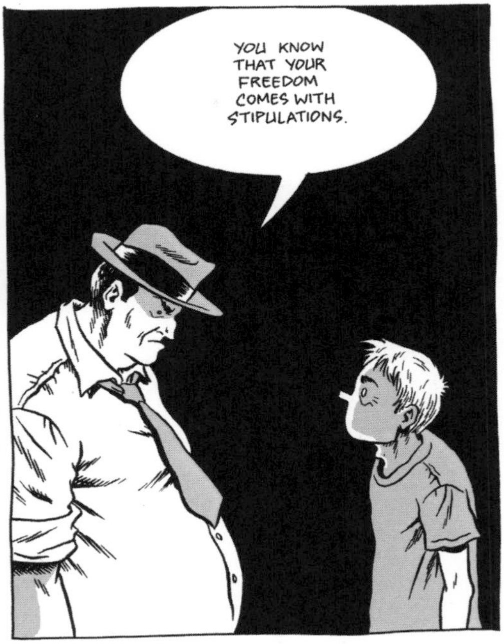
YOU KNOW THAT YOUR FREEDOM COMES WITH STIPULATIONS.

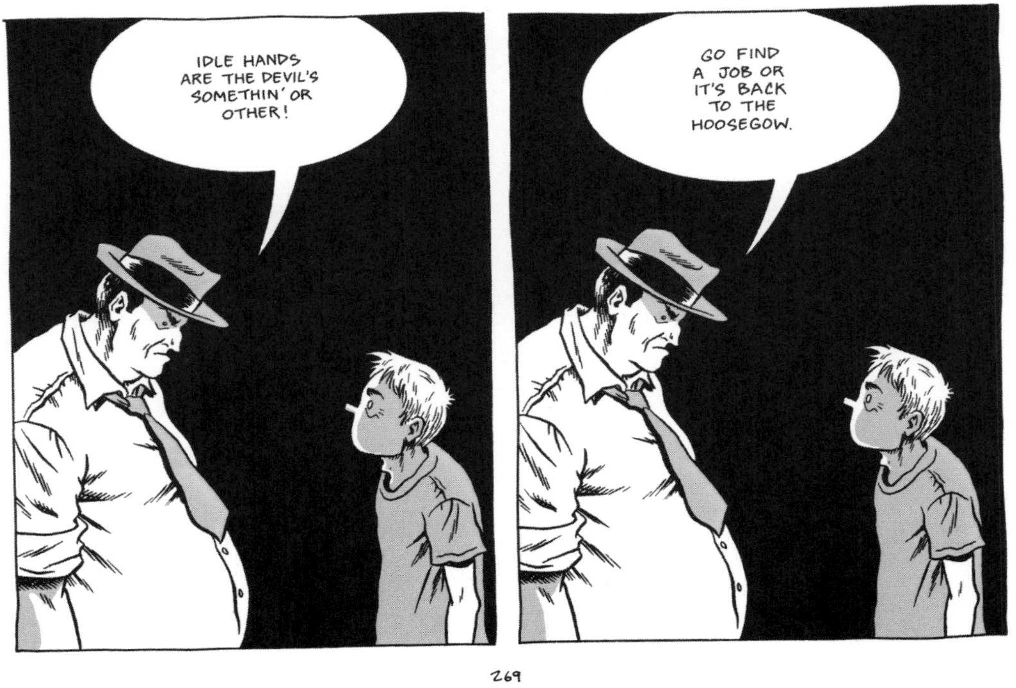
IDLE HANDS ARE THE DEVIL'S SOMETHIN' OR OTHER!
GO FIND A JOB OR IT'S BACK TO THE HOOSEGOW.

The Hunt

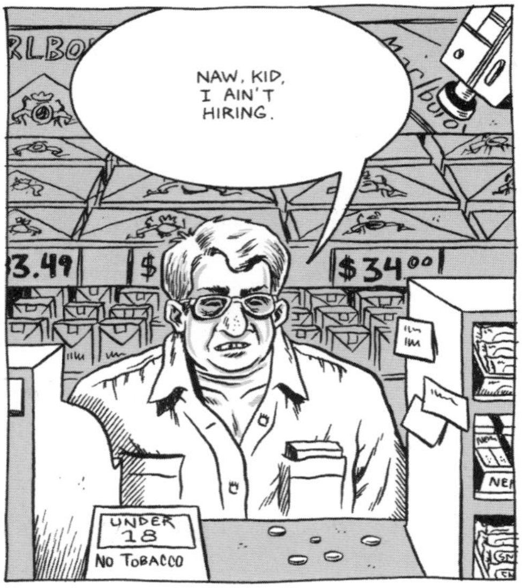
NAW, KID, I AIN'T HIRING.
$34.00
UNDER 18
NO TOBACCO

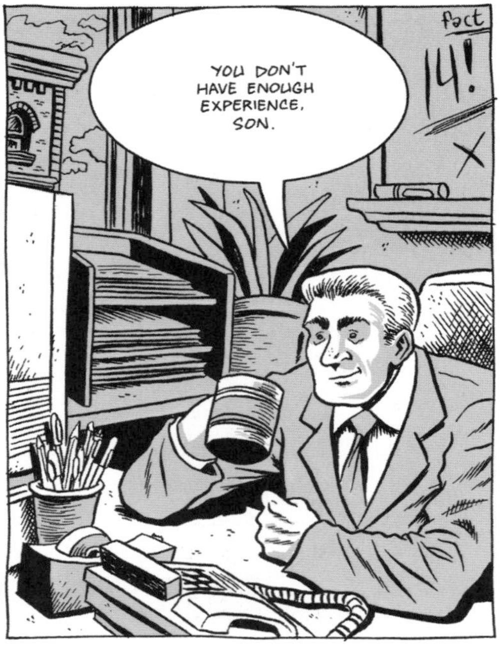
YOU DON'T HAVE ENOUGH EXPERIENCE, SON.
fact
14!

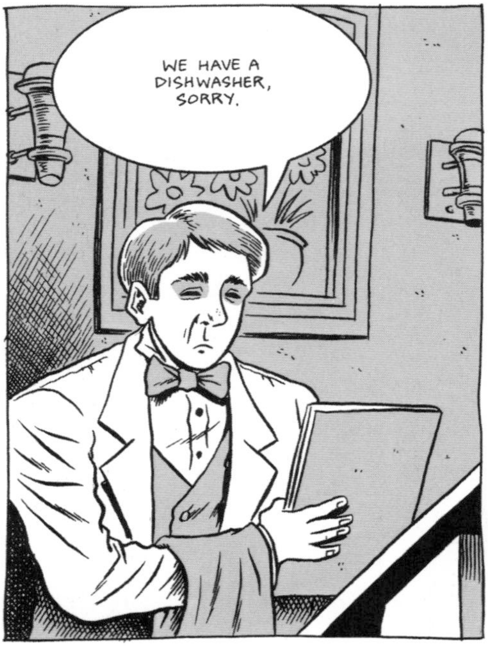
WE HAVE A DISHWASHER, SORRY.

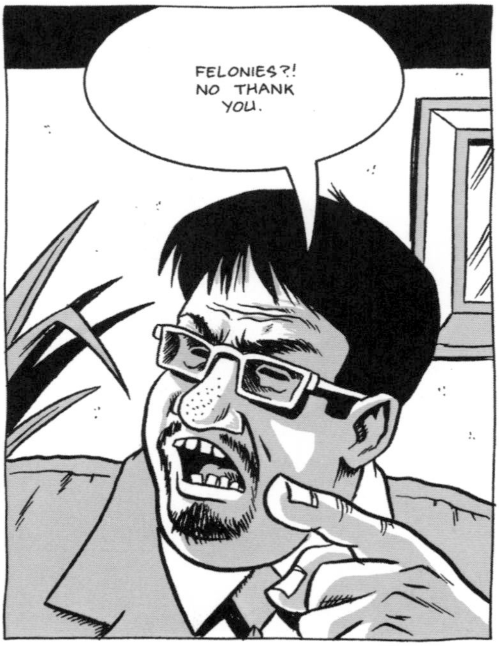
FELONIES?! NO THANK YOU.

The Next...

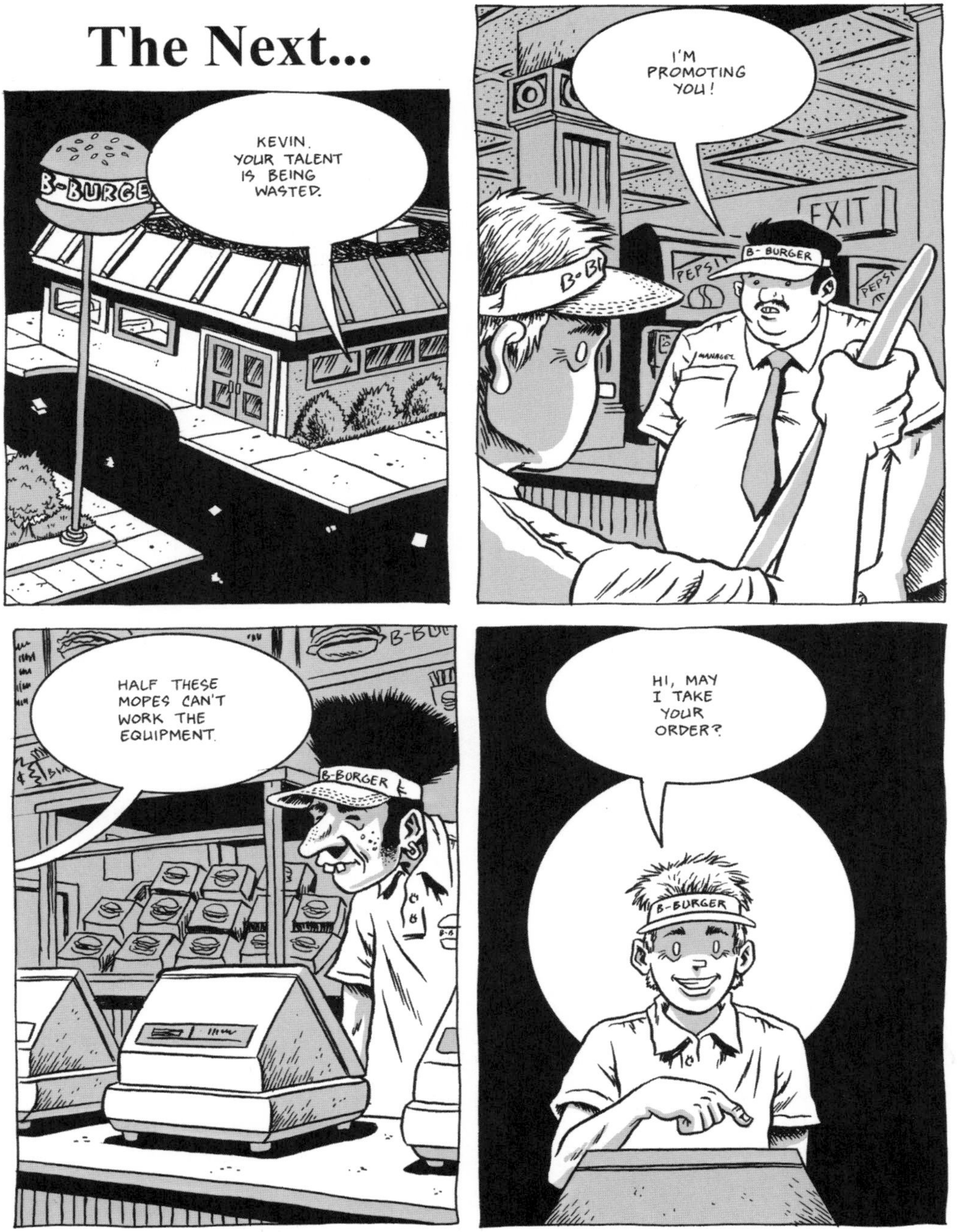
B-BURGER
KEVIN. YOUR TALENT IS BEING WASTED.
I'M PROMOTING YOU!
EXIT
B-BURGER
HALF THESE MOPES CAN'T WORK THE EQUIPMENT.
B-BURGER
HI, MAY I TAKE YOUR ORDER?
B-BURGER

The Result

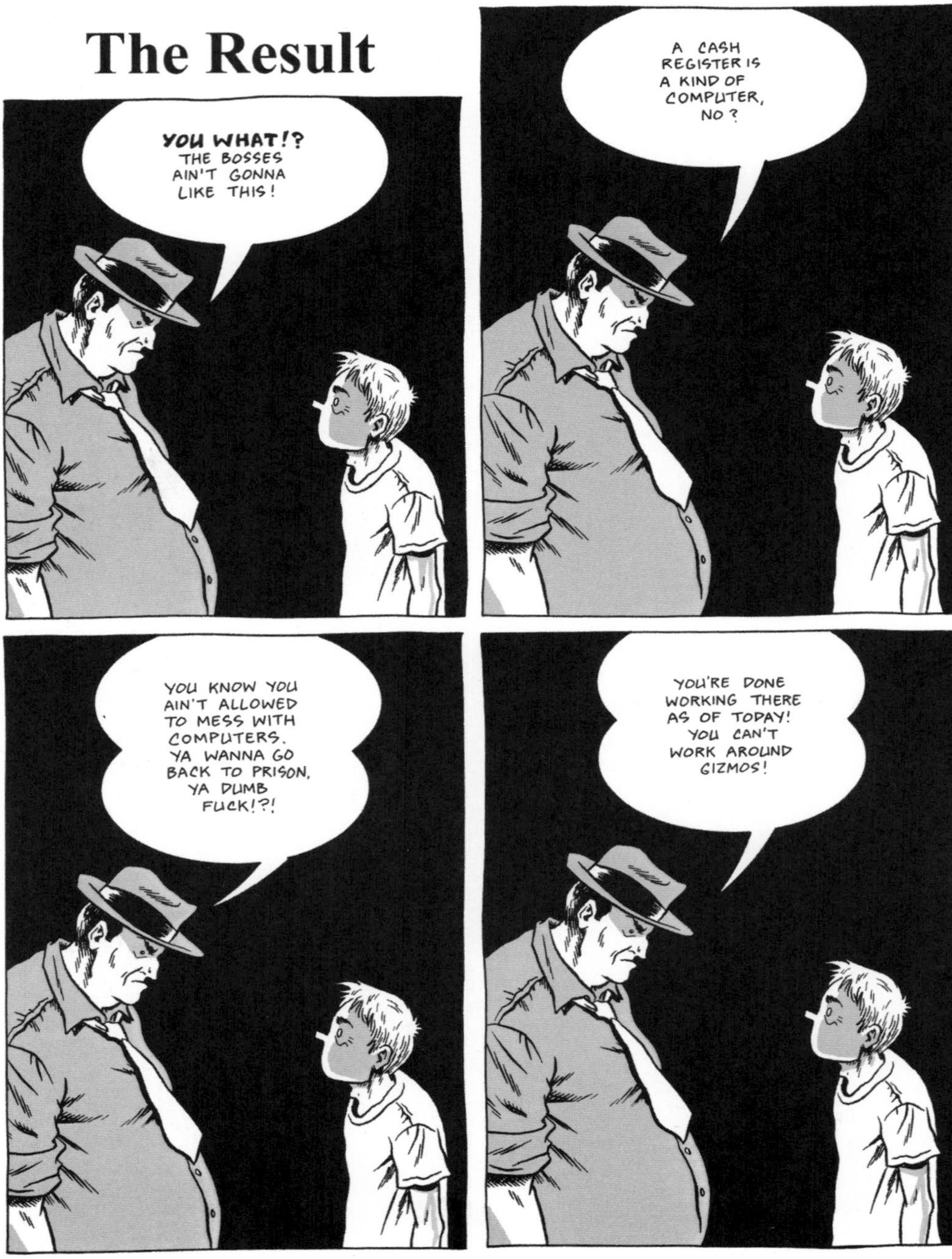
YOU WHAT!? THE BOSSES AIN'T GONNA LIKE THIS!
A CASH REGISTER IS A KIND OF COMPUTER, NO?
YOU KNOW YOU AIN'T ALLOWED TO MESS WITH COMPUTERS. YA WANNA GO BACK TO PRISON, YA DUMB FUCK!?!
YOU'RE DONE WORKING THERE AS OF TODAY! YOU CAN'T WORK AROUND GIZMOS!

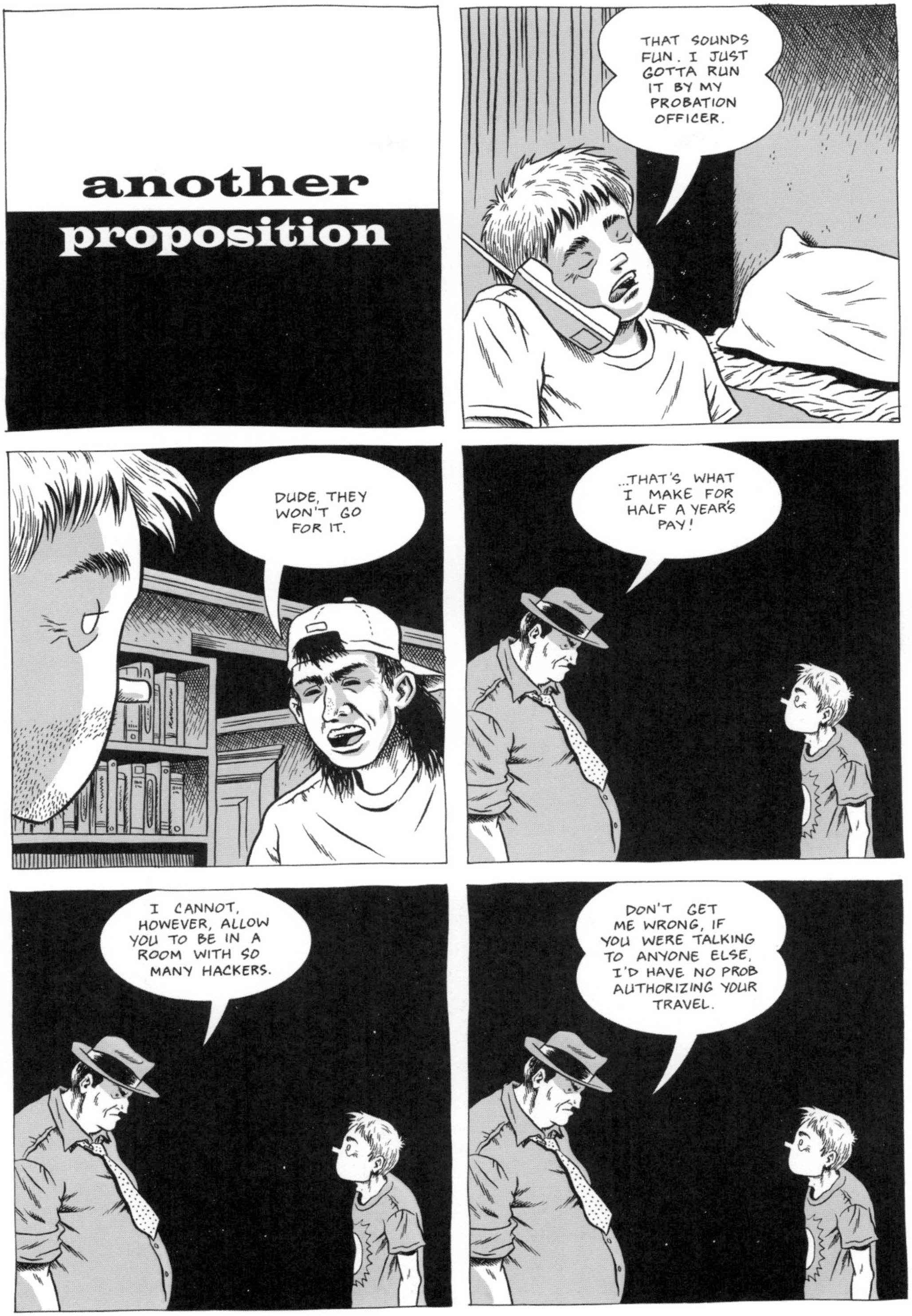
another proposition
THAT SOUNDS FUN. I JUST GOTTA RUN IT BY MY PROBATION OFFICER.
DUDE, THEY WON'T GO FOR IT.
...THAT'S WHAT I MAKE FOR HALF A YEAR'S PAY!
I CANNOT, HOWEVER, ALLOW YOU TO BE IN A ROOM WITH SO MANY HACKERS.
DON'T GET ME WRONG, IF YOU WERE TALKING TO ANYONE ELSE, I'D HAVE NO PROB AUTHORIZING YOUR TRAVEL.

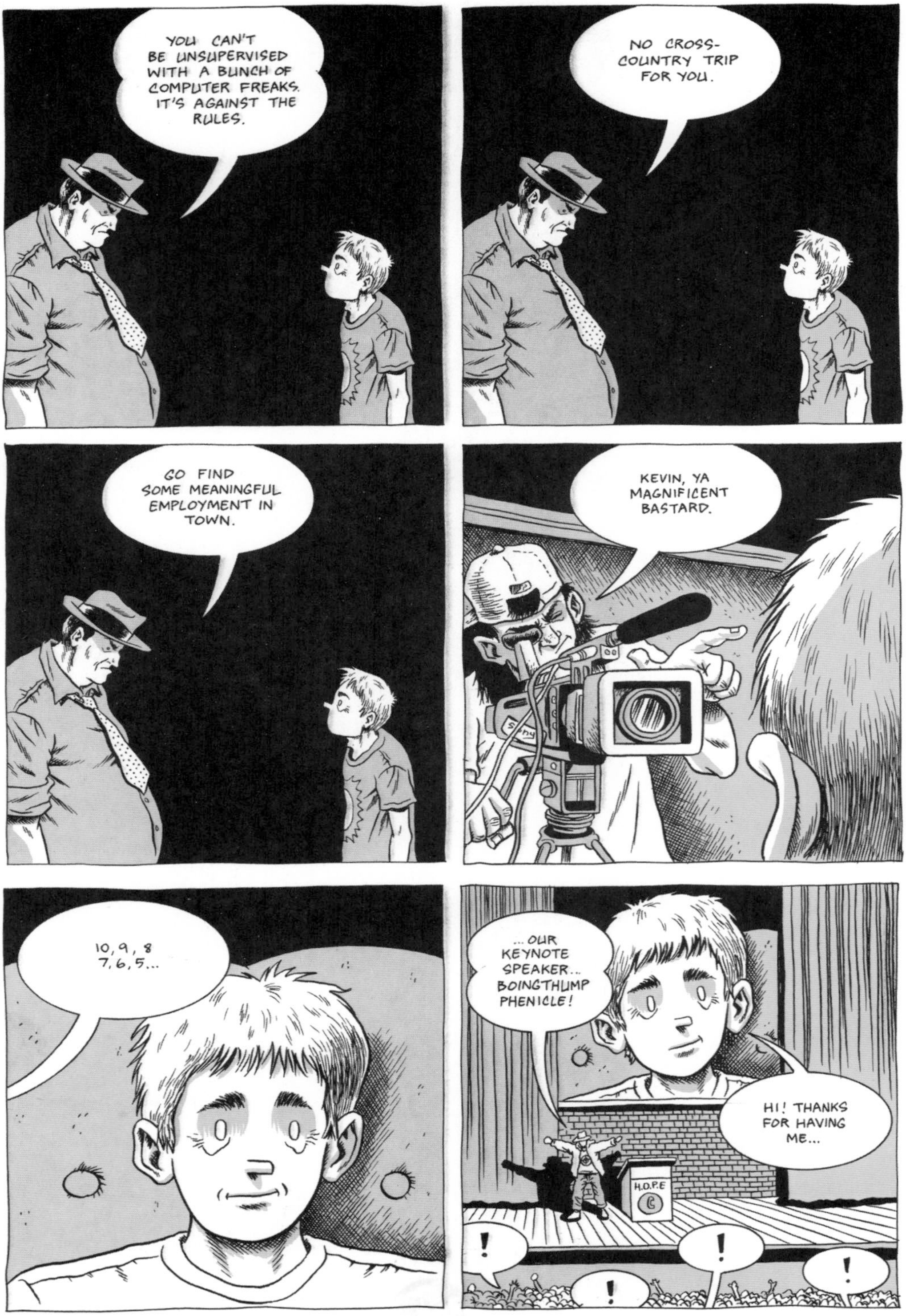
YOU CAN'T BE UNSUPERVISED WITH A BUNCH OF COMPUTER FREAKS. IT'S AGAINST THE RULES.
NO CROSS-COUNTRY TRIP FOR YOU.
GO FIND SOME MEANINGFUL EMPLOYMENT IN TOWN.
KEVIN, YA MAGNIFICENT BASTARD.
10, 9, 8 7, 6, 5...
...OUR KEYNOTE SPEAKER... BOINGTHUMP PHENICLE!
HI! THANKS FOR HAVING ME...
H.O.P.E
!
!
!
!

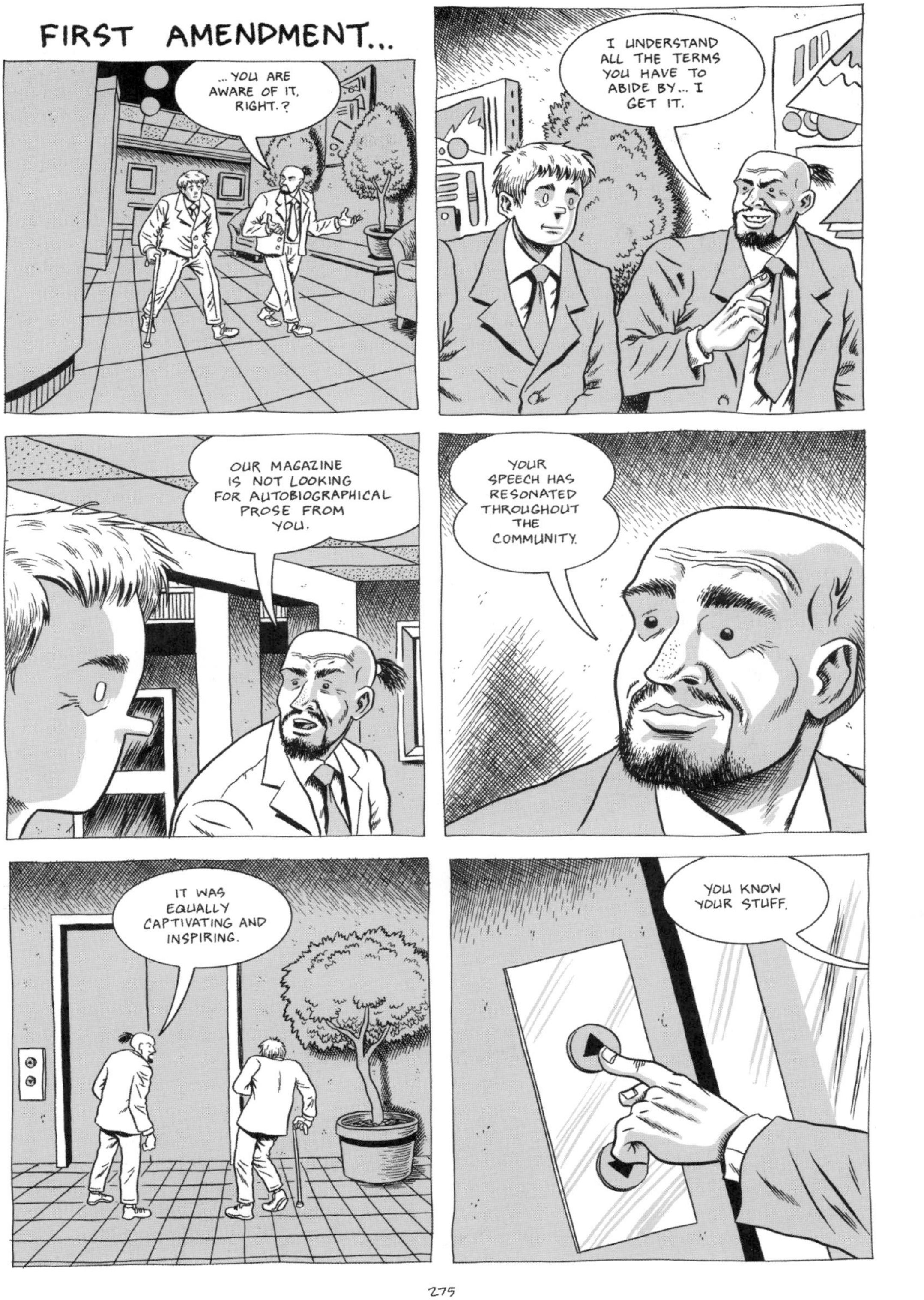
FIRST AMENDMENT...
...YOU ARE AWARE OF IT, RIGHT.?
I UNDERSTAND ALL THE TERMS YOU HAVE TO ABIDE BY... I GET IT.
OUR MAGAZINE IS NOT LOOKING FOR AUTOBIOGRAPHICAL PROSE FROM YOU.
YOUR SPEECH HAS RESONATED THROUGHOUT THE COMMUNITY.
IT WAS EQUALLY CAPTIVATING AND INSPIRING.
YOU KNOW YOUR STUFF.

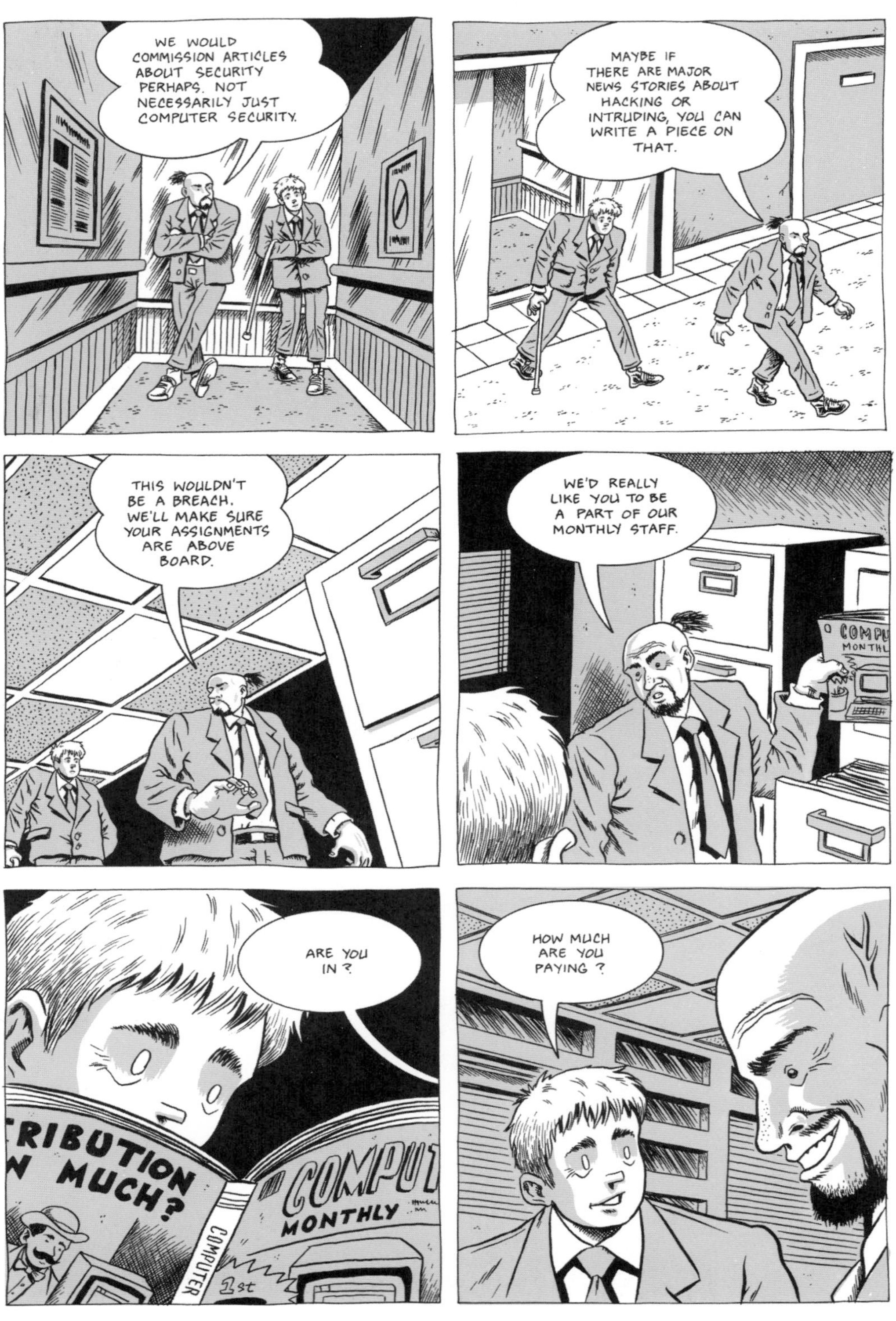
WE WOULD COMMISSION ARTICLES ABOUT SECURITY PERHAPS. NOT NECESSARILY JUST COMPUTER SECURITY.
MAYBE IF THERE ARE MAJOR NEWS STORIES ABOUT HACKING OR INTRUDING, YOU CAN WRITE A PIECE ON THAT.
THIS WOULDN'T BE A BREACH. WE'LL MAKE SURE YOUR ASSIGNMENTS ARE ABOVE BOARD.
WE'D REALLY LIKE YOU TO BE A PART OF OUR MONTHLY STAFF.
ARE YOU IN ?
RIBUTION
N MUCH?
COMPUT
MONTHLY
COMPUTER
1st
HOW MUCH ARE YOU PAYING ?

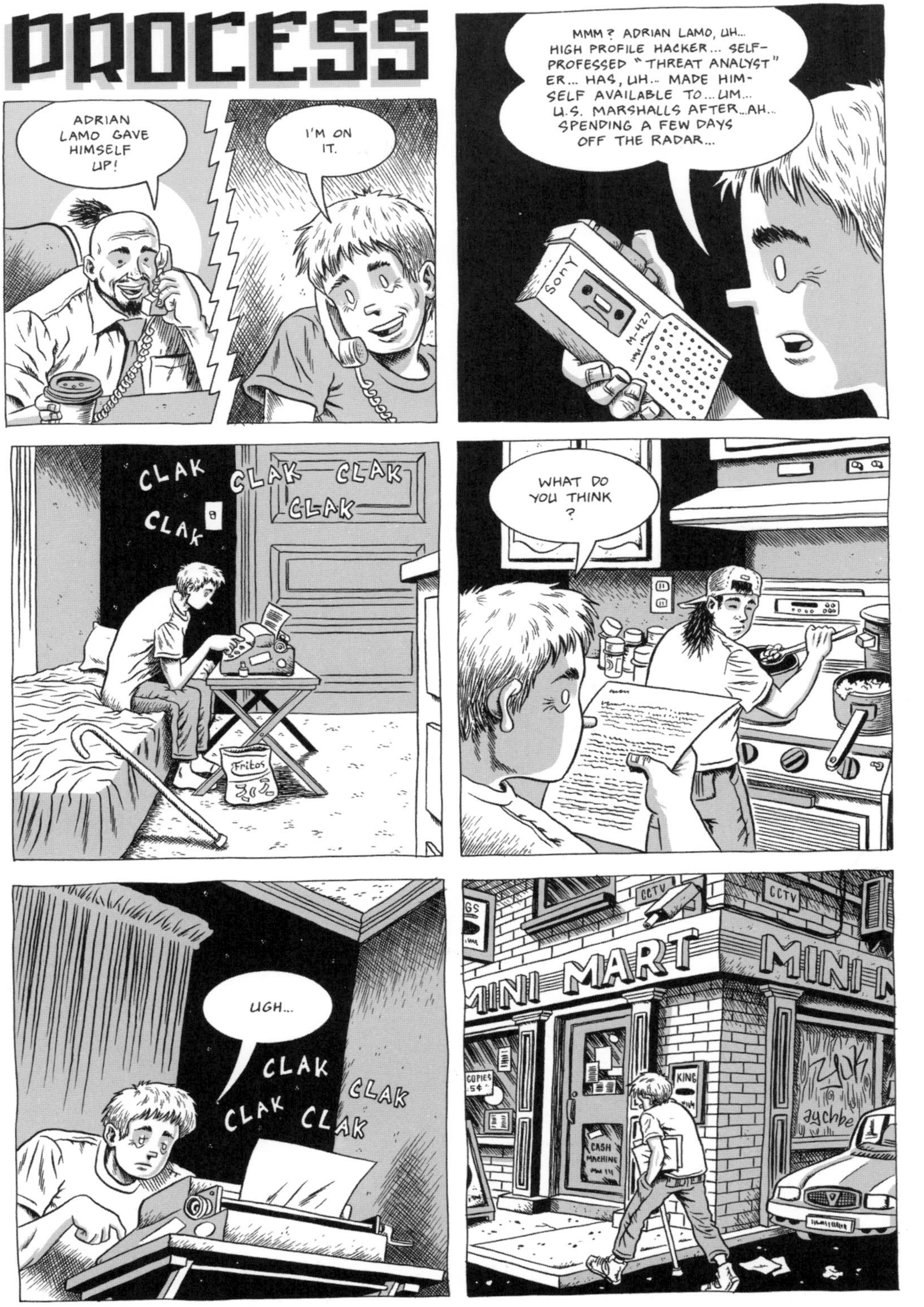
PROCESS
ADRIAN LAMO GAVE HIMSELF UP!
I'M ON IT.
MMM? ADRIAN LAMO, UH... HIGH PROFILE HACKER... SELF-PROFESSED "THREAT ANALYST" ER... HAS, UH... MADE HIMSELF AVAILABLE TO... UM... U.S. MARSHALLS AFTER...AH... SPENDING A FEW DAYS OFF THE RADAR...
SONY
M-427
CLAK CLAK CLAK CLAK CLAK
Fritos
WHAT DO YOU THINK ?
UGH...
CLAK CLAK CLAK CLAK
CCTV
CCTV
MINI MART
MINI
COPIES 5¢
KING
CASH MACHINE

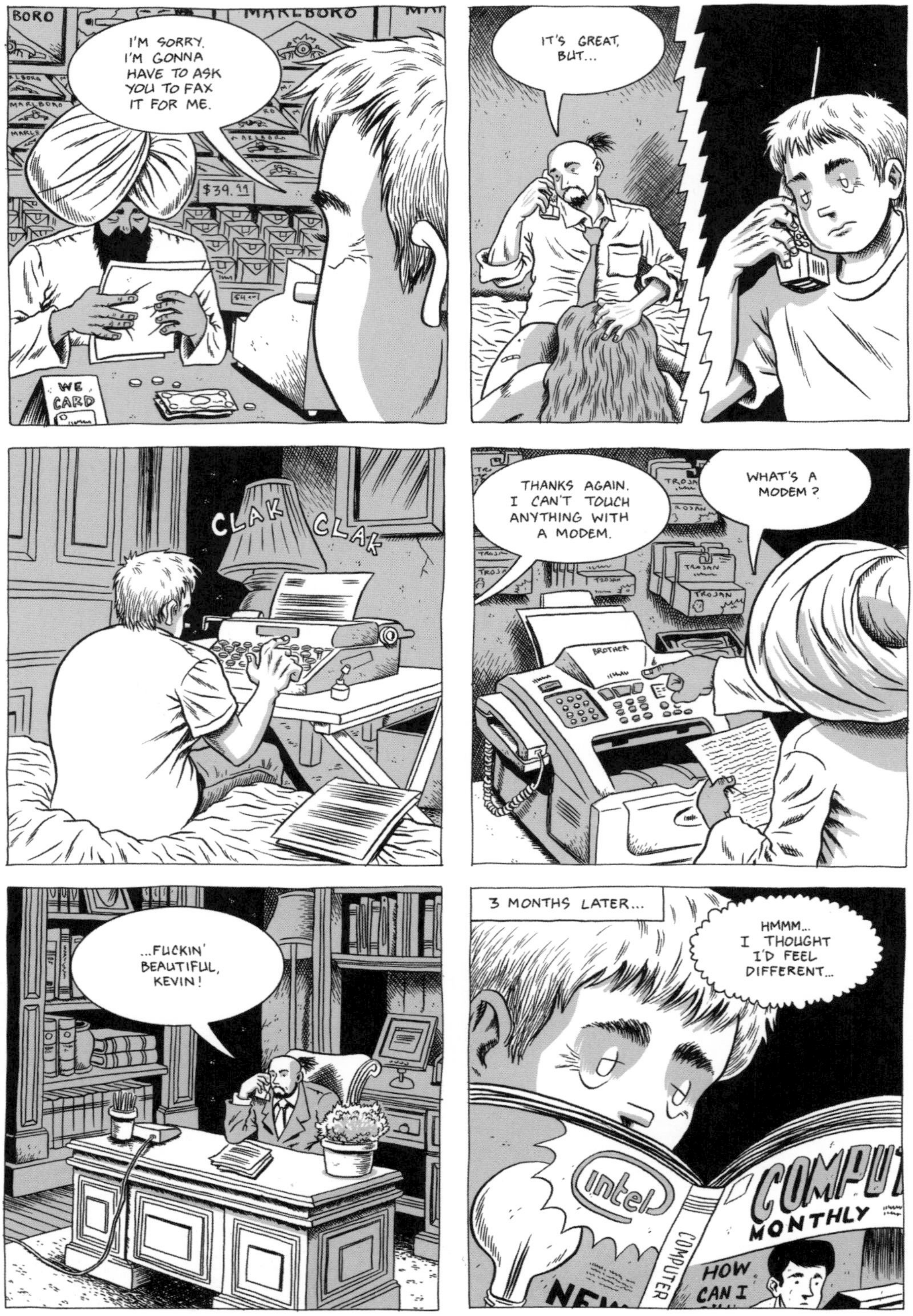
BORO
MARLBORO
I'M SORRY. I'M GONNA HAVE TO ASK YOU TO FAX IT FOR ME.
$39.99
WE CARD
IT'S GREAT, BUT...
CLAK CLAK
THANKS AGAIN. I CAN'T TOUCH ANYTHING WITH A MODEM.
WHAT'S A MODEM?
TROJAN
BROTHER
...FUCKIN' BEAUTIFUL, KEVIN!
3 MONTHS LATER...
HMMM... I THOUGHT I'D FEEL DIFFERENT...
intel
COMPUTER
MONTHLY
HOW CAN I

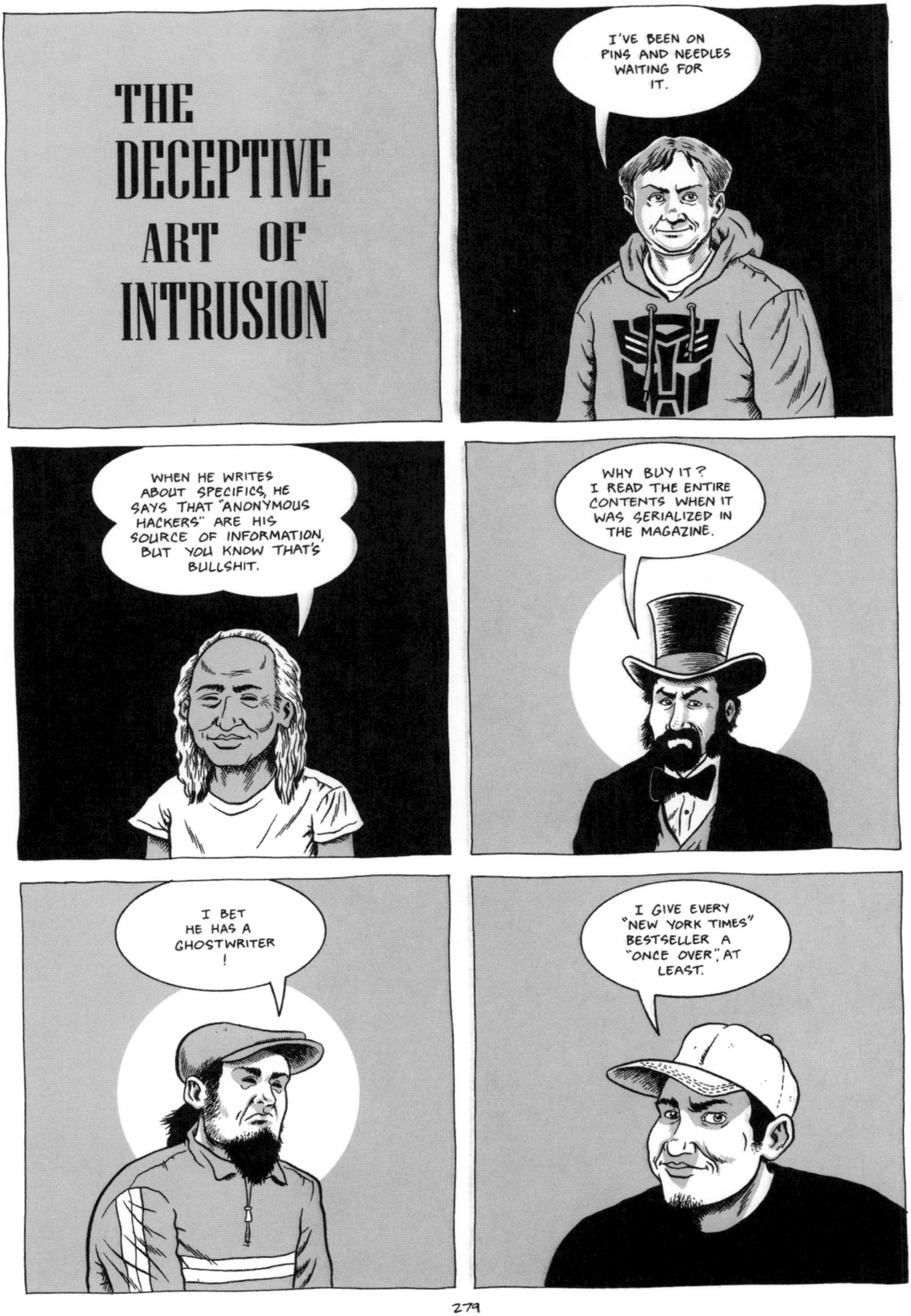
THE DECEPTIVE ART OF INTRUSION
I'VE BEEN ON PINS AND NEEDLES WAITING FOR IT.
WHEN HE WRITES ABOUT SPECIFICS, HE SAYS THAT "ANONYMOUS HACKERS" ARE HIS SOURCE OF INFORMATION, BUT YOU KNOW THAT'S BULLSHIT.
WHY BUY IT? I READ THE ENTIRE CONTENTS WHEN IT WAS SERIALIZED IN THE MAGAZINE.
I BET HE HAS A GHOSTWRITER !
I GIVE EVERY "NEW YORK TIMES" BESTSELLER A "ONCE OVER", AT LEAST.

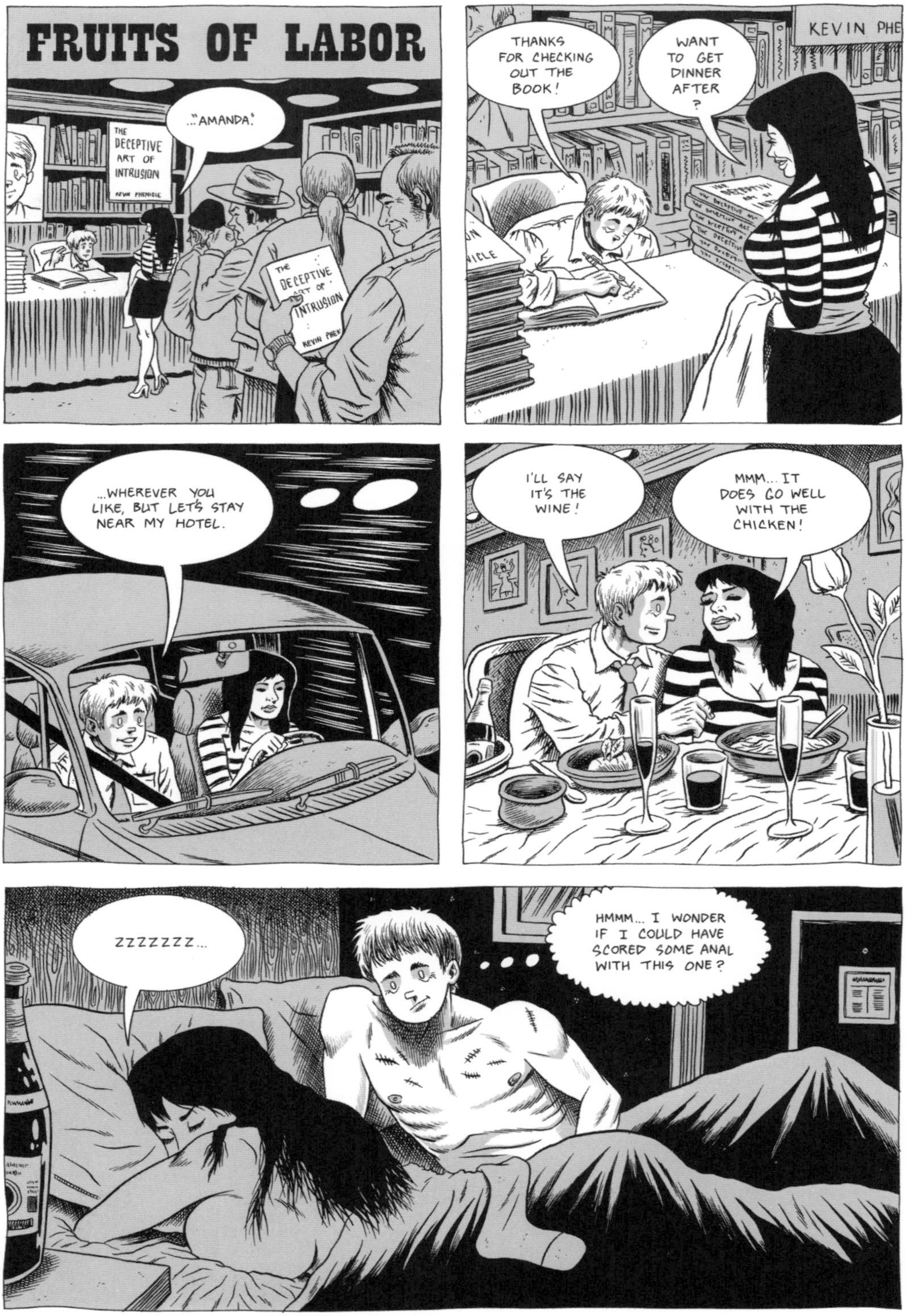
FRUITS OF LABOR
THE DECEPTIVE ART OF INTRUSION KEVIN PHENICLE
..."AMANDA."
THE DECEPTIVE ART OF INTRUSION KEVIN PHEN
KEVIN PHE
THANKS FOR CHECKING OUT THE BOOK!
WANT TO GET DINNER AFTER ?
...WHEREVER YOU LIKE, BUT LET'S STAY NEAR MY HOTEL.
I'LL SAY IT'S THE WINE!
MMM... IT DOES GO WELL WITH THE CHICKEN!
ZZZZZZZ...
HMMM... I WONDER IF I COULD HAVE SCORED SOME ANAL WITH THIS ONE?

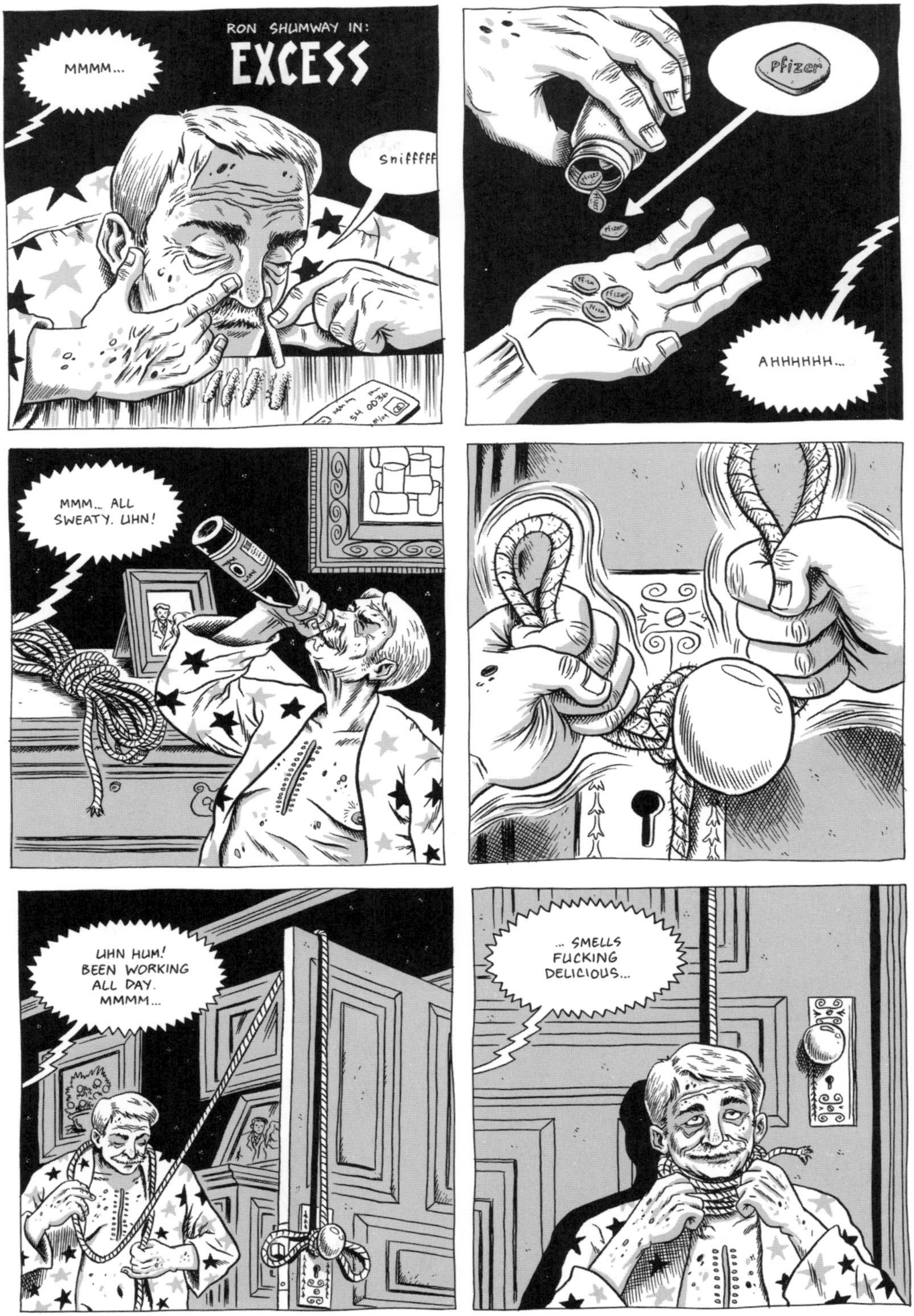
RON SHUMWAY IN:
EXCESS
MMMM...
sniffffff
Pfizer
AHHHHHH...
MMM... ALL SWEATY. UHN!
UHN HUM! BEEN WORKING ALL DAY. MMMM...
... SMELLS FUCKING DELICIOUS...

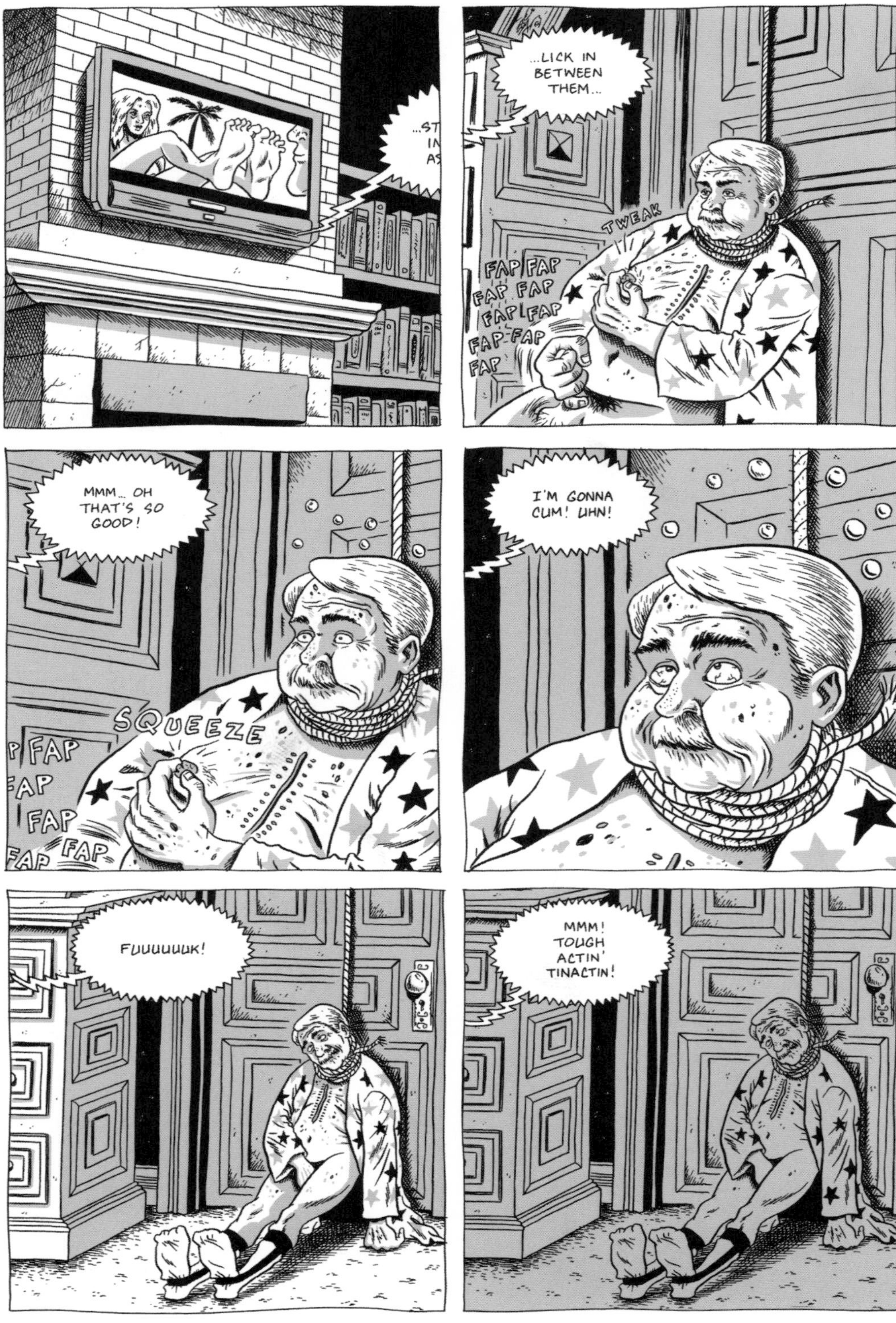
...ST
IN
AS
...LICK IN BETWEEN THEM...
TWEAK
FAP FAP FAP FAP FAP FAP FAP FAP FAP
MMM... OH THAT'S SO GOOD!
SQUEEZE
FAP FAP FAP FAP FAP
I'M GONNA CUM! UHN!
FUUUUUUK!
MMM! TOUGH ACTIN' TINACTIN!

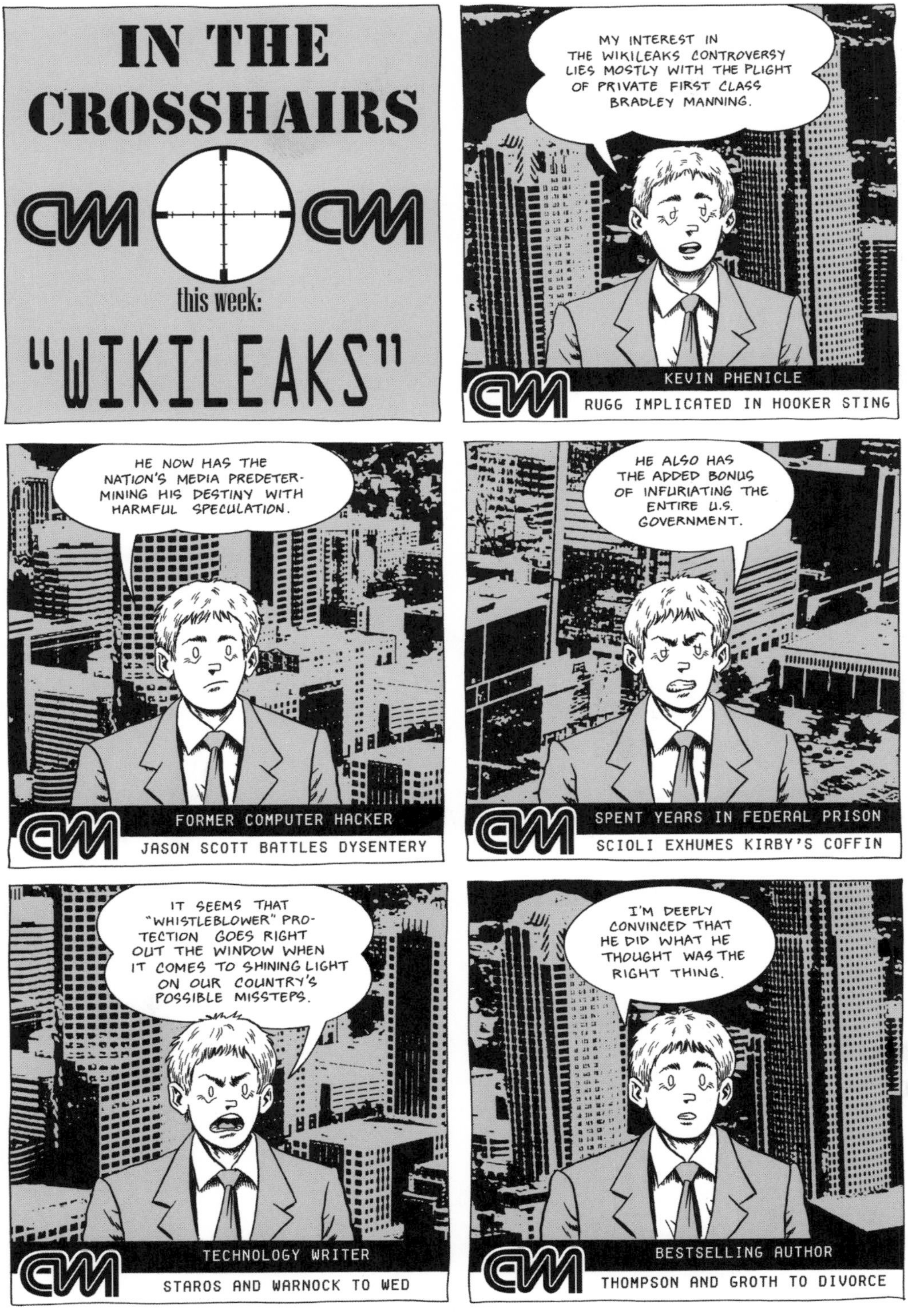
IN THE CROSSHAIRS
this week:
"WIKILEAKS"
MY INTEREST IN THE WIKILEAKS CONTROVERSY LIES MOSTLY WITH THE PLIGHT OF PRIVATE FIRST CLASS BRADLEY MANNING.
KEVIN PHENICLE
RUGG IMPLICATED IN HOOKER STING
HE NOW HAS THE NATION'S MEDIA PREDETERMINING HIS DESTINY WITH HARMFUL SPECULATION.
FORMER COMPUTER HACKER
JASON SCOTT BATTLES DYSENTERY
HE ALSO HAS THE ADDED BONUS OF INFURIATING THE ENTIRE U.S. GOVERNMENT.
SPENT YEARS IN FEDERAL PRISON
SCIOLI EXHUMES KIRBY'S COFFIN
IT SEEMS THAT "WHISTLEBLOWER" PROTECTION GOES RIGHT OUT THE WINDOW WHEN IT COMES TO SHINING LIGHT ON OUR COUNTRY'S POSSIBLE MISSTEPS.
TECHNOLOGY WRITER
STAROS AND WARNOCK TO WED
I'M DEEPLY CONVINCED THAT HE DID WHAT HE THOUGHT WAS THE RIGHT THING.
BESTSELLING AUTHOR
THOMPSON AND GROTH TO DIVORCE

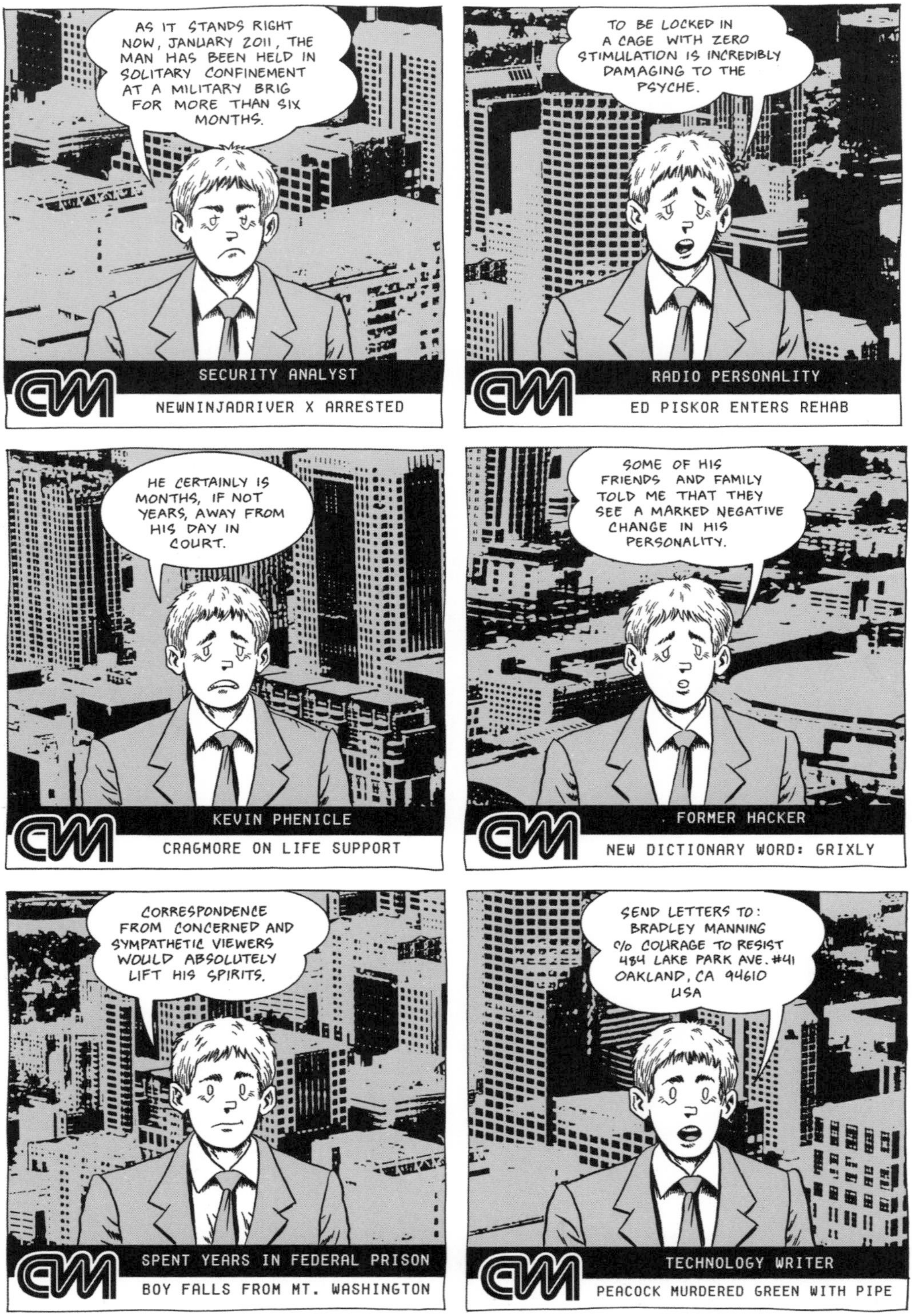
AS IT STANDS RIGHT NOW, JANUARY 2011, THE MAN HAS BEEN HELD IN SOLITARY CONFINEMENT AT A MILITARY BRIG FOR MORE THAN SIX MONTHS.
SECURITY ANALYST
NEWNINJADRIVER X ARRESTED
TO BE LOCKED IN A CAGE WITH ZERO STIMULATION IS INCREDIBLY DAMAGING TO THE PSYCHE.
RADIO PERSONALITY
ED PISKOR ENTERS REHAB
HE CERTAINLY IS MONTHS, IF NOT YEARS, AWAY FROM HIS DAY IN COURT.
KEVIN PHENICLE
CRAGMORE ON LIFE SUPPORT
SOME OF HIS FRIENDS AND FAMILY TOLD ME THAT THEY SEE A MARKED NEGATIVE CHANGE IN HIS PERSONALITY.
FORMER HACKER
NEW DICTIONARY WORD: GRIXLY
CORRESPONDENCE FROM CONCERNED AND SYMPATHETIC VIEWERS WOULD ABSOLUTELY LIFT HIS SPIRITS.
SPENT YEARS IN FEDERAL PRISON
BOY FALLS FROM MT. WASHINGTON
SEND LETTERS TO: BRADLEY MANNING C/O COURAGE TO RESIST 484 LAKE PARK AVE. #41 OAKLAND, CA 94610 USA
TECHNOLOGY WRITER
PEACOCK MURDERED GREEN WITH PIPE

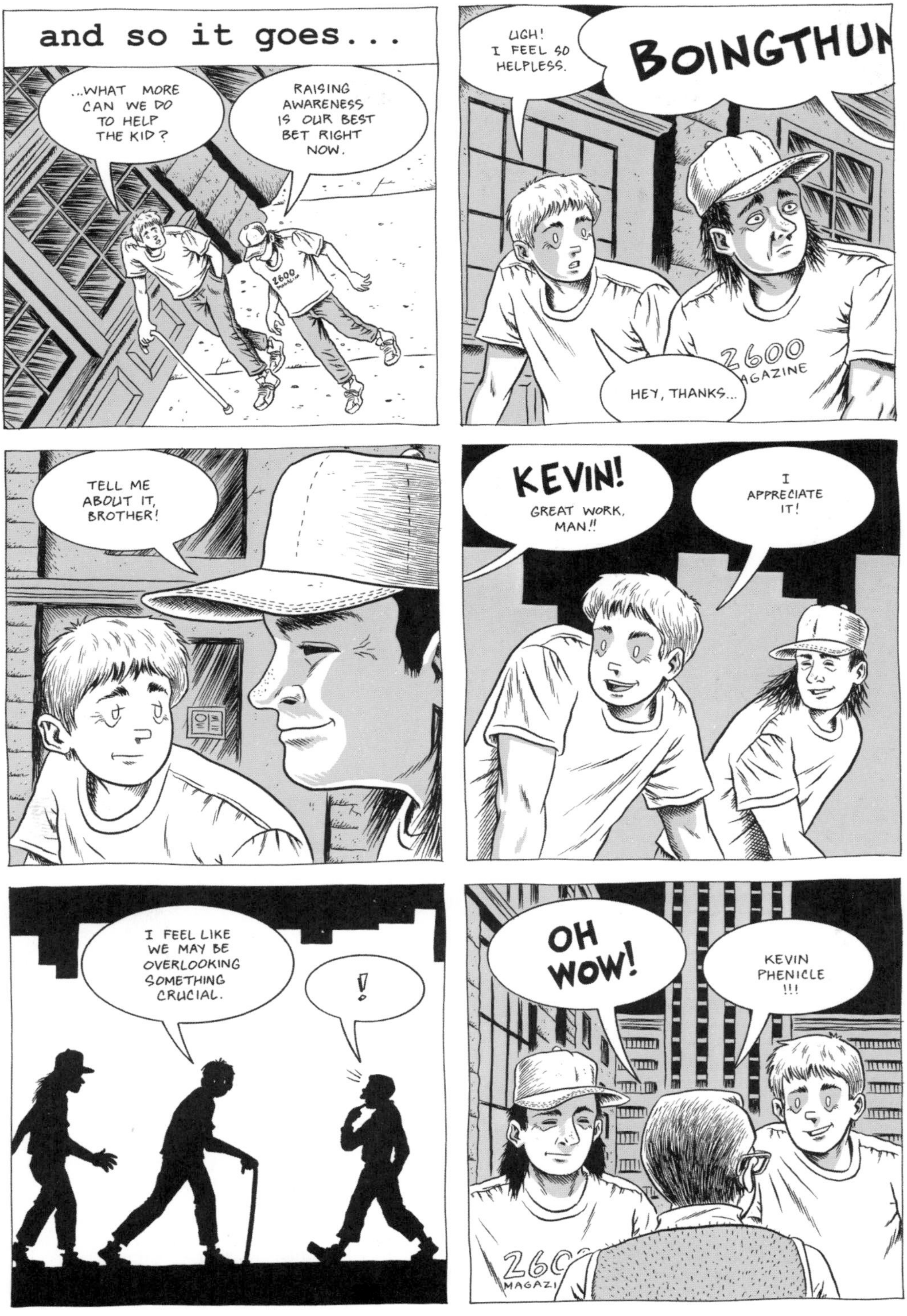
and so it goes...
...WHAT MORE CAN WE DO TO HELP THE KID?
RAISING AWARENESS IS OUR BEST BET RIGHT NOW.
UGH! I FEEL SO HELPLESS.
BOINGTHUN
2600 MAGAZINE
HEY, THANKS...
TELL ME ABOUT IT, BROTHER!
KEVIN! GREAT WORK, MAN!!
I APPRECIATE IT!
I FEEL LIKE WE MAY BE OVERLOOKING SOMETHING CRUCIAL.
!
OH WOW!
KEVIN PHENICLE !!!

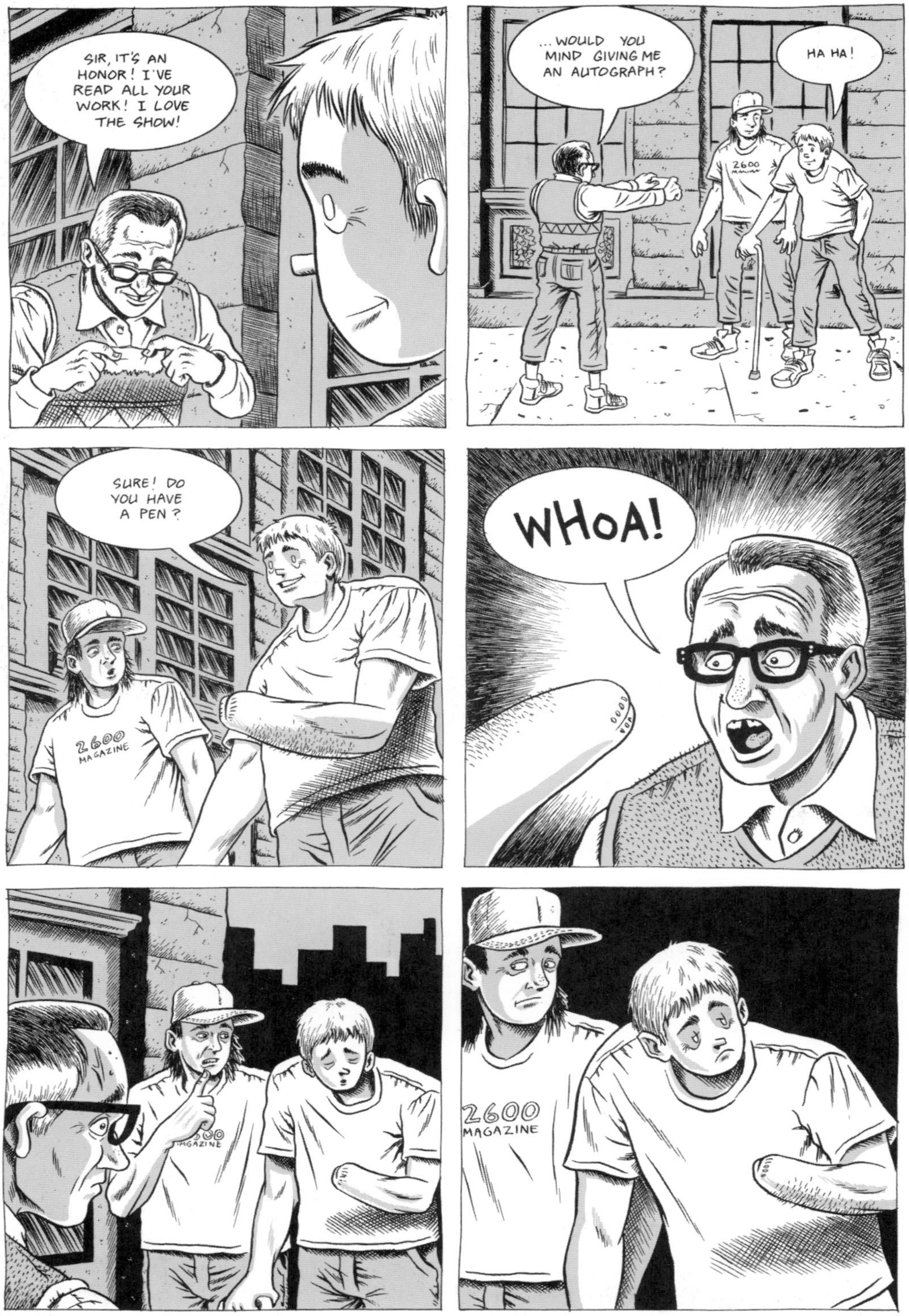
SIR, IT'S AN HONOR! I'VE READ ALL YOUR WORK! I LOVE THE SHOW!
...WOULD YOU MIND GIVING ME AN AUTOGRAPH?
HA HA!
2600
SURE! DO YOU HAVE A PEN?
2600 MAGAZINE
WHOA!
MAGAZINE
2600 MAGAZINE

KEVIN

FREE

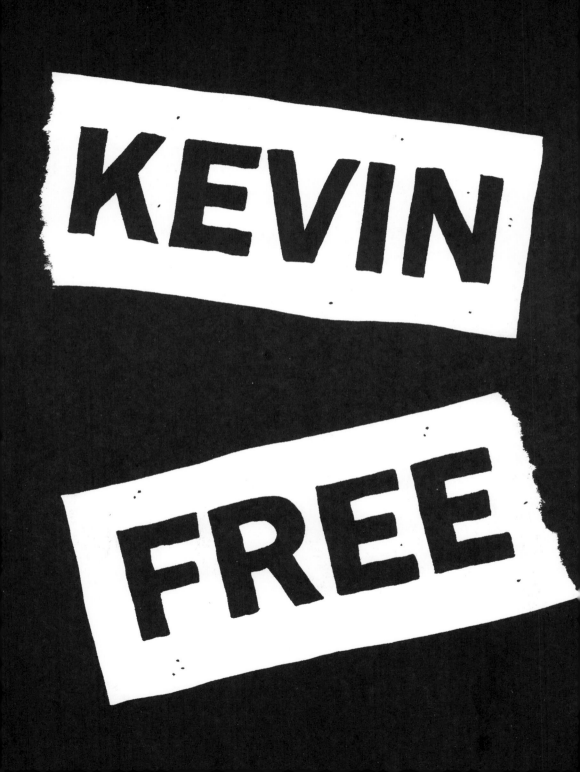

ABOUT THE
AUTHOR

"WIZZYWIG" IS ED PISKOR'S FIRST "REAL" SOLO
RELEASE. IN BETWEEN DOING THIS BOOK, HE HAS
DRAWN A FEW OTHERS, "MACEDONIA" AND "THE
BEATS". BOTH OF THOSE WERE WRITTEN BY
THE LATE, GREAT, HARVEY PEKAR. ED'S ALSO
DESIGNED THE CHARACTERS, AND PRODUCED
ART FOR AN ADULT SWIM SHOW ON CARTOON
NETWORK.

RIGHT NOW ED'S FINISHING ANOTHER, ALBEIT
LOOSER, BOOK CALLED "DELETERIOUS PEDIGREE"
WHICH CAN BE SEEN AT WIZZYWIGCOMICS.COM.
HE ALSO DOES/DID A WEEKLY COMICSTRIP
ONLINE AT THE NOTORIOUS HACKER-FRIENDLY
WEBSITE, BOINGBOING.NET, CALLED "BRAIN ROT."

ED'S EMAIL: WIMPYRUTHERFORD@GMAIL.COM
    TWITTER: @EDPISKOR
SNAIL MAIL: ED PISKOR
             4106 FAIRFIELD AVE.
             MUNHALL, PA. 15120

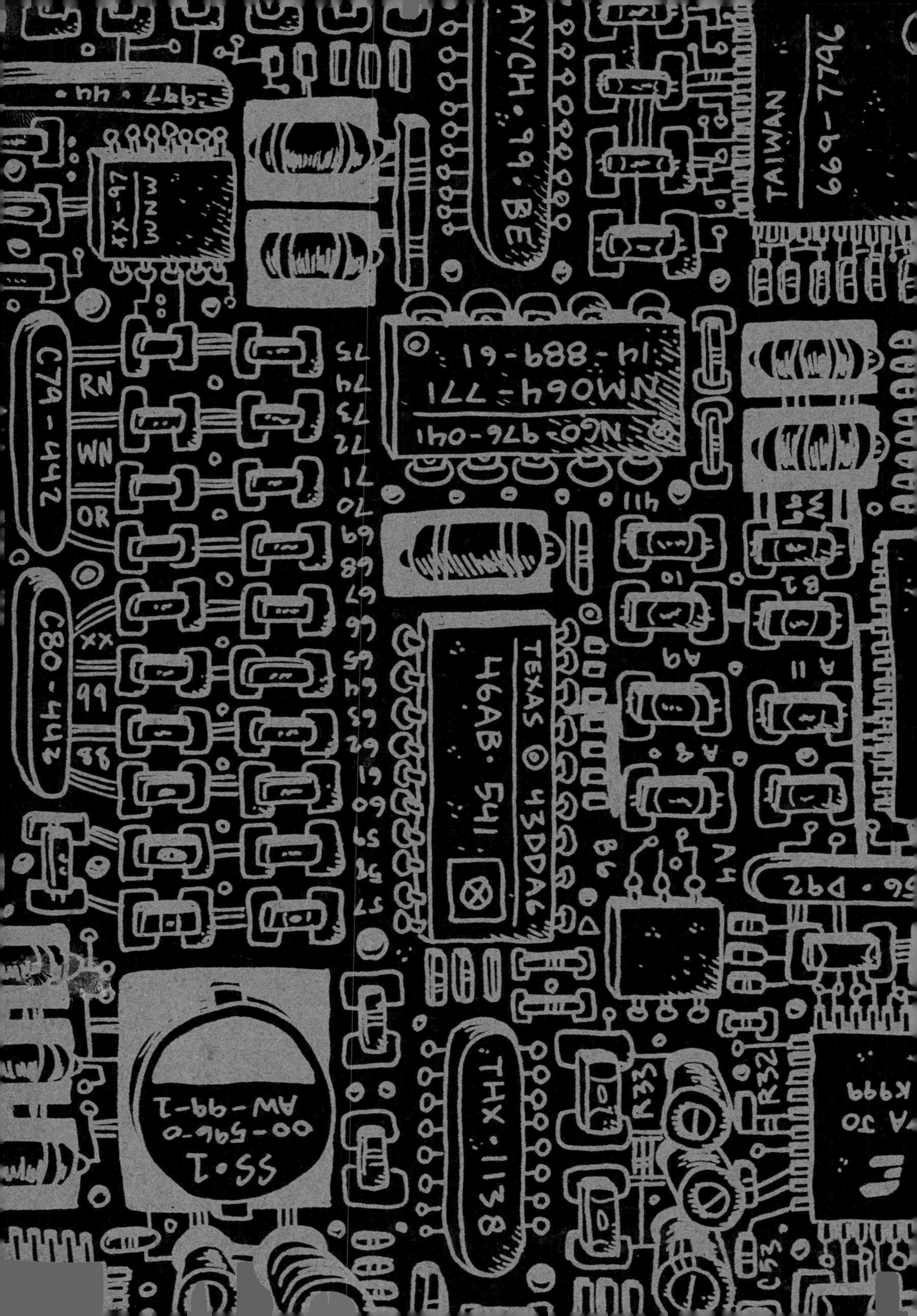